1987

BROADCASTING
IN AMERICA

Houghton Mifflin Company
Boston
Dallas Geneva, Ill. Lawrenceville, N.J. Palo Alto

BROADCASTING IN AMERICA

A Survey of Electronic Media

FIFTH EDITION

Sydney W. Head
University of Miami

Christopher H. Sterling
The George Washington University

with contributions by

Susan Tyler Eastman, *Indiana University*

Lemuel B. Schofield, *University of Miami*

Acknowledgments for photos on part opening pages:

Prologue: Peter Menzel/Stock Boston
Part I   Culver Pictures
Part II   Courtesy of the National Association of Broadcasters
Part III   Courtesy of Home Shopping Network
Part IV   Courtesy of *TV Guide*
Part V   Ulrike Welsch
Epilogue: NASA

Printed in the U.S.A.

Library of Congress Catalog Card Number: 86-81342

ISBN: 0-395-35936-8

BCDEFGHIJ-VB-8987

Cover photograph by Gorchev and Gorchev.

Brief Contents

Contents

Exhibits and Boxed Features

Preface

Even more than its predecessors, this edition of *Broadcasting in America*, which appears three decades after the first, has been heavily revised and updated — and this time restructured as well. These changes are due partially to our own evolving views of the field as well as to the substantial changes going on in the field itself. Starting with universally available broadcasting, we take a more unified approach to the many competing electronic media, dealing with them in an integrated fashion reflecting their true audience and marketplace interaction. Given the widespread use of broadcast content on newer delivery systems (most specifically including cable and videocassette recorders), "broadcasting" in this book's title and text now generally refers to all of the electronic media. Readers of past editions will note the following:

- We have rearranged the book and reduced the number of chapters to nineteen. Throughout, we have updated and tightened our discussion and grouped related topics together. For example, chapters on media impact and policy have been recast to reflect changes in the field and to make for clearer understanding of relationships.
- We lead off the book with historical background, somewhat condensed from previous editions, using it to lead into the technology chapters that follow. The present role of technology is more clearly seen if we first trace the development of knowledge and application of that technology.

- We have integrated treatment of public broadcasting and the newer technological rivals to radio and television, rather than dealing with each separately as in the fourth edition. We now feel it important to understand the changing interrelationships between broadcasting, cable, and home video (as well as other services with thus far limited audience penetration) all of which compete in the same market for the same potential audience.
- We have retained our approach in the chapters on technology of electronic media — stressing the fundamental physical and policy factors which are essential to a true understanding of how broadcasting and newer electronic media services work, and the different ways that each is limited.
- Economic aspects of the fast-changing electronic media have been given expanded treatment in the three new chapters which make up Part 3, contributed by Associate Professor Lemuel B. Schofield of the University of Miami. His extensive experience in television station supervisory roles, including that of general manager, combined with his legal training (he holds a J.D. from the University of Pennsylvania) add new insight to the treatment of station, system, and network organization and operation, as well as to advertising and the many other kinds of media financial support.
- Likewise, we have greatly increased the material on programming process and trends that now make up three chapters in Part 4, contributed by Dr. Susan Tyler Eastman, an

associate professor at Indiana University. Dr. Eastman is senior editor of *Broadcast and Cable Programming* (Wadsworth, 1985), among many other works, and has taught the "BIA course" for more than a decade. She deals with basic aspects of all programming before concentrating on network programs (Chapter 12) and nonnetwork, syndicated programming (Chapter 13).

• The material on electronic media research and consequences in Part 5 has been revised and tightened to cover both industrial and academic research efforts and findings. The chief and best known type of research, that on audience ratings, is now treated together with the analysis of media impact and consequences. The theoretical basis for the latter (Chapter 15) is totally revised for this edition.

• The regulatory chapters in Part 4 have been recast, reflecting the current deregulatory trend. Christopher Sterling, special assistant to an FCC commissioner during the transition from the Ferris to Fowler administrations (1980–82), highlights the regulatory differences between broadcasting and its newer rivals.

• For this edition, Dr. Norman Felsenthal, an associate professor at Temple University, has written the separately published *Instructor's Manual* (available to adopters) and a totally new *Study Guide*. He has worked closely with the authors so his work reflects the substantial changes in the revised main text.

Despite all these changes, our overall goal remains the same: to treat the electronic media within a broad academic perspective, touching on such traditional fields as the physical sciences, history, economics, political science, psychology, and sociology. This approach is rooted in our belief that for purposes of both general and professional education, electronic media should be studied as both the product of social forces and as social forces themselves. We seek to explain how broadcasting and more recent services developed, why they operate as they do today, and what part these services play in American society. We hope to spark readers to draw their own conclusions on the proper role of these services in the future.

As with previous editions, a number of colleagues gave valuable advice and suggestions. Among them were James Anderson (University of Utah) and Timothy Meyer (University of Wisconsin–Green Bay), who guided our revision of Chapter 15; Herbert Terry (Indiana University) and Erwin Krasnow (of Verner, Liipfert, Bernhardt & McPherson in Washington, and former general counsel of the NAB) who gave detailed comments and suggestions on Chapters 16–18; and Charles Clift (Ohio University); Peter Habermann (University of Northern Iowa); Darrel W. Holt (The University of Tennessee, Knoxville); Barry Litman (Michigan State University); George Mastroianni (California State University, Fullerton); Michael J. Porter (University of Missouri–Columbia); John A. Regnell (Southern Illinois University at Edwardsville); Ruth Schwartz (University of California, Los Angeles); David L. Smith (Ball State University); Donna Walcovy (Emerson College); and Judith B. Wallace (University of Miami). Naturally, we assume final responsibility for what we have done with their suggestions.

Sydney W. Head　　**Christopher H. Sterling**
Coral Gables, Florida　　Washington, D.C.

BROADCASTING
IN AMERICA

PROLOGUE

The World of Broadcasting

CHAPTER 1

Global Context

Broadcasting in America is best understood within the context of communications generally, both here and abroad. Telegraph, telephone, and radio ship-to-shore technologies led up to broadcasting. Its name came from the farmer's way of hand-sowing grain by *casting broadly*, letting seeds fall where they may. In a similar manner, news, entertainment, education, and other types of messages are cast into space to be picked up at will by the general public. In contrast, the older media sent private messages over predetermined paths to individual recipients.

Strictly defined, broadcasting is a technology that uses radio waves; cable television, which reaches people by means of wires, is therefore not broadcasting, though cable uses programs that are broadcast. Communication satellites use radio waves, but people who intercept the signals by means of back-yard antennas are not receiving true broadcasts because the programs are not intended for public reception — unless, of course, a direct-broadcast satellite is involved.

At one time this book might have confined itself to discussing broadcasting in the limited sense defined above, and to describing its use in the United States only. In recent years, however, revolutionary changes in tele-communication have made such a narrow perspective inadequate. One needs now to understand broadcasting in a global context, in both technological and geographic terms.

1.1 Convergence

This wider context is needed in part because of *convergence* — the blending together of many different services and technologies, such as satellites, cable television, videocassettes, computers, lasers, and telephones — into new configurations. Technological convergence has blurred the formerly sharp distinctions between wire and wireless communication, between private and public messages. Thanks largely to the computer's ability to manipulate images, sounds, and text, such varied modes of communication as the telephone, phonograph, motion picture, radio, and television now interact in novel ways.

Geographic convergence has also occurred, especially as satellite communication becomes more sophisticated. Cultural distinctions among nations and differences among their telecommunications systems erode as satellites make possible rapid exchange of programs and communication software throughout the world. In sum, the phenomenon of convergence requires that one view the specific medium of broadcasting in a *telecommunication* perspective, a perspective that includes all the wire and wireless technologies that have been said to turn the world into a "global village."

People tend to think of broadcasting parochially, in terms of their personal program preferences, limited by their own national system. To them the medium consists of their favorite programs, whether *Dallas, Masterpiece Theatre,* MTV, a rock station, or talk radio. Most audience members do not care who pays for the programs, when they started, where they came from, what technologies brought them to the receiver, or why those programs are scheduled instead of others. They might think it odd to start a book about broadcasting in America by talking about telecommunication instead of broadcasting and about foreign nations instead of the United States. Students of broadcasting, however, need to look beyond the receiving set and outward to the rest of the world.

Starting the study of these topics from the dual perspective of telecommunication and its international aspect prepares you to look at broadcasting in America more discerningly than you might if you approached it from the limited viewpoint of traditional broadcasting in a single country. This wide-angle lens should give you an enhanced awareness of the medium's infinite possibilities, enabling you to imagine future developments in this rapidly changing arena.

POTS and POBS   When new technical marvels revolutionized the telephone business, telephone experts adopted the wry term *POTS* to describe traditional telephony. POTS means "*p*lain *o*ld *t*elephone *s*ervice," distinguishing traditional telephony from the new jazzed-up kind that uses computerized switching, automated operations, communication satellites, fiber-optic transmission, telephones with memories, answering machines, and other innovations.

Now that broadcasting has reached a similar stage of development, we need a broadcasting equivalent of POTS; in this book we will use *POBS,* for "*p*lain *o*ld *b*roadcasting *s*ystem." POBS denotes the traditional medium as it existed before such technical developments as broadband cable television, satellite networks, direct satellite broadcasting, optical fiber links, videocassette recorders, and the like transformed the media landscape.*

In drawing this distinction between old and new, we by no means intend to imply the imminent end of POBS. Traditional broadcasting remains fundamental — still viable and still the most universally available telecommunication medium. Broadcasting faces many new sources of competition for audience attention, but it is also enhanced by many new resources.

In some sections of this book the term *broadcasting* refers only to POBS. In other places, *broadcasting,* along with such phrases as *electronic media* and *radio and television,* covers some of the wide range of old and new services collectively denoted by the term *mass communication media* as defined in the Communications Act of 1934: "television, radio, cable television, multipoint distribution service, direct broadcast satellite service, and other services, the licensed facilities of which must be substantially devoted toward providing programming or other information services within the editorial control of the licensee" [47 USC 309(i)(3)(C)(i)].

---

*Don't worry about the specific meanings of these terms if they are not familiar to you. Each will be discussed in relation to broadcasting later in this book.

Telecommunications Perspective As mentioned, convergence requires us to take an even wider view of broadcasting, that of *telecommunications*. Elsewhere you will sometimes find the term *telecommunications* used to mean primarily telegraphy and telephony. Here, though, we intend it to mean more: communication by means of electromagnetic energy, whether using wire, cable, radio, light, or other channels of transmission. This definition embraces many point-to-point forms of communication, as well as electronic mass communications.

The United States has been at the forefront of the world telecommunications revolution. For example, it made a decisive operational leap forward in 1964, when the International Telecommunications Satellite Organization (Intelsat) began relaying transatlantic communications traffic. Ever since, we have been able to see live televised scenes from distant overseas news events instantaneously.* More than a hundred countries share Intelsat ownership, but the United States originated it, owns the largest percentage of its shares, and until 1979 operated it on behalf of the rest of the consortium.

Intelsat makes possible instant worldwide distribution of not only television programs but also telephone conversations, news agency services, and business data. Intelsat, though primarily an international carrier, also offers its facilities at reasonable rates to Third World countries for domestic use. This en-

ables less developed countries to set up their own internal satellite relay networks. Many of these countries vaulted with the aid of Intelsat directly into the satellite era, and have been able to broadcast daily television news programs throughout their countries decades, even generations, before such national program distribution would have been possible using earthbound, presatellite networks.

As the United States forged ahead with new telecommunications technology, much of the world, aside from participating in Intelsat (and a much smaller USSR version, Intersputnik), generally stayed with POBS while cautiously experimenting with the new technologies — all the while watching the U.S. telecommunications transformation with both fascination and a certain amount of alarm. By the late 1970s, however, European nations, Japan, and some other countries began to join in, feverishly installing modern cable facilities and launching satellites. At the same time they began to reassess their traditional reliance on highly centralized, state-owned POTS and POBS.

True, Europe has had cable television for many years. However, cable in these countries merely extended POBS coverage, taking on the form of CATV (community antenna television) and MATV (master antenna television) systems. These small cable systems, mostly noncommercial, offered few program choices, no local origination, no advertising, and certainly no satellite-to-cable networks and pay-cable channels. They merely extended the coverage of ordinary television stations. Sky Channel, the first European satellite-to-cable network, did not start until 1982. It relays a pan-European service, delivering programs via a multinational satellite to cable systems in a growing list of countries. By that time, of course, U.S. cable television subscribers had long since become accustomed to numerous satellite-distributed cable program channels

---

*In the early days, before videotape recorders and Intelsat, the U.S. networks occasionally installed film processers in airplanes so that they could develop film of exceptionally newsworthy European events during the return trip across the Atlantic. Such strenuous efforts enabled U.S. television to show the coronation of Britain's Queen Elizabeth in 1952, for example, only a few hours after the event actually took place. This contrasts with coverage of the marriage of the Prince of Wales to Lady Diana in 1981, seen live, without delay, all over the world, thanks to the global satellite system Intelsat.

such as ESPN and HBO, as well as superstations such as WTBS.

Aside from the difficulty of constructing satellites, the communication industry faces the problem of launching them into orbit. Fighting the pull of gravity and resistance of the atmosphere to get satellites off the ground and into orbit some 22,300 miles above the earth is expensive and technically difficult. As another example of American pioneering, the U.S. National Aeronautics and Space Administration (NASA) was for years the only agency that sold satellite launch services to foreign countries. By 1984, however, a European-owned launch facility, Arianespace, had begun to challenge NASA's monopoly. The facility, named for Ariane, the rocket that launches the satellites, is located in French Guiana, on the northern coast of South America near the equator — a more convenient spot than NASA's Florida location for attaining equatorial orbit. In 1984 Arianespace launched communication satellites for Brazil and for a consortium of Middle Eastern Arabic-speaking countries called Arabsat.

Of course, other innovations have come from all over the world. For example, the USSR pioneered in space and was the first country to use satellites for relaying television programs. Japan has led in consumer electronics production and high-definition television development. British television engineers developed the transmission of text and graphic materials to television screens. The two British radio and television authorities, the British Broadcasting Corporation (noncommercial) and Independent Television (the British commercial program companies) began broadcasting teletext services in 1974. These textual and graphic materials are piggybacked onto regular television broadcast transmissions for display on home receivers equipped with special converters. In Britain, daily television listings published in the newspapers give Oracle, the

ITV's teletext, and the BBC's Ceefax as regular television offerings.

Standardization   Another aspect of convergence is the need to adopt universal technical standards. Standardization helps to prevent interference, to maximize efficient use of the electromagnetic spectrum, and to maintain quality of services. Moreover, common telecommunication standards greatly facilitate international exchange of technology and programs.

Whereas technology thus encourages internationalism, national chauvinism tends to impede it. If you take a portable radio receiver abroad, you can pick up stations almost anywhere you travel. But television receivers and most other items of video equipment do not share that characteristic. Fourteen sets of incompatible black-and-white technical standards and three color-television systems make it necessary to use converters when sets from one country are exported to others. International exchange of videotaped television programs, an ever-expanding trade, requires not only soundtrack dubbing to accommodate language differences but also conversions from one technical standard to another.

Nations sometimes find even domestic compatibility hard to achieve. In the United States, for instance, two incompatible types of home videocassette recorders, Betamax and VHS, compete for public acceptance; and doubts as to which of several recording methods will prevail have delayed adoption of AM stereo and the growth of teletext. In addition, the Federal Communications Commission refused to set standards for home satellite antennas when it authorized companies to prepare direct-broadcast satellite (DBS) services. Such reluctance to mandate national compatibility standards grows out of the now-dominant U.S. federal policy of minimizing government regulation.

Other nations do set their own national standards, but international commercial and political rivalries often prevent them from agreeing among themselves on world standards. Nations try to win consensus through their global regulatory agency, the International Telecommunication Union, but economic chauvinism too often prevails. The three color-television systems, for example, represent separate American, French, and German government choices. Each of the three countries lobbied frantically to persuade other governments to adopt its version, since adoption meant not only national prestige but also tremendous profits from international sales, both present and future, by manufacturers of equipment using the favored color television system.*

1.2 Common Grounds

Despite differences in standards for specific items of equipment, each country starts with identical potentials because telecommunications use a fundamental technology based on universal natural phenomena. Radio waves behave in California, Kenya, and Denmark according to the same physical laws that govern them in Maine, Singapore, and France. Countries exchange know-how, equipment, and programs on a worldwide scale, even though they may need to overcome differences in languages and technical standards. All nations must deal with the fact that the "airwaves" (actually electromagnetic radiations, which travel best in space, and have nothing to do with air) are a universally available resource.

---

*A new single-standard color-television system called MAC has been proposed for direct-broadcast satellites. They require a common international standard because they will often cover several countries. Immediately, however, many countries began advocating incompatible variations of MAC.

However, since electromagnetic radiations interfere with each other, regulation to prevent mutual interference is necessary. And beyond the technical realm, broadcasting has potentially dangerous political power because of its unique ability to go over the heads of leaders, instantly reaching an entire nation, and to surmount the political frontiers that otherwise set nations apart.

The Spectrum as a Public Resource

Governments consider the electromagnetic frequency spectrum, upon which all forms of wireless telecommunication depend, as a vitally important public resource, as part of their "national patrimony." No other communication medium depends for its very existence on a resource that cannot be manufactured or privately owned. This dependence imposes a duty on governments to administer radio frequency usage in the best interest of national sovereignty and public well-being. Naturally, interpretations of this duty vary with political philosophies.

Interference Prevention   Without regulation of power, location, and types of emissions, stations using the same or nearby frequencies will inevitably interfere with each other. In fact such interference occurred in the United States during the early 1920s, creating such discord among broadcasts that Congress belatedly passed the Radio Act of 1927, the foundation of present U.S. radiocommunication law. Not enough usable frequencies exist to avoid the need for sharing, both among services and among nations, obliging international cooperation on rules for apportioning the spectrum and governing its use:

One clearly cannot communicate by radio with another country without its cooperation as to frequency, time, power, and place of communication. In some cases one cannot even use radio within one's own boundaries without the forbearance of other nations. These and other limits on national discretion could be said to make the spectrum an international resource comparable in theory to airspace over the high seas, to international waterways, or even to migratory fisheries. (Levin, 1971: 37)

Political Controls   Revolutionaries attempting a coup make a nation's broadcasting facilities one of their first targets. Many countries, sensitive to this danger, install machine-gun emplacements guarding radio and television facilities. Authoritarian rulers go to great lengths to bar opposing political factions from using the airwaves. Solidarity, the militant Polish trade-union movement, made access to the nation's government-controlled broadcasting system a primary goal in its confrontation with the communist regime in the early 1980s. Even the most stable and democratic countries take care to prevent a single political party from exerting undue influence over broadcasting.

Although they share these common grounds, countries adapt the universal potentials of broadcasting to suit their own needs, circumstances, and limitations. As you will see in the following sections of this chapter, national broadcasting systems of the POBS variety tend to reflect national character, responding to fundamental political, cultural, geographic, historical, and economic imperatives.

1.3   Political Philosophies

Differing political philosophies produce differing systems of broadcasting control. The attitude a country's leadership takes toward its people gives a clue to the amount of control a nation exercises over broadcasting. The three basic orientations are, broadly stated, permissive, paternalistic, and authoritarian.

Permissive Orientation   Broadcasting in America furnishes the major example of a permissive system. Congress considered federal operation of the new medium only briefly before turning it over to private enterprise (including in some cases local public authorities such as municipalities, school boards, and state educational systems). Private entrepreneurs, the great majority of early licensees, soon settled on advertisers as the preferred source of funding. The profit incentive, when minimally hampered by government regulation, encourages reaching as many people as possible and catering to the program tastes shared by the largest number.

Operating within the permissive framework of the free-enterprise system, American commercial broadcasting took on the pragmatism, aggressiveness, materialism, expansionism, and free-swinging competitiveness of American marketing in general. Whatever critics may say (and many deplore the result), American commercialism achieves more lively, inventive, popular, and slickly produced broadcasting services than can be found elsewhere in the world. And despite criticism, American programs exported to other countries win popular acclaim virtually everywhere.

But many countries disagree with the extreme permissiveness of the American system's commercial component. They do not agree that popular acceptance and production slickness represent the best that can be expected of broadcasting; they deplore commercial motivations that emphasize what people *want* rather than what critics and national leaders think they *need*. In general, only countries influenced by the United States, such as those in Central and South America, have adopted similar permissive, profit-driven systems. Moreover, since the advent of television, even these countries have retreated from their former easy-going, permissive approach.

Paternalistic Orientation Most countries, lacking the American dedication to untrammeled free enterprise, feel strongly that programming cannot be left entirely to the interaction of supply and popular demand. Lacking also the avowed "melting pot" character of the United States, they feel impelled to ensure that broadcasting will play a positive role in preserving their national cultures, including those all-important bearers of cultural traditions, national languages. They also feel justified in mandating a balanced diet of program types. In particular, they stress the importance of children's programs, expecting them to meet the needs of children rather than those of advertisers, and to set positive examples while avoiding exploitative commercialism.

The paternalistic orientation aims at maintaining a balanced program diet, with neither too much cultural and informational spinach nor too much entertaining ice cream for social and personal well-being. Paternalists feel obliged to gratify popular mass tastes to some extent, but they also feel a duty to counterbalance such preferences with programs appealing to more cultivated tastes. They want both ethnic and intellectual minorities to receive program services relevant to their tastes and interests, whether or not it is commercially profitable to do so. They believe rural citizens should have the same access to program choices as urban residents.

Most non-communist industrialized countries provide varying degrees of paternalism. British broadcasting, the classic example, started with the deliberate goal of avoiding such American "mistakes" as commercialism. The British Broadcasting Corporation (BBC) replaced a short-lived private company in 1927 with a public, chartered, nonprofit corporation.* The BBC carries no advertising, deriving nearly all its funds from annual receiver-set license fees. The government appoints the BBC governing board but leaves its members free to supervise the operation without interference. Outsiders sometimes mistake the BBC for a government service, but its charter, as buttressed by the British unwritten constitutional tradition, assures its independence from both commercial and direct government controls.

True, the home secretary, the public official responsible for broadcasting and cable, has on paper certain "reserve" powers that could be used to justify government interference. Theoretically, the secretary could even go so far as to veto a particular program or class of programs, a power the Constitution as well as broadcasting law denies to any American official. Common law and powerful, long-standing traditions of government restraint protect the BBC's freedom. In a unique breach of this tradition, the home secretary asked the BBC governors in 1985 to cancel a scheduled television interview with an Irish politician alleged to be a leader of the Irish Republican Army (IRA), on the grounds that the BBC should not provide a platform for terrorists. (This request echoed statements many American observers had recently made criticizing U.S. network coverage of press conferences terrorists in Lebanon had staged concerning hijacked Americans.) As evidence of the unusual nature of the request, over two thousand BBC employees called a 24-hour news strike in protest, and the episode drew prominent notice in both Eastern and Western media. After some minor editing, the program was eventually run.

From its earliest days the BBC adhered to a philosophy of conscientious public service, stressing its obligation to the entire public, not just those segments most easily and cheaply

---

*In the United States, *corporation* implies commercialism, but the BBC chose that term for its noncommercial implications in Britain, where a "limited company" is comparable to the U.S. corporation.

reached or, as in commercial systems, those segments particularly interesting to advertisers. It aimed to "give a lead" by programming somewhat ahead of popular taste at least part of the time. Symptomatic of the BBC's paternalism was the lack of interest its officials took in conducting objective audience research to validate their conscientious personal judgments. Not until large segments of its supposedly loyal audience began tuning to popular music from European transnational commercial stations such as Radio Luxembourg did the BBC embark on systematic audience studies. As late as 1960, a BBC official could write:

The real degradation of the BBC started with the invention of the hellish department which is called "Listener Research." That Abominable Statistic is supposed to show "what the listeners like" — and, of course, what they like is the red-nosed comedian and the Wurlitzer organ. (Quoted in Briggs, 1965: 261)

Robert Silvey, hired in 1936 to organize the BBC audience analysis department, steadfastly refused throughout the thirty-two years he headed that department to issue program ratings. He said they imply that every program should aim at reaching the total audience and they ignore the factor of audience satisfaction (Silvey, 1974: 185). His reports always included, as does BBC research to this day, "Appreciation Indexes" as well as audience size measurements.

BBC research methods and BBC broadcast philosophy spread worldwide. Thousands of broadcasters from scores of countries went to the BBC's famous Broadcasting House in London for systematic training and indoctrination (Exhibit 1.1). It is fair to say that the BBC has been the single most influential and imitated POBS in broadcasting history. Yet no other country has come close to duplicating it. Too much of its special character arises from the special character of the British nation. In this way, every broadcast system uniquely reflects its national setting.

Exhibit 1.1   Broadcasting House, London

In pretelevision days, broadcasters from all over the world journeyed to this famous art deco building in the heart of London for training and observation. The sculpture above the entrance represents Prospero, the wise magician of Shakespeare's The Tempest, *with Ariel, a sprite whose lightning speed symbolizes radio. The BBC moved here from its original quarters on the bank of the Thames in 1932. Though Broadcasting House tripled the corporation's previous space, the new building proved too small for the BBC's activities even before completion. The giant BBC television center is located in a London suburb.*

Source: BBC copyright.

The advent of television and the turbulent political and social changes of the 1960s modified BBC paternalism. Moreover, after 1955* the BBC had to cope with a competing, advertising-supported service, albeit with strict limitations on advertiser influence over programming. More about this competing service and its relation to the BBC is covered later in §1.4.

Authoritarian Orientation Communist countries and many Third World countries take an authoritarian approach to broadcasting. The state itself finances and operates the broadcasting systems, along with other telecommunication services, harnessing them directly to implementation of government policies. This means that governments own and operate by far the greatest percentage of the world's broadcasting systems (Exhibit 1.2).

In the Soviet Union, a committee responsible to the top echelon of political power runs broadcasting. When challenged about their subservience to government controls, Soviet broadcasters are apt to dismiss the charge by replying, "We are not controlled by the government — we *are* the government." Marxist doctrine holds that private ownership of the media inevitably results in capitalistic exploitation, and that only the government can truly serve the masses. The writer of *The Great Soviet Encyclopedia's* entry for television (later chairman of the USSR central broadcast committee) contrasts capitalist with communist uses of the medium, asserting that capitalist countries use television "in the interests of the ruling monopolistic circles to propagandize bourgeois ideology." With unconscious irony, in view of this statement, the Soviet writer goes on to say:

In the USSR and other socialist countries, television is used to report the activities of communist and workers' parties, the actions of government bodies, and workers' participation in communist and socialist construction. It demonstrates individual features of the socialist way of life, molds public opinion, and helps provide the ideological, moral, and aesthetic education of the masses. (Lapin, 1973: 484)

Because communist ideology stresses the media's importance for mass political education, the Soviets embraced broadcasting early, embarking on a vigorous "radiofication" program. The Russian masses, however, failed to invest in home radio receivers as extensively as did Western audiences. Communist countries rely heavily on state-subsidized listening by means of *wired radio*. This seemingly contradictory term refers to an audio forerunner of cable television, a system that receives broadcasts at a local government redistribution center and forwards them by wire to speaker boxes in homes and public places. Redistribution centers sometimes have their own small studios for preparation of local material on a closed-circuit (nonbroadcast) basis to supplement programs received from a distant regional or national capital. People rent speakers for a nominal monthly fee or listen without cost at work or in public squares.

About 14 percent of the radio reception worldwide relies on speaker boxes; in Eastern Europe the proportion reaches nearly 40 percent (BBC, 1984). Lack of purchasing power and shortages of consumer goods no doubt account in part for this dependence on subsidized reception, but the government's desire to control information and the low motivational quality of didactic government programming also discourage people from purchasing radios.

In recent years Soviet television has paid increasing attention to production values and popular tastes. Even so, programming remains predominantly serious, emphasizing political commentary, documentaries, classical

*The enabling law went into effect in 1954; the last of the fifteen regional companies comprising the Independent Television Network began telecasting in 1962.

Exhibit 1.2   World Broadcasting Ownership

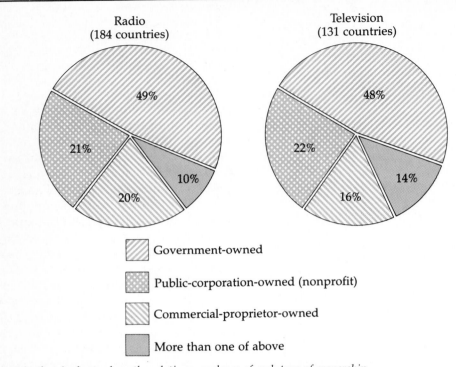

Radio
(184 countries)

Television
(131 countries)

Government-owned

Public-corporation-owned (nonprofit)

Commercial-proprietor-owned

More than one of above

Percentages in the pie charts show the relative prevalence of each type of ownership. Governments own about half of the world's broadcasting systems. The public corporation type of ownership implies noncommercial or limited commercial operation by a public body insulated from direct political control. Mixed systems combine two or more types of ownership, usually a public corporation plus private commercial ownership. This tabulation treats each national broadcasting system equally, regardless of its audience size. Relating type of ownership to the number of receivers reachable yields quite different figures. For example, government, public corporation, and mixed television systems each potentially reach about equal numbers of receivers, with mixed systems somewhat ahead of the others (36 percent of the potential receivers). Solely commercial systems reach less than 1 percent of the world's aggregate receiver potential.

Source: Based on data in UNESCO, *Statistical Yearbook, 1984* (UNESCO, Paris, 1984), Tables 9.1 and 9.3.

music, ballet, and theater. From a production standpoint, Soviet shows occasionally seen on Western television seem technically competent but constrained in comparison with surrounding programming. This is especially true of the Soviet prime-time newscast, *Vremya*, which American network news programs sometimes excerpt. It is not surprising, therefore, that television-set penetration in the USSR still lags far behind that of the United

States, which in 1985 had 603 receivers per thousand population, compared to 272 for the USSR.*

In ascribing low television receiver penetration to USSR programming, *Time* commented that "between the culture and the propaganda, there is little room for fun, and many Soviet viewers seem to long for more diverting fare" (23 June 1980). Even entertainment formats must serve ideological goals:

The quiz show, a popular item, is an example. One, called "Let's Go, Girls" ("A nu-ka, devushki"), is telecast once a month for an hour and a half. Everyone wins something, a small prize of flowers or books, and the object is not to get rich, but rather to popularize occupations and encourage good work. Recently, a group of policewomen performed on the show, marching and drilling to music with their nightsticks. They were asked ("quizzed") how to improve traffic rules, and they offered such suggestions as redesigning traffic signs. (Mickiewicz, 1981: 20)

In most Third World countries, woeful lack of purchasing power means even lower set penetration. Neither receiver license fees nor advertising can be counted on to support broadcasting. Out of necessity, Third World governments therefore usually own and operate their own broadcasting systems. In any event, leaders of these often-shaky regimes feel they dare not allow private broadcasters free rein in communicating with largely illiterate masses. In most cases, Third World authoritarianism thus rests more on pragmatic than ideological considerations, but its net effect on programming tends to resemble that of dogmatic Marxism.

---

*The quarterly periodical *Television Age International* publishes tables estimating current worldwide TV-set counts. Sets-per-thousand-population figures in this chapter come from the February 1985 issue.

1.4 Pluralistic Trend

The three prototype regulatory systems — permissive, paternalistic, and authoritarian — exist nowhere in pure form. Permissive systems impose some regulations, paternalism bows at times to popular demand, and even authoritarianism finds it expedient to conduct audience research to find out what people really want. Relatively few countries, however, have truly *pluralistic* systems.

Role of Motives   In the perspective of over half a century of broadcasting experience, pluralistic systems seem best able to assure optimum development of the medium. Such systems cultivate broadcasting's beneficial potentials to the fullest while minimizing its less desirable effects. Pluralism in this context means more than simply having many competing services, since if the same motivation drives all services, they tend merely to imitate each other. Pluralism means putting more than one motive to work in the production, selection, and scheduling of programs, with the profit-driven component on an approximately even footing with the public-service component.

Commercial motives alone, no matter how carefully regulated, constrict the range of programming. Though regulations may prevent advertisers from directly controlling programs, those responsible for schedules nevertheless will inevitably defer to advertiser interests, even if unconsciously. Commercial programmers imitate success, avoid controversy, concentrate on audience segments having the most buying power, and aim at the lowest audience common denominator. By the same token, a public-service monopoly risks bureaucratic complacency, lack of responsiveness to popular tastes, and deference toward the politicians and bureaucrats who control the purse strings. A healthy competition between differently motivated broadcasting organizations, on the other hand, can stimulate creativity and encourage innovation, giving audiences a range of genuine program choices instead of several versions of essentially the same type of program.

In the United States, broadcast pluralism suffers from the weakness of its noncommercial components, the public broadcasting radio and television services. Their low-level and uncertain funding, along with ambiguity as to their proper goal, prevents them from competing effectively with commercial broadcasting. The latter dominates in spectrum allotments, numbers of stations, hours on the air, financial resources, and the strength that comes from unambiguity of purpose.*

British Pluralism   Pluralism in Britain rests on a sounder footing. The BBC's monopoly began to end in 1954 with government authorization of a competing, commercially supported service known as Independent Television (ITV). Local commercial radio followed in 1972, though the BBC still retains a monopoly on network radio.

A nonprofit, chartered corporation, the Independent Broadcasting Authority (IBA), authorizes and regulates the ITV companies responsible for commercial programming. Like the BBC, the IBA owns and operates its own networks of television transmitters, so that commercial considerations do not control coverage. Unlike the BBC, the IBA has no programming function. Instead it empowers private commercial companies to do the programming and to sell advertising. Commercial programming comes mainly from fifteen re-

gional companies licensed and regulated by the IBA.* Regionalization prevents any one company from dominating the commercial field. The IBA even goes so far as to divide the lucrative London market between two companies, Thames Television (weekday programming) and London Weekend. Regional franchising also prevents broadcasters from neglecting regional interests in order to pursue profits in the national market. Thus Britain avoided the American commercial television pattern, which is dominated by an oligopoly of only three huge television networks, all similar and each national in scope.

Nevertheless, in order to realize the benefits of pluralism, commercial television services in Britain need to compete as a national network on a more or less equal basis with the BBC networks. For this reason, the IBA allows its fifteen regional (ITV) companies to join forces most of the time to provide a cooperative national network service. The five biggest companies furnish most of the network programs, though the ITV network relies on ITN (Independent Television News), a commonly owned, nonprofit subsidiary, for its national and international news programs.†

Until the 1980s the BBC still retained the advantage of two television networks (BBC-1 and BBC-2) against the single ITV commercial network. Though British viewers could choose among only three television programs, all three could be received nearly everywhere. Britain thus avoided the marked inequality of U.S. television distribution, by which eight or

---

*There has even been a shortsighted proposal to abandon what little pluralism exists in American broadcasting by permitting public stations to sell time, thereby leaving them with essentially the same motivation as commercial stations.

---

*The IBA also supervises subsequently authorized commercial programmers: a national television service, Channel Four; a "breakfast-time" television service, TV-am; and about 50 local radio stations.

†U.S. viewers have become familiar with the larger ITV company names through British programs seen on U.S. networks, such as Anglia Television's *Survival*, Thames Television's *The Benny Hill Show*, London Weekend's *Upstairs, Downstairs*, and Granada Television's *The Jewel in the Crown*.

ten over-the-air stations are available to metropolitan residents whereas only one or two (and sometimes none at all) reach small-town and rural dwellers.

Pluralism in Britain has been a success. When commercial broadcasting started there, it captured three-quarters of the audience, forcing the BBC to meet the competition by sharpening its scheduling strategies and paying more attention to popular tastes. Now the two major competing television services have about equal audience ratings. But the BBC maintains its dedication to offering alternatives to commercial programming and to serving cultural and intellectual minorities. BBC-1, its mass-appeal network, confronts the commercial competition, and BBC-2 aims at smaller, more specialized audiences. The BBC retains its monopoly on national and regional radio, operating four national networks plus regional services in Northern Ireland, Scotland, and Wales. Radio 1 features pop music, Radio 2 general middle-of-the-road programming, Radio 3 serious music and talk, and Radio 4 news and current affairs.

1.5 Legal Foundations

In the United States private owners operate the telecommunications facilities. In most other countries, the government retains ownership, especially of common carriers such as telephones, cable and microwave relay networks, and domestic satellites. Government post office, telephone, and telegraph agencies (PTTs) exercise central control. They often supply the broadcast transmitters and relay links even in countries where the programming functions remain in the hands of private entrepreneurs or nonprofit public corporations. The more nongovernment ownership and operation prevail, the more elaborate the domestic laws regulating transmitter licensing

and the conduct of telecommunication services tend to be.

International Law   Because radio waves do not respect political boundaries, the world has to cooperate in regulating use of the spectrum. Most nations belong to *The International Telecommunication Union* (ITU), an agency of the United Nations with headquarters in Geneva, Switzerland. Nations join the ITU by means of treaties, after which they meet in periodic conferences to agree on ITU regulations. Members do not surrender their individual sovereignty, so the ITU has no means of enforcing its rules. Nations may withhold agreement by making a "comment" on any rule they oppose, have doubts about, or simply do not understand.

The ITU adopts both wire and wireless communication rules, standardizing terminology and procedures for international information exchange. For example, it assigns each country specific letters of the alphabet as initial letters of station call signs (which is why U.S. broadcast call letters always being with *K* or *W*). Most important is the ITU's agreements as to which frequencies will carry which types of service. ITU members agree to *allocate* specific bands of frequencies to specific services. For example, AM radio, FM radio, television, and broadcast satellite services each have been allocated their own bands of frequencies, in accordance with the needs of each service. Frequencies within these bands are then allotted to specific countries, each of which *assigns* channels within its allotted bands to individual stations or locations.*

---

*The high-frequency (HF or short-wave) bands used by governments for international broadcasting are exceptions to the allotment procedure because of their transborder nature and because transmitters must switch channels frequently to match changing ionospheric conditions. Each country chooses its own short-wave channels within the allocated bands, advising the ITU's International Frequency Registration Board (IFRB) of these choices.

The ITU staff in Geneva makes no rules on its own initiative; it must await agreements reached by member states at regional or world conferences. In 1979 the ITU held a World Administrative Radio Conference (WARC) of great importance, addressing fundamental broadcasting regulations for the first time in twenty years. The more than seventy new sovereign countries that had joined the ITU since the 1959 WARC had their first opportunity to claim a share of the frequency pie. At the time, the developing countries used only an estimated 7 percent of the spectrum, yet represented 75 percent of the world's population. Of course these pre-industrial countries were not yet ready to expand their spectrum use dramatically, but they approached WARC '79 expecting to obtain guarantees that their future needs would be met as their telecommunications systems developed.

During preparations for WARC '79, observers anticipated that it might degenerate into a fruitless wrangle between haves and have-nots. However, true to ITU tradition (it is sometimes cited as the most pragmatically successful agency of world cooperation), conferees managed to compromise on most points of dispute — no mean achievement, considering that the conference debated fifteen thousand proposals. But WARC '79 may have only postponed the eventual showdown, for actual implementation of most of its agreements had to await further conferences scheduled throughout the 1980s.

Domestic Laws   Broadcasting in America falls under federal jurisdiction because U.S. law classifies it as a form of interstate commerce, in accordance with the Constitution (Article I, Section 8). However, national policy favors local rather than centralized station ownership and control. This policy reflects another constitutional provision, the First Amendment, which implicitly calls for the maximum possible diversity of information sources. In contrast, most countries prefer centralized control, with emphasis on national networks of repeater stations rather than on autonomous local stations, with or without network affiliation, but always with a residue of local programming.

U.S. regulation also reflects the Constitution's concern for due process of law. Broadcasters can invoke an elaborate machinery for review and appeal to preserve their freedom of expression and to protect themselves from arbitrary government action. Appeals can take years to settle. Again, the U.S. regulatory scheme differs from that of most other countries. It must deal with thousands of autonomous private licensees, each of whom can invoke rights to rehearings and appeals. American broadcasting has therefore spawned a legal library of amazing proportions. The basic law, the Communications Act of 1934, runs to about 150 pages, but Federal Communications Commission (FCC) regulations, based upon the act, occupy over two thousand pages, filling four volumes of the *Code of Federal Regulations*. The FCC's published decisions filled nearly 150 fat legal volumes by the end of 1984. Federal courts of appeal and the Supreme Court have handed down hundreds of legal opinions, and congressional committees annually publish numerous transcripts of hearings on electronic media issues.

Domestic broadcasting laws of most other countries are relatively brief and simple. For example, the charters and laws establishing the two British broadcasting authorities, the BBC and IBA, could be bound into a slim volume. Moreover, Britain has no written constitution to serve as the basis of court challenges to alleged curtailments of licensee freedoms. The two British authorities, the BBC and the IBA, can act quite arbitrarily, carrying out most functions without benefit of public hearings, reviews of decisions, or appeals to the courts. Autonomous, private licensees that control both programming and transmission functions of individual stations simply do not exist in Britain, or in most other countries, as they do in the United States.

In Europe, broadcasting cases infrequently arise in the courts, and those that do usually center on fundamental constitutional issues. In Italy, for example, the official broadcasting organization, RAI, went to court to suppress unauthorized private cable television operations that cropped up in the early 1970s. The case went eventually to the Constitutional Court, which ruled in 1975 that the RAI's legal monopoly covered only *network* broadcasting and so could not prevent local cable or broadcast operations by private owners. This ruling opened the floodgates to thousands of private radio stations and hundreds of private television stations. Ten years later they still operated without benefit of formal regulation, though a new comprehensive Italian broadcasting law was imminent.

Statutes adopted to govern only POBS, as this example suggests, proved inadequate to deal with the new technology and newly aroused interest in privately controlled broadcasting. In the United States, the FCC for years devised patchwork rules for cable television under the 1934 act. Finally Congress passed a special statute, the Cable Communication Policy Act of 1984. Similarly, Britain adopted a new cable act in 1984. Many countries, however, still wrestle with the problems of adapting their laws to deal with new technologies.

1.6 Access to the Air

People in most developed countries have equal access to such common-carrier facilities as the telephone, usually at fixed, government-approved rates. However, broadcasting is not a common carrier, and its power to inform, persuade, and cultivate values has always made access to the airwaves a jealously guarded prerogative. Traditionally, access has been reserved for professional broadcasters, for experts on subjects of public interest, for people currently in the news, and for politicians.

Political Access   In political systems that allow free elections, broadcasting plays a vital informational role. It can also pose a threat if the party in power takes advantage of its incumbency to monopolize broadcasting access, converting it into an instrument of political control. One critical task of regulation in democracies is to devise ways of preserving fairness in the political uses of broadcasting without inhibiting its legitimate role of informing the electorate.

U.S. law deals with the problem of candidate access in terms of *equal opportunities*. A station may (with some exceptions) give or sell unlimited time to a candidate, but doing so obligates the station to grant equal opportunities to all other candidates for the same office. Thus the weakest candidates and parties have a right to the same broadcast opportunities as the strongest, provided they can raise equal amounts of money to buy time. Moreover, the law requires stations to give or sell federal candidates "reasonable" amounts of time.

Few other countries allow candidates and parties to exploit broadcasting to this extent. Great Britain, for example, severely limits election broadcasting, emphasizing parties rather than individual candidates (in keeping with the parliamentary system, in which party membership plays a more important role than in the United States). The two broadcasting authorities, the BBC and the IBA, confer annually with representatives of the political parties to set up ground rules. In the recent past, only parties offering fifty or more parliamentary candidates have been granted television time. Each party is granted from one to five free broadcasts of five to ten minutes' duration.

Individual candidates may not make a broadcast campaign appearance "in which any other rival candidate neither takes part nor consents to its going forward without his taking part." Thus a candidate can forestall opponents' broadcasts simply by refusing to appear on the same platform with them. The British people thus escape the interminable merchandising of candidates so wearisome to American audiences. Moreover, British candidates have no need to collect huge sums to pay for broadcast advertising.

However, in Britain as in the United States, rules for candidates and incumbents do not inhibit coverage of them in legitimate news programs. In such appearances, journalists rather than politicians choose the formats and run the shows. Journalists must, however, use professional news judgment, taking care to give fair opportunities for all sides of issues to be aired.

Most continental European systems, though similarly restrictive about candidate appearances, are less successful in maintaining neutrality, even though it may be mandated by law. Political parties can often evade neutrality requirements by controlling appointments to the state broadcasting services, enabling infiltration by politically motivated personnel. When in 1985 Italy's RAI proposed a nighttime *nonpartisan* newscast, members of the ruling party opposed introduction of such a novel program. In France the party in power has long regarded the right to appoint the heads of the state networks and of the broadcast news organizations as one of the normal spoils of office. A comprehensive new French statute adopted in 1982 tried to eliminate this political sore-point by barring partisan programs from state-operated networks, but be-

cause of strong political controls over the broadcasting authority that appoints heads of services, it seemed to have only limited success.

In an attempt to achieve impartiality, the West German states use a system called *Proporz* ("proportion"), which requires that appointments to key broadcasting posts be apportioned so as to mirror the political complexion of the state legislatures. For example, the chief executive officer of a broadcasting unit would belong to the ruling party, and that officer's deputy would belong to the main opposition party. Italy's state-operated service, RAI, uses a similar balancing system, called *lottizzazione* (allotment). This kind of calculated balancing errs in the opposite direction: it may ensure political neutrality, but it also tends to promote undue reluctance to come to grips with political issues.

Public Access   During the restless 1960s, people increasingly began to question the traditional barriers that denied the general public access to broadcasting. They reasoned that if the electromagnetic spectrum really does constitute a common resource of all people, then more people should have access to it.

Abetted by numerous domestic and external pirate stations, the access movement became very widespread and vocal in the 1970s — so much so that the United Nations Educational, Scientific and Cultural Organization (UNESCO) commissioned a study to analyze the movement in several Western countries. The study identified five groups, in addition to minority party politicians, that demanded access to accomplish various ends:

• Social reformers, to influence public opinion
• Artists, to add to the media that could be used for self-expression

• Educators, to try out innovative teaching tools

• Private entrepreneurs, to capitalize on the technology for personal financial gain

• Futurists, to experiment with the brave new world of innovative technology

All these access seekers, said the editor of the UNESCO study, shared "a common mood and tone, at once romantic, radical, and missionary" (Berrigan, 1977: 15).

Access seekers could hardly expect the highly centralized systems of Europe to open their studios for messages of less than national importance. Development of local or community stations therefore became a goal of the access movement (community stations being smaller in scope than local stations). Only individual stations originating local programs can answer the needs of local advertisers, politicians, and other individuals. As one outcome of the access movement, community broadcast stations and cable systems have grown tremendously in recent years. France, for example, legitimized over a thousand small, privately owned FM stations following passage of its 1982 broadcasting law. Many started as pirate operations, subject to rigorous suppression by the French government. Italy has a flourishing private radio and television industry, the legacy of the previously mentioned 1975 court decision barring RAI from closing down nonnetwork private broadcasters and cable systems (§1.6).

Even some authoritarian regimes have responded to the demand for local outlets. China, noted for highly centralized control of broadcasting and widespread use of wired radio speaker boxes (65 percent of all receivers), has begun regionalizing and localizing its broadcast services. In much of the Third World, however, lack of trained personnel, tribalism, and the ever-present threat of political subversion tend to keep program control centralized in the capital city, with provincial transmitters functioning only as relays for the national network.

Group Access   Some countries seek to ensure access, if not to every individual, at least to every significant social group. One way of widening representation is to give groups a role in the national controlling bodies. The Netherlands has gone farther, actually turning over operation of most programming to social groups. Eight major sociopolitical groups share most of the time on the national facilities. Six have common religious or political bonds; two are nonideological. Even very small constituencies such as immigrant workers or people from former Dutch colonies can obtain small amounts of airtime. As a by-product of this system, groups have no obligation to practice fairness in their programming. Since each group has its own time on the air, each can promote its own viewpoint to the exclusion of all others.

Associations seeking recognition as regular daily broadcasters in the Netherlands set up nonprofit corporations, obtaining government-allotted funds from receiver license fees and generating income from their membership in the form of subscriptions to program guides. The associations sell no airtime but can sell advertising in their program guides (the system carries a limited amount of broadcast advertising, handled by a separate official agency). A coordinating unit, known as NOS, provides common studio facilities for the groups.

1.7 Economics

Economics is second only to politics in determining the nature of a country's telecommunication system. No country can afford the entire range of services that technology could provide if expense were no object.

Facilities   The world has some 220 broadcasting systems, nearly a quarter of which do not include television.* The number of transmitters and receivers within each system varies widely relative to population size. The United States leads in television-set penetration, as noted earlier, with 603 television sets per thousand population. Among other major countries, leaders in set penetration are Canada (493 television sets per thousand), the United Kingdom (399), Australia (387), Austria (375), Sweden (375), Denmark (355), and West Germany (354). U.S. leadership can be ascribed in part to economics — high living standards that make sets affordable to most of the population. However, another factor also plays a role: strong motivation for set purchasing, aroused by highly attractive mass appeal programming. Additionally, the national policy favoring numerous localized stations has stimulated interest by enabling some types of local access.

In Third World countries where low purchasing power, lack of attractive indigenous programming, and paucity of local stations minimize set-buying incentives, investment in transmitters and production facilities can be extremely uneconomic. It costs just as much in program and transmission expenses to reach a few scattered individuals as to reach the total population within a transmitter's reach. A poorly developed communications infrastructure (electric power, telephones, and interconnection facilities for networks) further impedes broadcasting growth in many Third World countries.

Revenue Sources   Most broadcasting systems depend primarily on government fund-

---

*This enumeration, based on listings in the *World Radio-TV Handbook* (Frost, 1985), includes dependencies as well as sovereign nations. Most of the fifty-one systems without TV are on small islands.

ing. Authoritarian regimes regard government support as natural, for in their view the media exist to serve the state. Third World countries, even if they would prefer to rely on advertising or receiver license fees to finance broadcasting, usually must use government funding because nongovernment sources, in the absence of mass purchasing power, cannot generate enough revenue. In contrast, industrialized democracies usually take pains to avoid direct government funding so as to insulate broadcasting from political control.

Government-imposed receiver license fees can provide such insulation. In Europe, where fees are almost universal, color-television-set licenses in 1984 ran from the equivalent of about $45 to as much as $100 a year. Receiver licensing imposes on fee-supported broadcasting organizations a strong sense of public responsibility. From the public's viewpoint, fees distribute the cost of a system fairly, provided the social setting encourages voluntary compliance and there is an efficient and cost-effective method of collection. At best, collection and enforcement are relatively costly. Great Britain has one of the more efficient systems, using the postal service as a collection agency; about 8 percent of the revenue goes to defray collection and enforcement expenses. NHK, Japan's equivalent of the BBC, is unique in employing its own collectors. They call personally on set owners and have little difficulty persuading the law-abiding Japanese to pay up.

With the advent of color television and its high production costs, systems relying on fees found themselves in financial trouble. As set penetration reached the saturation point, the revenue curve leveled off while operational costs continued to rise. Fees lag behind need because voter resistance makes increases a touchy political issue. Politicians, who always control fee levels, therefore delay authorizing increases as long as possible. Some European fee-supported systems have had to cut back production or turn to advertising for at least partial support. Even the staunchest holdouts against broadcast advertising welcome its support for modernized cable, subscription television, and direct-broadcast satellite services, while continuing to insulate POBS from the commercial marketplace.

As for the communist world, Marxist doctrine frowns on advertising as a capitalistic device for exploiting workers. In practice, however, communist countries find broadcast commercials useful for moving consumer goods that sometimes pile up because of central-planning errors. In the West, liberal and Socialist political parties usually oppose broadcast advertising and conservative parties favor it. Thus a Conservative British Parliament voted for the IBA's advertising-supported services, whereas the Labor opposition voted against it; in the United States, Democrats have been more generous in voting funds for public (that is, noncommercial) broadcasting than have Republicans. However, France, always a maverick, introduced private station ownership under a Socialist government; and rightist French politicians want to sell off the government television networks as well, to private businesses.

Founders of early national broadcast systems often looked toward the United States for the prime example of advertising's adverse social consequences. They abhorred the American system's permissiveness and what they viewed as its advertising excesses. Newspaper owners strongly opposed broadcast commercialism, especially at the local and regional levels. Some countries initially approved television advertising only on condition that part of the proceeds would be turned over to the press as compensation for lost advertising revenue.

In Europe, only Belgium, Denmark, Norway, and Sweden still bar advertising from POBS. Most European countries that do accept commercials try to insulate their programming from advertiser influence by strict regulations, including a ban on sponsorship* and limits on the percentage of revenue that may be derived from advertising. For example, in the early 1980s, the Italian parliament allowed RAI to rely on advertising for only 23.8 percent of its budget. Aside from a few transnational commercial broadcasters (discussed in §1.10), Spain permitted the highest proportion of advertising revenue, 75 percent. The public-service components of pluralistic systems also moderate the impact of commercialism. Thus Britain's BBC bans advertising, whereas the IBA companies totally rely on it.

Most European countries further limit the intrusion of commercials by scheduling them all in a few special time blocks devoted exclusively to advertising, leaving the rest of the schedule free of interruption. And Italy, France, and Holland, for example, have still another method of keeping the advertiser at arm's length: they create official advertising agencies with monopolies on the sale of commercial time.

Transborder Advertising   Severe European restrictions on advertising left a large, unsatisfied commercial demand in many countries. In response, two external advertising-supported sources of programs emerged: *offshore pirates* and *transborder commercial stations.*

Because of its permissive system, its ample localism, and its free-enterprise advertising, the United States has not experienced

---

*While Europeans are unanimous in forbidding out-and-out commercial sponsorship (in which advertisers schedule commercials within their own programs), there is a trend toward more liberal rules governing *program underwriting*, a limited form of sponsorship familiar to American viewers of public broadcasting.

pirate invasions of its airwaves except occasionally by youthful pranksters. Europe's less permissive systems have been plagued by pirates operating stations on small ships and offshore World War II forts in the English Channel and North Sea. Transmitting from beyond the territorial limits of their target countries, they violate licensing, copyright, and music performance laws with impunity. The first offshore pirate began broadcasting from a ship anchored between Denmark and Sweden in 1958. Often financed by U.S. companies and always frankly imitative of American pop-music formats, advertising techniques, and promotional gimmicks, the pirates quickly captured large and devoted youthful audiences. Some pirates made a lot of money, but only at great risk. They suffered from storms, raids by rival pirates, and finally from stringent laws penalizing land-based firms for supplying the pirates or doing any other business with them. Nevertheless, in spite of punitive laws, offshore pirates still crop up even today.

The pirates whetted appetites for pop music and radio advertising, forcing national systems to adapt their programming to hitherto ignored musical tastes and to reexamine their opposition to commercials. The BBC, as one example, reorganized its national radio network offerings, adding a pop-music network (Radio 1) imitative of the pirates. Some of the offshore disc jockeys ended up working for the BBC and other established broadcasters. After Holland revised its broadcasting system as a result of pirate influence, two pirate organizations even moved ashore to become legitimate broadcasters.

Several ministates in Europe have long capitalized on the demand for broadcast advertising, furnishing transborder commercial services beamed to neighboring countries. Like the pirates, they employ popular music formats, often supplemented by objective news programs, welcome in countries where the ruling political parties dominate broadcast news. The Grand Duchy of Luxembourg, at the intersection of Belgium, France, and Germany, has an ideal location for a peripheral station and earns much of its national income from international commercial broadcasting. *Radio-Télé-Luxembourg* (RTL) broadcasts commercial radio services in Dutch, English, French, and German and television services in German; it also plans direct broadcast satellite television aimed at Western Europe. Other notable transborder commercial stations operate in the German Saar (Europe No. 1), Monaco (Radio Monte Carlo), Cyprus (Radio Monte Carlo East), Morocco (Radio Mediterranean International), Yugoslavia (Studio Koper/Radio Capodistra), and Gabon (Africa No. 1).

Program Economics   Television consumes expensive program materials at such a rate that most countries, even highly industrialized ones with strong economies, cannot afford to program several different television networks exclusively with homegrown productions. In Europe, this shortfall has stimulated cable television growth, for in many small countries a half-dozen foreign signals can be picked up and redelivered via cable. Shortages also account for the lively international trade in syndicated programs. The bulk of these programs comes from the United States, and a relatively large number from Britain. However, communist and Third World countries increasingly display their wares at international program fairs. Most countries try to limit U.S. imports, but the quantity, low cost, and mass appeal of American programs make abstinence difficult.

One solution devised to ease the problem of program shortage, other than commercial syndication, is transnational sharing. For example, the European Broadcasting Union, an association of official broadcasting services in Europe and nearby countries, facilitates program sharing through *Eurovision*. It arranges regular exchanges among its members, primarily of news, sports, and entertainment items. In 1982 Eurovision transmitted nearly two thousand hours of television programming, including more than seven thousand news items (Eugster, 1983: 224–225). The East European communist countries have a similar association with their own program cooperative, *Intervision*. The East-West groups exchange programs with each other, most of the material flowing from Eurovision to Intervision. African, Arabic-speaking, Caribbean, and Asia-Pacific broadcasting unions also exist, but they have not yet developed their program exchanges to anywhere near the level of the Eurovision-Intervision operations.

1.8 Geography

A nation's size, shape, population distribution, and nearness to neighbors are factors that determine its broadcasting coverage. Efficient coverage of a country depends on the country's shape as well as its size. The continental United States, for example, consists of a relatively compact, unified land mass, surrounded mostly by large bodies of water — favorable factors from the viewpoint of broadcast coverage. The outlying states of Alaska and Hawaii, however, had to await satellite relays to enjoy coverage simultaneous with the rest of the country. Contrast the geography of Japan, an archipelago of mountainous islands spread over two thousand miles of ocean. Indonesia, another archipelago, presents a still more forbidding challenge to efficient coverage. It consists of six thousand or so widely scattered inhabited islands. Such difficult coverage problems could not be solved satisfactorily prior to satellite distribution of programs.*

---

*Indonesia launched *Palapa*, its own domestic satellite, in 1976, the first Third World country to have such a facility.

Geography insulates most American listeners and viewers from spillover programs originating in foreign countries, and relatively few of them listen to foreign stations on shortwave receivers. Treaties with Canada, Mexico, and the Caribbean islands minimize transborder interference. In recent years, however, Cuba has announced plans to put 500-kilowatt AM stations on the air, in defiance of international agreements. Such high-powered signals would interfere with U.S. stations in Florida and even cause skywave interference to stations as distant as Iowa (NAB, 1982).

Geography both helps and hinders European broadcasting. National systems suffer a great deal of interference from neighbors because of proximity and their numerous transmitters. On the other hand, as previously noted, the smaller countries count on foreign stations to supplement their own programming. Spillover sometimes creates odd situations, as in divided Berlin, whose West German television reaches into surrounding East Germany. Citizens on either side of the Berlin Wall enjoy each others' programs, though their governments are politically at odds and though they need to buy converters to match the different color systems. East German authorities, after trying fruitlessly to stop their citizens from viewing Western programs, have resigned themselves to living with the electronic invasion.

Because most of Canada's population lives along its border with the United States, Canada is ideally situated to pick up American radio and television signals. In addition, Canadian cable television companies deliver American programs to their subscribers, with the result that Canada has become one of the world's most cabled countries (about 60-percent penetration). Resenting the dominance of U.S. culture, Canada imposes quotas on the amount of syndicated programming that Canadian broadcasters and cable operators may import.

1.9 Programs and Schedules

One of the results of broadcasting's techno-economic and social nature is the use of the same basic program formats throughout the world. News, commentary, music, drama, variety, studio games, sports events — these genres appeal to people everywhere. However, there are marked differences in the details of program content, in the balance among program types, and in the length of program schedules from one country to another.

News and Public Affairs   National differences are especially evident in the treatment of news and public affairs. Daily news presentation is one of the most universally popular programs. However, each system has its own version of what has taken place. Parochialism, chauvinism, and ideological biases affect the choice, treatment, and timing of news stories.

TV Guide once compared a single week's television news as seen by six widely scattered systems. Not unexpectedly, each country stressed its own national happenings, few of which held the slightest interest for the rest of the world. When treating the same international story, each saw the event in a different light. For example, the American networks reported vigorous debates within the United States on a controversial arms-limitation summit meeting between the two superpowers. Viewers in the USSR heard only statements from the American Communist Party leader, who said there was no U.S. opposition to the treaty. Chinese television acted as if the meeting had never taken place, only to show the opening session a week later. Likewise, on the night Israeli television showed its basketball team defeating the USSR in a championship match, Soviet television showed an earlier contest between two East European teams. As for domestic news events, variety prevailed:

U.S. television news covered in depth American's energy crunch. Egyptian TV news pursued the runoff elections for the Egyptian parliament. Israeli TV news focused on a member of the Nigerian mission to the United Nations caught smuggling arms into Israel on behalf of the Palestine Liberation Organization. On Japanese TV, the major domestic news story was the payoff scandal rocking the Japanese parliament . . . Soviet TV news was fascinated by the marathon ordeal of Russian cosmonauts orbiting in the Salyut 6 space lab. Even China had a story to cover: the Second Session of the Fifth National People's Congress.

Yet no one — including the U.S. TV news — devoted anything but minimal coverage to the major domestic stories of any of the other five nations that week. (Kowet, 1979)

Third World leaders tend to take the same approach to news as the communist countries do. Having no need to compete with alternate domestic news sources, Third World journalists can afford to ignore timeliness, human interest, and Western news values. Political correctness and educational values come first. They play down or omit stories about crime, accidents, civil disorders, and the personal lives of political figures. If Third World governments were to allow broadcast employees to report and edit according to Western standards, they reason, the news could become depressingly downbeat, loaded with reports on food shortages, crop failures, black markets, industrial mismanagement, official corruption, breakdowns in public services, urban blight, and all the other horrendous problems that plague the less developed nations. Instead, most Third World leaders expect their journalists to look for news, or to devise news treatments, supportive of the government, praising its leaders, heralding the nation's accomplishments, and urging audiences to work hard at nation building.

Program Balance   Audiences everywhere prefer light entertainment to more serious content; accordingly, entertainment dominates most schedules. But aside from the United States, most industrialized nations regulate broadcasting to ensure a certain balance between light entertainment and news, information, culture, and education. Third World nations find regulating program balance more difficult because of the paucity of home-grown productions. This shortage makes inexpensive shows imported from abroad hard to resist, even though they may throw schedules out of balance and play up alien cultures.

U.S. dominance in the international syndication market has led to charges of "cultural imperialism." Spokespersons for Third World cultures, some of which are uncertain even of survival in the modern age, profess to find imported entertainment especially damaging. The images and values depicted in *Dallas* and *Three's a Crowd*, for example, tend to undermine indigenous cultures; moreover, every program purchased from abroad denies indigenous artists and craftspersons opportunities to develop their own talents and skills. Nor does the Third World monopolize these apprehensions; even highly developed nations with their own flourishing production resources impose import quotas, putting a ceiling on the amount of entertainment their national systems may import from the United States, as in the previously mentioned example of Canada.

Schedules   Eighteen- to twenty-four-hour broadcast days, though commonplace in the United States, occur in very few other countries. Many radio services go on the air for a short morning segment, take a midmorning break before a midday segment, and take another midafternoon break before the evening segment. Television services usually commence late in the afternoon and go off the air by 11:00 P.M. Even in such a highly developed system as Britain's, the BBC did not begin

twenty-four-hour radio until 1979, when Radio 2 filled in the previously blank hours of 2:00 to 5:00 A.M. "Breakfast television" began in Britain in 1983, when both the BBC and a new IBA-franchised commercial company began offering early-morning programs.

Audience Research   All broadcasting systems agree in principle on the importance of using audience research as a management tool in making program and schedule decisions. Not all systems, however, can afford continuous, systematic audience studies. The more a service depends on advertising for revenue, however, the more likely it is to allot funds for audience measurement.

U.S. commercial broadcasters, extremely research conscious, spend large sums on audience studies, but they emphasize audience size and composition more than audience opinions and reactions. Most foreign systems put emphasis on qualitative as well as on quantitative measurements. In Britain, as in many other developed countries, the law requires broadcasting authorities to conduct research on audience likes and dislikes as well as on audience size. As noted previously, the BBC stressed Appreciation Indexes from the outset of its in-house research. A survey of fifteen European systems revealed that two-thirds of them measure television audience appreciation (McCain, 1985: 75).

In the USSR, the government once frowned on social research, of which audience research is an applied example. It took for granted that whatever it put on the air would be heard or seen and sufficiently understood (Mickiewicz, 1981: 6). During the 1970s, however, Soviet authorities increased both the amount and quality of their audience research. More attractive programming seems to have followed, evidence of the role audience research can play in shaping broadcasting output, even under authoritarian systems.

Exhibit 1.3   Major External Broadcasters

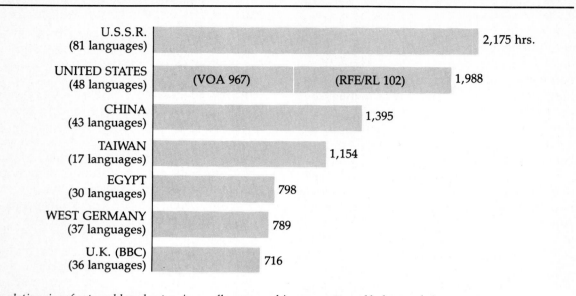

The relative size of external broadcasters is usually measured in aggregate weekly hours of air time in all languages, without taking into consideration repeat broadcasts. Adding the outputs of Radio Martí, a special service aimed at Cuba, and RIAS (Radio in the American Sector of Berlin), a special service aimed at East Germany, increases the U.S. total hours to a figure well above the USSR total.

Source: U.S. Advisory Commission on Public Diplomacy, *1985 Report* (Government Printing Office, Washington, D.C., 1985): 23.

1.10 Transborder Broadcasting

Broadcasting introduced a potent new factor in relations among nations. Never before had it been so easy to cross national boundaries and talk directly to a nation's people. Broadcasting can inform and persuade people in societies impossible to penetrate with in-person messages. Using mostly short-wave radio (because of its long range), *external broadcasting* — that is, official programming aimed at foreign countries, — has become an important ideological weapon, both during war and in times of peace. More than 80 countries operate external broadcasting services, though many

have little more than symbolic importance. In 1984, the USSR topped all external broadcasters in weekly time on the air, as shown in Exhibit 1.3.

External Service Origins   Colonial commitments abroad prompted the first external services. Holland and Germany started theirs in 1929, and France in 1931. After experimenting for several years, Britain's BBC formally launched its Empire Service in 1932. Broadcast entirely in English, it sought to maintain home-country ties with colonial expatriates and people in the dominions (independent ex-colonies such as Canada and

Australia). Later on, the use of foreign languages in external services shifted the focus toward diplomatic and propaganda roles. The BBC launched its first foreign language external broadcasts in 1938 on the eve of World War II, countering Italian radio propaganda in Arabic to the Near East. Soon Britain and the Axis powers became locked in a deadly war of words, using many languages.

The United States added its voice to the war when President Franklin D. Roosevelt appointed a popular radio newscaster, Elmer Davis, to head the Office of War Information (OWI). As a component of the OWI, the Voice of America (VOA) went on the air in February 1942. Wary of creating a propaganda agency that might be turned against the American people by the U.S. party in power, Congress forbade the VOA to release its programs in the United States, though anyone with a short-wave radio can pick up VOA programs aimed at overseas listeners. There is no such proscription in Britain; the BBC's external service, coming as it does from a nongovernment source, welcomes domestic listeners to its 24-hour World Service in English, which can be heard in Britain on regular AM radio sets.

The USSR, not having a colonial empire when broadcasting began, had different motives than the West for starting an external service. The Soviets were anxious to explain their recent revolution to sympathizers in Western Europe and to legitimize their regime among the family of nations. From the outset they recognized the importance of broadcasting in foreign languages as a means of gaining and influencing friends abroad. Radio Moscow began regular external services in 1929.

Voice of America   Today the VOA functions as an arm of the United States Information Agency (USIA), the federal unit responsible for informational and cultural contacts with the rest of the world as well as for the official international exchange of teachers, artists, students, and so on. In 1985, the VOA broadcast in over forty languages in addition to English, ranging from Albanian to Vietnamese (see Exhibit 1.3). Programs originate in Washington, D.C., and are sent to VOA short-wave transmitters in Greenville, North Carolina, and several secondary U.S. sites. Programs go overseas via both short-wave transmitters and leased satellite facilities. The VOA leases sites in about a dozen foreign countries where it maintains transmitters for rebroadcasting programs to listeners in nearby areas.

VOA programs use most of the formats familiar in domestic radio, including even a telephone talk show.* Entertainment programs feature materials about American culture. News and public affairs items naturally reflect official U.S. policies, but for the sake of credibility the VOA tries to observe the spirit of its original 1942 manifesto: "Daily at this time we shall speak to you about America. . . . The news may be good or bad. We shall tell you the truth." Despite some lapses for expediency's sake, truth-telling continues as VOA policy. Its news staff, which has civil-service status, has a keen sense of professionalism. It vigorously resists occasional efforts by partisan officials appointed by the U.S. party in power to bend the truth to suit political objectives.

The Republican administration that took over in Washington in 1981 called for vigorous exploitation of the VOA as a propaganda organ. Implementation of this policy caused dissension; some staff people felt that new

---

*The VOA launched "Talk to America," a 50-minute monthly call-in program hosted by Larry King, a Mutual radio network talk-show host, in October 1984. King interviewed ex-president Gerald Ford in the first program. During the program the VOA telephones, at its own expense, foreign callers who have left their numbers with an answering machine located in Washington.

Exhibit 1.4   Voice of America

Voice of America master control panel, which visitors to the VOA have been shown since 1954. It was due to be replaced in 1986 with a modern, solid-state, computerized facility, part of the Republican administration's multi-million-dollar updating of VOA facilities at home and abroad.

Source: Courtesy Voice of America.

directives tended to undermine VOA credibility as a reliable information source and as an effective external service. In keeping with their aggressive information policy, the Republicans undertook a major VOA improvement and expansion plan, committing $1.5 billion to updating long-neglected equipment and to building new facilities. They planned to add a dozen languages and to upgrade and increase the number of overseas relay transmitters, especially in the Caribbean and Central America, where the VOA has installed powerful standard AM transmitters in order to reach listeners with no access to short-wave receivers.

Because of its short range, television does not lend itself to external broadcasting. Instead, the USIA attempts to persuade the domestic television services of foreign countries to carry USIA-furnished programs. In the 1980s the agency took an innovative approach by setting up Worldnet — daily features, news feeds, and satellite teleconferences that enable journalists in foreign countries to interview important U.S. officials by satellite interconnection. The resulting coverage of U.S. official viewpoints in foreign media afforded more effective exposure than that arranged by direct USIA placement of tapes and films. USIA also gives visiting journalists generous assistance in sending their coverage of events in the United States back to their home media. It frequently arranges U.S. visits and tours for foreign broadcasters and other media people, enabling them to witness American elections, for example. In 1985 the VOA considerably expanded the training services it offers to foreign broadcasters — a device used by all the major external services to exert indirect influence.

Direct-broadcast satellites (DBS) could presumably enable a nation to deliver both radio and television programs to listeners and viewers anywhere in the world without intermediary relays. Many nations, both East and West, have expressed concern in the United Nations about this possibility, which they regard as much more threatening to national sovereignty than short-wave radio. They demand the right to prevent such electronic invasions, whereas the United States argues almost single-handedly for a "free-flow" policy. However, DBS technology, at least for the near future, requires expensive reception equipment and conspicuous receiving antennas. Presumably, a government wishing to suppress satellite reception of foreign programs could spot the antennas and take action against their owners.

Surrogate Domestic Services   In addition to conventional external services, the United States engages in a special type of external broadcasting designed to simulate domestic services within target countries. Authorities in communist countries censor their own domestic media, withholding or distorting information unfavorable to communist regimes or favorable to the West. Surrogate services seek to act as uncensored substitutes for domestic services, representing the sending countries' views of the facts. The two main U.S. services of this type, Radio Liberty (RL) and Radio Free Europe (RFE), aim at the USSR and the East European Communist states, respectively. They have studios and transmitters in Munich, West Germany, and additional transmitters in Israel, Portugal, and Spain.

RFE/RL originated after World War II, covertly supported by the Central Intelligence Agency. They aimed at stirring up dissent within, and undermining the credibility of, communist regimes. After the CIA connection became known publicly in 1973, Congress created a special agency, the Board for International Broadcasting (BIB), to supervise the operations. Congress funds them openly with annual appropriations.

RFE/RL scriptwriters rely on extensive research libraries in Munich. These libraries subscribe to many kinds of communist publications, obtain transcripts of communist domestic broadcasts, and collect information from travelers and defectors. Broadcasting entirely in the languages of their target countries, RFE/RL cover domestic and foreign news from the target countries' perspective. In contrast, the VOA covers U.S. news and foreign news from the United States' perspective.

The USSR deeply resents RFE/RL, claiming they violate international law by interfering in the internal affairs of the communist states. Congress has been of two minds about these operations. Some legislators feel they represent a counterproductive hangover from the 1950s Cold War. Others argue, as did the Republican administration of the 1980s, that the West should vigorously counteract the domestic propaganda of communist regimes on their home ground and help keep alive the spirit of dissent among their citizens.

In 1985 the United States introduced a new surrogate service, Radio Martí, aimed at giving the people of Cuba news and information free of Castro-regime bias. Anti-Marxist Cuban exiles in South Flordia zealously supported the Radio Martí scheme, but it ran into opposition from more objective observers. The latter contended that the multimillion dollar radio operation aimed merely at gaining the expensive satisfaction of tweaking Castro's nose. After all, they argued, the Cuban people can get ample outside news from regular VOA Latin American services as well as from U.S. commercial Spanish-language stations in south Florida, which are easily picked up on the island.* Moreover, U.S. broadcasters opposed Radio Martí, fearing that Castro would retaliate by stepping up interference with U.S. stations, already a problem in south Florida, where the FCC allowed some stations to increase their power to overcome Cuban interference.

After much debate, Congress declined to set up Radio Martí as an independent surrogate service like RFE/RL. Instead it was authorized as a special VOA service, transmitted from an existing VOA station at Marathon, in the Florida keys. Unlike other VOA services, however, Radio Martí has its own presidential advisory board. It started in May 1985, with an authorized staff strength of about 175. At first Castro reacted sharply, canceling an agreement to take back some unwanted Cuban immigrants. Later he ignored Radio Martí's existence. Supporters claim it has a strong effect, while opponents claim its only success has been to win an audience for an old Spanish-language soap opera. Some observers think that competition from Radio Martí has motivated the Castro regime to upgrade its own domestic services — in other words, that Cuban radio now benefits from inadvertent pluralism.

*See for example the arguments pro and con in a 1982 House Subcommittee on Communications hearing (USHR, 1982).

BBC   Foreign listeners generally regard the Voice Of America as a relatively objective source of news, but the BBC retains the highest credibility among external broadcasters. Throughout the world, listeners tune automatically to the BBC when in doubt about the authenticity of news sources. In times of local disorder, it is not uncommon for foreign government officials to turn to the BBC for vital information about the state of affairs in their own countries.

The BBC has a longer tradition than the VOA and greater insulation from government influence. Listeners know the VOA as a government agency, staffed by federal employees. Its news commentaries come from government spokespersons, whereas the BBC's come from university professors, newspaper correspondents, and other independent specialists speaking on their own behalf. True, the British Foreign Office reimburses the BBC for the cost of the External Services, but that ministry's main control over programming concerns only the choice of the languages used.

Radio Moscow   During the 1970s the Soviet Union forged ahead of the VOA to become the leading international broadcaster in terms of hours on the air (Exhibit 1.3). Radio Moscow uses fewer overseas relay stations than the major Western external broadcasters, though it does have one in Cuba aimed at the Americas. Radio Moscow, like the external services of all communist countries, tends to be relentlessly propagandistic. Western studies of audience reactions in a variety of countries always show Radio Moscow's appeal running well behind that of the BBC and the VOA. However, Moscow has tried to lighten the tone of its broadcasts. It initiated a 24-hour daily service in English, using the BBC's long-established title, "World Service." It departs from the traditionally solemn Soviet tone, even going so far as to make occasional jokes about itself.

Jamming   Ideally, truth should be the best rebuttal to propaganda. The truth often hurts both the teller and the listener, however, so nations sometimes resort to *jamming* foreign broadcasts instead of rebutting them. Jammers transmit programs or sheer noise on or near the offending program's channel, making listening difficult if not impossible. Communist countries jam more massively and persistently than any others, but most countries have occasionally resorted to jamming, despite its inefficiency and high cost.

Western sources estimated in the early 1970s that the USSR devoted three thousand transmitters to jamming operations, at an annual cost of $185 million. Willingness to devote so much equipment and money to jamming testifies to the effectiveness of external broadcasting, at least in the minds of communist authorities. But jamming never succeeds in completely overwhelming incoming signals:

The effectiveness of jamming varies: at times it can block a signal in a city and fail to do so a few miles away in the countryside; the use of high-power transmitters and several frequencies can overcome some jamming; and there are limited periods during the day when propagation conditions give a properly sited broadcaster virtual immunity. (President's Study Commission, 1973: 19)

The extent of jamming by the USSR and its allies serves as an East-West relations barometer. During the détente of the late 1970s, jamming almost ceased, only to soar again in 1980 with the Soviets' Afghanistan invasion and Solidarity's confrontation with the Polish government (the Solidarity issue gave RFE a wonderful opportunity to needle the Polish regime with news Poles could not obtain from their own domestic services). RFE/RL have al-ways been more subject to jamming than the VOA. News reports of the Polish turmoil, however, triggered jamming not only of VOA but of the BBC and West Germany's external services as well.

1.11 U.S. Dominance

Private U.S. program sources probably exercise far more influence on other countries than do the combined efforts of USIA and the surrogate services. The emergence of pay cable, over-the-air subscription television, and satellite-to-cable networks in Europe has created enormous new demands for program materials. This means new markets for American feature films and television series, exacerbating fears of American cultural domination.

As Europe began installing the new technologies, U.S. program providers started wheeling and dealing with large European publishing and telecommunication cartels, forming complex consortia to answer these new demands. Third World charges of U.S. cultural imperialism gained strength not only from the dominance of American programs but also from the worldwide impact of such American institutions and activities as its commercialism, its consumerism, its telecommunications manufacturing, its international news agencies, its RFE/RL broadcasts, its government-aid programs to developing countries, its invasion of foreign economies by multinational corporations, its preeminent position in maintaining data banks and controlling transborder data flows, and its dominant position as operator of Intelsat. The leading American critic of U.S. media behavior, Herbert I. Schiller, charged that

messages "made in America" radiate across the globe and serve as the ganglia of national power and expansionism. The ideological images of "have-not" states are increasingly in the custody of American informa- tion media. . . . The facilities and hardware of interna- tional information control are being grasped by a highly centralized communications complex, resident in the United States and largely unaccountable to its own population. (Schiller, 1971: 147)

Free Flow, Balanced Flow   U.S. policy ardently favors the *free flow* of communica- tions, both within and between countries. The phrase occurs in the 1946 United Nations Dec- laration on Freedom of Information: "All states should proclaim policies under which the free flow of information, within countries and across frontiers, will be protected." Free- dom of expression, a fundamental article of faith in American political philosophy, was in 1946 generally accepted as a sound principle. However, both the world and its means of communication have changed drastically since the UN voted to support that principle. Over seventy new nations have joined the UN, most of them extremely conscious of prior his- tories as colonial territories of the Western powers.

Third World nations complain bitterly that Western international news agencies domi- nate worldwide news flow. An estimated bil- lion people each day see and hear Associated Press stories, for example. Western editors and reporters, claim Third World critics, seek mainly negative stories in the less-developed countries, choosing riots, famines, natural dis- asters, and the antics of military dictators as far more colorful and interesting subjects than factories, dams, education, hospitals, agricul- ture, and the achievements of Third World intellectuals.

A United Nations bloc claiming nonalign- ment with either superpower is intensely pre- occupied with *neocolonialism*, which it sees as threatening to drag emergent countries back into dependent status. What value does free flow have for us, these countries ask, when it runs almost entirely in one direction — *from* the United States and a few other industrial-

ized countries *to* the Third World? We need not *free* flow but *balanced* flow, they say; we need news reporting that treats us qualita- tively fairly and quantitatively in proportion to our numerical significance. They demand ac- cess to the means of communication, charging that the West monopolizes access and uses the free-flow doctrine to maintain the status quo. As a former VOA officer summarized it, one- way flow means that

citizens of the less developed countries must depend on foreigners to a significant extent for the books they read, the television programs and films they watch, and the news stories they read. They rely on foreign foundations for scholarly research grants, depend on universities abroad for better-quality higher education, and, indeed, must even learn a foreign language, most often English, in order to avail themselves of desired information. (Read, 1976: 163)

UNESCO's Role   Third World opponents of the free-flow doctrine used their preponder- ance of votes to advance their views in the UN and in its specialized agencies, such as the In- ternational Telecommunication Union and the United Nations Educational, Scientific and Cultural Organization (UNESCO). The latter, which had made Third World communication a major subject of study and aid, became the main arena of debate.

After spending several years polishing draft documents, UNESCO adopted a resolu- tion in 1978 known as the Mass Media Decla- ration. Its intricate full title, "Declaration on Fundamental Principles Concerning the Con- tribution of the Mass Media to Strengthening Peace and International Understanding, to the Promotion of Human Rights and to Coun- tering Racialism, Apartheid and Incitement to War," was read by Western observers to mean that journalists should abandon professional objectivity in order to take active part in politi- cal disputes. In response to Western opposi- tion to implementation of the declaration, UNESCO set up a commission to attempt a definition of a *New World Information Order* (NWIO), a revised way of organizing and controlling the world's flow of news and of communications in general. Called the MacBride Commission, after its chairman, Sean Mac-Bride, a distinguished Irish statesman, it brought forth a report offering over 80 recommendations (UNESCO, 1980). They turned out to be relatively conciliatory, urging, for example, development of

• Third World broadcasting, especially localized radio
• National production capacity, to reduce dependence on syndicated material from foreign sources
• Mechanisms for dealing with consumer complaints about advertising
• Nonprofit means of information distribution and news dissemination, including curbs on advertiser influence
• Codes of journalistic ethics, self-generated by the profession
• Revised news values and standards for news processing
• More inclusive communication rights for the individual, including freer access to the media.

Although it toned down the more strident anti-Western NWIO demands, the report displeased many U.S. government and media leaders. Typical of U.S. reaction, the trade journal *Broadcasting* editorialized that the Mac-Bride report

is heavy with recommendations that go against the grain of press freedom. It advocates free access to news sources and professes to oppose censorship, but at the same time it urges news media to support — not merely report on, but support — social, cultural, economic and political goals set by governments. (Broadcasting 12 Jan. 1981)

The editorial concluded by recommending U.S. withdrawal from UNESCO, and four years later the United States did just that. Alleging that UNESCO was not only against the free-flow doctrine but was also politicized and given to spendthrift ways, the United States took the drastic step of canceling its UNESCO membership at the close of 1984, thereby deleting a quarter of the agency's budget. American defenders of UNESCO, including the private U.S. Commission for UNESCO, disagreed with this decision, pointing out the many beneficial aspects of U.S. membership and the inevitability of politics in such international agencies (USNCU, 1982). Critics of the U.S. action deplored the cutting off of American scholars from participation in important UNESCO projects in science, education, and the international copyright field.

The "Media Box"   A fundamental conflict between two ideologies, broadly identifiable as an aspect of the East-West conflict, lies at the root of the opposition between the NWIO movement and the free-flow doctrine. The Third World joined hands with communist ideologues on the issue, though not necessarily because of doctrinaire Marxist convictions. As mentioned earlier, Third World leaders generally find the Soviet media model less threatening than the Western free-enterprise, freedom-of-expression model. Most approve of state-controlled media devoted to educating the masses and to preserving the political status quo. The Western model, they fear, would endanger their struggle to stay in power and undermine their countries' chances to become economically viable and culturally autonomous. For its part, the USSR welcomes emulation and the chance to cultivate anti-Western attitudes among Third World nations.

Charges of cultural imperialism became most pronounced in the late 1960s and early 1970s, when television stations began to go on the air in the developing world. But evidence of Western dominance collected during that formative period, though dramatic, reflected an exceptional, one-time situation. Though most new Third World television systems at first depended entirely on foreign equipment, training, know-how, and program materials, many have since become more self-sufficient. In a study of the decline of American influence on Brazilian television, for example, a researcher concluded:

Imported programs occupy less viewer time. . . . Programming ideas once imported from the U.S. have largely been "Brazilianized" almost beyond recognition. American management concepts have been similarly "Brazilianized" and new commercial broadcasting ideas have been created to fit the looser Brazilian regulatory laws. (Straubhaar, 1982: 21)

Even though U.S. syndicated programming still dominates the world market, Third World production centers have sprung up, supplying programs to culturally similar countries.

Undoubtedly the NWIO agenda includes legitimate grievances; and the West has in fact made efforts at rectification. News agencies have become more sensitive to Third World feelings, and Western governments have increased their aid to development of Third World communications. In the matter of program exports, however, a look at the experience of Europe's small but well-financed systems suggests that television program autonomy cannot be realistically expected in countries of limited size, especially when they also lack the financial means, the appropriate cultural traditions, and the communications infrastructure demanded by television. They will always need to import a certain amount of programming. Viable cultures can survive the onslaught, but unfortunately not all cultures have the strength to remain viable in the modern world. Once their shell of isolation is broken, they are doomed, with or without television. A British media scholar, Jeremy Tunstall, wrote a book on the subject of media imperialism, *The Media Are American*. Though critical of many aspects of Anglo-American broadcasting influence, he rejects the position of Herbert Schiller, the American scholar quoted earlier. Schiller, he says,

attributes too many of the world's ills to television. He also has an unrealistic view of returning to traditional cultures, many of which although authentic are also dead. In my view a non-American way out of the media box is difficult to discover because it is an American, or Anglo-American, built box. The only way out is to construct a new box, and this, with the possible exception of the Chinese, no nation seems keen to do. (Tunstall, 1977: 63)

Ironically, since Tunstall wrote that comment, even China has stepped tentatively into the Anglo-American "media box." Following overthrow of the "gang of Four" in 1977 and abandonment of its devastating Cultural Revolution, China began cautiously to import Western television programs, advertising techniques, consumerism ideology, and even free-enterprise marketing.

Summary

• Convergence has brought technologies and countries together, causing new configurations and new associations. As a result, one needs to see American broadcasting in the wider perspective of telecommunications technology and of the other national broadcasting systems.

• The United States has led in private satellite and cable development, but the rest of the world, in which telecommunications tend to be state-operated and centralized, is now catching up.

• National pride and economic chauvinism interfere with adoption of universal technical standards, causing incompatibilities that complicate the international exchange of programs and equipment.

- The current U.S. domestic regulatory philosophy favors standardization by the marketplace rather than by government regulation.
- Each country must decide how to treat the medium as a national resource, how to prevent interference, and what political controls to impose.
- Responses to these challenges can be categorized as permissive, paternalistic, or authoritarian. The U.S. response is more permissive than most, the British system paternalistic, and communist and Third World systems authoritarian.
- Ideally, broadcasting systems are pluralistic, combining both commercial and public-service motivations. Relative to Britain's, for example, the U.S. system is only weakly pluralistic because its public broadcasting is inferior.
- The world shares common regulations through the ITU, but domestic regulations vary.
- The U.S. Constitution shields U.S. broadcasters, making regulation lighter and more subject to review and appeal than in most countries.
- Broadcasting systems respond in various ways to growing demands for access to the medium by politicians and by the general public.
- U.S. politicians have more access and spend more money on obtaining it than politicians elsewhere.
- Reception facilities vary greatly from one country to another, both because of economic constraints and because of varying ability of programs to motivate set purchasing.
- Revenue to support broadcasting systems comes from governments, receiver license fees, and advertising, often in combination.
- Economic and political considerations rule out advertising as a major source of support in many countries.
- International syndication flourishes in response to television's high program costs.

- Program formats are similar all over the world, but program content and scheduling varies from country to country. Few countries other than the United States use continuous schedules.
- All countries use audience research as a management tool, but not all can afford full-scale rating services, nor do all agree with the United States broadcasters' stress on audience size rather than on audience characteristics and the quality of programming.
- Political, military, and economic motives encourage transborder broadcasting. The USSR and its allies invest heavily in political transborder services and in jamming facilities to prevent their citizens from hearing Western services.
- The USIA provides both television and radio external services for the United States. The VOA is its radio external service.
- RFE/RL and Radio Martí, surrogate domestic services aimed by the United States at communist countries, have a more explicit propaganda purpose and so do not come under the USIA umbrella. Some critics oppose these services, believing they exacerbate relations with the communist world without realizing corresponding gains for the United States.
- U.S. media dominance has led the Third World, backed by the communist world, to demand a New World Information Order. Western governments and news media oppose this movement, seeing it as an attack on freedom of expression, the free flow of ideas, and the free-enterprise marketplace. This confrontation contributed to the United States' withdrawal from UNESCO, the United Nations agency most supportive of the NWIO demands.
- Despite the legitimacy of many Third World complaints, there seems little likelihood that Western communication dominance can soon be rectified, given the technoeconomic nature of telecommunications.

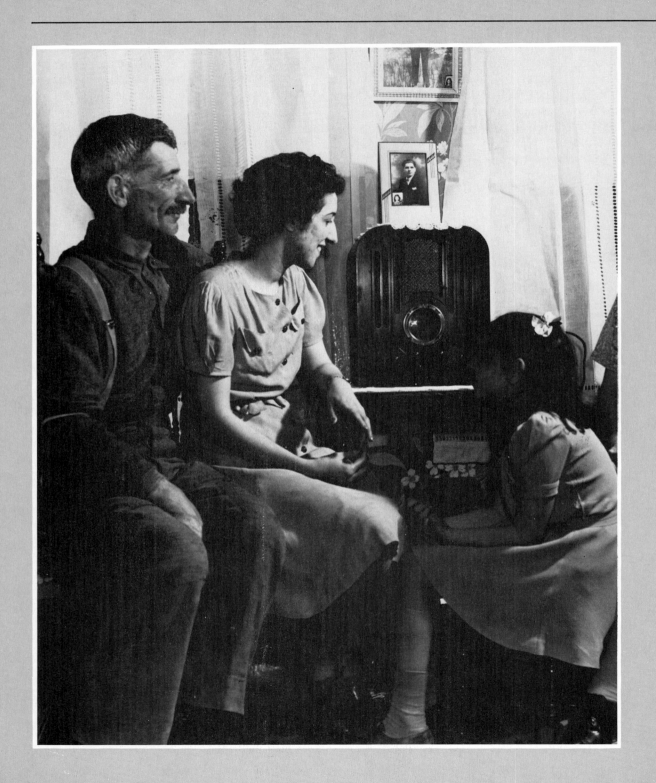

PART 1

Development

American broadcasting took a number of decades to develop into the widespread and varied system we know today. The next three chapters trace that evolution: the development of wireless and then radio to 1927 (Chapter 2); the heyday of radio and television for the next half-century (Chapter 3); and the development of competing electronic media services, mainly in the past decade or so (Chapter 4). We consider the inventors who made broadcasting possible, along with the business innovators who made it a universal reality, and follow the growth of system and content from the first tentative programs and hookups of the crystal-set era of the 1920s to the cornucopia of electronic media services available in the 1980s.

CHAPTER 2

The Rise of Radio

Broadcasting spread from a series of tentative local ventures to a recognized national service, more universal than bathtubs and refrigerators, in a very short time. To introduce photography into general use took a century, the telephone half a century; radio technology itself took thirty-five years to become widely used, but broadcasting took only about eight years. The preconditions for its emergence, however, had been evolving for at least a century. Several developments intertwine: (1) the emergence of social conditions favorable to the development of mass communication, leading to the habit of media consumption; (2) the corresponding growth of the appropriate industrial and business institutions able to provide consumer goods in quantity (including entertaining and informative media content); and (3) the progress of scientific know-how that made possible new ways of communicating that content.

2.1 Precedents

The habit of mass media consumption had already been cultivated by the popular press, the phonograph, and the motion picture long before broadcasting began. These older media arose from the mechanical inventive tradition of the nineteenth century and from fundamental social changes brought about by the Industrial Revolution (roughly 1750–1850). For centuries the primary occupations of the masses of people living in Western countries had been agricultural; but increasingly, industrial occupations began to draw people away from the land until, eventually, most people lived and worked in cities.

The concentrations of people in cities became the target of what we now call the "mass media" — those means of communication that use technology to reach large parts of the total population almost simultaneously with the kinds of news and entertainment that ordinary people find attractive and at a price that ordinary people can afford to pay.*

The Penny Press   Urban concentration, education, and more leisure all contributed to

*It is worth remembering that the word *media* is a plural noun (the media *are*), in spite of the fact that many writers use it as a singular. This is more than a petty usage error, for it implies that all the media — broadcasting, print, film, and the rest — are identical, obscuring the important fact that each medium has its own separate identity and unique characteristics. One of the goals of this book is to delineate the uniqueness of broadcasting as a medium among media.

changing the medium of print from a special amenity provided primarily for the elite to a commonplace product for the masses. The penny press was the most visible example of this transformation. In the 1830s the *New York Sun* led a new trend toward mass-oriented and mass-produced papers that were sold on the streets for a mere penny a copy. They sold in the thousands and eventually in the millions of copies.

Until that time newspapers had concentrated on news of commerce, party politics, and other such "serious" subjects. The popular press broadened the coverage, exploiting news of everyday events, sensational crimes, gossip, human interest stories, and sports — all presented in a breezy, colloquial style that contrasted with the flowery essay style of the past. Popular newspapers broadened their appeal by cutting across lines of party, class, sex, age, and cherished beliefs. By the 1890s some mass-oriented newspapers had circulations of over a million. This helped to create the habit of mass media consumption from which broadcasting would profit in the 1920s.

Vaudeville   The sound of 1920s broadcasting (§2.8) was heavily drawn from vaudeville, a traveling successor to minstrel shows. Immensely popular in the 1880–1920 era as the pinnacle of show business, vaudeville shows featured song-and-dance teams, blackface comics, Irish tenors, ethnic comics, and the like, and ran in established vaudeville theaters in cities large and small. New York had 37 vaudeville houses, Philadelphia 30, and Chicago 22. Hundreds operated in smaller towns across the country. A headliner would be preceded by perhaps a dozen other acts. By the turn of the century, vaudeville theaters would show short bits of novelty film while clearing the house between programs — "an ironic foreshadowing of impending doom" (Nye, 1970: 171). At its peak, the vaudeville circuit

was pulling in more of an audience than all other kinds of entertainment combined. But the greater revenue potential of movies and then radio helped the newer media take over vaudeville's content in the 1920s. Radio picked up many of the better people and acts, especially the song-and-patter teams. Such famous radio comics as Jack Benny and Fred Allen got their start in vaudeville, and Charlie Chaplin's immortal "Little Tramp" was based on a character that had long figured in vaudeville programs. The highly popular musical variety shows of network radio and, later, television are modern adaptations of vaudeville modes and routines.

The Phonograph   A late-nineteenth-century invention, the phonograph, combined with vaudeville to prepare the public for radio broadcasting. Owning a phonograph accustomed people to investing in a piece of furniture that brought entertainment into the home; it was an individual means of listening to the same material presented in vaudeville shows. Public appetite for this entertaining novelty was so great that by the end of World War I, on the eve of the introduction of broadcasting, some two hundred phonograph manufacturers were turning out over two million machines a year.

When radio began to develop in the 1920s, phonograph recording was still dependent on acoustic methods not fundamentally different from those used by Thomas Edison in 1878. This obsolete technology, competition from radio broadcasting, and the impact of the 1929 stock market crash devastated the phonograph industry. By 1933 "the record business in America was practically extinct" (Gelatt, 1977: 265). Ironically, not long after forcing many phonograph companies out of business, broadcasting began to help them revive. This came about partly as a result of the increased mass appetite for music that radio created and partly because of the dramatic improvement in recording methods made possible by the belated application of radio technology to the phonograph.

Motion Pictures   Closely paralleling the phonograph in its evolution was the motion picture. Edison's name is linked with both. His 1889 kinetoscope was the first commercially usable motion picture camera (though some people contend he merely placed his marketable name on the work of others). With slight modification it served also in the 1890s as a projection device that enabled one viewer at a time to see a brief film sequence as a peepshow.

Like the phonograph industry, motion pictures had achieved the status of a well-established industry by the time broadcasting began in 1920. The movies created a mass audience for information and entertainment (newsreels were an important part of movie theater presentations before television phased them out).

Nevertheless, as in the case of the phonograph, the motion picture had something to learn from radio technology — the ability to talk. Progress toward "talkies" was stymied by the need for *synchronized* sound (precise matching of sound and picture). Talkies finally began in earnest in 1928, with several rival sound systems competing for acceptance. One of these had been developed by RCA, an example of the many links between broadcasting and motion pictures that began in the 1920s, long before the advent of television.

2.2 Wire Communication

Although broadcasting benefited from the prior arts of sound recording and the motion picture, its direct technical and industrial descent was from the telegraph and the tele-phone — from point-to-point rather than from mass-oriented communications media. This means that electrical technology, rather than the mechanical technology of the early phonograph and the movies, led to the invention of radio and, eventually, to its application to public rather than private communication purposes.

The Land Telegraph   Most people did not feel any urgent need for instant communication beyond the horizon in times of peace until the era of the steam railroad. Then some means of signaling to distant stations became essential for safe and efficient rail operations. To meet this need, the British developed a form of *electrical telegraphy* in the 1820s.* Electrical impulses sent along a wire caused deflections of a pointer in a detecting device at the receiving end. An operator "read" the message by interpreting the movements of the pointer.

Crucial improvements were made by an American, Samuel F. B. Morse, after extensive experiments in the 1830s. His telegraph receiver had the great advantage of automatically making a permanent record of messages on strips of paper. We still use the term *Morse code* for the system that he and a partner developed for translating the letters of the alphabet into patterns of electrical impulses.

With the help of federal money, in 1844 Morse installed the first operational telegraph line using his system between Washington, D.C., and Baltimore. The first message over the 40-mile line suggests the awe with which the achievement was regarded: "What hath God wrought!"

In most parts of the world, governments still retain responsibility for operating national

---

*The word *telegraphy* ("distant writing") was already in use, referring to relaying semaphore (visual) messages by means of a series of line-of-sight signaling stations.

telegraphic systems. Congress, however, fearing the federal Post Office would lose money if the government competed with itself by running the telegraph as well, sold its interest in Morse's line to private investors, retaining only the right of government regulation. By the end of the Civil War, a single company, Western Union, had emerged as the dominant force in the telegraph field.

Submarine Cable   Laying telegraph lines underwater offered a more difficult challenge than overland telegraphy. Technological problems and the search for financial backing led to several frustrating attempts to cross the Atlantic Ocean with a telegraph cable. Regular transatlantic cable communication began in 1866, and soon all the major centers of the earth could exchange information in minutes instead of weeks or months. This brought profound change. The first breach had been made in the walls of international isolation, with far-reaching effects on trade, politics, diplomacy, and war.

Submarine cable and telegraphy had an early and lasting association with news. Even before the electric telegraph became available, newspapers had begun to share the costs of news gathering, which was, in effect, the first form of media syndication (§13.2). The British news agency Reuters "followed the cable" wherever it led around the globe, establishing what is today one of the five worldwide *news agencies* or *news wire services*. The others are Associated Press and United Press International (the two U.S. agencies), Agence France Presse (French), and Tass (Soviet).

Bell's Telephone   The next goal of inventors was to transmit speech itself, eliminating the tedious business of encoding and decoding telegraph messages. Sound, of course, involves a much more complex variation of electromagnetic waves (§5.4) than does the

simple "on-off" signal of the telegraph. The problem of the telephone centered on finding a sensitive *transducer*, a modulating device able to convert complex sound energy from one medium (air) to another medium (electrical current). Many investigators were struggling with this problem, and were approaching a solution, when Alexander Graham Bell filed for the key telephone patent in 1876.

Bell organized his original telephone firm in 1877, the year in which he secured his second essential patent. But the inventor and his friends could not raise enough capital to develop the new invention. Control over the patents soon passed to others who went on to develop the company known today as AT&T.

AT&T (The Bell System)   Rather than spread to ungainly proportions by trying to serve the entire country directly, AT&T adopted a policy of franchising regional operating companies. These firms received the exclusive and permanent right to use the Bell patents. They in turn gave AT&T substantial stock holdings. By the time the Bell patents ran out in 1893–1894, AT&T had controlling interests in the franchise companies. Furthermore, AT&T had developed the *long lines* connecting the central offices of telephone companies with one another. AT&T's supremacy in the long-distance field was assured by its acquisition of a key radio invention, the Audion (§2.4), in 1914, making coast-to-coast telephone service possible. With AT&T's 1881 purchase of Western Electric as its manufacturing arm, the whole process of manufacture, installation, and servicing could be kept within the Bell companies.*

---

*This very control led to the eventual breakup of the telephone monopoly. For several decades, AT&T operated as a *regulated monopoly* under supervision of the Federal Communications Commission. Development of microwave and later satellite technology, along with a general

This centralization of control and extensive electronic communication experience allowed AT&T to dominate broadcasting briefly in the 1920s when the company saw radio as closely related to telephony (§2.9). The need for long-distance terrestrial relay facilities used for network interconnections was the basis of AT&T's continuing role in broadcasting into the 1980s.

2.3 Big Business and Patents

Before turning to the development of wireless communication, we must briefly examine the industrial context for that development. We've examined the precedents in journalism, show business, and wire communication that laid the groundwork for broadcasting. In our discussion, we've noted the importance of patents in the control of technology. Understanding the basis of patents, and how companies were built around patents, is vital to understanding the development of wireless and radio.

Role of Patents   To be valid, a patent must describe a "novel" invention; it must introduce something genuinely new, not merely improve on a previous invention. One of the reasons inventor Lee de Forest would have so much trouble defending his Audion patent was that it built on a previous patent (§2.4). Such interdependence was characteristic of improvements in the radio field; as a result, the history of wireless invention in the first half of this century was marked by constant patent litigation.

As we shall see, the grand objective of wireless inventors was to carve out a self-sufficient system, independent of the need to get licenses from rival patent holders. The more the wireless art progressed, the more impossible that goal became. Literally thousands of patents were on the books in several different countries, and no patent holder was safe from suit.

A patent gives an inventor an exclusive property right to an invention for a period of seventeen years. During that time the inventor has a legal monopoly. The inventor can manufacture and sell the product himself or herself or can license others to do so. Patents are intended to provide economic incentive to encourage creativity. The Constitution, in Article I, Section 8, emphasizes the public interest in invention rather than stressing the private gain of inventors.

Patent control was at the core of the first huge telecommunications monopolies, Western Union and AT&T. Western Union, when first offered the fledgling Bell patent in 1877 for a mere $100,000, turned down the chance, figuring telephony was unimportant to their sure monopoly position. Yet in a few years, telephony's expansion carried AT&T to much greater size and scope than Western Union. Indeed, the telephone firm bought control of its older rival in 1910 and held it until pressured by the government to sell in 1913.

Electrical Manufacturing   During the early years of this century, AT&T's manufac-

trend toward electronic miniaturization, began to revolutionize the communications industry in the 1970s, and firms offering specialized long-distance communications began to compete with AT&T. The government grew wary of AT&T's monopolistic response to these competing firms and its apparent suppression of some promising technologies. In 1974 the Department of Justice brought suit to break up the Bell System on antitrust grounds. After years of legal wrangling, the case was settled with a 1982 "consent decree," wherein the defendant admitted no wrong but changes were made. AT&T agreed to divest itself of its local operating companies and to get out of the local telephone business entirely, retaining the manufacturing arm and the country's premier industrial research operation, Bell Laboratories. Each of the now-independent regional holding companies and the now-leaner AT&T provide communication services to the electronic media.

turing arm, Western Electric, was one of the largest industrial concerns in the country. With two other companies, General Electric and Westinghouse, it largely dictated the direction of the electrical industry and set the tone for the industry's reaction to early wireless communication.

General Electric was created by the 1892 merger of two earlier firms. GE took immediate interest in development of the vacuum tube, which would prove crucial to wireless innovation. The company also became a key investor in early radio broadcasting, and to this day it controls a group of stations that pioneered AM, FM, and television service. Its great rival, Westinghouse, was founded on the basis of control of the railroad air-brake patent control. It owned broadcast stations even before GE, including the pioneer station KDKA (§2.8), and now controls radio and television stations in a subsidiary known as Group W.

Increasing use of electrical power after 1900 made both Westinghouse and GE extremely profitable. Together with AT&T's Western Electric, they formed an invincible triumvirate in the fields of electrical lighting, power, and transport manufacturing, as well as in communication. Their patent control, economic power, and know-how were all to have a crucial impact on the emergence of wireless and broadcasting.

2.4   Invention of Wireless

The notion that it should somehow be possible to do the job of the telegraph and the telephone without using costly and confining wire connections stimulated the inventive juices of many scientists and tinkerers in the last quarter of the nineteenth century. Their goal was *wireless* communication — what we now call *radio*.

Conflicting Claims   Many inventors in many countries claimed to have been the first to solve the problem of wireless transmission. Most of those people who claimed the invention had common access to some critically important scientific knowledge about electromagnetic energy that had recently been published by two physicists: (1) an 1873 theoretical paper by James Clerk Maxwell, predicting the existence of invisible radiant energy similar to light; and (2) the report of a laboratory experiment by Heinrich Hertz, in which he proved Maxwell's theory by generating and detecting radio energy and measuring its wavelength.

Maxwell, a Scot, hypothesized that electromagnetic wave energy must exist. Using mathematical proofs and drawing upon observable facts about the behavior of light waves, he constructed a theory about electromagnetic energy, hypothesizing that this energy existed not only as light but also in forms invisible to the eye. Nearly twenty years went by before Hertz, a German physicist, succeeded in a laboratory demonstration that detected the invisible waves that Maxwell had predicted. His 1888 paper *Electromagnetic Waves and Their Reflection* led directly to the invention of radio within a few years of its publication. In recognition of the importance of his contribution, his name, abbreviated *Hz*, has been adopted internationally as the standard way to express the frequency of radio waves, with the meaning "one cycle per second."

Hertz sought to verify a scientific theory, not to invent a method of communication. He failed to realize the practical implications of his experiments.

Marconi's "Releasing Touch"   It remained for Guglielmo Marconi — more an inventor than a scientist — to supply the "right releasing touch," as a Supreme Court justice put it in an opinion on a patent case many years later (320 US 65, 1942).

Stimulated by Hertz's paper, as a young man Marconi experimented with equipment similar to Hertz's, first indoors and then on the grounds of his father's estate in Italy. End-less experiments with different shapes, sizes, and types of antennas, ground systems, and other components gradually improved the performance of his pioneering wireless sys-tem. Fortunately, Marconi had the leisure for experimentation and the money for equip-ment. Equally important, he had access through his family to high official and busi-ness circles.

As soon as Marconi had convinced him-self that wireless was more than a laboratory toy, he offered it to the Italian government, only to be rebuffed. His mother, who came from a well-known family of British whiskey distillers, was able to arrange introductions to important English postal and military officials, the most likely customers in Britain for the in-vention. Marconi went to London and regis-tered his patent in 1896. He was twenty two. In 1897 he launched his own company with the help of his mother's family. Its object was to manufacture wireless equipment and to of-fer wireless telegraphic services to the public.

To a remarkable degree Marconi com-bined the genius of the inventor with that of the business innovator. As an inventor he per-sisted tirelessly, never discouraged, even by hundreds of failed attempts at solving a prob-lem. As a businessman he had a flair for effec-tive public relations. In the early years of the century he repeatedly staged dramatic and convincing demonstrations to prove the use-fulness of wireless (Exhibit 2.1). In 1909 Mar-coni shared the Nobel prize in physics with Germany's Ferdinand Braun for achievements in wireless telegraphy.

Among Marconi's business ventures, the U.S. branch of his company, known as Ameri-

Exhibit 2.1   Guglielmo Marconi (1874–1937)

In a 1902 photo, the inventor examines the paper tape on which a radiotelegraphic message is inscribed in Morse code. At that time radio equipment was still very crude, but the already well-developed equipment of wire telegraphy was readily adaptable to the task of recording wireless messages. Seated: George Kemp, Marconi's most trusted engineering assistant.

Source: Courtesy Smithsonian Institution, Washington, D.C.

can Marconi, is of particular interest because it had decisive influence on the development of broadcasting in America. Founded in 1899, American Marconi finally began to realize sub-stantial profits in 1913 with its virtual monop-oly on U.S. wireless communication: it owned seventeen land stations and four hundred ship's stations. All these facilities used a wire-less extension of the telegraph principle — point-to-point communications between ships and shore stations, between ships at sea, and between countries.

Signal Generation, Detection, and Amplification   After years of experimentation with radio waves, the invention of the *vacuum tube oscillator* provided the means for transmitting a continuous signal. Only this *continuous* signal could provide effective transmission of speech via the new wireless technology. Early experimental versions were in use by the end of World War I, but at that time, the only effective means of long-distance wireless transmission (of telegraphy, not voice, signals) was by way of a huge, cumbersome device, the *Alexanderson alternator*, perfected at General Electric by Ernst Alexanderson for the experiments of Reginald Fessenden (§2.6).

Another key problem in the development of early wireless was achieving adequate *detection*, or sensing, of incoming signals. Marconi and later inventors worked on a variety of approaches to this dilemma. In 1904 Marconi obtained a U.S. *tuner* patent, which enabled his transmitters to restrict their radiations to a limited group of frequencies. Receivers could then select, or tune to, the desired frequencies, excluding simultaneous signals present in other parts of the spectrum.

Yet another early equipment drawback was lack of signal amplification, at both the sending and receiving ends. The electronic device that finally solved this problem, the Audion, also solved the generation and detection dilemmas, making possible radio as we know it today. For that reason, the Audion's inventor, Lee de Forest, felt justified in titling his autobiography *Father of Radio* (1950).

De Forest's Audion   After receiving a Yale Ph.D. in 1899, de Forest worked first as an engineer but soon began to devote all his time to developing his own inventions. Following the leads of Edison's electric light in 1883 and Marconi researcher Ambrose Fleming's vacuum tube patent of 1904, he experimented with the idea of creating a radio detector by using a glowing filament to heat gas within a glass enclosure. Edison and Fleming had both patented devices based upon the then-unexplained fact that an electric current would flow between the hot filament of an electric lamp and a nearby metal plate inside the lamp. Because such lamps or tubes had two elements, the filament and the plate, they were called *diodes*.

De Forest took the next crucial step by adding a third element to the tube, making it a *triode*. He positioned the new element, a *grid*, between the filament and the plate. A small voltage applied to the grid could control with great precision the flow of electrons from filament to plate. Thus a weak signal could become strong — amplification could occur. De Forest first used the triode, or *Audion*, as one of his associates dubbed it, in 1906.

Development of the Audion and the new circuits to go with it took more than a dozen years. Its first practical application was not to radio but to telephony. In 1913 AT&T bought telephone rights for vacuum tube repeaters (amplifiers in telephone lines) from de Forest, making the first long-distance service possible two years later.

De Forest and the Feedback Circuit   All the inventors of the wireless era engaged in constant patent litigation, but de Forest seemingly more than most. He filed over thirty patents in the pioneer years 1902–1906, and in all was granted over one hundred. His most bitterly fought suit had to do with the *feedback*, or regenerative, circuit — the subject of "the most controversial litigation in radio history" (Maclaurin, 1949: 78). This design feeds back part of a received signal on itself, greatly increasing signal strength. The circuit was of vital importance because it increased tremendously the sensitivity of radio receivers. In fact, it has been called "as historic as the first Bell telephone patent and as clearly decisive in the development of the modern world" (Lessing, 1956: 78).

Four powerful companies claimed to hold the controlling patent on this improvement, including AT&T, with the de Forest patent, and American Marconi, with a patent granted to Edwin Armstrong. This four-way battle moved in and out of the courts for twenty years. In 1934, after the contenders had spent millions of dollars in legal fees, the Supreme Court finally decided in favor of de Forest. Even the final court decision did not completely clear the atmosphere. Engineers today generally recognize Armstrong's claim, despite the court's award to de Forest.

This case shows how the growing complications of the wireless patent situation during the early twentieth century made substantial control of the new industry by the great corporations inevitable. They alone had the resources to build up patent strength, to withstand frequent court battles, and to undertake the developmental work that patents always need.

2.5 Initial Development of Wireless Services

During its first two decades wireless as a business made its money from supplying *communications services*. Wireless manufacturing was not yet a big industry because the market for the equipment was limited to the specialized needs of the few communications service companies. The mass market for millions of broadcast receivers and thousands of broadcast transmitters lay in the future. The main demand was for services that wire could not duplicate; therefore, overland wireless services were not at first important. The efficient network of existing telephone and telegraph lines already did the job.

Maritime Service   Ships at sea were the first commercial customers for radio communication. Now they could communicate with each other over long distances and with coastal stations far beyond the horizon. Wireless was used in a maritime disaster as early as 1898. In 1909, when the S.S. *Republic* foundered off New York, all passengers were saved by wireless-alerted rescue ships. In that same year wireless came to the rescue in other emergencies at sea, and each year the number increased (see Box, page 48).

Naturally, the naval powers of the world took an immediate interest in military applications of wireless. Both the British and American navies began experimenting with ship installations in 1899. The Japanese victory in the Russo-Japanese War in 1904–1905 is ascribed at least in part to the superiority of their Marconi equipment to that used by the Russian Navy.

Transoceanic Wireless   Long-distance radio communication across oceans held commercial promise as an alternative to telegraph cable, but because of technical limitations this radio service did not become strongly competitive until the 1920s. In the meantime, the Marconi company, which dominated the transatlantic wireless business, built several high-power coastal spark-transmitter stations in the United States and Canada prior to the outbreak of World War I, in 1914.

In 1917 GE installed a 200-kilowatt Alexanderson alternator in New Brunswick, New Jersey. The alternator, a huge and costly machine, put out a powerful very low frequency (VLF) signal of about 20 kHz.* It represented a major improvement in long-distance radio communication.

---

*For more about the division of the radio frequency spectrum into bands, see Exhibit 5.4.

The *Titanic* Disaster

In 1910 Wanamaker's Department Stores contracted with American Marconi to install wireless stations in its outlets in Philadelphia and New York. The Wanamaker stations exchanged messages between the two stores and ships at sea. By chance, the store's New York station played a bit part in radio history, for it was the first station to make contact with the rescue ships involved in the 1912 *Titanic* disaster. The young operator who ran that station was David Sarnoff (§2.10), later to become the preeminent industrial leader in broadcasting and electronics.

A luxury liner advertised as unsinkable, the *Titanic* struck an iceberg and sank in the mid-Atlantic on her maiden voyage from Britain to the United States. A heroic Marconi operator stayed at his post and went down with the ship. Some 1,500 people died — among them some of the most famous names in the worlds of art, science, finance, and diplomacy — partially because nearby vessels had but one radio operator each (as then required), who had turned in for the night. Only by chance

did a ship some fifty miles distant hear the distress calls and steam full speed to the rescue of about seven hundred survivors.

The fact that for days radiotelegraphy maintained the world's only thread of contact with the survivors aboard a rescue liner brought the new medium of wireless to public attention as nothing else had done. Subsequently, inquiries revealed that a more sensible use of wireless (such as a 24-hour radio watch) could have prevented the accident, or at least decreased the loss of life. Because of these findings, the *Titanic* disaster had an important influence on the worldwide adoption of stringent laws governing shipboard wireless stations. It also set a precedent for regarding the radio business as having a special public responsibility. This concept carried over into broadcasting legislation a quarter of a century later.

Sources: *Titanic*, courtesy United Press International/Bettman; Sarnoff, courtesy RCA.

During the 1920s the alternator was displaced by vacuum tube transmitters. They enabled development of the short-wave (high-frequency) portion of the spectrum (§5.1), which turned out to be much more efficient than the lower frequencies previously used for long-distance communication. A dramatic rise in transatlantic radio traffic followed.

Wireless in World War I   When U.S. direct participation in the war began in April 1917, the navy took over all U.S. wireless stations, commercial and amateur alike, and either dismantled them or ran them as part of the navy's own facilities, which included thirty-five shore stations.

The Army Signal Corps also used radio, as did the Air Service. However, U.S. combat participation was so brief, and the trench warfare in Europe so static, that radio's uses were limited. The navy, however, having the most urgent need for wireless, had been developing its use since the turn of the century. Some ten thousand soldiers and sailors received training in wireless. After the war they helped popularize the new medium. They formed part of the cadre of amateur enthusiasts, laboratory technicians, and electronics manufacturing employees that constituted the ready-made first audience for broadcasting.

In order to mobilize the total wireless resources of the country for war, the Navy decreed a moratorium on patent suits. Manufacturers agreed to pool their patents, making them available to each other without risk of suits for infringement. Such extraordinary measures were necessary because by that time the tangled web of conflicting patent rights had begun to strangle the progress of wireless manufacturing.

The wartime patent pool broke this stalemate. After the war, the radio industry profited from its wartime experience by voluntarily entering into patent-pooling agreements. These, as we shall see, had important implications for broadcasting in the 1920s.

Military purchases and a moratorium on patent suits greatly increased the quantity and sophistication of wartime wireless manufacturing. The war served as a transitional period. In prewar days the wireless industry had been dominated mainly by inventor-entrepreneurs, struggling to market their discoveries while at the same time feverishly experimenting on new ones (§2.6). After the war, big business took over. AT&T had added wireless rights to its original purchase in 1914 of telephonic rights from de Forest. General Electric was in the forefront with the powerful Alexanderson alternator and the ability to mass-produce vacuum tubes. Westinghouse, also a producer of vacuum tubes, was casting about for new ways of capitalizing on wireless.

2.6 Experiments with Radiotelephony

All the wireless services we have been discussing used *radiotelegraphy*, not voice transmissions. Throughout this early period, however, eager experimenters sought the key to *radiotelephony*, the essential precursor of broadcasting.

Fessenden's 1906 "Broadcast"   The first known wireless transmission using radiotelephony and resembling what we would now call a broadcast took place in 1906, and was made by Reginald Fessenden. Using an ordinary telephone microphone and his Alexanderson alternator to generate radio energy (§2.5), Fessenden made his historic transmission on Christmas Eve 1906 from Brant Rock, a site on the Massachusetts coast south of Boston (Exhibit 2.2). Fessenden himself played a violin, sang, and read from the Bible. He also

Exhibit 2.2   Reginald Fessenden (1866–1932) at Brant Rock

Fessenden (center) stands with some of his associates in front of the building where he made the historic 1906 broadcast. The column in the background is the base of his antenna.

Source: Courtesy Smithsonian Institution, Washington, D.C.

transmitted the sound of a phonograph recording. Ships' operators heard the transmission far out at sea, utterly amazed to hear actual voices and musical tones in earphones that up to then had reproduced only static and the harsh staccato of Morse code. In a sense this event marked the start of broadcasting, though of course it lacked the essential attribute of continuousness of service. Fessenden's historic transmission was merely the first in a long string of demonstrations that would culminate in the start of regular broadcasting services in 1920.

De Forest's Experiments   The prolific inventor who patented the Audion (§2.4) also felt the challenge of radiotelephony. Lee de Forest, a lover of fine music, naturally turned toward the idea of using radiotelephony to communicate sound. In 1907, hard on the heels of Fessenden, de Forest made experimental radiotelephone transmissions from a building in downtown New York City (Exhibit 2.3).

In 1916 de Forest began using his Audion as an oscillator to generate radio frequency energy. In doing so he opted for electronic means, rather than the mechanical means of the Alexanderson alternator. He set up an experimental transmitter that year in his Bronx home and began to transmit phonograph recordings and announcements. He even transmitted election returns in the fall of 1916, anticipating by four years a similar program on KDKA, now considered to be the oldest regular broadcasting station (§2.8).

The Fessenden and de Forest radiotelephone transmissions are examples of the many experiments that were conducted at university laboratories and in private research facilities throughout the United States and elsewhere in the world during the early years of the century.

Exhibit 2.3   Lee de Forest (1873–1961)

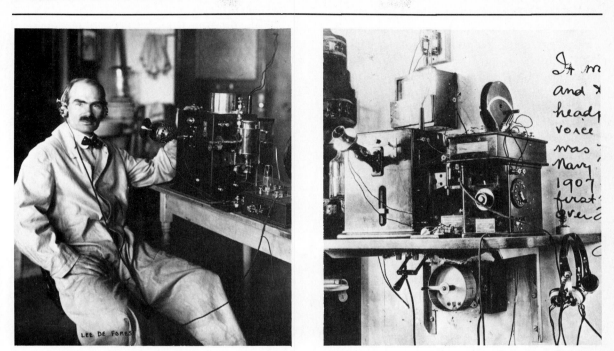

The inventor is shown in 1907 with a transmitter of the type used in his famous 1907 voicecast, along with a shipboard receiver of the type that picked up the transmission.

Sources: Courtesy Smithsonian Institution, Washington, D.C. and Culver Pictures.

2.7 Government Monopoly: The Road Not Taken

The Navy's Claims   World War I ended in November 1918, yet the navy did not relinquish control of radio properties until early in 1920. The critical decisions made during this delay of over a year affected the whole future of radio in the United States.

Was radio too vital to entrust to private hands? The U.S. Navy thought so. In fact, the navy had always asserted jurisdiction over radio as a natural right, assuming that it was destined to remain primarily a marine service. The navy supported a bill, introduced into Congress late in 1918, proposing in effect to make radio a permanent government monopoly. Despite strong arguments from navy brass at the congressional hearings, the bill failed to get out of committee. Its wartime powers over civilian radio having thereby lapsed, the navy reluctantly turned the stations it had seized back to private ownership early the next year.

The Alternator Issue   Restoration of private ownership meant, however, turning over most commercial wireless communication facilities in the United States to a foreign company, American Marconi. Moreover, that company seemed about to capture exclusive rights to use a most important American invention — the Alexanderson alternator that had greatly improved transoceanic radiotelegraphy during the war. Marconi had grasped the significance of the original alternator three years earlier and had started negotiations with GE for exclusive rights to its use. The talks had been interrupted by the U.S. entry into the war, but in March 1919 the negotiations were reopened. The navy was deeply disturbed at the prospect of American Marconi consolidating its U.S. monopoly by capturing the exclusive rights to the Alexanderson alternator.

British Marconi found itself caught in a squeeze play. The U.S. government made no actual overt move to expropriate British Marconi's American holdings. But with tacit government approval, negotiations for the sale of American Marconi were carried out privately by Owen D. Young, board chairman of General Electric. The Marconi company's position in the United States was plainly untenable.

RCA Founded   Under such pressures British Marconi agreed to sell its stock in its American subsidiary to General Electric, on condition that it be allowed to buy Alexanderson alternators for its own use outside the United States. GE thereupon created a new subsidiary in the fall of 1919 to carry on American Marconi's extensive wireless telegraphy business — the Radio Corporation of America (RCA). Under RCA's charter all its officers had to be Americans and 80 percent of its stock had to be in American hands.

RCA took over American Marconi's assets on November 20, 1919. Eventually RCA's name became closely linked with broadcasting, but in 1919 its first permanent broadcasting station was still a year away and its founders had no plans to enter that field.

Westinghouse and AT&T joined General Electric as investors in the new corporation. AT&T sold its RCA interest in 1923. RCA remained under the control of General Electric and Westinghouse until, in order to settle an antitrust suit, they sold their stock in 1932, making RCA an independent corporation, as it remained until repurchased by GE in 1986.

David Sarnoff had followed up the favorable notice he had won in connection with the 1912 *Titanic* disaster (see Box, page 48) by becoming assistant traffic manager of American Marconi's radiotelegraphic business. In 1919, when American Marconi became RCA, he stayed on with the new company, promoted to commercial manager. His role was to convert the company from a collection of small radiotelegraph firms into a major corporation presiding over numerous subsidiary companies. In 1930 he became president of the company and in 1947 chairman of the board, finally retiring in 1969. As *Time* said in its obituary in 1971, his was "one of the last great autocracies in U.S. industry."

Cross-Licensing: Phase 1   RCA's mission was more than to take over the half-dozen American Marconi wireless communication businesses. Each of its parent companies held important patents, yet each found itself blocked by patents held by the others. As GE's (and RCA's) board chairman, Owen D. Young, testified to a Senate committee, "It was utterly impossible for anybody to do anything in radio, any one person or group or company at that time [1919]. . . . Nobody had patents enough to make a system. And so there was a complete stalemate" (Senate CC, 1930: 1116). Young proposed that in RCA the major patent rivals could find common meeting ground. Accordingly, in the period 1919 to 1923 the contenders worked out a series of *cross-licensing agreements*, modeled after the World War I patent pool. These allowed the signatory companies to use one another's patents, dividing income.

In addition to resolving the patent stalemate, the cross-licensing agreements divided up the communications pie, giving each company exclusive rights in its special area of interest. General Electric and Westinghouse used the pooled patents to manufacture electronic goods. RCA acted as their sales agent. AT&T's exclusive right to manufacture, sell, and lease transmitters for commercial use was intended to ensure the telephone company's control over telephonic communication, whether by wire or wireless means. GE and Westinghouse were allowed to make transmitters for their own use but not for sale to others. Within a few years, however, these carefully worked out plans were thrown into utter confusion by the astonishingly rapid growth of a brand-new use for radiotelephony — radio broadcasting.

2.8 The "First" Broadcast Station

Amateur Beginnings   In 1920 Dr. Frank Conrad, an engineer with Westinghouse in Pittsburgh, operated an amateur radiotelephone station, 8XK, in connection with experimental work at the factory (Exhibit 2.4). Conrad fell into the habit of transmitting recorded music, sports results, and the like in response to requests from other amateurs. These informal programs built up so much interest that they began to get mentioned in the newspapers. None of this was particularly unusual; similar amateur transmissions had been made by other experimenters, in other parts of the world as well as elsewhere in the United States (§2.6). What made Conrad's 8XK transmissions unique was the chain of events they set in motion.

Horne's department store in Pittsburgh, noting the growing public interest in wireless, sensed an opportunity to develop a hitherto untried commercial sideline. Previously, wireless had been primarily the domain of engineers and earnest amateurs. Now it seemed the general public might be willing to buy ready-built receiving sets. Horne's installed a demonstration receiver in the store and ran a box in their regular newspaper display advertisement of September 22, 1920. It was headlined "Air Concert 'Picked Up' by Radio Here," and concluded: "Amateur Wireless Sets made by the maker of the Set which is in operation in our store, are on sale here $10.00 up."

Opening of KDKA   Westinghouse executives had been looking for a profitable entry into the consumer communications field; in fact they had already explored several possible new types of radio service. Thus they were alert to the implications of Horne's modest advertisement. They saw the possibility of a novel merchandising tie-up: Westinghouse could manufacture home radiotelephone receivers and at the same time create a demand for the new product by transmitting programs for the general public. Accordingly, Westinghouse Vice President H.P. Davis ordered conversion of a radiotelegraph transmitter for radiotelephony. It went on the air as station KDKA from an improvised studio on the roof of the Westinghouse factory in East Pittsburgh on November 2, 1920.

KDKA's opening was scheduled to coincide with the presidential election of 1920 so that the maiden broadcast could take advantage of public interest in the voting results. This first KDKA program consisted of news about the Harding-Cox presidential election, fed to the station by telephone from a newspaper office, interspersed with phonograph and live banjo music.

Exhibit 2.4   Conrad's 8XK and Its Successor, KDKA

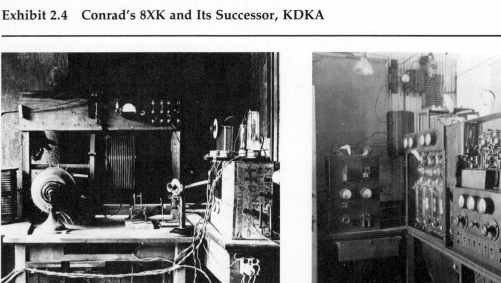

Frank Conrad's transmitter (left) is typical of the improvised setups used by wireless inventors and experimenters. It contrasts with the KDKA professional broadcasting facilities, from which the Harding-Cox election returns were broadcast on November 2, 1920.

Source: Courtesy Group W (Westinghouse Broadcasting Co.), Pittsburgh, PA.

The Listeners   Broadcasting would have developed much more slowly than it did had it not been for a ready-made audience of the thousands of amateur set-builders who created a demand for a type of radio service never before supplied commercially — entertainment.

In order to appreciate the fascination of the 8XK and early KDKA transmissions for listeners of the day, we have to remember that previously, with rare exceptions, the only signals on the air had been in code. To hear music and the human voice instead of the monotonous drone of Morse was a startling and thrilling experience for listeners.

The audience quickly expanded beyond the original nucleus of amateurs. Ready-made crystal sets were cheap, and many receivers were inexpensive homemade affairs.* Moreover, the experience of listening-in created an insatiable public appetite for bigger and better receiving equipment: first (after 1922) a detector vacuum tube, then another tube for an am-

*A homemade set consisted at the minimum of a hand-wound coil (a round Quaker Oats box was a favorite form on which to wind the coil) with a slide to make contact at various points along the coil as a means of tuning, a crystal, and a pair of earphones. A simple length of wire strung outdoors acted as an antenna.

plifier, then more tubes for a superheterodyne circuit, then a loudspeaker. Manufacturers could not keep up with the demand.

KDKA's Success   Because broadcast channels were as yet uncrowded, station interference did not exist and KDKA's sky wave (§5.6) could be picked up at great distances. Newspapers all over the country and even in Canada printed the station's program logs. To assist DX (long-distance) listeners, stations later observed a local "silent night" each week when they went off the air so as not to interfere with incoming signals from distant stations (Barnouw, 1966: 93).

In its first year of operation, KDKA pioneered in broadcasting many types of programs that later became standard radio fare: orchestra music, church services, public-service announcements, political addresses, sports events, dramas, and market reports (Exhibit 2.5). But one now-familiar type of broadcast material was conspicuously absent — *commercials*. Westinghouse did not sell advertising but rather bore the entire expense of operation as a means of promoting sales of its own products. It was taken for granted that each firm that wanted to promote its wares over the air would open its own station and do likewise.

KDKA meets five criteria that qualify it as the *oldest U.S. station still in operation*, despite earlier experiments, demonstrations, and temporary operations: KDKA (1) used radio waves, (2) to send out noncoded signals, (3) in a continuous scheduled program service, (4) which was intended for the general public, and (5) was licensed by the government to provide such a service (Baudino & Kittross, 1977).*

---

*There was of course no *broadcasting* license as such in 1920. KDKA received a license equivalent to the ones issued to commercial shore stations that exchanged messages with ships under the Radio Act of 1912 (§2.11).

Competition Begins   Westinghouse did not have the field to itself for very long. Broadcast station operation had strong appeal for department stores, newspapers, educational institutions, churches, and electrical equipment supply dealers. The number of stations increased slowly in 1920, with 30 licenses issued by the end of the year. In the spring of 1922, however, the new industry began to gather momentum. In that year alone 100,000 sets were sold. By May over 200 stations had been licensed, and the upward trend continued the next year, reaching 576 early in 1923.

Among these early stations, however, mortality was high. Would-be broadcasters hastened to get in on the ground floor of — they knew not quite what. Inadequately backed stations soon fell by the wayside. Educational stations were particularly heavy losers in this process of elimination.

2.9 Radio Broadcasting vs. Radiotelephony

No such problems of money or managerial support bothered the two leading New York stations, representing major groupings in the patent-pooling consortium — WJZ, flagship station of the Radio Group (General Electric, Westinghouse, and RCA), and WEAF, flagship of the Telephone Group (AT&T and Western Electric). They represented two opposing philosophies of broadcasting.

Radio Group Station   Westinghouse opened WJZ in October 1921. That station, like KDKA, started in a Westinghouse factory, this one in Newark, New Jersey. Westinghouse transferred ownership of WJZ to RCA, which moved it across the river to Manhattan as the flagship station of the Radio Group. As manufacturing companies, the Radio Group at first saw WJZ as a sales-promotion device, a good way to stimulate interest in their

Exhibit 2.5   KDKA's Studio in 1922

Before development of the modern acoustic wall treatments, heavy drapes were used to dampen reverberation. The producer Robert Saudek visited this studio as a boy, remembering it as "very much like the inside of a burlap-lined casket. Burnt orange, a favorite decorator color in 1922, was chosen for the draped silk meringues that billowed from the ceiling" (Saudek, 1965: 25).

Source: KDKA Radio Photo, Pittsburgh, PA.

own products. Attractive programming was needed to motivate people to buy receivers. WJZ therefore accepted from the start the responsibility for producing its own programs.

Telephone Group Station   AT&T's WEAF went on the air August 16, 1922. The company spared no expense because WEAF served as a laboratory for experimenting with ways of making a profit out of the new medium. As the country's leading communication firm, AT&T gave WEAF every technical advantage.

Programming was a different matter. AT&T explained that it would "furnish *no programs whatsoever* over that station" (Dept. of Commerce, 1922:7, italics supplied). In other words, telephone company officials thought of broadcasting as a *common carrier*, as a new form of telephony. In a 1922 press release about WEAF, AT&T emphasized the point:

Just as the company leases its long distance wire facilities for the use of newspapers, banks, and other concerns, so it will lease its radio telephone facilities and will not provide the matter which is sent out from this station. (Quoted in Banning, 1946: 68)

It soon became clear, however, that the idea of filling the schedule entirely with leased time simply would not work. Not only were there not enough customers at first, but more important, advertisers were not prepared to fill their leased time with program material capable of attracting listeners. The telephone company therefore found itself forced into show business after all — a decidedly uncomfortable role for a regulated monopoly extremely sensitive about maintaining a serious and dignified public image.

Rival Theories   Thus the two groups started with opposing theories about the way broadcasting should work. In the end it turned out that each group was partly right, partly wrong. The idea of the Radio Group that each advertiser would own a separate station devoted exclusively to promoting that advertiser's goods was not practicable. The Telephone Group correctly foresaw that the number of stations would have to be limited, and that each station would be used by many different advertisers. It miscalculated, however, in placing the primary emphasis on message *senders* rather than on the interest of the general public, whose good will had to be earned. In this matter the Radio Group's concept — to accept responsibility for providing a service to the receiving public, emphasizing the public's own needs and wishes — prevailed. It took about four years for these conflicting ideas to sort themselves out.

"Toll" Broadcasting   WEAF called advertiser-leased time "toll" broadcasting. Its first lease of facilities for a toll broadcast occurred on August 28, 1922. A Long Island real-estate firm paid a $50 toll for ten minutes of time, during which it explained the advantages of living in Hawthorne Court, an apartment complex in the Jackson Heights section of New York.

True to the telephone company's concept, WEAF at first allowed advertisers to fill entire segments of leased time with promotional talk. The idea that advertising messages would occupy only occasional one-minute-or-less announcements in programs consisting mostly of entertainment came later.

AT&T thought in terms of *institutional* advertising, the type it used itself. Nothing so crass as price could be mentioned. In 1923 the first weekly advertiser appeared on WEAF, sponsoring a musical group it called "The Browning King Orchestra" — a handy way to ensure frequent mention of the sponsor's name. The fact that Browning King sold clothing, however, was never discussed.

AT&T Monopoly on Radio Advertising
Even had it wished to, WJZ was not in a position to sell time to advertisers, as did WEAF. A clause in the patent cross-licensing agreements (§2.7) gave AT&T the exclusive right to sell radio transmitters that used patents in the pool. AT&T refused to sell to radio stations that planned to offer broadcast time for sale, unless those stations paid it a license fee for that right.

AT&T foresaw that if every firm that wanted to advertise bought its own station, interference would become intolerable. It had already received no less than sixty requests for delivery of transmitters from would-be broadcasters in the New York area alone. Shared use of facilities by advertisers, therefore, seemed essential.

The effect of AT&T's policy on commercial operation was soon reflected in the relative economic positions of WJZ and WEAF. Within a few years, WJZ was costing the Radio Group $100,000 a year to operate without realizing any direct income whatever, while WEAF was grossing $750,000 in advertising revenue annually.

AT&T was not so successful in preventing other stations from infringing on its patent rights. By early 1923, 93 percent of the 576 stations on the air were selling time in violation of AT&T restrictions (Banning, 1946: 134). Worried about the charges of monopoly, the telephone company was reluctant to take aggressive action against the infringers. Rather than let its rights go by the board completely, AT&T reluctantly issued licenses to the transmitter owners, permitting them to operate commercially.

"Chain" Broadcasting

AT&T also interpreted the cross-licensing agreements as giving it the right to prevent other broadcasters from connecting broadcast equipment to its telephone lines. WEAF soon began to capitalize on this advantage.

In 1923 the first permanent interconnection was set up, between WEAF and WMAF (South Dartmouth, Massachusetts), the latter owned by a rich eccentric who operated WMAF for his own amusement but who had no means for programming the station. He persuaded WEAF to feed him both toll (commercial) and nontoll (sustaining) programs, paying a fee for the latter and broadcasting the commercial programs without additional cost to the advertisers.

AT&T gradually added to its "chain" (network) of stations. By October 1924 it was able to set up a temporary coast-to-coast chain of twenty-two stations to carry a speech by President Calvin Coolidge. The regular WEAF network at this time, however, consisted of only six stations, to which WEAF fed three hours of programming a day. Interconnection was by regular AT&T telephone lines. But by 1926 the telephone company began setting aside permanently equalized circuits for the exclusive use of its radio network.

Meanwhile WJZ, already prevented by the cross-licensing agreements from selling advertising, was also refused network interconnection by AT&T. The Radio Group's station turned to the telegraph lines of Western Union, but telegraph wires pass such a narrow band of frequencies that these lines were far less satisfactory for broadcast programs than AT&T's telephone lines. Despite these difficulties, WJZ in 1923 opened a station in Washington, D.C., and by 1925 it had succeeded in organizing a network of fourteen stations.

New Cross-Licensing Agreements

The rivalry between WEAF and WJZ was not the only source of irritation among the companies that signed the patent-pooling agreements of 1919–1923 (§2.5). The market for broadcasting equipment, and in particular the mass market for receivers, upset the delicate balance of commercial interests that cross-licensing had devised.

The fad that Horne's department store anticipated in 1920 had really caught on: "The public appetite for sets was insatiable and not to be filled for years. Queues formed before stores that had any sets or parts. Dealers were a year catching up on orders" (Lessing, 1969: 111).

Between 1923 and 1926 continual behind-the-scenes negotiations went on aimed at settling the differences among the cross-licensees. A federal suit, alleging that the pool violated antitrust laws, added urgency to the need for action. By 1926 the telephone company was ready to admit that it had been mistaken in its original concept of broadcasting as just another branch of telephony.

Accordingly, the signatories of the cross-licensing agreements finally arrived at a revised set of three agreements in July 1926. The new agreements redistributed and redefined the rights of the parties to use their commonly owned patents and to engage in the various aspects of the business that grew out of the patents. Briefly summarized, the following terms directly affected broadcasting:

1. AT&T was granted exclusive control over wire telephony and *two-way wireless* telephone (that is, nonbroadcast radiotelephony).
2. Telephony was defined in a way that left AT&T in control of both wire and future wireless *relays* used for broadcasting.
3. RCA agreed to lease *network relay facilities* from AT&T.
4. Western Electric was barred from competing with the Radio Group in the *manufacture* of radio receivers.
5. AT&T surrendered its exclusive right to use the pool patents to control the manufacture of broadcast *transmitters*.
6. AT&T agreed to *sell WEAF* and all its other broadcasting assets to the Radio Group for a million dollars.
7. AT&T agreed *not to reenter* the broadcasting field. RCA received the right to carry on *commercial broadcasting*.

It would be difficult to overestimate the significance of the 1926 cross-licensing revisions to the future of broadcasting in America. As long as the two groups of major communications companies disagreed about fundamental policies, broadcasting's economic future remained uncertain. The 1926 agreements removed this uncertainty.

2.10 Evolution of Radio

NBC Organized   A few months after the 1926 settlement, the Radio Group, under David Sarnoff's leadership, created a new subsidiary, the National Broadcasting Company (NBC). NBC was the first company organized solely and specifically to operate a broadcasting *network*. Its four-and-a-half-hour coast-to-coast inaugural broadcast took place on November 15, 1926. The twenty-five stations in the network reached an estimated five million listeners on that occasion. Not until 1928, however, did coast-to-coast network operations begin on a regular basis.

Starting with the new year in 1927, RCA organized NBC as two semiautonomous networks, the Blue and Red. WJZ (later to become WABC) and the old Radio Group network formed the nucleus of the Blue; WEAF (later to become WNBC) and the old Telephone Group network formed the nucleus of the Red. This dual network arrangement arose because NBC now had duplicate outlets in New York and other major cities. By tying up two of the best stations in major cities, and by playing one network off against the other, NBC gained a significant advantage over the rival networks that had begun to develop.

Paley and CBS   The second network followed soon after NBC, in 1927. It began as United Independent Broadcasters (UIB), launched by an independent talent-booking agent who wanted an alternative to NBC as an outlet for his performers. Off to a rocky start, the UIB network went through rapid changes in ownership, picking up along the way the name Columbia Phonograph Broadcasting System as a result of an investment by a record company. The latter soon withdrew, but UIB retained the right to use the Columbia name.

The network's future remained uncertain until September 1928, when William S. Paley purchased the "patchwork, money-losing little company," as he later described it. At that point it had only twenty-two affiliates. Paley quickly turned the failing network around with a new affiliation contract. In his autobiography a half-century later he recalled:

I proposed the concept of free sustaining service . . . I would guarantee not ten but twenty hours of programming per week, pay the stations $50 an hour for the commercial hours used, but with a new proviso. The network would not pay the stations for the first five hours of commercial programming time . . . to allow for the possibility of more business to come, the network was to receive an option on additional time.

And for the first time, we were to have exclusive rights for network broadcasting through the affiliate. That meant the local station could not use its facilities for any other broadcasting network. I added one more innovation which helped our cause: local stations would have to identify our programs with the CBS name. (Paley, 1979: 42)

The Paley innovations outlined in the above passages became standard practice in network contracts, though some of the more restrictive terms were later banned by the Federal Communications Commission.

Paley also simplified the firm's name, calling it Columbia Broadcasting System (the corporate name was later further simplified to CBS, Incorporated), and bought a New York outlet as the network flagship station (now WCBS). From that point on CBS never faltered, and Paley eventually rivaled Sarnoff as the leading executive in the history of broadcasting in America (see Box, page 61).

Doubts About Commercialism   Paley's enthusiasm for the exploitation of radio as an advertising medium was not universally shared in the 1920s. At the First Radio Conference, called by Secretary of Commerce Herbert Hoover in Washington in 1922 (§2.11), the sentiment against advertising had been almost universal.

At the Fourth Radio Conference, in 1925, broadcasters still considered direct advertising objectionable, recommending good-will announcements only. Two years later the author of a book titled *Using Radio in Sales Promotion* could write, "the broadcast listener regards any attempt at radio advertising as an affront" (Felix, 1927: 211). As the book's title implies, the author saw radio only as a supplement to direct advertising: "clearly it is not an advertising medium, useful in disseminating sales arguments and selling points" (8). The same concept had governed WEAF's early experiments with toll broadcasting, described in §2.9.

But only a year or so later, under the pressure of rising operating costs and advertiser interest, advertising became more acceptable and much more common. Because stations themselves had not yet developed the production and programming skills needed for mass appeal entertainment, advertising agencies moved in and took over the programming role, introducing the idea of *sponsorship*. Sponsors did more than simply advertise: they also brought to the networks the shows that served as vehicles for their advertising messages. Advertising agencies thus became program producers, and during the height of network radio's popularity most major entertainment shows were controlled by agencies on behalf of their advertiser clients.

The agencies evaded early network rules against frequent mention of sponsors by tacking trade names to performers' names. Audiences of the late 1920s heard "The Cliquot Club Eskimos," "The A&P Gypsies," "The Ipana Troubadours," and so on. An opening "billboard" from this period manages to add four indirect product mentions to the permissible single direct mention of sponsor name and product name:

Relax and smile, for Goldy and Dusty, the Gold Dust Twins, are here to send their songs there, and "brighten the corner where you are." The Gold Dust

Sarnoff and Paley

Both these pioneers of network broadcasting came from immigrant Russian families, but there the similarity ceases. Sarnoff (left) rose from the direst poverty, a self-educated and self-made man. In sharp contrast, Paley (right) had every advantage of money and social position. After earning a degree from the Wharton School of Business at the University of Pennsylvania in 1922, he joined his father's prosperous cigar company.

The differences between Sarnoff and Paley extended to their personalities and special skills. Sarnoff was "an engineer turned businessman, ill at ease with the hucksterism that he had wrought, and he did not condescend to sell, but Bill Paley loved to sell. CBS was Paley, and he sold it as he sold himself" (Halberstam, 1979: 27).

Sarnoff had been introduced to radio by way of hard work at the telegraph key, Paley by way of leisurely DX listening: "As a radio fan in Philadelphia, I often sat up all night, glued to my set, listening and marveling at the voices and music which came into my ears from distant places," he recalled (Paley, 1979: 32).

Paley's introduction to the business of radio came by way of sponsored programming. After becoming advertising manager of his father's cigar company in 1925, he experimented with a program on WCAU (Philadelphia). Impressed with the results, he explored radio further. The rest is history.

Sources: Sarnoff, courtesy RCA; Paley, courtesy CBS.

Corporation, manufacturer of Gold Dust Powder, engages the facilities of station WEAF, New York, WJAR, Providence, WCAE, Pittsburgh, WGR, Buffalo, WEEI, Boston, WFI, Philadelphia, and WEAR, Cleveland, so that listeners-in may have the opportunity to chuckle and laugh with Goldy and Dusty. Let those Gold Dust Twins into your hearts and homes tonight, and you'll never regret it, for they do brighten the dull spots. (Quoted in Banning, 1946: 262)

Anyone not already aware of the product could hardly guess that the commercial refers to laundry soap powder.

Most commercial programs were musical variety shows, sponsored by advertisers of batteries, radios, soft drinks, bread, and candy. Even though such down-to-earth details as the mentioning of price were still banned, advertising was already well on its way to becoming the dominant factor in broadcasting in America.

A Still Small Voice   The federal government had licensed many of the earliest broadcasting stations to universities, outgrowths of experiments in their science and engineering laboratories. Though usually operated noncommercially, educational AM stations held the same kind of licenses as commercial stations, since the Radio Act of 1927 (§2.11) made no provisions for a separate noncommercial service. As channels increased in commercial value, most of these educational stations lost their assignments to commercial interests. Only a score survived, representing a still, small voice crying out for broadcast pluralism in the ever growing commercial wilderness (§4.6).

2.11   Government Regulation

There remains one final foundation block to put in place before the story of broadcasting's emergence is complete: the passage of legislation capable of imposing order on the new medium.

Regulation of Wire   The government's decision to return radio to private operation after World War I (§2.7) did not mean abandonment of government oversight. Since the beginning of telegraphy, governments throughout the world had recognized that both national and international regulation were essential to fair and efficient operation of telecommunication systems. In 1865, twenty-five European countries drew up the International Telegraphic Convention, precursor of the International Telecommunication Union that now provides a cooperative world forum for administration and allocation of wire and wireless communication. Thus prior experience in the regulation of the wire services set a pattern for radio regulation.

Maritime Wireless Regulation   The first international conference specifically concerned with wireless communication took place in Berlin in 1903, only six years after Marconi's first patent. Its main object, in fact, was to deal with the Marconi Company's refusal to exchange messages with rival maritime wireless systems. It was agreed at the conference that humanitarian considerations had to take precedence over commercial rivalries when human lives were at stake in maritime emergencies. Three years later, at the Berlin Convention of 1906, nations agreed to require ships to be equipped with suitable wireless gear and to exchange SOS messages freely among different commercial systems.*

---

*The international distress, or SOS, frequency was set at 500 kHz. This decision had a bearing on the eventual allocation of the broadcasting band. It would have been more efficient to start the AM band lower in the spectrum, but this was prevented by the need to avoid interference with the 500-kHz distress frequency.

Finally, prodded by the terrible lesson of the *Titanic* disaster (see Box, page 48), Congress confirmed the 1906 convention rules by passing the Radio Act of 1912. This was the first comprehensive U.S. *radio* (not broadcasting) legislation, replacing earlier piecemeal enactments, including a wireless act passed in 1910. The 1912 act remained in force during the period of broadcasting's emergent years.

Failure of the 1912 Act   The new law worked well enough for point-to-point services. Broadcasting, however, introduced unprecedented demands on the spectrum never imagined when the 1912 act was written. That act directed the secretary of commerce and labor to grant licenses to U.S. citizens "upon application therefor." It gave no grounds on which the secretary could *reject* applications. In 1912 the demand for channels was so limited that Congress had no reason to anticipate the need to reject applicants. Presumably all who had a good reason to operate radio stations could be allowed to do so.

Secretary of Commerce Herbert Hoover at first made all broadcast stations share time on the same channel. Then in 1921 he allocated the carrier frequency 833 kHz for "news and entertainment" stations and 618 kHz for "crop and weather report" stations. The practice of time-sharing worked well for ships' stations, which needed to make only occasional exchanges of specific messages and could wait in line to get access to a shared channel. But broadcast stations, with their need to transmit uninterrupted program services, demanded continuous access to their channels.

The rapid growth in the number of stations soon created intolerable interference. Adding more channels helped not at all, for stations multiplied faster than ever. Some station owners took matters into their own hands and began to change frequency, power, times of operation, and location at will — all in violation of their licenses. These changes created even worse interference, of course, so that intelligible reception became impossible. (Exhibit 2.6)

National Radio Conferences   Herbert Hoover, a Republican and an ardent believer in free enterprise, hoped that the industry would be able to discipline itself without government regulation. To that end he called a series of four national radio conferences in Washington. At the first, in 1922, only 22 broadcasters attended; by 1925 the number had risen to 400.

In 1924 Hoover optimistically called the national radio conferences "experiments in industrial self-government" (Dept. of Commerce, 1924: 2), but even at that time he must have suspected the hopelessness of the experiment. He commented repeatedly on the fact that here was an industry that actually *wanted* government regulation. From year to year the radio conferences grew more explicit in their suggestions for government regulations.

Zenith Decision   Finally, a 1926 court decision completely undermined the secretary's power of enforcement. A Zenith Radio Corporation station, WJAZ (Chicago), had operated at times and on frequencies different from those authorized in its license. The secretary of commerce brought suit under the Radio Act of 1912 to enforce compliance, but the court found in favor of the station, stating, ". . . Administrative rulings cannot add to the terms of an act of Congress and make conduct criminal which such laws leave untouched" (12 F 2d 618, 1926).

The Zenith case illuminates a fundamental concept of the American system of "government by laws, not men." No government official is granted unlimited authority. Paradoxically, by failing to limit the secretary's discretionary powers to enforce the radio act,

Exhibit 2.6   Hoover vs. the Evangelist

An example of the bizarre problems faced by the secretary of commerce was the station owned by Aimée Semple McPherson, a popular evangelist of the 1920s. She operated a pioneer broadcast station from her "temple" in Los Angeles. The station "wandered all over the wave band." After delivering repeated warnings, a government inspector ordered the station closed down. The secretary of commerce thereupon received the following telegram from the evangelist:

PLEASE ORDER YOUR MINIONS OF SATAN TO LEAVE MY STATION ALONE. YOU CANNOT EXPECT THE ALMIGHTY TO ABIDE BY YOUR WAVE-LENGTH NONSENSE. WHEN I OFFER MY PRAYERS TO HIM I MUST FIT INTO HIS WAVE RECEPTION. OPEN THIS STATION AT ONCE. (Hoover, 1952: II-142)

Evangelist McPherson, after being persuaded to engage a competent engineer, was allowed to reopen her station.

Source: United Press International/Bettmann.

Congress left him with such unconstitutionally broad powers that he became powerless.

In less than a year, two hundred new broadcast stations took advantage of the government's inability to enforce licensing rules. Meaningful reception had become impossible in most places. "Co-channel interference became so bad at many points on the radio dial," reported the Federal Radio Commission later, "that the listener might suppose instead of a receiving set he had a peanut roaster with assorted whistles" (FRC, 1927: 11). Thirty-eight stations created bedlam in the New York area, as did forty in the Chicago area. Sales of radio sets declined noticeably. In his message to Congress in December 1926, President Calvin Coolidge said, "The whole service of this most important public function has drifted into such chaos as seems likely, if not remedied, to destroy its great value. I most urgently recommend that this legislation should be speedily enacted" (Coolidge, 1926: 32).

Radio Act of 1927   Coolidge was referring to the proposed new radio law, which Congress finally passed on February 23, 1927. The Radio Act of 1927 embodied the recommendations of Hoover's Fourth Radio Conference and so can be said to represent what most of the broadcasters themselves wanted.

The act provided for a *temporary* Federal Radio Commission (FRC) to put things in order. After two years, though, it became clear that broadcasting and other radio services would in fact need continuing and detailed attention, and so Congress made the FRC a permanent body.

The FRC was not in a position to wipe the slate clean by canceling existing licenses and assigning channels from scratch, but it did take immediate steps to reduce interference. It temporarily limited license periods to only sixty days (the law allowed a maximum of three years), continuing an earlier edict of Congress. The commission defined the broadcast band, standardized channel designation by frequency instead of by wavelength, closed down portable broadcast stations, and cut back on the number of stations allowed to operate at night. At last investors in broadcasting could move ahead with assurance that signals would not be ruined by uncontrollable mavericks on the airwaves. The passage of the Radio Act of 1927 and the start of continuing supervision by the FRC meant that the final foundation stone of broadcasting as a new communication service was in place. The period of emergence was over and the period of stable growth could now begin.

Summary

• Among the preconditions for development of broadcasting were the general late-nineteenth-century trends toward urbanization, education, and development of major industries. The penny-press newspaper, vaudeville, the phonograph, and the motion picture gave rise to patterns of mass media production, distribution, and consumption that would soon be followed by radio broadcasting.

• The industrial context for radio was the electrical industry, dominated by AT&T's Western Electric, by General Electric, and by Westinghouse, all of which controlled important patents. The immediate technical precursors of wireless were the land telegraph of the 1840s, the submarine cable of the 1860s, and the telephone of the 1880s.

• The theories of James Clerk Maxwell in the 1860s led to the experiments of Heinrich Hertz two decades later, and provided the impetus for Guglielmo Marconi's development of a working wireless system in the 1890s.

• Wireless was first applied to maritime and transoceanic telegraphic communication early in this century. Only after development of the vacuum tube in 1904 by Ambrose Fleming, and its major improvement in 1906 by Lee de Forest with the Audion, did practical radiotelephony become possible.

• World War I accelerated the development of radio technology, bringing about the pooling of crucial wireless patents and the development of radio manufacturing and trained radio personnel. The U.S. Navy took over control of most radio transmitters for the 1917–1920 period.

• Under protest, the navy in 1920 handed back nonmilitary transmitters to private hands. General Electric formed RCA to take over and operate the holdings of American Marconi. Major manufacturing firms entered patent cross-licensing agreements in the 1919–1923 period to allow wireless development. All of this, however, was aimed at furthering the application of wireless to point-to-point long-distance services.

• The foundation for broadcasting in America was laid between 1919 and 1927, a period of time that brought about (1) the concept of broadcasting to entertain a general audience, (2) the acceptance of advertising as the means of radio's financial support, (3) the development of competing national networks of stations, and (4) the federal regulation and licensing of stations.

• The development of broadcasting, with its market for receivers and advertising time, brought conflict between the Radio and Telephone groups of broadcasters. RCA, GE, and Westinghouse stations comprised the former, and AT&T stations the latter. Disagreements centered on use of pooled patents, rights to sell advertising on the air, and the use of telephone lines for networking.

• In 1926 cross-licensing agreements drawn up prior to the development of broadcasting were replaced. AT&T withdrew from broadcasting, except to provide network interconnection. The rival networks came under RCA control. RCA formed NBC Red around WEAF, which it had purchased from AT&T, and NBC Blue around WJZ. A rival firm, CBS, was formed in 1927 and came under the control of William Paley two years later.

• A wireless act passed in 1910 and other piecemeal legislation were replaced by the Radio Act of 1912, which was not designed to control broadcasting. By 1926, despite the efforts of Secretary of Commerce Hoover, radio had fallen into a chaotic unregulated state. Congress finally passed the Radio Act of 1927 to control broadcasting, the final step in establishing the foundation of broadcasting in America.

CHAPTER 3

From Radio to Television

For nearly three decades AM radio dominated the broadcasting business. While other technologies were slowly developing in laboratories, broadcasting grew within lines that had been established in the 1920s. Changes were evolutionary as networks matured, the number of stations and receivers increased, and radio became part of the American fabric of life.

These were radio's "golden years" of expanding popularity and success with audiences and advertisers. Yet they were years of extreme social stress — the Great Depression, followed soon by the Second World War. For millions of listeners, radio provided both entertainment that provided an escape from reality and news that described the changing world. Changes in older print, film, and recorded media became evident in the 1930s and accelerated rapidly with the inception of commercial television. This chapter relates the important transition from radio to television, setting the stage for the even more dramatic changes of recent years.

3.1 Radio During the Great Depression (1929–1937)

During the early 1930s, for the first time in broadcasting history, the number of stations on the air actually decreased (Exhibit 3.1). This decline occurred both because of the efforts of the Federal Radio Commission to clear up interference among stations and because of the shortage of investment funds during the Depression years. By 1937, however, three-quarters of all U.S. homes had radios and the number of stations had again begun an upward climb that has continued ever since.

During these years from 1929 to 1937 a third of American workers lost their jobs and national productivity fell by half. Suffering was intense, for none of the welfare programs that now cushion the effects of unemployment and poverty were in place. In this time of great trial, radio entertainment came as a godsend, the one widely available distraction from the grim realities of the daily struggle to survive. As little as $15 could buy a vacuum tube receiver. Listener loyalty was so intense it became "almost irrational," according to historian Erik Barnouw:

Destitute families, forced to give up an icebox or furniture or bedding, clung to the radio as to a last link to humanity. In consequence radio, though briefly jolted by the Depression, was soon prospering from it. Motion picture business was suffering, the theater was collapsing, vaudeville was dying, but many of their major talents flocked to radio — along with audiences and sponsors. Some companies were beginning to make a comeback through radio sponsorship. In the process, the tone of radio changed rapidly. (Barnouw, 1978: 27)

Coming into office early in 1933, Franklin D. Roosevelt proved to be a master broadcaster, the first (and some still think the most skillful) national politician to exploit the new medium to its full potential in presidential politics. The nation's spirit was lifted during his inaugural address by the ringing phrase "The only thing we have to fear is fear itself," broadcast throughout the country by both CBS and NBC (still the only national networks on the air in 1933).

Soon Roosevelt's distinctive, patrician voice became familiar to every listener who tuned in to his "fireside chats," the term used to suggest the informality, warmth, and directness of these presidential radio reports to the people — a brand-new phenomenon in American politics. "It was in the most direct sense," wrote David Halberstam, "the government reaching out and touching the citizen . . . Roosevelt was the first professional of the art" (1979: 15).

Creation of the FCC   Roosevelt also had an important impact on the regulation of communications. Uncomfortable with the confusion and overlap among the several agencies then dealing with telegraph, telephone, and radio operations, he sent a message to Congress early in 1934 urging formation of a *communications* commission to pull together the different pieces under one roof. Based on that request, plus its own study of the situation, Congress passed the comprehensive *Communications Act of 1934* (§16.2). The act created a seven-member Federal Communications Commission to regulate all interstate electrical communication, including broadcasting. The old FRC was abolished, but much of the Radio Act of 1927 survived, its text incorporated as part

of the 1934 act. The FCC began operation in mid-1934, one of the many agencies established in the flurry of New Deal government activity. A half century later, FCC Chairman Mark Fowler would often refer to the agency as the last of the New Deal dinosaurs.

Broadcast Conservatism   Major stations and networks of the 1930s maintained standards of deportment that today would seem absurdly formal. Network announcers were expected to wear dinner jackets in the evening and to speak literate English. Broadcasters and advertisers were sensitive to radio's status as a guest in the home. A public furor erupted in 1937 over some lines read by Mae West in a comedy dialogue with Charlie McCarthy, Edgar Bergen's ventriloquist dummy (now in the Smithsonian Institution):

West: *Why don't you come home with me? I'll let you play in my woodpile. . . . You're all wood and a yard long. You weren't so nervous and backward when you came to see me at my apartment. In fact, you didn't need much encouragement to kiss me.*
Charlie: *Did I do that?*
West: *You certainly did, and I got marks to prove it, and splinters, too. (Quoted in* Broadcasting, *1970: 119)*

The FCC responded to outraged complaints by lecturing NBC on its obligation to maintain proper standards of taste and propriety.

Another aspect of broadcast conservatism was its refusal to permit all-out advertising. The networks continued their ban on mentioning prices until 1932. A prime mover in overcoming radio's reticence about direct advertising was William Benton, who cofounded the Benton and Bowles advertising agency in 1929. Benton realized that to be effective on radio, advertising had to make two adaptations: it had to break away from the print-media style of copywriting and compensate for radio's lack of visual cues. When Benton started

Exhibit 3.1   Growth of Radio Stations, 1920–1985

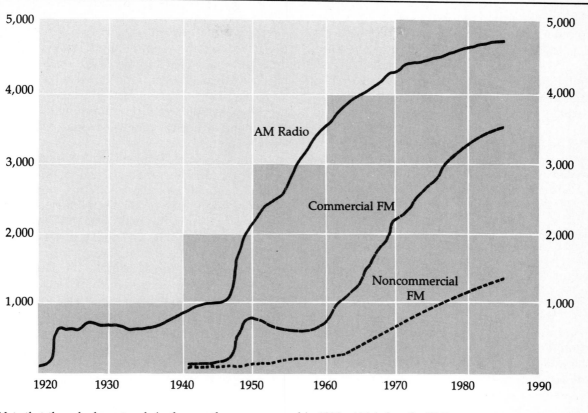

Note that the only down-trends in the growth curves occurred in 1930s AM (when the FRC was imposing order on the pre-radio act chaos) and in 1950s FM (when its initial promise seemed not to be paying off). The sharp upward trend in the AM growth curve in the late 1940s occurred after removal of World War II's restraints on consumer goods.

Sources: Adapted from *Stay Tuned: A Concise History of Broadcasting,* by Christopher H. Sterling and John M. Kittross. Copyright 1978 by Wadsworth Publishing Co., Inc. Reprinted by permission of Wadsworth Publishing Company, Belmont, CA. 1985 data from *Broadcasting* (21 Jan. 85), p. 105.

writing advertising copy for radio, a commercial consisted of someone simply reading an announcement. Benton changed all that, as he later recalled: "I *staged* commercials, you could hear the spoons, people clinking cups of coffee, everything acted out" (quoted in Whitman, 1973, emphasis added). Besides helping

to revolutionize commercials, Benton developed consumer research techniques, launched some of the most successful radio network shows of the period, introduced live studio audiences as an acoustic setting (using audience reaction cue cards), and popularized the singing commercial.

Programming Excesses   Side by side with the self-conscious correctness and conservatism of network radio, however, there existed another, quite different standard of broadcasting. All across the country radio proved irresistibly attractive to a variety of raffish, offbeat individualists who exploited it as a personal mouthpiece. As pioneer radio critic Ben Gross recalled it:

Tailors, preachers, loan sharks, swamis, and physical-culture men, merchants, nostrum dispensers and frenzied advocates of odd ideas, such as Colonel Henderson of Shreveport, Louisiana, who combined primitive theology with hatred of chain stores, indulged in a saturnalia of "free speech." . . . In a steady procession, there came before the microphones newscasters who merely read word-for-word items from the daily papers, owners of diploma mills, crystal-gazing fortune-tellers, installment furniture men, conductors of matrimonial bureaus, fakers, nuts and dreamers making merry carnival. (Gross, 1954: 68)

In most cases the Federal Radio Commission (FRC) was able to correct abuses without withdrawing licenses (which at first had to be renewed at six-month intervals). But in two notorious instances in the early 1930s the commission did administer the ultimate penalty. In one case the FRC objected to the broadcasting of medical advice by a "Dr." J. R. Brinkley on his station, KFKB, in Milford, Kansas. Brinkley was not a qualified physician and yet prescribed drugs that he packaged himself and sold by number, rather than by name. The FRC refused to renew KFKB's license, saying Brinkley conducted the station only in his personal interest, not in the interest of the public.

The second case involved a religious crusader alleging municipal corruption. The Reverend Dr. Shuler of the Trinity Methodist Church (South) broadcast in Los Angeles over KGEF, a small, shared-time religious station. His fire-and-brimstone personal attacks drew the biggest radio audience in Los Angeles when he was on the air. When KGEF's license came up for renewal in 1931 some ninety witnesses appeared in opposition. The FRC turned down the renewal application.

Both the KFKB and the KGEF renewal denials withstood court appeals, establishing in the early 1930s the commission's legal right to review a station's past programming in deciding whether license renewal would be in the public interest.

The fact that Brinkley and Shuler were broadcast *licensees* made them vulnerable. Most personal exploiters of radio, however, simply bought time on the air. Notable among this group during the 1930s was the Reverend Charles E. Coughlin, a Catholic priest with a charismatic radio appeal. From the unlikely base of a small parish church, the Shrine of the Little Flower, in a suburb of Detroit, Father Coughlin built up a fanatically loyal national radio following. His vitriolic sermons against communism, Wall Street, Jews, labor unions, and other targets generated millions of dollars in small donations from his devoted followers. Because of his pro-Nazi sympathies his opponents called his church "the Shrine of the Little Führer." He was finally silenced in 1940, not by his political opponents directly or his church superiors, but by the refusal of networks and most larger stations to continue selling him time (Brown, 1980). With U.S. entry into World War II imminent, his tirades had become an embarrassment to the broadcasting industry.

Brinkley, Shuler, and Coughlin were examples of the more extreme consequences of radio's innate susceptibility to misuse. Their downfall did not put other exploiters out of business; it merely caused most of them to lower their profile. Spellbinders, quacks, cultists, zealots, and get-rich-quick schemers have always been part of the broadcasting scene. They cannot be completely suppressed without violating the First Amendment's guarantees of freedom of expression and of religion and the constitutional separation of church and state.

Network Development   William Paley's upstart rival network, CBS, struggled for years to overcome its image as the number-two chain, laboring in the wake of NBC. Big advertisers and star performers automatically preferred NBC to CBS whenever they had a choice, regardless of CBS's growing popularity. "We were at the mercy of the sponsors and the ad agencies," wrote Paley. "They could always take a successful show away from us and put it on NBC" (1979: 174).

NBC remained a wholly owned RCA subsidiary while RCA itself developed into a giant diversified corporation with worldwide interests in communication services and manufacturing. NBC, reflecting the parent company's high corporate status, tended to assume the role of a dignified elder among the networks. Its image was further enhanced in 1933 when NBC moved into its new headquarters in the seventy-story art-deco-style RCA building, part of New York's famed Rockefeller Center.*

The Mutual Broadcasting System started on a different premise from the older networks. Only two major-market radio stations on clear channels had remained in the early 1930s without affiliation with CBS or NBC, WGN-Chicago and WOR-New York. They arranged in 1934 to form a network organization to sell time jointly with WXYZ-Detroit and WLW-Cincinnati. The four stations started the

network by exchanging programs on a regional network basis. Their chief program asset at the start was *The Lone Ranger*, a series that WXYZ had introduced in 1933.

Radio Comedy   The first network radio entertainment program to achieve addictive popularity was a prime-time, five-days-a-week situation comedy, *Amos 'n' Andy*. Charles Correll ("Andy") and Freeman Gosden ("Amos") came to radio as a song-and-patter team, a format much esteemed in early radio. At a station manager's suggestion they tried their luck at a comedy series. The two white performers developed a black dialect show in fractured ghetto English, featuring the ups and downs of the "Fresh Air Taxicab Company of America, Incorporated."

Amos 'n' Andy became the top network show in the early 1930s. Traffic would stop on the main streets of towns across the country and movies would be halted in midreel at 7:00 P.M. so that people would not miss their nightly fifteen minutes of chuckles over the antics of Amos, Andy, the Kingfish, Lightnin', Madam Queen, and a host of minor characters, most of whom Correll and Gosden played themselves.

Today the impersonation of blacks by white actors using exaggerated dialect and comedy situations based on ghetto poverty could not be seriously proposed. A Pittsburgh newspaper asked the FCC to ban the series in 1931, alleging racism, but its defenders had a convincing argument: most blacks seemed to enjoy the program just as much as whites.*

---

*CBS did not achieve its own architectural monument until 1965, when it moved into splendid new headquarters at the corner of 52nd Street and Avenue of the Americas, two blocks from NBC. Sheathed in elegant dark granite, the CBS building came to be known as Black Rock. In 1986, NBC announced plans to move elsewhere in New York City.

*Opposition became more general in the 1950s. CBS ran a television version of *Amos 'n' Andy* (with black actors) from 1951 to 1953, but dropped it because of opposition from the National Association for the Advancement of Colored People. Syndicated showings continued until 1966, but the syndicator finally agreed to withdraw the series from both national and international syndication (Brown, 1977: 16).

3.2 Radio Controversies

Live Music Era   Both networks and the larger stations relied heavily on music from the very beginning of radio. In the mid-1930s over half of all radio programming was music, and three-quarters of it was carried on a sustaining (nonsponsored) basis. Most large stations had their own musical groups, and the networks even had their own symphony orchestras.

In CBS's early years, a quarter of its entire schedule was devoted to music. NBC began regular broadcasts of the Metropolitan Opera in 1931, carrying it mostly on a sustaining basis until 1940. Thereafter Texaco, Inc., underwrote the Met broadcasts and has continued to do so ever since — "the longest continuous commercial underwriting of the same program by the same sponsor in the history of radio" (McDowell, 1979). Texaco, which now organizes a special ad hoc 300-station radio network to carry the programs, abstains from commercial interruptions, inserting brief sponsor identifications only at intermissions.

All this had tremendous impact on the musical world, creating vast new public appetites for all sorts of music, old and new, classical and popular. While expanding the market for music, however, radio also created copyright and union-rights problems never before faced by the creators and performers of musical works.

Music Performing Rights: ASCAP and BMI   Under the copyright law* the playing of a recording in public for profit is regarded as a performance. As such it obligates the user (in this case the radio station) to pay the copyright holders (who may include composers of the music, lyricists, and music publishers) for *performing rights.*

Music copyright holders cannot possibly monitor personally all the tens of thousands of commercial establishments where music is performed, including concert halls, hotels, nightclubs, and other such public places as well as broadcasting stations. Instead they rely on *music licensing* organizations to act on their behalf in collecting copyright fees for performances of both live and recorded music. The first U.S. organization of this type, the American Society of Composers, Authors and Publishers (ASCAP), was founded in 1914. It checks on the public performances of music copyrighted by its members, collects royalty fees, and distributes the net income to the copyright owners.

When radio began, no one could be sure what impact this new way of performing music would have. Would repeated radio performances quickly kill off interest in new musical works, or would they enhance the market for sheet music, recordings, and in-person performances? As early as 1922, ASCAP began making substantial demands for payments by broadcasters for the use of musical works in its catalog, whether broadcast live or from recordings. These demands imposed a new and unexpected financial burden on radio stations. In 1923 station owners formed the National Association of Broadcasters (NAB) to deal with ASCAP's demands on an industry-wide basis. Nevertheless, as radio grew the fees collected by ASCAP also grew, and soon broadcasting was contributing the major share of the association's royalty collections. Effective resistance to ASCAP's demands was impossible because it was the sole U.S. licensing organization and controlled virtually all contemporary American music, along with contemporary arrangements of older compositions on which original copy-

---

*The present law, the Copyright Act of 1976 (17 U.S. Code), replaced the 1909 law that was in effect when radio broadcasting began. (Details of the 1976 Act are discussed in §16.5.)

rights had expired. Radio stations found it impossible to produce listenable music programs without infringing on ASCAP copyrights.

Finally broadcasters moved to break the ASCAP monopoly. When ASCAP proposed yet another substantial fee increase in 1937 the broadcasters rebelled, forming their own cooperative music-licensing organization, Broadcast Music, Inc. (BMI). The new organization started business in 1940. Its first "affiliates," as the copyright owners are called, were composers of country, western, and "race" music (black popular music), most of whom had never registered with ASCAP. Eventually, BMI built up a comprehensive library representing over a million musical works owned by some 55,000 publishers and writers.

Union Battle Against Recordings

Although broadcasting created many new jobs for musicians, they saw its increasing reliance on recorded music (especially the electrical transcriptions then used for syndicated programs) as a threat. If stations and networks made use of recordings, many musicians would lose their jobs. Each of the major networks, and many larger stations, had full-time orchestras, which would become redundant if records were used heavily. In 1922 an implacable opponent of radio's use of recordings, James Caesar Petrillo, had become president of the Chicago chapter of the American Federation of Musicians (AFM).

"Little Caesar," as Petrillo was called, first built a strong political base locally in Chicago, then went on to become national AFM president in 1940. He threatened to close down transcription makers, forcing syndication firms to pay substantial extra fees for every broadcast transcription made, the money going to a union slush fund that Petrillo alone controlled. He succeeded in forcing broadcasters to hire professional musicians as "platter turners" in the control rooms and as

librarians in the station record libraries of his hometown, Chicago. He demanded that stations increase musicians' pay as much as fivefold. With unprecedented bravado, Petrillo defied the National War Labor Board, President Roosevelt, the Supreme Court, and the Congress of the United States.

Congress finally passed the Lea Act in 1946, amending the Communications Act of 1934 specifically to bring Petrillo under control. The Lea Act forbade stations to hire unneeded personnel to satisfy union demands, banned union restrictions on the use of transcriptions, and forbade unions from preventing broadcasts by amateur musicians.

Press-Radio "War"   News, no less than broadcast entertainment, depends on syndication (§13.2). Newspapers share material by means of *press associations* — or *wire services*, as they were traditionally called, referring to the fact that they flourished with the telegraph (§2.1).

Radio disturbed the vested interests of the news agencies and their customary clients, the newspapers. Radio, in bypassing the written word, seemed to threaten the very future of news publications. Who would want to buy a paper to read news already heard on the radio? Who would want to buy advertising space in papers whose news was already stale? The newspapers recognized that the key to suppressing radio competition was control over broadcasters' access to the output of the major established news agencies. At the time, these were the Associated Press (AP), which was owned cooperatively by newspapers themselves, the International News Service (INS), and the United Press (UP).

NBC's Blue Network inaugurated regular fifteen-minute nightly newscasts by Lowell Thomas in 1930, a sign that radio might soon assume a serious competitive role. In response to threats that news agency services would soon be cut off, CBS began forming its own newsgathering organization. To defuse possible competition, the newspaper publishers proposed a truce in 1933. The result, known as the Biltmore Agreement, set up a Press-Radio Bureau designed to protect the papers' interests.*

According to the terms of the agreement, CBS suspended its own newsgathering, and the two networks agreed to confine themselves to two 5-minute press-wire news summaries a day from the Press-Radio Bureau. These could be aired only after the morning and evening papers had appeared, could be used only on a sustaining (non-sponsored) basis, and had to be followed by the admonition, "For further details consult your local newspaper(s)." The bureau agreed to issue additional special bulletins on events "of transcendent importance," but they had to be written "in such a manner as to stimulate public interest in the reading of newspapers" (quoted in Kahn, 1983: 103).

In practice, however, the Press-Radio Bureau never worked effectively. Only about a third of the existing stations subscribed to it, and several independent radio news services sprang up to fill the gap. Broadcasters also took advantage of escape clauses in the agreement that exempted news commentaries. In consequence a great many radio newscasters became instant commentators.

United Press broke the embargo in 1935, soon to be joined by International News Service. The Press-Radio Bureau finally expired, unmourned, in 1940 when the Associated Press began to accept radio stations as members of the association.

As broadcast news matured it became evident that, contrary to the expectations of the newspaper publishers, radio coverage actually stimulated newspaper reading instead of discouraging it. The press services eventually acquired even more broadcasters than publishers as customers and began to offer services especially tailored for broadcast stations, including audio feeds ready to go directly on the air.

3.3 Television and FM Radio

As they tuned in to radio entertainment and news, listeners in the 1930s began to hear and read more about radio-with-pictures, or television, experiments. There were also rumors of a new kind of radio that eliminated static. While highly promising, both developments were to take far longer to reach commercial fruition than their backers then suspected.

Why TV Took So Long   The idea of wireless transmission of pictures occurred to inventors as early as did the idea of wireless sound transmission. However, even after sound broadcasting became a reality, television still remained in the experimental stage.

This delay was partly because of the more sophisticated technology that television required, but even more because of the need for *compatibility*, the need to adopt a single national standard specifying the details of the television signal. The act of standardizing such technical details as frame- and line-frequency (§6.6) would freeze development at a particular level. If it turned out later that standards should have been set at a higher level, tremendous waste would occur because millions of receivers and much studio and transmitter equipment would be outmoded.

Setting television standards involved finding a compromise among the conflicting interests of patent holders, manufacturers, and government bureaucracies, all with their own

---

*CBS and NBC were parties to the agreement, but not the nonaffiliated stations. The relevant parts of the document are reprinted by Kahn (1984: 101).

economic and political concerns. For these reasons, in the years before 1948 television moved forward in fits and starts as standards were improved bit by bit and FCC permission was won to try the improvements out on the public.

This technological evolution went through two phases: that of mechanical scanning and that of electronic scanning. The latter began to take the lead in the early 1930s and had just begun to reach a satisfactory level when World War II interrupted further development. Accordingly, widespread introduction of modern television occurred only after the conclusion of the war.

Experimental television existed for decades before television became a mass medium. Early systems worked, but the pictures were far too crude to be regarded as anything but curiosities. The problem was basically one of getting a clear enough picture, or what television engineers refer to as sufficient *resolution* (§6.6). A standard at least as good as home movies was needed for widespread public acceptance.

Mechanical TV   The mechanical era in television began with development of the *scanning wheel* or disc, invented in 1884 by Paul Nipkow in Germany. A large flat metal disc, perforated with a ring of small holes in a spiral pattern, the scanning wheel was central to experiments with television through the 1920s. Early experimental TV depended on the rapid spinning of synchronized discs in both camera and receiver to reproduce a crude picture made up of about 30 lines (compared to the all-electronic system of 525 lines we use today; see §6.6 and Exhibit 3.3).* Charles Jenkins in

the United States and John Logie Baird in Britain demonstrated mechanical systems, and both briefly manufactured and sold receivers. Baird's persistent efforts, along with the competing all-electronic system of the Marconi-EMI concern, culminated in late 1936 with the BBC's introduction of the first high-definition television service.* Mechanical television had by the late 1930s reached the peak of what it could offer, and electronic systems, even in the crude stage they were in at that time, provided far better transmission and reception and much clearer pictures. The BBC soon dropped Baird's mechanical apparatus and concentrated on electronic developments. Though German experiments with television continued sporadically during World War II, the BBC closed down its service when the war began.

Electronic Television   The names most prominent in U.S. television developments after Baird's mechanical system was abandoned were those of two inventors of widely different backgrounds, Philo T. Farnsworth and Vladimir Zworykin. Farnsworth, an American genius who was virtually self-taught, developed an electronic (nonmechanical) scanning system he called "image dissection." He is credited with the invention of the basic methods still used for suppressing retrace path and for inserting synchronizing pulses (§6.6–6.8).

Zworykin emigrated to the United States from Russia in 1919 and worked as an engineer for Westinghouse. In 1923 he applied for patents covering the basic all-electronic television system, but he immediately found himself embroiled in a seven-party patent interference suit. One of the seven parties was Farnsworth, who finally won a key decision on his electron optics patent in 1934. RCA

---

*A variant of this mechanical system of television provided the first pictures of man on the moon in 1969. Scientists reverted to the older system because of its ruggedness, which was desirable under the conditions of broadcasting from space.

High-definition television is characterized by pictures that consist of at least 200 scanning lines (§6.6).

Exhibit 3.2   Vladimir Zworykin

The inventor holds the 1923 invention for which he is most famous, the iconoscope camera tube. RCA made Zworykin an honorary vice president of the company upon his official retirement in 1962, but he was still active in his late 80s at the company's Princeton, N.J., research laboratories. He died, age 92, in 1982.

Source: Brown Brothers.

acknowledged Farnsworth's victory by paying him a million dollars for the rights to use his discoveries. In the interim Zworykin won lasting fame as the inventor of the *iconoscope*, the electronic camera pickup tube, for which he was granted a patent in 1928 (Exhibit 3.2).

In 1930 Zworykin became head of a celebrated research group of more than forty engineers at the RCA laboratories in Camden, New Jersey. Formed from a merger of the television research programs of General Electric

and Westinghouse as well as that of RCA, the Camden team mounted a systematic investigation of all aspects of television development, aimed at solving not only technological problems but also the subjective problem of setting the specific standards of picture quality that would be needed to win full public acceptance. The RCA studies made it clear that much higher resolution than had been obtained in the early 1930s was essential.

During the 1930s the Camden team tackled and solved all the outstanding problems. They progressed to higher and higher line frequencies, year by year, from the 60-line standard of 1930 (Exhibit 3.3) to 441 lines in 1939. They increased image size and brightness, introduced interlace scanning (§6.7), adapted equipment to use the newly opened VHF band, and introduced sets into homes on an experimental basis.

By 1939 the Camden group felt ready for a major public demonstration. RCA chose the 1939 New York World's Fair, with its "World of Tomorrow" theme, as a suitably prestigious and symbolic launching pad for the 441-line RCA television demonstration. For the first time the general U.S. public had a chance to see (and to be seen on) modern television.

Nevertheless, the Federal Communications Commission withheld permission for full-scale commercial operations pending industry-wide agreement on engineering standards. This came with the recommendations of the National Television Systems Committee (NTSC), representing the fifteen major electronics manufacturers. In 1941 the FCC adopted the NTSC standards for black-and-white television, including the 525-lines-per-frame and the 30-frames-per-second standards still in effect today (§6.6).

Within the year the United States was at war. Production on civilian consumer electronics came to a halt and television development had to be shelved for the duration.

Exhibit 3.3   First U.S. Television Star

A 12-inch model of Felix the Cat (a popular cartoon movie character of the 1920s), posed on a revolving turntable, was used at the RCA laboratories as a moving subject to televise during the development of electronic television. The image at left shows how Felix looked on television in 1929 when picture definition was still only 60 lines per frame.

Source: Photos courtesy of the National Broadcasting Company, Inc.

FM's Troubled Origins   For its first quarter century, the word *broadcasting* meant only one thing, amplitude-modulated (AM) radio. Edwin Armstrong (Exhibit 3.4) invented a much improved alternative system using frequency modulation (FM) in 1933, but for almost thirty years it languished as a poor relation of the established AM system.

Initially, Armstrong delayed making a public announcement of his invention because of his friendship with David Sarnoff, to whose RCA he gave a first option. Unknown to Armstrong, Sarnoff was about to commit RCA to a multimillion-dollar investment in the development of electronic television. Moreover, FM threatened the continued high profitability of the AM system and its networks. RCA did collaborate with Armstrong for two years in carrying out tests, but in the end, it turned down the chance to pioneer FM development.

RCA's failure to take up the cause of FM increased Armstrong's bitterness at having lost the long court battle over paternity of the regenerative radio circuit to de Forest in 1934 (§2.4). Now he started another frustrating suit, this time against RCA for patent infringements.* Armstrong saw himself as the victim

---

*The suit was not settled until 1954, after the inventor's suicide, for the same million-dollar settlement offered by RCA in 1940 when the suit was brought.

Exhibit 3.4   Edwin Armstrong (1890-1954)

The inventor is shown on the catwalk of his 400-foot experimental FM antenna, built in 1938 on the Palisades high above the Hudson River at Alpine, N.J. He opened station W2XMN at this site in 1939, the first high-powered FM station, the only previous one having been a low-powered amateur station used for demonstration purposes.

Source: Courtesy *Broadcasting*.

of a conspiracy to kill FM, to frustrate his second chance at fame.

Costly changes in spectrum allocations, favoring television over FM, seemed to Armstrong still more evidence of conspiracy. First, in 1939 the FCC allocated 19 VHF channels to experimental television, only 13 to FM. The next year the FCC authorized commercial FM

operation in the VHF band, 42–50 MHz, but only thirty stations had gone on the air when further development was frozen in 1942 by World War II. At the close of the war, on the basis of controversial engineering advice, the FCC took away FM's prewar channels, moving FM up to its present location at 88–108 MHz. This 1945 move made obsolete the half million FM receivers that had been built up to that time.

Many major AM station owners nevertheless obtained FM licenses, simply as insurance against the possibility that FM might catch on and make AM obsolete. They made no attempt to take advantage of FM's superior quality or even to program it as a separate service. Instead they merely "simulcast" their AM programs on FM transmitters. In the absence of high-fidelity programming, listeners had little incentive to buy, and manufacturers had little incentive to develop, high-fidelity receivers.

The interest in FM stations, mostly planned as minor partners in AM/FM combinations, peaked in 1948, when over a thousand were authorized. But in that year television began its rapid climb to power, and FM was pushed into the background. In 1949 alone, 212 commercial FM stations went off the air, and total authorizations continued to decline until 1958 (Exhibit 3.1).

Program Recordings   When radio began, phonograph recordings were still relatively primitive. They ran at 78 revolutions per minute, allowing time for only three or four minutes to a side. Sixteen-inch ETs (electrical transcriptions), running fifteen minutes to a side at 33 1/3 rpm, were introduced in 1929 specifically for radio program syndication and for subscription music libraries. The latter provided stations with a basic library of music on ETs, supplemented at regular intervals by additional recordings.

The radio networks, however, scorned recorded programs. They regarded their ability to distribute *live* programming to their affiliates as a major asset.

ABC, formed in 1945 (§3.5), was the first network to do away with the recording ban completely, in order to lure Bing Crosby away from NBC in 1946. The singer hated the tension and risks of real-time broadcasting, which were compounded by the need to repeat each live program in New York a second time for the West Coast to compensate for time-zone differences. Crosby himself financed a company to make tape recorders, based on magnetic tape recording technology developed by the Germans during World War II. As soon as broadcast-quality audio tape recorders became available Crosby insisted on recording his weekly prime time program. CBS and NBC soon followed the ABC lead.

Development of LP Recording   Meanwhile, by the mid-1940s CBS had assigned Peter Goldmark, head of the network's research laboratories, to explore ways of improving the technology of disc recording. Goldmark took the entire process apart, piece by piece, from the recording microphone to the playback speaker, analyzing each component and the relationships of one to another. By 1948 CBS was able to announce its new long-playing (LP) 33 1/3-rpm records and new playback equipment to go with them.

CBS's arch-rival, RCA, countered with the 45-rpm "extended play" recording, but soon had to accept the longer-play CBS system as well. Both systems used a vinyl disc, which is light, flexible, and durable, a great improvement over the old 78-rpm shellac. More grooves per inch and slower turntable speeds enabled dramatic increases in playing time. For the first time music lovers could hear long pieces played back without interruption. Well-designed electronic components greatly improved quality and reduced noise. These improvements soon started a boom in high-fidelity music, which in turn increased public interest in the "hi-fi" capabilities of FM broadcasting.

3.4 Broadcasting at War (1938–1946)

The last shackles of the Great Depression fell away only when the country began to increase production in response to the growing threat of war in Europe and the Pacific. Radio developed the first live overseas reports of events in Europe, relayed by short wave back to New York, and thence to network affiliates. Hitler's annexation of Austria in 1938, the invasion of Poland a year later, and finally the 1941 Pearl Harbor attack were all brought into American homes by radio reporters on the scene.

During World War II, radio escaped direct military censorship by complying voluntarily with common-sense rules. For example, man-on-the-street and other live interviews were avoided and weather reports were discontinued.* In 1942 President Roosevelt appointed a well-known CBS radio newscaster, Elmer Davis, to head the newly created Office of War Information (OWI). The OWI coordinated the mobilization of domestic broadcasting and initiated the external broadcasting service that eventually became the Voice of America. By 1944, even though broadcasting had been declared an essential industry and therefore exempt from the draft, half the broadcast

---

*During World War I private radio stations had been closed down (though this was before the broadcasting era). During World War II the president refrained from using his right, under §606 of the Communications Act of 1934, to assume sweeping controls over all federally regulated wire and radio communications. Currently, broadcasting stations voluntarily participate in the Emergency Broadcasting System, a set of standby procedures that can be put into immediate effect in case of national emergency.

employees of the country had joined the armed forces.

Although wartime restrictions on civilian manufacturing, imposed in 1942, cut back on station construction and receiver production, during this period the number of stations on the air more than doubled, reaching just over a thousand by the end of 1946 (Exhibit 3.1). Moreover, the lack of civilian goods actually worked to radio's advantage. The government allowed manufacturers to write off advertising costs as a business expense, even though they had nothing to advertise. This stimulated manufacturers to spend freely to keep their names before the public. They were willing at times to invest in first-rate programming, because they were not under competitive pressures to maximize audiences with sure-fire, mass appeal material.

The networks, too, invested in creative programming, particularly drama. The most sensational radio play for this period, "The War of the Worlds," was a production of *The Mercury Theater on the Air*, a series directed by Orson Welles and John Houseman. The play presented an imaginary invasion from Mars in the form of a series of radio news reports. It caused widespread panic among listeners, many of whom began to flee the imaginary Martians even though the play had been clearly identified as a Halloween prank. One reason for the extraordinary impact of the play may have been that it was broadcast on October 30, 1938, only a month after radio reported the month-long Munich Crisis.

Radio developed many of its own playwrights, notably Norman Corwin and Arch Oboler, who won their chief literary fame in broadcasting. CBS commissioned Corwin to celebrate the great moment of Allied victory in Europe with an hour-long radio play, "On a Note of Triumph."

"On a Note of Triumph" climaxed an extraordinary flowering of radio art — original writing of high merit, produced with consummate skill and always live, for the networks still banned recordings. With the end of the war years and the artificial support for culture, competitive selling resumed and this brief, luminous period of radio creativity came to an end.

Radio News   Anxious to outdo NBC's developing European news operation, CBS decided on a bold stroke, a full half-hour devoted to a CBS foreign news "roundup" on the Nazi invasion of Austria, originating live from key points: London, Paris, Rome, Berlin, Vienna. The problems of coordination and precise timing were tremendous, because of the networks' ban of recordings. In that historic half-hour, which was anchored by Robert Trout and featured reports by William Shirer, Edward R. Murrow (see Box, page 81), and others, "radio came into its own as a full-fledged news medium" (Kendrick, 1969: 158).

Later in 1938 came the Munich Crisis. The Allies abandoned Czechoslovakia to Hitler, climaxing eighteen days of feverish diplomatic negotiations among the great powers. During these tense days and nights, pioneer commentator H. V. Kaltenborn achieved fame and fortune by extemporizing a remarkable string of eighty-five live broadcasts from New York, reporting and analyzing news of each diplomatic move as it came in by wire and wireless. News staffers at CBS would shake Kaltenborn awake (he slept on a cot in a studio) and hand him the latest bulletin; he would go on the air immediately, first reading the bulletin, then ad-libbing his own lucid, informed commentary. "Even as I talked," wrote Kaltenborn, "I was under constant bombardment of fresh news dispatches, carried to my desk from the ticker room. I read and digested them as I talked" (Kaltenborn, 1938: 9).

Thanks to CBS's early start, Paley's enthusiastic support, and his good luck in assem-

Edward R. Murrow

Murrow is seen here walking not far from the BBC's Broadcasting House in downtown London during the war. He and other American reporters used a tiny studio located in a sub-basement. Once when the building took a hit during a German bombing raid, Murrow continued his live report as stretcher bearers carried dead and injured personnel past the studio to a first-aid station (Kendrick, 1969: 212). First employed by CBS in 1935 as "director of talks" in Europe, he came to the notice of a wider public through his memorable live reports from bomb-ravaged London in 1940, and later from even more dangerous war-front vantage points. Unlike other reporters, he had a college degree in speech rather than extensive newspaper or wire-service experience. The British appreciated his realistic and often moving word-and-sound pictures of wartime, and American listeners appreciated what William Paley termed his radiation of "truth and concern" (1979: 151). He was widely admired and became the core of the CBS wartime and postwar news organization. He served briefly as a CBS news vice president, but resigned the administrative post to resume daily newscasting. As an on-the-air personality, he survived the transition to television better than others, moving on to still greater achievement. Murrow died in 1965.

Source: Photo CBS News.

bling a superlative staff of news specialists, CBS set a high standard for broadcast journalism during the war years, establishing a tradition of excellence that has lasted to this day.

Television During and After the War

During the war six experimental stations remained on the air, located in New York City (two stations), Schenectady, Philadelphia, Chicago, and Los Angeles. They devoted their brief schedules (they were required to be on the air only four hours a week) primarily to civilian defense programs. About 10,000 sets were in use, half of them in New York City.

The end of the war in 1945 did not, as some expected, bring an upsurge in television activity, despite a backlog of 158 pending station applications. Investors held back for several reasons. The 1941 decision on standards (§3.3) had left the issue of color television unresolved, and many experts believed that all-out development should await adoption of a color system. Moreover, potential investors wondered whether the high costs of sets would repel buyers who were accustomed to inexpensive radios, and whether the major advertisers would be willing to pay the higher cost of television programming. Owners of successful radio stations, accustomed to making money with the greatest of ease, were reluctant to take on the formidable complexities of an unknown new medium.

Two favorable developments had occurred shortly after the war, however: (1) the *image orthicon* camera tube, introduced in 1945, had improved camera sensitivity, eliminating the need for the uncomfortably high levels of studio light that the iconoscope had required; and (2) AT&T had begun to install intercity coaxial cable links (§7.4) to enable network interconnection, starting with the New York–Washington, D.C., link in 1946. In the summer and fall of 1947, the long-predicted rush into television finally began.

3.5 Radio Networks: Development and Decline

The year 1948 marks both the highwater mark of network radio and the beginning of the end. Radio networks grossed more revenue than ever before or since that year, excluding profits from their owned and operated stations (§8.2). For better than fifteen years, the networks had dominated radio. Yet dramatic changes were fast approaching, developments in television that would undo the commanding radio network role.

Chain Broadcasting Investigation   Back in 1938, radio stations representing 98 percent of the total nighttime wattage were affiliated with either NBC or CBS. This included virtually all of the major stations in the country. Then as now, the great majority of affiliated stations were tied to their networks not by ownership but by contract.

As we have seen, NBC had the advantage of deploying a double network, NBC Red and NBC Blue, against CBS. This meant that NBC tied up the two best stations in many markets and could afford to use the weaker of its line-ups, NBC Blue, as a kind of loss leader to undercut CBS.

In 1934, the Mutual Broadcasting System (MBS) began to emerge in the Midwest. Frustrated in its attempts to expand from a regional into a national network, MBS complained to the Federal Communications Commission that the older chains unfairly dominated the network field. The FCC initiated a major inquiry. After more than three years of investigation, the FCC issued a set of "Chain Broadcasting Regulations" aimed at relaxing the hold of the older networks over affiliates and talent, to free affiliates to program for local needs and interests. Among other things, the new rules forbade dual networks covering the same markets and forced both CBS and NBC to give up the talent-booking agencies they had developed as sidelines. The rules also forbade the networks to force stations to carry programs they did not wish to accept, or to infringe in other ways on the autonomy of affiliates.

CBS and NBC were outraged at these intrusions into their business affairs. Predicting total collapse of the network system if the regulations went into effect, they fought the case all the way to the Supreme Court, but in 1943 the Court finally settled the argument in favor of the FCC (319 U.S. 190).* The most tangible immediate outcome was the end of NBC's dual network operation, with the sale in 1943 of its Blue network, which later became the American Broadcasting Company (ABC). The predicted collapse of network broadcasting failed to materialize and Mutual began to expand rapidly. Thus emerged radio's four-network pattern, which endured until the 1960s.

CBS vs. NBC   After the war, CBS's William Paley launched an all-out attack on NBC's leadership. "I would grant NBC its greater reputation, prestige, finances, and facilities," said Paley, "but CBS had and would continue to have the edge in creative programming" (1979: 174). By 1948 CBS was packaging twenty-nine sponsored radio programs, two of which were in the top ten. Paley's next target was a bigger prize — NBC's superstars.

The ensuing CBS "talent raid" used a secret weapon, the discovery that star performers could increase their income by incorporating themselves, then selling their corporations to a network instead of taking salaries. Profits on corporate sales were taxed as capital gains at only 25 percent, whereas the tax on a correspondingly high salary was 77 percent (Paley, 1979: 193).

With this leverage, Paley went after Jack Benny in 1948, and Benny moved over to CBS. Within a short time Bing Crosby, Red Skelton, Edgar Bergen, George Burns and Gracie Allen, Groucho Marx, and Frank Sinatra all deserted NBC for greener fields at CBS.

By the fall of 1949 Paley finally achieved his dream of taking the lead away from NBC,

a lead CBS held for the brief remaining life of big-time network radio.

Mutual Broadcasting System   The network whose complaints against CBS and NBC had precipitated the chain broadcasting investigation, MBS, signed up several of the smaller regional networks that had developed in the 1930s and, in the post-World War II period, offered a haven for the newly emerging small stations that began to go on the air in great numbers. By 1948 MBS affiliations had passed the five hundred mark, and it was advertising itself as "the world's largest network." The significance of the number of affiliates in a network has to be judged in terms of their power, however, and most of MBS's affiliates were in the lower power classes, many located outside the major urban centers. Mutual took on a somewhat conservative political tone. Lacking the prestige and corporate resources of the older networks, it had to scramble to stay alive. It tended to be less choosy about both its programs and their sponsors than the older networks and carried many paid religious and politically right-wing programs that would have had difficulty finding time on the more prestigious networks.

Under the pressure to survive, MBS introduced innovative business practices, such as network *cooperative advertising*. This is a means of using local advertisers to support network programming, originally the exclusive domain of national advertisers.

Such expedients never succeeded in making Mutual financially stable, however, and its whole history has been marked by frequent changes in ownership. During a four-year period in the 1950s its ownership changed six times.

American Broadcasting Company
When NBC was forced to sell one of its two networks in 1943 as a result of the chain

---

*The Chain Broadcasting Regulations were later extended in 1946 to television networks. In 1977, after radio networks had ceased to play a dominant role, most of the original chain regulations were lifted for radio. (For details see §8.2.)

broadcasting investigation, it naturally chose to sacrifice the weaker of the two, NBC Blue, which had descended from the old WJZ Radio Group network of the 1920s (§2.10). Thus the new owner of the Blue network (who renamed it American Broadcasting Company in 1945 and dropped the historic WJZ call letters in favor of WABC) faced a difficult competitive situation, running well behind both NBC and CBS.

A second government-decreed corporate breakup resulted in ABC's rescue in 1953. Earlier the Justice Department had forced "divorcement" on the Big Five motion picture companies. This meant that the major Hollywood production studies had to sell off their extensive theater chains. One of the spin-off companies, Paramount Theaters, merged with ABC, injecting much-needed funds into the radio network and also establishing a link with Hollywood that eventually paid off handsomely when ABC went into television. But these developments came after the period of network radio dominance; during it, ABC ran third to NBC and CBS, with MBS trailing even further behind.

Network Decline   During their heyday, radio networks supplied a full schedule of programs much as television networks do today. Advertisers sponsored entire programs, rather than buying scattered spot announcements as they now do in television (§9.4). But this very identity of sponsors with network programs and stars led to the precipitous decline in radio network fortunes after 1948, as television rapidly captured the mass audience, luring away major advertisers and with them the major performers. By the early 1950s, the complacent pretelevision days were over. William Paley, who led CBS through this transition, recalled:

Although [CBS's] daytime schedule was more than 90 percent sponsored, our prime-time evening shows were more than 80 percent sustaining. Even our greatest stars could not stop the rush to television. Jack Benny left radio in 1958; Bing Crosby left nighttime radio in 1957 and quit his daytime program in 1962. It was sad to see them and other old-timers go. Amos 'n' Andy, which had been on radio since 1926 and on a network since 1929, left the air in 1960. (1979: 227)

The ultimate blow came when radio stations actually began refusing to renew network contracts — a startling change, considering that previously a network affiliation had always been regarded as a precious asset. But rigid network commitments interfered with the freedom that stations needed to put their new tailor-made, post-television program formulas into effect. Only a third of the stations had network affiliations by the early 1960s. Networks scaled down their service to brief hourly news bulletins, short information features, a few public affairs programs, and occasional on-the-spot sports events.

3.6 Television at Last

After several false starts, American commercial television finally began its explosive growth in 1948. That year, the number of stations on the air increased from 17 to 48. The FCC reported an "unprecedented surge in the number of applications for new television stations." The number of cities served by television went from 8 to 23. Set sales increased more than 500 percent over the 1947 level and by 1951 had already surpassed radio set sales. Increased opportunities for viewing in 1948 multiplied the audience in one year by an astonishing 4,000 percent.

In 1948 coaxial cables for network relays became available in the Midwest as well as on the East Coast, and regular network service began. Important advertisers started experimenting with the new medium and large-scale programming emerged.

Freeze Imposed (1948–1952)   Television's growing pains were not yet over, however. The FCC's go-ahead for commercial television had made only fourteen VHF channels available to serve the entire United States.* As more and more stations began to go on the air it became obvious that (1) the demand for stations would soon exceed the supply of channels, and (2) the FCC had not required enough geographical separation between stations on the same channel to prevent serious co-channel interference.

To forestall a potentially chaotic situation, the FCC on September 29, 1948, abruptly imposed a freeze on processing of further applications. The freeze did not affect applicants whose permits had already been approved; thus they were able to go ahead with construction of stations. As a result, for the nearly four years of the freeze, 108 "pre-freeze" stations had an enviable monopoly.

Enough stations were on the air throughout the freeze years so that television's forward surge was not seriously inhibited. During the freeze the number of sets in use rose from a quarter-million to over 17 million. After heavy losses at the outset, by 1951 stations began to earn back their investment. The coaxial cable and microwave networks joined the East Coast to the West Coast in 1951, inaugurating national network television, which soon reached 60 percent of American homes.

Sixth Report and Order (1952)   Meanwhile, the FCC had been holding a series of hearings to settle the engineering and policy questions that had brought on the freeze. The long-awaited decision, the charter of present-day U.S. television, came on April 14, 1952, in the historic FCC *Sixth Report and Order* (41 FCC

148).* The new rules expanded the number of channels by supplementing the twelve existing VHF channels with seventy new channels in the UHF band (the feasibility of using this higher range of frequencies had been demonstrated during World War II; see §6.9).

A table of 2,053 allotments awarded the use of one or more channels to each of 1,291 communities — a sharp contrast with the prefreeze plan, which had allotted channels to only 345 cities. Over 66 percent of the allotments were UHF. About 10 percent of the total were reserved for noncommercial educational use, mostly in the UHF band. Exhibit 3.5 shows how co-channel allotments are spread around the country to avoid interference and also gives an example of individual city allotments. The table of allotments has been amended many times, one of the more significant changes being an increase in educational reservations to about 35 percent of the total.†

Tremendous pressures for new stations had built up during the freeze. In less than a year after the thaw, all outstanding uncontested applications had been granted. Then began the long-drawn-out process of deciding among competing applicants for the few, immensely valuable remaining channels in the most desirable markets. The number of stations more than tripled in the first postfreeze year (Exhibit 3.6).

However, the new channel allotment plan had serious defects. For one thing, there still

*When faced with complex decisions the FCC often issues preliminary "reports and orders" for public comment before arriving at a final version. The fact that it took six such reports to decide on the television allotment plan is evidence of the complexity of the problem.
†Other major changes include reallocating channel 37 to radio astronomy and, in 1970, channels 70–83 to land-mobile use. In 1980 the FCC proposed over a hundred additional VHF channel allotments, to be made available as "drop-ins." These would be shoehorned into the allotment plan by reducing co-channel mileage separations and using directional antennas. In the end, only four such allotments were added.

*Originally there were thirteen channels, but channel 1 experienced too much interference from adjacent frequencies. It was reassigned in 1948 to land-mobile communication. The rest were the same VHF channels, numbered 2 through 13, still in use today.

Exhibit 3.5   TV Channel Allotment Plan

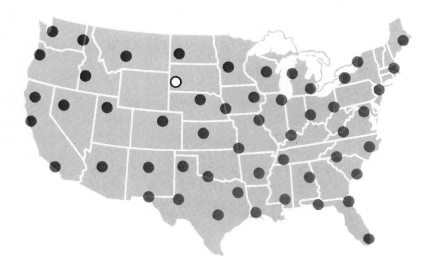

The map shows the occupied *channel 7 allotments (except for Anchorage, Alaska; Wailuku, Hawaii; and Ponce, Puerto Rico). They are scattered relatively evenly throughout the country, separated from each other by a minimum of 170 miles. The list of all channels available in one of the cities to which channel 7 has been allotted is shown below. Rapid City's UHF channels have not been activated, but it gets service from translators that bring in signals of several stations allotted to other cities in that region.*

Status of channel allotments in Rapid City, S.D. (shown by white dot on map)
3 — Occupied by KOTA (NBC/CBS affiliate)
7 — Occupied by KEVN (ABC affiliate)
9 — Occupied by KBHE (noncommercial, licensed to state ETV system)
15 — Not occupied
21 — Not occupied

were not enough channels to give viewers in every market an equal number of choices. Ideally, every viewer would eventually have the choice of being able to tune in at least five *local* stations: an affiliate of each of the three commercial networks, a noncommercial station, and at least one independent station.

In practice 70 percent of the television *households* in the country can receive nine or more stations off the air (not counting cable TV). But only 8 percent of the *markets* in the

country have five or more local stations. The entire state of New Jersey, for example, had no VHF station until the 1980s, and only four or five UHF commercial stations.* Yet New Jersey was flooded with signals from two ma-

---

*WOR-TV, channel 9, was reassigned to northern New Jersey from New York City in response to strong Congressional pressure in 1982. In return, the licensee, RKO General, achieved license renewal amidst some controversy (§17.3).

Exhibit 3.6   Growth of Television Stations, 1948-1985

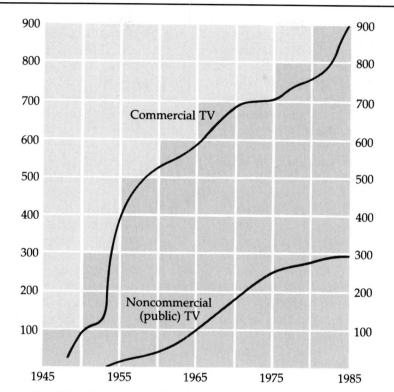

The modern TV era started in 1948, with sixteen stations on the air. Just over a hundred stations had been authorized when the 1948-1952 freeze imposed a temporary ceiling. After the thaw the number shot up remarkably until about four hundred was reached in 1955. Growth began to slow down at that point, but has never actually stopped. Noncommercial stations grew more slowly, starting with the first two in 1954.

Source: Adapted from *Stay Tuned: A Concise History of Broadcasting,* by Christopher H. Sterling and John M. Kittross. Copyright 1978 by Wadsworth Publishing Company, Inc. Reprinted by permission of Wadsworth Publishing Company, Belmont, CA. 1985 data from *Broadcasting* (21 Jan. 85), p. 105.

jor neighboring markets, New York and Philadelphia. In several of the biggest cities, New York, Los Angeles, and Philadelphia among them, the maximum feasible number of VHF channels had already been licensed before the freeze, so that it was impossible to designate noncommercial VHF channels in those cities in the allotment table.

UHF Dilemma   The inequities of channel distribution were increased by the FCC's decision to allot television to both VHF and UHF channels and, moreover, to *intermix* the two in many localities. The commission had tried originally to ensure equal coverage potentials for both VHF and UHF allotments by authorizing UHF to use much higher power, hoping in this way to overcome the inherent propagation weakness of UHF waves as compared to VHF waves. Even if added power could have had the desired effect, however, years went by before maximum-power UHF transmitters became available.* UHF transmitters cost more than VHF to install and operate, and at first there were no UHF receivers on the market. To pick up UHF stations, set owners had to buy converters. Long after UHF was introduced, manufacturers continued to build VHF-only receivers because of the low demand for all-channel sets. Viewers had no incentive to buy UHF receivers in areas where they could pick up VHF signals, because in such markets UHF stations had little to offer in the way of attractive programming.

Faced with such overwhelming disadvantages, UHF television began to slip backward. From an initial high point of 120 stations in 1954 soon after the freeze was lifted, the number of UHF licenses steadily declined until the low point of only 75 stations was reached in 1960. The FCC tried a variety of measures to encourage the failing stations. In Fresno, California, for example, it deleted the one VHF channel, making Fresno a five-station all-UHF market. But this *deintermixture* option could not be widely adopted without making a shambles of the entire allotment table.

In 1961 and 1962 the FCC financed a model station in New York to demonstrate the viability of a well-engineered UHF operation. The most useful step, however, was to compel manufacturers to equip all receivers with UHF tuning. This legislation became effective in 1964, creating an amendment to Section 303 of the Communications Act of 1934. Television

receiver manufacturers at first undermined the rule by installing continuous tuners, which the public found difficult to use. Not until the late 1970s was this problem resolved by the introduction of "click-stop" tuners. In 1980 the FCC was still struggling with the UHF problem. In that year it released a special study on how to improve UHF reception, stressing the importance of upgrading receiving antennas.

By 1965 some of the FCC's efforts had taken effect, and UHF began a steady, though not spectacular growth. FCC financial reports indicate that until 1974 UHF stations as a group continued to lose money. Thereafter their profit margin increased each year.

In practice it appears that at present UHF stations can achieve only 80 to 85 percent—at best—of the coverage enjoyed by competing VHF stations, though UHF proponents still have hope that improved receivers and antennas — as well as carriage of UHF stations on cable television — will some day equalize coverage with VHF except in areas of rough terrain and in cities with many tall buildings.

Color Rivalry   RCA's leadership in the original development of black-and-white television gave NBC a substantial head start over the other networks. CBS saw an opportunity to counter NBC's advantage by taking the lead in color. During the 1940s, CBS developed a partially mechanical color television system that was *incompatible*, meaning that viewers would have to buy separate receivers to pick up color programs. Meanwhile, RCA continued working on its own compatible all-electronic color system.

The competition between the rival networks and their systems shifted from the laboratories to a series of FCC proceedings that ran from 1946 to 1953. Eventually tired of the expensive wrangling, all parties accepted new standards proposed by the National Televi-

---

*The pioneer commercial UHF station, KPTV (Portland, Oregon), went on the air in September 1952, using an RCA experimental transmitter. The first maximum-power (5 million watts) UHF transmitter did not go on the air until 1974.

sion System Committee (NTSC) for an electronic system patterned closely on RCA's, and thus compatible with sets already in use. This meant black-and-white receivers already on the market could pick up color signals in monochrome.

But color telecasts on a large scale were slow to develop, because of high costs of receivers and lack of advertiser interest. Five years after the 1953 FCC adoption of the NTSC standards, only NBC was producing programs in color. Full network color production in prime time came only in 1966. By 1972 half the country's homes had color television sets. With the exception of small portables, virtually all sets manufactured today are color sets.

3.7 The TV Age Begins

Television grew far more rapidly than had radio two decades before because developers of the new medium could build on the knowledge and capital they had attained from the old. But the shoestring operations sufficient to get small radio stations on the air were no longer possible: the very nature of television programming favored the network approach. True television networking had to await development of special coaxial cable and microwave relay links built by AT&T.

The first regular intercity relay circuit, running between New York and Washington, D.C., was operating by 1946, and the first transcontinental links came only five years later. Until the early 1950s, however, many television stations had to survive without a direct network connection. The recorded alternative was a filmed version, called a *kinescope*, of the television picture as it appeared on the face of a receiver tube. These filmed recordings of network programs were available in 1948 but were poor in quality and thus little used. Only in 1956 did the Ampex Corpora-

tion demonstrate a successful *videotape* process, which saw its first practical use that fall on CBS. In a rare spirit of cooperation, competing manufacturers put aside their rivalries, opting for a compatible standard from the outset of the new technology.

Three Networks   Several factors kept the number of national commercial television networks to three: limitations on the availability of suitable and sufficient programming, on advertiser support, on hours available at affiliated stations, and most crucial of all, on the number of channels available in urban areas. To be competitive, a full-service commercial network must have access to affiliates of approximately equal coverage potential in all major markets. The FCC's 1952 *Sixth Report and Order* effectively limited television to three network services, since too few cities were allotted more than three channels. Even if all the independent commercial stations in the country today were to combine forces in a fourth network, it would only be able to reach about 85 percent of the population, whereas the three existing networks can reach better than 95 percent of television homes.

Nevertheless, there have always been pressures for, and candidates to be, a fourth network, if not some lesser alternative between the extremes of independence and network affiliation. When television networking began, the Mutual radio network was too weak to consider branching into television. But from 1946 to 1955 a fourth chain *did* exist, the DuMont Television Network. Founded by Allen B. DuMont, a developer and manufacturer of cathode ray tubes and a pioneer receiver manufacturer, DuMont survived only while the lack of live interconnection facilities kept networking somewhat localized, for it could not compete with the larger and older networks. Its demise helped to strengthen ABC's position against CBS and NBC.

It also prompted the FCC's second investigation of networks in 1955-1957. Under attorney Roscoe Barrow, the inquiry concluded that the television networks held too much economic power over their affiliates (House CIFC, 1958). While not a landmark like the first network report of 1941 (see §3.5), the Barrow study did lead eventually to substantial rule changes (see Box in Chapter 13).

Weaver's Innovations at NBC   Most of NBC's early programming strategies sprang from the fertile imagination of Sylvester "Pat" Weaver. Weaver resigned his job as the broadcasting chief of a major advertising agency in 1949 to become NBC's vice president for television. He left NBC only six years later as chairman of the board, but in those few formative years made a permanent mark on television programming. Though assuredly an intellectual, Weaver had the common touch in mass entertainment without being common. Most presumed television "experts" at that time simply tried to adapt radio or the theater to television. Weaver's special talent was the ability to free himself of preconceived media habits and to look at television with a fresh vision.

He foresaw, for example, that the single-sponsor show, the hallmark of big-time network radio, simply could not last in television. Program costs would eventually become far too high for any but a few rich, highly prestigious corporations to bear, and even they would be able to afford full sponsorship only occasionally. Instead, Weaver introduced *segmented sponsorship*, which enabled a number of different advertisers to share the spotlight in a single program, and the *magazine format*, which combined a number of separate features within the framework of a single program. Disregarding conventional wisdom about the inviolability of established viewing habits, he disrupted regular schedules to run occasional one-time "spectaculars," 90 minutes long. The other networks refused to take such risks at first, but eventually, under the name "specials," Weaver's spectaculars became common practice on all networks.

Weaver, as well as William Paley at CBS, wished to recapture control of commercial entertainment from the advertising agencies, who had taken command during radio days (§2.10). He recognized that advertiser control meant conservative, no-risk programming. Only the networks, Weaver said, could "gamble on shows, on talent, on projects; and we will lose in doing this all too often. But only a great network can afford the risk, and that is essentially why the great network service is so important to this country" (1955). As production costs rose, fewer advertisers could afford to supply programs. A study of prime-time program sources in the period 1957 to 1968 showed that advertisers declined as a source from 33 percent of the total to 3 percent. Independent program packagers (§11.2) increased during the same period, producing 81 percent of all regularly scheduled prime-time programs by 1968 (Little, 1969: 1).

Despite Weaver's success with specific innovations, however, CBS steadily gained in the *overall* ratings race with NBC during Weaver's tenure. In consequence, NBC let Weaver go.

CBS Leadership   William Paley's struggle to prevail over prestigious NBC started to pay off in 1953 when CBS Television first became profitable — after a start-up investment of $60 million. By 1955 CBS achieved number-one place in the ratings, holding undisputed leadership for twenty-one years.

Paley had become chairman of the board of CBS in 1946, but he continued to act as the master programmer. On CBS's fiftieth anniversary, when Paley was 76, he still reportedly saw every program pilot, read many new scripts, and expected to have a say in the details of program decision making and scheduling. His instincts must have been right, for "no corporation can trace as long and unbroken an ascent to prosperity under the unquestioned control of a leader on active duty" (*Broadcasting*, 19 Sept. 1977).

ABC Seizes the Lead   As the networks entered the television age in 1948, ABC Television found itself in somewhat the same position that CBS had occupied in the early days of network radio. Top advertisers and performers automatically turned to CBS or NBC, regarding ABC only as the last resort. ABC began to pay more attention to demographics, tailoring prime-time shows to the young, urban, adult segments of the audience. In practice, this policy meant emphasizing action, violence, and sex, and abandoning any serious attempt to offer the more balanced range of programming that the older networks had always thought essential to their national images.

ABC was aided by its link with the motion picture industry, an association that had begun with the ABC–Paramount Theaters merger in 1953 (§3.5). In 1954 Walt Disney, the first of the major studio leaders to make a deal with television, agreed to produce a series of programs for ABC called *Disneyland* (1954–1957; then other various titles on NBC until finally dropped in 1981). The ABC deal was an exceptionally good one for Disney, who got free advertising for his theme park (just then opening) and for Disney feature films.

The "Live Decade": 1948–1957   If we look back with nostalgia to radio's "golden era" of the 1930s and 1940s, we may justifiably feel the same way about television's first decade. The networks put first priority on stimulating people to buy sets. Only attractive programs could provide the necessary stimulus:

It was the only time in the history of the medium that program priorities superseded all others. If there was an abundance of original and quality drama at the time . . . it was in large part because those shows tended to appeal to a wealthier and better-educated part of the public, the part best able to afford a television set in those years when the price of receivers was high. (Brown, 1971: 154)

Most programming, local and network, was necessarily live — a throwback to the earliest days of radio. Videotape recording had not yet been invented. Original television plays constituted the most memorable artistic achievements of television's live decade. "Talent seemed to gush right out of the cement," wrote the pioneer *New York Times* critic, Jack Gould (1973: 6). Robert Alan Aurthur, a young playwright at the time, recalls the challenge of producing fifty-two live, original plays a year — no network reruns in those days.

It is easy to become oversentimental about the live decade. A more realistic appraisal, perhaps, is that of Robert Saudek, producer of *Omnibus*, a prestigious series initiated in 1952 with Ford Foundation support as an experiment in high-quality television. Asking himself if the strain of live production was really worthwhile, Saudek concluded:

Any sane observer would have to say no, because it is both efficient and economical to put shows on film or tape. Not only does it provide profitable reruns, but also . . . the scheduling of crews, studios, lights, cameras, sound and all the other hardware can be computerized. In that way a whole season of shows can be frozen and stored away like TV dinners to be retrieved and served up on demand. (Saudek, 1973: 22)

In short, the economics of television drove it unrelentingly toward syndication and therefore toward recording. This was equally true at both the local and the network levels.

Production Moves to Hollywood   Television programs could, of course, have been

Exhibit 3.7   Early TV Shows

What's My Line? *exemplifies the half-hour panel show (in this case celebrity panelists tried to identify mystery guests' careers) and the heavy presence of early advertisers.* Lassie *was a long-running Sunday evening program aimed at children.* Mary Martin as Peter Pan, *on NBC in 1955, was an early example of the "spectacular" or special program.* The Honeymooners, *starring Art Carney, Jackie Gleason, and Audrey Meadows was an early success as a half-hour situation comedy built around a plumber (Carney) and a bus driver (Gleason).*

Sources: What's My Line, Lassie, The Honeymooners *courtesy of CBS;* Peter Pan *courtesy of NBC.*

recorded from the very beginning by making them originally on motion picture film. Economic, technical, and social barriers delayed adoption of this solution.

First, the slow and cumbersome single-camera production method traditional in Hollywood was far too expensive for television. Time was needed to adapt film technology to the physical limitations of television, with its lower resolution, its smaller projected picture area, and its much more restricted range of contrast. Solutions to these problems were slow in coming because the motion picture industry regarded the upstart television medium with a mixture of overt contempt and secret fear. Moreover, many television specialists and critics wanted television to stay clear of the movies, counting on it to bring about a new breed of mass entertainment, independent of the familiar Hollywood fare.

The two points of view were as far apart as their two centers, television in New York and film in Los Angeles. But the economics of the two media drove them ever closer together. Inexorably, as the technical barriers to producing television programs on film were overcome, the production base for entertainment programming shifted to the West Coast.

In the 1956–1957 season, 63 percent of all network programming was still being produced in New York, nearly all of it live, with most of the West Coast production on film. But in 1958 NBC moved *Studio One*, which for a decade had been the most prestigious of the New York live television drama series, to Hollywood. *Studio One* died within months, symbolizing the demise of the live decade.

Television's live production methods brought about changes in Hollywood's traditional production techniques. Live television usually employs three or more cameras running at the same time, taking shots from different angles and at different focal lengths. The live action unfolds continuously, while the director edits simultaneously, selecting optional shots from the several cameras. The result is continually recorded on videotape for possible further editing. Adaptations of this technique to film make possible much faster, more economical shooting than the traditional Hollywood method of staging and lighting each short scene separately for a single camera. In the traditional method, after filming many "takes" of the same scene, the camera had to be moved to a new setup and the scene relighted before the next shot was taken.

Feature Films   In a replay of the newspapers' earlier fears about the inroads radio might make on the news business (§3.1), Hollywood withheld its better and more recent theatrical feature films from television for a dozen years. Only pre-1948 films were released to television, except for some foreign imports, and even these were released grudingly by the film companies in fits and starts. The cutoff year was 1948, because after that year feature-film production contracts contained restrictive clauses taking into account the possibility of release to television.

During the early 1950s, then, television stations had to content themselves with old "B" grade movies produced by minor companies. Somewhat in the spirit of early radio, when networks disdained to use recorded sound, television networks in the 1950s disdained to use feature films. For the time being movies served only as fillers in locally programmed hours. For example, the WCBS-TV (New York) movie series *The Late Show*, which started in 1951, was one of the longest-running feature-film series on television. Its producer recalled that the first break in the major studios' united front came in 1955. By 1956 most of the big Hollywood studios had begun to offer him "packages" of films culled from their vaults (Broder, 1976). Only in the early 1960s did Hollywood conclude that the television bane could also be a boon because of the substantial prices that the networks would pay for "post 48s" films that had no further theatrical value.

3.8   Radio Responds to Television

Predictions of what the growth of television would do to radio were dire in the 1950s, with some observers predicting the demise of radio entirely. Others felt that, despite its shaky beginnings, FM would at last supersede AM. Public and industry attention was on television, with radio seemingly relegated to a backwater, though it was radio revenue that had made expansion into television possible.

Radio's Identity Crisis   As radio stations continued to expand in number and shrink in revenue, they faced a growing problem of *anonymity*. Cast adrift from their network program moorings, stations floundered in a sea of sameness. Networks had given their affiliates ready-made personalities, and unaffiliated stations were few enough in number to have relatively little difficulty in creating recognizable independent public images. But with the loss of star talent to television and the cutback in network program schedules, all stations became very much alike.

Declining income told the story in a nutshell. In 1948, the year television began its phenomenal growth, the radio networks and their few owned-and-operated stations earned $18 million. By 1958 network income had dropped to zero. Total income of the rest of the stations dropped in the same period from $46 million to $41 million, but by 1958 twice as many stations claimed a slice of the pie. On an average, each station earned only half as much in 1958 as it had in 1948.

The Role of Rock   If music had been important to radio during the pretelevision era,

after television began it became all-important. With the loss of network dramas, variety shows, quiz games, and documentaries, radio programming fell back essentially to music and news/talk, with music occupying by far the majority of time on most stations. Providentially for radio, this programming transition came at a time when a new musical culture was arising, one that was to find in radio an ideally hospitable medium.

Early in the 1950s, a Cleveland DJ named Alan Freed gained national recognition:

[Freed] began playing a strange new sound. A sound that combined elements of gospel, harmony, rhythm, blues, and country. He called it "rock and roll." And people everywhere began to listen. . . . It transcended borders and race. It was enjoyed down South as well as in the North. The music was no longer segmented. Both blacks and whites were able to listen. . . . Rock and roll sang to the teen-ager; it charted his habits, his hobbies, his hang-ups. (Drake-Chenault, 1978: 1)

Radio proved to be the perfect outlet for this new form of expression. Rock lyrics spread the slogans of the disenchanted and the disestablished in a coded language, in defiance of the stuffy standards that broadcasting had previously sought to maintain.

Top-40 Radio   The answer to radio's identity crisis came in the late 1950s in the form of "Top-40" programming. The name referred to the practice of rigidly limiting DJs to a prescribed *playlist* of currently best-selling popular recordings. Gordon McLendon (Exhibit 3.8), a colorful sportscaster and station owner, is one of those credited with launching the format.

Another pioneer, Todd Storz (Exhibit 3.8), applied the Top-40 formula to group-owned stations. Such innovators frequently moved bottom-ranked stations to the first rank in their markets in a matter of months. An hour's monitoring of a Storz Top-40 station in the late

Exhibit 3.8   Top 40 Radio Pioneers

The two most important innovators of formula music radio programming in the 1950s were Todd Storz (left) and Gordon McClendon (right), both of whom experimented with varied combinations of hit music, short newscasts, spot advertising, and "personality" disk jockeys.

Source: Photos courtesy of *Broadcasting*.

1950s yielded the following statistics: 125 program items in the single hour; 73 time, weather, promotional, and other brief announcements; 58 repetitions of call letters; a three-and-a-half-minute newscast featuring accidents and assaults, each item averaging two sentences in length. The overall effect was loud, brash, fast, hypnotic — and memorable. The station acquired an instantly recognizable "sound." No other station on the dial in a Storz market sounded anything like the newly programmed Storz station.

The dramatic success of the Top-40 formula came as much from its ruthlessness in repelling listeners as in its skillfulness in attracting them. To formula programmers, consistency was of the utmost importance. They defined a specific audience *segment* (in terms of age and musical taste), programmed relentlessly for that segment no matter how many other segments took offense, and fulfilled the established formula with unwavering consistency.

The second ingredient in Top-40 success came from an equally single-minded dedication to ceaseless promotion and advertising. Everything possible was done to imprint call letters and dial position indelibly on the listener's mind (§13.9).

FM's Triumph   The resurgence of FM that began in 1958 continued at an accelerated pace. This success was attributable not only to the inherent physical advantages of FM in terms of sound quality but also to the drying up of AM channel availabilities and to a deliberate FCC policy of encouraging FM licensees. In the earlier years, when FM stations had difficulty in persuading advertisers to use their facilities, their financial survival was helped by the sale of Subsidiary Communications Authorization (SCA) services. In effect, the FM licensee could provide a regular public broadcast service plus a separate broadcast service for subscribers renting special receivers. Muzak, a firm providing background music for offices and stores, became an early customer for SCA (§10.3).

Important to the rapid expansion of FM in the 1960s was FCC approval in April 1961 of technical standards for FM stereo transmission. Following the pattern of its previous decisions on black-and-white and color television, the commission followed the advice of an industry testing committee that recommended a specific standard, which would allow stereo broadcasting without harming SCA income. The combination of the new stereo capability with FM's greater frequency response (§6.4) provided a substantial advantage over AM sound, and came just as public interest in high-fidelity stereo recording was rising to a peak. FM rode that technical lead to become the fastest-growing broadcasting medium of the 1960s.

A series of related FCC decisions in mid-decade contributed greatly to FM's success. The commission's *nonduplication rule* required AM/FM owners in major markets to program FM operations independently of AM sister stations at least half the time, giving an important stimulus to independent FM programming. The rule was gradually expanded to cover smaller markets and more station time. Resisted at first by the radio industry, the decision proved crucial in transforming FM from

a shadow of AM to an independent service with as much format specialization as AM. One indication of this change was a trend toward adoption of separate call letters for FM operations, away from the use of hyphenated call signs based on AM call letters. The nonduplication rule was dropped in 1986 (§4.6).

Another FM limitation that was overcome was the relative scarcity of FM receivers compared to AM radios. The development of *transistor* radios in the 1950s had assisted AM in becoming a truly portable medium. Further, the important morning and afternoon "drive time" audiences were dominated by AM stations, since few cars had FM receivers. Though FM spokespersons lobbied Congress for an "all channel" bill similar to that passed for television (§3.6), audience demand for access to both radio services eventually accomplished the same end without legislation. Receiver cost came down and quality improved. By 1974 the majority of all radios had FM capability, and two years later most car radios could also receive FM signals (Sterling, 1984: 225). By the 1980s few radios were sold that did not have both bands, many with the new AM stereo service (§4.5).

3.9 Ethical Crises

The explosive growth of broadcasting and the potential for vast profits created considerable temptation for networks and stations to cash in on the situation by any means possible. A series of ethical crises occurred in the 1950s: fraudulence in programming (including *payola*, payoffs to radio DJs for playing certain records), political blacklisting, and malfeasance in office by FCC commissioners. By the end of the decade, soul-searching by broadcasters and their critics was giving rise to concerns about social responsibility.

Quiz Scandals   In the mid-1950s, high-stakes television quiz programs captured national attention. They dominated prime-time ratings and became almost an obsession for audiences and programmers alike. The first big-time quiz show, *The $64,000 Question*, premiered on CBS in 1955 and was followed in 1956 by NBC's *Twenty-One* and then dozens of others. At the height of the fad, five new quiz shows were introduced in one day.

Producers milked the contests for the last possible drop of suspense. Thousands of dollars hung in the balance as audiences awaited crucial answers from contestants enclosed in "isolation booths" to prevent prompting. Most glamorous of the contestants on *Twenty-One* was Charles Van Doren, a bachelor in his twenties and a faculty member at Columbia University (see Exhibit 3.9). For fifteen breathless weeks, Van Doren survived the challenges of other contestants. By the time he was finally defeated he had won $129,000 and had become a media supercelebrity. But the worm in this apple was that Van Doren, and most of the other contestants, had been faking all the time, conniving with program producers to rig the outcome. Advertisers interested in the largest possible audiences had supplied the impetus for the quiz rigging in order to keep appealing contestants on the air over long periods.

The first hints of quiz rigging began to surface in 1956, when several unsuccessful contestants began to speak out about what was going on. Amid pious disclaimers from other contestants, producers, advertisers, and network officials, the New York district attorney began an investigation late in 1958. Ultimately ten persons pleaded guilty to having perjured themselves by denying complicity in quiz rigging. By the time official confirmation of fraud came in July 1959, the quiz craze had run its course, having earned millions of dollars for drug and cosmetic sponsors. Van

Exhibit 3.9   Quiz Scandals

Former Columbia University instructor Charles Van Doren speaks before press after a New York grand jury hearing. In the investigation of rigged quiz shows, Van Doren was given a suspended sentence after pleading guilty to charges of perjury.

Source: Wide World Photos.

Doren and others indicted by the grand jury received suspended sentences.

The ripples spread far and wide. President Dwight D. Eisenhower requested a report from the U.S. Attorney General, and Congress investigated. As a result, Section 509 was added to the Communications Act of 1934, threatening fines and/or jail for complicity in rigging "contests of intellectual knowledge, intellectual skill or chance." Also, the networks moved to take back some degree of programming control from advertisers — a move reinforced by the rising cost of television time, which discouraged advertisers from paying for total program control and forced them to share expenses of the medium. For a time, network officials spoke in glowing terms of an increase in public-affairs and documentary programming. The industry set up a Television Information Office to give broadcasting a better public image.

The quiz scandals dramatized divergent views of the role of broadcasting. To some, the quiz deceptions seemed a massive betrayal of public trust, a symptom of widespread moral decay. But to others, the rigging seemed no more fraudulent than a stage pistol with blanks rather than real bullets. In response to an opinion survey taken just after the disclosure of the quiz rigging, a quarter of the respondents saw nothing at all wrong with the deception (Kendrick, 1969: 130).

Blacklisting   The social role of broadcasting came into question from another perspective during the late 1940s and 1950s. This was the period of the Cold War, when some Americans feared imminent Russian takeover. One reaction in the United States was an intensive hunt for evidence of procommunist, subversive influences. People in the news and entertainment media became favorite targets of the hunters. Many performers and writers suspected of leftist sympathies found themselves on *blacklists* — privately (and sometimes publicly) circulated rosters compiled by zealous investigators. These list makers searched through newspaper files and other records for evidence of people's associations with certain causes and organizations that were suspected to have subversive intentions.

People whose names appeared on such lists lost their jobs suddenly and thereafter found themselves unemployable, usually with no explanation or opportunity for rebutting the evidence. Actors were especially vulnerable because a few years before, during World War II, they had often been asked to appear at benefit performances and rallies in support of various aspects of the war effort. Because Russia was a wartime ally of the United States, these conspicuous appearances were often misinterpreted as evidence of communist leanings.

After news of a few cases of arbitrary dismissals became embarrassingly public, little more was heard about them. This meant not that the blacklisting had let up but that the networks and advertising agencies had "institutionalized" it in order to avoid unfavorable publicity. According to a study commissioned by the Fund for the Republic, they assigned top executives to comb through blacklists and to compile their own "black," "gray," and "white" lists as guides to safe casting and job-assignment decisions (Cogley, 1956). They found plenty of names in such publications as *Red Channels: The Report of Communist Infiltration in Radio and Television*, published by Counterattack in 1950. Scores of writers, performers, newspersons, and other broadcast employees found their careers abruptly halted. Many innocent people were permanently damaged, and some even committed suicide.

Proving that accusations were false (as many of the accused did), showing that circumstances were entirely innocent (as many did), or disclaiming any communist leanings (as many tried to do) did not suffice to "clear" names once clouded. Mere innocence was not enough. Private anticommunist "consultants" demanded that suspects purge themselves of "dangerous neutralism." AWARE, Inc., one of the self-appointed blacklist groups, published *The Road Back: Self Clearance*. It advised those who wanted to clear their names to actively "support anti-Communist persons, groups, and organizations" and "subscribe to anti-Communist magazines, read anti-Communist books, government reports and other literature." Religious conversion was suggested as a favorable sign of political redemption (quoted in Cogley, 1956: 136).

The broadcasting industry knuckled under with scarcely a murmur of public protest. However, when the Fund for the Republic polled broadcasting executives it found that only 11 percent considered the blacklisters as "sincere and patriotic." Other executives referred to them as "misguided," "crazy," "profiteers," and "pathological." Sixty-seven percent of the industry members interviewed believed the blacklisters were motivated by professional jealousy. But still no one wanted to be quoted by name (Cogley, 1956: 242).

Among the talent unions, only Actors' Equity took an antiblacklisting stand. The American Federation of Television and Radio Artists (AFTRA) was nearly torn apart by controversy. Even though a problacklist group of officers was shown to represent only a minority of the members, AFTRA still failed to come to the aid of its accused members, who were facing the most serious crises in their careers.

The Faulk Case   One AFTRA member who fought back was John Henry Faulk, a successful radio and television personality at CBS. He had helped to organize an antiblacklist (but also anticommunist) ticket for the New York AFTRA chapter, winning election as second vice president. The problacklist faction included several officers of AWARE, Inc. Following the defeat of its slate in the AFTRA election, AWARE published a report accusing Faulk of seven instances of activities it considered politically suspect.

He brought suit against the blacklisters in June 1956. Late in 1956 CBS abruptly discharged Faulk while he was out of the country on vacation. Upon his return he found his ca-

reer suddenly at an end. Alleging a malicious conspiracy to defame him, Faulk proved in court that each of AWARE's seven charges against him was false. The viciousness of the libel so appalled the jury that it awarded even more damages than Faulk asked — a total of $3.5 million. On appeal, the defendants received another stinging rebuff when a five-judge New York appellate court unanimously upheld the guilty verdict, remarking that "the acts of the defendants were proved to be as malicious as they were vicious." The court did, however, reduce the damages to $550,000 (19 AD 2d 464, 1963), most of which Faulk was never able to collect. Louis Nizer, Faulk's lawyer, concluded his own story of the case by saying, "One lone man had challenged the monstrously powerful forces of vigilantism cloaked in super patriotism" (1966: 464).

In point of fact the blacklisters only *seemed* monstrously powerful. They gained their strength from the timidity of the broadcasters, advertisers, and agencies who generally surrendered meekly in order to avoid controversy.

Murrow Confronts McCarthy   Acceptance of broadcasting's journalistic responsibility was exemplified by another episode in the 1950s. The best-known exponent of the blacklisting approach to patriotism was Senator Joseph R. McCarthy. As chairman of a Senate subcommittee on investigations, McCarthy staged a series of flamboyant witch hunts. So notorious were his methods that the term *McCarthyism* has since entered the language as a synonym for public character assassination based on unfounded accusations.

One of those who took the risk of openly opposing McCarthy was Edward R. Murrow, a CBS newsman (see Box, page 81). In television documentaries and radio commentaries Murrow had criticized specific instances of McCarthy's unfairness, but not until March 9,

1954, did he mount a direct attack on McCarthy's methods as a whole. That night, Murrow devoted his entire *See It Now* program to a devastating critique of McCarthyism (Exhibit 3.10).

To create the program, Murrow and his producer, Fred Friendly, needed to do little more than draw upon their film files. McCarthy was so outrageously inconsistent, illogical, opportunistic, and devious that he condemned himself. McCarthy accepted CBS's offer of rebuttal time, filming his reply on a Fox Movietone soundstage at a cost of $6,000, which CBS paid. With his usual wild rhetoric, McCarthy called Murrow "the leader and the cleverest of the jackal pack which is always found at the throat of anyone who dares to expose individual Communists and traitors" (quoted in Friendly, 1967: 55). Later in 1954, television dealt another blow to McCarthy by broadcasting in full the 36-day hearings of his Senate subcommittee, during which he attacked the patriotism of the U.S. Army.* As in the *See It Now* broadcast, on camera McCarthy turned out to be his own worst enemy.

Murrow himself never claimed that the *See It Now* analysis played a decisive role in McCarthy's subsequent decline. But press criticism was on the rise, and the mood of the country was changing. In any event, within the year McCarthy's career was effectively brought to an end when the Senate passed a motion of censure against him.

In doing its part to expose McCarthy, broadcasting to some extent redeemed itself for having given in so tamely to the demands of the blacklisters. Nevertheless, as Murrow said, looking back five years after the event,

"the timidity of television in dealing with this man when he was spreading fear throughout the land is not something to which this art of communication can ever point with pride. Nor should it be allowed to forget it" (quoted in Kendrick, 1969: 70).

FCC Payoffs   Concern over the identification of regulators with the industry they regulate is a recurring issue; but it came to a head in the late 1950s when two members of the FCC were forced to resign under pressure. In March 1958, Commissioner Richard Mack resigned when it became known he had accepted a bribe to vote for a particular applicant for a potentially lucrative television license in Florida. Two years later, FCC chairman John Doerfer was pressured out of office after having accepted cruises on the yacht of a group broadcaster and having submitted double and triple billing for official travel.

These and other FCC transgressions led to a series of intensive Congressional investigations of FCC operation. Part of the problem was the quality of appointments made to the FCC (and other agencies of government). But the problem was also due in part to a too-close industry-regulator relationship. This problem became largely irrelevant by the 1980s when regulators adopted industry viewpoints on minimizing regulations (§17.2).

Summary

• Over the four decades covered in this chapter, broadcasting expanded from a small prewar business of 800 AM stations to a modern industry of some 10,000 radio and television stations. Throughout, first in radio and after 1948 in television, the three national networks dominated broadcast programming and economics. Early concern about broadcasting's competitive impact was evident in 1930s' battles over music licensing, union battles against

---

*In those days the networks, especially the weaker ones, could find time for such extended coverage without undue sacrifice. Both the DuMont network and ABC carried the 187 hours of hearings in full, though ABC did not at that time have complete coast-to-coast coverage. NBC carried a few days of the hearings and CBS showed film clips in the evenings.

Exhibit 3.10   Murrow vs. McCarthy on *See it Now*

CBS journalist Edward R. Murrow (see Box, page 81) detailed the investigative methods of Senator Joseph R. McCarthy (R-Wis) on See it Now in March 1954. The senator replied with a strong attack on Murrow three weeks later on the same program. The two telecasts, along with the Army-McCarthy televised Senate hearings later that spring marked the beginning of the end of McCarthy's political career.

Source: Murrow, courtesy of CBS; McCarthy, UPI/Bettmann.

use of recordings, and the brief press-radio war.

• RCA spearheaded the U.S. television system finally approved by the FCC in 1941. FM radio, the brainchild of inventor Edwin Howard Armstrong, was also approved for commercial operation in 1941 but saw only limited growth until the 1960s.

• Though the radio industry grew little in size during World War II, it gained enormously in stature as it reported from the world's battlefronts, laying the ground for postwar broadcast journalism.

• Postwar network radio reached the height of rivalry as CBS surpassed NBC in popularity. ABC, which developed from the sale of NBC Blue, continued to struggle and Mutual developed its small market affiliations.

• Commercial television began in earnest with the inception of network service in 1948, though coast-to-coast interconnection did not come until 1951.

• Demand for station assignments became so heavy that the FCC was forced to re-evaluate its entire allotment scheme. A freeze on licensing was implemented from 1948 to 1952, ending with the *Sixth Report and Order*, which opened up UHF frequencies and set aside reserved assignments for noncommercial operation. Channel assignment, and the problems of limited UHF coverage, were dominant industry issues in the 1950s.

• After years of developmental work by CBS (on a mechanical system) and RCA (on an electronic system), the FCC approved color television operations late in 1953. But color did not take off commercially for another decade, largely because of its high cost.

• Patterned on the radio model, networks dominated the first decades of television operation. Though NBC pioneered many original programs, CBS soon dominated audience ratings. ABC struggled in a weak third place; and

DuMont, a fourth network attempt, failed in 1955, since too few markets had four stations.

• Production of network programming moved from New York to the West Coast, providing a closer alliance with the film industry. In 1956 videotape was introduced, making possible greater production and scheduling flexibility.

• As viewers and advertisers flocked to television, the old radio network system fell apart. The development in the mid-1950s of rock music, formula Top-40 radio formats, and portable transistor radios helped to build a new identity for radio.

• FM radio became the fastest growing broadcasting medium of the 1960s, encouraged by FCC decisions that allowed SCA services to generate income, that established stereo standards, and that required separate AM and FM programming from owners who operated both kinds of stations. In addition, the general overcrowded nature of AM contributed to FM's growth.

• Rapid change and expansion of the broadcast industry, and the potential for fast and vast profits, led to several ethical crises late in the 1950s. Rock radio was shaken by DJ payola, popular TV network quiz shows turned out to be largely rigged, political blacklisting was widespread, and two FCC commissioners were forced to resign due to malfeasance in office. Yet the industry showed what impact television could have as CBS's Edward R. Murrow took on demagogue Senator Joseph McCarthy in a hard-hitting documentary that helped end the senator's reign of political terror.

• Throughout this period, broadcasting had little competition, except from established newspapers. Radio and television stations were often money machines for owners. Network-dominated television appeared likely to dominate leisure time for decades to come. But dramatic changes were in the offing.

CHAPTER 4

Era of Electronic Media

Through the 1970s, traditional television and radio broadcasting continued to develop and prosper. Though not much changed in outline from a decade or two earlier, broadcasting in 1970 was a bigger and more complicated business. Network-dominated television and local music-radio formats continued their evolution based largely on earlier patterns. But major competition on the horizon would dilute the dominance of radio and television with new delivery options.*

4.1 The Limits of Television

Unfulfilled Demand   The seeds of future change had already been sown in the 1952 *Sixth Report and Order* (§3.6). The television channel allotments set up by that watershed decision severely limited the number of television signals that could be received in even the largest cities. Minority groups and people in rural areas demanded more video signals than the allotment plan could provide. Some wanted more specific types of programs, others a wider choice of channels than the three to five most homes could receive. Some wanted to watch distant stations, and others called for more cultural, educational, or children's programs.

Interim Services   The 1950s and 1960s saw a number of experiments intended to expand signal availability. Mountain states with poor reception supported establishment of mini-TV stations tied directly to main transmitters. Low-power transmitters called *boosters* filled holes in VHF and UHF station coverage. They boosted weak signals, using the same channel as the main transmitter. *Translators* also strengthened signals but used a different channel for the "fill-in" station, to avoid interference. *Satellite* stations provided some local independent programming but generally rebroadcast programs from an originating station under the same ownership, much in the way of a network affiliate. The aim of all these stations was to provide an interim service to underserved areas.

But none of these options, some quite controversial at the time,* provided more or

---

*The technical details of the services that appear in this chapter are discussed further in Chapters 5 through 7, especially the latter.

*At first, these small operations were not licensed, since they didn't fit into the scheme of the *Sixth Report*. The FCC tried to force them off the air, but the governor of Colorado, Edwin Johnson, formerly an influential senator, used his contacts in Congress to force the FCC to license the boosters and translators retroactively.

different service; they merely expanded coverage of existing stations, one signal at a time. As we will see, however, they laid the technological groundwork for a new service of the 1980s, *low-power television* (LPTV).

Basis for Change   Audience demand for more viewing options coalesced in the 1970s with the development of technological alternatives to broadcasting, and with a combination of political and economic thinking that stressed marketplace choice rather than government regulation, to create the fast-changing electronic media scene of the 1980s. By the mid-1980s, alternative media delivery technologies were becoming commercial competitors with broadcast stations.

Such alternative means of delivery can be regarded as parasitic. Demand for broadcast television created a nation of homes with TV sets, the essential home-viewing devices on which the newer services depend. Yet the new media do not contribute anything to the profitability of the broadcasters who made universal ownership of TV sets possible (though it can be argued that program production has been substantially increased as a result of the demands of these newer services).

4.2 Rise of Cable Television

Origins   Community antenna television (CATV) emerged soon after broadcast television began commercial service. One of the first systems began operation in 1950 at Lansford, PA, miles from the nearest large market, whose stations Lansford residents could not receive because of hilly terrain. The system picked up three stations from Philadelphia with a large antenna on a nearby hilltop, delivering the signals to subscribers via cables.

During its first decade, cable remained primarily a local concern. Initial regulation came from municipal governments, from which permission was needed to run cables over or under public property. Municipal authorities granted cable operators *franchises* to install and operate their systems for a fixed number of years. These early systems carried only a few channels, usually five or six, virtually all of them occupied by off-the-air television signals of stations in nearby larger cities. Most served from a few dozen to a few hundred subscribers. Few systems in the 1950s reached more than a thousand homes. CATV was a small business in every way.

Cable Augmentation   After their initial success at answering existing demand for better reception of broadcast television, cable operators began to seek ways to augment this service in order to make subscriptions more salable. After a system repaid its installation costs, new services could be added at small additional cost.

Augmentation takes several forms. One approach is simply to increase the number of available programs by importing more distant signals via microwave relay. Another type of augmentation is *local origination*, whereby systems supply original programming on one or more cable channels at no extra subscriber cost. And a third type, eventually crucial to cable development, is the provision of feature films, sports, and special events, at extra cost to subscribers, usually without advertising (§4.4).

But augmentation developed slowly. For years, cable simply extended the coverage of over-the-air stations. As long as cable acted as a neutral redelivery system, filling in coverage "shadow" areas, beefing up fringe reception, and overcoming local interference, broadcasters welcomed it. Some stations found their signals carried by dozens of cable systems, reaching substantially larger audiences than before.

Big-City Cable Cable found initial success in small communities, where it brought good television reception for the first time or increased viewer choice. But when cable pioneers began to look for ways to expand their business, the obvious direction was toward larger towns and cities where large concentrations of potential subscribers could be found. Big-city dwellers, despite ample local over-the-air service, would often experience direct-reception difficulties because of various kinds of interference. Cable operators could sell them clearer reception, but they wanted to sell them more — importation of distant signals, local origination, and sometimes extra-cost services.

Cable augmentation and the invasion of big-city markets created complex new legal and economic problems. By the mid-1960s, broadcasters began to wonder if cable was becoming a dangerous predator rather than a benign parasite. The growing practice of importing signals tended to obliterate the fixed market boundaries previously imposed by the limitations of over-the-air broadcasting. A network affiliate might find its network programs duplicated in its viewing area on a cable-carried distant station, thus dividing its audience. Cable tended to fragment audiences, leaving broadcast stations with lower ratings and thus with far less appeal for advertisers.

Protectionist Regulation Broadcasters began to appeal to the Federal Communications Commission for help. Several times in the 1950s, the FCC had declined to regulate cable, since cable was not strictly broadcasting and therefore not subject to existing law. The FCC saw cable systems merely as extensions of the viewer's own antenna. As cable's potential economic impact on broadcasting increased, however, the FCC felt obliged to intervene. Having nurtured UHF television

for years, the commission could not afford to see UHF's shaky foundation threatened by cable expansion, which hurt the weakest stations first. Even educational stations expressed concern about imported noncommercial signals from other markets, claiming cable was unfair competition for their small audiences.

The FCC based its initial foray into regulation on cable's use of microwave relays to import distant signals, since the FCC licenses interstate wire communications. In 1962 the commission began to impose case-by-case restrictions on cable systems applying for microwave licenses. In 1966 regulation was extended to all cable systems, beginning a period of pervasive cable regulation.

Cable systems now were told they must carry all local television stations and must not duplicate network programs on the same day the network presented them. No new signals could be imported into any of the top hundred markets without a hearing on the probable effect of such importations on existing television stations. On appeal in 1968, the Supreme Court upheld the FCC's expanding jurisdiction (*Southwestern Cable*, 392 US 157).

A period of intense effort to create a comprehensive system of cable regulation followed, with extensive negotiations between the FCC and broadcast and cable trade associations. The debate centered on cable development in the top hundred television markets. Broadcasters feared unrestricted invasion by augmented cable. They spread scare stories of viewers soon having to pay a monthly fee to obtain theretofore "free" television and warned of the demise of network-supported news and local-station public-service programs if cable were allowed to cut deeper into broadcaster revenues.

1972 Rules The result was the issuance in 1972 of so-called definitive FCC regulations governing cable television. The order (36 FCC 2d 143) incorporated an industry compromise of conflicting views, with cable severely restricted in the type and number of signals it could bring into the largest cities. Commission concerns included the desire to avoid excessive division of the broadcast audience, protection of syndicated television programming from being freely imported by cable, and the economic health of UHF stations. In other words, the economic interests of the existing service were to govern expansion of the newer competing option. Further, cable now had to provide, on request, "access" channels for local government entities, educational institutions, and the general public. As long as cable served primarily to expand coverage of television stations, or provided new kinds of viewer access, it would be allowed, if not encouraged, by the FCC to develop further.

The heavy hand of regulation at both federal and state levels (some states had established franchise standards to be administered by public utility commissions) slowed the expansion of cable development. Blue-sky predictions of a "wired nation" made in the early 1970s now seemed highly unlikely. But the regulatory cage built to contain cable began to come apart in short order.

Deregulators   Only five years after the FCC rules appeared, a Court of Appeals decision (*Home Box Office*, 567 F 2d 9, 1977) held that the commission "has in no way justified its position that cable television must be a supplement to, rather than an equal of, broadcast television." This rebuff, plus a change in administration (both at the White House and in the FCC chairmanship), led the FCC to reconsider its approach to cable. Under court orders, and also on its own initiative, the commission removed itself step-by-step from cable regulation. No longer would the FCC oversee local cable franchise standards, nor

did systems have to meet federal standards of construction or number of channels provided. A requirement that large cable systems originate at least some programming was also dropped.*

Amidst the court actions, the commission initiated a massive investigation of the economic relationship between cable and television broadcasting. After compiling considerable statistical evidence, the commission concluded that cable penetration (see Exhibit 4.1) would likely have little impact on audiences or revenues of broadcast stations.
the face of lasting broadcaster opposition, the

In response to these findings, though in the face of lasting broadcaster opposition, the FCC in 1980 dropped two important and limiting cable programming rules. These rules had banned the importation of most distant signals and had mandated protection of some broadcast syndicated programming from cable competition. Under the triple pressures of court review, its own economic analysis, and a changed political sense of its own proper function, the commission had turned completely around in its perception of cable's role.

At the same time, the advent of satellite-distributed services allowed previously local cable systems to become outlets for an increasingly wide choice of national program services. This increase in program diversity coincided with longtime FCC broadcasting objectives. Consequently, the commission no longer sought to protect broadcasting from cable, but rather encouraged competition between the two.

---

*The impact of this regulatory cycle shows up best in FCC employment records. With the promulgation of the 1972 rules, the commission established a new bureau to oversee cable, and within a year the bureau had grown to some three hundred employees. A decade later, the decline in the FCC's role had left but thirty persons working on cable television, and these employees were joined with the FCC's Broadcast Bureau to form a Mass Media Bureau (§17.1).

Exhibit 4.1   Cable Growth Indicators: 1960–1985

Year	Number of systems	Number of subscribers	Average subscribers per system	Percentage of homes with cable	Percentage of systems with 13 or more channels*
1960	640	650,000	1,016	1.4	na
1965	1,325	1,275,000	962	2.4	na
1970	2,490	4,500,000	1,807	7.6	3
1975	3,506	9,800,000	2,795	14.3	22
1980	4,225	16,000,000	3,787	20.0	29
1985	6,500	35,000,000	5,385	41.1	29

*Data on system channel capacity for 1980 and 1985 actually reflect data for 1979 and 1984, respectively.

The major trend in cable TV has been the increasing size of individual systems, followed by greater channel capacity. Pay cable spurred the dramatic growth of basic cable penetration after 1975.

Sources: Christopher H. Sterling, *Electronic Media: A Guide to Trends in Broadcasting and Newer Technologies*, pp. 28, 30. Copyright © 1984 by Christopher H. Sterling. Reprinted and adapted with permission of Praeger Publishers; 1985 data, National Cable Television Association, citing *TV Factbook.*

4.3   The Cable Establishment

Deregulation was accompanied, and to some degree pushed, by expanding options in cable delivery. Though cable was in only 10 percent of the nation's homes in 1972, its major growth would come in the next decade (Exhibit 4.1). How cable expanded in the face of initial regulatory intransigence is a story of technological advances and entrepreneurial risk.

Domsats   To understand the dramatic development of cable and its competitors in the 1980s, we must briefly review the creation of the domestic communications satellite, or *domsat*. Developed for and funded largely by commercial and military interests, international communication satellites had been in use since the 1960s. U.S. domsats date to a 1972 "open skies" decision by the FCC to allow free entry into the business by any firm with the financial and technical ability to provide a satellite for the National Aeronautics and Space Administration (NASA) to launch (35 FCC 2d 844). Western Union's Westar I, launched in 1974, was the first American domsat.

The FCC regulates satellite operators as common carriers (point-to-point rate-regulated communication services). Carriers lease or sell transponders (combination receiver-transmitters) to program distributors and many nonmedia services. Reception of satellite signals is a different matter, however. Development of inexpensive television receive-only (TVRO) satellite antennas for stations and cable systems was a crucial factor in conversion to satellite distribution. Mass production brought down costs of these TVROs (Exhibit 4.2 and §10.4). Late in 1979 the FCC, faced with a sharply rising demand for licenses just as it was relaxing its approach

Exhibit 4.2   TVRO Earth Station

The most important technical development in the use of satellite distribution of video signals was the relatively small and inexpensive receive-only earth station, or TVRO. The dish collects and focuses the weak satellite signal for processing and boosting at the TV station, cable system, motel, or residence. Such dishes, thousands of which were in use in the early 1980s, are usually aimed at a single satellite (to cover two or more would add greatly to ground station costs).

Source: Eric A. Roth.

toward regulation of the antenna business, dropped its requirement that TVROs be licensed, thus eliminating a cumbersome and expensive licensing process. Lack of regulatory barriers combined with dropping prices opened the way for widespread use of satellite distribution.

The Entrepreneurs: HBO and Turner

The story of satellite-to-cable networks can be told in terms of two companies, Home Box Office (HBO) and Turner Broadcasting System.

HBO started in 1972 in Wilkes-Barre, Pennsylvania. It supplied pay-channel movies to several cable systems in the Northeast, delivering its programs to cable companies by mail or by microwave relays. Lack of an interconnected affiliate system restricted pay cable companies to a few thousand subscribers, and limited income in turn limited the ability to purchase programming.

In 1975, HBO announced it had leased a transponder on RCA's Satcom I and would offer its programs to any system in the country able to buy or lease a TVRO antenna. Satellite delivery sharply reduced distribution costs and enabled national promotion of the service because of simultaneous scheduling. This move transformed the cable business at a stroke:

Rarely does a simple business decision by one company affect so many. . . . In deciding to gamble on the leasing of satellite TV channels, Time, Inc. [by then the owner of HBO], took the one catalytic step needed for the creation of a new national television network designed to provide pay TV programs. (Taylor, 1980: 142)

HBO charged a flat monthly payment rather than the complicated pay-per-view charge used in earlier experiments. At first, subscribers complained about the quality of its films, but after 1978 HBO began to make a profit and was able to improve programming. HBO promotion escalated audience demand for pay cable services, stimulating other entrepreneurs. Whereas fewer than 200 cable systems had TVROs in 1977, some 8,000 antennas were in place by 1983 (many systems using two or more to cover different satellites). Only a quarter of all cable systems carried pay cable in 1977, but by 1983 over three quarters did (Sterling, 1984: 33–34).

In 1970, wealthy sportsman Ted Turner (see Box, page 276) purchased the fifth-ranked television station in Atlanta (which only had five stations), an independent UHF on channel 17. In 1976 Turner contracted with South-ern Satellite Systems (SSS) to relay WTBS programming to RCA's Satcom I for distribu-tion to cable systems. He enticed cable sys-tems to invest in TVRO's to carry WTBS (the call letters stand for Turner Broadcasting Sys-tem) by offering its sports and movie pro-gramming practically for free: systems paid SSS only 10 cents per subscriber (Turner's rev-enue came from higher advertiser rates, which were charged starting in 1979). Turner had in-vented the superstation. WTBS programs went up on Satcom I in December 1976 for re-lay to about twenty systems. By the end of 1978, more than two hundred systems re-ceived his signal, and a year later, ten times that many did. Changing TVRO technology, which made the dishes smaller and thus less expensive, helped Turner to expand.

The models provided by HBO and Turner were soon copied. By the 1980s, cable compa-nies could choose from dozens of basic, pay, and superstation cable services (§8.4). The in-creasing number of such services in the late 1970s, virtually all distributed by satellite, en-couraged cable expansion and experimentation.

In 1985, NBC became the first commercial broadcast television network to distribute pro-gramming to its affiliates by satellite. CBS and ABC soon followed suit. PBS, the major cable program services, and some program syndica-tors (for *Donahue* and *Entertainment Tonight*) al-ready were using satellites.

The Interactive Experimenters   The po-tential of cable to provide many program channels inspired predictions of specialization unthinkable in traditional broadcasting. Some writers in the early 1970s predicted a multi-tude of exotic cable services, including one al-lowing viewers literally to talk back to their television sets.

In 1977 Warner Cable, one of the large multiple system operators (MSOs), began to offer a service called "Qube" on its Columbus, Ohio, system. Warner selected Columbus as a test market because its demographics paral-leled those of the country at large. Qube pro-vided ten special channels over which viewers could respond, by means of a touch-pad con-trol, to questions aired during programs. At the height of the experiment, Qube asked viewers to respond to questions about ten times a day.

In 1980 American Express bought a 50-percent share in the MSO, and Warner-Amex announced plans to provide expanded Qube-type services in other cities where it had franchises. But the difficult economic condi-tions of the early 1980s brought an end to such expansion and to the Columbus experiment, which in three years of operation had never broken even. Too few in the viewing audience had made enough use of the option to warrant its cost.

Numerous other two-way experiments took place, often supported by research grants from federal or local government. These usu-ally utilized the basic cable network to provide intracommunity communication among such groups as the elderly. But when government or foundation support lapsed, most of these experiments also ended. Simply because tech-nology makes a new service possible does not guarantee consumer appetite or advertiser support for that service.

4.4 Pay Television

The notion of paying to receive special kinds of programming is not new; it dates back at least to experiments with radio in the 1930s. Pay television can be categorized by means of delivery or by number of channels provided. Delivery is either wired (cable) or wireless (all other systems). The number of channels pro-vided can be single or multiple. But all pay television is built around the idea of presenting feature films or sports events without advertising. Audiences pay either a flat per-month fee, as pioneered by HBO (§4.3), or, more rarely, a per-view fee. Generally accepted today as a part of modern electronic media, pay television was a matter of considerable controversy for decades. The different means of delivering pay television have had varying degrees of success (Exhibit 4.3).

Rise and Fall of STV   Zenith and other firms pioneered the theory and technology of *subscription television* (STV), or over-the-air pay television, in the late 1940s. But broadcasters and theater owners, fearful of new competition, lobbied the FCC and Congress to delay authorization of the new service. News media devoted much time and space to reports of fears that pay television would "siphon" programming, especially big-ticket sporting events, away from "free" television. This was not in the public interest, critics argued, because soon viewers would have to pay for what they then received free, and many could not afford to pay. But broadcasters were split on STV's role, since weak independent UHF stations saw STV as an alternative source of income.

After years of scattered and inconclusive STV experiments, the FCC finally adopted STV rules in 1968. They were so restrictive that no one rushed to begin service. Only in 1977, as part of its general deregulatory thrust (§17.2), did the FCC start to eliminate most STV rules. The eased regulatory situation prompted the first STV stations to go on the air in 1977 in Los Angeles and New York; 27 stations were in operation by 1983, with another 20 in various planning and financing stages. They served about two million viewers, only one-tenth the number of pay cable viewers. Ironically, the newer service of pay cable was most responsible for audience de-

Exhibit 4.3   Growth of Pay TV Subscribers, 1977 and 1985

	1977	1985
Pay Cable		
subscribers	1,174,000	29,966,000
as percentage of homes passed	11%	50%
as percentage of homes with basic cable	23%	88%
average monthly charge	$7.81	$10.08
Multipoint Distribution Service (MDS)		
subscribers	65,000	438,600
as percentage of homes passed	21%	3%
number of systems	22	86
average monthly charge	$10.39	$15.24
Subscription TV Stations (STV)		
subscribers	5,000	622,000
as percentage of homes passed	4%	3%
number of stations	2	12
average monthly charge	$14.98	$18.43

The data given here are for June 1977 and December 31, 1984. Among the pay services available, only pay cable reaches a substantial population, despite the fact that all three services have grown since 1975. "Percentage of homes passed" here means homes passed by a cable system, or within the coverage area of MDS or STV signals — that is, potential subscribers. STV was already in decline and would disappear by the middle of 1986. Single-channel MDS was also down from subscribers highs of a year before, as system owners got ready to convert to multichannel MDS in the face of pay cable competition. Subscriber data and percentages are rounded.

Source: *The Cable TV Financial Databook* (Carmel, CA: Paul Kagan Associates), June 1985, p. 16. Used by permission.

mand for pay services and created a temporary market for STV in those cities not yet wired for cable's multiple signals.

Single vs. Multiple Channels   The bottom soon fell out of STV. As cable service expanded rapidly in the 1980s, markets in which single-channel STV could compete declined accordingly; the last STV operations closed down in 1986. The decline and failure of STV brings into sharp focus the chief division within the pay-television business: one-channel versus multichannel services. Broadcasters pioneered pay television, but as a broadcast service an STV station could provide only one program channel at a time. Cable television can provide many channels simultaneously, giving viewers a welcome choice among programs.

The dichotomy between multiple- and single-channel systems has become sharper as large-capacity cable systems begin to appear in major markets. Some offer viewers the potential of more than a hundred channels, though many of the channels are not activated for years. But even older and smaller cable systems provide more viewing options for about the same price as a single-channel STV service. Two other services, MDS and SMATV, demonstrate what has been happening.

MDS and MMDS   Operating far higher in the frequency spectrum than traditional television channels, *multipoint distribution service* (MDS) is a specialized kind of television broadcasting operation (Exhibit 4.4 and §7.6). As its name indicates, it is able to transmit from one place to multiple points of reception, where those leasing special *down-converter* devices convert the high-frequency MDS signals to normal television frequencies viewable on any set. First authorized only for common-carrier (mainly business-oriented) service in 1962, MDS channels were widened eight years

later by the FCC to allow the transmission of television signals. Two such channels were made available in each of the fifty largest U.S. cities. MDS service began to expand in the 1980s, sparked by increasing demand for movies and special events offered on a pay-television basis in cities with little or no cable service.

Because MDS is regulated as a common carrier, holders of licenses may not themselves provide programming. Instead, the program function is contracted out, often to HBO or some other pay cable provider. MDS is the only electronic medium in which the owner does not directly program the service. The common-carrier classification, however, allows for simpler regulation and faster entry for new services, since FCC procedures are less cumbersome. Also, construction costs are lower for MDS than for cable.

Yet until 1983, MDS, like STV, remained a single-channel service, limited to a few large market areas, facing multichannel competition from expanding cable services. Several firms proposed to the FCC a *multichannel MDS* (or MMDS) service in major markets, which would allow MDS operators to offer several pay channels in competition with cable. The most logical source of additional channels was the list of frequencies reserved for the noncommercial *Instructional Television Fixed Service* (ITFS). After FCC approval in 1983 of additional MDS channels, interest in the medium boomed. Faced with an avalanche of applications (16,000 for the approximately 1,000 MMDS channels available), the FCC announced plans to choose licensees by lottery (§17.3). The first MMDS service, Capital Connection of Arlington, Virginia, began operations in December 1985.

SMATV   The first *satellite master antenna television system* (SMATV) operations began to appear around 1980, as a result of the FCC

Exhibit 4.4   MMDS

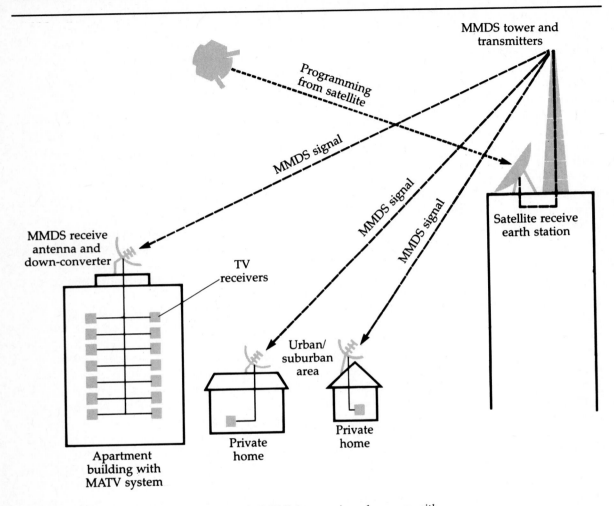

Multichannel multipoint distribution services (MMDS) serve major urban areas with programming picked up from satellites and transmitted on high frequencies to apartments (using their master antenna television or MATV systems), and private homes where the signal is "downconverted" to frequencies tuned by regular television sets. MMDS systems cover much smaller areas than full-power broadcast television stations.

Source: Copyright COM/TECH Report Series National Association of Broadcasters, Washington, D.C. 20036.

deregulation of TVROs. SMATV is similar in concept to cable, but operates on private property, usually large apartment buildings, com-plexes, and motels or hotels, and is limited to servicing that property. This fact exempts SMATV from the government controls im-

Exhibit 4.5   SMATV

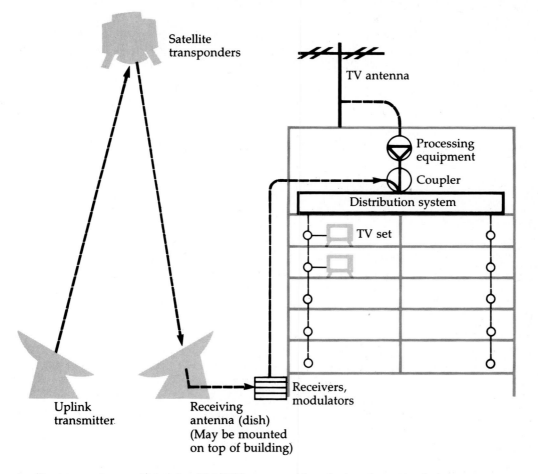

Satellite Master Antenna Television (SMATV) systems pick up basic and pay signals from satellites, as well as off-air broadcasts using a building-top antenna, and then distribute them to individual apartments by means of a cable distribution system. SMATV systems thus provide multiple channels like cable, but are usually not subject to local franchising as the system is entirely on private property.

Source: Program on Information Resources Policy, Harvard University, Cambridge, MA 02137.

posed on cable television systems that string cables over or under public rights of way. A rooftop TVRO (Exhibit 4.2) brings satellite-distributed signals to the building(s) for a monthly viewer subscription fee. The TVRO may tie into an existing master antenna television system (MATV) already in place, or cabling may be needed (Exhibit 4.5).

There is considerable controversy surrounding SMATV. Naturally, cable-system operators want access to all households in their franchise areas and fear competition from SMATV inroads in heavily populated building complexes. Applicants for cable television franchises often pressure the governmental unit granting the franchise either to dismantle existing SMATVs or to require that cable operators be given equal access to SMATV buildings. MMDS and SMATV compete head-to-head, each with several channels of pay programming. And both of these services compete with single-channel STV and regular television broadcasting, yet are not subject to broadcast-type regulation.

4.5 Traditional Broadcasting

Amidst all the rising competition (and further potential developments discussed below), traditional broadcasting after 1975 has been marked by several trends. The number of radio and television outlets has continued to grow, but at a slower rate (Exhibits 3.1 and 3.6). Technical developments have been highlighted by satellite program distribution inspired by cable television. And noncommercial radio and television underwent fundamental reorganization on the national level as federal support increased temporarily. But most important, broadcasters in the 1980s face a growing cadre of competitors for access to the home television screen.

Regulatory Parity   In the late 1970s broadcasters called for dismantling of much of the regulatory structure that had been built up since the 1920s. Faced with competition from less heavily regulated cable systems and newer delivery systems, broadcasters argued for regulatory parity. Yet traditional content and behavioral controls on radio and television stations persisted, despite the weakening of a prime rationale for those regulations — the scarcity of channels. As discussed further

in §17.2, the FCC and Congress began to come around to the broadcasters' thinking in the late 1970s, responding to changing political ideology, economic theory, and the new options created by technology. The quest for further deregulation has remained the top industry priority in the 1980s.

Television Network Competition   During the 1970s, ABC finally achieved competitive equality with the CBS and NBC television networks. ABC had long had the fewest and weakest affiliates; lacking funds, it was last to expand its evening news to a half-hour and was late getting into color. Only late in the 1970s, with a new network management team in place, did ABC climb to equal status with — and for a time surpass — both CBS and NBC. Network president Fred Pierce and program chief Fred Silverman forged popular entertainment series that grabbed audience ratings. ABC's entertainment-program success paid off in the marketplace, as the network picked up greatly increased advertising revenue plus about thirty new affiliates, some wooed from the other networks.*

These gains supported ABC's upgrading of its news. Sports wizard Roone Arledge, a proven ratings success, was assigned responsibility for improving the quality and visibility of the ABC news division. Some journalists feared that ABC's "happy talk" and entertainment approach would dilute its news content, but critics praised what quickly became a viable third network news voice.

Building on his success at ABC, Fred Silverman moved with considerable fanfare to the NBC presidency in 1978. He thus became the only person to occupy top-level program roles at all three networks (he had been day-

---

*By 1985 each television network served from 206 to 210 affiliates (the number varying a bit from year to year). Before 1980, ABC had 20 to 30 fewer stations than either CBS or NBC, and thus had lower ratings and lower advertiser appeal.

time program chief at CBS prior to joining ABC). Silverman's earlier magic did not work a third time, and NBC remained in third place, losing millions in revenue to the other networks from advertisers seeking the top-rated shows. NBC eased Silverman out in 1982, replacing him as network president with a respected independent producer, Grant Tinker. By the 1985–86 season, Tinker's NBC team moved to prime-time ratings supremacy.

CBS's story in the 1970s and early 1980s is largely that of a search for William Paley's replacement. After a half-century at the helm, Paley (still the largest single stockholder in the firm) brought in a string of potential sucessors, only to tire of each and force him out. Finally, when Paley retired in 1983, Thomas Wyman, a proven executive in several non-broadcast firms, was brought on board to become only the second chief executive officer in the network's history.

FCC Network Investigation   In 1978 the FCC began its third investigation into the role of national networks (see §3.7), this time studying the potential for a fourth television broadcast network. The study had been prompted in part by complaints from affiliates of excessive network profit-taking at their expense. The Department of Justice had previously settled, with consent decrees, antitrust suits against all three networks, contending that the networks had too much control over independent programmers. In light of the Justice settlements and rising complaints from some affiliates that they received too little of the networks' revenue, the commission undertook careful research on the impact of its own network rules.

The Network Inquiry Special Staff* issued nearly twenty detailed study reports in 1979–

*Suggesting the interplay of legal and economic factors in network behavior, the inquiry was headed by attorney Thomas Krattenmaker and economist Stanley Besen.

1980. The staff concluded that most FCC rules that limited network behavior had little value, merely restricting normal business interaction between networks and affiliates without providing any real protection for the stations. It also found that only three national television networks existed not because of network greed but because of allotment decisions made in the 1952 *Sixth Report* (§3.6). As a result of the 1952 allotments, markets given three commercial television channels could, as a group, reach virtually all of the country's population, whereas larger markets allotted four stations, taken as a whole, could reach only about 75 percent of the population, and markets with more stations could reach even smaller proportions of people. Thus possible fourth or fifth networks could never have achieved parity with the existing three.

The FCC, said the staff, lacked the expertise and personnel to closely monitor or tightly control network business practices, and they recommend dropping the prime-time access rule (§13.2) and most other rules. Further, the study found that the rise of competing delivery technologies made the broadcast networks' role less crucial than it had been at the time the FCC originated its network rules. The network study staff concluded:

The Commission presently faces a clear choice. It can attempt to continue to deal with network dominance through what we regard as a vain search for effective regulation. Or it can try to deal with the source of that dominance by reducing or eliminating barriers to the entry of new networks. (FCC, 1980: 29)

Radio Expansion   Radio continued to grow as the number of FM stations increased to match that of AM by the early 1980s (Exhibit 3.1). Indeed, projections indicate that by the late 1980s, FM will surpass AM in number of stations, as it already had by early in the decade in overall audience popularity, if not advertiser response. Continued demand for new stations led the FCC to "drop in" (that is, to add within the existing allocation) about six hundred potential new FM allotments for smaller towns, especially in the South and West.

Facing increased competition from FM stations, AM broadcasters petitioned the FCC to allow stereo transmissions on their stations. Five stereo systems competed for acceptance, however, and neither the industry nor FCC engineers could choose any one of them as best. Thus in 1981 the commission approved AM stereo, but declined to set any standard. This set a precedent, as hitherto the FCC had always set national standards for new technologies. The commission argued that the marketplace should set the standard, and that individual stations should decide which system they wanted to use. Consumers could then purchase AM stereo sets for whatever system broadcasters might adopt. The FCC would get involved only if interference resulted. Broadcasters argued that lack of a required standard would delay the spread of AM stereo, and unsuccessfully urged the commission to reconsider its marketplace approach. The broadcasters were right. Three years after the go-ahead, only a handful of AM stations had started to broadcast in stereo, though the number of viable competing systems had dropped to two.

4.6 Public Broadcasting

Origins   Faced with the decline in AM educational radio (§2.10), the FCC had established reserved channels for noncommercial FM (1941) and television (1952) stations. Growth was slow. By 1960, there were only 162 educational FM and 44 educational television stations on the air. The problem was lack of funding. Prior to the 1960s, educational radio and television depended for financial support on state and local governments, foun-

dations, and some business underwriting.*
Hard pressed to raise the money to build and operate television stations, educational interests had been slow to activate the channels reserved for them in the *Sixth Report and Order* (§3.6). Beginning with the Kennedy administration, the federal government began to provide grants and loans to speed development of noncommercial television.

In 1967 the Carnegie Commission on Educational Television (CCET) issued its watershed report calling for a stronger national organization of what they termed "public" television, to be aided by greatly increased federal funding. Use of the term *public* underlined the CCET's belief that a viable alternative system had to reach beyond narrowly defined educational content.

National System   The Public Broadcasting Act of 1967 created the Corporation for Public Broadcasting (CPB) as a nongovernmental organization to funnel federal funds to individual stations and to create public radio and television networks. CPB established the Public Broadcasting System (PBS) to arrange network facilities for linking noncommercial television stations nationally. Unlike PBS, National Public Radio (NPR), which the CPB also established, not only arranged interconnection of some two hundred of the larger public radio stations (by the 1980s) but also produced programming.

During the early 1970s, the CPB, PBS, and NPR jockeyed for power as PBS and NPR tried to limit the programming input and general oversight role of the CPB. Public radio and television stations, not used to the highly centralized network approach to programming and funding, chafed at the new structure.

---

*From 1951 to the early 1980s, the Ford Foundation was the largest nongovernmental funding source for educational television stations, providing some $300 million in grants. Ford began to phase out this support in the 1970s, moving on to other projects.

Out of this matrix of forces emerged conflicting views of the nature and proper role of the noncommercial service. Some felt public television and public radio should serve a broad cultural and informational role, but others saw a narrower instructional priority. Some wanted to stress high culture through intellectually stimulating programs, and others wanted programming of interest and value to children, ethnic minorities, and the poor. The issue of whether the national organizations or the local stations were to be dominant in this debate added to the confusion. Arguments over the long-range financing of the expanding public broadcasting system provided the grist for further debate (§10.6).

Satellite Distribution Public broadcasting gave electronic media a major improvement in the technology of program distribution. Since their inception, broadcast networks had used AT&T telephone lines, coaxial cables (§7.4), or microwave to relay their signals to affiliates. These relays were expensive and limiting, since stations could generally get but one signal from their networks at a time.

PBS pioneered a new approach by switching from landlines to satellite. In 1978, 280 public television stations began receiving their network feeds via the Westar I. Satellite delivery provided better-quality transmission; quicker flexibility to send programming east, west, or within specific regions; greater choice of programming (because PBS fed four different signals, stations usually carried one signal and recorded others for later use as needed); and, over time, a substantial cost saving. Six regional ground stations send programming to the satellite, and some 150 receive-only antennas allow all PBS members to pick up programming.

NPR developed satellite delivery for its radio interconnection in 1980, programming four audio channels and paving the way for commercial network satellite use (§4.3).

4.7 Home Video Center

Even more dramatic than the rise of new delivery systems has been the increasing ability of home viewers to control their immediate electronic media environment. Home video systems allow viewers to purchase and use programs of their individual choosing, rather than having to accept common signals sent at one time to a large, widely separated audience. Home video and other developments of the past decade are based on the *integrated circuit.*

The Chip We left the evolution of the electronic age at the stage where de Forest's improvement of the electronic tube had opened the way to broadcasting (§2.4). De Forest's thermionic device has since been supplanted by a far more efficient means of manipulating electrons, the *transistor.* It replaced the fragile, bulky, power-hungry tube with a tiny solid block of crystal — hence the term "solid-state device" for the transistor and its later offspring. Such devices are less expensive, smaller, lighter, cooler, more rugged, and faster working than any electronic tube.

A trio of Bell Laboratory engineers — John Bardeen, Walter Brattain, and William Shockley* — invented the transistor in 1947, and collectively received the Nobel Prize in Physics for it in 1956. In a very few years, the transistor transformed the electronics industry. The transistor radio, one of the first mass-produced products based on the transistor, appeared first in 1954 and quickly became the best seller in consumer product history.

The transistor made possible the development of the prime electronic artifact of the modern age, the computer. Early experimental computers used electronic tubes, but they

---

*Shockley's name is the best known of the three because of his later espousal of controversial theories about intelligence and race.

needed thousands of them, plus miles of wires. The tubes generated so much heat that attendants had to stand by to replace the ones that blew out. Transistors solved this problem, making computers with greater speed and capacity a practical reality.

Small computers could not be constructed, however, so long as thousands of separate transistors had to be meticulously wired together with hand-soldered connections. True miniaturization became possible with the invention of the *integrated circuit*, or computer "chip." Two engineers working separately arrived at this solution six months apart, Jack Kilby in 1959 and Robert Noyce in 1960. Each one's version had an advantage over the other, but Kilby won the rights to the invention in a lengthy patent suit in 1969 (416 F 2d 1391). Today the two regard each other in friendly fashion as co-inventors of the chip. Curiously, these heroes of modern electronics remain unsung:

Twenty-five years after they came up with the idea that changed the world and launched the microelectronic revolution — a revolution that has become a part of daily life for everyone on Earth — both Robert Noyce and Jack Kilby are cloaked in almost total obscurity. (Reid, 1984: 195)

Their epochal invention uses a single crystalline material, often silicon (hence the name Silicon Valley for the area south of San Francisco where much of the computer industry is concentrated), to make each of the main electrical components needed in most circuits. A single chip no bigger than a baby's fingernail can contain hundreds of separate resisters, capacitors, and other components, all linked together electrically by a circuit etched on the surface of the chip. Zenith first used such chips commercially in a miniature hearing-aid amplifier marketed in 1964. The concentration of functions in the chip makes possible computers of all sizes, digital watches, hand-held calculators, cable TV remote-control pads,

TV electronic graphics — and home video recording.

Home Recording The idea of modern home video recording dates back at least to 1972, when Sony introduced the first video-cassette (VCR) machine, the U-Matic standard, for the educational and business market. Three years later the same firm marketed its Betamax machine for the home, at an initial retail price of $1,300. Pundits predicted a new video revolution, now that consumers could not only choose *when* they would view something but could also choose *what* they would view from broadcast, prerecorded, or their own home sources.

For two years, Sony had the market to itself, selling some 50,000 units. Its monopoly ended in 1977 with Matsushita's introduction of a technically incompatible cassette format, the VHS system, also developed in Japan. The new system had a longer recording time (though the Beta machines soon matched it) and gradually acquired about 70 percent of the home VCR market. Various "bells and whistles" were added to both types of VCR as companies here and abroad competed for market share. Increased sales volume brought prices down from an average of over $1,000 to less than half that amount, and encouraged further sales (see Exhibit 4.6).

Discs The videodisc, yet another alternative for home playback, was first marketed by Magnavox in 1978. Though technically limited (it did not allow for home recording), it was less expensive than VCRs and offered a superior picture. Several incompatible formats, using either a laser or capacitance (nonlaser electronic) technology, were soon on sale. RCA bet on the latter format, introducing its "Selectavision" with considerable fanfare in 1981.

Both disc players and prerecorded discs were cheaper per unit than their VCR counterparts, at least initially. But mass marketing

Exhibit 4.6 The VCR Comes Home

Year	VCRs sold	Average price	VCRs in use	Titles available
1978	402,000	$1,200	200,000	na
1980	805,000	$1,080	1,200,000	3,000
1982	2,035,000	$900	4,500,000	4,000
1984	7,616,000	$680	15,000,000	7,000

By 1986, videocassette recorders were in about 30 percent of the nation's homes. Sales shot up as prices dropped, and by early 1986 it was possible to buy basic models for well under $200. Of the thousands of tape titles available, most were rented, not sold.

Source: Data from Electronic Industries Association. Reprinted by permission.

brought VCR prices down faster than expected, wiping out the cost advantage of videodiscs. Coupled with the inability of discs to record off the air, this proved fatal to the home-market potential of videodisc machines (though they continue to play an important role in training for schools and businesses). In 1984 RCA pulled out of the home consumer videodisc market, taking a loss of some $500 million.

VCR Boom   By 1985 several trends combined to create the long-promised home video revolution. Sufficient numbers of VCR machines had been sold to lower prices of basic units below $200, thus widening the potential audience. Indeed, sales of VCRs since 1975 have closely paralleled the "take-off" years of color-television sales, from 1959 to 1966. As the penetration of VCRs rose, Hollywood recognized a new market for motion pictures. Soon hundreds of films could be bought or, more likely, rented for home showing. This increase in available films also encouraged VCR sales.

Perhaps more fundamental to the boom in VCR sales has been the change in how movies and other prerecorded materials are marketed. By 1983, rentals (for as little as $1 a night) were far more common than sales (given retail prices of about $50 for first-run films). VCR users had discovered how easily a tape could be duplicated, so that one purchased copy was often widely duplicated, at a charge, for friends of the purchaser (§16.5). Film distribution methods changed to meet the threat of illicit copying, as chains of outlets opened to rent films at just a dollar or two a night — cheaper than copying. The opportunity of such inexpensive rentals encouraged still more people to buy VCRs.

Impact   Experts predict VCR penetration of half of all television homes by 1990, though the explosive growth in sales that occurred between 1983 and 1985 is not likely to continue. Such widespread availability of this technology has naturally raised the concerns of both broadcasters and cable system operators, as the attention of their audiences becomes increasingly divided.

VCRs encourage *timeshifting*, or recording programs for viewing at a later time. Research shows that daytime soap operas are the most heavily recorded programs (often by people who are at work during the original broadcast), but that between 20 and 25 percent of all programs recorded are never played back at all (*Newsweek*, 6 Aug. 1984)! Nonetheless, the fact that VCRs allow viewers to control what they see, and when, gives VCRs an important psychological effect. Furthermore, the machines make it fairly easy to cut out commercials during recording and playback, thus limiting viewer exposure to advertising — a selling point for VCRs, but a great concern to both broadcasters and advertisers.

Cable interests also see VCRs as competitors. HBO and the other pay services have seen little audience growth in the mid-1980s,

4.7   Home Video Center

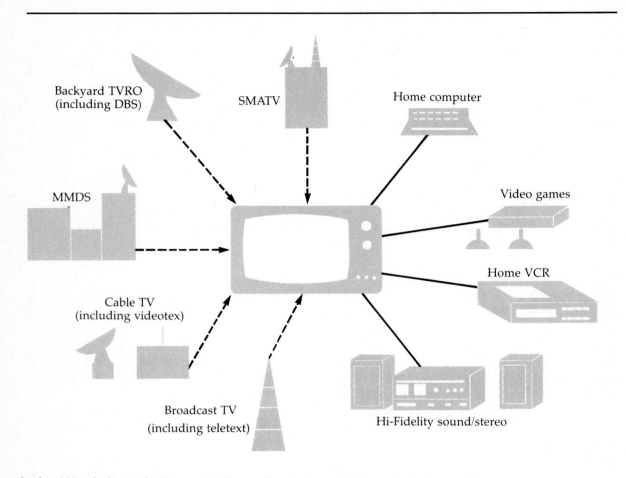

In the 1980s, the home television receiver became the reception center for an increasing variety of video distribution channels including such out-of-home sources (left, with dashed lines) as off-air broadcasting, backyard TVROs, MMDS systems, cable television, videotex/teletext experiments; and in-home inputs (right), with solid lines) including home computers, video games of various kinds, high-fidelity sound, and, most important, home videocassette recorders.

partially because of the competition VCR film rental offers cable film presentations. (Other reasons for pay cable's slackening appeal include repetition of films among the competing services and the perceived low quality of most films shown.)

Audience diversion from broadcasting and cable is only in part due to VCRs, of course, for many homes have video games and some have home computers. Video games and computers often use home television sets as display screens. Thus far, relatively little research has been done to determine how much television "viewing" in such homes has nothing to do with broadcasting or cable (Exhibit 14.9). These nonbroadcast options help illustrate the central role the receiver plays as more inputs become available (Exhibit 4.7).

Additionally, the home VCR appears to be expanding the amount of program material available to rural viewers. Often able to receive only one or two off-air television signals, and sometimes beyond the reach of any cable system, such homes in the past were largely isolated from mainstream electronic media. Now, through mail or nearby retail outlets as well as TVROs, rural dwellers are able to enjoy the variety of material long available to city residents.

4.8 Developments to Come

Several further video-related developments are being claimed as constituting the next revolution of the 1980s.

Teletext and Videotex   Broadcast teletext and wire- or cable-delivered videotex systems provide means of delivering print and graphic materials to home and office television screens. Developed first in Britain, with improved systems appearing in France and Canada by the late 1970s, these twin technologies were subject to numerous experiments in the United States. The lack of technical standards among the competing systems arose from disagreement over whether these services are best aimed at homes or at institutions.

Some experts tout teletext as the core of a developing home information utility built around the television or computer screen. Whether delivered over the air (teletext) or by wire (videotex), these print and graphic systems are a kind of pay television, in that subscribers pay a monthly connection fee, plus an amount determined by the number of information "pages" screened (§7.6 and §7.8). A decoder on the television set provides access to the teletext information, much in the way the decoder used for closed captions for the deaf does (Exhibit 4.8).

Common-carrier firms usually control the videotex delivery system, selling access or page space to information providers who fill their pages with specialized kinds of data, such as weather, news, sports scores, catalog-ordering, consumer information, games, education, cultural and theater guides, and advertising. Though such information is of course widely available in other formats, both teletext and videotex offer in-the-home instant retrieval. Early in 1986, however, the two largest videotex services aimed at home consumers closed up shop within two weeks of one another, having lost some $90 million because of insufficient consumer and advertiser appeal. By then, it appeared that the home computer would be used more frequently than the television set for interactive information retrieval services such as CompuServe and The Source.

DBS   One of the most exciting and glamorous proposed new technologies was the *direct-broadcast satellite* (DBS). At first widely touted, but fading in popularity by 1985, DBS promised to make land-based delivery systems obsolete by sending programming direct from producer to consumer, without benefit of an intervening television station or cable system. In theory, each subscribing home (for this is another means of delivering pay television) would use a TVRO antenna to receive signals directly from specially designed high-power domsats (Exhibit 4.9).

In 1980 a subsidiary of the Communications Satellite Corporation (Comsat) applied to the FCC for permission to launch a DBS system providing three channels of programming

Exhibit 4.8   Teletext and Closed Captions

Broadcast transmission of text and graphics to the home or office TV receiver makes use of the vertical blanking interval (VBI) lines between TV pictures. The various systems can produce a variety of effects in multiple colors. Simple lists or computer graphics are the least expensive approach. The transmission of closed captions for the deaf (shown at right) uses the same basic technology and VBI lines (see §7.6).

Source: Courtesy CBS Television Network.

for the eastern part of the United States. The service was designed for those unable to get cable or off-air service, mainly rural residents. Construction cost estimates ran from $250 to $750 million, including satellite design and launch fees and initial program expenses. Eight other firms soon announced similar plans.

After a lengthy proceeding, the FCC authorized commercial DBS operations in June 1982. In 1983, a landmark year for DBS, United Satellite Communications (USCI) inaugurated America's first DBS service in Indianapolis, albeit using temporary facilities. Debate ensued as to whether DBS should be regulated as a broadcasting service or a common carrier. Economists claimed that DBS aimed only at a rural audience would never be able to recoup its costs, and others argued that DBS offered nothing not already available

from existing broadcast and cable services or, for those outside their range, from videocassette recordings.

When USCI expanded beyond its initial market area in 1984, it was said to have committed $178 million for equipment, marketing, programming, and customer service. But in that same year, some of the biggest names in electronic communication decided *not* to continue their investment in this new technology. Western Union, CBS, and Comsat all backed away from earlier DBS plans. The Comsat decision was critical to USCI, which had hoped for a lifesaving infusion of fresh capital through a partnership with Comsat. With only about seven thousand subscribers in 1985, USCI managed to stay alive for a time, thanks to new money pumped in by Tele-Communications, Inc., the nation's largest cable MSO. But it was not enough. USCI, unable to meet

Exhibit 4.9   A Direct Broadcast Satellite System

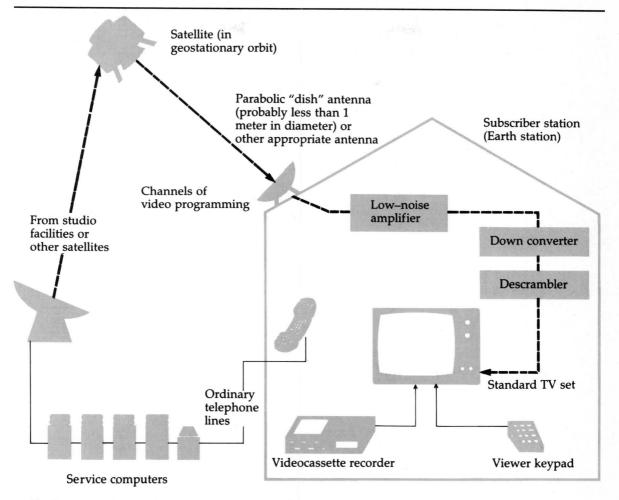

Unlike the present-day use of satellites to transmit programs to cable systems or even local TV stations, a DBS system sends signals directly to viewer homes, each of which is equipped with a small receive-only antenna. Such services are likely to be offered on a pay basis, with subscribers buying the equipment and paying a monthly reception fee for the right to decode scrambled signals.

Source: Federal Communications Commission.

its bills, shut down on April 1, 1985. Estimated losses from DBS endeavors included $140 million by Comsat and $68 million by Prudential Insurance Company, the principal investor in USCI. This dismal performance, plus the rapid

expansion of cable systems and home VCR sales, made DBS prospects dim indeed.

But despite these losses, others still planned to launch some form of DBS services. These included RCA Americom, Hughes

Communications, and Advanced Communications Corporation. Another, United States Satellite Broadcasting, a service of Hubbard Broadcasting, had been in the planning stages for several years and was scheduled to begin DBS service in 1988 with a mixture of advertiser-supported and pay television. Nonetheless, far more attention overall has been paid to DBS technology than to services. And in the United States, at least, DBS seemed to offer nothing sufficiently different from other media to make it likely to succeed.*

HDTV and Stereo TV   Meanwhile, laboratories in Japan had announced impressive improvements in the television receiver. Demonstrated in Washington in 1981, *high-definition television* (HDTV) provided a picture resolution of 1,125 lines, rather than the standard 525 lines — a picture as good as 35mm motion-picture film. Japanese HDTV initially required a 36-MHz channel, which is the equivalent of six regular television channels (§6.9). By mid-decade, it appeared that HDTV might first be used in cinemas and for home video recording, where spectrum limitations, broadcast transmitters, and existing home television receivers — all designed to operate on the existing 525-line standard — would not be a barrier.

Another improvement, multichannel or *stereo television*, seemed more likely to reach the marketplace. In 1984, acting on petitions from the industry, the FCC approved the idea of stereo TV, leaving details of the technical system to the marketplace. Manufacturers who had already generally agreed upon a technical standard announced availability of decoders to pick up the stereo sound, and the

first network programs providing stereo transmissions appeared in the 1984–1985 season. To receive the signals, however, consumers either had to invest in one of the new receivers or hook up a decoder to their existing audio system.

Too Much Technology?   Development of new delivery systems and improvements on older systems raised a number of questions for manufacturers, broadcasters, cable-system operators, and critics. For one thing, what should be concluded from the highly expensive failures of the 1980s, such as RCA's videodisc and Comsat's DBS? Some argued that too much technology was chasing too little program creativity and too few audience dollars. Were consumers being offered a real choice or simply different means of receiving the same content long provided by plain old broadcasting? Were marketplace pressures encouraging the wrong kind of media investment — overlapping services providing nothing really new?

A widespread preference for marketplace rather than government control became increasingly evident after 1970. Services developed since then — pay cable, MMDS, SMATV, DBS, and videocassette recordings, for example — have little or no regulatory oversight. The FCC, beginning with its AM stereo "nondecision," abandoned its traditional role of helping to shape electronic media by controlling application of technology through mandated standards.

In this new competitive arena some services will survive and others will fall by the wayside. But thus far, all the technological jockeying has offered only a variety of delivery systems rather than a real choice of new and different program options. Diversity of channels has not been matched by comparable variety in content. The chapters that follow provide more detail on why this is so.

---

*Plans for DBS service in several other countries continue to evolve. In Western Europe, for example, where there are fewer delivery options available, several regional DBS projects are being planned. A number of developing regions are likewise pressing ahead with DBS options.

Summary

• The years since 1970 have been marked by dramatic expansion in the number and type of delivery systems competing with radio and television broadcasting. This expansion grew out of limitations in television coverage, some of them traceable to the 1952 FCC *Sixth Report* decision on television allocations (§3.6).

• Community antenna television (CATV) began in several mountain communities in Pennsylvania in the late 1940s, using a common antenna and direct cable connections to subscriber homes.

• Cable service was augmented with original program channels and distant signal importation by the 1960s, and with pay channels by the late 1970s. This augmented competition concerned broadcasters, who pressured the FCC to regulate cable. In addition, several states set up cable commissions, and operators had to negotiate with local government franchise authorities.

• The late 1960s and early 1970s saw the peak of FCC activity in controlling cable. But the 1972 FCC rules unraveled over the next several years, under pressure of both judicial review and revised economic thinking, and nearly all had been lifted by 1980.

• Cable continued to expand, despite regulatory confusion, because of the opportunities provided by use of domestic satellites. The decisions of Home Box Office and Ted Turner to use domsats to deliver programming nationwide opened the door to other operators.

• By the 1980s, it was clear that single-channel pay television systems, such as over-the-air subscription television (STV) and multipoint distribution systems (MDS), were losing the competitive battle with multichannel services: pay cable, multichannel multipoint distribution systems (MMDS), and satellite master antenna (SMATV) systems.

• Traditional broadcasting continued to thrive in the 1970s and 1980s, despite the new competition. Broadcasters argued for less regulation to match the virtually unregulated new delivery systems. The FCC conducted its third investigation of networks and concluded that most existing rules limiting television network behavior should be eliminated.

• Educational radio and television stations developed slowly for a lack of funds until the 1960s. In 1967 Congress, following most of the recommendations of the Carnegie Commission, established the Corporation for Public Broadcasting (CPB), which in turn set up the Public Broadcasting Service (PBS) and National Public Radio (NPR). The noncommercial system suffered considerable financial and organizational tensions in the 1970s as it sought long-range funding.

• Following the lead of public radio and television, broadcast networks took to using satellite delivery, ending decades of landline use. Live satellite-delivered news reports were common by the early 1980s.

• Based on development of the integrated circuit, or computer chip, the home videocassette recorder (VCR) by 1986 was in a quarter of the nation's homes, was changing film distribution patterns, and was limiting the growth of pay cable networks.

• Several technologies remain in the wings, not yet beyond the market experimentation stage. These include teletext, direct-broadcast satellites (DBS), and high-definition television (HDTV). By 1985, it appeared that development of a successful DBS system in the United States was highly unlikely because of cost and competition from cable and other services.

• Many critics argue that we have plenty of technological options in the 1980s, but nowhere near enough original programming ideas or new applications of the technology to meet societal needs.

PART 2

Technology

To understand broadcasting and related media you must understand something of their physical nature. Stubborn physical facts dictate where and how far electromagnetic signals travel and how much information they carry. Propagation factors affect transmitter placement, limiting how many transmitters can operate in any one locality. Technology calls for standardizing of systems, equipment, and procedures, demanding a high degree of international coordination. To avoid interference, users must cooperate in ways unique to electronic communication.

The next three chapters survey in lay terms the basic concepts involved in using radio energy for communication (Chapter 5); the technology of POBS, the traditional broadcasting system (Chapter 6); and the supporting distribution and recording technologies, along with the newer methods of electronic communication and their interaction with traditional methods (Chapter 7).

CHAPTER 5

Basic Physical Concepts

The ability to radiate through empty space and to travel in all directions without benefit of any vehicle is electronic communication's most dramatic advantage over other modes of communication. Radio* waves can leap over oceans, span continents, penetrate buildings, pass through people, go to the moon and back, and reach the earth from the farthest star.

5.1 Electromagnetic Spectrum

In the context of this chapter, radio must be understood as a form of energy, belonging to the same class of energy as visible light, X rays, and cosmic rays. Collectively, such phenomena constitute the domain of *electromagnetic* energy. All forms of this energy share three fundamental characteristics: (1) they all travel at the same high *velocity*; (2) in traveling, they assume the properties of *waves*; and (3) they *radiate* outward from a source, without benefit of any discernible physical vehicle.

Radiation can be explained in terms of

*As used in this chapter, the word *radio* refers not only to sound broadcasting but to the wireless *method* of communicating. In this sense, radio conveys not only sounds and pictures but streams of coded data and many other types of content — even sheer noise.

light. Turn on an electric bulb, and light radiates into the surrounding space. Light rays, fundamentally the same as radio waves, travel at a velocity of 300 million meters (186,000 miles) per second. The two forms of energy differ, however, in the length and frequency of their waves: light has much shorter waves and higher frequency. All electromagnetic energy has an *oscillating* (vibrating or alternating) motion, depicted in terms of waves. The number of separate wavelike motions produced in a second determines a wave's frequency — a key concept because differences in frequency determine the varied forms that electromagnetic energy assumes.

A large number of frequencies visualized in numerical order constitutes a *spectrum*. The keyboard of a piano presents one version of a spectrum, starting with keys that produce low sound frequencies at the left end and progressing through higher and higher frequencies toward the right end of the keyboard. You can see a visible spectrum when a rain shower, acting as a prism, breaks up sunlight into its component colors (sunlight, though seemingly colorless, actually combines "all the colors of the rainbow"). Humans perceive the lower frequencies of light as red in color and, as frequency increases, see light as yellow, green, blue, and finally violet. Above the fre-

Exhibit 5.1   How the Electromagnetic Spectrum Is Used

Electromagnetic phenomena	Examples of uses	Approximate frequency ranges	Typical wavelengths
Cosmic rays	Physics, astronomy	10^{14} GHz and above	Diameter of an electron
Gamma rays	Cancer therapy	10^{10}-10^{13} GHz	Diameter of smallest atom
X rays	X-ray examination	10^8-10^9 GHz	Diameter of largest atom
Ultraviolet radiation	Sterilization	10^6-10^8 GHz	1 hundred millionth of a meter
Visible light	Human vision	10^5-10^6 GHz	1 millionth of a meter
Infrared radiation	Photography	10^3-10^4 GHz	1 ten thousandth of a meter
Microwave radio waves	Radar, microwave relays, satellite communication	1-300 GHz	1 centimeter
Radio waves	UHF television	470-806 MHz	1/2 meter
Radio waves	VHF television, FM radio	54-216 MHz	3 meters
Radio waves	Short-wave radio	3-26 MHz	30 meters
Radio waves	AM radio	535-1,605 kHz	3,000 meters

Note that frequency decreases as wavelength increases (reading from the top down). As frequency increases, the manifestations of electromagnetic energy become more dangerous to man (though not necessarily less useful). Even frequencies as low as those used in radar and microwave relays can damage humans exposed to long-term, high-level radiation. Microwave ovens can also pose a hazard if not properly shielded. Not mentioned in the usage examples are the many nonbroadcast and auxiliary broadcast applications of radio communication. The table does not mention the lowest frequencies, which manifest themselves as radiant heat and electric power.

quency of visible violet come *ultraviolet* frequencies; below the frequency of visible red come *infrared* frequencies.

Exhibit 5.1 shows at what frequencies the various types of energy in the spectrum occur. Note that as frequency *increases*, wavelength *decreases*. Frequencies usable for radio communication occur near the lower end of the electromagnetic spectrum. As frequency increases, the practical difficulties of using electromagnetic energy for communication purposes also increase, until finally it can no longer be used. As communication methods improve, the limit to usable frequencies has been pushed higher and higher. The higher the frequency, the more radio waves behave like light. Today communication satellites use frequencies near 14 gigahertz (14 billion oscillations per second). This is still far below light frequencies, but in the enclosed environment of fiber-optic cable, light itself can be used for radio communication.*

5.2 Sound Waves

Although sound energy differs in fundamental ways from electromagnetic energy, it pro-

---

*Of course light as such has long been used to communicate by means of semaphores, lighthouses, and other devices.

vides a useful analogy because sound, too, has an oscillating motion and can be depicted as traveling in a wavelike manner. Sound therefore serves as a means of illustrating the characteristics of waves in an understandable way, because we can perceive sounds.

Wave Motion

Using the example of a conversation between two people at a party, consider what happens in terms of wave motion. A speaker's vocal cords vibrate, producing word-sounds; these oscillations of the vocal cords set molecules of air in wavelike motion; sound waves travel through the air to the eardrums of a listener, which respond by vibrating in step with the wave motion of the air molecules. Eardrum vibrations stimulate nerve fibers leading to the listener's brain, which interprets the vibrations as words.

The chief wave-motion concepts can be deduced from this sequence of events. At each step in the sequence, vibration (alternation, oscillation) occurs. Vibration in one object (vocal cords) causes corresponding vibratory motion in other objects (air, eardrums). The medium of vibrating air molecules carries meaning from one point to another.

Wave Motion Analyzed

To break wave motion down into its components, consider the motion of a point on the perimeter of a revolving wheel, as depicted in Exhibit 5.2. A tracing of that motion renders a waveform that has *amplitude, length, frequency,* and *velocity.* Distance above and below the level of the axle represents *amplitude,* which in the case of sound is perceived as loudness. We can measure the distance the wheel travels in one revolution, which tells us the *length* of the wave. We can count the number of revolutions the wheel makes in a second, which tells us the *frequency* of the wave, perceived in terms of sound as pitch. Finally, the distance traveled in a unit of time (in this case a second) yields a measure of *velocity.*

Phase

As the wheel in Exhibit 5.2 goes through its first half revolution (180 degrees), the waveform rises to a maximum and then drops back to its starting level; then, during the second half of the wheel's revolution, the waveform goes through an opposite phase. Each half of the entire cycle of motion is in fact called a phase, so that a complete wave involves two opposite phases.

These opposing phases of a wave cycle may be regarded as positive (plus) and negative (minus) aspects of the wave. If the positive aspects of two simultaneous waves coincide, their energies combine to make a larger total amplitude at that point. If, however, a negative and a positive aspect of two waves coincide, the smaller subtracts from the larger, making a smaller total amplitude at that point. When two waves of the same frequency exactly coincide they are said to be "in phase." If they have the same amplitude, their combined amplitude is double the amplitude of each one.

Phase plays an important role in many practical applications throughout electronic systems. Two or more microphones fed to the same amplifier must be phased correctly to prevent their signals from interfering with each other; and television relies on phase differences in processing color information. Also, some directional antennas use phase reinforcement and cancellation to strengthen radiation in one direction and to weaken it in another.

Overtones

Phase also has an important bearing on sound quality. A sound having a perfectly smooth, symmetrical waveform consists of a single frequency, a pure tone. Pleasing musical tones and natural sounds, however, consist of many different frequencies of varying amplitudes, all produced at the same time. When these frequencies combine, their phase differences result in complex

Exhibit 5.2   Wave Motion Concepts

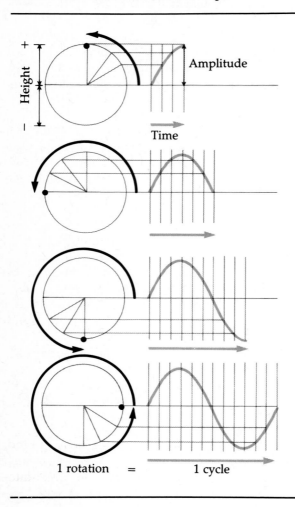

Tracing the rise and fall of a spot on the rim of a revolving wheel illustrates the wave-motion concepts cycle, phase, amplitude, and velocity. The spot starts at the level of the axle, moving first up, then down, then up again. The changing distances of the spot above and below the axle level represent changes in amplitude. One complete revolution of the wheel represents one cycle of wave movement. If we regard movement above the level of the axle as positive and that below the axle as negative, we can say that each cycle consists of two opposite halves, or phases. The distance covered during the time the wheel takes to make one revolution can be used to calculate its speed-of-travel, or velocity. For example, a wheel that revolved ten times a second and travelled four feet for every revolution would have a velocity of 10 × 4, or 40, feet per second.

Source: Adapted from John R. Pierce, *Signals: The Telephone and Beyond* (W. H. Freeman & Co., San Francisco, 1981), p. 35.

waves that have irregular patterns, as shown in Exhibit 5.3.

Complexity in sounds comes from *overtones*, or *harmonics*. The frequency we hear as the pitch of a sound is its *fundamental*. The fundamentals of human speech are quite low — from 200 to 1,000 hertz (cycles per second) for women, from 100 to 500 hertz for men. Overtones, which give voices their distinctive timbres, are higher frequencies, multiples of the fundamentals. Thus middle C, with a fundamental of 264 hz, may have overtones at 528 hz, 792, 1,056, and so on. Differences in the distribution and amplitudes of overtones account for qualitative differences between sounds having the same pitch. One can distinguish a violin from a clarinet, even when they are producing exactly the same note at the same volume, because their overtones differ. For high-fidelity sound reproduction, over-

Exhibit 5.3 Complex Waves

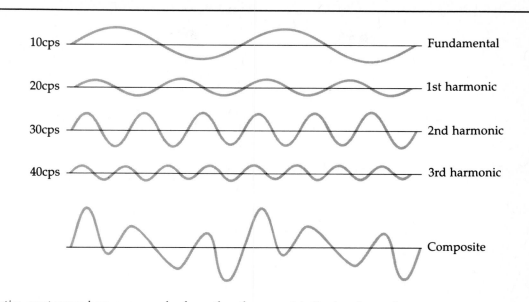

10cps — Fundamental

20cps — 1st harmonic

30cps — 2nd harmonic

40cps — 3rd harmonic

Composite

In practice, most waves have more complex forms than the symmetrically shaped wave in Exhibit 5-2. Overtones in a musical note, for example, markedly alter the shape of its fundamental wave as they interact with it. The smooth fundamental 10-cps wave at the top, combined with its shorter-wave-length 1st, 2nd, and 3rd harmonics, results in the complex composite wave at the bottom. Cps = cycles per second.

Source: Adapted from Paul Davidovits, *Communication* (Holt, Rinehart & Winston, New York, 1972), p. 129, Fig. 11–1.

tones, having relatively high pitch by definition, require equipment able to reproduce the higher sound frequencies.

Acoustic Environments Sound waves, once launched into a given environment, begin to *attenuate*, gradually losing their energy as they travel. Draperies, human bodies, and other soft, irregularly shaped objects tend to *absorb* sound energy, increasing the rate of attenuation. Hard, flat room surfaces *reflect* sound waves, causing reverberations or echoes (*reverberations* are echoes so closely spaced in time that they are not heard as separate sounds). Excessive sound absorption

gives a room a "dead," uninteresting sound; reflections produce "live," bright sounds. Acoustic engineers design studios and auditoriums with the optimum degree of reverberation. Often they provide adjustable reflective and absorptive panels to enable the increase or lessening of reverberation, according to the specific needs of particular performers and instruments.

The shorter the waves, the more easily they are blocked by small objects. Long waves tend to "bend" around objects in their path. You can verify this fact by listening to music in another room or from around the corner of a building. As soon as you turn the corner into the area where the music originates, the sound you hear immediately becomes brighter. You begin hearing the shorter-wave (that is, higher-pitched) sounds that were unable to get around corners as readily as the longer-wave sounds.

5.3 Radio Waves

Like sound waves, radio waves behave in characteristic ways, depending on their frequency and phase relationships. Radio waves attenuate, can be absorbed or reflected, and produce echoes. Visual echoes resulting from reflected signals account for the "ghosts" sometimes seen as double images in television pictures. Keep in mind, however, that radio waves differ fundamentally from sound waves, especially in terms of frequency, velocity, and mode of travel. Limitations of the ear confine audible sound to a frequency range of about 16 to 20,000 cycles per second (individual hearing acuity varies greatly, especially at the upper frequencies). In comparison, the frequency range of the radio spectrum is vast, running from a few thousand cycles per second into the billions. Radio waves travel with the speed of light, about 900,000 times the speed of sound in air. Finally, radio waves need no intervening medium in which to travel, such as air. Indeed they travel best in a total vacuum. Sound, on the other hand, must have air, water, or some other physical conduit through which to travel.

Frequency-Wavelength Relationship

The phrase "cycles per second" has been shortened by international agreement to the term *hertz** (abbreviated Hz), meaning a frequency of *one cycle per second*. The numbers of

---

*So named to honor the pioneer radio physicist, Heinrich Hertz (1857–1894). His contribution is discussed in §2.4.

Exhibit 5.4   Divisions of Radio Frequency Spectrum into Bands

Name of band	Frequency range
Very low frequency (VLF)	3-30 kHz
Low frequency (LF)	30-300 kHz
Medium frequency (MF)	300-3,000 kHz
High frequency (HF)	3-30 MHz
Very high frequency (VHF)	30-300 MHz
Ultra high frequency (UHF)	300-3,000 MHz
Super high frequency (SHF)	3-30 GHz
Extremely high frequency (EHF)	30-300 GHz

By international agreement, the radio frequency spectrum has been divided into large groups of frequencies called bands. *Various radio services occupy parts of these bands. The bands become progressively larger as frequency increases, necessitating changing the nomenclature to avoid excessively long numbers. A kilohertz (kHz) = 1,000 hertz (Hz, or cycles per second); a megahertz (MHz) = 1,000 kilohertz; and a gigahertz (GHz) = 1,000 megahertz.*

hertz in the higher-frequency radio waves rise into the billions, making for awkwardly long numbers. Prefixing the term *hertz* with the standard metric multipliers *kilo-* (thousand), *mega-* (million), and *giga-* (billion) simplifies the numbering system. Exhibit 5.4 shows the use of these metric terms in identifying the radio-frequency spectrum's major subdivisions (or bands) and the abbreviations such as VHF and UHF used to identify them.

As Exhibit 5.1 indicates, the location of any wave in the electromagnetic spectrum can be stated either in terms of its frequency or its wavelength. The term *microwaves* identifies a group of waves by their length, but the term *VHF* identifies a group by frequency. If one knows the length of a wave in meters, one can easily find its frequency in hertz by dividing its length into 300 million, which is the velocity of radio waves in number of meters per second. For example, a wave with a length of 300 meters would have a frequency of 1 million hertz (1 MHz). Conversely, one can determine the wavelength by dividing frequency into velocity; thus a wave with a frequency of 100 million hertz would have a length of 3 meters. Looked at another way, velocity (treated as a constant of 300 million meters per second) is the product of wavelength times frequency.

Because of the fixed relationship between wavelength and frequency, one can identify the position of a radio station within its band by either the frequency or the length of its carrier wave. Usually frequency is used. The number 600 (often abbreviated 60) on a standard (AM) radio receiver dial identifies a carrier frequency of 600 kHz; an FM station's dial number gives frequency in megahertz (98.9, for example, means a carrier frequency of 98.9 MHz). Television stations, however, have different carrier frequencies for their video and audio components; for the sake of convenience, television stations are identified by channel number rather than by wavelength or frequency. For example, it is easier to say "channel 6" than to speak of a station having a video carrier-wave frequency of 83.5 MHz and a sound carrier-wave frequency of 88.75 MHz.

Carrier Waves   Recall that sound production needs some physical *vibrating* object — vocal cords, drum head, saxophone reed, guitar strings, or the like. Radio-wave production, too, depends on vibration (oscillation), but of an electrical current rather than a physical object. An oscillating current can be envisioned as power surging back and forth in a wire, rising to a maximum in one direction (one phase), then to a maximum in the other direction (the opposite phase).

When current alternates in any electric circuit, even in the wiring of one's home, it releases electromagnetic energy into the surrounding space. The 60-cycles-per-second oscillation of household electrical power causes radiations that a broadcast receiver would pick up and reproduce as a 60-cycle audible hum, were it not for shielding that cuts off the emissions. The tendency of alternating current to radiate energy increases with its frequency; the higher the rate of alternation, the more radiation. Dangerous radiations occur at the higher frequencies.

A broadcast transmitter generates radio-frequency energy for radiating into space via the transmitting antenna. The basic emission, the transmitter's *carrier wave*, oscillates at the station's allotted frequency, radiating energy at that frequency continuously, even though no sound or picture may be going out at the moment.

5.4 Modulation

The next basic concept, *modulation*, concerns the method by which information is impressed on a transmitter's carrier wave.

Energy Patterns   We can modulate a flashlight beam merely by turning it on and off. A distant observer can decode a modulated light beam according to any agreed-upon meanings: a pattern of short flashes might mean "All O.K." and a series of short-long flashes might mean "Having trouble, send help." Thus modulation produces a *signal*, a meaningful pattern. Any perceptible physical variation can become a signal — light changing from green to red, a head nodding up and down, a finger pointing.

In terms of waves, sounds consist of amplitude patterns (loudnesses) and frequency patterns (tones, or pitches). A microphone, responding to variations in air pressure, translates these pressure patterns into corresponding electrical vibrations — a sequence of electrical waves having amplitude and frequency variations approximately matching those of the sound-in-air pattern. Next, those electrical variations modulate a transmitter's radio-frequency carrier, causing its oscillations to assume the same pattern. Thus we have a radio signal — patterned variations that convey information by means of a carrier wave.

Note that radio modulation involves frequencies in two widely different ranges: that of the signal (for example, sound frequencies) and that of the carrier wave (radio frequencies). In order to reproduce the signal-frequency pattern, the carrier wave's own frequency must be much higher than that of the signal. Exhibit 5.5 shows how several cycles of the carrier wave are needed to represent the pattern of *each* cycle of the signal wave.

Transduction   At each point where a transfer of energy takes place, a *transducer*, literally a "leader across," does the job. A microphone as a transducer changes sound patterns into electrical patterns. A television camera transduces light patterns into electrical patterns. A transmitter transduces electrical frequency patterns into a higher frequency domain, that of *radio-frequency* (RF) energy. Even the keyboard on a computer is a transducer, changing the physical energy of striking the keys into electrical pulses.

Sidebands   The single radio frequency that identifies a carrier wave can carry only a very small amount of information each second. Modulation affects adjacent frequencies, both above and below the specific carrier frequency. These additional groups of frequencies constitute *sidebands*. The more information

conveyed, the larger the sideband.

Either the upper or the lower sideband suffices to convey all the information imposed on a carrier wave. Many radio communication services nevertheless transmit both sidebands, because suppressing one of them adds to equipment costs. Some services, however, economize on spectrum usage by suppressing one sideband, either fully or partially. Suppression results in *single sideband* (SSB) transmission. AM and FM radio use double-sideband transmission, but television is an example of a service using only one sideband, as shown later in Exhibit 6.3.

Channels   As indicated, the existence of sidebands requires the allotment of a bundle of frequencies to each station. This bundle is referred to as a station's *channel*. A channel can be visualized in terms of a water-supply pipe. A very thin pipe could eventually fill a big reservoir with its trickle of water, but a gush of water from a large-diameter pipe is essential to fill the reservoir rapidly.

In broadcast communication, we are usually interested in large pipes, or channels, because we want immediate, "real time" results. Some nonbroadcast services, however, trade slow delivery for economy in channel width. Certain pictorial news services, for example, deliver video information over very narrow channels, taking ten seconds to build up a single black-and-white still picture. On the other hand, broadcast television needs channels wide enough to show pictures in color and in motion as the events they depict occur.

AM and FM   The chief methods for imposing patterns on broadcast carriers vary either *amplitude* or *frequency*. Exhibit 5.6 shows how they work. Standard radio is called AM because it uses *amplitude modulation*, and FM radio is so called because it uses *frequency modulation*. Television uses both methods, AM for the video signal, FM for the audio signal.

Exhibit 5.5 Amplitude Modulation

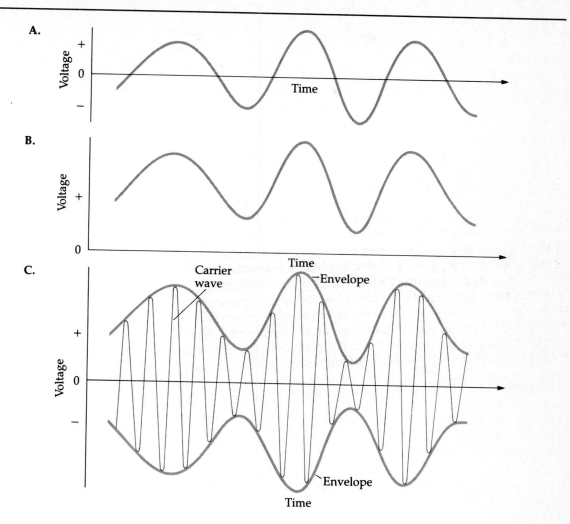

A. The wave representing a portion of a sound signal that a microphone might produce is called the base-band *signal*.

B. In preparation for modulating the station's carrier wave, the base-band voltages (amplitudes) are artificially increased so that the entire signal consists of positive voltages.

C. This voltage pattern, when imposed on the carrier wave (whose frequency remains constant), shapes the carrier with an envelope, producing an amplitude-modulated wave. The lower half of the modulated carrier automatically mirrors the upper half. Note that in order to form an envelope, the carrier wave must have a higher frequency than the base-band wave.

Source: John R. Pierce, *Signals: The Telephone and Beyond* (W. H. Freeman & Co., San Francisco, 1981), p. 61.

Exhibit 5.6   Amplitude vs. Frequency Modulation

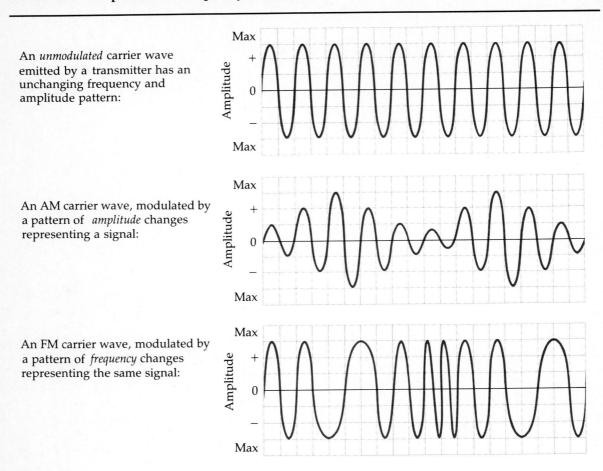

An *unmodulated* carrier wave emitted by a transmitter has an unchanging frequency and amplitude pattern:

An AM carrier wave, modulated by a pattern of *amplitude* changes representing a signal:

An FM carrier wave, modulated by a pattern of *frequency* changes representing the same signal:

In AM, frequency remains constant, amplitude varies; in FM, amplitude remains constant, frequency varies. The patterns of change, whether of amplitude or frequency, represent the energy patterns of the transmitted signal.

Source: Federal Communications Commission.

Recall that modulation means imposing a meaningful pattern of variations on an otherwise unvaried stream of energy. To visualize the process, picture a transmitter being fed a sound having the pitch of middle C — in other words, acoustic vibrations of 264 cycles per second. Such a sound would cause an ampli-tude-modulated carrier wave to change its amplitude, or level of energy, 264 times a second. The same sound would cause a frequency-modulated carrier wave to change its frequency 264 times a second.

Because amplitude modulation depends on *amount* of energy received, its signals are vulnerable to electrical interference. AM radio receivers pick up random bits of energy, such as those caused by lightning or electrical machinery. These meaningless pulses interact with the transmitted RF (radio frequency) energy, distorting the modulation pattern. Listeners perceive such distortions in the received signal as noise or static. FM carriers, relying on frequency rather than amplitude patterns, are relatively immune to electrical interference. Unwanted amplitude variations of the modulated carrier can be clipped off the wave peaks without disturbing the essential information pattern.

5.5 Digital Signal Processing

AM and FM signal patterns are called *analogue* patterns, because, when depicted as waves, their shapes are analogous to the waveforms of the original sound signal. Traditional clocks and watches, with their continuously rotating hands, represent an analogue method of telling time. *Digital* watches on the other hand, give the time directly in numbers, jumping from one number to the next.

Analogue signal processing reproduces patterns by means of *continuous* change, corresponding (or *analogous*) to the continuous flow of sound or images that impinge upon a microphone or a television camera pickup tube. This continuous pattern is inherently fragile, susceptible to various sources of distortion. The previously mentioned example of static is just one of many distortion-causing influences that limit the ability of analogue systems to process information with fidelity.

In contrast, digital signal processing breaks down an incoming signal into a stream of separate, individual pulses of energy. Rapid *sampling* of the analogue incoming signal, at such high speeds that the resulting digitized version *seems* continuous to an observer, en-

ables conversion of the signal into a stream of simple pulses of energy. Each pulse is represented by a number, hence the term *digital*.

Digital Encoding   For example, signals picked up by a microphone consist of continuously varying electrical amplitudes (voltages). A digital processor breaks down this continuous amplitude pattern into a series of small, discrete steps. An encoder *quantizes* each momentary energy level by assigning it a number, employing the *binary code*. This is the familiar number system employed by computers, based entirely on two digits, 0 and 1. Strings of zeros and ones can be used to signify any number (Exhibit 5.7). The signals representing such numbers consist of nothing more than a pattern of "power off" signals (zeros) and "power on" signals (ones).

The extreme simplicity of digitized signals protects them from the many forms of distortion that affect analogue signals. Repeated recording, relaying, and other manipulations of analogue information inevitably cause quality loss because each new manipulation of the signal introduces its own distortions. But digital signals, being simply numbers, are immune to distortion as long as the elementary difference between "off" and "on" is maintained. Exhibit 5.7 shows how a single cycle of a complex analogue wave can be sampled, with the amplitude of the wave at each sampling moment assigned a binary number. The final output consists exclusively of "off" and "on" signals of varying length.

Bit Speed   In digital signal processing, the minimum item of information conveyed by the difference between 0 and 1 is called a *bit* (binary digit).* Bit speed — the number of bits

---

*A group of bits conveying a letter of the alphabet or a number in the decimal system is called a *byte*, a term familiar to computer users.

Exhibit 5.7   Digital Signal Processing

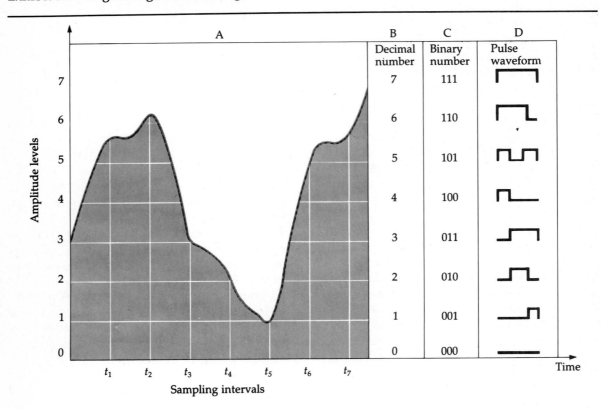

	B Decimal number	C Binary number	D Pulse waveform
	7	111	
	6	110	
	5	101	
	4	100	
	3	011	
	2	010	
	1	001	
	0	000	

Pulse amplitude modulation, long used in telephony, is one form of digital signal processing. The wave-form at A represents an analogue signal of varying amplitude. At the intervals marked t_1 t_2, and so forth, the signal is "quantized" by taking sample amplitude readings. Amplitude levels, varying from a minimum of zero

amplitude to a maximum of 7, are listed under B as ordinary numbers. At C they are converted to binary numbers, that is, numbers consisting exclusively of combinations of 1 and zero. At D the binary numbers modulate a digital signal, with the number 1 representing "signal on" and zero representing "signal off."

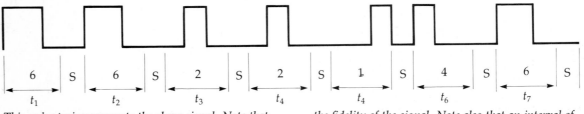

This pulse train represents the above signal. Note that quantizing involves some rounding off; thus the level at t_1, though actually about 5.5, is rounded to 6. This means that the higher the rate of sampling, the higher

the fidelity of the signal. Note also that an interval of zero amplitude occurs between each sample (indicated by s in the diagram); this interval keeps the pulses from blending into one another.

Source: Graham Langley, *Telecommunications Primer*, 2nd ed. (Pitman Books, London, 1986). Used by permission.

a channel can handle each second — becomes the measure of channel capacity. A digital telephone circuit, for example, needs a bit speed of 64,000 bits per second.

Complex information requires very high bit speed, which translates into the need for very wide frequency channels. Digital methods were first applied to technologies that use relatively simple signals and hence do not require extraordinary channel width: data processing, telephony, and experimental satellite communications are examples. The need for high-capacity channels has delayed the application of digital processing to broadcasting transmission and reception. However, digital methods employed in sound and video recording have revolutionized prebroadcast phases of production, enormously increasing the range of tools available to the video director. Moreover, digital processing has been applied to numerous consumer items, notably compact disc (CD) audio recordings.

5.6 Wave Propagation

However processed, modulated broadcast signals go from the transmitter to its antenna, the physical element from which signals radiate into surrounding space. The traveling of signals outward from the antenna is called signal *propagation*. In traveling, radio energy attenuates, growing progressively weaker as it covers a larger and larger area.

Coverage Contours   Under ideal conditions, a transmitter would cover a circular geographic area. Assuming an omnidirectional antenna, radio energy radiates evenly in all directions. In practice, however, the varying conditions that waves encounter affect the distance they travel and hence the shapes of coverage areas. Conditions influencing coverage patterns include weather, physical obstructions (both natural and artificial), the nature of

the soil, the time of day, and even seasonal sunspot changes. Waves may be affected by *refraction* (bending), *reflection, absorption, interference*, and *ducting* (unusually long-distance propagation of waves that normally reach only to the horizon). As a result of these and other variables, coverage patterns usually assume irregular shapes. Engineers use field measurements to determine a station's actual coverage contours.

How much and in what ways specific conditions along a signal's wave path affect signal propagation depend in major part on which frequency band the signal occupies. Just as the spectrum's electromagnetic radiations taken as a whole differ markedly in their behavior from one range of frequencies to another, so do different bands of radio-frequency energy vary in behavior. Description of frequency-related differences in propagation behavior can be summarized by dividing waves into three types: direct waves, ground waves, and sky waves.

Direct Waves   Line-of-sight waves occur in the VHF frequencies and above. Called *direct waves*, they follow a straight path from transmitting antenna to receiver antenna, reaching only to the horizon. Beyond that point, most of their energy flies off into space (Exhibit 5.8). Line-of-sight distance to the horizon depends on antenna height: the higher a radiating element, the farther it can "see" before reaching the horizon. By the same token, raising a receiving antenna can extend the horizon limit. FM radio and both VHF and UHF television use direct waves and therefore cover areas limited by the horizon distance. Satellites also use direct waves, but because of their tremendous height above the earth's surface the signals they send can cover nearly a third of the globe before reaching the horizon.

Obstructions in the paths of waves cast "shadows" if the objects are wider than the length of the waves. Waves used for television, and higher frequency waves, have such

Exhibit 5.8   Wave Propagation

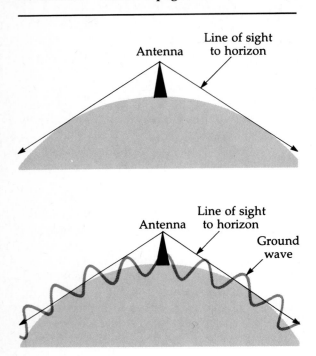

Direct waves *travel like light rays, straight out from small radiating elements atop the antenna structure. The line-of-sight angle to the horizon limits their radius of coverage. TV antennas have directional characteristics to prevent energy radiating at an angle above the horizon so that it will not be lost in space.*

Ground waves *travel through the atmosphere along the surface of the earth but are affected by the electrical conductivity of the soil over which they pass. Given sufficient power and soil conductivity, ground waves can outdistance direct waves, travelling well beyond the horizon. The entire antenna structure radiates energy. Although the antenna is insulated from the earth, it has a ground component consisting of many wires buried in the earth, radiating out from the antenna base. Exhibit 5.10 pictures an antenna tower and the radial pattern of its ground system.*

Ground Waves   Because ground waves propagate along the surface of the earth, they can follow its curvature and so can travel beyond the horizon, as shown in Exhibit 5.8. Ground waves therefore have the potential for covering a wider area than direct waves. In practice, however, the distance a ground wave travels depends on several variables, notably transmitter power, conductivity of the soil surrounding its antenna, and the amount of interference from distant stations on the same channel. Dry, sandy soil conducts radio energy poorly, whereas damp, loamy soil conducts it well.* Because ground waves occur at medium frequencies, AM (standard) broadcast signals, which are of medium frequency, often reach well beyond the horizon, even in the daytime.

Sky Waves   Time of day affects propagation because of sky-wave phenomena. Most radio waves, when allowed to radiate upward toward the sky, lose much of their energy through atmospheric absorption. Any remaining energy dissipates into space. Waves in the medium-frequency and high-frequency bands, however, tend to bend back, forming *sky waves*. This bending effect occurs when waves encounter the *ionosphere*, a high, stratified layer of atmosphere. Bombarded by high-energy radiations from the sun, the ionosphere takes on special electrical properties, causing sky waves to refract (bend) back toward the earth. Under the right conditions, these refracted waves bounce off the surface of the earth, travel back to the ionosphere, bend back again, and so on, following the curvature of the earth and travelling thousands of miles (Exhibit 5.9).

short lengths that even relatively small objects can interfere with their propagation. In the higher frequency bands, objects as small as raindrops cause blockage.

*The FCC publishes a map showing soil conductivity throughout the United States (47 CFR 73.190). The most conductive soils are 30 times as conductive as the least conductive. Salt water, by far the best conductor, sometimes helps to propagate signals for long distances along shore lines.

Exhibit 5.9   Sky Wave Propagation

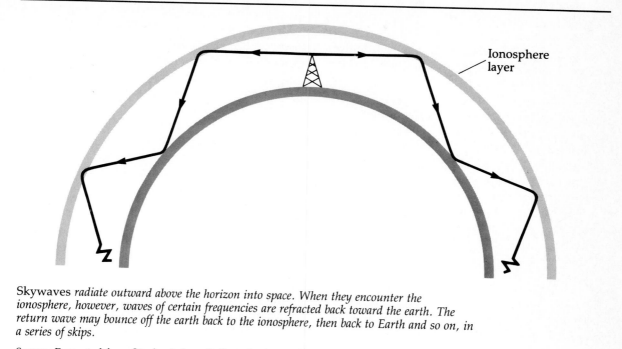

Ionosphere layer

Skywaves *radiate outward above the horizon into space. When they encounter the ionosphere, however, waves of certain frequencies are refracted back toward the earth. The return wave may bounce off the earth back to the ionosphere, then back to Earth and so on, in a series of skips.*

Source: Excerpted from Stanley Leinwoll, *From Spark to Satellite*, copyright 1979 by Stanley Leinwoll. Reprinted with permission of Charles Scribner's Sons.

The ionosphere refracts medium-frequency waves, the kind used by AM radio, only after sundown. At night, therefore, AM stations can produce sky waves, reaching out to areas far beyond their daytime coverage contours. Unless protected from co-channel interference, however, AM stations do not necessarily get improved nighttime coverage from sky waves. Indeed, sky waves from distant co-channel stations may intrude, shrinking an AM station's nighttime coverage.

International radio services depend primarily on sky waves. They use the short-wave (high-frequency) band, whose waves tend to be refracted by the ionosphere both day and night. Unlike domestic AM stations, short-wave international services are allowed to switch frequency from time to time throughout the day. They need this latitude because the ionosphere rises and falls with temperature changes. Angles of refraction change, and different ionospheric layers become refractive under the sun's influence. By switching frequencies, short-wave stations can provide continuous sky-wave service to distant areas for listeners willing to retune their sets as the frequencies change.

Propagation and Frequency in Summary

Following are several generalizations about frequency and propagation:

• Ground waves are most useful for communication at the lower frequencies (LF, MF), sky waves in the middle frequencies (MF, HF), and direct waves in the higher frequencies (VHF and above).

• For transmissions through the atmosphere, the higher the frequency the more power it takes to generate a usable signal. Thus a station channel located at a lower point in the frequency spectrum is always preferable, other things being equal, to one at a higher point. At a given power and with equivalent surroundings, an AM channel at 540 kHz has better coverage than one at 1,600 kHz and a television station on channel 2 has better coverage than one on channel 12.

• The shorter the wave length, the more highly directional propagation is and the more easily waves are blocked by obstructions.

5.7 Antennas

Antennas serve both to launch signals at the transmitting end and to pick them up at the receiving end. Small, built-in receiving antennas are adequate to pick up strong signals, but the higher the frequency the more elusive the signal and the more essential it becomes to have an efficient outdoor antenna. Thus indoor rabbit ears may suffice to pick up VHF television signals in many locations, but UHF signals may require a more efficient antenna.

Length   Antennas vary greatly in size, because to work efficiently their length must be mathematically related to the length of the waves they radiate or receive. The usual length for the radiating elements of broadcast transmitter antennas is one-half or one-quarter of a wavelength. Waves at the lower end of the AM band (540 kHz) are about 1,823 feet long; at the upper end of the AM dial (1,600 kHz) they are only 593 feet. And the waves at channel 48 of UHF television are less than 2 feet long.

AM Antennas   AM stations usually employ quarter-wavelength antennas. For example, the aforementioned 1,823-foot waves of a 540-kHz signal could best be radiated by a tower about 456 feet in height. The entire steel tower acts as the radiating element. In choosing sites for AM antennas, engineers look for good soil conductivity, freedom from surrounding sources of electrical interference, and locations away from the flight paths of aircraft approaching and leaving airports. Because ground waves propagate through the earth's crust, AM antennas must be extremely well grounded, with many heavy copper cables buried in trenches radiating out from the base of the antenna tower. Exhibit 5.10 shows an array of AM antennas as construction nears completion.

FM and TV Antennas   For FM and TV antennas, engineers seek the highest possible locations, such as mountaintops and the roofs of tall buildings. Rather than themselves acting as radiating elements, direct-wave antenna towers simply support small radiating elements, in keeping with the shortness of VHF and UHF waves. Both transmitting and receiving elements are positioned horizontally with reference to the ground below, because the United States has established *horizontal polarization* as the standard for broadcast FM and television propagation.

Polarization refers to the fact that radio waves oscillate back and forth *across* their propagation paths. Antenna orientation determines the direction of the oscillations. FM reception in automobiles loses efficiency because whip antennas, usually oriented vertically, do not match the polarization of the FM broadcast signal.

Short-Wave Antennas   Antennas designed for long-distance short-wave (HF) broadcasting to foreign audiences are con-

Exhibit 5.10   Antennas

A. The entire steel tower of an AM radio antenna serves as its radiating element. Efficient propagation depends on soil conductivity, which in turn necessitates an exceedingly good ground system for the tower. The photo shows an array of several antennas (for obtaining directional propagation). Heavy copper ground cables are buried in the trenches that radiate out from the bases of the towers.

B. Because height is important to maximize direct-wave coverage, Boston's WQTV (TV) chose the 55-story Prudential Center's roof as its antenna site. A helicopter had to be used to lift the antenna assembly into place. The circularly polarized antenna's radiating elements are mounted in a spiral pattern around the supporting column.

C. HF antennas for external broadcasting differ from both television and domestic radio antennas. The radiating elements are hung between the steel towers. Each VOA transmitter site has many antennas to enable using several different frequencies. Antennas are also variously positioned to beam signals toward selected target areas.

Sources: A. Courtesy of Stainless, Inc., North Wales, PA. B. CETEC Antenna Corporation. C. Courtesy Voice of America, Washington, D.C.

B.

A.

C.

structed quite differently from domestic AM, FM, and television antennas. Large towers support extensive arrays of radiating elements in the form of cables. Though short compared to MF waves, HF waves used in broadcasting are nevertheless quite long, varying from 11 to 130 meters. Ideal radiating elements must therefore also be long, as suggested by Exhibit 5.10, which shows part of a Voice of America HF antenna. VOA antenna sites occupy hundreds of acres because the service uses many different frequencies, each requiring its own antenna; moreover, the antenna structures are complicated by the need to incorporate reflecting elements for directional propagation.

Directional Antennas   In most cases propagation of radio signals in all directions, upward as well as outward, would be wasteful, because receivers are not found in all directions. Moreover, it may be desirable to control propagation so as to prevent interference with other stations or to beam the signal toward inhabited areas. Radio waves can be directed in a desired direction, just as light from flashlights and headlamps can be focused by reflectors. Directional antennas reinforce and block radiations, helping to prevent interference with other stations, to match coverage contours with population-distribution patterns, and to avoid sending valuable energy into space.

Concentrating radiant energy increases its effective strength. This increase, called *antenna gain*, can be very great. For example, a microwave relay antenna concentrates its energy into a narrow beam, aimed at a single reception point. Such beams can achieve a gain of 100,000 times the effective radiated power of an omnidirectional antenna. Indeed, because microwave signals attenuate rapidly, they would be of little use without the high gain that enables them to punch through the at-

mosphere. Highly focused beams are also essential for the operation of both uplink and downlink satellite transmissions. Exhibit 5.11 shows how dish and horn antennas focus microwave radiations.

Television antennas direct their radiations at a low angle toward the surrounding terrain, redirecting rays that would otherwise shoot off into space. The resulting beefed-up signal strength is expressed in terms of ERP (effective radiated power), which is much higher than antenna input power.

AM directional antennas use the principles of phase interference and reinforcement (§5.2). Several towers simultaneously radiate the station's signal. Spaced so as to produce the desired phase relationships, the towers reinforce radiations in some directions and cancel them in others. As many as ten towers are used in AM directional antenna arrays.

5.8 Spectrum Conservation

A huge and ever-growing number of radio transmitters of many different kinds (over seven million in the United States alone, not counting military stations) must share the electromagnetic spectrum. The threat of interference among stations, the demands of new services for spectrum allocations, and the growth of established services make efficient spectrum management vital.

Frequency Allocation   Through the International Telecommunication Union, national communication authorities agree on worldwide division of the spectrum among the various telecommunication services. This process, called *allocation*, involves designating specific segments (bands) of the spectrum for the use of specific services, sometimes on a shared basis.

Exhibit 5.11 Microwave Antenna Design

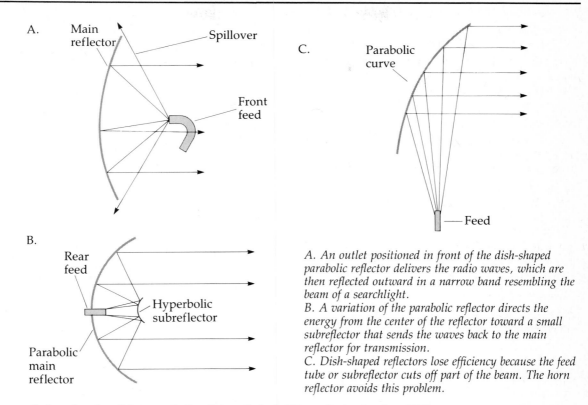

A. An outlet positioned in front of the dish-shaped parabolic reflector delivers the radio waves, which are then reflected outward in a narrow band resembling the beam of a searchlight.
B. A variation of the parabolic reflector directs the energy from the center of the reflector toward a small subreflector that sends the waves back to the main reflector for transmission.
C. Dish-shaped reflectors lose efficiency because the feed tube or subreflector cuts off part of the beam. The horn reflector avoids this problem.

Source: Graham Langley, *Telecommunications Primer,* 2nd ed. (Pitman Books, London, 1986).

Allocation strategies seek to match the needs of a service to a part of the spectrum that has the appropriate propagation characteristics. Thus terrestrial long-distance services need allocations in the HF band in order to capitalize on sky waves, whereas services that need to make only line-of-sight contacts can use VHF or higher frequencies. Some services require exclusive use of bands for around-the-clock communication, and others require only occasional use. Some, such as radiotelephony, can use narrow channels; others, such as television, must have very wide channels.

Demands on Spectrum It is important to realize that frequency allocations must be made for many services other than broadcasting. These include personal services (citizens' band radio, for example), private land-mobile services (ambulances, newsgathering units), marine services, aviation services, public safety services (police, fire), common carriers (radiotelephones, microwave relays), land transportation (taxicabs, railroads), and satellite services. Broadcasting, though it represents less than one percent of all transmitters authorized in the United States, is especially demanding. There are more than ten thousand radio and television stations in the United States, and they need continuous access to relatively large channels. Moreover, broadcasters use many auxiliary facilities, such as subsidiary repeaters (translators), studio-transmitter links, and remote pickup transmitters. On the average, three to four of these auxiliary transmitters support every primary broadcast station. Broadcasting uses over 80 percent of the radio spectrum below one gigahertz — that is, in the region of the spectrum most in demand for terrestrial communication.

Conservation Measures   The need to conserve radio frequencies encourages spectrum-saving technologies. One of the most common, *multiplexing*, allows the transmission of two or more independent signals within the same channel. One type of multiplexing, *frequency-division* multiplex, divides the channel into two or more subchannels, each with its own carrier and signal. Another type, *time-division* multiplex, rapidly samples each of several signals, sending them in short bursts through the same channel; this method enables filling in otherwise wasted time — the small pauses, for example, that occur between words and phrases in speech.

Stereophonic FM sound picks up "right" and "left" versions of the sound source, keeping them separate by transmission on different subcarriers within the standard FM channel. Some FM stations transmit still other materials on subcarriers, such as subscription background music or readings for the blind. Television channels necessarily have two subcarriers, one for video information and one

for audio, and can use additional subcarriers in both video and audio portions of the channel. An extra video subcarrier may be used for teletext, for example, and an extra audio subcarrier for stereophonic sound and for alternative-language soundtracks. Color information in the video signal is conveyed by a form of time-division multiplexing that relies on phase differences. Finally, subcarriers used by AM radio channels permit stereophonic sound and remote monitoring of transmitter meter readings.

Ordinary single-carrier receivers cannot detect subcarriers. Special sets or adapters are needed for stereo reception, for picking up subcarrier background music, for listening to readings for the blind, and for using other specialized subcarrier services.

Another, more sophisticated measure, known as *band compression*, economizes on frequencies by selective omission. For example, in any video transmission, pictures do not change completely from frame to frame; some picture elements remain the same over a series of frames. One method of band compression transmits information only about elements that *do* change, thus reducing the average amount of new information that has to be processed each second. In the future, such methods may enable broadcasters to transmit better-quality television pictures without expending more frequencies.

Guided Waves   Many problems of spectrum conservation can be sidestepped by propagating radio energy through guides or pipes, such as coaxial and fiber-optic cables (§7.4). This confinement within a *closed circuit* eliminates the need for antennas, the problems of co-channel interference, and the varying behaviors of direct, ground, and sky waves. But the nature of radio energy remains unchanged in enclosed systems. Cable television, a conspicuous example of a closed-circuit system, uses the same modulated carrier waves and channels as broadcasting. It has the advantage of avoiding the problems of interference and the vagaries of open propagation paths, but it sacrifices the unique asset of open-circuit communication — the ability to reach audiences without the aid of physical connections.

Summary

- It is important to understand the physical bases of electronic communication because so many of its attributes and problems arise from its physical nature. Moreover, new media are introducing drastic changes that can be appraised only if one understands their underlying technology.
- Radio communication (including sound, pictures, and other types of material) employs a form of electromagnetic energy that has some of the characteristics of sound and visible light.
- Like sound, radio energy originates from an oscillating source and can be described in terms of waves that have length, frequency, amplitude, phase, and velocity. These waves are subject to attenuation, refraction, reflection, absorption, interference, and sometimes ducting.
- It is essential, however, to realize that sound waves differ significantly from radio waves and light waves as to velocity, frequency, and mode of travel.
- Radio frequencies occupy part of the electromagnetic spectrum, the characteristics of which vary according to frequency range. International agreements have grouped waves within the radio-frequency range into bands, designated by frequency: low (LF), medium (MF), high (HF), very high (VHF), and so forth. Waves have characteristic behaviors specific to each band.
- The basic emission of a broadcasting station is known as its carrier wave. Modulation imposes information on a carrier wave, creating sidebands collectively occupying a group of frequencies called a channel. The more information a channel must deliver simultaneously, the wider it must be.
- Traditional broadcasting modulates either the amplitude (AM) or the frequency (FM) of a carrier wave, and as such is an analogue method of signal processing.
- Digital signal processing converts continuous, analogue signals into discontinuous pulses of energy. Digitally processed signals, though more resistant to distortion and highly manipulable, require wider frequency channels than analogue signals.
- Carrier waves may be propagated as direct waves (reaching only to the horizon), ground waves (reaching beyond the horizon), or sky waves (reaching long distances because of ionosphere refraction).
- Modulated carrier waves, upon being piped to an antenna, radiate as electromagnetic energy. An antenna's radiating element varies in length according to the length of the waves it radiates. Directional antennas control the spread of signals, increasing signal intensity in desired directions.
- Because demand for radio frequencies exceeds supply, spectrum management practices must efficiently match service needs to the characteristics of the various frequency bands. Multiplexing helps conserve frequencies by making possible the modulation of more than one carrier in a single channel. Band compression is another conservation measure.
- Broadcasting shares the spectrum with many other radio services. It consumes much spectrum space, requiring continuous access to relatively wide channels. Moreover, primary broadcasting stations depend on a variety of auxiliary transmitters, adding to the burden the medium imposes on the spectrum.

CHAPTER 6

Technology of
Traditional Broadcasting

This chapter briefly describes applied telecommunication technology as it relates to the traditional broadcasting services: AM radio, FM radio, and television. It assumes that you already understand the basic nature of radio waves and their propagation, as described in the preceding chapter.

6.1 Gaining Access to the Spectrum

Use of the spectrum for communication requires adherence to formal access rules. These rules seek to minimize interference among users and to ensure that the spectrum is used as efficiently as possible.

Spectrum Regulation   Most countries belong to the International Telecommunication Union (ITU), the body that coordinates radio-frequency spectrum use. The ITU recognizes three steps in parceling out frequencies. First it *allocates* groups of frequencies for the use of one or more specific communication services. Although allocations differ somewhat accord-

ing to the three ITU regions (roughly the Americas, Europe-Africa, and Asia), ITU allocations are essentially worldwide in scope.

Next the ITU breaks down allocated frequency bands into channels, smaller frequency groups suitable for the use of individual stations. These it *allots* to individual countries or groups of countries. Finally, countries *assign* their allotted channels to individual stations, usually by means of licensing procedures.

U.S. Channel Allotment   In the United States, the Federal Communications Commission compiles allotment tables designating specific FM and television channels for use in specific communities. A would-be licensee would look through the allotment tables to find out whether an unused channel exists in the proposed service area.* The FCC assigns AM channels on an ad hoc basis, however. A would-be licensee for a station on an unoccu-

---

*The allotment tables can be found in 47 CFR 73.202 and 73.606.

pied AM channel must make an engineering study in the proposed service area to find out whether the channel could be activated without causing interference to existing stations. So many AM stations are on the air nowadays that activation of new channels rarely occurs.

Channel Capacity   In deciding on channel size, planning authorities must consider the information capacity needed to fulfill the purpose of the service. They must balance the desire for optimum information capacity against the costs of communication, both in terms of physical apparatus and the number of frequencies used. Efficient spectrum management requires that channels have the minimum bandwidth needed to perform the essential functions of the service.

Radiotelephony requires a bandwidth of about 2,500 Hz. This width allows a level of fidelity sufficient for voice intelligibility but is far too limiting for sound broadcasting, which must attain not merely intelligibility but also the aesthetic aspects of speech and music and the realistic rendering of sounds. Ideally, this would mean using broadcast channels wide enough to encompass the full range of sound frequencies detectable by the keenest ear — a bandwidth of about 15,000 Hz, six times the telephone bandwidth.

Because so many factors enter into determining the appropriate channel width for each broadcast service, there are no worldwide standards. The United States uses 10-kHz AM channels, but many countries use only 9 kHz.* U.S. television channels have a 6-MHz bandwidth, but those of other countries range in width from 5 to 14 MHz.

6.2 Interference

Channel-assignment and station-licensing authorities must take into consideration the factor of mutual interference among stations. This factor severely limits the number of stations that can be licensed in any particular market. The primary troublemaker, *co-channel* interference, comes from other stations on the same channel. *Adjacent* channel interference also occurs, but only among stations with transmitters in the same locality.

Co-channel Interference   Two stations operating on the same channel must be sufficiently far apart geographically to prevent their coverage contours from overlapping. Signals too weak to provide reliable service may nevertheless be strong enough to interfere with a co-channel station; a station's interference zone therefore extends far beyond its service zone. For example, the usable service area of a channel 2 television station might have a radius of about 60 miles, but if it is located in the southern United States it must be at least 220 miles from any other channel 2 station.* The protection of AM stations from co-channel interference is complicated by their changing daytime and nighttime coverage areas, which is caused by sky-wave propagation at night. The FCC tries to control coverage by requiring most AM stations to use lower power at night.

Co-channel interference could be prevented simply by licensing only one station on each channel, but this would too drastically limit the number of available stations. One U.S. regulatory goal is to allow as many communities as possible to have their own local

---

*Increasing the number of AM channels by reducing channel separation to 9 kHz was considered at ITU regional conferences in 1980 and 1982, but the U.S. delegation reversed its position favoring the change, under pressure from U.S. broadcasters.

---

*For purposes of setting TV co-channel separations, the FCC divides the United States into three geographic zones and the channels into two groups, VHF and UHF. For details of these rules, see 47 CFR 73.609.

stations; the FCC therefore makes co-channel separation rules as liberal as possible.

Adjacent Channel Interference   In the vicinity of a transmitter, where power output is extremely high, sidebands spread beyond nominal channel limits, spilling over into adjacent channels above and below the station's assigned channel. Distance rapidly attenuates the signal, however, so that adjacent-channel stations need be separated only by about the radius of their service areas. For example, for VHF television, the FCC imposes an adjacent-channel separation distance of only 60 miles. The possibility of adjacent-channel interference does, however, limit the number of stations that can be assigned to any one locality.*

6.3   AM Stations

As the first broadcasting service to develop, AM radio came to be designated "standard broadcasting." Bear in mind, however, that AM refers specifically to a type of modulation used by many different services. The video component of television, for example, is amplitude-modulated.

Channel Location and Size   By international agreement, AM radio channels occupy a segment of the MF band. In the United States the AM band runs from 535 to 1,605 kHz, affording a total bandwidth of 1,070 kHz. AM channel spacing of 10 kHz allows for 107 channels (that is, 1,070 divided by 10). A station's carrier-wave frequency identifies its channel, expressed in kilohertz: 540, 550, 560, and so on up to 1,600 kHz.*

Modulation generates sidebands on each side of a carrier frequency. All the information in a channel is contained in either sideband, the other being a mirror image (§5.4). Therefore the nominal information capacity of an AM broadcast channel is only half its channel width, or 5 kHz, whereas sound covers a range of about 15 kHz. This limitation makes AM less than ideal as a medium for music; hence the development of FM as the preferred music medium. It is true that the 10-kHz limit refers to channel *spacing* rather than to maximum channel width. And AM stations may modulate beyond 5 kHz on both sides of their carrier frequencies if they can do so without causing interference. But for most listeners this wider channel does not result in improved sound, because inexpensive AM receivers usually have low-fidelity components, especially loudspeakers, incapable of handling an audible range beyond 5 kHz.

Channel Classes   The FCC classifies some of the AM stations as *local* (assigned to 6 channels), *regional* (assigned to 41 channels), and *clear* (assigned to 60 channels). By defining varying areas of coverage according to need, channel classification helps the FCC to license the maximum number of stations. Local-channel stations serve small communities or parts of large metropolitan regions; regional-channel stations serve metropolitan areas or rural regions; and clear-channel stations serve both large metropolitan areas and, at night, distant rural listeners. These latter channels have been "cleared" of interfering co-channel nighttime signals to enable sky-wave reception in remote areas.

---

*Though numbered consecutively, television channels 6 and 7 can operate in the same locality. They are not truly adjacent channels, because the FM radio band and other services intervene between them. A smaller band of frequencies intervenes between channels 4 and 5 allowing them, too, to operate in the same area. Exhibit 6.4 shows these discontinuities in the VHF television band.

---

*The ITU extended the upper limit of the AM band to 1,705 kHz in 1979, but implementation awaited a further conference.

Station Classification   Again in the interest of licensing the maximum possible number of outlets, the FCC divides AM stations into classes, designated I, II, III, and IV. Class I stations (about 1 percent of the total) have "dominant" status on clear channels.* Secondary stations on clear channels, designated as Class II (about a third of the total), must avoid interfering with the Class I stations whose frequencies they share. Class II stations avoid interference mainly by means of their wide geographic separation from co-channel Class I stations, but often they must also restrict their output by using directional antennas (sometimes with different patterns for night and day) and by either reducing power or closing down entirely at night.

Class III stations (about 46 percent of the AM total) occupy regional channels, and Class IV occupy local channels. Although only 6 of the 107 AM channels are local, the Class IV stations assigned to them amount to about 22 percent of the AM stations on the air. They have such low power (and hence such short range) that many can use the same channel without interfering with one another.

Power   Transmitter power plays an important role in AM radio. High power not only improves the efficiency of both ground-wave and sky-wave propagation, but also overcomes static. Furthermore, station owners find the claim of high power psychologically useful in persuading advertisers that their stations have strong audience impact.

Power authorizations for domestic U.S. AM broadcasting run from 250 watts for the smaller Class IV stations to a maximum of 50,000 watts (50 kW) for Class I and Class II stations. The 50-kW ceiling, which is low relative to the maximum in some other countries, permits licensing of more stations and prevents those with high power from gaining too much of a competitive edge on those with less power.

Carrier Current   Low-power AM signals fed into the steam pipes or power lines of a building radiate for a short distance into the surrounding spaces. Such systems, used by *carrier-current* stations, combine elements of both wire and wireless propagation. Familiar carrier-current applications include stations that serve dormitories and other buildings on college campuses. As long as the radiations do not interfere with licensed spectrum users, carrier-current stations need not obtain broadcast licenses and, unlike educational FM stations, may sell advertising.

A licensed carrier-current service, Travelers Information Service (TIS), uses radiations from wires strung or buried alongside highways to supply traffic information to motorists approaching airports and similar congested areas. Road signs instruct motorists to tune to the relevant AM channel.

6.4 FM Stations

Channels   In the United States, frequency-modulation broadcasting occupies a block running from 88 to 108 MHz in the VHF band. The FCC has designated 200 kHz (0.2 MHz) as FM channel width, allowing for 100 channels. These channels are numbered 201 to 300, but licensees prefer to identify their stations by mid-channel frequency rather than by channel number, using 88.1 for channel 201 and so on.

---

*Originally, the FCC gave dominant stations on clear channels nationwide protection from interference, but the proliferation of AM stations, the demand for still more licenses, and the spirit of deregulation have led to erosion of the clear-channel principle. Since 1980, Class I stations on clear channels have been subject to sharing their frequencies with other primary stations in distant parts of the country. For lists of channels by class and the classification of stations on each channel, see *Broadcasting/Cablecasting Yearbook*.

The FCC has reserved the first twenty FM channels (88–92 MHz) for noncommercial, educational use.

Coverage

Since stations using the VHF band radiate direct waves, FM reaches only to the horizon. Because of this limitation, FM evades the nighttime sky-wave problem that complicates AM station licensing. An FM station has a stable coverage pattern night and day, its shape and size depending on the station's power, the height of its transmitting antenna above the surrounding terrain, and the presence or absence of obtrusive terrain features or buildings that block wave paths. The fact that FM signals blank out interference from other stations much more effectively than do AM signals also contributes to coverage stability. An FM signal needs to be only twice as strong as a competing signal to override it, whereas an AM signal needs to be twenty times as strong.

Station Classes

Because of FM's coverage stability and uniformity, the FCC needs no elaborate channel and station classification systems such as it uses for AM. The commission simply divides FM stations into three groups according to coverage area: Classes A, B, and C, defined in terms of both power and antenna height. Class A station power-height combinations enable coverage of a radius of about 15 miles, Class B about 30 miles, and Class C about 60 miles.* The maximum power-height combination permits 100,000 watts of power (twice the maximum AM station power) and 2,000-foot antenna height.

Signal Quality

Good FM receivers with suitable loudspeakers can reproduce sound frequencies as high as 15,000 Hz. For the discriminating listener, this frequency range gives FM a major advantage over AM radio, since, as previously noted, high frequencies are important to sound quality because of overtones (§5.4). Moreover, in areas subject to heavy atmospheric interference (mainly in the south), FM's freedom from static is highly prized.

FM radio also scores higher than AM in terms of *dynamic range*, which is the difference between the weakest and the strongest reproducible sounds. Sound-reproducing systems do not easily match the human ear's capacity to accept extremes of loudness and softness. Very soft sounds tend to get lost in the electron noise of the apparatus, and very loud sounds overload the system, causing distortion. AM broadcasting even sacrifices some of its already limited dynamic range by artificially compressing the signal in order to maximize average power output.

Multiplexed Services

FM's generous 200-kHz channel width, twenty times that of AM radio, enables it to furnish stereophonic sound.* Parallel sets of equipment, corresponding to a listener's left and right ears, pick up and amplify two versions of the sound source. One component modulates the regular FM carrier wave, the other a subcarrier within the FM channel. A stereophonic receiver, also equipped with parallel sound channels, separates the signals for delivery to left and right speakers.

---

*A fourth class, D, consists of very low power (10 watt) FM educational stations, but since 1980 the FCC has sought to displace them if other, full-powered candidates for their noncommercial channels exist. The 10-watt stations have several options for moving to other channels if they do not interfere with full-power stations. See 47 CFR 73.512 for details.

---

*AM radio has also achieved stereophonic sound, but its narrow channel makes the technology more difficult. The FCC declined to choose among several competing methods when it authorized AM stereophony in 1982. In the absence of a standardization method, most stations' owners were reluctant to convert (§4.5).

FM's wide channel also allows for multiplexing *Subsidiary Communications Authorization* (SCA) services. Examples of SCA services include background music for stores and offices, readings for the blind, paging services, and slow-scan-video still pictures. These added signals cannot be detected by ordinary home receivers, requiring special receivers or adapters for SCA subscribers.

6.5 Short-Wave Stations

Propagation   International radio services designed to reach long distances use AM broadcasting on short (high-frequency) waves. The ITU has designated parts of the HF band for international short-wave services. With the ionosphere's help, high-frequency sky waves can be propagated over great distances both day and night. This does present some technical challenge, however, since the ionospheric layers continually change their electrical properties under the impact of the sun's rays and also lose altitude as they cool off at night. For these reasons, a frequency that works well propagated at a given angle over a given wave path at ten in the morning might be entirely useless by four in the afternoon. Seasonal changes also occur, such that frequencies usable in the spring may no longer work in the summer or fall. Propagation theory predicts ionospheric shifts, enabling short-wave engineers to schedule frequency changes throughout the day and from season to season.

Because of the need to switch frequencies, international stations, unlike domestic AM stations, may feed their outputs to several different antennas, each designed to radiate a different frequency. Short-wave antennas are directional, enabling users to beam signals toward specific target areas. The antennas themselves consist of suspended cables rather than steel towers, as shown in the Voice of America antenna depicted earlier (Exhibit 5.10).

U.S. Short-Wave Stations   The United States uses short-wave stations for international but not for domestic services, though many foreign countries do have domestic HF transmitters.* Only a few U.S. privately operated international short-wave stations exist, mostly evangelistic religious outlets operated noncommercially. Elsewhere in the world a number of international commercial stations use short waves, however, and a trend toward such stations may be emerging in the United States. Recently WRNO, an international short-wave commercial station located in New Orleans, began targeting commercial messages to Canada and Europe. It can, of course, also be heard by listeners with short-wave receivers in the United States.

The U.S. government's main official external service, the Voice of America, operates more than thirty short-wave transmitters at several domestic sites.† They send programs overseas either for direct reception by foreign listeners or for intermediate reception by strategically located overseas relay stations that rebroadcast the programs on either short-wave or medium-wave stations to nearby audiences.

6.6 Pictures in Motion

Before turning to television, it is helpful to consider first how the simpler technology of cinematography works.

---

*The ITU allocates certain HF bands for domestic broadcasting in the tropics, where standard AM radio is largely ineffective because of atmospheric noise during the rainy season.
†An exception to the general rule designating MW stations exclusively for domestic services is Radio Martí, the special U.S. government international station aimed at Cuba, which uses a MW VOA station at Marathon in the Florida keys (§1.10).

Resolution   Most photographic systems represent scenes by breaking reality down into many tiny *pixels* (picture elements). Basically, the size and distribution of pixels govern picture *resolution*, or *definition*. These terms refer to a photographic system's fineness of detail, specifically how well it distinguishes between two small, closely adjacent objects. Resolution in photography is analogous to information capacity in radio communication. High-resolution pictures demand a broadband channel, one able to handle a great many pixels each second.

The information capacity of a cinematic system not only depends on degree of resolution but also on the picture area available for each frame in the film strip, and on the rate (stated in frames per second) at which the film moves through the camera. Three size standards have emerged, identified by film width: 35 millimeter, 16 millimeter, and 8 millimeter. Along with some larger formats for widescreen projection, 35mm film is the professional theatrical standard. The intermediate size, 16mm film, originally represented the amateur standard, but television, with its great appetite for film, stimulated the evolution of less expensive 16mm film into a professional medium. Thus 8mm, along with an improved small format, Super 8, became the amateur, home-movie standard.

In all cinematic formats, some film area must be reserved for sprocket holes, between-frame spaces, and soundtrack. Some of a television channel's frequencies must similarly be reserved for sound and auxiliary information.

Frame Frequency Standards   In cinematography, what appears to be motion actually consists of still pictures (frames) projected in rapid succession. Each frame freezes the action at a slightly later moment than the preceding frame. A useful tendency of the human eye to retain the image of an object for a brief moment after the object has disappeared (called *persistence of vision*) blends the successive frames together. Thus the motion depicted by motion pictures is actually a visual illusion.

A satisfactory illusion of natural motion occurs if a projector displays at least 16 frames per second (fps). For that reason, the motion-picture industry adopted 16 fps as the standard for silent films. With the development of sound-on-film, the soundtrack was positioned along the edge of the film. But at 16 fps, the film passed too slowly over the projector's sound-pickup head to allow for adequate sound quality; thus the industry adopted the higher frame frequency of 24 fps for motion pictures with sound. This difference between standards for silent and sound films accounts for the comic jerkiness of silent films shown on modern projectors, which increase the original projection rate by 50 percent, speeding up the action to an unnatural degree.

Prevention of Flicker   Although 24 fps gives the illusion of continuous action, at that projection rate the eye can still detect that light falls on the screen intermittently. After each frame flashes on the screen, a moment of darkness ensues while the machine pulls the next frame into position for projection. The eye reacts more sensitively to these gross changes from complete illumination to complete blackout than to the smaller changes in positions of objects within frames. A sensation of *flicker* results. In fact, early movies were called *flicks* because their low frame frequency made them flicker conspicuously.

Increasing the frame frequency can overcome the flicker sensation, but because the 24-fps rate gives all the visual and sound information required, such an increase would be wasteful. Therefore, increased expenditure of film is avoided by *projecting each frame twice*. When the projector pulls a frame into place, it flashes the picture on the screen, blacks out the screen, then flashes the same frame again before blacking out to pull the next frame into position. It projects only 24 separate pictures while illuminating the screen 48 times per second, thereby suppressing the flicker sensation. Television uses a similar trick, illuminating the screen twice as many times as the number of complete pictures shown each second.

6.7 Electronic Pictures

The foregoing analysis of cinema suggests that an electronic analogue of film must be able to do four things: (1) break pictures down into electronic pixels; (2) generate enough frames per second to create the illusion of motion; (3) suppress the sensation of flicker without increasing information load; and (4) provide a channel wide enough to transmit all this information, including simultaneous sound and auxiliary signals, in real time (that is, without perceptible delay).

Camera Picture Tube   The heart of the television system, the camera's picture, or pickup, tube breaks down each image into thousands of pixels. The pixels start as bits of light energy distributed throughout the image; the camera picture tube detects them in systematic order, converting them into a stream of electrical impulses (voltages). A conventional camera lens system focuses on the face of the pickup tube the live or filmed scene to be televised. Thereafter, electrons take over. Without the speed and exquisite precision of electrons, television with satisfactory definition would be impossible.

Picture tubes come in various shapes and sizes, as shown in Exhibit 6.1. In principle they work as follows: Visual information in the form of light patterns passes through the

Exhibit 6.1   TV Pickup Tubes

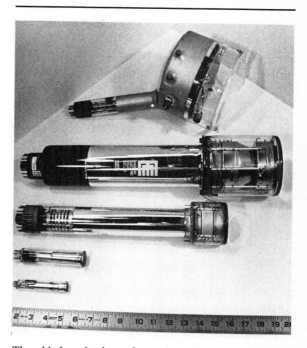

The odd-shaped tube at the top is an iconoscope, *the type first used in commercial broadcasting. It was replaced by the* image orthicons *with 3-inch and 4.5-inch diameter faces. These in turn have been replaced by smaller tubes, such as* vidicons *and* plumbicons, *varying from 1¼-inch to ⅔-inch diameters.*

Source: Photo by Frank Sauerwald, Temple University.

tube's glass face, falling upon a *target plate* within the tube. The target plate, representing a single picture or frame, is covered with many thousand specks of photoconductive material. Each speck converts the light energy that falls upon it into an electrical charge of corresponding intensity. Each of the thousands of pixels on the target plate takes on an electrical charge proportionate to the amount of light it has stored. Next, each of these charges momentarily stored on the target plate is released, one at a time.

Electrons come into play as the releasing agent. At the opposite end of the tube an *electron gun* shoots a stream of electrons toward the back of the target plate. As the electrons fly down the length of the tube they pass through magnetic fields generated by external *deflection coils* surrounding the body of the tube. Magnetic forces attract and repel the electron stream, making it move systematically in a *scanning* (reading) motion, left to right, line by line, top to bottom. The electron beam "reads" the information on the target plate.

As the scanning electron beam strikes a pixel stored on the target plate, it releases the light energy of that pixel in the form of an electrical voltage. The string of voltages, representing the energy in a sequence of pixels, is the picture tube's output. Picture output thus consists of an amplitude-modulated analogue electrical waveform, as shown in Exhibit 6.2.

The pickup tube has no moving parts. Its electron gun remains fixed. The scanning movements of the electron stream are controlled by special circuits that send appropriate electrical messages to the deflection coils. A film camera must have a revolving shutter to interrupt the scene each time it draws a new film frame into place for exposure. A television camera, however, needs no shutter, for the video picture never exists as a complete frame, only as a sequence of pixels. Television relies on persistence of vision to blend the pixel sequence into a seemingly unbroken image in the mind's eye.

Scanning Standards   Recall that motion pictures have two frequency standards, 24 fps for continuity of motion, and 48 fps for continuity of illumination (to eliminate flicker). Television might have been able to avoid some problems in reproducing motion picture film had it adopted the same standards. Instead, the corresponding frequencies in television

are 30 (frame frequency) and 60 (field frequency).

U.S. engineers chose these numbers to take advantage of a precise timing standard already available throughout the country, the 60-Hz alternating electrical current in homes. For television pickup of motion picture films, the mismatch between film and television field-frequency standards is solved as follows: special television film projectors display every fourth frame an extra time, thus adding 12 projections per second to film's normal 48 fields to bring the projection rate up to television's 60-field standard.* One reason for international differences in television technical standards is that in much of the world 50-Hz AC house current is the standard rather than 60. Accordingly, television frame and field frequencies in such areas have been standardized at 25 and 50.

Inasmuch as the television camera does not "take" a complete picture, it cannot use the antiflicker strategy developed for film, that of repeating each entire frame twice. Instead, television splits each frame into two parts by scanning first the odd-numbered lines, then the even-numbered lines. Each scanning sequence, called a *field*, illuminates the receiver screen from top to bottom, but each field picks up only half the pixels in the frame. This method, known as *offset* or *interlace* scanning, causes the electron beam to scan line 1, line 3, line 5, and so on to the bottom of the field, then fly back to the top of the field to fill in line 2, line 4, line 6, and so on.

---

*Still other frequencies are sometimes used: 16mm film cameras adapted to shoot at 30 fps yield pictures almost equal in quality to 35mm film. Variable-speed television film-projection cameras are available to handle such nonstandard film. Standards experts have discussed adopting the 30–60 standard for film generally. RCA has developed a solid-state television camera using a charged coupled device (CCD) with shutter speed up to 1/500th of a second, useful for slow-motion sports coverage.

Exhibit 6.2   TV Pickup Tube Output

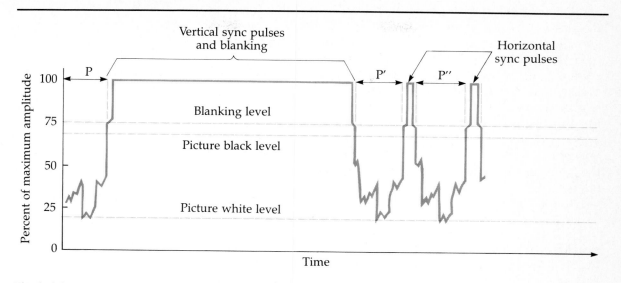

The dark line represents in simplified form the voltage output (amplitudes) generated by a pickup tube as it delivers the last line of a field (P), the vertical blanking information, and the first two lines of the next field (P' and P''). Note that, as a result of reverse modulation, the lowest amplitude represents white in the picture and the highest amplitude black. This means that electrical interference will show up as stray black images in a picture. Reverse modulation enables hiding blanking and other auxiliary information by transmitting it at a higher amplitude level than the blackest part of the picture, hence the term "blacker than black" for these invisible signals.

Source: Based on FCC specifications in 47 CFR 73.699.

6.8   The TV Signal

You can see from the foregoing description that television reconstructs an electronic picture consisting of pixels arranged in lines, fields consisting of lines, and frames consisting of fields. All this requires the utmost precision in timing, made possible only by electronic means.

Picture Definition   The number of lines per frame makes a convenient index of a system's resolving, or definition, capacity. The U.S. standard of 525 lines per frame determines the *vertical resolution* of the resulting pictures. The 525-per-second line-frequency standard is only nominal, however, because part of the channel must be devoted to the accompanying sound and auxiliary information. In practice, only about 340 lines per frame effectively convey black-and-white picture information.*

---

*The color component consists of even fewer lines, about 280. By way of comparison, a theatrical-quality 35mm film frame has the equivalent of 1,000 lines. However, high-definition television, discussed in §6.11, will exceed the film standard.

Auxiliary Signals   One source of line loss is the time the electron beam takes to fly back diagonally from the end of one line to the beginning of the next, and from the bottom of a field back to the top. During these breaks in scanning, called *blanking* or *retrace* intervals, special auxiliary signals cut off picture pickup so that the electron beam's retrace paths will not destroy the orderly scanning pattern. During the blanking intervals no picture information can be transmitted, though the longer of the two types of breaks, the vertical blanking interval (VBI), is used to multiplex teletext and other additional information (discussed in §6.11).

Other auxiliary signals, the *sync pulses*, synchronize camera scanning with scanning by the television receiver. This is the equivalent of "registration" in cinema, the exact positioning of film in the camera and projector, accomplished by means of sprockets engaged in holes along the edge of the film. Television sync pulses, originated by a special timing device in the studio (see Exhibit 6.5), ensure that each pixel and each line will appear on the receiver screen in the same location they had in the pickup tube. Even a slight loss of synchronization renders received pictures unusable. For this reason, lightweight portable television equipment could not be used outside the studio until a remote means of maintaining synchronization could be devised — the time-base corrector (§6.11).

Sound   In U.S. television, the sound carrier, located in the upper part of the television channel (Exhibit 6.3), is frequency modulated; the video carrier is amplitude modulated.* No synchronizing signals are needed to keep sound and picture in step, inasmuch as both are sent in real time, that is, simultaneously and without perceptible delay.

Color   A key goal in devising a color system for television was *compatibility*, making sure that people who owned monochrome receivers would continue to receive pictures after transmitters converted to color. At the same time, the system had to be capable of adding color information without requiring enlargement of the monochrome channel. A committee of major U.S. manufacturers met these criteria with the system known as NTSC (National Television System Committee) color.* Multiplexing enabled adding color without enlarging the television channel, fulfilling the compatibility criterion. Exhibit 6.3 shows the location of the color subcarrier.

The color aspect of the television signal relies on the mixture of three primary-color signals to produce all other colors. Filters in the television camera separate the primary-color information (red, blue, and green) before the image reaches the camera tube. In addition to *hue* (what we perceive as color), all colors have a brightness attribute, *luminance*. The sum of the luminance components of all three primary colors supplies the fine detail of color television pictures. Monochrome receivers interpret color pictures in terms of the luminance signal alone. In the highest quality studio cameras, separate tubes pick up luminance and each primary color; smaller portable color cameras use fewer tubes.

A special auxiliary signal called the *color burst* synchronizes the processing of the pri-

---

*Amplitude modulation of the video signal enables sending auxiliary signals at the "blacker-than-black" level of modulation — that is, at an artificially enhanced voltage, above the amplitude that yields "picture black." Exhibit 6.3 shows how this works. Some national systems use AM for television sound, but most chose FM for its quality advantages.

*Nearly three-quarters of foreign television services use the rival color systems PAL (West German) and SECAM (French). PAL is the most widely used. However, for future direct-broadcast satellite services, broadcasters are considering a common, digitized color system, known as MAC (multiple analogue component), developed by British IBA engineers.

Exhibit 6.3   TV Channel Architecture

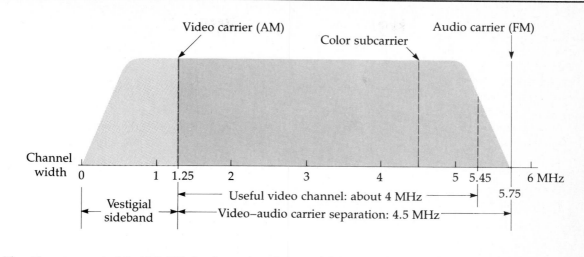

The video component of the U.S. TV signal occupies only part of the 6 MHz channel. Other parts of the channel must be devoted to the vestigial lower sideband and the audio channel. In addition, a small buffer zone above the frequencies occupied by the audio signal separates the upper end of the channel from the next higher contiguous channel.

Source: Adapted from FCC specifications in 47 CFR 73.699.

mary colors, which are kept apart by means of phase differentiation. Though some overlap occurs between the modulated monochrome (luminance) and color carriers, *interleaving* minimizes the conflict. Uneven distribution of frequencies carrying the luminance signal makes such interleaving possible. If the teeth of a comb stand for the frequencies occupied by the monochrome information, the spaces between the teeth would represent the color-information frequencies.

6.9 The TV Channel

Television's heavy information load requires a broadband channel 6 MHz in width, which is 600 times the width of an AM radio broadcast channel. Indeed, all the AM and FM broadcast channels together occupy less spectrum space than only four television channels.

Channel Architecture   As Exhibit 6.3 shows, NTSC television channel architecture allots 4 MHz of each 6 MHz channel to picture information (including auxiliary signals). The vestigial lower sideband, the audio channel, and guard bands (buffer zones to prevent side-by-side signals from interfering with each other) occupy the remaining 2 MHz.

Picture Resolution   The 4-MHz television channel capacity allows for only mediocre picture resolution in comparison with the standards of theatrical motion pictures and good-quality still photography. The average home television receiver displays about 150,000 pixels per frame. A projected 35mm

Exhibit 6.4   Summary of Broadcast Channel Specifications

Broadcast service	Channel width	Number of channels	Band	Channel identification numbers	Allocated frequencies
AM (standard) radio	10 kHz	107	MF	[b]	535–1605 kHz[a]
FM radio	200 kHz	100	VHF	201–300	88–108 MHz
TV	6 MHz	3 } 12 2 7) 56[d]	VHF UHF	[c]2–4 5–6 7–13 14–69	54–72 MHz 76–88 MHz 174–216 MHz 470–806 MHz

This table brings together scattered information in the text to enable comparing the main main channel specifications of the three broadcast services, AM radio, FM radio, and television.
[a]*International plans exist for expanding the AM band upward to 1705 kHz.*
[b]*AM channels are identified by their midpoint frequencies at 10-kHz intervals throughout the band, that is, 540, 550, 560, and so forth up to 1600. Receiver dials often omit the last zero, numbering channels 54, 55, and so on.*
[c]*Originally a television channel 1 existed, located at 44–50 MHz. Because television on that channel interfered with other services, the FCC in 1948 reallocated the 44–50 MHz frequencies to nonbroadcast services; however, it retained the old numbering system, making channel 2 the lowest television channel in the spectrum.*
[d]*Not all the 56 UHF channels are available in all areas: channel 37 is reserved for radio astronomy, and in some areas channels 14–20 are used by land mobile services.*

film displays about a million per frame, and an 8- x 10-inch photoengraving about 2 million. Magnifying the television picture by projection makes it possible to sit farther from the screen but adds no detail — in fact, some of the detail is lost in the process of projection.

Current television resolution standards represent compromises based on research identifying the lowest quality that most viewers can tolerate. Any better quality would use up too much of the radio frequency spectrum. But not every nation has made the same compromise. Great Britain pioneered in 1936 with a 405-line television system, but later found its quality not up to emerging world standards. Eventually Britain replaced its first system with a 625-line system. Since the frame fre-

quency is only 25 fps (because of European 50-Hz AC house current), the British system's 625 lines convey about the same net amount of information per second (15,625 lines) as the United States' 525-line system (15,750 lines).

The channel capacity specified for home television reflects the need to deliver sufficiently detailed moving pictures in real time. An exceedingly narrow channel can be used if viewers are willing to wait for the slow building up of delayed still pictures one at a time, as in the case of slow-scan pictures multiplexed on FM channel subcarriers (§6.4).

Location in Spectrum   When the time came to allocate frequencies for television, much of the most suitable spectrum region, the VHF band, had already been allocated to other services. Room remained for only twelve VHF channels, and even they had to be broken up into three different blocks of frequencies (Exhibit 6.4). When the twelve channels proved inadequate to satisfy the demand for stations, the ITU allocated additional channels in the UHF band.

6.10 TV Transmission and Reception

Studio   As Exhibit 6.5 indicates, a major component in the television studio control room is the *sync generator*, a device to ensure synchronization of pickup and receiver tubes. This component generates the timing signals for driving the camera's deflection coils and inserting the blanking signals. The sync generator similarly controls timing of such additional video sources as remote cameras, tape recorders, videodisc recorders, computer memories, film projectors, and network feeds. An independent set of equipment handles the sound component of the program.

Transmission   The studio section's video and audio signals are fed independently to the station's transmitter section; there the two signals modulate separate audio and video transmitters. Because of its greater information load, the video component needs up to twenty times as much power as the audio. A station's wattage is usually stated in terms of the effective radiated power (ERP) of its video signal.

The two transmitters feed their signals to a *diplexer*, which combines them into a composite output to the antenna. As related in §5.7, television radiating elements atop the antenna tower are relatively small, in keeping with the shortness of VHF and UHF waves. They propagate a directional signal, aimed at

the terrain between the antenna and the horizon.

UHF waves behave somewhat differently from VHF waves. Being shorter, they are more directional and more easily blocked by objects in their path. Moreover, they attenuate more rapidly than VHF waves. For these reasons, the FCC allows UHF stations to use very high power (up to 5 million watts) to help compensate for their coverage limitations.*

Reception   Television coverage depends on the efficiency and height of the receiving antenna, as well as on terrain features, transmitter frequency, and power. Ordinarily, within about 20 miles of a powerful transmitter, indoor antennas are sufficient for reception. At about 30 miles outdoor antennas become essential. For commercial and regulatory purposes, television station coverage is described in terms of Grade A and Grade B contours. Grade A contours enclose areas where there is satisfactory reception 90 percent of the time; Grade B, areas where satisfactory reception exists 50 percent of the time.†

A transmitting antenna can be sized ideally for its channel, but receiving antennas must be designed to pick up either all channels or all channels in one of the bands, VHF or UHF. Because they are highly directional, receiving antennas must be oriented toward the transmitters. In locations where transmitters are located at widely different points of the compass, a rotatable outdoor antenna may be necessary.

Like transmitters, receivers process the video and audio parts of the signal separately.

---

*As in the case of FM, the FCC, in setting television power limits, uses a formula that takes antenna height into consideration. For details, see Fig. 3, 47 CFR 73.699).

†These contours have no meaning for cable television subscribers, who receive their local television stations, as well as cable-specific programming, via cable and so no longer depend on their own antennas. Antennas do become desirable, however, during cable system outages.

Exhibit 6.5   TV System Components and Signals

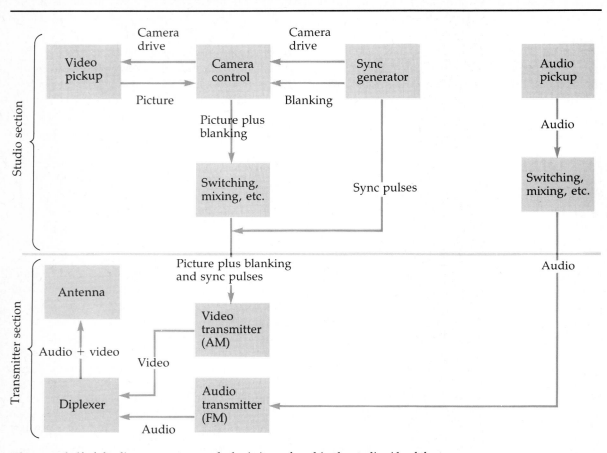

The upper half of the diagram represents the basic items found in the studio side of the operation, the lower half the ones found in the transmission side. Each block stands for a function that in practice may involve many different pieces of equipment. Note that the audio portion of the signal is handled separately until the output of its transmitter is combined with the video transmitter output in the diplexer for delivery to the antenna as a composite signal.

Source: Harold E. Ennes, *Principles and Practices of Telecasting Operations*, Howard W. Sams, Indianapolis, 1953.

In conventional receivers, the video information goes to a type of cathode ray tube (CRT) called a kinescope. A phosphorescent layer coating its inside face glows when bombarded with electrons. Within the neck of the kinescope, an electron gun, a larger analogue of the one in the pickup tube, shoots electrons toward the inside face of the tube. Guided by external deflection coils, the electron beam delivers pixels of varying intensity, laying them down line by line, field by field, and frame by frame. The synchronizing signals originated by the sync generator in the studio activate the deflection coils, keeping the receiver's scanning sequence in step with scanning by the picture source.

Phosphors that glow in the three primary colors coat the insides of color kinescopes and are arranged either in narrow parallel stripes or triads of dots. Receiver circuits decode the video signal into components representing the energy levels of the three primary colors, delivering each one to the tube face separately by means of one or more electron guns (Exhibit 6.6). Only the primary colors appear on the kinescope. The eye blends the mix of primaries represented by varying energy levels in the color tube outputs, giving the illusion of many hues. If you look at part of a color picture on the face of a receiver with a small magnifying glass, however, you will see only the three primary colors.

In principle, the kinescope displays only one pixel at a time, but because it takes a while for the activated phosphor to lose its glow, several pixels remain visible at any given instant. Considering that the eye blends the momentary primary-color pixels, lines, fields, and frames into the illusion of realistic moving pictures, comfortably viewable without distracting flicker, the achievement of television is truly remarkable.

6.11 Technical Innovations

Improvements in this remarkable performance nevertheless continue to come thick and fast. Following are a few examples of technical innovation.

Miniaturization   Starting in the 1950s, the changeover in electronics from dependence on vacuum tubes to the use of solid-state devices has profoundly affected television technology, as it has all media. Vacuum tubes (so called

Exhibit 6.6   Color Kinescope Tube Design

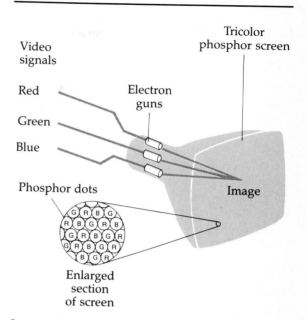

Some receiver tubes use three electronic guns and tricolor phosphor dots. Varying amplitudes in the modulated currents fed to each of the electron guns cause the dots to glow with varying intensities; though only the red, green, and blue primary colors appear on the kinescope face, the eye blends them together to make all the various hues.

Source: Paul Davidovits, *Communication* (Holt, Rinehart & Winston, New York, 1972), p. 114.

because they provide an enclosed space for the manipulation of electrons in a near vacuum) are bulky, power-hungry, hot, and easily damaged. A rack of equipment containing scores of tubes takes up a great deal of space and has to be artificially cooled.

Solid-state devices eliminated these problems in most applications, though some vacuum tubes persist, notably the CRT, of which the television kinescope (picture) tube is the best-known example. The solid-state revolution started with transistors, which made possible the manipulation of electrons in a small piece of solid material instead of within the relatively large vacuum chamber of an electron tube.

The next generation of solid-state devices, silicon chips, has become familiar from use in microcomputers. The latest version of this technology is the Very Large Scale Integrated Circuit (VLSIC), which enables the etching of complex circuits, incorporating hundreds of transistors and other components, on a single chip an eighth of an inch in diameter. By 1985, 256,000-bit chips had evolved, with million-bit chips on the horizon. Integrated-circuit technology marries ideally with digital signal processing (§5.5), which is rapidly displacing analogue processing methods. Miniaturization, microprocessing, and digital techniques have been applied extensively to the field of sound and video recording, which is discussed in the next chapter.

Remote Equipment

ENG (electronic news gathering) and EFP (electronic field production) are examples of benefits made possible by miniaturization. To cover news events held outdoors or to produce on-location program segments and commercials, television crews at one time had to use cumbersome *remote vehicles* (Exhibit 6.7). Miniaturization has resulted in lightweight, portable equipment easily carried and operated by one or two persons. The key to this development was the *time-base corrector*. This microcomputer device supplies synchronizing information that enables remotely-operated portable equipment to eliminate time-base errors, which occurred whenever recording equipment was not controlled by the studio sync generator. Such errors showed up as jittery pictures, skewing, and color breakup.

Introduction of news gathering by satellite (NGS) mobile earth stations in the mid-1980s made possible relay of television news pictures (or complete reports) from any location away from a studio. NGS-equipped stations (Exhibit 6.7) affiliate with a satellite firm to obtain access to Ku-band (§7.5) satellite transponder time. One such company, Conus Communications, originated NGS operations with the initial satellite news-exchange cooperative.

Receiver Improvements

Solid state devices have made broadcast receivers lighter, cooler, less demanding of power, and less expensive to operate than they were in the vacuum tube era. The next major breakthrough will be new methods of displaying the picture, which will involve discarding the bulky, power-hungry kinescope tube in favor of a flat, solid-state picture device that affords a much larger display. This technology has already been applied to tiny portable receivers. For larger-size receivers for the home, however, current resolution standards will have to be increased.

Progress in this direction has been made by high-definition television (HDTV), several versions of which have been proposed. Japan pioneered the best-known of these, an 1,125-line system with a wider screen, 5 units wide by 3 units high, as compared to the present 3×4 aspect ratio. This system surpasses the quality of theatrical motion pictures and therefore lends itself to projected display. For 525-line television, the ideal viewing distance is six times the picture height; closer viewing causes eyestrain, because the viewer strives to see detail not present in the picture. HDTV enables comfortable viewing at a distance of only three times the picture height; it can also be viewed at a much wider angle from the screen plane than can ordinary television.

However, HDTV would probably outmode all present receivers and transmitters and require two or more times the present 6-MHz channel width. Since additional spectrum space in the present terrestrial television

Exhibit 6.7   ENG and NGS Units

A. The unwieldy remote vehicle in the background contrasts with the compact, lightweight ENG (electronic news-gathering) van in the foreground. The machine-gun-like object on top of the van is an antenna for relaying pictures to the studio by means of microwaves.

Source: Photo courtesy of WTVJ-TV, Miami, FL.

B. News gathering by satellite (NGS) greatly expands the ENG idea by using mobile earth stations that overcome the short-distance, line-of-sight limitations of terrestrial relays.

Source: Photo courtesy of WTVT, Tampa, FL.

bands is no longer available, a possible option for HDTV is direct-broadcast satellite (DBS) transmission, discussed in the next chapter. The Japanese have experimented extensively with this option. In the United States, CBS has proposed a compatible HDTV system occupy-ing two standard 6-MHz channels, so configured that conventional sets could receive a picture on one of the channels while special sets would receive high-definition pictures utilizing both channels. Neither of these HDTV systems seems likely to become operational in the United States within the near future, however; the tolerability of the present television standard inhibits the build-up of strong demand and consequent financing for a radically improved system.

Ancillary Signals   Several possibilities exist for multiplexing additional signals within the existing 6-MHz television channel. For example, no picture information is transmitted during the vertical blanking interval (VBI), the time during which the pickup tube's scanning beam returns from the bottom of the picture to the top to start scanning a new field (Exhibit 6.2). That interval occupies about 8 percent of the 60th of a second devoted to each field, amounting to the equivalent of 21 picture lines. VBIs are represented on the television screen by the black bars between frames seen when a set's vertical picture is mistuned.

Teletext, one of the several users of the VBI, delivers textual matter (including maps and drawings). For teletext, the television transmitting station stores up to several hundred pages (picture frames) of information in digital form, transmitting them in rotation during the VBI. At the home receiver, the user requests specific pages by means of a key pad. The key pad activates a minicomputer that "grabs" the requested frames as they are transmitted in rotation, displaying them on the home television screen. Teletext pages can either temporarily displace the television picture or they can be superimposed over the picture. *Closed captioning*, a specialized form of teletext, superimposes captions over regular television programs for the benefit of the hearing impaired. It is called "closed" because only viewers with a decoder can display the captions (Exhibit 4.8).

Teletext technology has not been standardized, leaving several rival systems to compete for acceptance. In the United States, two formats have been tried, NABTS (North American Basic Teletext Specification) and WST (World System Teletext). NABTS resembles systems developed in Canada and France, and WST is based on the Britain's BBC and IBA systems, which pioneered the technology.

Another ancillary television signal, an audio subcarrier enabling the telecasting of stereophonic and bilingual sound, was authorized and used experimentally in 1984. Receivers that had the necessary double speakers were already coming on the market at the time; they featured MPX (multiplex) terminals on the back for plugging in the converters needed to extract the subcarrier signal.

These are but a few of the many innovations brought about by new technology's explosive growth — or, more accurately, by the growth of new applications of existing technology. If technological capacity alone controlled growth, many more new services, as well as improvements on old services, would have already emerged. But technology must wait for consumer demand, awakened by creative entrepreneurial activity.

Summary

• Each broadcasting service is allocated certain frequency bands, within which each station is licensed to use a specific channel. Co-channel stations can interfere with each other, as can, at lesser distances, stations on adjacent channels.

• The FCC classifies channels and stations according to rules calculated to maximize the number that may operate without causing mutual interference. These classifications take into consideration the propagation characteristics of the frequency band in which each service operates.

• FM radio and television coverage, which depends on frequencies that do not propagate sky waves, is easier to control than AM coverage.

• The wide channels of FM and television readily accommodate multiplexing of additional information on subcarriers. Stereophonic sound and SCA services such as background music are examples of FM subcarrier services; teletext is an example of a television subcarrier service.

• Short waves are used for distant coverage by means of sky waves. Unlike domestic stations, international short-wave stations usually use several different frequencies and correspondingly different antennas in order to adjust to varying sky-wave behavior throughout the broadcast day.

• Television technology is analogous to cinematography, in that it uses similar strategies for creating the illusion of motion and continuity of screen illumination. Electronic pictures consist of pixels, lines, fields, and frames, transmitted one pixel at a time in terms of amplitude-modulated analogue signals. U.S. standards call for 525-line frames, transmitted at the rate of 30 per second, with interlaced fields transmitted at the rate of 60 per second.

• The sound and vision aspects of television rely on separate equipment components, both in the studio and in the television receiver. The sound signal modulates an FM subcarrier within the television channel, while the video signal modulates an AM carrier.

• To reduce information load, color information is based on only three primary colors. When mixed in appropriate proportions, they depict all the different hues. These three primaries are multiplexed in the same-size channel as that used for monochrome television, thus permitting monochrome receivers to pick up color transmissions in black and white.

• Television channels are allocated in both the VHF and UHF bands. Because UHF waves attenuate more quickly than VHF, UHF stations generally have smaller coverage areas, despite the increased power the FCC allows UHF as compensation.

• Television receivers repeat the scanning sequence of the camera pickup tube, kept in step by synchronizing signals. The picture is displayed on the face of a kinescope tube. An electron scanning beam activates the tube's phosphorescent coating.

• Teletext uses an otherwise idle part of the television signal, occurring in the vertical blanking interval, to transmit text and graphics to home television receivers equipped with special decoders.

• Current technological innovations in television include miniaturization of receivers and production equipment through the use of solid state devices; stereophonic sound; and the prospect of high-definition television, offering projected images equal in quality to theatrical film.

CHAPTER 7

Delivery, Distribution, and Storage

Technology has entered an innovative and confusing era, constantly offering new options for combining traditional broadcasting with nonbroadcast media. It helps to start with some basic concepts that furnish a perspective from which to view this cornucopia of innovation.

Think of electronic communication as providing the means for carrying out three basic functions: *delivery*, *distribution*, and *storage*. If we view traditional broadcast stations as a delivery mechanism, it follows that distribution and storage give stations the potential for delivering programs of near universal appeal. Without benefit of these technologies, broadcasting could never have become the world's most popular mass communication medium.

7.1 Basic Concepts

Delivery   Stations function basically as mechanisms for program delivery to consumers. Most programs come from wholesale sources, external to the station, which does not, as a rule, produce its own offerings. By their very nature, stations are essentially *local*. Without networks and recordings, most stations would be limited to presenting live pro-

grams based on purely local resources.* Few, if any, could attract large audiences. There would be no national programming, no costly productions, no superstar performers.

Syndication   To rise above the limitations of their local resources, all mass media depend on some means of storing centrally produced program materials and of distributing them nationally and internationally. The techno-economic device for harnessing centralized production and exploiting storage and distribution technologies is *syndication*. This chapter explains the technological aspects of syndication. Later chapters discuss its economic aspects and its products.

Syndication is a means of wholesaling program materials, by dividing the costs of ex-

---

*Like most broad generalizations about broadcasting, this statement needs qualification. A few radio stations featuring talk shows do some of their own programming (extensively supplemented, however, by outside news services and telephone interviews with distant celebrities). Class I (clear-channel) radio stations furnish some nighttime service to communities remote from their cities of license. And a few so-called television superstations distribute their programs to cable systems in distant markets; however, they depend heavily on recorded material and function not merely as stations but as headquarters for cable-network operations.

tremely costly products among many local delivery systems that pass the materials on to end-users. The classic and pioneer syndicator is the international news agency. It enables stations, cable television systems, and newspapers all over the world to furnish consumers with expertly reported and edited news gathered from the far corners of the earth. Centrally processed for use by local delivery systems and pre-edited for easy incorporation into those systems' offerings, the news agency product is tremendously expensive. It involves maintenance of worldwide networks of reporters, editors, and communication channels and is affordable only because thousands of outlets share in defraying production and distribution costs. Symptomatic of technology's key role, news agencies first burgeoned with the emergence of the pioneer electronic communication medium, the telegraph (§2.2).

Storage   Syndication is facilitated by the technological capacity to program materials for release and rerelease long after production. Means of storage include disc and tape recordings, still and motion-picture films, and computer memories. Except for news, live sports, and some special events, virtually all broadcasting is prerecorded. In order to compensate for time differences among geographic zones, national networks often record even "live" materials for *delayed broadcast*. Affiliates also sometimes record live network feeds for later release. Most programs, even timely ones, thus go through one or more recording steps before reaching the public.

Distribution   The broadcasting network is not usually looked upon as a syndication device, but from a technoeconomic viewpoint, it introduced a novel form of syndication — instant program distribution, which was different from the news, motion-picture, and music

distribution methods already in existence when broadcasting began. A network can bind any number of local voices into a single, unified, national voice. Broadcast stations can function at times as affiliates of networks and at other times as independent, local outlets. This ability to function locally, regionally, nationally, or indeed even internationally, and to switch instantaneously from one type of coverage to another, gives broadcasting great flexibility.

A broadcast network, reduced to its simplest terms, consists of two or more stations *connected* to each other so as to be able to put identical programs on the air in more than one market *simultaneously*. Thus networks take advantage of broadcasting's unique ability to deliver programs instantaneously. They use this attribute best when covering real events in real time. Simultaneity is valuable even for recorded material, however, because it makes networks unique among media and enables efficient national promotion of network offerings.

Relays   The "net" of a network is its interconnecting *relay* links. A relay station passes on an electronic signal, much as a relay runner passes on the baton at a track meet, using wire, cable, microwave, or satellite intermediaries. Normally, relayed signals are not open to public reception, though intelligence services routinely gather information by intercepting relay traffic.

Relay systems and the firms that operate them are called *common carriers*. Common carriers sell the use of their facilities to all comers on a first-come, first-served basis, at fixed, government-regulated rates. Telephone firms are the most familiar example. They remain neutral toward communication content, merely forwarding calls from one address to another without having any control over what callers say. Broadcasters, in contrast, have an undelegable legal responsibility for content (that is, their programs), and commercial broadcasters may charge users (advertisers) any rates they wish.

Convergence   New technology opens up possibilities for combining old and new functions into innovative configurations. This *convergence*, or coming-together process, blurs traditional distinctions between delivery, distribution, and storage functions, as well as between common carriers and broadcasters. For example, the "superstation" combines four elements: (1) a local-delivery unit (the originating television station), (2) a satellite relay interconnection, and (3) the broadcast network principle — but (4) with cable television systems rather than with stations. As further evidence of convergence, the viewing screens of television broadcast receivers have become general-purpose display terminals for cable television, teletext, videotex, satellite downlinks, videocassette recorders, video games, home videocameras, and computers.

Computers play a vital role in convergence, handling complex switching and other interactions among the elements of hybrid systems. Small computers that incorporate digital signal processing and large-scale integrated circuits on microchips bond different elements together into the new configurations. Thus computers at the sending and receiving ends, respectively, store and retrieve the pages of teletext that some television stations broadcast along with their regular programs. Much of what you see in current broadcast programs has been modified by computers built into production equipment.

7.2 Sound Recording

Turning now to specific storage technologies, we start with the first to emerge, the prebroadcast art of sound recording. Phonographs had wide public acceptance in the two decades before broadcasting, and phonograph recordings furnished much of broadcasting's earliest programming (§2.1).

Discs   In conventional phonograph disc recording, a sound source causes a *stylus* to vibrate as it cuts a spiral groove in a revolving master disc. The stylus transfers the frequency and amplitude patterns of the sound source into corresponding patterns in the form of minute deformations in the sides of the grooves. Molds derived from pressings of the master disc can be used for mass production of copies.

In playback, the grooves cause vibrations in a pickup-head stylus, which converts the movements into a modulated electrical current. These analogue voltages, after suitable amplification, complete the operation by causing vibrations in a loudspeaker. The fidelity with which conventional discs store sound information depends on many variables, among them the sensitivity of the recording and pickup styluses, the accuracy of the styluses in tracking grooves in the disc, the speed with which the disc revolves, and the quality of the electronic components. All these factors cause imperfections in the sound.

The distortions inherent in the analogue method of disc recording just described can be avoided by digital signal processing, the principles of which were described in §5.5. In addition, the substitution of *laser** beams for mechanical tracking by styluses eliminates the wear and tear inflicted by the physical contact

---

*A laser (*l*ight *a*mplification by *s*timulated *e*mission of *r*adiation) produces coherent light, a highly concentrated beam at a single frequency (or very few frequencies). In addition to their role in videodisc production and playback, lasers supply light for transmission through fiberoptic channels and make possible experimental three-dimensional television.

Exhibit 7.1   Compact Disc (CD) Playback System

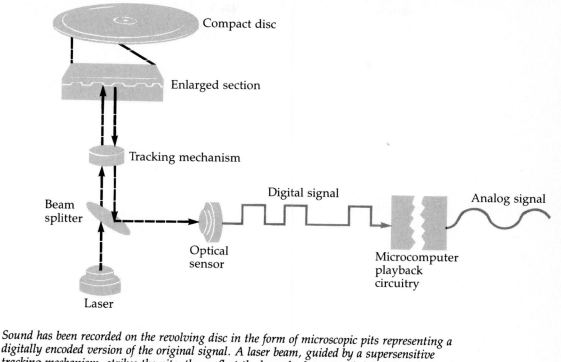

Sound has been recorded on the revolving disc in the form of microscopic pits representing a digitally encoded version of the original signal. A laser beam, guided by a supersensitive tracking mechanism, strikes the pits; they reflect the beam back as a modulated digital signal to an optical sensor. The sensor feeds its digital output to a microcomputer that has a transducer for converting the digital information into analog form for delivery to the audio reproducing system.

of stylus on disc. Digitally processed sound in *compact disc* (CD) format will probably eventually replace stylus recording and playback (Exhibit 7.1). CDs are sealed in plastic covers, making them impervious to damage. They have enormous storage capacity, storing an hour's worth of sound on a 4¾-inch disc, which is smaller even than a 45-rpm recording.

Tape   Another way of avoiding the distortions inherent in revolving turntables and stylus-and-groove contact is magnetic-tape recording. This method eliminates some of the mechanical operations and greatly improves portability and convenience. In magnetic recording, the usual storage medium consists of plastic tape coated with minute particles of a metallic compound. The smallness of the particles and the number available per second of running time, as determined by the tape's width and velocity, define storage capacity. Master sound recordings on quarter-inch tape usually call for a tape speed of 15 inches per second (ips). In broadcasting, a playback speed of 7½ ips usually suffices. Much lower speeds can be used when quality matters less, as in office dictation and station-output monitoring. Multitrack master recording and other specialized tasks call for wider tape stock.

In magnetic-tape recordings, the amplified modulated electric current from a microphone varies a magnetic field in a recording head over which the tape passes. Magnetic-field variations induce patterned arrangement of the metallic particle molecules on the tape. On playback, the tape passes over another electromagnetic head, in which the magnetic patterns induce a modulated electric current that goes to amplifiers and the loudspeaker. Running the tape over a third electromagnet, the erase head, rearranges all the molecules, neutralizing the stored magnetic patterns so that the same tape can be used repeatedly. Like disc recording, tape recording is being converted to digital processing, with consequent improvement in quality. Digital tape can be copied many times in the course of editing or mass production without the losses that occur in duplicating analogue tapes.

Originally, all tape recorders had a reel-to-reel configuration, each reel separate and accessible. Now, however, most users find enclosed tape cassettes or cartridges both more convenient and more protective of the tape. The cassette incorporates two hubs, for feed and takeup reels, within a single housing; after playing, the cassette must be rewound or, if the recording uses only one half the width of the tape, the cassette may be flipped over to play a second "side." The cartridge, commonly referred to as a "cart," has a single hub and contains an endless tape loop that repeats itself. Carts are especially convenient for use in automated radio stations. A large number can be loaded, each cart containing a single program item. Inaudible cues recorded on the tape tell the playback unit to stop at the end of the item and to cue up the tape for subsequent replay (Exhibit 13.2).

7.3 Picture Recording

Adaptation of tape technology to the recording of television pictures required a vast increase in information capacity. This need for a more sophisticated technology delayed the evolution of disc and tape video-recording. Videotape recording, the first method to evolve, came on the market in 1956.

Kinescopes   Surviving recordings of the earliest television shows exist only as filmed versions known as *kinescope recordings*. These were made by using a film camera, especially adapted for television's field frequency, to photograph programs by focusing on the face of a black-and-white picture (kinescope) tube. Kinescope recording lost much of television's already skimpy detail: played back, the programs looked flat and hazy, far from satisfactory for reuse on the air. Broadcast quality had to await the adaptation of magnetic tape to picture storage.

Videotape   That adaptation came with the first quadruplex videorecorders, developed by Ampex. The chief technical hurdle was to increase the speed at which tape passes over the head, in order to process the large amount of information entailed in the pictures and sound signals. Ampex ingeniously solved this problem by mounting *four* recording heads on a revolving drum (hence the name *quadruplex*). The drum rapidly rotates *transversely* (across the width of tape), while the tape itself moves longitudinally, as it does in sound recording. Suction holds the two-inch tape against the curvature of the revolving drum to maintain head contact, as shown in Exhibit 7.2. The combined movements of heads and tape produce an effective head-to-tape speed of 1,500 inches per second. If the tape itself moved at that speed, it would quickly wear out the

Exhibit 7.2 Videotape Recording Formats

A. Transverse Quadruplex Format.

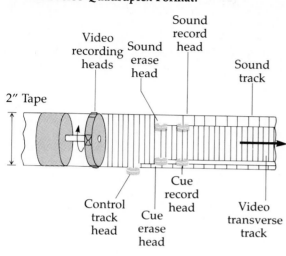

2″ Tape

Video recording heads — Sound erase head — Sound record head — Sound track — Control track head — Cue erase head — Cue record head — Video transverse track

B. Helical Format.

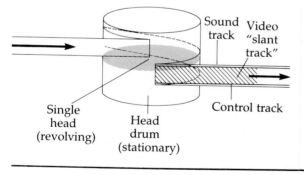

Single head (revolving) — Head drum (stationary) — Sound track — Video "slant track" — Control track

C. One-inch Format.

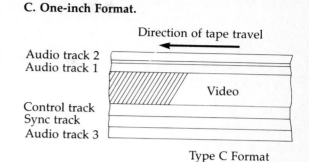

Direction of tape travel

Audio track 2
Audio track 1
Video
Control track
Sync track
Audio track 3

Type C Format

A. Transverse Quadruplex Format. *Four video recording heads mounted on a rapidly spinning wheel, shown at the left, lay down transverse tracks across the width of the two-inch tape. Sound is recorded longitudinally along one edge, auxiliary information along the other edge.*

B. Helical Format. *The tape spirals around a large, stationary drum. Within the drum, the videorecording head spins on a revolving disc, making contact with the tape as it slips over the drum's smooth surface. Because of the spiral wrap the tape moves slightly downward as well as lengthwise, so that the combined movements of tape and recording head produce a slanting track, as shown. Some helical recorders use two heads, some use different wraparound configurations.*

C. One-inch Format. *This is an example of one of the smaller formats. Still narrower VTR tapes are used — ³/₄-inch, half-inch, 8-mm, and even ¹/₄-inch.*

Source: Courtesy Ampex Corporation.

---

pickup heads and would require such enormous spools of tape as to be impracticable.

Subsequently, simpler and less expensive videotape recorders using one-inch and narrower tape stock have come on the market. They retain the principle of combining head and tape movements but use fewer heads. Instead of laying down the track transversely, the heads cross the tape at an angle, producing a *slanted* track, as shown in Exhibit 7.2. A

slanted track allows the head to make a longer sweep than it could if it moved across the narrow tape transversely. Slant-track recorders are called *helical*, because the tape wraps around a stationary drum, or capstan, in a spiral (helical) path while a spinning disc inside the drum brings each head in contact with the tape as it passes by.

For portable videotape equipment, broadcasters opted first for three-quarter-inch tape (called U-matic), but as tape technology improved, half-inch, 8mm (about one-third of an inch), and even quarter-inch video formats evolved. Lack of standardization among competing equipment manufacturers delayed widespread professional adoption of the smaller formats, despite their greater convenience and reduced cost.

VCRs   Competing videocassette recorder (VCR) formats designed for home use confuse the consumer market as well. The leading contenders, Beta and VHS (video home system), are incompatible, even though both use one-half-inch, slant-track tape. Older models record sound along the edge of the tape, as in the formats shown in Exhibit 7.2. More recent models incorporate high-quality stereophonic sound, using slanted tracks for sound as well as for picture.

VCRs depend on the user's home television set for playback display, but they contain their own tuners for recording off the air while the user watches the program, or a different program, on the set. They can also record the output of home videorecorders and can display rented or purchased feature films. Equipped with many sophisticated computer-assisted features, such as the options of programming days in advance to pick up a sequence of shows on different stations, modern VCRs are among the most versatile and popular of the ancillary consumer electronic products.

Laser Video   Laser video recorders play back with better quality than do VCRs, with improved freeze-frame and slow-motion functions. They use the same laser pickup technique to record pictures as compact discs do to record sound. In fact it is possible to buy a combination laser playback unit that reproduces both CDs and laser videodiscs of movies and other materials sold in video stores.

Laser technology may eventually displace most other types of home information storage, including the magnetic floppy discs used in home computers. One laser disc has a 600-megabyte capacity,* many times that of a floppy disc. With the development of a simple technique for home recording on laser discs, they could fully rival the versatility of videotape and floppy discs.

Role of Computer Memories

Computers rely on huge numbers of semiconductor memory elements, each of which "flip-flops" to register either "one" or "zero" (that is, an electrical charge or no charge). As previously noted, computers now play an ever-increasing role in communications, and all electronic information processing is moving away from analogue toward digital as the standard mode. However, it will take time to displace the billions of dollars' worth of existing analogue television receivers and transmitters.† In the meantime, many of the individual functions of both home and studio equipment have been converted to the digital mode and taken over by computers.

Notable among these are production aids such as character generators, electronic frame stores, and digital effects units. These computer-based aids enable the electronic insertion of text and graphics into ongoing programs and the manipulation of images to produce an endless repertoire of visual transformations, now familiar especially in the title sequences that introduce television programs.

---

*In a striking demonstration, Grolier Electronic Publishing recorded the text of a 21-volume encyclopedia on a single CD, with plenty of space left over for recording both graphic and audio illustrations. A special CD drive allowed random access to the encyclopedia, which could be read out on a personal computer screen.

†A television receiver already on the market can reprocess the received picture digitally, clean it up, and convert it to analogue form for display on the kinescope tube.

Dissection of pictures into digitized pixels offers unlimited possibilities for shifting the elements around innumerable times, because the simple "off-on" signals are so immune to distortion.

7.4 Terrestrial Relays

In addition to means of storage, syndication depends on means of distribution. These include interconnection facilities for networks and remote pickups. Formerly, such interconnection depended on earthbound systems, using land-based transmitters and receivers. Later, satellites furnished relay stations in space, enabling far more flexible interconnection.

Interconnection   Point-to-point relay circuits, usually furnished by AT&T or other common carriers, provide the interconnection for network broadcasting. Relays perform a distribution function, feeding centrally produced and scheduled materials to stations for simultaneous delivery to consumers.

Any point-to-point wire or radio circuit can function as a relay. The channel capacity of the circuit determines which types of relays can be used for specific types of material. Ordinary telephone circuits (usually especially equalized to compensate for more rapid attenuation of higher frequencies over distance) suffice for radio programs but not for television.

Coaxial Cable   When fed through ordinary copper wire, the energy in a wide band of frequencies such as that needed by television tends to be lost by radiation. *Coaxial cable* prevents this loss, trapping the energy and conducting it through an enclosed space. Coaxial cable consists of two conductors — a solid wire running down the center of a

Exhibit 7.3   Coaxial Cable

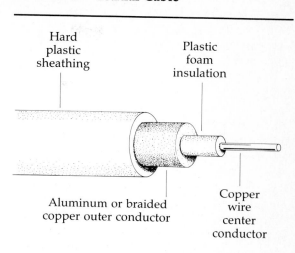

Hard plastic sheathing

Plastic foam insulation

Aluminum or braided copper outer conductor

Copper wire center conductor

Coaxial cable gets its name from the fact that it has two conductors with a common axis, a solid central conductor surrounded by a tubelike hollow conductor. The radio energy travels within the protected environment of the space between the two conductors. Cable television relies on this type of conductor, as do many terrestrial relay links that convey television signals, telephone calls, data, and other types of information.

Source: Adapted from illustration in Walter S. Baer, *Cable Television: A Handbook for Decision Making* (The Rand Corporation, Santa Monica, CA, 1973), p. 4.

hollow metal tube. The wire and the metal tube are insulated from each other by air or a nonconductive material, as depicted in Exhibit 7.3. Attenuation occurs, as it must when any radio signal travels; but it can be compensated for by amplifiers, usually inserted about every third of a mile.

Coaxial cable is bulky, expensive to manufacture, and costly to install. Cable relays must be buried in underground trenches outside of cities and in utility tunnels beneath the streets within cities. In rugged mountain terrain, cable installation can become prohibitively expensive. Nevertheless, television networks in the United States originally reached their affiliates by means of nationwide coaxial cable links. AT&T supplied the coaxial facilities, just as it had the telephone-wire facilities for network radio.

Microwave Relays   Later, after techniques for efficient transmission of very short waves had been developed, AT&T supplied microwave relay facilities for TV networking. Microwaves, located in the UHF band and above, range in wavelength from one meter down to a millimeter. Waves this short attenuate in the atmosphere so rapidly that they seemed at first unusable for communication over long distances. When focused into a narrow, concentrated beam, however, microwave power can be increased by a factor of a hundred thousand. With this much strength, microwaves can punch through thirty miles of atmosphere, and because of their short length they require relatively small sending and receiving antennas (Exhibit 5.11).

A typical microwave relay station receives signals from a preceding station and passes them on to the next station. Relay towers must be spaced within sight of each other. Each repeater station reamplifies and retransmits the signals it receives. It takes over a hundred such repeaters to span the United States from coast to coast.

Microwave relay networks have the advantage over coaxial cable of not requiring continuous right-of-way easements. Rugged terrain actually favors microwave transmission by providing high points that help in laying out line-of-sight transmission paths. Prior to the advent of the space relays, all network television was relayed by microwaves, except for short local coaxial links.

Optical Fiber Cable   Recently, however, for some relay applications cable has come back into favor in a new form, *optical fiber* conductors. The hair-thin strands of extremely pure glass used in optical fiber cable can transmit modulated light. Its tremendously high frequency provides a bandwidth in the thousands of megahertz. Thus a thin filament of glass has the capacity of many bulky coaxial cables.

The bundle of frequencies present in ordinary light will not travel efficiently through an optical fiber. Instead, lasers or light-emitting diodes, known as LEDs (the source of number images on digital watches), must be used to provide a "coherent" light source. The modulated light does not run straight down the glass fiber as does water through a pipe but is reflected at an angle back and forth within the fiber. For this reason, the glass must be devoid of impurities that would randomly change the angle of reflection.

Optical fiber cables have many advantages for relay links, especially those bearing very heavy traffic. The cables are small and lightweight; they neither radiate energy to interfere with other circuits nor receive interference from the outside; and they are made of one of the cheapest and most abundant natural materials. Some European governments plan to install national fiber-optic networks for cable television. In the United States, fiber-optic links were used for intercommunication at the 1984 Los Angeles Olympic Games and have been permanently installed on certain heavy-traffic telephone routes.

7.5 Space Relays

The physical limitations of microwave relay networks prevent them from spanning oceans to distribute programs worldwide. The existing transoceanic cables have been too busy with telegraph and telephone traffic to devote their limited capacity to the relay of the broad frequency bands that are always needed by television.* Because of these limitations, transatlantic television became possible only with the advent of communication satellites functioning as relay stations in space. Far beyond the earth's attenuating atmosphere, a single satellite can have line-of-sight access to almost a third of the globe's surface before encountering the horizon (Exhibit 7.4).

Advantages of Space Relays   Communication satellites are often likened to microwave repeater towers thousands of miles in height. This analogy can be misleading. One must remember that a microwave repeater links one specific location with only two others, the next sending and receiving points in the relay network. A satellite, however, links a single repeater station (the satellite itself) to an *unlimited number* of receiving earth stations, located at *any distance* from the satellite within its coverage area. The addition of receiving stations adds nothing to transmission costs as it does in microwave networks. Thus satellites are referred to as "distance insensitive."

Microwave signals lose quality over the course of many reamplifications by successive repeater stations. Satellite relays, however, handle a signal only once before sending it down to its destination. HF sky-wave propagation can achieve long-distance terrestrial relays, but sky waves suffer from fading and sunspot disruptions, which satellite relays are immune to.

Geostationary Orbit   It is desirable to keep satellites constantly in view of their targets in order to have 24-hour service and to

avoid the need for costly tracking mechanisms that point receiving antennas at a moving signal source. To accomplish this, communication satellites should ideally be held stationary above their target areas. A satellite in *geostationary* (or *geosynchronous*) *orbit* stays in the same position relative to the earth, because the centrifugal force tending to throw the satellite outward and the gravitational force tending to pull it back to earth are kept in equilibrium. Geostationary orbit is an imaginary circle 22,300 miles above the equator. Though satellites actually move very rapidly through space, from the perspective of an observer on Earth they appear to stay in one place, because they keep in step with the earth as it rotates. A satellite in *nonsynchronous* orbit, on the other hand, appears to move across the sky as do the sun, moon, and planets. Small jet thrusters aboard the geosynchronous satellite enable ground-controllers to make minor adjustments to keep it from drifting out of its prescribed orbital position.* Through the ITU nations have agreed to allot each country one or more specific slots in the geosynchronous orbit. Positions are identified in degrees of longitude, east or west of the prime meridian at Greenwich, England.† Exhibit 7.4 shows the U.S. orbital slots.

---

*However, plans are under way for supplementing existing undersea copper cables with fiber-optic cables in the late 1980s. AT&T scheduled its fiber-optic TAT-8 for 1988. Tele-Optik, a non-common-carrier fiber-optic transatlantic link, was scheduled for completion the following year. Such facilities could compete with satellite systems such as Intelsat as providers of transatlantic television relays.

---

*It would take too much fuel to keep satellites *exactly* in geosynchronous orbit; actually they drift in and out of position very slightly, describing a figure-eight pattern.
†The meridians, imaginary lines dividing the earth's surface, run north and south, meeting at the north and south poles and crossing the equator. They divide the earth's surface into segments, like those of an orange. The circle of the equator is divided equally into 360 degrees, with each degree representing a meridian position. The meridians are numbered 1 to 180 degrees east and 1 to 180 degrees west of Greenwich, a location near London, England, that is called the prime meridian. The geostationary orbit extends the equator as an imaginary circle in space, 22,300 miles above the terrestrial equator. ITU orbital slot allotments take into consideration the ability of a satellite in a given orbital position to look down on its intended target area.

Exhibit 7.4   The Geostationary Satellite Orbit

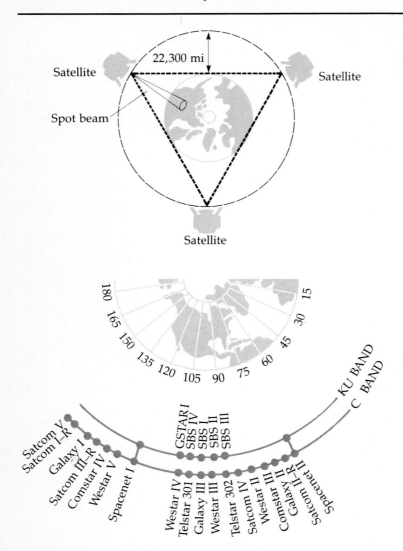

A. *Looking down from space on the earth's north pole, one can see how three equidistant satellites poised above the equator could "see" most of the earth's surface (only "most" because their signals fade out at polar latitudes). Signals can be intensified when concentrated in a "spot beam" directed at a specific region. The satellites appear to remain stationary with reference to the earth when positioned at a height of 22,300 miles. INTELSAT, the West's worldwide international satellite system, maintains such satellites over the Atlantic, Pacific, and Indian Oceans.*

B. *Each satellite has its assigned position, expressed in degrees of a half-circle either east or west of the prime meridian at Greenwich, in the segment of the geosynchronous orbit approximately above the target area. Because the orbital segment allotted to the United States is so crowded, Ku-band satellites are shown at a different height than the C-band satellites; actually, all occupy the same orbit, 22,300 miles above the equator. Note that the Satcom V occupies the position farthest west, at 143° west; Spacenet III occupies the position farthest east, at 69° west. The linkages between bands for Spacenet I and Spacenet II indicate that those satellites carry both Ku-band and C-band transponders. The drawing shows the U.S. satellites and their positions as of early 1986.*

Source: *Broadcasting-Cablecasting Yearbook 1986*, Broadcasting Publications, Inc., Washington, D.C., p. E-2.

Each degree of arc in the 360-degrees of the geostationary orbit represents a separation of 470 miles. How closely satellites can operate in orbit without interfering with each other depends on several factors, such as their power, the directionality of their antennas, and the sensitivity of Earth-station antennas. U.S. standards originally called for spacing satellites at least 4 degrees apart, but in order to crowd more satellites into the usable segment of the orbit, spacing was reduced to two degrees. Even so, the demand for allotments is so high that it creates a potential problem of orbital-slot scarcity analogous to spectrum scarcity.

Spectrum Allocations   Like Earth-based transmitters, satellite transmitters occupy ITU-allocated channels. Broadcast satellites use two bands, one in the 4–6 GHz region (called the C band) and one in the 11–15 GHz region (called the Ku band). Most existing operational satellites use the C band; newer and more powerful satellites that were originally planned for direct reception on small home antennas use the higher Ku band. C-band signals, being in the microwave range, are subject to reception-point interference on Earth from the many terrestrial services that use microwaves. Ku-band signals avoid this drawback, but the extreme shortness of their waves means they can be blocked by small objects, such as raindrops in a heavy downpour.

Each satellite needs two groups of frequencies, one for uplinking (reception) and one for downlinking (transmission). These frequency groups must be separated well enough so there is no interference between uplink and downlink signals. Thus satellite bands are referred to in pairs: 4/6 GHz, 12/14 GHz, and so on. The downlink frequency groups must be large enough to accommodate a number of different channels for simultaneous transmission by the satellite's *transponders* (combination receive-transmit units). Most recently launched satellites carry twenty-four transponders; by using polarized signals, each transponder can transmit two channels, for a total of forty-eight channels per satellite.

Reception   A satellite's downlink antennas can deliver *broad* beams, each covering al-

most a third of the earth's surface, or they can deliver directional *spot beams* that make relatively small footprints (satellite coverage areas). Generally, the smaller the footprint the stronger the signal, because of the gain obtained by directional antennas (§5.7).

The conspicuous feature of most satellite Earth stations is a bowl-shaped antenna, varying in diameter from over a hundred feet down to less than three feet. The larger antennas, usable for both transmission and reception, represent a deliberate trade-off. Massive Earth stations made possible lightweight satellites, important because of limitations on the weight rockets could launch. As launch capabilities improved, enabling the lofting of heavier vehicles into orbit, satellites grew more powerful and ground antennas grew smaller. Today, television receive-only antennas (TVROs) of the type used by cable systems to pick up their satellite-fed programs are usually 12 to 15 feet in diameter. Reception points near the margins of footprints need larger-diameter receiving antennas because of signal attenuation (see Exhibit 4.2).

An unexpected bonanza for TVRO manufacturers occurred with the rapid growth of "backyard" dishes operated by hobbyists and high-tech enthusiasts. About a million 6- to 10-foot dishes had been installed in the United States by 1985, and the demand remained high despite uncertainty about the legality of reception. Home dishes can pick up as many as 150 different programs from domestic satellites, some of them private relays, such as news feeds not intended for public consumption (see §16.5). These home pickups are called "C-band direct," because the C-band satellite transmissions were not intended for direct-broadcast reception by consumers. Originally, consumers were expected to wait for the launching of Ku-band DBS (direct-broadcast reception) satellites, which require smaller dishes. TVROs in many foreign countries intercept U.S. satellite traffic; by the same token, several U.S. universities have installed special converters for routinely intercepting Russian broadcast satellite signals.

Other major receiver components include special *low-noise amplifiers* (LNAs) capable of magnifying the extremely weak satellite signals that reach the antenna (increasing them by a factor as high as a million); tuners to select the desired transponder channels; and down-converters to translate satellite frequencies into the range usable by television receivers.

Construction and Launch   The principal components of a communication satellite are shown in Exhibit 7.5. Solar panels collect electrical energy from the sun's rays, but satellites also carry batteries, vital for supplying power during the brief periods when the earth shades them from the sun. Relative to most terrestrial transmitters, satellites have extremely low power and hence extremely weak signals.* Telemetry signals report the satellite's vital signs to the control station on Earth, which remotely controls many functions aboard the vehicle.

NASA (the National Aeronautics and Space Administration) has launched most U.S. and many foreign satellites, though competition comes increasingly from the European launch facility, Arianespace, located in French Guiana, on the north coast of South America. Exhibit 7.5 shows two NASA satel-

lite launch sequences, one initiated by a rocket, the other by the space shuttle, itself launched into low orbit by a rocket. The shuttle can carry a satellite to an altitude of two or three hundred miles, beyond the earth's atmosphere and most of its gravity; after release from the shuttle, the satellite's own rockets take over. When the rockets of a satellite launched from a shuttle fail to ignite, $70 million dollars worth of hardware is stranded in low orbit. In a remarkable rescue, astronauts on a shuttle mission in 1984 retrieved two such errant vehicles, stowed them aboard the shuttle, and returned them to Earth for repairs and eventual reuse.

7.6   Over-the-Air Hybrids

In traditional broadcasting, relays functioned as nonpublic links between network headquarters and stations. Relay providers were public utilities, not broadcasters. Under the impact of technological convergence (§7.1), however, broadcasting increasingly finds itself involved in, or affected by, nonbroadcast or quasi-broadcast enterprises. Individual production, delivery, storage, and distribution technologies can be regarded as versatile building blocks, capable of being assembled into many different configurations and adapted to serve many different purposes. Such cross-fertilization, highly characteristic of contemporary electronic communication, results in the formation of *hybrids*, configurations that are the subject of the rest of this chapter. In this context, the term *hybrid* has no pejorative implication; it merely identifies technologies that blend together hitherto distinct and separate functions.

Rebroadcasting   Though not a recent development, *rebroadcasting* illustrates hybridiza-

---

*It may seem paradoxical that satellites send signals such great distances and yet have very low power. Remember, however, that attenuation of radio signals occurs mainly because of atmospheric absorption. For most of their 22,300-miles-plus journey, satellite signals travel through the vacuum of space. When they do encounter the earth's relatively thin atmospheric envelope, they pass almost straight down through it. Terrestrial radio signals, in contrast, travel nearly parallel to the earth, impeded by atmospheric absorption along their entire route.

Exhibit 7.5A   Satellite Structure

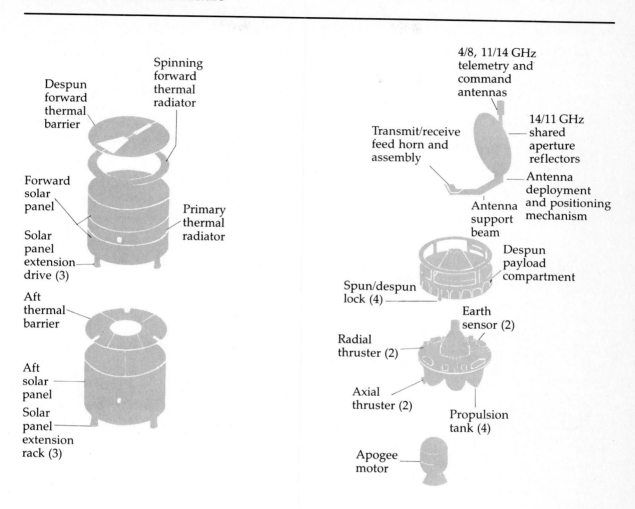

The essential components of a communication satellite include the launch motor, small thrusters to adjust its position in orbit, solar panels to collect electrical energy for storage in batteries, a means for stabilizing its position with reference to the sun and its target area, receiving and sending antennas, telemetry transceivers, and transponders (the receive-transmit channels that do the actual communicating).

Source: Stan Prentiss, *Satellite Communications* (TAB Books, Blue Ridge Summit, PA, 1983), p. 4, 5. Diagram is of SBS spacecraft by Hughes Aircraft.

Exhibit 7.5B   Satellite Launch Stages

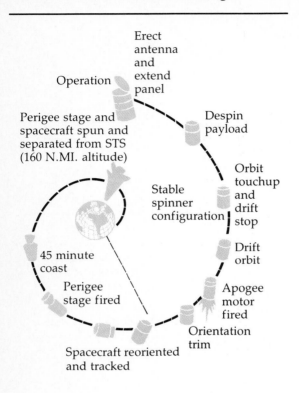

Erect antenna and extend panel

Operation

Perigee stage and spacecraft spun and separated from STS (160 N.MI. altitude)

Despin payload

Stable spinner configuration

Orbit touchup and drift stop

Drift orbit

45 minute coast

Perigee stage fired

Apogee motor fired

Orientation trim

Spacecraft reoriented and tracked

Satellites are launched either directly from the earth's surface by means of powerful rockets or from space shuttles orbiting a few hundred miles above the earth's surface. In either case, the biggest job is to overcome the initial drag of gravity and of the atmosphere as the vehicle leaves the earth. Thereafter smaller rockets aboard the satellite power it into geostationary orbit.

Source: Stan Prentiss, *Satellite Communications* (TAB Books, Blue Ridge Summit, PA, 1983), p.4, 5.

tion by combining the delivery and relay functions in a single operation. For example, broadcast station B would pick up station A's broadcast signal and retransmit it at B's own frequency; station C would pick up B's signal and retransmit it at C's frequency; and so on.

Some regional FM networks dispense with relays by rebroadcasting each other's signals.

Using rebroadcasting in place of separate relay facilities has serious drawbacks. Each time a program goes through the broadcast-receive-rebroadcast cycle, it loses some of its original quality; a series of such losses can degrade the signal below the standard expected of broadcasting. Also, broadcast stations are usually not ideally spaced geographically to act as relay stations, leaving gaps where stations are too far apart for successful rebroadcasting. Another drawback of rebroadcasting is that it provides no *private* means for the network headquarters to communicate with its affiliates. Moreover, while network affiliates air local programs, networks often use their idle relay facilities to send information, preview material, and programs to record for later broadcast, an amenity impossible if the interconnection is by rebroadcasting.

Translators   A specialized type of rebroadcasting extends the coverage of television stations and, to a lesser extent, FM stations. Low-power, unattended repeater stations called *translators* may be used to fill in dead spots in a station's coverage area or to reach isolated communities beyond its normal reach. Using a sensitive receiver located at a high point in the terrain, the translator picks up its parent station's broadcast signal and rebroadcasts it in an otherwise uncovered area. Sometimes, if too distant for direct rebroadcast, translators are linked to the originating station by microwave relays. Translators are so called because they transfer the main station's signal to a different channel to prevent co-channel interference between the rebroadcast signal and the parent station's signal.

Local groups that want to receive television programs in remote areas usually build and maintain translators, though consent of the originating station must be obtained. Of the more than five thousand translators in the United States, many are found in sparsely settled, mountainous areas. KREX-TV in Grand Junction, Colorado, for example, benefits from the added coverage provided by no less than fifty-one translators.*

ITFS and MDS The FCC originally allocated 28 microwave channels (later reduced to 20) at the high end of the UHF band to *instructional television fixed service* (ITFS), for noncommercial television use by educational authorities.† Most licensees use ITFS for relaying programs from one campus to another, though some address programs to diverse reception points, in a quasi-broadcast manner. Coverage radius is usually limited to about twenty-five miles. Parochial schools are one of the chief users of ITFS, but universities have also sometimes found innovative uses for it. Stanford University, for example, offers local commercial firms released-time training programs for their employees. Silicon Valley firms located within line-of-sight range of the Stanford ITFS transmitter can arrange to receive instructional programs on their own premises, relayed by ITFS.

The term "wireless cable," sometimes applied to multipoint distribution service (MDS), suggests the hybrid nature of this commercial counterpart of ITFS. At reception points within line-of-sight distance of the transmitter, special rooftop antennas pick up the MDS

signal, down-convert it to frequencies tunable by television receivers, and send it on by cable to customers' sets. Users pay program suppliers installation and monthly subscription fees for MDS, which is well adapted to serving apartment and office buildings in which a single antenna can serve a group of subscribers. MDS has also been used for individual home subscription in isolated areas lacking cable television services.

Multichannel MDS, a planned spinoff from plain, single-channel MDS, would allow the operator to use four channels, making the service somewhat more like cable television by offering subscribers program choices. Two groups of four channels each have been made available in each major market for MMDS. The FCC obtained these channels by reducing ITFS from 28 to 20 channels (Exhibit 4.4).

Teletext Teletext is another hybrid service, blending some elements of television broadcasting and print media. It consists of screenfuls (called "pages") of low-definition textual and graphic matter. Because of the poor definition, only a few lines of print can be used per screen, supplemented by relatively crude drawings or images. Page data are transmitted in short bursts sixty times a second during the television vertical blanking intervals (VBIs). (For more details on the VBI, see §6.11.)

At the transmission end, a computer stores up to a few hundred pages of teletext. The viewer uses a touch pad to order up specific pages, selected from index pages. This command operation makes teletext seem like an interactive system, but the viewer is actually only signaling the home decoder, telling it to "grab" a designated page as it goes by in rotation. This means that there can be some delay until the desired page turns up; the number of pages the computer can store is

---

*A special class of television stations, *low-power television* (LPTV), uses the same kind of transmitters as translators. Unlike translators, LPTV stations are permitted to originate their own programs. Limited to power of 10 watts (1,000 watts if UHF), LPTV stations have secondary status —that is, they must not interfere with full-power television outlets.
†The FCC permits educational licensees to lease the excess capacity of their ITFS systems (time not needed for educational programs) to commercial users.

limited to about four hundred, inasmuch as a very large number would cause too much delay in answering the viewer's requests.

DBS   Although first used only as relay facilities, communication satellites also have the potential for hybridization by combining relay and delivery functions. The satellite's uplink leg constitutes a broadcast relay, and the downlink leg delivers the signal directly to consumers, without the intermediation of a ground station. The higher a satellite's power, the smaller its earth-station receiving antennas can be. A direct-broadcast satellite (DBS) therefore has relatively high power, permitting lower-quality (hence cheaper) LNAs and receiving antennas only two to three feet in diameter. Also facilitating small antenna size is the fact that DBS satellites have been allocated to the Ku band, where waves are extremely short (Exhibit 4.9).

7.7 Cable Television

The hybrids discussed in the previous section are subjected to all the problems of spectrum crowding and interference inherent to radio communication conducted over the air. Coaxial cable, however, creates an artificial, enclosed environment (Exhibit 7.3). Within it, the frequency spectrum can be exploited without causing external interference or receiving interference from external signals. Coaxial cable technology was originally designed to serve broadband *distribution* needs, such as the need for television network relays. Cable television changed this concept, blending the distribution and delivery function into a new, hybrid service.

The Cable TV System   The translators mentioned earlier in this chapter afforded only a partial solution to the problem of extending

television station coverage. Each translator rebroadcasts only a single channel, whereas viewers demand a choice of channels. Community antennas feeding homes via coaxial cable gave viewers a choice, at first among four to six channels and then in ever-expanding numbers (§4.2).

Cable systems assemble programs from various sources at the system's *headend*, delivering them via cable to subscriber homes. Program sources include over-the-air signals from local and distant* television stations, locally produced material, and program services relayed by satellite-to-cable networks, such as ESPN (Entertainment and Sports Programming Network). Besides reception facilities, a headend usually contains local-origination facilities and equipment for reprocessing the incoming materials, equalizing them and feeding them to a modulator for transmission over the system's coaxial cable delivery network, and assigning each program source to a specific cable channel.† The delivery network assumes a "tree-and-branch" pattern. As Exhibit 7.6 shows, *trunk cables* branch to lighter *feeder cables* that carry the signals to clusters of homes, where still lighter *drop cables* link feeders to individual homes. A headend can feed programs over a radius of about five miles; to cover wider areas requires subsidiary headends, which receive programs via special supertrunk cables or microwave relays.

Radio-frequency energy attenuates in cable much more rapidly than in the atmos-

---

*The FCC has authorized a special microwave relay service, CARS (Community Antenna Relay Service), to enable cable television systems to make their own arrangements for picking up distant stations. In addition, a few broadcast superstations feed numerous cable systems nationally via satellite.

†The cable operator can assign programs to channels arbitrarily, without reference to the channels over which stations broadcast. For this reason, subscribers often receive television stations on cable-channel numbers different from the stations' over-the-air channel numbers.

Exhibit 7.6   Cable Television System Plan

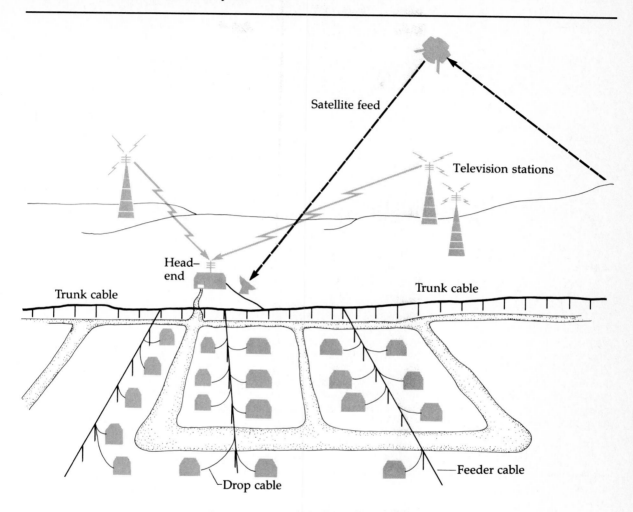

The headend of a cable system contains the amplifiers and local origination facilities of the system (if any). Feeding the headend are off-the-air TV station signals picked up by special antennas and possibly also signals from more distant stations fed by microwave relay. The most important input adjunct is a small earth-station receiving antenna for picking up satellite signals relayed from a variety of program sources. Trunk and feeder distribution cables, shown mounted on poles in the sketch, would often be run underground within cities.

phere, and the higher the frequency the more drastic the attenuation. In the VHF frequency range used by cable, signals lose half their strength traveling a mere two hundred feet. Booster amplifiers and equalizers (to compensate for the varied rates of attenuation at dif-

Exhibit 7.7   Cable TV Spectrum Architecture

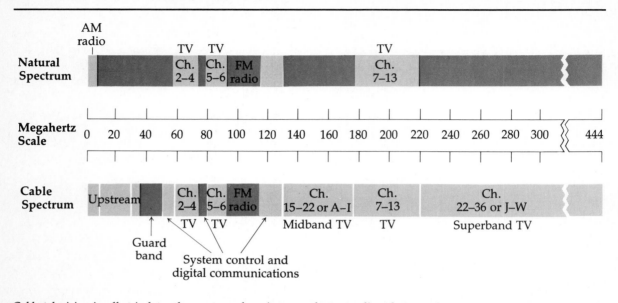

Cable television in effect isolates the spectrum from its natural surroundings by operating within the confines of coaxial cables. This insulation from nature eliminates the possibility of interference, always a serious problem when using the natural spectrum; it also enables cable to use segments of the spectrum allocated to nonbroadcast services. Note that cable retains the VHF channel frequencies and numbering system, but positions what it calls "midband" channels (numbered 14 to 22) and "superband" channels (numbered 23 to 60) in frequency bands allocated in the natural spectrum to nonbroadcast services, below the frequencies allocated to over-the-air UHF television. Cable can manipulate signals more easily at these lower frequencies.

Source: Adapted from Thomas F. Baldwin and D. Stevens McVoy, *Cable Communications* (Prentice-Hall, Englewood Cliffs, NJ, 1983), p. 28.

ferent frequencies) must be inserted in the cable at frequent intervals to keep the signals up to strength and at the same level on all channels. The battle against attenuation therefore adds considerably to the already high cost of the cable itself. Other major capital costs include cable installation and obtaining rights of way. Where possible, cable firms mount cables on existing utility poles, but within cities the cables must go underground in conduits and tunnels, at even greater expense.

Cable Channels   Exhibit 7.7 shows the breakdown of the broad band of frequencies able to pass through a 60-channel coaxial cable. Systems with only 12 channels rely on the VHF tuners in subscribers' television receivers. Systems with more channels must supply customers with an adapter unit that has its own tuning facility. In effect, the adapter contains an expanded VHF tuner to avoid resorting to the receiver's UHF tuner. UHF signals attenuate too rapidly to be practicable for cable use, but within coaxial cable's closed environment additional VHF channels not available for over-the-air television transmission can be used. These channels are not available for over-the-air use because their frequencies have been assigned to other services.

Cable television assigns no television channels to the segment of the VHF band allocated to FM radio (Exhibit 7.7), retaining these frequencies for delivery of audio services. Cable firms can obtain audio programming for delivery over their systems from subcarriers on satellite-delivered television channels as well as from radio broadcast stations.

7.8 Special Cable Features

Other products of convergence emerged as variations on basic cable technology, such as pay cable, interactive cable, MATV/SMATV, and videotex.

Pay Cable   Introduced when cable systems began offering expensive, nonbroadcast programming such as recent movies and prime sports events, pay cable requires some means of screening out subscribers who have not contracted for the extra-pay channels. The pay signals can be interdicted by electronic traps, installed at the points where subscriber drop cables leave feeder cables. Alternatively, they can be encrypted (scrambled) in any of several ways, for example by tampering with the sync pulses (Exhibit 6.2). At the receiver, a converter decodes the scrambled signal for pay-cable customers.

Interactive Cable   Still another, thus far less widely used, technique for controlling pay channels is the *addressable* converter, which enables cable companies to bill subscribers on a *pay-per-view* (PPV) basis. A minicomputer in the home converter relays the viewer's request to the headend and in turn receives instructions from the headend to release the channel. Or the viewer's request can be relayed to the headend by telephone, though this method can lead to delays when calls pile up just before the start of a popular program.

A fully interactive system allows viewers to send other kinds of messages upstream, for example to conduct banking operations or to order goods from stores. Interactive systems use a block of frequencies at the lower end of the coaxial-cable frequency band for the return (upstream) messages, shown in Exhibit 7.7. There are several methods for returning messages, all of which depend on microcomputers to carry on the dialogue between the subscriber's converter and the headend. Subscribers communicate via key pads linked to the minicomputers in converters attached to their receivers.

MATV/SMATV   Referred to sometimes as "private cable," an MATV (*master antenna television*) installation is a mini-cable system confined to the premises of a single building such as an apartment house or a hotel. MATVs offer resident-subscribers programming on several channels, usually not more than five. Most MATVs receive feeds from satellite-to-cable networks, in which case they are called SMATVs (Exhibit 4.5).

Cabletext   Many cable systems use character generators to formulate one-way, full-channel text services, sometimes called *cabletext*. Cable can also use a subcarrier to emulate teletext, though teletext normally goes out over the air via television station subcarriers (§7.6). Cabletext services can be automated to convey a continuous cycle of alphanumeric (letter and number) displays. Some cable systems have *frame-store* channels for continuously reporting news or weather. Specialized program suppliers feed slow-scan television pictures by satellite subcarrier or telephone wire to the cable systems' headends. It takes ten seconds to build up a single slow-scan frame (page); while the consumer reads one frame another one is building up for transmission from the frame-store memory.

Videotex   European telephone authorities developed the two-way text-and-graphics medium called *videotex* as a means of deriving more income from existing wire networks. Videotex is a hybrid service melding wire with print communication, just as teletext marries broadcasting with print. Interactive cable systems can employ videotex, but so far it has more often been supplied via telephone lines.

At videotex origination centers, computers loaded with many "pages" of textual and graphic material send specific pages on request to subscribers, who can use their terminals to call up desired pages by number or subject matter. The pages can be displayed on a regular television set or on a home computer screen. Since videotex has full access to its wire channel, it is not as limited as teletext in the number of pages it can handle; moreover, the interactive feature of videotex has the potential for enabling users to access many different data bases. In some systems, videotex subscribers can use the return circuit only to request pages but also to conduct business such as banking and shopping (Exhibit 4.8).

Summary

• Broadcasting stations function as local delivery mechanisms, highly dependent on storage and distribution technologies for syndication of mass-appeal programming. These technologies include disc and tape recording, computer memories, terrestrial relays, and space relays. All of these technologies are increasingly moving away from analogue processing and into digital signal processing.

• Compact disc audio recording, which uses laser light and digital processing, represents a major advance over conventional disc and tape recording.

• Kinescope recording, the earliest means of television picture storage, gave way to recording on two-inch quadruplex magnetic tape. For portable videotape recording, professionals use smaller, slant-track formats. The latest home videocassette recorders have stereophonic sound and other advanced features. Computer-based television text and graphic production aids are stored in digital form.

• Networks use relays for program distribution, usually on a leased basis. Terrestrial distribution systems employ telephone wire (for radio), coaxial cable, and microwave relays. Optical fiber is replacing coaxial cable in heavy-traffic circuits.

• Space relays by satellites in geosynchronous orbit have advantages over terrestrial relays. Such satellites need orbital-slot allotments and separate frequency allocations for uplink and downlink legs. Cable television systems and backyard-dish owners use 6- to 15-foot receive-only antennas; 3-foot dishes suffice for direct-broadcast-satellite reception. NASA launches most U.S. satellites, either by rocket or via the space shuttle.

• Convergence of technologies produces hybrid over-the-air systems. Relay-delivery over-the-air hybrids include rebroadcasting, translators, ITFS, MDS, MMDS, teletext, and DBS.

• Cable television, a wire hybrid, uses a relay facility, coaxial cable, as a delivery mechanism. Frequent repeaters (booster amplifiers) are required to overcome attenuation in cable delivery systems. Cable operators use electronic traps, scramblers, or addressable converters to control customer access to extra-pay channels.

- Cable television employs part of the VHF spectrum in the closed environment of coaxial cable. A single cable can handle many television channels, along with audio and response channels.

- MATV, a cable system that uses master antennas, serves limited numbers of subscribers in multiple-unit dwellings. When programs are fed to such systems by satellite they are called SMATVs.

- Cable systems offer alphanumeric services such as news and weather. The textual and graphic material may derive from character generators or frame stores.

- Videotex, a two-way alphanumeric service, usually employs telephone lines to deliver pages to home television receivers or computers. Customers can send return messages over the same lines.

PART 3

Economics

Broadcasting and other electronic media in America are, first and foremost, businesses. As we see here, the electronic media business is different from other business enterprises in many ways. We have already said a good deal about the development of broadcasting (Part 1), and explained how its structure is defined to some degree by the physical laws of nature (Part 2). Here we look more closely at how the industry is organized and financially supported. We begin in Chapter 8 with a description of the basic entities of electronic mass media: stations, systems, and networks. Chapter 9 then details the major fuel that supports the system: advertiser purchase of time on broadcast and cable facilities. Finally, in Chapter 10, we review the economics of electronic media, focusing on financial support other than advertising, investment in and ownership of electronic media properties, and the long-controversial topic of how best to fund public broadcasting.

CHAPTER 8

Stations, Systems, and Networks

The business of broadcasting and cable is conducted by means of a complex array of structures and relationships. Stations, networks, and systems operate in much the same way as other businesses, performing many of the same basic functions but with their own unique concerns. Each entity strives for success in a paradoxical world of both intense competition and profound interdependence.

8.1 The Commercial Broadcast Station

In the United States, a commercial broadcast station (the traditional radio or television station with which most of us are most familiar) might be formally defined as an entity (individual, partnership, corporation, or nonfederal governmental authority) that:

- is licensed by the federal government to organize and schedule programs for a specific community in accordance with an approved plan.
- transmits those programs over the air using designated radio facilities in accordance with specified standards.

- is permitted to carry commercial messages, promoting the products or services of profit-making organizations, for which the station receives compensation.

Although individual owners may legally control more than one station, every station is licensed separately to serve a specific community. Moreover, each license encompasses both transmission and programming functions. A station therefore normally combines four facilities: business offices, studios, transmitter, and transmitting antenna. Often the offices and studios are located separately from the transmitter and antenna, because each may work best in a different environment, but all come under common ownership (although in a few cases transmission facilities are leased).

Station Organization Broadcasting stations vary enormously, conforming to no standardized table of organization. Nevertheless, all stations need to perform four basic functions: (1) general and administrative, (2) technical, (3) programming, and (4) sales. These functions are so basic that they are performed at noncommercial as well as at commercial stations, though in the former the money-gathering function is called development instead of sales.

Exhibit 8.1 shows some of the subordinate functions that fall under the four main headings. References to contractual services in the chart are reminders of the extent to which stations depend upon syndication in its various forms (Chapter 13). Not only are program materials obtainable from external sources but so too is the expertise of consultants on problems of finance, management, programming, promotion, sales, and technical operations. Over a thousand firms offer such program and consulting services. But regardless of whether accomplished internally or with outside assistance, the following functions are performed by all radio and television stations:

1. *General and administrative* functions include the services that any business needs to provide an appropriate working environment. Services of a specialized nature peculiar to broadcasting are most likely to be obtained by contract with external organizations such as engineering-consultant firms and program syndicators. For a network affiliate, the main such external contract is with its network.

Broadcasters are untiring joiners. The timely nature of their work requires keeping constantly up-to-date with new developments. Management is likely to join trade associations such as the National Association of Broadcasters, the Television Bureau of Advertising, and the Radio Advertising Bureau. There are specialized station associations for independent television, UHF, and state networks, and for farm, religious, and Spanish-language broadcasters. Individuals can join associations of engineers, program executives, promotion specialists, pioneer broadcasters, and women broadcasters.

2. *Technical* functions center on transmitter operation, which has been subject to strict FCC rules — though some of these are now being relaxed. Technical operations are headed by a station's chief engineer. In the smallest stations the chief engineer may be the only staff member with technical expertise, but in most cases he or she supervises a staff of operational and maintenance personnel. Chief engineers at large television stations spend most of their time on administration and on keeping up with the rapidly developing technology of the electronic media.

3. *Programming* functions divide into planning and implementation phases. Major program planning decisions usually evolve from interplay among the heads of programming, sales, and management. Because in most cases relatively little programming is locally produced, a major role of the program department is the selection and scheduling of prerecorded material — music, in the case of radio stations, and syndicated series on film or tape or by satellite, in the case of television. Implementation of program decisions is the role of *production*, which has the day-to-day task of putting the programming on the air.

News, although a form of programming, is usually treated as a separate department, with its own head, reporting directly to top management. This separation from entertainment programming arises because of the timely nature of news and the special responsibilities it imposes on management. The news department is usually also in charge of station editorials and public-affairs programming.

4. *Sales* departments have their own staff members for selling time to local advertisers, but to reach regional and national advertisers most stations contract with a national sales firm to represent them in out-of-state centers of business. A network affiliate benefits from a third sales force, its network.

The sales operation and its coordination with programming require the processing of a vast quantity of detail, which is performed by

Exhibit 8.1   Station Functional Organization

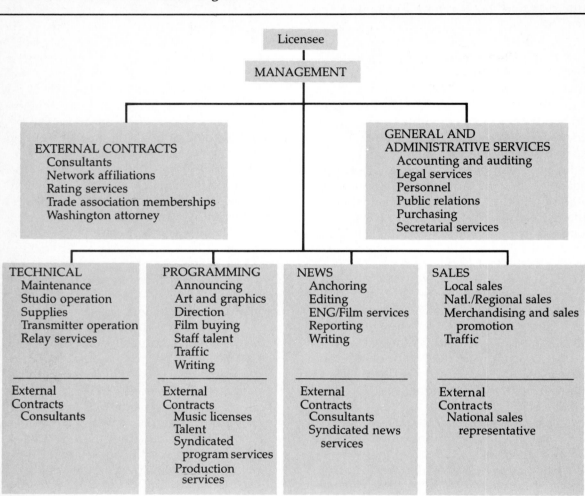

The chart does not represent any particular station but rather depicts major functions usually performed by all stations. In smaller operations, several functions are often carried out by a single employee. Stations also vary widely as to the types and the extent of the services they obtain under contract from outside sources.

the *traffic* department. The traffic department prepares the daily *program pre-log* (or, at most stations, simply *program log*), which schedules facilities, personnel, programs, and announcements. As the broadcast day progresses, operators in the station's control room make entries on the pre-log to record when the scheduled events actually take place; this function is called "keeping" the log. At the end of the day, the official program log — actually the pre-log, with any schedule changes that have occurred incorporated — is completed. Traffic personnel make sure that commercial contracts are fulfilled and that schedules are stopped and started on time; they also arrange for *make-goods* of commercials that are missed or technically inadequate. In addition, the traffic department maintains a list of *availabilities*, which informs sales personnel of commercial openings in the schedule as they become available for advertisers. Traffic personnel usually fill unsold openings with public-service or promotional announcements. At many stations, computers handle much of the complex work of the traffic department, including producing the program pre-log, and, in some control rooms, computers keep the log as well.

Low-Power Television   Low-power television (LPTV) stations operate at substantially lower power than traditional stations,* and consequently their geographical coverage area is much smaller, only about 12 to 15 miles in radius. Some LPTV owners elect to organize and operate their stations in traditional fashion, though with fewer employees. Others serve simply as translators, retransmitting the signal of a full-power station (§7.6). Others may affiliate with specialized low-power networks, and still others may belong to a commonly owned group of LPTV stations all of which carry the same programming simultaneously — perhaps distributed by satellite. Only at a station operating as a traditional television facility is it likely that there would be a full-time staff whose duties are limited solely to that station.

An LPTV station's role determines its organization. If it operates as a competitor to other stations in its market, or if it is a "mother" station, providing services for its

satellite or retransmitting stations, it is usually structured along traditional lines. If it operates simply as a translator, its entire staff might consist of a single, outside contract engineer who maintains the station's technical facilities.

Group Ownership   As do other enterprises, broadcasting businesses benefit from "economies of scale." Ownership of several stations enables a company to buy programs, supplies, and equipment in bulk; to spread the cost of using consultants across several stations; to better use and promote employees through transfer; and more generally to share experiences and new ideas.

Were it not for legal constraints, large chains of commonly owned stations would doubtless have evolved, just as in the newspaper business. For reasons of public policy, however, individual broadcast ownership is limited by regulation to a maximum of 12 AM, 12 FM, and 12 television stations (§17.7). Even with such limitations, group owners have "traded up" — that is, they have sold stations in smaller markets and bought in larger cities in order to increase the economic potential of their groups by increasing the size of the audience.

There are over 450 commonly owned station groups, each consisting of three or more radio stations and/or two or more television stations (licensees of single AM/FM or AM/FM/TV combinations are not considered group owners). Most of the groups consist of three to five small stations, but a few, such as the network-*owned-and-operated (O&O)* groups, are very powerful combinations. However, excluding the O&O groups, common ownership does not necessarily mean that all members of a group are affiliated with the same network.

Television network O&O groups serve the networks in several ways: (1) O&Os are extremely profitable, each group reaching approximately 20 percent of the nation's television households and providing over a third

---

*LPTV stations operate at 10-watt maximums on VHF frequencies, 1000 watts for UHF. Full-power stations, on the other hand, may at times reach as high as 316,000 watts on VHF and 5 million watts on UHF.

of network revenue; (2) they give the networks their own prestigious outlets in major markets; and (3) like other powerful groups, O&O stations benefit from economies of scale in dealing with suppliers.

Networks administer their O&O groups separately from their network operations. Each O&O station is headed by a vice president who, as general manager, has a good deal of autonomy in operating the station. This ensures compliance with the FCC requirement that each station must serve its own community of license. Independence is sufficiently real to enable the general managers of O&O stations to reject network programs that they judge would be contrary to the interests of their local communities, a power rarely but occasionally exercised.

Among the best known of the large nonnetwork group owners, each with several radio and television stations, are Cox Broadcasting, Taft Broadcasting, and Westinghouse Broadcasting (known as Group W). Westinghouse, noteworthy for leading attacks on what it regards as network encroachments on affiliates, was responsible for initially proposing the prime-time access rule (§13.2).

Group W also led in efforts to use the leverage of group ownership to produce local programs. In 1976, one member of the group, KPIX-TV in San Francisco, started a locally produced magazine program called *Evening*, designed especially for access-time scheduling. Group W stations in four other major cities adopted the format, with each station contributing its own local segments (many of which were shared with the other stations) to make up a composite magazine and each station having its own host-and-hostess team. In this way production costs and creative demands were spread over several stations rather than concentrated in one. *Evening* was so successful that in 1978 Group W began syndicating the series to stations outside its own

group, but on a *cooperative* rather than one-way basis. Each purchaser agreed to contribute its own locally produced segments to the show, rechristened *PM Magazine*, as well as to use segments from other cooperating stations. By the early 1980s *PM Magazine* had become one of the most successful programs in television syndication.

8.2 Commercial Broadcast Networks and Affiliates

Two or more stations interconnected by some means of relay (wire, cable, terrestrial microwave, satellite) so as to enable simultaneous broadcasting of the same program constitute a minimal network in the legal sense. In the early years of radio, networks provided local stations with hours of soap operas, dramas, comedies, and newscasts. By the 1950s, radio had succumbed to television's inroads, and network offerings were largely limited to sports and other special events and to newscasts and other short-form programs. Radio networks continue today (§12.8) but have been joined by radio syndicators in providing programming to local stations (§13.9). Like television networks, radio networks usually provide programs to their affiliates free in exchange for the stations' agreement to carry network commercials, and even *pay* network compensation to some stations in large markets.

In addition to the major national television networks there are over a hundred smaller networks. These are mostly part-time or occasional hookups, usually designed to share programs within a region or single state. Some have common program orientation, such as religion (the CBN Cable Network), language (the Spanish International Network), or sports (Hughes). Those formed for a limited time or time or special purpose are often referred to as *ad hoc* networks.

Some station groups (such as Tribune) and some program syndicators (such as LBS Entertainment and SFM) have established limited networks for special programs and feature films or for specific parts of the broadcast day. Our concern here, however, is with the national *full-service television networks*.* And because networks contribute only about 5 percent of radio's total revenue, our interest lies with the three major commercial television networks, ABC, CBS, and NBC, which generate over 50 percent of commercial television's total revenue.

Network Organization Like stations, networks vary in their organizational structure, yet each must fulfill the same four basic functions as stations: administration, programming, engineering, and sales. Networks enjoy the luxury of a much higher degree of specialization than do stations. NBC, for example, has separate units, each with its own president, for entertainment, news, sports, and the television network (NBC's O&O stations division makes do with an executive vice president).

The networks are notorious for appointing droves of vice presidents. NBC, for example, has well over a hundred. In NBC sales there are vice presidents for the central, eastern, and western regions, and even one just for Detroit;

other vice presidents for sales concentrate on sports, daytime, and special programs. In NBC Television's Entertainment Division, vice presidents supervise units specializing in children's programs, daytime programs, movies, series, and miniseries; others head story, drama, and comedy development units.

Distinctive network responsibilities include arranging the relay facilities that deliver programs to stations and maintaining good relations with the affiliates. NBC's Affiliate Relations Department keeps six vice presidents busy. In addition, separate advisory boards representing NBC's radio and television affiliates help maintain the working relationship. Every spring each television network organizes a plush convention for its affiliated stations, at which it shows pilots of new shows and unveils program plans for the coming season. These efforts at building affiliate morale and creating an atmosphere of loyalty are vital to the networks' long-term success.

Affiliation vs. Independence About three-fourths of all commercial television stations are affiliates of a major network. Most are *primary affiliates*, serving as the sole affiliate of ABC, CBS, or NBC in their markets. *Secondary affiliates* share affiliation with more than one network. For example, Scottsbluff, Nebraska, has only two stations, one a primary affiliate of CBS and a secondary affiliate of ABC, the other a primary affiliate of NBC. A few markets have only a single station. Affiliates in Twin Falls, Idaho, and Presque Isle, Maine, for example, have the unusual privilege of picking and choosing programs from all three networks. Each of the three networks has over two hundred affiliates through which it can reach virtually all the television homes in the United States.

Affiliation does not mean that a network owns or operates its affiliates. ABC, CBS, and NBC do, of course, own radio and television

---

*The FCC uses varying definitions of *network* depending on the context. What we are calling a full-service network is referred to by the FCC in its rules dealing with television affiliation agreements as "a national organization distributing programs for a substantial part of each broadcast day to television stations in all parts of the United States, generally via interconnection facilities"; and in its rules dealing with the prime-time access rule as an entity "which offers an interconnected program service on a regular basis for 15 or more hours per week to at least 25 affiliated television licensees in 10 or more states" (47 CFR 73.658).

stations. But, to their hundreds of other affiliates, affiliation is a contractual relationship whereby the network agrees to offer its programming to the affiliate before offering it to another station in the same market. The station may agree to carry each offered program, may decline to carry it, or may offer to carry it at a time other than the time of network origination, an arrangement to which the network may or may not agree. In most cases, networks pay affiliates for each program carried.

Networks must have affiliates in order to reach an audience. In exchange, a broadcasting network offers five basic services to affiliated stations: (1) a structured *program service*; (2) a means of *program distribution* so that the service can be received by all affiliates at the same time; (3) an *advertising environment* appealing to local advertisers; (4) *monetary compensation* to the stations based on audience size; and (5) a *sales organization* that finds national advertisers to purchase part of the affiliates' commercial time.

Nearly three hundred stations, most of them UHF, are *independents*, meaning they have affiliation with none of the three major networks, though they may affiliate with smaller networks. For years, most independent stations had an economic struggle. They were unable to compete successfully with the network affiliates in attracting comparable audiences. As a group they lost money until 1975, when they first reported a small profit.

Though independents still have not reached parity with affiliates, they have dramatically improved their lot in recent years. During the 1977–1978 television season, independent stations attracted a total of only 9 percent of the viewing audience. By the 1985–1986 season that proportion had reached 21 percent. With audience growth came markedly improved economics: independents grew from a $20 million loss in 1970 to a $200 million profit in 1983.

Several factors influenced this increase in audience appeal and profitability. Independents benefited from the introduction of the *prime-time access rule* (PTAR) in 1971. The rule forbids affiliates in the top fifty markets from clearing more than three prime-time hours for network entertainment (for a more detailed discussion of how this works see §13.2). PTAR weakened network affiliates' early ("fringe") prime-time programming (7:00 P.M.–8:00 P.M. Eastern and Pacific time), giving independents a chance to counter-program effectively with off-network syndicated programs denied the affiliates by PTAR. Though PTAR gave independents a significant advantage, most of their audience increases have come about in other time periods. Two developments account for this: first, the increased willingness by many independents to compete with affiliates for expensive syndicated program series; second, expanded coverage by independents of live sporting events, made possible by satellite distribution.

Also helpful was the establishment of the Association of Independent Television Stations (INTV) in 1972. In 1977 INTV sponsored an Arbitron study that provided much-needed favorable evidence about the size and character of the independent stations' audience and that helped to overcome the negative image of independents common in the minds of advertising-agency time buyers. In addition, cable television assisted independent stations by carrying their programming. This made the signals of otherwise weaker UHF stations seem equal in the eyes of the cable viewer to the normally more powerful VHF affiliates.

Some independents have enhanced their viability by specializing in Spanish or religious programming. Some have even tried all-music-video formats. But despite gains by independents in audience size and in profits, network affiliates continue to dominate television viewing hours and advertising revenue.

Exhibit 8.2   Commercial Television Networks and Organizations

In addition to those for the three major, commercial television networks, other industry logotypes (or logos) include those for the National Association of Broadcasters, the National Association of Television Program Executives, the Association of Independent Television Stations, and the Television Bureau of Advertising.

Source: Logos courtesy of their respective organizations.

Affiliation with a national network remains one of the most valuable assets a television station can have.

Network-Affiliate Contract   The economic link between a television network and an affiliate is formalized in an *affiliation contract*, by law renewable every two years. At the heart of the contract is the clause that defines the terms on which the network will pay the station in return for the right to use the station's time. Called *network compensation*, this payment represents in effect a discount price conceded by the affiliate in consideration of the network's services in obtaining and promoting programs, selling advertising, and relaying both to the station.

Each television network uses a slightly different formula for calculating compensation, but they all arrive at about the same rate of payment. The contract assigns a hypothetical base value to an hour of each affiliate's time. This rate varies from station to station, reflecting differences in market size, station popularity, and other factors. Each of the New York City flagship stations of the three networks is valued at approximately $10,000 per hour. Rates go as low as $50, and some affiliates receive no compensation at all.

The actual amount a network pays for each network program an affiliate carries is determined by applying a rather complex formula to the station's base hourly rate. That formula takes into account (1) the fraction of an hour occupied by the program, (2) the number of commercials sold by the network within the program (compared to the total commercial time available for sale), and (3) the time of day the program airs. The last factor reflects the fact that audience potential varies drastically from one time of day to another. NBC, for example, pays as little as 4.5 percent of the base rate for some late-night programming, but 30 percent for programs carried between 6 P.M. and 11 P.M. On the average, network compensation to affiliates — the amount in dollars actually received by the stations — equals only about 15 percent of their theoretical network hourly base rates. The three networks combined pay their affiliates about $400 million a year to broadcast their programs.

Some programs require special compensation adjustments. For example, NBC pays no direct compensation for the two-hour early-morning *Today* program. Instead, affiliates sell advertising in the first and third half-hours, retaining all the income; the network in turn keeps all the income from sales that it makes in the second and fourth half-hours.

On the average, network compensation represents about 9 percent of the gross revenues of network-affiliated stations. But stations measure the value of affiliation not only in terms of compensation but also in terms of the audiences that network programs attract. Affiliates profit spectacularly from the sale of spots during the ninety seconds or so the network leaves open for affiliate station breaks in each prime-time hour of network program-

ming and during the seven or eight minutes made available at other times. And audiences for the stations' own programming (whether locally produced or syndicated) are of course much enhanced by the attraction of popular and widely promoted network programs.

Regulation of Network-Affiliate Contracts

Ever since the late 1930s, the FCC has been busy trying to counteract the inevitable tendency, of first radio, then television, networks to exert what the government perceived as undue control over affiliates, programming, and other aspects of the industry. Regulation of the business relationships between networks and their affiliates began in the radio era (§3.5) and was later extended to television. Unable to control networks directly (because networks are not licensed), the FCC exercises control indirectly through rules governing the affiliation contract.

The rules forbid stations from entering into contracts with networks that would restrict affiliates' freedom of action in several areas, the most critical of which are:

1. *Exclusivity.* A network contract may not include *exclusivity rules* aimed at preventing an affiliate from accepting programs from other networks; nor may an affiliate prevent its network from offering rejected programs to other stations in its market. In practice, independent stations often enter into agreements with networks to have first call on programs that affiliates in their markets reject.

2. *Length of affiliation contract.* Affiliation agreements must be renewed every two years and must bind the two parties equally (previously the radio networks had tied up affiliates for five years but themselves for only one).

3. *Network ownership.* A network may not own two or more networks covering the same territory (aimed at the NBC Red-Blue network combination).

4. *Program rejection*. A network may not coerce an affiliate in any way to ensure clearance of time for its programs. The allowable reasons for rejection are broad: "unsatisfactory or unsuitable"; "contrary to the public interest"; time needed for another program "of outstanding local or national importance." In effect, the affiliate has complete freedom of choice.

5. *Rate control*. A network may not influence an affiliate's nonnetwork advertising rates (at one time the radio networks tried to ensure that network advertising would be more attractive to national advertisers than spot advertising arranged by direct contracts with stations).

6. *Sales representation*. A network may not function as national spot (nonnetwork) sales representative for any of its affiliates other than its O&O stations.

In 1977, recognizing that the original chain broadcasting rules no longer had much relevance to modern radio networks, the FCC freed the radio networks from most of the old rules,* with the main exception of the exclusivity rule. At the same time, the commission broadened the definition of *radio network* to include the audio news services offered on an interconnected basis by news agencies (63 FCC 2d 674, 1977). While giving radio networks more freedom, however, the FCC retained its control over television networks and imposed still more restrictions on them (such as the prime-time access rule), again through regulation of the network-affiliate agreement.

Network-Affiliate Relations Networks and their affiliates experience a somewhat un-

---

*Radio networks may now offer more than one service in the same market. ABC, for example, offers six different news services — Information, Entertainment, Contemporary, Direction, Rock, and FM — targeted to different demographic groups, plus Talk Radio.

easy, paradoxical sharing of power, complicated by political and economic factors too subtle for contracts to define. In one sense the networks have the upper hand. Affiliation is vitally important to the success of some television stations. Although the law states that a network may not coerce stations into accepting programs, the threat of nonrenewal of network contracts, though rarely carried out, is an ever-present reality. When CBS ended its 23-year relationship with KXLY-TV in Spokane in 1976 because the station repeatedly rejected CBS programs and frequently delayed broadcast of accepted programs, the decision came as a shock to most in the industry.

On the other hand, without the voluntary compliance of affiliates, a television network amounts to nothing but a group-owner of a few stations instead of the main source of programming for two hundred stations. In that sense affiliates have the upper hand, and woe to the network that fails to please them. The defections from other networks that occurred when ABC forged into the ratings lead in the late 1970s showed what could happen. In a three-year period ABC not only equaled or topped its rivals in audience size, it also met them in number of affiliates by picking up more than thirty stations.

Not all affiliation switches result from programming considerations, however. A network may want to have its programming carried by a stronger station in a particular market. ABC, for example, was able in the early 1980s to move from WJKS-TV, a UHF station in Jacksonville, Florida, to WLTV-TV, a VHF station in the same city. Much of ABC's success in recent years in gaining affiliates may be credited to its offering of substantially higher compensation, rather than to affiliates' dissatisfaction with network program performance.

Audience reaction to affiliation changes is not always predictable. In 1982, for example, when NBC was experiencing some of the lowest ratings in its history, it picked up KCBJ-TV, a UHF station in Columbia-Jefferson City, Missouri, after ABC dropped it in favor of a VHF station, KOMU-TV. The unexpected result in the first rating period following the switch was that the new NBC affiliate increased its share of prime-time audience in that market by a surprising 22 percent.

The fulcrum of the balance of the complex relationships between networks and their affiliates is the act of *clearance*. This is the voluntary agreement by an affiliate to keep clear in its program schedule the time needed to run network programs. But even after an affiliate has cleared time for a network series, it still has the right to *preempt* the time of scheduled episodes and to substitute programs from other sources.

Networks rely on affiliates not only to carry their programs, but to carry them *as scheduled*. Delayed broadcasts by affiliates reduce a network's immediate audience for the delayed programs, in consequence reducing their national ratings. Moreover, networks need simultaneous coverage throughout the country in order to get the maximum benefit from their efforts at promoting and advertising their program offerings. These efforts are vitally important to network success.

In practice, affiliates accept about 90 percent of all programs offered by their networks, most of them on faith. Stations feel no need to preview all network offerings, despite the fact that they as licensees, not the networks, have the ultimate legal responsibility for programs. Because most television programs come in series, however, their general tone is already well known, so that the acceptability of future episodes can usually be taken for granted. Questionable or controversial programs can be screened in advance for affiliates, but previewing is not a universal practice.

Thus, realistically, affiliates have little or no influence over the *day-to-day* programming decisions of their networks. In the long run, however, they do exert a powerful influence. Network programming strategists take very seriously the feedback that comes from their affiliates. It comes to them from the affiliate-relations departments, station advisory boards, annual affiliate conventions, and individual contacts with managers and owners, reinforced by the statistics of affiliate refusals.

An affiliate might fail to clear time or preempt already cleared time for several reasons. Often a station simply wants to increase the amount of commercial time available for local sale beyond that which is available within network programs. To accomplish this, the station preempts one or more network programs and instead carries a syndicated program or a movie. Such preemption occurs especially during the year-end holiday period, when advertiser demand is highest. Sometimes stations opt to skip low-rated network programs in favor of syndicated materials, to keep audiences from flowing to competing stations. At other times affiliates want to protect their local audiences from what they regard as morally or politically offensive network offerings. Less frequently, affiliates take the risk of offending their networks and losing audience members for the sake of being able to schedule locally produced programs in desirable time normally cleared for their network.

One study of affiliate preemptions suggested that the dominating motive is to increase sales: more than half the replacement programs in a sample month of preemptions were either syndicated shows (35 percent) or movies (21 percent). Sports replacements ranked third (16 percent). Local programs were at the bottom of the list, representing only 9 percent of the replacements for network programs (Osborn, et al., 1979).

Low-rated network programs traditionally consist, almost by definition, of public-affairs and other nonentertainment offerings, which therefore are the ones most often denied clearance. One of the reasons ABC's evening news used to run such a poor third to CBS and NBC news in the 1960s and early 1970s was that over a score of ABC's major affiliates failed to clear time for it, which in turn guaranteed continued low ratings by denying ABC's news access to some 14 percent of the network's potential audience. CBS could persuade less than half its affiliates to clear time even for the highly respected, though often controversial, news documentaries of Edward R. Murrow (see Box, page 81).

A new temptation for affiliates to preempt network time emerged in the 1970s and grew stronger in the 1980s with the development of first-run syndication series designed to compete with networks for prime time (§13.4). For example, the twenty-five major affiliates that preempted network time to run the presponsored miniseries *Edward the King* received about 25 percent more payment for the time than they would have from their networks. CBS lost time worth $5 million or more because of defections by 19 affiliates to carry this series (Bergreen, 1979).

The foregoing description of the network-affiliate relationship suggests that the image of network programmers as all-powerful dictators, imposing their will on helpless affiliates, is a myth. Far from being helpless, affiliates in the final analysis have the upper hand when they mobilize their collective strength. It might be argued that in refusing to carry certain network programs, station licensees are doing no more than their undoubted duty to be responsible to their local audiences. This argument carries little conviction, however, when the pattern of nonclearance indicates that the real motive is money. Responding to

the claim that networks shift the blame for the cancellation of high-quality programs to the audience, Les Brown suggested that the real culprit is "the unwillingness of affiliates to clear for them; it was not that the shows were rejected by *people* but that they were *prerejected* by stations" (1971: 359, emphasis added).

8.3 Noncommercial Broadcasting

The most obvious difference between commercial and noncommercial broadcast stations is suggested by the nomenclature. The former do and the latter do not carry commercial messages (in the traditional sense, at least) that advertise the products or services of profit-making organizations, for which the station receives compensation. Thus, whereas the noncommercial station must address three of the same needs as the commercial station — general and administrative, technical, and programming — such is not the case with the fourth, sales. But even though noncommercial-station operators are not concerned with profit, they still are very much concerned with money. The cost of building and operating radio and television stations must somehow be met. The term most commonly used to identify the noncommercial fund-raising functions analogous to sales in the commercial structure is *development*.

But there are other differences. The relationship between noncommercial affiliates and their networks differs dramatically from the commercial pattern. The structure of ownership and control of noncommercial stations also differs. There are four distinct types of noncommercial television station ownership, and two very different classes of public radio stations. And their priorities not only differ from one to another but also often conflict.

Television Stations   The four broad categories of public television stations are: (1) state- or municipal-controlled stations, (2) college and university stations, (3) public school system stations, and (4) community stations.

More than 120 stations (about 41 percent of the total) fall under state or municipal control, and many of these are organized into state-operated networks. One city, New York, owns and operates a station (WNYC-TV) as a municipal service. Among the statewide networks, typically one station, often located in the state capital, does most of the programming; the other stations serve, in effect, as auxiliary transmitters of that signal. Alabama began what became a network of nine stations in 1955, and Georgia, Kentucky, Mississippi, Nebraska, South Carolina, and others soon followed its example. In some states, such as Pennsylvania, an informal state network exists, as the stations are actually licensed to different (usually local) groups.

Over seventy-five public television facilities (about 26 percent) are licensed to institutions of higher learning, nearly all of which are publicly supported. These were among the earliest public television stations on the air. They usually have close ties to college curricula and often to previously established university educational radio stations (the University of Wisconsin's WHA-TV on Channel 21 in Madison, for example, went on the air in 1954, building on four decades of radio experience). University stations, often heavily staffed by students or others on internships, become training grounds in addition to offering program services. College stations, although usually supported by state taxes, have an intervening layer of university administration between station decisions and the funding process. Most universities respect academic freedom and do not directly meddle in station affairs. One striking exception, however, was the reaction of the University of Houston to the Public Broadcasting Service program *Death of a Princess*, a 1980 documentary about the execution for adultery of an Arabian princess and her commoner lover. The university's vice president for public information canceled a scheduled telecast of the program on the university's public television station, despite the objection of station management. When viewers challenged the action, an appellate court upheld the university's decision and found no violation of viewers' First Amendment rights. The danger of supervisors remaining too remote, however, is illustrated by the case of the University of Pennsylvania's WXPN-FM in Philadelphia, for years operated mainly by and for students, with little supervision. When the FCC investigated complaints and discovered lewd and explicit language on call-in talk shows, as well as lack of licensee control, it ordered WXPN off the air. Only on appeal did the university manage to retain the license, promising far stricter control of programming.

Stations operated by, or as auxiliaries of, local school systems or school boards constitute by far the smallest category of public television broadcasters (about 5 percent). The prime role of such operations is naturally the development of in-school instructional programs, many of them produced by and for the school system. In recent years, several such stations have left the air (or have been transferred to other licensees) as school board budgets have become tighter.

Organizations made up of representatives from various community groups, including schools, colleges, art and cultural organizations, and the like, control about 29 percent of public TV stations. These nonprofit operations do not usually receive direct tax support; rather, they operate on foundation, business, and listener funding.

These four differing ownership structures strongly influence public television funding and programming. They also affect each station's basic philosophical view of the role public broadcasting should play. The school- and university-run stations have the strongest educational/instructional approach, as one might expect, whereas the community stations are most dedicated to providing a broad mix of cultural, entertainment, and educational programs for a general audience. (For details on the influences of funding on public broadcasting, see §10.6.)

Radio Stations   Technically, public radio licensees fall into the same categories as public television stations, with universities and schools holding about 60 percent, community groups about 30 percent, and states and municipalities about 10 percent of all "CPB-qualified" licensees. But the phrase "CPB-qualified" is the most important classification factor in radio, breaking the better than 1,100 noncommercial radio stations into a fairly small "have" class and a much larger "have not" group.

The Corporation for Public Broadcasting (CPB) decided to select a cadre of professionally run full-service radio stations on which to build a centralized system, using National Public Radio (NPR) as a core service. Thus arose a means of separating potentially stronger stations from hundreds of small operations. To be CPB-qualified, radio stations must meet minimal standards: FM power of at least 3,000 watts; at least one production studio and a separate control room; at least five full-time employees; an operational schedule of 18 hours per day; a total operating budget of at least $80,000 a year; and some general strictures concerning local and generalized public-service programs. In 1985 only about 275 stations met or exceeded those standards and thus qualified for CPB grants and affiliation with NPR. The other 900-plus stations generally fell outside the CPB-NPR axis and provided strictly local and often very limited service.

A major stumbling block to NPR's announced intention to expand the number of CPB-qualified stations in the 1980s results from an earlier FCC decision to license 10-watt noncommercial FM stations. Several hundred of these very low power stations were on the air by the 1970s, taking up frequency space and providing "electronic sandboxes" rather than serious broadcast training or service. With the expansion of demand for public radio service, the FCC in 1978 began to reverse its course, ordering all 10-watt stations either to raise their power to a minimum of 100 watts or to assume a secondary status on a commercial frequency, with the possibility of having to give way to an applicant for full-power service. By 1985 about half of these stations had applied to the FCC for power increases, about 25 percent had elected to move outside the noncommercial frequencies, and the status of the remaining stations awaited resolution.

In 1985 NPR established a new membership class for stations serving coverage areas with less than 150,000 population. To qualify, a station must have an annual gross income of $50,000; have the ability to receive NPR programming by satellite; and have at least one, but not more than four, full-time staff persons. These stations are eligible to receive NPR programming for which they contribute funds, but are not eligible for CPB grants, nor can they vote in the NPR membership organization.

But the "two-class" system of public radio stations persists. Funding grants go to the qualified stations, while the remaining stations operate in a kind of never-never land, not quite "public" but certainly not commercial. Whereas virtually all public television station licensees have a part and often a voice in PBS decisions, the majority of public radio stations are not even part of the system, and do not have a say in its development. This exclusive club atmosphere naturally helps to assure

NPR's dominance over affiliates, with a minimum of the frictions that have afflicted public television.

The Corporation for Public Broadcasting

Section 396(g) of the Public Broadcasting Act of 1967 (47 USC 396–398), which amended the Communications Act of 1934 and created the Corporation for Public Broadcasting, lists the following among the purposes and activities of the corporation:

- Facilitating "full development of educational broadcasting in which programs of high quality, obtained from diverse sources, will be made available to noncommercial educational television or radio broadcast stations, with strict adherence to objectivity and balance in all programs or series of programs of a controversial nature."
- Assisting in setting up network interconnection so that all stations "that wish to may broadcast the programs at times chosen by the stations." Common carriers are authorized to give free service or reduced rates to such networks, subject to FCC approval.
- Carrying out its work "in ways that will most effectively assure the maximum freedom . . . from interference with or control of program content or other activities."
- Making contracts and grants for production of programs.
- Establishing and maintaining a library and archives.
- Encouraging development of new public broadcasting stations.
- Conducting research and training.

In carrying out these functions, the corporation dispenses federal funds for public broadcasting, but may not own or operate any broadcast facilities itself — an important factor in its creation of two other public broadcasting entities: the Public Broadcasting Service and National Public Radio (§4.6).

The PBS-Affiliate Relationship

In its operational structure the Public Broadcasting Service (PBS) differs sharply from commercial network television. Affiliates contract with PBS to pay varying amounts of dues according to each affiliate's overall budget and market size. Rather than being paid by the network for their time, as is the case in the commercial system, public television stations pay the network for the programs.

Unlike the commercial networks, PBS has no program production of its own. Rather, it provides a delivery service for programming produced by others and largely selected by the affiliate stations. This occurs through a funding mechanism called the Station Program Cooperative (SPC). PBS offers affiliates a list of proposed programs for the coming season. Some are fully paid for by national underwriters, some are only partially funded, and some lack funding of any kind. The partially funded and unfunded programs will be carried by PBS only if sufficient stations "vote" for those programs in a series of rounds in which stations commit their programming dollars. Program cost is perhaps the major factor stations consider when choosing partially funded and unfunded programs.

An ancillary but by no means insignificant service provided by PBS, at additional cost to those stations using it, is fund-raising assistance. Through its Station Independence Program (SIP), PBS helps stations with their on-air appeals for private and corporate funds. Among other things, it gives advice on the selection of special programs to run during those campaigns that must draw the attention of the public but may sometimes irritate viewers.

National Public Radio

In 1970, CPB set up National Public Radio, both to interconnect stations (as PBS does) and to produce programs (unlike PBS). As a second Carnegie

Exhibit 8.3   Noncommercial Broadcasting Organizations

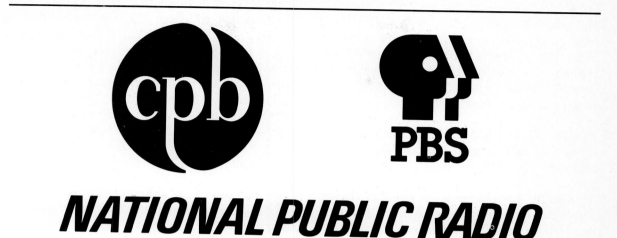

Logos for noncommercial broadcasting entities include those for the Corporation for Public Broadcasting, the Public Broadcasting Service, and National Public Radio.

Sources: Logos courtesy of their respective organizations.

Commission report (*Carnegie II*) noted:

NPR, therefore, now combines national production and distribution capability with political representation, in a way which many feel is unthinkable for television. In addition, the production activities of NPR are funded directly by CPB and are not, therefore, entirely controlled by the licensee. Unlike the situation in public television, the public radio stations have been quite willing to have national program production and distribution centralized and under the financial oversight of CPB. Public radio stations supported the creation of NPR from the beginning, and they retain control over it through its board. Sorely underfinanced, the stations have recognized the benefits of centralizing program functions. (CCFPB, 1979: 61)

NPR provides only about 20 percent of daily programming for its member stations, and members are not required to carry any NPR programs. Two additional services provided by NPR are station representation before Congress, the FCC, CPB, and others, and satellite interconnection coordination.

By 1985 the future of NPR was in doubt. Faced with a substantial deficit in 1983, the network borrowed operating funds from CPB and, through staff reductions and budget cutbacks, struggled to keep its operation alive. (See §10.6 for details of the NPR crisis.)

NPR is not, however, the only public radio network. American Public Radio (APR), founded in 1982, claimed in 1985 to be the largest distributor of public radio programming, providing more than ninety hours of programming each week to more than three hundred affiliates nationwide. In addition to distributing such series as *A Prairie Home Companion* and the broadcast season of the Los Angeles Philharmonic, APR also distributed nearly seventy-five other offerings, including an automated overnight music service.

8.4 Cable Systems and Networks

For our purposes a cable television system may be defined as an entity, franchised by a local government, that provides television programs by wire rather than over the air, on several channels simultaneously, to subscribers who pay for the service.

System Organization   By the mid-1980s there were more than 10,000 cable systems operating in the United States. Less than one percent of all systems offered fewer than 5 channels, about 35 percent offered between 6 and 12 channels, nearly 60 percent offered between 13 and 53 channels, and just under 5 percent offered 54 or more channels (some of these offered over 100). This diversity makes it nearly impossible to generalize about system organization and structure. But whether small with few subscribers or large with thousands, each system performs the same four basic functions as do broadcast stations.

1. *General and administrative* functions are much the same in cable as in radio, television, or any other business. However, the franchise agreements under which cable systems operate and the ongoing relationships with franchising authorities (§17.6) hold special concern for most cable operators. Also, rather than having an affiliation agreement with only one major television network (or at most three), cable systems often contract with many cable networks in order to feed their numerous channels. As do radio and television, the cable industry has its trade associations, the largest of which is the National Cable Television Association (NCTA).

2. *Technical* functions at cable systems differ somewhat from those at broadcast stations. First, of course, there is no transmitter. There is, however, a complex array of equipment used to receive at the headend signals from program suppliers and to send those and other signals, simultaneously, through a network of coaxial cables to homes throughout a system's service area (§7.7). Broadcast technicians finish their jobs when they have done everything possible to ensure that a good signal leaves the transmitter; they normally have no concern with the receivers at the other end of that signal. Not so with cable, which typically places in each subscribing home some sort of *converter* that provides an interface between the subscriber's receiver and the system's wired network. Because of concern for the integrity of the entire sending and receiving system, cable organizations often have *inside* and *outside plant* personnel; the first group concerns itself with equipment in the cable system's studio and headend, and the second group handles installation and service of subscriber equipment.

3. *Programming* functions at cable systems differ from those at broadcast stations, at least in scope. A radio or television station is concerned with programming a single channel. The cable system, on the other hand, programs a multitude of channels. At smaller systems, the general manager may make program decisions, usually in consultation with the director of marketing. Multiple system operators, which own more than a single system, may divide the programming function into specific areas such as satellite programming and local origination, often under the direction of a marketing vice president.

Some cable systems produce local programming, much of it on channels programmed by community or educational organizations. Although some cable companies, such as Colony Communications, headquartered in Providence, Rhode Island, have made a commitment to locally produced news, most systems have so far deferred to broadcast radio and television in this expensive and personnel-intensive area.

4. *Sales* at a cable system is better called *sales and marketing*. Though some systems do sell commercial time on some of their channels (§9.4), the marketing of the cable service to subscribers is a more important function. Monthly fees paid by subscribers represent the principal source of any cable system's revenue. These fees range from as little as $2 to $30 or more per month, depending on system rate structure, program options, and subscriber choice (§10.3). The marketing department has the task of trying to convince nonsubscribers to subscribe and subscribers not to *disconnect*. Subscriber turnover — new customers signing up for service as others cancel — is called *churn*. Cable operators calculate churn by dividing a current month's disconnects by the prior month's total subscribers and multiplying the result by 100. The rate of churn for basic services may run from as low as 5 percent per year for established systems in stable neighborhoods to over 60 percent for newer systems or those in areas with a more transient population. The average churn for pay-cable networks is about 33 percent.

Customer service representatives (CSRs) working within the marketing department have daily contact with present and potential subscribers. CSRs answer telephones eight or more hours a day, responding to complaints from subscribers and questions from potential customers. The ability of a system to handle these calls can have a profound effect on its financial success — even on whether it keeps or loses its franchise. In 1985 Boston's Office of Cable Communications cited customer service difficulties as the major reason for threatening Cablevision of Boston with fines and even with franchise revocation (*CableVision*, 4 March 1985).

System Interconnection   Individual cable systems interconnect for several reasons. First, the franchising authority may require a system to interconnect with others in a common geographical area (a county, perhaps) so that certain programs originated by one system may be carried by the others. This would be common, for example, in areas where a public school system or college produces material of interest to people throughout the area. Such an interconnection would most likely be an electronic (so-called *hard* or *true*) interconnection, whereby systems link by cable or microwave.

A second reason for interconnection is to facilitate the sale of advertising. Systems within a region may find it more efficient to sell advertisers their facilities by combining with others (§9.5) to offer coverage comparable to that of television stations in the same market. Such an arrangement might also be electronic,* or it might be *simulated* (or *soft*), with materials and information distributed among the systems but not by means of physical interconnection.

Multiple System Operators   Small systems, often serving only a few hundred subscribers in a small town, typified cable for many years. But these "mom-and-pop" outfits (commonly run as sidelines to other businesses, recalling the early days of radio) gave way in the 1960s as cable penetrated larger markets and the profit potential became apparent. The trend to ownership of more than one cable system by multiple system operators (MSOs) was caused in part by the franchising of companies to serve large urban areas, and their resultant need for very large amounts of construction capital. Small operators sold out to the MSOs, repeating the pattern seen earlier in other media. Unlike radio and televi-

---

*The cable industry's first electronic advertising interconnect, begun in 1983, was Videopath, a microwave network centered in McCook, Illinois, serving thirteen cable companies with a total of 376,000 subscribers.

sion, cable has no limit on the number of systems or subscribers that may be served by a single MSO.

In all, there are more than 180 MSOs in the United States. Exhibit 8.4 shows the top ten MSOs in number of subscribers. Impressive though these numbers may be, it should be noted that even the largest MSO serves less than 10 percent of all U.S. cable homes and less than 5 percent of all television homes. By contrast, the largest television station groups can reach more than 20 percent of all television homes.

Among the top MSOs are those owned by broadcasters (Cox, Storer), by television program producers and distributors (Viacom), by magazine and newspaper publishers (Time, Times Mirror, Newhouse), and by conglomerates (Warner Amex). Over 38 percent of all cable systems have ties with broadcast interests, almost 21 percent with program producers, and approximately 33 percent with newspapers.

Cable Networks

Cable systems carry a variety of programming, limited only by channel capacity and economic considerations. All offer the signals of local television stations, and some import the signals of other more distant stations; local programs produced by the system itself or by others occupy other channels. These services may be as many as the smaller systems can handle. But as channel capacity increases, so does the need for additional program sources. Three principal types of cable program services have developed to meet this need: (1) basic cable networks, (2) pay cable networks, and (3) superstations. As television networks do for their affiliated stations, cable program services offer benefits to their affiliated systems: basic cable networks offer structured program services, simultaneous program distribution, and, in many cases, advertising environments appealing to local

Exhibit 8.4   Top 10 MSOs

Rank	Multiple system operator	Basic cable subscribers*
1	Tele-Communications, Inc.	3,778,621
2	American Television and Communications Corp.	2,500,000
3[†]	Group W Cable	2,162,000
4	Storer Cable Communications	1,521,000
5	Cox Cable Communications	1,466,033
6	Warner Amex Cable Communications, Inc.	1,158,805
7	Continental Cablevision	1,100,000
8	Times Mirror Cable Television, Inc.	996,606
9	United Cable Television	949,000
10	Newhouse Broadcasting	927,000

*Subscriber counts are based on 1985 data.

†Sold in 1986; see p. 279.

Although there are nearly two hundred cable multiple system operators in the United States, the ten largest MSOs together serve more than 45 percent of all cable subscribers.

Source: From *CableVision*, March 3, 1986. Used by permission of International Communications, Inc.

advertisers; pay-cable networks provide the first two benefits and supply direct revenue to cable systems in the form of monthly subscription fees; superstations also offer the first two benefits and add to the cable system's package of services, potentially improving audience appeal and thus increasing subscribers. Following is a more detailed examination of each of the three principal types of cable programming services.

Basic Cable Networks   Cable systems typically include the programming of basic cable networks in the regular monthly subscription price. Most such services are *advertiser-supported* and depend on the sale of commercial time for the bulk of their revenue (§9.4). In some cases, the cable systems pay a per-subscriber fee to the network for the right to carry network programming. Such fees range from one or two cents up to about 25 cents per subscriber per month. Ad-supported networks usually make about two minutes per hour available to the cable system for sale to local advertisers. Basic cable religious networks look to viewer donations as well as advertising to meet their operating expenses. A few cable programming services pay the cable operator to carry their programming; SIN (Spanish International Network), for example, in order to ensure access to its target audience, pays cable systems 10 cents a month for each subscriber who has a Spanish surname; and each system carrying Home Shopping Network receives a percentage of all sales generated by that program service through that cable system. Exhibit 8.5 lists some of the better-known cable services.

Advertiser-supported cable networks organize along much the same lines as broadcast television networks, but they differ in a number of ways. First, they are much smaller than ABC, CBS, or NBC. Second, while they do maintain sales departments for the sale of commercial time, they must also sell themselves to cable systems. Though there is often competition among broadcast television networks for certain affiliates, in most cities enough stations exist, and network affiliation holds such value, that each network is assured of at least some outlet in almost every market. This is not the case with cable. One cable network might affiliate with several cable systems operating within the same market. Conversely, others might find that in some markets they have no outlet at all because competing networks have taken up all available channels. And some systems, even with

channels available, simply elect to carry some program services and not others. The program service's marketing department must address these problems and persuade cable systems to carry its programming.

Another way in which cable networks contrast with broadcast television networks is that the cable networks, whether ad-supported or otherwise, do not produce and present news (with the exception of the Cable Network News services and, to a lesser extent, CBN Cable Network). Avoiding the enormous costs of putting together a national news service enables cable networks to increase their profit potential.

Pay Cable Networks   Subscribers must pay a monthly fee or *premium* in addition to the fee paid for the basic cable service in order to receive pay cable networks. The amount of that fee varies from system to system and network to network but averages about $10 per month for each of the more popular networks. The cable operator consults with the program supplier to set the fee, and they split revenue on a negotiated basis, usually about 50-50.

HBO, the first pay cable network, owned by Time, Inc., began by offering commercial-free theatrical motion pictures (§4.3). It entered into movie-rights purchasing in a big way, buying the rights to hundreds of old and new Hollywood feature films, as well as short films. With its dominance of pay cable and its national circulation, HBO can all but dictate film prices to the Hollywood producers. Prices are calculated on the basis of a certain amount of money per subscriber (usually about 20 cents), plus a flat fee determined by the value of the specific film to HBO. Hollywood producers have long felt that HBO pays too little for film rights, but there is little they can do (aside from withholding films from sale), since HBO was long the only customer big enough to make such purchases.

Exhibit 8.5 Examples of Satellite-distributed Program Services

BASIC CHANNELS

	NAME, OWNER (Launch date)	MEANS OF SUPPORT	HOMES REACHED (MILLIONS)	CONTENT
(ESPN)	**Entertainment & Sports Programming Network (ESPN)** ABC Video Enterprises; Nabisco (9/79)	System pays 19¢ per subscriber; advertising	36.5	NHL hockey, college football and basketball, auto racing, boxing, golf, and tennis. Sports updates several times daily. Business news
CNN	**Cable News Network (CNN)** Turner Broadcasting (6/80)	System pays 15¢-22¢ per subscriber; advertising	33.1	Continuous hard news reporting; live coverage of breaking stories; interviews; documentaries; special features
USA NETWORK	**USA Network** Time Inc; Paramount Pictures; MCA Inc. (9/77)	System pays 7¢-10¢ per subscriber; advertising	30.6	Broad-based entertainment: prime-time sports, *Night Flight* (video art and music), news magazines, children's health and comedy shows, syndicated programming, movies, USA-produced programming
CBN CABLE NETWORK	**CBN Cable Network** Christian Broadcasting Network (4/77)	Advertising	29.7	Family programming including classic films, comedies, westerns, children's shows, game shows, inspirational shows
MTV	**Music Television (MTV)** MTV Networks Inc. (8/81)	System pays 10¢-15¢ per subscriber; advertising	27.3	On-air vee jays, rock videos, concerts, interviews, music news (Pay for exclusive rights to some premiere videos)
C·SPAN	**Cable Satellite Public Affairs Network (C-SPAN)** Nonprofit corp. of cable companies (3/79)	System pays 3¢ per subscriber	21.5	Live coverage of U.S. House of Representatives debates, congressional hearings; national call-in shows; profiles of public figures and current issues.

SUPERSTATIONS

SuperStation WTBS GREAT AMERICAN TELEVISION	**WTBS** Turner Broadcasting System, Atlanta (12/76)	System pays 10¢ per subscriber; advertising.	34.8	Network reruns, sports, movies, news, women's shows, music videos, documentaries
WGN Chicago superchannel	**WGN** The Tribune Company, Chicago (10/78)	System pays 10¢ per subscriber; advertising.	16.1	Network reruns, sports, movies, news

PAY SERVICES

	NAME, OWNER (Launch date)	SUBSCRIBERS (MILLIONS)	CONTENT
HBO	**Home Box Office** Time Inc. (9/75)	14.5	Movies, sports, family shows, made-for-pay movies, mini-series, specials
SHOWTIME	**Showtime** Viacom (7/76)	5.4	Movies; Broadway productions, music specials, made-for-pay movies, comedy and dramatic series, mini-series, family programming
cinemax	**Cinemax** HBO Inc., a subsidiary of Time Inc. (8/80)	3.3	Feature movies, comedy and music specials
THE MOVIE CHANNEL	**The Movie Channel** Viacom (1/80)	3.1	Feature films, film festivals, movie marathons
	The Disney Channel Walt Disney Productions (4/83)	2.1	Family-oriented programming including made-for-pay and Disney movies; classic cartoons. 6 A.M.-1 A.M.

Source: *Channels' Field Guide to the Electronic Media*, 1986, "A Guide: Satellite Channels," pp. 57-66.

The formation in 1978 of Showtime, which also uses satellite transponders to distribute its films and other special events, somewhat weakened HBO's bargaining power. In 1979, Viacom, the operator of Showtime, sold a half-interest in the network to the then-leading MSO, Teleprompter, providing more cable systems for the new service and more financial clout (and since 25 Teleprompter systems had been contracted to carry HBO, the loss to HBO was direct). But despite aggressive marketing, Showtime remained second to HBO.

In 1980, in part to offset the impact of Showtime, HBO began a second service, Cinemax, and the following year expanded its own schedule to 24 hours a day. Cinemax offered programming somewhat different from HBO's and closer to Showtime's. The second service also served to satisfy the demands of some cable systems for a pay service in addition to HBO. In 1982 HBO joined with Columbia Pictures and CBS to form a new motion-picture production company called Tri-Star Pictures. Continuing its efforts to compete with HBO, Showtime in 1983 merged with another pay cable network, The Movie Channel, although the two continued to operate as separate services. The merger somewhat improved the combination's ability to obtain programming, but HBO still dominated in the mid-1980s with about one-and-a-half times as many subscribers as Showtime and The Movie Channel combined.

Some pay cable networks take advantage of cable's multi-channel facility to target specific audiences. Among these are the Disney Channel and Home Theatre Network (both with all-family programming), the Playboy Channel (adult fare), Bravo (cultural programs), American Movie Classics (a sister service of Bravo offering classic films), and Galavision (a Spanish-language programming network.).

Like the advertiser-supported cable services, pay cable networks do not yet have staffs the size of those of ABC, CBS, and NBC. HBO, for example, has about 1,700 employees, compared to about 4,000 at each of the broadcast networks. Unlike the ad-supported networks, pay cable services do not, of course, have sales forces calling on advertisers and agencies to sell commercial time. They do, however, have extensive marketing departments that sell the network's service to cable operators and, often in partnership with the cable systems, convince potential customers to subscribe. As with the broadcast television networks, outside companies produce most programs, even original series, carried by pay cable networks.

Superstations   Independent television stations whose signals are distributed by satellite to cable systems throughout the country are called superstations. Ted Turner's Atlanta UHF station, WTBS, was the first such superstation (§4.3). Cable systems that buy the WTBS satellite feed pay only a few cents per subscriber per month for the service and include it in their basic package. The money goes to pay for the satellite uplink in Atlanta and for the use of the transponder, not to support WTBS. Turner counts on getting his share of the pie through higher advertising rates on WTBS, justified by the increase in audience represented by the cable subscribers.

What is the secret of Turner's programming strategy? Simply sports and movies, 24 hours a day. Of course WTBS also schedules other entertainment, as well as public-service programs and news, to serve its own community. But it carries far more sports and feature films than most UHF stations in a market the size of Atlanta would normally schedule. And the strategy works. By 1986 more than 10,000 cable systems serving over 35 million subscribers — more than one-third of all U.S. television homes — carried WTBS.

Other superstations include WGN, Chicago, owner of the Chicago Cubs baseball

Exhibit 8.6   Satellite Distribution of Superstation Programming to Cable TV Systems

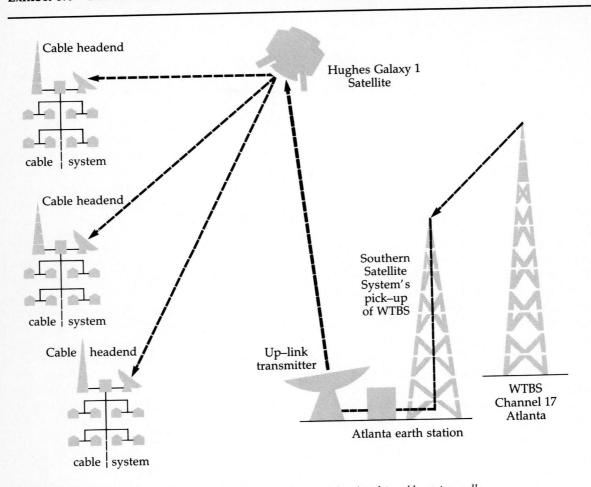

Cable headend

cable system

Cable headend

cable system

Cable headend

cable system

Hughes Galaxy 1
Satellite

Southern
Satellite
System's
pick–up
of WTBS

Up–link
transmitter

Atlanta earth station

WTBS
Channel 17
Atlanta

This diagram illustrates how Atlanta "superstation" WTBS gets its signal to cable systems all over the United States. The programming is picked off air by the satellite carrier, in this case Southern Satellite System, and is sent to a Hughes Galaxy satellite transponder by means of a large uplink earth station about nine miles from the television station. The signal is then beamed down by the transponder for pickup at receive-only earth stations located near the headends of cable systems across the country.

Source: Turner Broadcasting Systems.

team; WOR, New York, which carries more sports than any other station in the country; WPIX, also in New York, which features Yankee baseball games; and WTVT, Dallas. (Some cable systems also carry the signals of *radio* superstations, the most notable of which is classical music station WFMT, Chicago, heard on systems in about three hundred cities in

Exhibit 8.7   Employment

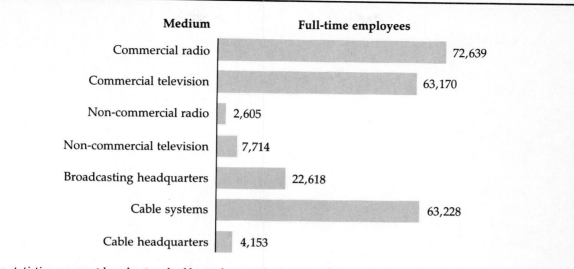

Medium	Full-time employees
Commercial radio	72,639
Commercial television	63,170
Non-commercial radio	2,605
Non-commercial television	7,714
Broadcasting headquarters	22,618
Cable systems	63,228
Cable headquarters	4,153

These statistics represent broadcast and cable employment in 1984 and are based upon reports from only those units that have five or more full-time employees.

Sources: FCC, *Equal Opportunity Trend Reports*, Washington, D.C., 30 Nov. 1984 (broadcast) and 5 Feb. 1985 (cable).

forty states. Subscribers can often receive such stations, as well as other audio services, at an extra fee, through a special connection to high-fidelity stereo systems.)

In addition to the financial arrangements between cable systems and superstations, cable systems also must pay a fee to the federal Copyright Royalty Tribunal for the right to carry copyrighted material into areas not covered by the superstation's payments for use in their own local markets (§16.5).

8.5   Employment

Size of Work Force   The broadcast and cable industries employ a relatively small number of people, about 300,000 full-time employees. This contrasts with General Motors, for example, a single corporation with over 700,000 employees. A large part of industry-related work is done by highly specialized outside firms that produce materials ranging from station identification jingles to prime-time entertainment series. These firms offer most opportunities for creative work — performing, writing, directing, designing, and so on. Many other types of related work take place in advertising agencies, sales representative firms, program-syndicating organizations, and the motion-picture business.

Aside from the major television networks, most broadcast and cable organizations have small staffs. The number of full-time employees at radio stations ranges from fewer than 5 for the smallest markets to about 60 for the largest; the average is 18. Television stations have between 20 and 300 employees, with a typical station employing about 90 full-time people.

Exhibit 8.8   Broadcast and Cable Average Annual Salaries

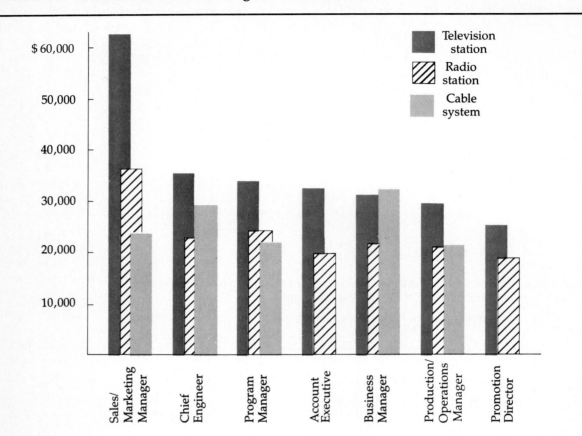

With the exception of business manager, all jobs at television stations command higher average annual salaries than comparable positions at radio stations and cable systems.

Sources: Based on data in *Television Financial Report*, National Association of Broadcasters (Washington, D.C., 1985); *Radio Financial Report*, National Association of Broadcasters (Washington, D.C., 1984); *Careers in Cable*, National Cable Television Association (Washington, D.C., 1983); and *Times-Mirror Corporate Survey of Cable Television Salaries*, National Cable Television Association (Washington, D.C., 1985).

Cable systems average about 30 full-time employees but range from the family-run system in a small community (even as late as 1984, over half of all cable systems operated with fewer than 5 employees) to large-city systems with staffs of well over 100. Cable MSO headquarters units average about 55 full-time employees. Cable networks, too, vary in staff size, depending on such factors as subscriber count, the amount and type of original programming offered, and whether or not the service is ad-supported. HBO, before some belt-tightening in 1984, had 24 vice presidents.

Salary Scales   The huge salaries reported in gossip columns are limited to top talent, creative persons, and executives working mostly at network headquarters and the production centers of New York and Hollywood. Average salaries for jobs at most stations and cable systems are moderate at best, the result of basic laws of supply and demand. Typically, those working in sales receive the highest pay at broadcast stations. It is not uncommon for some sales executives to have incomes higher than many in management. At the department-head level, general sales managers are usually the highest paid and promotion managers tend to be the lowest paid, with program managers' salaries falling somewhere between the two.

News jobs are among the better-paying nonsupervisory positions in television. A survey conducted by the National Association of Broadcasters found that in 1983 the median annual salary for a television news reporter was $16,600; anchors earned $30,000 and sportscasters $24,000. Radio pay was a good deal less, with reporters at $13,200 and sports directors at $15,000. Median annual salaries for television and radio news directors showed the same disparity, with television at $34,600 and radio at $16,000 (NAB, 1983, Table 1).

Women in Broadcasting and Cable   The FCC enforces Equal Employment Opportunities (EEO) Act standards for broadcast stations, cable systems, and headquarters operations with five or more employees. These standards require the submission of an annual report (FCC Form 395) classifying employees according to nine major job categories and according to sex and minority status.

In its annual employment study of broadcast stations with five or more employees, the FCC reported that in 1984 women occupied 36 percent of all jobs, up from 32 percent in 1979. Perhaps more important, women represented 29 percent of the employees classified as Officials and Managers (up from 23 percent in 1979) and 43 percent of those classified as Sales Workers (up from 31 percent in 1979).

A survey by the Radio-Television News Directors Association (*Broadcasting*, 30 July 1984) showed that in 1983 women constituted 31 percent of the work force in both radio and television news, the same as in 1982. But the stature and responsibility of women were on the rise. The survey found that women represented 11 percent of the news directors at commercial television stations (up from 8 percent in 1982 and from less than 1 percent in 1972) and 20 percent of the radio news directors (up from 18 percent in 1982 and from 4 percent in 1972).*

FCC reports for cable systems with five or more employees in 1984 reveal some similarities with broadcasting. Again, women constituted about 36 percent of all employees and nearly 32 percent of officials and managers. However, the potentially lucrative area of sales did not keep pace — women held barely more than 30 percent of those jobs.

---

*A widely publicized sex-discrimination case involved Christine Craft, hired in 1980 as co-anchor at KMBC-TV, the Metromedia station in Kansas City, Missouri. Craft claimed that although she had been assured her position depended on journalistic talent and not on her appearance, her bosses spent most of their time picking apart her makeup and clothes. The station replaced her in 1981, explaining, she claimed, that she was "too old, too unattractive and not deferential to men." Craft sued for $3.5 million and in 1984 won $225,000 in actual and $100,000 in punitive damages. The award was based on a finding of fraud; she lost on her claims of sex discrimination and equal-pay violations. In 1985 an appellate court overturned the award, and in 1986 the U.S. Supreme Court refused to hear Craft's appeal. Only one Supreme Court justice — Sandra Day O'Connor, the sole woman on the court — voted to hear the case.

A Woman's Place Is in the Newsroom

The path for women to equal job opportunity in telecommunications has been bumpy and long, but some progress has been made.

In 1948 ABC hired Pauline Frederick as the first woman network news correspondent. She remained the sole female hard-news network reporter for the next twelve years. In her early years, when assigned to interview the wives of presidential candidates at national political conventions, she was also required to apply their on-camera makeup. Later she became famous for her coverage of the UN, first as a correspondent for ABC, then with NBC.

In 1976 ABC hired Barbara Walters as the first woman anchor on a weekday evening network newscast. She shared the anchor desk with Harry Reasoner. Her salary: $1 million a year ($500,000 for anchoring and $500,000 for producing and hosting four entertainment specials a year), plus perquisites (a private office decorated to her taste, a private secretary, a makeup consultant, and a wardrobe person). Walters had established her reputation as co-host of NBC's *Today* show and as a successful, if sometimes controversial, interviewer of famous personalities as diverse as Princess Grace of Monaco, Fred Astaire, Ingrid Bergman, and Fidel Castro. Her tenure as anchor ended in 1977, and she moved on to more celebrity interviews and to ABC's news magazine *20/20*.

After earning a journalism degree in 1969, Connie Chung worked at a Washington, D.C., independent station. In 1971 she was hired by CBS as a Washington correspondent. Five years later she became news anchor at CBS's O&O station KNXT in Los Angeles and was reportedly the highest paid local anchor in the country. She joined NBC in 1983 as early morning anchor and took over the Saturday *Nightly News*.

Sources: Wide World Photos (Frederick and Chung); © 1986 ABC, Inc. (Walters).

FREDERICK   WALTERS   CHUNG

Minorities   EEO rules also require stations to report on their efforts to upgrade the employment opportunities of minority group members. Their progress in broadcasting has been slower than that of women. The FCC reported that in 1984 minorities represented more than 15 percent of all broadcast employees, an improvement of only one percentage point over 1979. The percentage of minorities holding sales jobs increased from just over 8 percent in 1979 to just under 9 percent in 1984. The report for officials and managers was somewhat better in terms of progress, if not in terms of numbers: in 1983, 9.6 percent were minorities, up from just under 8 percent in 1979.

FCC enforcement of EEO rules has been somewhat less vigorous for cable than for broadcasting. Still, the industry has kept pace in this area, at least in terms of its total work force. Of all workers at cable systems in 1984, about 17 percent were minorities, compared to less than 12 percent in 1979. Of those classified as officials and managers, just over 9 percent were minorities, an increase from less than 7 percent five years earlier.*

Unions   Unionization in broadcasting and cable is substantial at the networks and the national production centers, less so at the station and system level. The industry fragments into so many units — mostly, as we have seen, with relatively small staffs, involving personnel performing more than one type of job — that unionization at the small-station level is

not usually practicable. For example, a small radio station cannot afford to hire two employees to record interviews, paying one as a technician to operate the equipment and the other as a performer to do the talking, when the job could just as easily be done by one employee.

Unionization of the cable and broadcast industries is also affected by the fact that the medium draws upon personnel from older established electrical, musical, motion picture, stage, and newspaper industries that already have their own unions. Most of the 40-odd unions that affect broadcasting and cable therefore cover workers in other media as well. Thus the American Federation of Musicians, whose marathon battle to control the use of recorded music is described in §3.2, represents every kind of professional musician, from players in symphony orchestras to pianists in bars.

People who work in broadcasting and cable can be grouped into two broad categories — the creative/performing group and the crafts/technical group. Unions for these groups divide along similar lines; the former usually avoids the word *union*, calling itself a guild, association, or federation.

The first purely broadcasting union to arise was the American Federation of Television and Radio Artists (AFTRA), which was formed originally (as AFRA) in 1937 to represent that universal radio performer, the announcer. Most of the creative/performing unions, however, came from the stage and motion pictures. Examples are the Writers Guild of America (WGA), the American Guild of Variety Artists (AGVA), and the Screen Actors Guild (SAG). When videotape came to rival film as a medium of production, SAG and AFTRA both claimed jurisdiction over the new medium. The dispute was finally settled in favor of AFTRA. Many actors now belong to both unions, each of which has about sixty thousand members.

---

*Broadcasters and cable system operators are also prohibited from discriminating on the basis of age. In 1980 a 51-year-old Illinois radio disc jockey was fired after his station had changed its format from beautiful music to MOR/adult contemporary. He had been with the station for nine-and-a-half years. Claiming he had been terminated because of his age, he brought suit against the station. The jury in his 1984 trial agreed and awarded him $194,000 in damages, double the amount of his back pay (*Broadcasting*, 19 Nov. 1984).

The creative unions have played a significant role in forcing adaptation of contract terms to take belated account of developments in technology. Feature films were initially kept off television in the 1950s because filmmaking contracts had no provisions covering performance in the new medium. SAG went on strike in 1960 (when Ronald Reagan was president of the union) to force higher scales for *residuals*, which are payments made to performers and others for repeated showings of recorded programs on television. SAG has collected residuals on behalf of its members since 1954, much as ASCAP and BMI collect copyright payments on behalf of composers (§16.5). In fact, some performers lucky enough to be in particularly popular syndicated series have become known as "residual millionaires" (Henderson, 1979). New technology also triggered strikes in 1980–1981 that involved several unions. This time the issue was the sharing of income realized from the sale of recorded programs to the pay-television, videocassette, and videodisc markets. Videocassette revenue again figured in a 1985 Writers Guild strike.

Technical unions became active in broadcasting early in its history. The first successful strike against a broadcasting station may have been one in St. Louis in 1926 that was organized against a CBS-owned-and-operated radio station by the International Brotherhood of Electrical Workers (IBEW), a technicians' union founded in the late nineteenth century by telephone linemen (Koenig, 1970: 22). The IBEW later obtained a network contract with CBS.

In 1953, NBC technicians formed a separate association of their own that ultimately became the National Association of Broadcast Engineers and Technicians (NABET), the first union purely for broadcasting technicians. Later the word *Engineers* was changed to *Employees* to broaden the union's scope. Competi-

tion between NABET and IBEW caused many jurisdictional disputes. A third technical union, an old rival of IBEW, the International Alliance of Theatrical Stage Employees and Moving Picture Machine Operators of the United States and Canada (IATSE), entered the television scene from the motion picture industry.*

Employment Opportunities   Surveys of students enrolled in college electronic media programs indicate that most want to work in either on-camera and on-mike positions or in creative behind-the-camera positions. These jobs are the *least* accessible to beginners, because of the oversupply of candidates. The delegation by broadcast stations and cable systems of creative work to outside production companies means that such creative work concentrates in a few centers where competition is fierce and where unions control entry.

The news field, the one field in which *local* production still flourishes, offers an exception to this rule. Nearly all broadcast stations and many cable systems employ news specialists. Surveys by the Radio and Television News Directors Association (RTNDA) indicate that three-quarters of all commercial radio stations employ at least one full-time newsperson, and the median television news staff size is 17 persons. Moreover, a substantial number of news personnel are hired directly out of college (Stone, 1978). A 1984 RTNDA survey of future job opportunities predicted that the amount of local television news produced and the

---

*Other unions not normally associated with broadcasting occasionally look to radio or television for new members. In 1974 the NBC affiliate in Chattanooga, Tennessee, was organized by the locally powerful Teamsters Union. The union contract covered all employees at the station, except management and a security guard. This included not only engineers and technicians but also the clerical staff, news reporters, and even sales people. After some early stormy years during which several strikes occurred, employee support diminished, and by the early 1980s the union was gone from the station.

Advice for Job Seekers

A survey of broadcasting employment in the state of Virginia was unusual for achieving responses from every one of the 222 radio and television stations in the state. Virginia's 2,593 broadcasting jobs broke down as follows:

Primary job (percentage of total)	Total positions	Proportion held by women
Announcing (21)	545	6%
Sales (19)	485	18%
Traffic-Clerical (18)	419	46%
News (13)	340	12%
Management/ Administration (10)	270	5%
Engineer (10)	253	1%
Other (11)	281	12%

Asked to predict personnel needs ten years in the future, Virginia broadcasting executives gave top priority to *news* (59 percent expected increase), second priority to sales (53 percent increase). As to education, 40 percent of the chief executives and 24 percent of the staff had college degrees. The staff category with the highest percentage of college graduates was news (61 percent).

As always in such surveys, the broadcasters differed in their assessments of the value of college training for their field, but they did agree on the importance of getting *practical experience*. Executives who favored college training gave such advice as:

• "Study the 'people' subjects carefully. Psychology, sociology are good, and English composition is a must."
• "Get plenty of education — it's a highly competitive field. And above all, *learn the English language*."
• "Get as broad an education as you can. You've got to have at least a surface knowledge of many things to be a successful communicator. You can *never* know enough."

From the anti-college executives came such blunt advice as:

• "Get out of broadcasting courses. Every one I've seen, the student leaves with unrealistic attitudes, with rose-colored glasses."
• "Forget the college stuff. I'll hire one year of experience before a doctor's degree."

Source: Gordon A. Sabine, "Broadcasting in Virginia: Benchmark '79," Blacksburg, Va.: Department of Communications Studies, Virginia Polytechnic Institute and State University, 1980. Used with permission.

number of jobs at the local level would increase over the ensuing 10 years. That survey also saw a growing need for television news-promotion specialists. For radio, the major job growth was predicted to be at the outside program supplier level rather than at the local level with substantial growth in specialty radio networks (*BM/E*, Oct. 1984).

A group of broadcast executives had earlier predicted news as a field of employment likely to expand (see Box, above), and placed sales a close second on the list. All commercial networks and stations, and now a growing number of cable systems, employ people in the sales area; moreover, the highest managerial positions historically have been filled from the ranks of sales personnel (although, in recent years, more and more general managers, particularly at the network O&Os, have come out of news). Nevertheless, one of the most frequent complaints personnel directors have about college-trained job applicants is that they fail to comprehend the financial basis of the industry and its profound influence on every aspect of operations.

The field of *promotion* represents another area of potential growth. Stations, systems, and networks promote themselves both to the public and to potential advertisers. Cable networks also use promotion in their efforts to have their programming included in cable system offerings. As technologies proliferate and competition intensifies, so does the need for creative and effective promotion.

Although approximately two-thirds of all jobs in cable are technical, with an emphasis on electronics and engineering, there are other high-priority areas. Marketing, marketing research, and advertising stand at the top of this list. The need for creative people will also increase, as more cable systems gear up for public-access and local-origination programming.

But if applicants look only to broadcasting and cable and their suppliers for jobs, they will seriously underestimate their opportunities for employment. Telecommunication has become so pervasive that virtually every large organization that has any contact with the public uses the electronic media in one form or another. Opportunities exist with retail firms, religious institutions, educational and health organizations, foundations, government agencies, and the armed services.

Many such organizations make extensive in-house use of closed-circuit television. Some, such as Eastern Airlines in Miami, have sophisticated facilities for production of video materials. Eastern not only produces its own videotapes for training (of aircraft mechanics, for example) and for employee-corporate rela-

tions but also conducts workshops in television production for employees of companies from around the world. Some firms, such as IBM, have extensive teleconferencing networks.

These and other positions in the rapidly growing field of *industrial video* apply broadcast techniques to job-skills training, management development, sales presentations, and public relations. Such nonbroadcast uses of television require trained personnel for production, direction, writing, studio operations, program planning, and other tasks that originated as occupational specialties of broadcasting.

Summary

• There are four broadcast station functions: general and administrative, technical, programming, and sales. Station organization follows the same pattern, with subheadings for news, production, traffic, and other specialized functions.

• Stations differ according to whether they are network affiliates or independents and have single or group ownership.

• Networks are organized along lines similar to stations, with added responsibilities for program distribution and affiliate relations. Most affiliates are not owned by networks; rather, they have a contractual relationship with networks. Each network has a few highly profitable owned-and-operated stations.

• The most important provision of affiliate contracts specifies station compensation for time used for network programming. Such compensation amounts to only a small percentage of affiliates' revenues.

• Affiliates have the legal right to refuse to clear time for network programs and in fact are limited by the prime-time access rule in the amount of prime time they may clear for network programs.

• Most noncommercial television stations are operated either by state and municipal governments or by community organizations that exist solely to operate public broadcast stations.

• Public radio stations are similarly owned and fall into two categories: about 220 actively participate in national funding and affiliation; 900 much smaller stations subsist on local community support.

• The Corporation for Public Broadcasting acts as the federal funding agency for public broadcasting. It dispenses funds from annual congressional appropriations to PBS, to NPR, and directly to individual stations.

• Unlike commercial networks, PBS does not compensate affiliates; instead, the stations pay PBS for programs produced by others. NPR, however, both produces and distributes programs to its affiliates, who usually have little voice in program decisions.

• Cable systems perform the same four functions as commercial broadcast stations, and also market their own services to subscribers. The programming function is more extensive than at broadcast television stations because of cable's multiple channels.

• Cable networks are of two types: advertiser-supported (or basic) and pay. Subscribers usually receive ad-supported networks at no additional cost, as part of a system's basic package of programming, and pay an extra monthly fee for commercial-free pay cable networks.

• Many cable systems also carry the programming of superstations, independent television stations that distribute their signals by satellite throughout the country.

• Relative to their extensive social impact, the broadcasting and cable industries have small work forces.

• The percentage of broadcasting jobs held by women and minorities has increased in recent years but still falls far short of the percentage held by white males.

• Broadcast employees are unionized at the network level and in the major production centers, but most stations and cable systems are not targets for unionization because their employees are few in number and often perform several jobs.

• News and sales offer the best employment chances for newcomers to broadcasting. Technical and marketing people are most in demand in the cable industry. Other opportunities exist in nonbroadcast industrial video.

CHAPTER 9

Broadcast and Cable Advertising

Although they were late starters, first radio and then television quickly earned places among the top five advertising media. Today, only newspapers surpass television in total advertising volume, but television leads in national advertising. Radio comes fourth, after direct mail but ahead of magazines. Advertising on cable, although rapidly increasing, is still small relative to the other media (Exhibit 9.1).

Public broadcasting relies on governmental and business underwriting and foundation and citizen support to meet its expenses. Cable systems and pay cable networks look to monthly subscriber fees as their major source of revenue. But advertising is the single largest revenue source supporting national broadcast networks, thousands of commercial radio and television stations, and many cable program services.

This chapter examines the advantages and disadvantages of broadcast and cable media as advertising vehicles, as well as how advertising is sold and scheduled. A final section looks at some controls, governmental and otherwise, that can affect electronic media advertising.

9.1 Advantages of Broadcast Advertising

Access to Consumers Because virtually all homes have radio and television receivers, broadcasting has unrivaled access to all family members under the changing circumstances of daily living. At the same time, car radios and portable radios allow broadcasting to compete with magazines and newspapers as a medium that can travel with the consumer outside the home. Above all, the constant availability of broadcasting as a companion that provides entertainment and information gives it a great psychological advantage.

Timeliness Then, too, programming *unfolds* continuously. This attribute offers advertisers a unique advantage, letting them time their messages to coincide with activities relevant to their products. For example, commer-

Exhibit 9.1   Advertising Volume of Major Media, Local vs. National

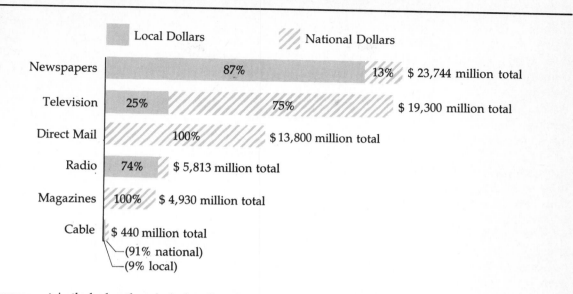

Newspapers retain the lead as the principal medium for local advertising, television leads in nonlocal advertising, and cable is far behind all other media in both categories.

Sources: Based on data prepared by Robert J. Coen, McCann-Erickson, Inc., in *Broadcasting Marketing and Technology News* (NAB, Washington, August 1985).

cials for household products can be shown at a time of day when consumers of those products are actually using them, and sportswear commercials can be aired while sports fans are engrossed in watching or listening to their favorite events.

Ability to Demonstrate   Advertisers find an asset in television's ability to show how a product works and how it affects the consumer. For example, they can "prove" claims made for their products by means of vivid demonstrations. Color adds to the effectiveness of demonstrations, as does participation by celebrity endorsers.

Entertainment Value   Commercials often take the form of tiny plays that exploit all the entertainment values of the theater — charac-

ter, conflict, suspense, and resolution. There is some truth in the wry comment that commercials are often more entertaining than programs. They have to be, for they have only a minute or less to make their point. If the skill, craftsmanship, attention to minute detail, and lavish expenditure of money that go into creating the best commercials went into the production of programs, the "vast wasteland" of television might be made to bloom. Unfortunately, multiplying the cost of making a top-quality commercial (typically $2,500 per second) by the number of seconds in programs would make an ordinary situation comedy as costly to produce as the movie *Star Wars*.

Attention-Holding Value   A great deal of research and planning goes into planting commercial messages at precisely the right moments to maximize their chances of being seen or heard. The newspaper reader can skip over advertisements, the commuter can ignore billboards, and mail addressed to "occupant" can be dropped unopened into the wastebasket. But listeners or viewers, once their attention has been engaged, find skillfully placed broadcast commercials hard to evade.

Status Value   The very fact that a product is advertised in a major medium confers a certain status. Some of the feeling of confidence that people have in a medium may be unconsciously transferred to the products it advertises. Taking advantage of this transference, advertisers sometimes use the phrase "As seen on television" in supermarket point-of-sale displays and newspaper ads.

Flexibility of Coverage   In addition to its psychological advantages as an advertising medium, broadcasting has the physical advantage of functioning almost equally well as either a local or a national and regional advertising medium. The same stations that at one moment serve as local outlets may at another moment serve as outlets for national or regional networks. Broadcast advertising is typically categorized as (1) local, (2) network, or (3) national spot.

1. *Local advertising*. All stations, even network affiliates, are by their nature essentially *local* media, covering single markets, though their individual coverage areas vary a great deal. As Exhibit 9.2 shows, radio depends for most of its revenue on local advertising, whereas television derives nearly half of its revenue from national spot advertising. This difference reflects the historical fact that television captured most of the national advertisers, driving radio to cultivate local sources of revenue. Moreover, since radio is a much less expensive medium, small local businesses find it more affordable than television.

Daily newspapers, broadcasting's chief rival for local advertising dollars, have far less flexibility of coverage. Almost all communities are one-paper towns. Daily newspapers do attempt to adapt their coverage to advertisers' needs by using add-on neighborhood supplements; but in many a one-newspaper town, local advertisers may choose from among two dozen or more radio and television stations with varying coverage areas.

The chief local clients for broadcast advertising are fast-food restaurants, department and furniture stores, banks, food stores, and movie theaters. Many local firms act as retail outlets for nationally distributed products. In such cases the cost of local advertising may be shared between the local retailer (an appliance dealer, for example) and the national manufacturer (the maker of television sets). This type of cost sharing, known as local *cooperative advertising*, or simply *local co-op*, is a major source of radio revenue, so much so that some stations appoint a special staff member to coordinate cooperative advertising.

2. *Network advertising*. When a station throws the switch that connects it to a network, the station instantaneously converts itself from a local to a national advertising medium. For advertisers of nationally distributed products, network advertising has five significant advantages.

First, in a single transaction the network advertiser can place messages on several hundred stations of known quality, located strategically to cover the entire country. Second, network advertisers can have centralized control over their advertising messages, and assurance that they will be delivered at the times and in the program environments of their choice. Third, network advertisers benefit

Exhibit 9.2   Broadcast Station and Cable System Revenue Sources

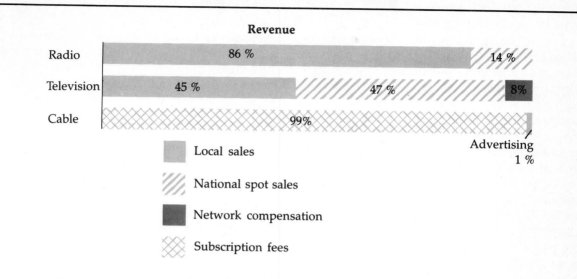

Subscription fees include payments for basic and pay program services, home security, pay-per-view events, and installation charges.

Sources: Based on data in *Broadcasting*, 30 Jan. 1984, *Telemedia*, Nov./Dec. 1983, and *The Cable TV Financial Databook*, Paul Kagan Associates, Inc., Carmel, CA, 1985.

from sophisticated audience research by their networks. Fourth, networks provide convenient centralized billing for commercial-time costs. And fifth, advertisers benefit from the prestige that attaches to the very fact of being network advertisers.

Traditionally, two basic ways of presenting network messages were available to advertisers. They could either *sponsor* entire programs, inserting their messages where and how they chose, or they could buy *participations* in network programs over which they had no control. Sponsorship, once the principal type of network advertising, had the advantage of giving advertisers considerable control over, and identification with, the programs and their stars. But sponsorship all but disappeared from network radio after television drained away national advertising; and it faded from television during the 1960s, when programs became too expensive for most advertisers to sponsor and when other advertisers, for strategic reasons, decided to scatter their messages over several programs. The term *sponsor* now usually means *any* advertiser, though historically it meant only those who assumed responsibility for an entire program. Today sponsorship in the original sense survives only for some daytime programs and for occasional specials, underwritten by large corporations that desire a particular type of image-building exposure. One example of the latter was the formation of Red Oak Production Company by five of the nation's largest advertisers — AT&T, Armstrong, Ford, Gillette, and Xerox. Red Oak was to produce five high-quality prime-time programs for the 1986-1987 network television season and ten more shows in seasons thereafter.

Participating advertising is sold as announcements ("participations") scheduled in slots made available by the networks within their programs. Most advertisers use *scatter-buying* strategies, distributing their ads over a number of different programs. In this way, they avoid risking too much on any one program and also gain the advantage of exposure to varied audiences.

3. *National spot advertising.* This is the alternative to network advertising for clients who need to reach national audiences. The major difference between spot and network advertising is that the stations that participate in national spot advertising do not constitute a true network of *interconnected* stations. Working through their advertising agencies and the stations' national sales representatives (§9.6), national spot advertisers use ad hoc collections of nonconnected stations chosen to suit their particular needs. Advertisers may choose network affiliates (of one or more networks) as well as independents to participate in national spot campaigns. The commercial announcements are sent out by mail or, more recently, by satellite to each of the chosen stations. This means, of course, that spot advertisers lack some of the centralized control of message, timing, program environment, and billing that is available to the network advertiser.*

The national spot advertiser assembles the combination of stations that best fits the needs of the advertised product or service. But rather than negotiating directly (over long distances) with several local television stations,

the advertiser may place an order with two or three national reps (who have offices in or near the advertiser or agency's city) for commercial time on perhaps 100 individual stations handled by those reps. Moreover, spot advertisers may select any advertising vehicles that suit their needs. This could mean station-break spots within or between network programs, sponsorship of either local or syndicated programs, or participating spots in such programs. In this way national spot advertising can capitalize on *local* program interests, something the network advertiser cannot possibly do. Most of the largest national advertisers (Procter & Gamble is by far the biggest) use spot and network advertising in combination, as shown in Exhibit 9.5, to achieve better coverage than either method could yield on its own.

9.2 Disadvantages of Broadcast Advertising

Television, with its unique combination of sight, sound, movement, and color, is usually considered the most effective and persuasive of all advertising media. But television and, in many cases, radio also have disadvantages that make other media more attractive for some messages.

Inflexibility of Coverage   Although, as we have seen, the broadcast media offer wide flexibility in terms of local, network, and national spot options, their very structure presents other limitations that frustrate advertisers. Networks cover virtually the entire country through a fixed number of affiliates. Yet some advertisers would rather concentrate their messages in certain regions. A company might have limited distribution of its product or might wish to introduce a new line in specific test markets. In some circumstances (re-

---

*One of the attractions of barter syndication (§13.4) as a form of national spot advertising is that it gives bartering advertisers control over the environment in which their commercials appear.

gional feeds of football games, for example) an advertiser may be able to limit the geographical exposure given to its commercial. But in most cases the client must take all stations in the network lineup or take none at all.

Local advertising and national spot advertising offer one solution, but even they sometimes force an advertiser to pay for superfluous audiences. The owner of an appliance dealership in a suburban mall, for instance, cannot realistically expect customers to come from the entire metropolitan area. Yet the store's commercial, seen or heard throughout a broadcast station's coverage area, will reach thousands of people who never visit that mall. In such cases, other advertising methods are more efficient, such as cable, suburban newspapers, neighborhood inserts in metropolitan dailies, or direct mail brochures addressed to appropriate zip codes.

Cost   The combination of limited commercial inventory, high demand, and large audience delivery puts television commercial prices beyond the reach of many advertisers. A 30-second announcement in the 1985 Super Bowl telecast cost $525,000 — obviously affordable by only the largest national advertisers. Even at the station level, television commercials, particularly those within or adjacent to programs delivering large audiences, cost too much for small- and medium-sized businesses. Radio and some independent television stations offer lower-priced availabilities, but with the cheaper cost comes a smaller audience.

Transience   A 30-second television commercial has 30 seconds in which to sell its product or service. Once run it is gone. The viewer cannot linger over the advertisement, pondering whether or not to buy; cannot clip out the ad to consult it later, say, to check the store's location.

The trend of *zapping* commercials makes the short lifespan of broadcast advertisements even more of a drawback. With remote-control devices for television sets and "pause" and "fast forward" features on videocassette recorders (VCRs), viewers avoid commercials by switching channels or muting sound, by putting their VCRs in pause while the ads run, or by intermittently speeding up their machines during playback. A 1984 study of VCR usage conducted by the A. C. Nielsen Company reported that 36 percent of those responding said they deleted commercials three-fourths or more of the time; only 14 percent said they never did (*Broadcasting*, 7 May 1984). Advertisers paying high prices for television commercials must be concerned about that portion of the audience for which they pay but that never sees their ads.

Commercial Limitations   Most radio commercials are 60 seconds long. The greatest number of television commercials are 30 seconds, and an increasing number are only 10 seconds; just a few are one or two minutes in length. Even the longest cannot duplicate the impact of a large-display department store ad or a supermarket ad with clip-out coupons. Nor can broadcasting compete effectively with the classified sections of newspapers. Some broadcasters and cable systems have offered "want-ad" segments in their programming, but they lack the convenience of newspapers: viewers must sit through all the announcements to find one of interest.

A broadcasting station has only 24 hours of "space" each day. And because only so many commercials may be scheduled within any given program, without risking audience objection, only a limited number of advertisers may be accommodated. Print media, on the other hand, can, at least theoretically, expand space indefinitely by adding pages. Nor does broadcasting have anything comparable to the multipage inserts that advertisers buy in newspapers and magazines.

Also, the three major television networks and many local stations have standards that forbid acceptance of advertising for some products (X-rated movies, for example) and limit the presentation form of others (§9.7). As a result, advertisers failing to meet those standards look to alternative media as outlets.

Clutter   Advertisers became concerned about the marked increase in television *clutter* that started in the late 1960s. *Clutter* refers to the feeling of disorder and confusion that arises from long strings of commercial, quasi-commercial, and noncommercial announcements. Clutter increased because of several developments, including the decline of program sponsorship, the change from 60 seconds to 30 seconds as the standard length for network commercials, and an escalation in the intensity of program promotion.

During the 1970s complaints about clutter steadily mounted. Advertisers objected because clutter undermined the effectiveness of commercials. A 1978 study, for example, confirmed that the longer the string of non-program items, the less people can remember about commercials in the middle of the string (Ray & Webb, 1978).

The increased use of 10-second commercials in the 1980s heightened the clutter problem. One observer counted seventeen messages during the closing break of a movie (*Broadcasting*, 21 May 1984). Clutter increased still more in 1984 when the networks and several group owners of television stations, faced with legal action by advertiser Alberto-Culver, reluctantly agreed to drop their restrictions against so-called split 30s, or 30-second spots that independently advertise two or more un-related products. In an effort to improve the situation, some broadcasters began to charge higher prices for commercial messages ap-pearing alone in "island" positions or in clus-ters with a limited number of messages.* Stations justified the higher rates by pointing to their reduced commercial inventories, and some advertisers agreed to pay the higher prices in order to achieve the enhanced expo-sure for their commercials.

9.3 Broadcast Commercials and Announcements

Sponsor Identification   Section 317 of the Communications Act of 1934 requires that commercials on radio and television be recog-nizably distinct from programs. Disclosure must be made as to the source of anything a station puts on the air for which it receives payment, whether in money or some other "valuable consideration." This *sponsor identifi-cation* is intended to prevent deception of the public, which might otherwise be subjected to propaganda or "disinformation" from un-known sources.

Of course ordinary commercials make their sources self-evident. Anonymity is the last thing commercial advertisers desire. But propagandists who use *editorial advertising* (sometimes called "advertorials") may not al-ways be so anxious to reveal their true iden-tity; nor do those who make under-the-table payments to disc jockeys or others for on-the-air favors wish to be identified. Thus the integration of commercial matter into pro-gramming must be handled in systematic ways to ensure its proper identification and to prevent violation of the Communications Act, as well as for the convenience of sales departments.

---

*Legal action by the Justice Department had earlier ended the broadcast industry's own attempts, through the NAB code, at organized though voluntary control of clutter (§16.7).

Trafficking of Commercials After sales have been made to advertisers, the station's traffic department is responsible for scheduling commercials in accordance with contracts. For this reason the practice of scattering commercials throughout the broadcast day is referred to as *trafficking* commercials.

Because the placement of commercials in relation to programs, other commercials, and other types of announcements is of the greatest interest to both advertisers and programmers, the trafficking of commercials takes on considerable importance. It requires identifying specific, predictable points at which commercials can be logically inserted into the flow of programming.

Avoiding Product Conflicts Part of the job of scheduling commercials involves ensuring that announcements for competing products do not appear next to each other. A Buick dealership, for example, does not want its commercial immediately followed (and thus diluted) by an ad for Chevrolets. This concern applies also to *antithetical* products, which may be considered to conflict with one another even though they are not directly competitive (beer and milk, for example). Today, at least at the larger stations, computers make these and many other complex scheduling decisions.

Sponsored Programs Sponsored programs allowed advertisers to control when and how commercials were inserted, and they could shape programs so as to integrate commercials smoothly and logically. In the few instances of fully sponsored programs that now occur, the sponsor often clusters commercials at the beginning and end so as not to interrupt program flow.

Participation Programs When stations took over the responsibility for programs from advertisers, they at first maintained the fiction of sponsorship by referring to advertisers whose commercials appeared during program breaks as "participating sponsors." For this reason the term *participations* (or *participating spots*) was adopted. Vestiges of this concept survive in the *billboards* shown at the open and close of some television programs, during which "participating" advertiser names are thrown in at no added cost as an incentive to spot buyers. Billboards often introduce major sports events, for which spot buyers pay premium prices; the higher prices entitle them to special treatment, such as the extra exposure they get from billboard listings.

Today most broadcast advertising is sold simply as *spot announcements* (or, more briefly, *spots*). Some types of programs have natural breaks, allowing for insertion of spots without interrupting the flow; the breaks between rounds of a boxing match or between record cuts on a radio show are examples. In other cases the break must be artificially contrived. Part of the art of writing half-hour situation comedies lies in building the plot to a suspenseful but nevertheless logical break-off point partway through, for insertion of commercials.

Opinions on what qualifies as a "natural" break can differ. The industry now regards breaks between stories in newscasts as natural, but originally the interruption of news with commercials was regarded as highly unprofessional and not at all natural. Certainly, viewers often complain about the arbitrary breaks made in theatrical feature films, which were not, of course, written with seemingly natural climaxes in the action every ten minutes where breaks would be appropriate. Others object to the "television time-outs" taken during football games for the convenience not of players but of advertisers.

Sustaining Programs Programs neither sponsored nor subject to participating spot advertising are called *sustaining* programs, and are now limited almost exclusively to public-affairs programs of a type that could not be commercialized without a serious breach of taste. Presidential addresses and state funerals are examples. Occasionally, programs too controversial for commercial advertisers (the episode of *Maude* dealing with abortion, for example) air on a sustaining basis.

Station Breaks   Partly as a matter of law and partly as a matter of custom, stations insert *identification announcements* (IDs) between programs and between the major segments of very long programs.* Because ID announcements represent breaks in the program sequence they are called station-break announcements. They open convenient slots into which to insert commercials for advertisers other than sponsors.

Networks observe the ID requirement by interrupting their program feeds periodically to allow affiliates to make station identification announcements. Thus developed the practice of scheduling network programs a bit short to allow affiliates time not only for ID announcements but also for one or more commercial announcements.

Promotional and Public-Service Announcements   Also figuring in programming at the junctures where commercials normally appear are two quasi-commercial types of announcements, promotional and public service.

Promotional announcements (promos) call attention to future programs of networks and stations. Although not technically commercials, they do advertise stations and networks. Most broadcasters consider on-air promotion their most effective and cost-efficient audience-building tool (Webster, 1983: 193).

Public-service announcements (PSAs) resemble commercials but promote noncommercial organizations and causes. Stations and networks broadcast them without charge. They give broadcasters a way of fulfilling some of their public-service obligations and, along with promos, also serve as temporary fillers for unsold commercial openings.

9.4 Cable Advertising

Some early cable systems used primitive monochrome cameras pointed at hand-crafted studio cards to advertise local businesses — much as early television had decades before. Today the cable industry uses network-quality equipment, computers, and satellites to handle commercials. In 1985 total cable advertising revenue was about $440 million. National cable networks generated about 85 percent, local systems only 15 percent.

But cable still had a long way to go to challenge the older media. In 1985 broadcasting and newspapers each accounted for more than one-fourth of all advertising expenditures in all media. Cable received less than one percent.

Cable Advertising Advantages   Cable shares many of television's advantages and disadvantages, with some variations of its own.

• *Flexibility of coverage.* Cable offers a variety of advertising opportunities. One local firm

---

*The FCC rule requires IDs, consisting of station call letters and the name of the community of license, at sign-on and sign-off and at hourly intervals, or at a "natural break" if a program runs longer (47 CFR 73.1201). When regulation began, ID requirements were more stringent, making it easier to track down improperly operated and unauthorized stations. Today, some radio and television stations, as a promotional device, air many more IDs than legally required. Sometimes extra television IDs are used to reduce viewer confusion over which stations they are watching on cable systems that carry stations on channel numbers other than their own — a particularly important point for viewers keeping rating diaries.

may run its commercials in a cable system's locally originated programs. A firm with several retail outlets can have its message carried by several interconnected systems. Others might run their ads in slots that ad-supported cable networks make available for local spots. National advertisers have more than twenty-five national cable networks and superstations from which to select.

• *Lower cost.* Because cable has a smaller audience than broadcast television, its rates are commensurately lower. But rates may, in some cases, be comparable to radio (§9.5).

• *Targeted audiences.* Most studies describe the cable subscriber as typically better-educated and more "upscale" than the average television viewer. Moreover, cable advertisers can target audiences with desired demographic characteristics — ESPN's avid sports fans, MTV's younger music-oriented audience, CNN's news viewers, and so on (§14.6).

• *Variable commercial lengths.* Although most cable commercials conform to traditional broadcast lengths, cable offers some opportunities for longer messages giving detailed product explanation or demonstration, to help viewers reach buying decisions. These "infomercials" may run 2, 5, or even 30 minutes.

Cable Advertising Disadvantages   As does any medium, cable has its disadvantages. Cable has suffered from an understandable yet prolonged wariness on the part of advertisers and agencies and, consequently, has grown less rapidly as an advertising medium than expected.

• *Viewer resistance.* Cable originally promised viewers "uncut, uninterrupted, commercial-free" television. Generally, only pay cable networks have kept that promise, and the temptation to carry advertising, and thus increase revenues, may eventually prove too great for even them to resist. Surveys have indicated that a majority of subscribers would accept commercials *if the cost of the service were reduced.* So far HBO and other pay networks have denied plans to carry commercials.

• *Commercial production concerns.* Larger advertisers accustomed to producing commercials for traditional television can easily supply them to cable as well. But small local firms may have difficulties producing commercials, even simple ones, and if done poorly they can be counterproductive. Longer "infomercials" require the expense and effort of special production. To alleviate this problem, some cable systems offer local companies quality commercial production free or at reduced cost as an inducement to advertise.

• *Commercial origination difficulties.* Radio and television stations can easily insert local commercials at the proper points in their single channels of programming. But a cable system faces the challenge of running different messages in different program services, for locally originated channels as well as for advertiser-supported networks that provide time for local commercials. Broadcasters usually assign an operator to integrate commercials and programming, but it would be economically unrealistic for a cable system to have one such person for each channel that carries commercials. To solve the problem, cable systems use automated equipment triggered by special electronic signals originated by cable networks. But such hardware is expensive and cable operators have often found the equipment imprecise and unreliable, rolling commercials late or not at all.

• *Inadequate audience measurement.* The lack of complete and reliable statistical information about cable's audience is perhaps the greatest impediment to the growth of cable advertising. Most advertisers calculate the efficiency of their advertising not simply by the cost but by how many and what kind of people see or hear the ads. Nielsen, Arbitron, and other organizations that conduct regular audience surveys throughout the country provide advertisers with demographic information about broadcast station and network listeners and viewers (§14.6). The Audit Bureau of Circulation offers much the same information for newspapers, and Verified Audit Circulation does so for magazines. But cable's multiplicity of program choices so fractionalizes its audience that few channels attract viewers in sufficient numbers to produce statistically valid rating results. Rating services make some information available for the more popular national cable networks,* but not for most cable channels.

Interactive Cable Systems   Early predictions for two-way, or *interactive*, cable as an advertising and marketing medium envisioned the homeowner "shopping at home" by watching advertisements on the television screen and simply pressing a button to order desired products. An electronic impulse would travel upstream to a computer that would register the order, perhaps charging it to the subscriber's credit card, and arranging for delivery of the product to the customer's door (§4.3).

With intense competition among MSOs for franchises, more and more applicants promised interactive systems. However, as economic reality settled hard on some segments of the cable industry in the mid-1980s, many franchisees asked to be relieved of their promises to build the very expensive two-way systems. The few interactive "home shopper" services that did exist generated little enthusiasm. Furthermore, two-way service can also be accomplished through videotex systems using telephone lines. In recent years the burgeoning home computer industry, with its ties to videotex services, has begun to replace

cable television as the provider of electronic shop-at-home options (§4.8).

9.5 Advertising Rates

Putting a price tag on advertising time is complicated by the fact that time has value to advertisers only in terms of the audiences it represents. Audiences constantly change in size and vary widely in demographic composition. As a result, so does the value of time to the advertiser.

Pricing Factors   The most stable factors that affect the prices advertisers pay for broadcast time are *market size*, *station facilities* (frequency, power, antenna location, and other physical factors that influence coverage), and *network affiliation* (if any). Within a given market and within limits imposed by a station's facilities, the major variable is audience availability. Audiences change with time of day, day of week, and season of the year. Station managers have no day-to-day control over any of these factors.

The major dynamic variables — the ones that make one station successful and another less so — are *programming*, *promotion*, and *sales*. Good management can lure demographically desirable audiences away from competitors by offering attractive programming supported by effective promotion, and an efficient sales department can lure advertisers away from competitors with persuasive arguments and solicitous attention.

There is no standard way of factoring all these variables into a formula for setting appropriate broadcast rates. Market forces, however, eventually tend to bring the prices charged for advertising to an economically rational level. One test of the reasonableness of a price is *cost per thousand* (CPM), which is the cost of reaching 1,000 households or people

---

*Nielsen requires that a cable program service reach at least 12.5 million households in order to qualify for national audience ratings.

Calculating CPM

The standard measure of the cost of commercial time is CPM, which means cost per thousand (the M being the Roman numeral for 1,000). A commercial in television Station A's evening news might, for example, cost $800; in Station B's evening news the price might be $900. But this does not necessarily mean that Station A is the preferred advertising buy. Station B might have a much larger audience than its competitor, so that, even at the higher price, its commercial is more *cost efficient*.

The only way to make a valid comparison is to calculate the cost of reaching the same number of people or homes or desired demographic groups on each station. Here is the formula:

$$\frac{\text{commercial cost}}{(\text{average audience delivered} \div 1,000)}$$

Thus, if Station A's news had an average audience of 200,000 homes, the CPM for a commercial in that program would be:

$$\frac{\$800}{(200,000 \div 1,000)} = \frac{\$800}{200} = \$4$$

By comparison, if Station B delivered 300,000 homes, the CPM for a spot in its newscast would be

$$\frac{\$900}{(300,000 \div 1,000)} = \frac{\$900}{300} = \$3$$

Using this calculation, the greater cost efficiency of a commercial on Station B becomes readily apparent.

Here is an example from real life: ABC estimated that 116 million people watched the 1985 Super Bowl. A 30-second commercial in that event cost $525,000. Although an ad costing over half a million dollars seems expensive, the price is not quite so overwhelming when stated in terms of what it cost to reach 1,000 people (the CPM): $4.53. This represented an increase over the $4.29 CPM commanded by the 1984 Super Bowl and the 1982 Super Bowl's CPM of $3.24.

or people (or any targeted group such as men or teens or women aged 18 to 34). As shown in the box above, you calculate CPM by dividing the audience (in thousands) reached by a commercial message into the amount the broadcaster is charging for that commercial.

CPM helps in comparing one medium with another, one station with another, and even one program with another. CPM measurements do, however, have their limitations: they can be no better than the research on which they are based, and in any event are normally based on past, not future, performance. (Occasionally sales are made "on the come," whereby a station predicts and in some cases even guarantees CPMs.) Nevertheless, in the long run advertisers and advertising agencies will bypass a station whose CPM is seriously out of line with the CPM of competing stations.

Radio Station Rates   Broadcast advertising depends for its effectiveness on cumulative effect. Spots are therefore bought not singly but in groups (a *spot schedule* or a specially priced *spot package*). Thus the *Broadcasting/Cablecasting Yearbook*, in listing sample rates of radio stations in its directory, gives the rates for one-minute spots scheduled twelve times a week in four different day parts. For example, a small, rural station in Georgia charges $4 per spot in any day part, whereas a metropolitan station in Ohio varies its charges from a high of $95 per spot in the 6 A.M.–10 A.M. day part (morning *drive time*) to a low of $35 in the 7 P.M.–midnight day part.

The small station does not bother to price day parts differently because it would hardly pay to keep track of different rates when the basic charge is so low. The larger the station and market, the more expensive the time and the more refined rate differences become, reflecting even hour-to-hour changes in audience size and composition.

For detailed radio rate information, buyers consult either individual station rate cards or *Spot Radio Rates and Data*, a bi-monthly publication of Standard Rate and Data Service (SRDS). This publication, especially valuable to national spot time-buyers, gathers rate card information from stations all over the country, presenting it in a standardized format. Exhibit 9.3 includes a typical SRDS radio entry. In addition to rates, rate cards contain such information as the following:

• *Time classes.* Typically, radio stations divide their time into specific day parts, and even into subclasses of day parts, with different prices for each.

• *Spot position.* Subclasses within day parts are usually based on the way spots are scheduled. *Fixed-position* spots have an assured place in the schedule and are sold at a premium rate. *Run-of-schedule* (ROS) spots may be scheduled anywhere within the time period designated in the sales contract. Some stations *rotate* spots, both *horizontally* (over different days) and *vertically* (through different time

Exhibit 9.3   Sample SRDS Listings

WKSE (FM)
1946
NIAGARA FALLS

ncb

Media Code 4 233 1759 3.00   Mid 012404-000
Porter Broadcasting Corporation
2692 Staley Rd., Box 364, Grand Island, NY 14072.
Phone 716-773-1714.

PROGRAMMING DESCRIPTION

WKSE (FM): Contemporary Hit Radio, incl Rock, Soul & Pop. Contact Representative for further details. Rec'd 4/2/85.

1. PERSONNEL
Vice-Pres. & Gen'l Mgr.—Bruce A. Biette.
General Sales Manager—Roger L. Bertolini.

2. REPRESENTATIVES
Hillier, Newmark, Wechsler & Howard.

3. FACILITIES
ERP 46,000 w. (horiz.), 46,000 w. (vert.); 98.5 mhz. Stereo.
Operating schedule: 24 hours daily. EST.
Antenna ht.: 380 ft. above average terrain.

4. AGENCY COMMISSION
15/0; 30 days.

5. GENERAL ADVERTISING See coded regulations
General: 2a, 2b, 3a, 3b, 3c, 3d, 4a, 4d, 5, 6b, 7b, 8.
Rate Protection: 10h, 11h, 12h, 13h, 14g, 15b, 16.
Basic Rates: 20b, 21d, 22a, 23b, 24c, 25c, 26, 27, 28b, 29a, 30, 31, 32b, 33d.
Contracts: 40a, 41, 42b, 43, 44b, 45, 46, 47a, 48, 49, 50, 51a.
Comb.; Cont. Discounts: 60b, 61c.
Cancellation: 70a, 71a, 72, 73a.
Prod. Services: 80, 81, 82.

TIME RATES
No. 2 Eff 10/1/84—Rec'd 11/12/84.

AAAA—Mon thru Fri 5-10 am & 3-7 pm.
AAA—Mon thru Fri 10 am-3 pm; Sat 5 am-7 pm.
AA—Mon thru Sat 7 pm-midnight; Sun 5 am-midnight.
A—Mon thru Sun midnight-5 am.

6. SPOT ANNOUNCEMENTS

WEEKLY

GRID:	1 min AAAA	AAA	AA	A	30 sec AAAA	AAA	AA	A
I	73	66	59	20	58	53	47	16
II	62	57	50	17	50	46	40	14
III	53	48	43	15	42	38	34	12
IV	45	41	37	13	36	33	29	11

10 sec: Use 30-sec rate.

7. PACKAGE PLANS

TAP—5 DAY MINIMUM ROTATION, 1/3/AAAA, 1/3AAA, 1/3AA

GRID:	I	II	III	IV
1 min	51	43	37	31
30 sec	41	34	29	25

BEST BUY—MON THRU SUN 5 AM-MIDNIGHT

	I	II	III	IV
1 min	44	37	31	26
30 sec	35	30	25	21

Exhibit 9.3   Sample SRDS Listings (continued)

WGRZ-TV
(formerly WGR-TV)
(Airdate August 14, 1954)
BUFFALO

Katz American

nab   **TvB**

Media Code 6 233 0400 3.00   Mid 007612-000
WGRZ-TV Inc.
259 Delaware Ave., Buffalo, NY 14202. Phone 716-856-
   1414, TWX, 710-522-1729.

1. PERSONNEL
Vice-Pres. & Gen'l Mgr.—Lyn P. Stoyer.
General Sales Manager—Raymond P. Maselli.
National Sales Manager—James C. Vickery, Jr.

2. REPRESENTATIVES
Katz Television, American.
Canada—Radio-Television Representatives, Ltd.

3. FACILITIES
Video 100,000 w., audio 20,000 w.; ch 2.
Antenna ht.: 1,000 ft. above average terrain.
Operating schedule: 24 hours daily. EST.

4. AGENCY COMMISSION
15% to recognized agencies on time charges; no cash
discount.

5. GENERAL ADVERTISING See coded regulations
General: 2a, 3a, 3d, 4a, 5, 6b, 7b, 8.
Rate Protection: 14c, 15, 16, 16a, 17.
Contracts: 20a, 21, 22a, 22c, 22d, 24a, 25, 26, 27e, 28,
   29, 30, 31a, 31b, 31c, 32a, *32d, 33, 34b.
Basic Rates: 40a, 41a, 41b, 41c, 41d, 42, 43a, 43b, 44b,
   45a, 46, 47a, 47d, 49, 50, 51, 52.
Comb.; Cont. Discounts: 60a, 60c, 60d, 60e, 60f, 61a,
   61b, 61c, 62a, 62b.
Cancellation: 70b, 70i, 71, 72, 73b.
Prod. Services: 80, 81, 82, 83, 84, 85, 86, 87a, 87b, 87c.
(*) 72 hours.
Affiliated with NBC Television Network.

6. TIME RATES
   No. 2 Eff 12/25/85—Rec'd 2/3/86.

7. SPOT ANNOUNCEMENTS

30 SECONDS-DAYTIME

MON THRU FRI, AM:	1	2	3	4
6:30-7, NBC News At Sunrise	65	55	45	35
6:55, Today in Buffalo Sponsorship	80	70	60	50
7-9, Today Show	110	95	85	75
7:25/8:25, Today In Buffalo				
Sponsorship	115	110	100	90
9-noon, AM Rotation	95	85	75	65
PM:				
Noon-12:30, Noon News	50	40	35	30
12:30-3, PM Rotation	110	95	85	75
3-3:30, She-Ra	275	230	190	160
3:30-4, He-Man	350	275	230	200
3-4, She-Ra/He-Man	300	240	200	170

EARLY FRINGE				
4-4:30, Three's Company	235	205	185	165
4:30-5, MASH	235	205	185	165
4-5, Three's Company/MASH	215	195	175	155
5-5:30, Newscenter 2 Local	275	225	200	175
5:30-6, People's Court	325	275	250	225
6-6:30, Newscenter 2 Local	300	250	225	200
7-7:30, Entertainment Tonight	500	450	400	350
7:30-8, PM Magazine	500	450	400	350
7-8, Rotation	475	425	375	325
6-6:30/11-11:30 Mon thru Sun,				
News Combo	700	600	550	500
5-5:30/6-6:30 Mon thru Sun, News				
Combo	1000	800	750	675

LATE FRINGE				
11-11:30 Mon thru Sun, Newscenter				
2	450	375	350	325
11:30-12:30 am, Tonight Show	325	275	250	225
12:30-1:30 am Mon thru Thurs,				
David Letterman	175	125	100	75

10. PROGRAM TIME RATES

	1 hr	1/2 hr
Daily 7-11 pm	15000	9000
Weekends noon-6 pm	10000	6000

11. SPECIAL FEATURES

SPORTS & SPECIALS
NBC Baseball 375

INFORMATIONAL PROGRAMS

PER WK:	1 tl	2 tl	3 tl	5 tl
Sign-on-noon 5 min	750	700	625	500
Noon-6 pm 5 min	1250	1150	1000	800

Stations pay SRDS to list their rates and other
information of interest to advertisers and agencies in its
national directory. In these examples WKSE (FM),
Niagara Falls, and WGRZ-TV, Buffalo, indicate that
they both are members of the NAB, that the radio station
is a member of the Radio Advertising Bureau and that
the television station belongs to the Television Bureau of
Advertising.

Listings conform to standard SRDS pattern,
represented by the numbered sections. Section 1 for each
station lists top management; section 2 names the
national (and for WGRZ-TV the Canadian) sales reps;
section 3 describes station facilities; and section 4
indicates that both stations allow the standard 15
percent commission to advertising agencies. To save
space, SRDS uses a number code for the various policies
and contract terms listed in section 5. For example, the
code number 4a in section 5 of each listing means that
both stations accept beer and wine advertising; 6b means
that neither station accepts sponsored religious
programs.

The actual rates charged by WKSE, listed as dollar
amounts without the dollar signs in sections 6 and 7,
vary according to spot length, time of day, and level of
preemptibility; a spot bought by one advertiser at a lower
rate may be preempted, or replaced, by another
advertiser willing to pay a higher rate for that spot.

WGRZ-TV's rates, for television's standard 30-second
commercial, also vary by time of day and level of
preemptibility. As examples, Daytime and Early and
Late Fringe rates are listed above in section 7. Section 10
gives rates for full program sponsorships and section 11
offers pricing for special features.

Source: Reproduced with permission from Standard Rate
and Data Service, Inc., *Spot Radio Rates and Data*, Vol. 68,
No. 3, 1 Mar. 1986, p. 447, and *Spot Television Rates and
Data*, Vol. 68, No. 3, 15 Mar. 1986, p. 182.

periods) to give advertisers the benefit of varying exposures for their commercials.

• *Preemptibility.* Another basis for varying the price of spots is the degree of *preemptibility* risk they face. Preemptible spots, sold at a rate lower than that for fixed position spots, can be canceled by a station when a higher-paying customer wants that commercial position. Spots sold as preemptible with no advance notice are offered at a rate even lower than spots preemptible with advance notice. Advertisers do not, of course, pay for a spot that is preempted. Often, when a preemption does occur, the station will try to get the preempted advertiser to accept a spot at another time. When this happens (or if a commercial does not air for technical reasons and the advertiser agrees to run it at a later time), the rescheduled spot is called a *make-good.*

• *Package plans.* Radio and television stations offer a variety of *packages* that may include several spots scheduled at various times and on various days or may, for example, include announcements on both an AM and a co-owned FM station. The total cost of such a package is less than the sum of the individual spots, a feature often emphasized by salespersons negotiating with small local firms that have little broadcast advertising experience.

• *Special features.* Spots associated with particular programs are often sold at a higher rate. Many stations list a number of such features, such as live sporting events, including both local and network programs in which stations are entitled to sell spots.

TV Station Rates   Listings in the SRDS *Television Spot Rates and Data* books are similar to those for radio (Exhibit 9.3). Many stations decline to list their rates. Most listing stations have rates far more variable than typical of radio. It is not uncommon for a station to list over a hundred different prices for spots, using a device known as a *rate grid.* For example, a station might list twenty different time periods or program titles down the left side of its grid. Across the top it might list six different rate levels, numbered I through VI. This arrangement would create 120 cells, or boxes, into which specific prices can be entered. The rate levels can be defined quite arbitrarily, enabling the station to quote six different prices for essentially the same spot. Such a grid gives sales personnel great flexibility in negotiating deals without having to resort to under-the-table rate cutting. The grid also permits the use of the same rate card over longer periods of time, despite changes in audience or in advertiser demand, because sales management can simply direct salespersons to negotiate within one area of the grid rather than another. The station sells spots at a higher-priced grid level when advertiser demand is strong, and at a lower level when it is not. Grids also help in setting levels of preemptibility at which a commercial is likely to "hold" and not be preempted by a higher-paying advertiser.

Brief information on some television station rates can also be obtained from the *Broadcasting/Cablecasting Yearbook*'s station directory, but most stations prefer not to quote hard-and-fast rates for entire day parts, especially in a publication that comes out only once a year. In fact some television stations refrain from publishing rates in *any* form, relying instead on their sales personnel to negotiate rates with each individual client. For an idea of the range of television rates, examine Exhibit 9.4, which compares prices for television spots in markets of varying size.

TV Network Rates   Extreme differentiation in rates is especially true of network television. The rate for the same spot position in the same program changes even over the course of a single season, if the audience for the program changes significantly. In 1985 the cost for one showing of a 30-second network

Exhibit 9.4   Influence of Market Size on TV Rates

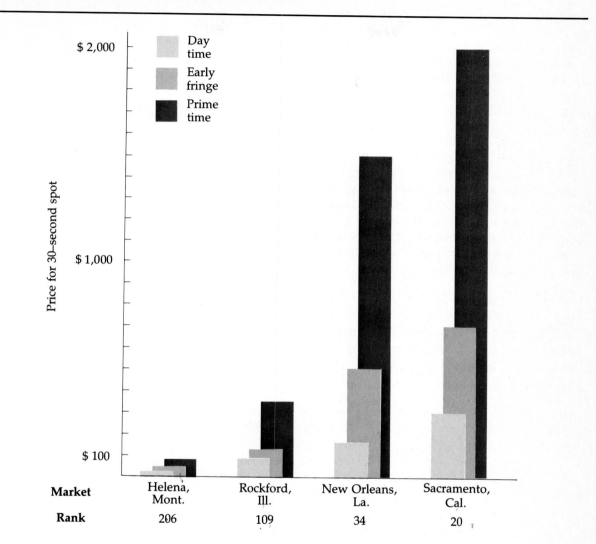

Prices are quoted for a specific station in each market and refer to rates for national advertisers. The graph shows the strong correlation between market size and rates. Because TV audiences vary more in size according to day part than do radio audiences, TV rates vary more widely by day part than do radio rates. Unlike small-market radio stations, even very small-market TV stations vary rates according to day part.

Source: Based on data in station directory in *Broadcasting/Cablecasting Yearbook, 1984*, Broadcasting Publications, Inc., Washington, D.C., 1984. Reprinted with permission.

spot in a regular prime-time television program averaged about $80,000; low-rated programs commanded about $50,000 per spot, and high-rated shows sold at $200,000 or more. Remember that these are *average* rates. Rates for specific spots in specific time slots vary widely. The rates cover only time charges and do not include commercial production costs.

SRDS also publishes a booklet on network rates and data, covering both radio and television networks, including the nonwired radio networks operated by some of the large advertising agencies and national sales representatives. However, none of the major radio or television networks releases details on rates to SRDS, preferring to remain flexible, free to negotiate each sale individually.

Cable Television Rates   As with broadcasting, the principal determinant of cable advertising rates is the size and composition of the audience exposed to the commercial. Although there are wide variations in audience within each of the three levels of the industry — local cable systems, interconnected systems, and cable networks — the most clear-cut pricing distinctions are found between those levels.

• *Local cable systems* offer many advertising opportunities in both locally originated programs and national program services. Rates for 30-second commercials range from as little as $2 to as much as $400 or more. The *Broadcasting/Cablecasting Yearbook* indicates which cable systems accept advertising and estimates annual advertising revenue but does not list advertising rates.

• *Interconnected cable systems* (§8.4), whether the connection is physical or simulated, combine to deliver a cumulative audience throughout a geographic region. The area covered by such a group of systems is called a *cable market*

of opportunity (CMO) and may represent anywhere from about 120,000 subscribers in the Syracuse, New York, CMO to nearly 1 million in the New York City Metro CMO. Rates may run from as low as $75 for several spots in selected advertiser-supported cable network programs in Syracuse to nearly $1,000 for a single spot in a sporting event shown in New York City. The Cable-television Advertising Bureau publishes a directory of interconnected (but not individual) systems with their rates and sales representatives (§9.6).

• *Cable networks and superstations*, although national in nature, do not necessarily command the highest advertising prices. Again, audience size and composition are the major determinants. In 1985 a 30-second spot on Cable News Network cost as little as $150 during the 1 A.M.–6 A.M. day part and as much as $5,000 during the network's Saturday morning *Moneyweek* program. Commercials on MTV averaged $1,200, and on MTV's second music channel, VH-1, $300. Superstation WTBS charged anywhere from $780 to $6,500.

Variant Rate Practices   Three types of commercial practices, used by both broadcasters and cable operators, fall outside normal rate practices: trade deals, time brokerage, and per inquiry.

In the most common of *trade deals* (also called *tradeouts*), stations exchange commercial time for advertiser goods and services. These might include such items as office space, office supplies, news department vehicles, and so on.

In a more specialized type of trade deal the advertiser exchanges game-show prizes for 7- to 10-second mentions (or *plugs*) during the show. In exchange for costly prizes the advertiser receives one or more short plugs; in exchange for less expensive prizes the advertiser must additionally pay a fee to receive a single plug.

Another special type of trade deal, *barter syndication*, is the trading of commercial time for programs. Barter programming is described in Chapter 13.

Stations that practice *time brokerage* sell time in blocks to brokers who then resell it at a markup. Foreign-language programming is often brokered in this way. Time brokerage was once regarded as a somewhat questionable practice, because it often meant surrender of licensee control over programming, in violation of one of the FCC's most emphatic rules. However, in its 1981 report affirming radio deregulation (§17.2), the FCC approved of time brokerage as a means of giving groups access to air time. Those who cannot afford to operate a station might at least be able to afford a few hours of their own air time each week.

Per inquiry (PI) deals, favored by mail-order firms on some cable networks and in cut-rate, late-night time periods on television stations, commit the advertiser to pay not for time but only for the number of inquiries or the number of items sold in direct response to PI commercials. Among the most successful PI promotion items have been Slim Whitman record albums and Veg-a-matic food slicers. Most broadcasters and cable operators oppose PI advertising in principle because it underrates the value of broadcast advertising. The worth of advertising cannot be judged fairly by direct sales alone, because a well-presented ad can also result in unmeasurable benefits: creating a favorable image of the advertiser and product, imprinting trade names in the audience's consciousness, and leading indirectly to sales at a later time.

9.6 Selling Advertising

Local Sales Departments   The stars of commercial broadcasting may seem to be the performers the public sees and hears, but in the broadcasting and cable business the real stars are the sales people who generate the revenue to pay the performers.

Indeed, salespeople (sometimes called "account executives") typically receive the highest pay among radio and television employees. Salespersons usually work on a *commission* basis, keeping a percentage of all advertising dollars they bring in. This arrangement gives them both an incentive to sell as much commercial time as possible and the opportunity to enhance their personal income without depending on annual salary increases. One variation of the straight-commission plan, called *draw against commission*, pays the account executive a stipulated weekly sum in anticipation of future sales. Some companies treat this arrangement as salary, and others consider the payments to be true advances, repayable by the employee if commissions don't measure up. Some stations pay the commission when a sale is made, and others wait until the commercial actually airs. Still others pay only when the station gets paid by the advertiser.

Most sales departments consist of a general sales manager, a local (and sometimes a national) sales manager, account executives, and support staff. The number of account executives varies from station to station; about six sales people are usually adequate for a medium-market station. Support staffs also vary; some stations employ one secretary to do all the support work, and others employ research people and commercial writers.

In addition to hiring, firing, managing, and training employees, sales managers assign each salesperson to specific advertisers and ad agencies. Beginning salespeople sometimes start without benefit of an *account list* (except, by industry tradition, the telephone yellow pages) and must build their own by making *cold calls* on potential new advertisers.

The account executive's major sales tool, aside from the personal qualities needed for success in any sales job, is audience research (Chapter 14). He or she must reduce the myriad numbers contained in rating reports to terms understandable to a client and present them so as to show the station in the best possible light. Armed with these data (often printed up in attractive brochures), along with a list of commercial availabilities supplied by the traffic department, the local rate card (if there is one), and information on the advertising needs and history of each prospect, the salesperson sallies forth to do battle.

Radio stations compete among themselves for "radio dollars," and television stations do the same for advertising budgets earmarked for television. But intermedia competition also occurs. The cable salesperson tries to convince broadcast advertisers to allocate portions of their budgets to cable. The broadcast salesperson suggests to newspaper advertisers that more efficient use of advertising dollars calls for fewer columns of newspaper ads and allocation of the money saved to radio or television commercials.

Selling aids available to the local sales department include the services of the Radio Advertising Bureau (RAB), the Television Bureau of Advertising (TvB), and the Cable-television Advertising Bureau (CAB). These New York–based organizations supply sales ammunition such as specialized audience and product data and sales-promotion materials for their respective subscribers.

In a sense the salesperson's real job begins *after* a client signs the first contract. Thereafter the salesperson nurses the client's interest in the medium through *account servicing*, seeking to ensure renewal of the first contract and, better still, to bring in bigger contracts in the future. Such servicing includes ensuring timely station receipt of the client's commercial materials, advising the client whenever a commercial airs improperly, and informing the client of special advertising opportunities.

Regional and National Sales   Stations gain access to national advertising business through *national sales representative* firms (*reps*, for short) and also, in the case of affiliates, through network sales departments. Some stations also have *regional reps* for nonnational sales outside the station's service area. A rep contracts with a string of stations (the top firms represent about one hundred stations each), selling their clients' time in the national and regional markets and functioning as an extension of the stations' own sales staffs. Television reps have only one client station within a market, whereas radio reps often have more than one. Some radio reps sell their client stations' time to national spot advertisers as a group, referring to them as *nonwired networks.*

Cable systems also use sales representatives. Specialized cable reps sell local or regional advertising on individual and interconnected systems. Others, as with radio and television, sell local systems to national spot advertisers.

Reps perform many services other than sales. Their national perspective provides client stations or systems with a broader view than that of merely local markets. Reps often advise clients on programming, conduct research for them, and act as all-around consultants. In return for their services, rep companies collect a commission of from 8 to 15 percent on the spot sales they make for their clients.

Network sales staffs and national reps are natural rivals. Major national advertisers use many different media, so that one medium must persuade advertisers and their agencies to divert as much of their advertising budgets as possible in its direction. Exhibit 9.5 shows how the nation's 5 largest advertisers, with

Exhibit 9.5   How Top Advertisers Spread Their Budgets

Rank	Advertiser	Ad budget (millions)	Percentage of budget allocated to:								
			Net TV	Spot TV	Net radio	Spot radio	Net cable	News-paper	Maga-zines	Out-door	Other media
1	Procter & Gamble	$872	47	27	*	*	3	*	6	*	17
2	General Motors	$764	30	5	*	4	*	14	13	*	34
3	Sears, Roebuck	$747	23	4	1	1	*	0	3	*	68
4	Beatrice	$680	16	8	*	*	*	2	6	*	68
5	R. J. Reynolds	$678	14	7	0	*	*	15	29	13	22

*Less than 1 percent

Four out of these five premier advertisers chose network television for their major expenditures. R. J. Reynolds, prohibited from advertising its tobacco products on radio or television, turned to magazines (including heavy use of TV Guide*) and billboards. So far, from this list, cable has succeeded in attracting large advertising dollars only from Procter & Gamble.*

Source: Based on 1984 data reported in *Advertising Age*, 26 Sept. 1985. Reprinted with permission. Copyright 1985 by Crain Communications, Inc.

annual expenditures of over half a billion dollars each, allotted funds to the major media. Allocations differ widely, but no advertiser puts all its advertising money into a single medium. Deciding on the right *media mix* is the task of advertising agency media directors.

Advertising Agency Functions   All regional and national advertisers, and most large local advertisers, deal with the media through *advertising agencies*. Some firms have their own in-house agencies, but most rely on independent agencies staffed with specialists able to handle a number of clients (Exhibit 9.6).

Advertising agencies employ a variety of specialists who advise clients on how to get the most out of their advertising dollars. They conduct research; design advertising campaigns; create commercials; buy time from cable systems, broadcast stations, and cable and broadcast networks; supervise the implementation of campaigns; and pay the media on behalf of advertisers. Agencies become intimately familiar with each client's business problems, sometimes even assisting in the development of new products or the redesigning and repackaging of old ones.

Large advertisers rely almost entirely on advertising agencies for creating commercials. Indeed, designing and producing commercials are an agency's most crucial functions. Anyone who doubts that making commercials is a highly developed art need look no further than the homemade commercials aired on small radio and television stations for evidence. The most convincing proof can be found in commercials that star local advertisers in person. Though the weird performances of used-car dealers and discount store owners sometimes achieve a kind of bizarre local notoriety, these commercials are testimony that the creation of advertising requires a special kind of talent.

Financial Role of Agencies   Ad agencies traditionally receive a 15-percent commission on *billings* — the amount charged by the advertising media. An agency bills its client the full amount of advertising time charges, pays the medium 85 percent and keeps 15 percent as payment for its own services. Variations in payment method arise, because a firm's own advertising department may do some of the work or may retain specialist firms to do specific jobs such as research, time-buying, or commercial production. Some agencies accept less than 15-percent commission or charge fees in addition to commission; some work on a straight fee basis, some on a cost-plus basis.

In any event, the fact that the media allow a discount on business brought to them by agencies creates an odd relationship: the agency works for its client, the advertiser, but is paid by the medium in the form of a discount on time charges. The travel business operates similarly: a travel agency works, at least theoretically, for the traveler, but is paid by the hotel or airline in discounts on charges. The fact that the ad agency actually makes the payments for time to the medium (as an agency service, but also in order first to deduct a commission) can create problems if an agency falls on hard times. In the 1970s a large agency collected money an advertiser owed CBS, but before passing on the payment due to the network the agency went bankrupt, leaving CBS empty-handed. A court ruled that CBS could not collect from the advertiser, and the network had to write off the debt. Learning well from the CBS case, the media now require the signature of both the advertiser and the agency on all contracts made with agencies deemed less than solid.

Exhibit 9.6   Top Advertising Agencies and Broadcast Billings

Rank	Agency	Annual broadcast billings as percentage of agency total
1	Young & Rubicam	64
2	J. Walter Thompson	71
3	Batten, Barton, Durstine & Osborn	71
4	D'Arcy, Masius, Benton & Bowles	77
5	Leo Burnett	67
6	Ogilvy & Mather	70
7	Dancer Fitzgerald Sample	78
8	Foote, Cone & Belding	76
9	Grey Advertising	56
10	McCann-Erickson	63

Note: By mid-1986, several agencies had merged.

"Billings" refers to the amounts billed to clients by the agencies for their services. The top two agencies billed over a billion *dollars in a single year.*

Source: Based on 1985 data in *Broadcasting*, "Broadcasting's Top 50 Advertising Agencies," 10 Feb. 1986, p. 42, reprinted by permission of Broadcasting Publications, Inc.

The CBS incident reinforces the point that the agency works *for the advertiser*, not for the advertising medium. That being the case, it may seem odd that a medium would be willing to accept lower payment for its services when the business is brought to it by an agency. But there is good reason for this seeming generosity. Many agency services would otherwise have to be done by the media, which are not equipped with the specialists and facilities to do the agency's jobs, or which simply would prefer not to do the work. Another way this method of payment benefits the media is that the agency assumes the burden of judging an advertiser's ability to pay. Some media compensate for the discount on agency-supplied advertising by paying their own sales executives a lower commission for sales made through agencies than for *direct* sales, those made directly to the advertiser.

Proof of Performance Advertisers and their agencies need evidence to show that contracts have been carried out. Although the FCC in 1984 deleted its rule requiring broadcast stations to keep daily program logs, those logs continue to be the most universal documentation of broadcast performance. Logging the time, length, and source of each commercial serves as documentary proof of contract fulfillment. A station's sales department relies on logs when preparing proof-of-performance warranties to accompany their billing statements. At many stations today, computers do the logging automatically. Some stations also make slow-speed audio recordings of everything they air, in the event of a dispute.

Following the FCC's deletion of its logging rules, Young & Rubicam, a major advertising agency, announced it would audit commercial performance itself. It planned unannounced visits to stations by members of the agency's staff — this despite an earlier survey by the agency indicating that nearly all responding stations planned no changes in their logging procedures.

Advertisers and agencies can gain independent confirmation of contract fulfillment by subscribing to the services of Broadcast Advertising Reports (BAR), a firm that conducts systematic studies of radio and television commercial performance. BAR checks on commercials by recording the audio portion of television programs in seventy-five markets, sending the recordings to central offices for processing, and actually viewing commercials

in some markets.

Two new commercial tracking systems were announced in 1985. The A. C. Nielsen Company planned to launch its Monitor-Plus service in ten markets in 1986 and to expand to seventy-five markets over succeeding years. Monitor-Plus would use computer technology to recognize each television commercial's unique combination of images and sounds. The other system, Ad Audit, planned to operate in 210 television markets. It would also rely on computers, but, in this case, the computers were to read electronic codes that had previously been recorded on the commercials.

9.7 Advertising Standards and Practices

Evolution of Standards Time and taste standards for commercials constantly evolve, reflecting changing conditions in society as well as within the broadcast and cable industry. As society becomes more permissive, the industry becomes more competitive. Ads for products that could not have been shown on television before the 1970s (feminine hygiene aids, for example) have become routine. Others (such as for contraceptives) did not appear until the 1980s. Increased competition demands increasingly flexible standards.

A constant tension exists between the urge to cram ever more commercial material into the schedule and the need to avoid alienating audiences by intolerable levels of interruption. At the same time, the desire to exploit every tactic of persuasion and to capitalize on every available source of advertising income collides with the need to stay reasonably close to socially accepted standards of taste.

These are not struggles between crass commercialism and pure idealism. Rather, they are pragmatic encounters between the points of view of sales directors and program directors, aimed at maximizing present income without endangering future income by driving away the audience.

No Mandatory Time Standards

Contrary to what many people think, the FCC does not, and never has, set a maximum number of commercial minutes per hour of programming. True, the commission once proposed to start regulating commercials, but, faced with severe broadcaster pressure, it quickly dropped the idea when a bill to forbid such regulation was introduced into Congress (House CIFC, 1963).

Broadcast license applications and renewal forms once required applicants to state the number of commercial minutes per hour they planned to allow, or had allowed in the past. Applicants who exceeded the industry's own time standards might then be asked to justify the excess. Thus the FCC tacitly endorsed the industry standards without officially adopting them, leaving open the possibility of case-by-case variations.*

The FCC also once prohibited what it called "program-length commercials." The term referred to productions in which the noncommercial segments of a program were so closely interwoven with the sponsor's commercial messages that the program as a whole promoted the sponsor's product or service.

But the FCC's move to *deregulation* (§17.2) did away with the program-length commercial prohibition and even the tacit endorsement of industry time standards. The FCC removed

the commercial time guidelines for radio in 1981, for television in 1984. The commission argued that the marketplace, not the government, could best control the amount of commercial time. FCC chairman Mark Fowler was quoted as saying, "What's really at issue here is whether the government trusts the common man to make up his own mind about what to watch or not to watch. If a half-hour TV shop-at-home service is an annoyance, he will choose to watch — or do — something else" (*Broadcasting*, 2 July 1984). No commercial time limits have ever been set for cable.

Voluntary Time Standards

The industry standards tacitly accepted by the FCC were those adopted by the National Association of Broadcasters. The NAB, in its radio and television codes, had set up voluntary time standards both for advertising and for programs (§16.7).

But even these NAB codes no longer exist, because the Justice Department charged that industry efforts to set guidelines for the conduct of its business violated antitrust laws. Some broadcasters continue to use the now-defunct codes as general guidelines for their operations. Others, including networks, set their own time limits. NBC, for example, permits a maximum of 10 minutes per hour of nonprogram material (including commercials, promos, and billboards) during prime time, 16 minutes per hour during all other time periods, and 16 minutes during sports programs whatever the time of broadcast.

Standards of Taste

Many perfectly legal products and services not usually advertised on the electronic media are nevertheless advertised in the print media.* This double standard of taste is more evidence of the special

---

*Although there were exceptions and qualifications, the nominal limits on commercial material per hour were as follows: 18 minutes for radio; $9\frac{1}{2}$ minutes for prime time and 16 minutes for all other time aired by network-affiliated television stations; and 14 minutes for prime time and 16 minutes for all other time aired by television independents.

---

*For example, federal law prohibits advertising cigarettes and smokeless tobacco on radio and television.

obligations society imposes on broadcasting (and, to a somewhat lesser degree, on cable) because of its special nature as home media accessible to all.

The most conspicuous example of self-imposed advertising abstinence is broadcasting's policy of not advertising hard liquor. Beer and wine ads have always been accepted, although various organizations over the years have tried to remove even them from the air. One of the most ambitious, called SMART (Stop Marketing Alcohol on Radio and Television), conducted a nationwide campaign in 1984 and 1985, collecting thousands of signatures to pressure Congress into banning all alcohol ads. Though the campaign attracted a great deal of attention and represented the most serious challenge to such ads in years, it did not lead to any action either by Congress or the FCC. It did, however, result in increased industry self-restraint and a public-service announcement campaign, organized by the NAB, to combat alcohol abuse.

On rare occasions hard liquor ads have been broadcast, though the NAB codes prohibited liquor ads, and distilling-industry codes still do. Even after the NAB codes were dropped, most broadcasters declined to carry liquor ads for fear of giving added ammunition to opponents of wine and beer advertising. CBS departed slightly from NAB code standards in 1983, announcing it would accept wine commercials showing people actually sipping the beverage — an indiscretion that had been forbidden by the broadcast code.

Another broadcast advertising taboo has been the display of the human body. Broadcasters generally feel that although nudity may be acceptable in a National Geographic special, it is not in an ad for women's lingerie. But this barrier, too, has begun to crumble. In the fall of 1983 the first United States television commercial with nudity premiered on the USA and Cable Health networks; it showed a nude young woman, back to the camera, donning her $16 bra and $9 panties and then rising and turning to reveal the sponsor's product. This commercial seemed to predict cable's further departure from broadcast advertising standards, and raised the question as to whether television will ease its standards in order to meet cable competition.

In any case, in the absence of voluntary industry codes and externally applied regulation, individual broadcasters and cable programmers are left to gauge the tastes of the audiences they serve and to set their standards accordingly.

Industry Standards and Practices   The three major television networks, as well as some group broadcasters, set and enforce both program and advertising standards through separate departments, variously called *Continuity Acceptance*, *Broadcast Standards*, or *Program Practices*.

At NBC, for example, the Broadcast Standards Department has reviewed program and commercial materials since 1934 to maintain standards of taste and propriety, and publishes detailed guidelines for both programs and advertising. In a typical television season, department editors make judgments on more than 2,000 entertainment outlines and scripts. The staff reviews every step of the program production process, from inception to broadcast.

Regarding commercials, the department's concerns include deceptive advertising, as well as matters of taste. Advertising agencies that produce commercials cooperate in the self-regulation program and, in most cases, submit commercial ideas to NBC at a very early stage, either as script or story-board. Each ad is assigned to a network staff member responsible for that particular category of advertising, such as automobiles, food, toys, or drugs. Agencies must supply documentation that supports claims made in a commercial ("Eight out of ten doctors prefer . . ."). When a new product is introduced, the editor requests a sample, including the package and label, to ensure that the product and its use are accurately described. Product demonstrations require advertiser or agency affidavits that include descriptions of how the demonstration was conducted and assurances that products were not altered from those a purchaser would find in a store. If a commercial mentions a warranty or guarantee, NBC obtains a copy.

Of the approximately 48,000 radio and television commercials submitted to NBC each year, one-quarter require substantiation of claims. The Broadcast Standards Department returns more than 7 percent to the agency or advertiser for revision. The number of television commercials that reach the film or tape screening stage totals more than 18,000 yearly. The experience at ABC and CBS is much the same.

Advertising self-regulation comes also from the National Advertising Review Board (NARB), which evaluates complaints about media advertising that are forwarded to it by the National Advertising Division of the Council of Better Business Bureaus. The NARB was formed in 1971 in response to growing public cynicism about the truthfulness of advertising claims. It does not review advertising in advance, as do the networks, but examines charges brought against advertisements after broadcast or publication.

Deceptive Advertising and the FTC

Prosecution for outright deception in advertising falls under the jurisdiction of the Federal Trade Commission (FTC) rather than that of the FCC. However, use of fraudulent advertising by a broadcaster can be cited by the FCC as evidence of lack of character qualifications required of licensees. The FTC's responsibilities extend to all media and to all types of unfair trade practices, of which deceptive advertising is only one.

Instances of possible false advertising may be brought to the FTC's attention by consumers, competitors, or the commission's staff. Under its *Advertising Substantiation Program*, the FTC may require the advertiser to provide proof — often based on scientific testing — of the correctness of its advertising claim. If the proof satisfies the FTC, the matter is closed. If not, the FTC may proceed with various sanctions.

The FTC settles most cases of alleged deceptive advertising by *stipulation*, an informal (and hence time-saving) way of getting advertisers to drop objectionable practices voluntarily. If a formal complaint becomes necessary, the FTC can seek a *consent order*, another nonpunitive measure, under which the advertiser agrees to stop the offending practice without admitting guilt. Actual guilt has to be proved before the FTC can obtain a *cease and desist order* forcing compliance with the law. These orders can be appealed to the courts, which usually means considerable delay in bringing the objectionable advertising to a halt.

In the early 1970s the FTC introduced a new penalty, designed to go beyond merely forcing false advertisers to cease and desist. Called *corrective advertising*, it requires offending advertisers (if they wish to continue advertising the products in question) to devote some of their advertising budgets to setting the record straight. The FTC has imposed the corrective penalty in very few cases since the first case in 1971, and the rectifying messages have been so skillfully worded that probably few consumers recognize corrective advertisements as admissions of prior misrepresentations. Nevertheless, corrective advertising represented a positive move in the direction of consumer welfare by an agency that had previously been regarded as ineffectual in this area of its responsibility.

However, the Reagan administration's drive to deregulation and the 1981 appointment of James C. Miller as FTC chairman appeared to reverse that direction. Miller made clear his belief that government regulation is not needed in most situations, and that market forces lead business to work for the benefit of the consumer. In 1983 the FTC revised its policy on deceptive advertising by requiring proof that a "reasonable consumer" had actually been harmed before an advertiser could be charged with deceptive advertising practices. It was no longer enough that the advertising was in fact deceptive.

Former FTC chairman Michael Pertschuk, upon leaving the agency in 1984 after serving as a member for seven years, attacked the FTC in a 273-page report to the House Energy and Commerce Committee, which has jurisdiction over the agency, writing, "Today the agency is crippled; tomorrow, under the same choking reins, it will be moribund." He accused the commission of being "consumed with a single-minded determination to undo the past — not just the immediate past — but the very foundations of antitrust and consumer protection law." He went on to say that the agency had an "ideological blindness" that led to a "new era of regulatory nihilism, and just plain nuttiness." Responding to Pertschuk's attack, Miller, who earlier had promised vigorous enforcement of consumer protection laws, found the report "riddled with factual errors and distortions of varying degrees: unsubstantiated claims, half-truths, misrepresentations and faulty logic" (*Broadcasting*, 3 Sept. 1984).

After Miller was named director of the Office of Management and Budget in 1985, continuation of his approach to advertising regulation seemed assured with President Reagan's appointment of commissioner Terry Calvani as acting FTC chairman. Said Calvani: "In my view, Jim Miller has really turned this agency around. It's pointed in the right direction; it's going at the right speed, and my principal responsibility is to see that the Miller initiative, the Miller direction, is continued" (*Broadcasting*, 14 Oct. 1985).

Children's-Advertising Standards Consumer groups such as Action for Children's Television (ACT; §12.5 and §15.3) contend that because young children have not yet learned to understand the difference between advertising and entertainment, they need special protection from commercial exploitation. After conducting hearings on this and related questions, the FCC issued a statement of policy in 1974 regarding children's programming (§12.5) and recommended that broadcasters voluntarily adopt special standards for children's advertising in four areas:

1. *Time standards.* Nonprogram material in children's non-prime-time programs should be limited to 9½ minutes per hour on weekends and to 12 minutes on weekdays.
2. *Separation.* Care should be taken so that commercial and program materials are clearly separated from one another.
3. *Host selling.* The host of a children's show should not deliver commercials within that program.
4. *Product tie-ins.* Gratuitous product mentions within children's programs should be avoided.

In 1983 the FCC watered down those portions of the 1974 policy statement dealing with broadcasters' obligations to carry children's programming but left children's-advertising standards intact. The FCC's 1984 deregulation of television eliminated all commercial time guidelines, including those applicable to children's programs, but had no effect on the other standards for children's advertising.

Meanwhile, in 1978 the FTC had begun separate proceedings aimed at restricting advertising to children. Proposals included limits on commercials for foods with high sugar content and an outright ban on all ads aimed at preschool children. Broadcasters, advertisers, and ad agencies registered their opposition. Some members of Congress threatened to cut FTC appropriations unless the inquiry was dropped. Producing no new regulations, the investigation ended in 1981 after the FTC's activist chairman, Michael Pertschuk, responding to allegations he was not impartial on the issue, voluntarily removed himself from the proceedings. Reagan administration appointments of succeeding deregulation-minded FTC chairmen made it unlikely that the agency would soon again consider limitations on children's advertising.

Continuing its campaign, ACT in 1984 complained to the FCC about programs such as *He-Man* and *G.I. Joe* that, according to ACT, were designed more to sell dolls and accessories than to entertain children (Exhibit 12.5). The organization also objected to program syndication deals, such as that used with *Thunder Cats*, whereby stations carrying the program share profits from the sale of Thunder Cat products — a motivation ACT suggested was incompatible with the public interest. In 1985 the FCC, noting the absence of any evidence that these practices in fact produced any harm, rejected ACT's complaints. In the same year the FCC denied yet another ACT request by refusing to require broadcasters and cable operators to insert signals into their programming that would activate special devices to delete commercials directed at children.

Loudness   Style as well as length affect commercial salience. Harsh voices, rapid delivery, excessive repetition, and loudness are stylistic aspects of commercials often deliberately used to make them more obtrusive.

One of the most persistent subjects of complaints to the FCC and to broadcasters is the perceived loudness of commercials. After more than one study of the subject, the FCC

in 1984 decided not to impose any regulations in this area, saying its studies led it to conclude that "loudness" was too subjective to regulate (FCC, 56 RR2d 390, 1984).

Unethical Business Practices   Several areas of commercial abuse in broadcasting have been the subject of FCC and even congressional action. Four types of unethical deals have been particularly troublesome: plugola, payola, fraudulent billing, and clipping.

1. *Plugola.* Conflict of interest occurs when a station or one of its employees uses or promotes on the air something in which the station or employee has an undisclosed financial interest. This practice, called *plugola,* usually results in an indirect payoff. A disc jockey who, on his program, publicizes a flying school in which he has part ownership would be one example.

2. *Payola.* Direct payments to the one responsible for inserting plugs is known as *payola.* It occurs most frequently in the form of under-the-table payoffs by recording company representatives to disc jockeys and others responsible for putting music on the air (§3.9).

The legal basis for banning both plugola and payola is the sponsor identification law (§9.3). A 1959 congressional investigation uncovered a wide range of both plugola and payola practices. As a result of these disclosures, Congress in 1960 strengthened the sponsor identification law, adding Section 507 (formerly 508) to the Communications Act, prescribing a $10,000 fine or a year in jail (or both) for each payola violation. Despite these efforts, payola scandals continue to erupt every few years.

3. *Fraudulent billing.* Local cooperative advertising (§9.1) sometimes tempts stations into fraudulent *double-billing* practices. Manufacturers who cooperate in paying for local advertising by their dealers are easy targets for such deception. Being far away, they must rely on

their local dealers to handle co-op advertising Dealer and station may connive in sending the manufacturer a bill for advertising that is higher than the one actually paid by the dealer. Station and dealer then split the excess payment. In the past, some stations have lost their licenses for double-billing frauds compounded by misrepresentations to the FCC.

4. *Clipping.* Network *clipping* occurs when affiliates cut away from network programming prematurely, usually in order to insert commercials of their own. Clipping once violated FCC rules and also constitutes fraud, since networks compensate affiliates for carrying programs in their entirety with all commercials intact (§8.2).

Continuing its practice of deregulation, the FCC in 1986 eliminated its policies dealing with fraudulent billing and network clipping. The agency said that complaints about billing were civil or criminal matters, not the business of the FCC, and that clipping was a matter between the networks and their affiliates. The FCC did say, however, that it would consider the falsification of billing statements when judging a licensee's character during any licensing proceeding.

Summary

• Broadcasting achieved relatively rapid success as an advertising medium because of its unique psychological advantages and its great flexibility in serving local, regional, and national advertisers.

• Commercial practice has shifted from program sponsorship to the insertion of spots within and between programs over which advertisers have no direct control.

• The effectiveness of broadcast advertising is offset for some users by its cost, by the fact that it often reaches more people than desired, and by limits on commercial length.

• Clutter, an impression created by the pile-up of announcements, worries the advertising community because it decreases the effectiveness of commercials.

• A station's traffic department schedules commercial announcements, preventing back-to-back advertising of competitive products.

• Cable enjoys many of television's advantages but suffers two major disadvantages: the difficulty of inserting commercials in its numerous channels and the absence of audience research comparable to broadcast rating reports.

• Advertising rates reflect the fact that advertisers buy time only as a means of getting access to audiences. Because audiences change with programs and services as well as with times of day and times of year, prices for spots tend to change accordingly.

• Sales representatives and (for affiliates) network sales organizations supplement broadcast and cable sales departments in reaching some advertising clients.

• Advertising agencies plan most advertising campaigns and select media outlets.

• The media provide proof of performance by means of their daily program logs, but agencies also hire specialized firms to check the fulfillment of advertising contracts.

• No laws limit the amount of commercial time inserted in and between programs. Formal industry guidelines fell with the NAB codes, so that today only individual station and network standards and market pressures limit advertising time.

• Standards of taste continue to evolve with changes in competition and the attitudes of society.

• The Federal Trade Commission has authority over deceptive advertising practices.

• Offenses that can jeopardize station licenses include plugola and payola.

CHAPTER 10

Other Economic Aspects of Electronic Media

With some exceptions (public broadcasting and cable's C-SPAN network, for example), broadcasting and cable are designed to be profit-making businesses. As we have seen in the preceding chapter, radio and television attempt to accomplish this goal primarily through the sale of advertising time.

But other financial aspects affect the profitability of the electronic media and even form the foundation of some of them. This chapter first places the industry in an economic setting and then examines some of those other considerations: program acquisition costs and procedures; subscriber fees, the principal revenue source of cable television and some other media; the investments required to construct stations and systems; the purchase, sale, and merger of broadcast stations and cable systems and networks; and the economic bases of public broadcasting.

10.1 Financial Framework

A Money Machine?   Broadcasting seems so profitable that critics have called it "a license to print money." This is only a partial truth as far as stations are concerned, al-though the dominant forces in the industry, the television networks, have been both highly profitable and relatively immune from the financial ups and downs that affect most businesses. In 1983, for the first time, each of the three major commercial broadcast networks generated revenues in excess of $2 billion. In 1984, ABC became the first to exceed $3 billion. In 1985, although revenues fell slightly for the first time since 1971, the three networks attracted more than $8.3 billion in advertising and produced profits exceeding $1 billion.

A survey by the National Association of Broadcasters found that in 1983 the typical network-affiliated television station had a pretax profit of about $1.4 million, and the typical independent station a profit of just under $1 million (NAB, annual). But whereas the typical radio station showed a 1982 pretax profit of $51,100, about 33 percent of all responding radio stations failed to show any profit at all (NAB, annual).

There are two major reasons an unprofitable station continues to operate. First, many so-called losses exist only on paper. Because corporate income taxes are paid on profits, not on revenues, owners avoid such taxes by keeping profits to a minimum. "Creative" deductions from income for such items as depreciation, amortization, and payments to owners may result in a deliberate "loss" for tax purposes, even though the station may have a positive cash flow. Second, even genuinely unprofitable stations tend to hang on because the owners or prospective owners are optimistic about an eventual payoff. Despite these considerations, however, in 1984, for example, fifty-one radio stations, as well as thirteen television stations (including low-power, subscription, and translator stations), performed so poorly that they were forced to file for bankruptcy.

The profitability of most FM radio and UHF television stations after years of losing money shows that in broadcasting it often pays to keep trying against formidable odds. Failing broadcast properties attract investors for three related reasons. First, owners have confidence that losing stations can be turned into money machines if only the right formula can be found. Second, owners who wait long enough may eventually realize profits from selling their stations. Third, station ownership satisfies an owner's ego by conferring a certain aura of glamour and community prestige.

The cable industry, which went from a $200 million loss in 1982 to an estimated $800 million profit in 1984, also has its share of winners and losers. Newer systems with high construction costs and low subscriber penetration experience sizable losses, at least initially. But many of the smaller, established systems regularly generate handsome profits. In the mid-1980s, 12-channel cable systems averaged the highest profit margins, $9.15 per subscriber before taxes and depreciation; 35-channel systems, with higher operating costs, averaged $8.80 per subscriber; and systems with 55 and more channels averaged per-subscriber profits of only $5.85 (*Broadcasting*, 19 Dec. 1983).

Multiple system operator (MSO) profits and losses vary widely. Tele-Communications, Inc. (TCI), the nation's largest MSO, had a 1985 net income that was about 41 percent lower than its net income for 1984. On the other hand, Adams-Russell, the forty-eighth largest MSO, enjoyed 1985 profits that were 21 percent higher than in 1984.

One reason for the poorer showing by the larger systems was that during the franchising process, when several companies were bidding competitively for the franchise, applicants proposed to build unrealistically expensive systems, agreeing at the same time to charge unrealistically low subscriber fees. In 1982 the city of Baltimore's *Request for Proposals* (RFP) demanded a 100-channel interactive (two-way) system. In 1983 several firms seeking Philadelphia franchises proposed as many as 130 channels, and subscriber rates as low as $1.95 per month for a 36-channel basic package; in 1984 the city granted permits to four regional systems with mandatory 82-channel capacity. In Sacramento the bidding frenzy reached new heights, with the winner promising to plant 20,000 trees throughout the city.

Some franchise winners, having saddled themselves with unrealistic requirements, attempted to renegotiate their franchises. Warner Amex, for example, first proposed a dual-cable, 108-channel system for Milwaukee but later asked the city's permission to cut back to a 54-channel, single-cable system. The company also sought to eliminate all previously promised local origination facilities, to reduce the number of local access channels from eighteen to six, and to raise subscriber rates. Cable operators for systems serving Detroit and Washington, D.C., sought similar concessions. As the cable industry matured, mergers and consolidations occurred. Bill Daniels, a pioneer cable operator and a major cable broker, predicted that by 1995 the twenty-five largest MSOs would own 80 to 90 percent of the cable systems in the country (Welch, 1985).

Among pay cable networks, Home Box Office continues to lead with about 15 million subscribers — more than those of Cinemax, Showtime, and The Movie Channel combined. HBO demonstrated its ability to compete with the major broadcast television networks for the first time in December 1982, when one of its programs outranked ABC, CBS, and NBC in prime-time ratings in homes that subscribed to its service: the feature film *On Golden Pond* attracted over half of HBO households, while ABC, CBS, and NBC combined drew just over 40 percent. During the months of June and July, when the networks run mostly repeat programming, HBO often outperforms them with its first-time-on-television feature films.

By the mid-1980s pay cable networks experienced a drop in the growth rate of new subscriptions, and some even suffered a net loss in total subscribers. The home videocassette recorder (VCR) loomed as the principal cause (§4.7). Though the total effect of VCRs on the broadcast and cable industries was yet to be determined, it was likely that pay cable would feel the greatest impact, because videocassettes offered the same first-run, unedited movies as pay cable, and offered them sooner. About 22 million prerecorded videocassettes were sold in 1984, and countless more were rented for as little as a dollar a day — strong competition for the cable operator trying to market premium channels at $10 a month. By 1986, in fact, more American homes (about 30 percent of all television households) owned VCRs than subscribed to a pay cable service (21.6 percent). One pay program service, The Movie Channel, elected to compete with videocassette rental stores by special scheduling of movies (for example, a different film daily at 3:00 A.M.) to attract VCR owners and

encourage use of their machines' automatic timers.

Many cable systems still operate only twelve or fewer channels. This limited channel capacity restricts such systems to offering only a few program services, and a cable network service carried by only a few systems cannot reach enough people to attract advertisers. According to Kay Koplovitz, president of USA Network, for an ad-supported service to succeed it needs to be carried by cable systems having 25 million subscribers and should attract between 8 and 10 percent of that potential audience (*Broadcasting*, 2 Aug. 1982). By 1986 few of the forty or more such networks had achieved those results. MTV and CBN were in the black by 1984. And although superstation WTBS had been profitable for several years, the other Turner Broadcasting services, CNN and CNN Headline News, remained in the red until 1986. Many of the other cable networks struggle to survive.

Almost every week the lineup of ad-supported cable networks changes. Even networks with solid financial backing and entertainment expertise sometimes fail. CBS Cable, which offered quality cultural programming but which was able to attract no more than thirty advertising sponsors, went dark in 1982 after only one year of operation, losing an estimated $30 million. Others sold out or merged with surviving services (§10.5).

Role of Broadcast-Market Size   Profitability in broadcasting depends on market size, which affects all aspects of an enterprise. The larger the market, generally speaking, the larger the station staff, the higher the salaries, the longer the program day, the more network programs are carried, and the more local production occurs — and of course the higher the sales revenue and, therefore, the profits. Exhibit 10.1 compares markets of widely differ-

Exhibit 10.1   Television Station Income and Market Size

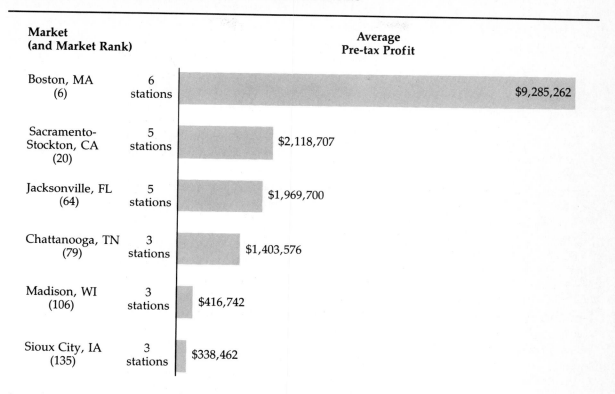

Market (and Market Rank)		Average Pre-tax Profit
Boston, MA (6)	6 stations	$9,285,262
Sacramento-Stockton, CA (20)	5 stations	$2,118,707
Jacksonville, FL (64)	5 stations	$1,969,700
Chattanooga, TN (79)	3 stations	$1,403,576
Madison, WI (106)	3 stations	$416,742
Sioux City, IA (135)	3 stations	$338,462

As market rank (in terms of number of television households in the market) goes down, so does the average income for television stations.

Sources: Arbitron market ranks from *Broadcasting/Cablecasting Yearbook 1984* (Washington, D.C., 1984), pp. C-201–C-204; average pre-tax profit calculated from National Association of Broadcasters data reported by *Broadcasting*, 5 Mar. 1984, pp. 41-42. Reprinted with permission.

ing size, showing, for example, that the average television station in the 6th market earns more than twenty-seven times as much as the average station in the 135th market.

This is not to say that the correspondence between market size and profitability is absolute. Economic conditions vary among markets, as does the efficiency of broadcast managements. For example, Wilkes-Barre–Scranton, Pennsylvania, a somewhat de-pressed area, ranks as the 50th largest market, but the average television station there made a profit of under $600,000 in 1982. By contrast, in upscale Salinas-Monterey, California, which is ranked 110th, the average station that year had a pretax profit of over $1 million, nearly twice that of the much larger market.

Influences on Profit   The larger the organization, the more likely it is to achieve a profit margin* higher than smaller organizations. A company may raise its profit margin by increasing revenue and/or by reducing expenses. Group owners, and to a lesser extent MSOs, often achieve savings through bulk purchase of equipment, supplies, and programs and by sharing of employees and ideas. Thus, they realize *economies of scale*.

Broadcasters, ad-supported cable networks, and some cable systems also benefit from the fact that what they sell, air time, is intangible. Expenses do not increase in step with sales. For example, if an appliance dealer buys a television set for $500 and sells it for $750, the dealer makes a $250 profit. Selling a second set yields another profit of $250. For every $750 in sales, the dealer must spend $500 in order to make the $250 profit. By contrast, if it costs a television station $500 to run one episode of *Gilligan's Island*, and if one 30-second commercial within the program sells for $750, the station makes a $250 profit. But a second spot sold at the same price does not incur a second expense: the cost of the program has already been accounted for, so the entire $750 in revenue is profit. A third $750 sale is again all profit. And so on.

This simplistic hypothetical example does not, of course, account for the many elements other than direct costs that constitute expenses, such as overhead and sales commissions. But it illustrates the advantage broadcasting has over businesses that incur additional costs with each sale. NBC's 92-percent increase in profits in 1985, on only a 10-percent increase in sales, offers a dramatic real-world example.

---

*Profit margin is that percentage of net revenues (after sales commissions but before operating expenses have been deducted) represented by pre-tax profit. Thus, for example, if a television station has net revenues of $2 million and a pre-tax profit of $400,000, it would have a profit margin of 20 percent ($400,000 divided by $2 million).

10.2 Program Economics

All program activities face the ever-present and ever-increasing problem of costs. Only by applying the parsimony principle (§11.1), which holds that program materials must be conserved by shared and repeated use, do broadcasters keep the problem manageable.

Local Station Programming and News
Average program and production department expenses at a typical radio station and at a network-affiliated television station amount to about 23 percent of total station expenses. In dollars, however, there is a dramatic distinction. A radio station spends about $112,000 annually on nonnews programming, whereas a television affiliate spends nearly nine times as much.* Personnel costs account for most radio programming expenses. Distributors usually supply music to stations at no charge in exchange for the promotion their albums and tapes receive from air plays. Television stations, however, must commit enormous sums to the acquisition of syndicated program series and feature films.

Comparing the costs of radio and television news presentation illustrates even more clearly the greater expense for television. Nearly all radio stations broadcast at least some news; a number of them, particularly on the AM band, provide news or news/talk 24 hours a day. Though some television stations, usually independents, offer little or no news, most network affiliates typically present at least an hour of local news each day, and many greatly exceed that amount. The typical radio station allocates about 5 percent of its total expenses to news; the network-affiliated television station, on the other hand, allocates

---

*Financial data in this section, unless otherwise attributed, are based on surveys conducted by the National Association of Broadcasters (NAB, annual).

over 15 percent. Translated into dollars, this means about $26,000 for the average radio station and about $680,000 for the typical television outlet. Television news requires a much larger staff (on the average, 17 full-time and 2 part-time people) than does radio (fewer than 3 people in all), as well as sophisticated and expensive electronic news gathering (ENG) and news gathering by satellite (NGS) equipment and supplies.

Broadcasters once considered news a necessary but unprofitable part of their business. News was necessary in order to meet a station's license obligations, but early audiences were small and advertisers were reluctant to lend much support. In 1963, however, a nationwide survey revealed that, for the first time since the biennial survey began in 1959, more respondents named television than named newspapers as the source of most of their news. Advertisers soon agreed not only to place their commercials within television newscasts and even to become segment sponsors but also, in many cases, to pay premium rates for access to the generally upscale and better-educated news viewers. Television has continued to be the primary news source for most people, followed by newspapers, with radio placing third (Roper, 1985).* With this acceptance of broadcast news by audiences and advertisers has come economic viability. A 1984 survey by the Radio-Television News Directors Association found that 81 percent of the responding radio news directors and 89 percent of television news directors reported their departments were making money or at least breaking even (*Broadcasting*, 29 Apr. 1985).

Local Production   Local television program production is confined almost exclusively to news programs. Simple economics makes it infeasible for local broadcasters to produce entertainment programs that compare to syndicated or network shows. Nor are advertisers usually willing to support locally produced programs, which traditionally attract small audiences.

Stations in large markets with better-than-average resources do somewhat more local production than others. Some, for example, produce a weekly *access-time** series. Few, however, accomplish as much as Boston's WCVB, which in 1984 produced 30 percent of its programs locally, compared to a national average of about 10 percent. Its innovative programs included *Chronicle*, the nation's only locally produced live nightly newsmagazine aired in access time.

Many local cable systems offer locally originated programs. The 1985 *Broadcasting/Cablecasting Yearbook* estimated that 3,700 systems, about a third of all systems, originated an average of 23 hours of programming a week. Much of this, such as simple newscasts, information programs, exercise shows, and coverage of city commission meetings is low-budget product. Cable systems often defray studio production costs by leasing studio facilities and air time to community organizations and local businesses, and some systems dedicate channels to public schools and to colleges and universities.

Syndicated-Program Acquisition   Television stations, independents much more than network affiliates, rely on *syndicated* programs

---

*Because it is commissioned by the broadcast industry, the Roper Report's validity is at times questioned. However, a 1985 study commissioned by the American Society of Newspaper Editors showed the same results (*Broadcasting*, 15 Apr. 1985).

---

*Access time refers to that part of a television affiliate's broadcast day unavailable to networks because of the prime-time access rule (§13.2). Depending on context, access time is either 7:00 P.M. to 8:00 P.M. or 7:30 P.M. to 8:00 P.M. (Eastern and Pacific times).

to fill many of their broadcast hours. Syndicated shows are those licensed on a station-by-station basis for local telecasting. Program series first seen on ABC, CBS, or NBC are referred to as *off-network*, or simply *off-net*, programs when in syndication. Programs that are shown first on local stations are known as *first-run* syndicated shows. The nature of these programs is described in §13.4.

To obtain the right to show a syndicated program, a station enters into a contract with the distributor of the program. For a negotiated fee paid to the syndicator, the station receives a *license* to broadcast the program in its local market. In industry parlance this is referred to as "buying" a program, though the program is in fact "rented" for a specific length of time, not bought. The license usually gives the station the right to show each episode in a series — each *title** — several times over a period of years. For example, a station contracting for reruns of the old off-network series *Bewitched* might agree to pay $1,000 for each of the 252 episodes in the series, for a total of $252,000. For this payment, the station might gain the right to run each episode six times over a six-year period. Thus each *run* of the program would cost $166.67 ($1,000 per title divided by six runs). In 1984, a New York City station paid $80,000 per title for ten runs of *Cheers* — a per-run cost of $8,000 for each episode. Agreeing to buy at least ninety-four *Cheers* episodes, the station committed over $7.5 million to acquire the series.

In view of the large sums involved, most stations negotiate with the distributor to pay a maximum of 10 percent of the total contract price at the time of signing the contract, with the balance paid in monthly installments over a number of years.

The prices stations pay for syndicated programs reflect such considerations as the popularity of and demand for the program, the size of the station's market, whether or not the series has already run in syndication in the market, and recent prices paid for other programs in that market. Ideally, the per-run price a station pays for a 30-minute program would equal the amount the station plans to charge for two 30-second commercials within the show. As media competition for programming increases, however, it becomes more difficult for program buyers to achieve that ideal. The success of NBC's *The Cosby Show*, for example, was expected to result in some stations paying as much as 70 percent of their anticipated revenue from the series just to obtain it and to keep it from running on a competing station.

Contributing to the price inflation of syndicated programs is the fact that in recent years few series have continued on the network sufficiently long to warrant syndication. Because stations usually *strip* (§11.5) off-network series on a Monday-Friday basis (that is, run an episode of the series daily at the same time), and because stations want to avoid repeating titles too frequently, sixty-five episodes is regarded as the bare minimum for successful syndication, with over a hundred preferable. The traditional network order is for only twenty-two new episodes of a series per year, so series require several years to reach a marketable total.

The scarcity of very popular network series has caused many stations to risk some of their program budgets by bidding for highly rated sitcoms and dramatic series years before enough episodes are produced to support a strip schedule (called bidding on *futures*). The bidding can start after a series has run on a

---

*Producers give specific titles, or names, to each episode of every syndicated series. Sometimes episode titles are used on the air (often with hour-long crime dramas, for example) and sometimes episodes are broadcast without mention of titles (typically the case with half-hour situation comedies). In either case, broadcasters use the terms *episode* and *title* interchangeably when talking about buying syndicated programming.

network for as little as two or three years and is common practice after four years. If the series fails to reach the ideal number of episodes or fails to achieve the desired ratings in rerun, the station runs the risk of having overbid for the program. In some cases, in exchange for stations' commitments to buy a program, production companies agree to produce new episodes after the network run of a series has ended (*Fame* and *Too Close For Comfort* are examples).

This scarcity of off-network series has also resulted in some record-breaking prices in major markets, as well as some record-breaking sales for distributors. It was expected, for example, that the initial sale of *Dallas* in syndication would produce total revenues of about $100 million, with repeat sales between $50 million and $60 million. *Magnum, P.I.* was expected to exceed $200 million in initial syndicated sales. A look at some of the per-episode prices reportedly paid for off-network series by stations in Los Angeles gives an indication of the cost of such programming in a major market: *Cheers*, $60,000; *Gimme a Break*, $70,000; *Magnum, P.I.*, $125,000. *The Cosby Show* was expected to sell for as high as $150,000 per title. By 1986, television program syndication was generating $500 million annually and was expected to reach $1 billion in total sales by 1990.

Another business arrangement under which stations may acquire program rights is *barter*. In a barter deal the station pays no money for the program but allows the syndicator to retain some of the commercial time slots within the program. The syndicator keeps whatever revenue is received from its sale of that time. Among the most successful shows "sold" on a barter basis have been *Hee Haw*, *Lawrence Welk*, and *Wild Kingdom*. A hybrid form of barter syndication is *cash/barter*, wherein the syndicator receives cash for the program but also retains some commercial time within the program for sale to national advertisers.

Network-Program Procurement   Broadcast television networks, like stations, obtain most of their programming from outside their own organizations. The networks spend several billion dollars a year for the rights to use programs for a limited number of plays. In the mid-1980s the license fee for a one-hour prime-time drama or action-adventure averaged $750,000 to $800,000 per episode for the original telecast and $65,000 to $70,000 for repeats. It should be noted that these are *averages*. Some series were priced as low as $600,000 and others (NBC's *Miami Vice*, for example) cost over $1 million per hour.

Thirty-minute shows cost somewhat less than 50 percent of the price of 60-minute shows, averaging about $325,000 per episode for the first run and between $30,000 and $35,000 for repeats. The principal reasons for the lower cost of half-hour shows are that (1) most 30-minute shows are on videotape rather than film, a savings of about $100,000 per show, and (2) they are usually produced on permanent in-studio sets with few location scenes.

High as these prices may seem, they rarely cover the full cost of production. In 1981, for example, it was estimated that each episode of *Hill Street Blues* cost about $175,000 more to produce than NBC was paying the producer, MTM; by 1985 the gap had widened to about $200,000, resulting in a cumulative deficit for MTM of some $25 million. Producers are willing to license prime-time entertainment series — the only ones with high residual value for syndication — to networks at cost or even below cost, counting on subsequent syndication fees to bring in the profits. This maneuver, known as *deficit financing*, capitalizes on the peculiar dynamics of the syndication market. Initial network showing enhances the future value of a series because such exposure gives the series the prestige and track record it needs to attain syndication in both foreign and domestic markets.

The average network cost for leasing a made-for-TV movie in the mid-1980s was about $2.5 million for two runs over four years, and about $3 million for theatrical features. Daytime serial dramas cost about $550,000 per week (for five episodes), and game shows between $120,000 and $150,000 per week.

Part of a network's program budget goes to purchasing rights to sports events. Examples include the $1.2 billion agreement signed in 1983 by ABC and NBC for rights to major league baseball in the years 1984 through 1989; the $2.1 billion contract signed by all three networks for five years of NFL professional football; ABC's agreement to pay $309 million for the exclusive broadcast, cable, pay television, and videocassette rights to the 1988 winter Olympic games in Calgary, Canada (more than three times the price the same network paid for the same rights to the 1984 games in Sarajevo); and NBC's "risk-sharing" deal for the 1988 summer games in Seoul, South Korea, which required the network to pay $300 million plus as much as $200 million more, depending on its advertising revenue from the games.

As do local television stations, the networks allocate considerable sums to their news operations. In 1985, CBS was expected to spend nearly $280 million in this area. Of that total, $189 million was for so-called hard news (for example, the *CBS Evening News*); $36 million for public affairs, (including *60 Minutes, West 57th*, and documentaries); $7 million for special and unscheduled events (such as disaster coverage); $5 million for political coverage (this figure increases enormously in presidential election years); $11 million for worldwide distribution of shows; and $31 million for staff, including management, whose salaries are not attributable to any particular program.

Cable networks also rely primarily on outside sources for their programming. Although they often compete directly with the television networks for theatrical motion pictures and some sporting events, their program budgets do not yet approach those of ABC, CBS, and NBC. HBO's total program budget for 1983 has been estimated at $350 million, compared to the annual $1.5 billion each for the three broadcast television networks. Of HBO's total commitment, $290 million went to feature-film rights, $10 million to films made especially for HBO, and $50 million to original made-for-cable programming and sports rights.

Production-Cost Allocation   The main variables affecting program costs are the production method used (taping performances before a studio audience is least expensive; single-camera film is most expensive) and cast salaries. Production expenses are divided for budgeting purposes into two categories, *above-the-line* and *below-the-line*. The "line" represents the division between the creative aspects and the craft aspects of the production. Typical above-the-line items are salaries for writers, performers, and directors. Typical below-the-line items are payments for scenery, costumes, props, lights, camera operators, editing, film and/or tape stock, film processing, and facilities rental or overhead. Although proportions vary from show to show, above-the-line items usually account for about 45 percent of a program's budget, and below-the-line 55 percent.

Program Guides   One concern shared by stations, systems, and networks, once programs have been produced or purchased, is informing potential viewers when and where they may see those programs. Program dollars will be wasted if no one watches the shows.

Television stations and broadcast networks consider on-air promotion announcements the most cost-efficient way to advertise their programs. Some cable systems dedicate one channel to program listings, while cable networks promote upcoming material between and within their programs. Cable systems also send subscribers printed program information (often supplied by cable networks), sometimes in magazine form, sometimes in brochures included with the customer's monthly bill.

Daily newspapers and Sunday supplements carry television and cable program listings. Some newspapers gather the data themselves, and others hire outside organizations to do the job. The most widely recognized source for program information is *TV Guide*. But as the box on pages 264-265 points out, even that magazine is unable to provide full details on all available programming in today's multichannel world.

10.3 Subscription and Other Supports

Substantial segments of the broadcast and cable industries look to means of support other than advertising. In fact, monthly fees paid by subscribers represent about 99 percent of cable television revenue. C-SPAN, cable's public-affairs network, looks to the cable industry itself to meet that network's expenses. Public broadcasting relies on viewers, government, and businesses for its support (§10.6).

Cable Subscription Fees   The economic base of every cable system is the monthly fee subscribers pay to receive the system's services. Some small systems charge a single monthly rate. Others offer several levels of

program service, called *tiers*, with a separate fee for each level.

Most systems offer a *basic* service that includes all local television stations, perhaps one or more distant superstations, and some advertiser-supported cable networks. The monthly fee for this basic package can vary from a few dollars to $25 or more. Industry expert Paul Kagan estimated that in 1984 the average rate for basic services was $8.92 per month.* Some systems with larger channel capacity break their basic service into two tiers. For example, some of the more popular ad-supported networks (such as MTV and ESPN) may be pulled out of the basic package and offered separately as an *expanded-basic* service at extra cost. The estimated 1984 average expanded-basic monthly fee was $4.58.

The next level of service includes pay cable channels such as HBO, Showtime, and Disney.† Usually, subscribers must pay a separate fee for each pay service they select. Such fees range from $2 or so to $20 or more, with the average about $10. In some cases, two or more pay services are packaged and offered at a price less than the cumulative price for the individual networks. A system in Carlsbad, California, for example, offered a 1985 package consisting of Cinemax, Bravo, American Movie Classics, and a choice of Disney or Playboy for $15.95, compared to the usual price of $9.95 each. By 1985 about 31 million homes subscribed to pay cable, with the average subscriber signing up for 1.3 pay channels.

In the mid-1980s, the average cable subscriber who took a basic and expanded-basic

---

*Estimates of cable fees and subscribers in this section are from *The Cable TV Financial Databook*, Paul Kagan Associates, Inc., 1984.

†Pay cable is one type of pay television, a term that also describes such services as subscription television, multipoint distribution service, master antenna television, and direct-broadcast satellites (§4.4 and §7.6).

TV Guide: **A Powerful Influence on the Electronic Media**

Every week about 20 percent of all U.S. television households turn to *TV Guide* to see what's on television, to decide what to watch, and to read articles and gossip about the television and cable industries. *TV Guide* comes in a distant third, behind newspaper weekly TV supplements and newspaper daily listings, as the most frequently cited source of program information; but these local publications cannot match *TV Guide*'s estimated readership of 43 million.

TV Guide is the creation of publisher-broadcaster Walter Annenberg (later a U.S. ambassador to Great Britain), who combined three local weekly television program guides to produce the first edition of *TV Guide* on April 3, 1953. It started with 10 regional editions and a circulation of 1.5 million. By 1985 the magazine offered 107 regional editions with a circulation of about 17 million (down from its 1977 peak of nearly 20 million). More than half of all copies are sold at newsstands, mostly in supermarkets. Each of the 107 regional editions offers the same national pages of articles and news, plus special pages for that particular region containing program listings for cable services and local stations only.

The publishers of *TV Guide* design the magazine for their readers, not for electronic media. Indeed it is not uncommon for the magazine to include editorials critical of the industry. The publishers stress that the publication is not a fan magazine, dwelling not so much on personalities as on television's relationship with, and impact on, society. A look at some of the contributing authors supports the claim: Arthur Schleslinger, Jr., Pulitzer Prize-winning historian; Lee Loevinger, former FCC commis-

LUCY'S $50,000,000 BABY

TV GUIDE

COMPLETE PROGRAM LISTINGS—April 3-9
15¢

DESIDERIO ALBERTO ARNAZ IV

package and one pay channel paid a monthly bill of nearly $24. If that subscriber were one of 5,000 served by a given system, the monthly revenue of that system would be about $120,000, and the annual income nearly $1.5 million. In practice, of course, not all systems have three (or more) tiers, not all charge the average prices, and not all subscribers make identical selections. Overall, the average total monthly revenue per cable subscriber in 1984 was only about $19. But even at that rate, a 5,000-subscriber system generates more than

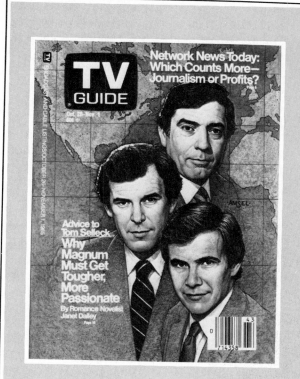

gram changes before the network's affiliates do —an occasional source of embarrassment to the stations and a common subject of network/ affiliate discussions. The magazine's computers store summaries of more than a quarter of a million syndicated episodes and some 28,000 movies. When a station or network tells *TV Guide* it plans to show a certain episode of a series on a certain day, the editors call up the appropriate summary for inclusion in the listings.

TV Guide does not list all stations and never lists some cable program services. A new station must acquire a substantial audience before it can get its program schedule included, a dilemma frustrating to many station operators. As for cable, dozens of systems, many with thirty or more channels, may operate within a region covered by a single *TV Guide* edition, making it impractical for the magazine to include everything. It therefore lists programming not by *channel* but by *service*. But again there are more cable networks and superstations than could reasonably be listed in a magazine of acceptable size and price. The magazine solves this problem by simply including only the most-watched services. Rarely, for example, does it offer program information for Modern Satellite Network, National Christian Network, The Learning Channel, or Black Entertainment Television. It never listed RCA's Entertainment Channel, now out of business, because the service attracted only about 50,000 subscribers. If viewers don't know that a service exists, or what its programs are, the service has little chance of survival.

sioner; Alvin Toffler, author of *Future Shock* and *The Third Wave*; Alexander Haig, Jr., former secretary of state.

Each week television stations throughout the country send in future program schedules, and each week editorial representatives of the magazine call stations to update program information. The publication has a three-week lead time, hence the disclaimer printed in each edition: "Channels and networks reserve the right to make last-minute changes." Often, through its direct contacts, *TV Guide* learns of network pro-

$1.1 million in fees each year. By contrast, the average monthly advertising revenue of cable systems was estimated in 1984 to be 30 cents per subscriber; at this rate, our hypothetical 5,000-subscriber system would realize only $18,000 in annual advertising income.

Cable systems with *addressable* converters (§7.8) offer special programs on a pay-per-view (PPV) basis (Exhibit 8.5). With PPV, the subscriber pays a one-time charge to see a single program, either a movie or a special event, such as a boxing match or a rock concert. In

1984 approximately 1.6 million PPV subscribers paid an average of $15 for each such program. The per-program price was expected to drop to as little as $2.50 as PPV became more widespread.

PPV programs are arranged in one of two ways. First, individual cable systems — so-called *stand-alones* — can negotiate for, and themselves originate, a PPV event. Second, national program services can acquire PPV rights to movies and other programs and distribute them to cable systems under a fee-splitting arrangement. Examples of the latter include EventTeleVision, a joint venture of several leading cable MSOs, and Request Television, owned by television producer Norman Lear and present or former cable executives. Cable networks also plan to enter the PPV arena. Showtime/The Movie Channel experimented with PPV in 1985 by supplying some programs to stand-alones and announced intentions to launch its full service in 1986. Also in 1985, Playboy tested its Private Ticket PPV service on three cable systems. HBO had already distributed some of its feature films on a limited PPV basis to some cable systems and explored the possibility of setting up a second tier of its pay cable service, initially called Festival, but denied plans to offer PPV on any full-scale basis. The early absence of electronic hardware, both to accomplish distribution of programs to paying subscribers and to handle the flood of last-minute, impulse telephone orders, slowed the growth of PPV. It was expected that reliable equipment to meet these needs would be available, and economical, by the late 1980s.

One variation on PPV is Video Jukebox. First begun in Miami in 1986, this cable service first offers viewers a *menu* of music videos, each with its own 2-digit code shown on the screen. The selection is made by calling Video Jukebox, using a touch-tone phone to enter the video's code. A computer registers the request, programs the channel, and eventually plays the video. Each request costs $1, charged to the viewer's telephone bill; the telephone company keeps 30 cents and 70 cents goes to the program service. The concept is limited, however, by available air time: during peak hours, 3-hour waits for videos to appear are common.

A few cable systems offer ancillary services, such as burglar and fire alarm protection, by wiring home doors and windows and installing heat and smoke sensors to detect entry or possible fire. In some systems, when a sensor is triggered, a signal alerts an operator at the cable headend who, after calling the homeowner for verification, notifies the police or fire department. In others, signals go directly to the appropriate authority. In 1984 there were about 75,000 subscribers to these security services, paying an average of $19 per month.

In addition to monthly fees, most cable systems also charge a one-time installation fee. There may also be a "connection" charge when a subscriber elects to add a new pay cable channel. To induce homeowners to sign up, cable operators frequently offer these charges at a reduced rate or waive them entirely.

Control of Subscription Rates   Historically, the amount of money that a cable system charged subscribers for its various services was determined by a combination of market conditions and negotiations with the city under whose franchise the system operated. In many cases franchise agreements spelled out exact prices for installation, for the basic packages, and for the pay channels. Further, the franchising authority retained the right to approve any proposed rate increases. Effective in 1987, however, the Cable Telecommunications Act of 1984 reduced most of the control cities had over cable-system rate structures. (For legal and other controls on cable, see §17.2 and §17.6.)

Other Subscription Services

Other fee-dependent media include multipoint distribution service, satellite master antenna television, and direct-broadcast satellite.*

Multipoint distribution service (MDS) offers a single channel of cablelike programming but is carried by microwave signals rather than broadcast television signals. The introduction of multichannel MDS (MMDS) enabled services to offer four channels of over-the-air programming (§7.6). In the mid-1980s, the average MDS monthly subscriber fee was about $15, plus installation, perhaps low enough to make it competitive with some cable systems (Exhibit 4.4).

Satellite master antenna television (SMATV) operates much like a cable system, but on private property (§7.7). In addition to local stations, typical SMATV systems provide three to five satellite-distributed services, including superstations and cable networks. Many operators divide the programming into a basic service and one or more tiers. Basic subscriptions usually range from about $6 to $20 per month, with the full package of basic service and added tiers priced at around $35 per month. Between 30 and 50 percent of the families living in a multiple-dwelling unit generally subscribe to SMATV, depending on the number and quality of signals available. Some building owners operate SMATV systems themselves, rather than using independent suppliers, and offer the service free or at cost to entice new tenants (Exhibit 4.5).

High per-house wiring costs discourage cable operators from constructing systems in rural areas with low population densities, and few MSOs are willing to build where there are fewer than twenty homes per mile. Some entrepreneurs saw direct-broadcast satellite (DBS) as a service that could fill this void, but as of early 1986 no DBS services were in operation (§4.8 and Exhibit 4.9). Other entrepreneurs tried using direct satellite feeds to beam X-rated programming to subscribers who already owned TVROs (Exhibit 4.2). The Pleasure Channel charged $350 to lease a descrambler, plus $100 a year for the service; Fantasy Unrestricted Network (FUN) asked $275 for the first year of service and $160 for subsequent years.

Meanwhile, satellite-distributed program services began to scramble their signals so that backyard-dish owners would be unable to watch without paying a fee. HBO and Cinemax were first with full-time scrambling in January 1986. The networks plan to market their services to TVRO households, directly and through local cable system affiliates. About 1.3 million home dishes had been sold by 1986, and although scrambling slowed sales considerably, new ones were being sold every month, thus creating a potentially lucrative market for the pay cable networks, if they could convince TVRO owners to pay for what they had been receiving free.

Industry-Supported Cable

One cable network has the distinction of being neither wholly advertiser-supported nor dependent upon subscriber fees: C-SPAN (Cable-Satellite Public Affairs Network) was started in 1979 as an expression of good will on the part of the cable industry. System operators view the service as good for their image, both in Washington, D.C., and in their local communities. Operating 24 hours a day, it carries live coverage of proceedings of the U.S. House of Representatives and, as of 1986, the U.S. Senate, as well as congressional committee hearings, interviews, call-in shows, conferences, and other public-interest programming.

---

*The technical bases of these services are described in §7.6.

About two thousand participating cable systems with 23 million subscribers meet most of C-SPAN's $8 million annual budget by paying four cents or less a month per subscriber to carry the service. About 10 percent of C-SPAN's revenue comes from advertising, corporate underwriting, and other services (such as production of videotapes and sublease of satellite transponder time). The network does not accept product advertising but does allow corporate image messages, usually 10 to 15 seconds long, between programs. Centel Communications, one of the nation's largest MSOs, was the first to agree to carry C-SPAN on all of its systems, and continues to offer additional support in the form of equipment donations and $50,000 a year in underwriting funds.

All in all, C-SPAN manages to provide remarkably varied programming for relatively few dollars. According to John P. Frazee, Jr., president of Centel and 1985 chairman of C-SPAN's board of directors:

[In 1984] 82 C-SPANers — 78 of whom are under the age of 30 — produced more than 4,000 hours of first-run public affairs programming. In all, C-SPAN transmitted 8,760 hours of quality cable programming to its affiliates [in 1984] at a cost per television hour of just $622. [For comparison,] in 1983 ABC offered its affiliates less than half that much programming at a cost per hour of $598,800. (C-SPAN Update, 1 Apr. 1985).

SCAs and VBIs   Radio and television station signals can be used to deliver secondary services. In a series of actions in the early 1980s, the FCC made it possible for broadcasters to profit from these services, and since 1982, AM stations have been permitted to multiplex inaudible secondary signals on their channels. For example, electric-power companies have arranged with AM stations to send multiplexed signals to special receivers at various business locations that would briefly turn off air-conditioning units when power demands were high. Two years later, authorization for secondary service was extended to any use that did not interfere with a station's program signal, such as uses already available on FM channels through subsidiary communications authorization (SCA) services.* Early utilization of SCAs was largely limited to Muzak and other background-music services, and a few stations offered farm news or business and financial information. Public radio stations use SCAs to transmit special programming for the visually impaired and some foreign-language material.

The FCC further expanded SCAs in 1983, permitting FM stations to use three subcarriers. Stereophonic sound usually occupies one, leaving two available for lease. A growing SCA user is the paging business. One company, Reach, Inc., headquartered in Lincoln, Nebraska, employs a national network of mobile electronic paging receivers, using FM subcarriers as its transmission medium. To belong to the network, a station must install the necessary transmitting equipment (costing about $2,500) and pay an affiliate fee ranging from $6,000 to $35,000 annually, depending on market size. The station makes its profit by selling time on the network to local customers and by leasing or selling the pagers themselves.

Another system, DataSpeed, based in Burlingame, California, sends out stock quotations using Quotrek, a technology incorporating a portable radio receiver with two-way capability. The portable unit, which subscribers lease, features LCD (liquid crystal display)

---

*The term has been officially changed to *subsidiary communications services* (SCS), but most of the industry continues to refer to it as SCA.

Exhibit 10.2   Subcarriers

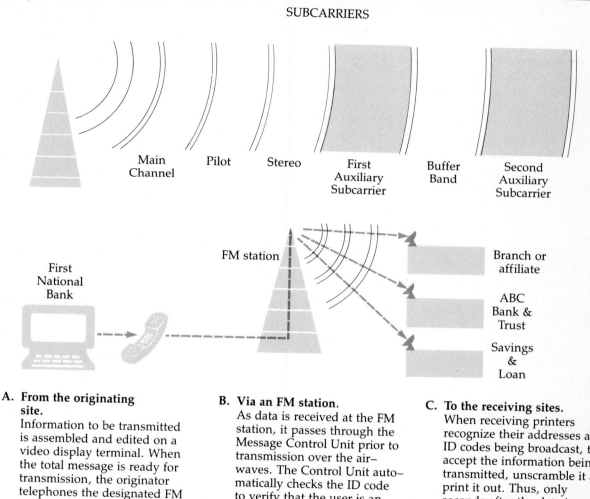

SUBCARRIERS

Main Channel   Pilot   Stereo   First Auxiliary Subcarrier   Buffer Band   Second Auxiliary Subcarrier

First National Bank

FM station

Branch or affiliate

ABC Bank & Trust

Savings & Loan

A. From the originating site.
Information to be transmitted is assembled and edited on a video display terminal. When the total message is ready for transmission, the originator telephones the designated FM station, and sends the data to the station over standard telephone lines.

B. Via an FM station.
As data is received at the FM station, it passes through the Message Control Unit prior to transmission over the air-waves. The Control Unit auto-matically checks the ID code to verify that the user is an authorized customer.

C. To the receiving sites.
When receiving printers recognize their addresses and ID codes being broadcast, they accept the information being transmitted, unscramble it and print it out. Thus, only seconds after the data is sent from the originating site, printed copies are available at each remote location.

FM subcarriers can be used for many nonbroadcast purposes, including transmission of business data from a central point to many receiving sites.

Source: © COM/TECH Report Series, National Association of Broadcasters, Washington, D.C., 20036, based on information from Bonneville Radio Data Systems, Inc.

readouts and stores stock symbols in its memory. The user enters into the unit the symbols for a desired stock quotation, and the unit displays the latest transmission it has received for that stock. DataSpeed transmits its information to participating radio stations by satellite and pays a flat fee to the broadcasters for carrying the service. Other DataSpeed applications of SCA technology include Informa, an electronic mail and information system, and Modio, a service providing data base access to computer owners.

Physicians Radio Network (PRN), in operation for several years, transmits medical information in forty cities, pays stations about $2,000 a month for subcarrier lease, and sells advertising time to pharmaceutical and other companies that offer products and equipment to physicians. A similar project, Lawyers Radio Network (LRN), offers subscribers 24-hour-a-day legal news, categorized by legal specialty.

The use of SCAs for transmission of slow-scan video is gaining increased attention. This service transmits still pictures to educational and other institutions, for teleconferencing and for instruction and information distribution. Broadcasters either lease subcarriers to producers of slow-scan video or become producers themselves.

As broadcasters' experience of SCA utilization increases, the potential revenue from the service may be as high as $10,000 a month for stations in the largest markets and as low as a few hundred dollars in small markets. Broadcasters considering this ancillary business must evaluate that potential in light of the start-up and operating expense and effort.

In 1983 and 1984 the FCC authorized television stations to exploit their unused signal capacity, making possible television stereophonic sound and simulcasts of foreign-language audio to accompany English-language television programming (§6.11).

Television stations have the further option of using their vertical blanking intervals (VBIs) to transmit closed-captioned subtitles to the hearing impaired (§6.11). Stations derive no direct revenue from their closed-captioned signals but rather see this activity primarily as a public service. In addition, some stations have experimented with teletext; but by the mid-1980s most operators had failed to find an economic base for it, although some continued to offer the service (§4.8 and §6.11).

Production as a Revenue Source   Students often have other expectations, but once employed they soon discover that most broadcasters and cable operators prefer to keep both program and commercial production to a minimum. The simple explanation is economics.

Rather than serving as sources of added income, most locally produced programs add to expenses. Only a very small portion of the materials carried by stations, systems, and networks is produced in-house. Most programs come from independent production companies or syndicators. As for commercials, a few television stations and cable systems have production departments that pay for themselves and sometimes even earn a profit. But commercials are usually produced at a loss or on a barely break-even basis; the service is considered a necessary cost incurred to induce the advertiser to buy time.

10.4 Capital Investment

One does not become the owner of an electronic mass communication business casually. Both legal and financial qualifications are involved. The broadcast and cable industries, though not as capital intensive as some other fields, nonetheless require a very high initial investment, either for constructing new facilities or for acquiring existing ones.

Broadcasting   The most valuable asset a radio or television station owner has is the FCC license permitting operation of the facility. To use a license an owner must buy equipment to receive, originate, and transmit programming, along with associated buildings and office facilities.

Radio station construction costs range from $50,000 for a simple, small-market AM or FM station to several million dollars for a sophisticated radio facility in a major market. A station in the low-power-television class (§7.6) that has local program production capability may, under ideal conditions, cost no more than $300,000, but a full-power television facility may cost ten times that much. Stations that plan to originate secondary services such as teletext need to invest an additional $200,000 for that technology alone.

Unlike most other media, broadcasting and cable count on the general public — the consumer — to supply the largest part of their basic capital equipment, the broadcast receivers. The public's capital investment in broadcasting amounts to many times the total investment of the industry itself. In fact, some estimates place the public's investment at more than 90 percent of the total. The extent of this public involvement forms much of the basis for the broadcast industry's unique obligation to its audiences.

Cable   On a cost-per-home-served basis, a cable system costs even more to construct than a broadcast facility. This is because each home must be physically connected to the cable system. A spokesman for Capital Cities Communications reported that for some of its new systems (*new builds*), which were anticipated to cost $600 per home to wire, it was actually paying $1,200 per home (*Broadcasting*, 11 April 1983). Costs of installing cable on existing utility poles range from $10,000 per mile for rural areas, to $20,000 per mile for urban areas, and up to $100,000 per mile for underground cable. Media analyst Jeff Greenfield claimed that systems in major metropolitan areas were paying as much as $1 million per mile (ABC, 21 Dec. 1984). Two-way cable costs considerably more than one-way, with additional expenses at the headend alone amounting to $30,000 to $50,000 per system.

As with a television station, the equipment investment for local cable origination will depend on the facility's operating philosophy and desired level of sophistication. A simple monochrome studio may be constructed for as little as $30,000, but a reasonably equipped color facility will cost $200,000 or more. In 1986 the cable industry was expected to spend a total of more than $1.2 billion for new construction and hardware, including about $12 million for commercial insertion equipment.

Satellites   Because they are more efficient and cost-effective than ground-based relay facilities, communication satellites have reduced the operating costs of stations, systems, and networks. Satellites, more than any other technology, have made it possible for modern cable and the other alternative media to flourish.

Though more economical for long-distance signal relay than traditional telephone lines and microwave relays, satellites and the equipment associated with them are not inexpensive. For example, Hughes' Galaxy I satellite, reserved for cable industry use, cost about $30 million to construct, plus another $40 million to launch and insure against possible loss. (This $70 million total was more than offset, however, by the sale of transponders for a reported total of $195 million.) Early satellite launches by NASA rockets cost about $70 million each. Later launches by the space shuttle brought launch costs down to about $30 million each.

The life expectancy of a geosynchronous satellite is eight to ten years. RCA Americom's Satcom I, the satellite that sparked the enormous growth of cable in the late 1970s, was launched in December 1975. After nearly nine years, Satcom I's twenty-four transponders were still working, but the fuel needed to keep the satellite in its synchronous position was running out. In June 1984, to make room for a replacement and prevent interference, the satellite was boosted into a higher, nonsynchronous (and useless) orbit.

It is not necessary, of course, for all those who wish to use a satellite to own one. Single transponders are available through outright sale or on long-term lease, usually for seven years, for between $10 million and $13 million. Occasional use (for example, by a television-station news department to bring home live coverage from the state capital) costs as little as $200 for one hour.

Earth stations that send signals up to satellites (the uplink) range in price from about $600,000 to $750,000. As is the case with transponders, those who do not have sufficient need of transmission facilities to warrant owning their own may rent uplinks from others. Satcom International is one of several companies with transportable earth stations. These mobile uplinks may be rented for about $4,000 a day plus travel charges of $250 per day and $1 per mile.

*Receive dishes** that cable systems, television stations, or other users employ to receive satellite signals (the downlink) are called TVROs if used only to receive and not to transmit. The cost of TVROs varies from as little as $1,000 for simple units for residential use to $40,000 or more for professional models capable of "looking at" several satellites.

*Although still referred to as "dishes," many satellite receiving antennas no longer have that characteristic shape.

SMATV   Satellite master antenna television construction costs vary widely, depending on the size of the multiple-dwelling unit and the sophistication of the installation. An average 300-unit system might cost about $80,000, including $35,000 for earth station equipment but excluding cabling. Cable and connection costs are often determined by the age and construction of the building (many new complexes are prewired for cable) and by the number of tenants subscribing.

10.5 Buying and Selling Properties

In the thirty-one years from 1954 through 1984 more than 11,000 radio stations and nearly 1,000 TV stations changed ownership. The total value of these transactions was pegged at over $13.6 billion. Every week the industry publication *Broadcasting* lists stations and cable systems for sale and others already sold.

The buying and selling of electronic media properties takes place for many reasons. Some owners of losing or marginal operations despair of ever making a profit and get out while they can. Broadcast group owners and cable MSOs expand their holdings or *trade up* (sell smaller, less desirable properties to buy larger ones) to improve their economies of scale and profit ratios.

The most common reason for acquiring a broadcast station or cable system is that the buyer perceives it as a better opportunity to make more money than is possible in many other fields. Supermarkets, for example, have a notoriously low *profit margin* of perhaps 1 or 2 percent. Most broadcast station profit margins exceed that level, with some at 50 percent or higher. For this reason, large, multifaceted *conglomerates*, many of which have no prior broadcast ownership, often choose to invest in the industry. Conglomerates prefer, however, to participate in several types of businesses rather than concentrating on just one or two. In this way, should one of their industries suffer setbacks, the effect on the conglomerate would be limited.

Ownership and Trafficking Rules

There are no limits on the number of cable systems one company may own, and in 1984 the FCC revised its "Rule of 7s" for broadcasting. Today a single entity may own as many as 12 AM radio stations, 12 FM stations, and 12 television stations, provided that the 12 TV stations do not together reach more than 25 percent of all U.S. television households (§17.7). The first station group to go beyond the earlier limit of seven was Universal Broadcasting, when it announced in September 1984 that it planned to buy an eighth AM station, WATI in Indianapolis. The first to go to twelve television stations was Taft Broadcasting, with its 1985 acquisition of the Gulf Broadcast Group properties. The expanded group produced a potential reach of slightly more than 11 percent of U.S. television homes.

In 1982 the FCC eliminated most of its twenty-year-old *trafficking* rules (in no way related to, and not to be confused with, station traffic departments). Those rules, designed to prevent trading in stations at the expense of service to the public, had required the holder of a license to keep it a minimum of three years before transferring it. Still remaining is the requirement that construction permits for new stations be held for one year before being transferred.

Before any sale of a radio or television station can become final, it must receive the approval of the FCC. In some cases a municipality exercises control over the sale of a cable system operating under that community's franchise. (For details on legal controls and other influences on sales of broadcast and cable properties, see §17.7.)

Sales of Broadcast Properties Though not all radio and television licensees sell at a profit, those that sell at a loss are exceptions. In 1984 David E. Schutz, an independent broadcast consultant on mergers and acquisitions, analyzed 207 radio station sales made in 1983. Of those 207, 143 (69 percent) sold for the same or for a higher price than was originally paid for the station; 64 (31 percent) sold at a lower price, most of them AM *stand-alones* (that is, without co-owned FM stations). In recent years AM stations as a group have declined in value compared to FM or AM/FM combinations. The 207 transactions showed that station values had increased at a 14 percent annual compounding rate. Excluding stations sold at a loss, the remaining stations increased in value 25 percent (*Broadcasting*, 3 Dec. 1984).

Brokers handle most station sales. Like real estate agents, they bring buyers and sellers together. Station brokers receive a standard commission of 5 percent of the selling price, but earn somewhat less on major transactions.

Pricing Broadcast Properties There are no fixed, reliable formulas for determining the appropriate selling price of a station. Several factors influence what a buyer should pay or a seller should ask: market size, market location (depressed industrial area or expanding Sunbelt area), radio format or television network affiliation, equipment, competitive position within the market, financing arrangements, and so on.

There are, however, some rules of thumb by which to estimate a ballpark price for a broadcast property. The selling price of an FM

Exhibit 10.3   Radio and Television Station Trading

	Radio		Television	
	Number	Average price	Number	Average price
1976	413	$437,442	32	$3,389,364
1978	586	$565,797	51	$5,680,804
1980	424	$801,024	35	$15,261,428
1982	597	$788,480	30	$17,589,180
1984	1,008	$1,192,333	82	$15,268,582*

*Of the eighty-two television transactions in 1984, thirty-one involved only construction permits, not operating stations. If the former (valued at less than $1 million each) are discounted, the average price per station was nearly $24.6 million.

Not included in these data are the relatively few combined radio/television transactions. Prices for individual stations vary widely, depending on market size and such other factors as whether a radio station is AM or FM (in 1984 the average AM sold for $533,380; the average FM for $1,271,584; the average AM/FM combination for $2,196,994), and whether a television station is VHF or UHF, affiliate or independent.

Sources: 1976–1982 data from *Electronic Media* by Christopher H. Sterling. Copyright 1984 Christopher H. Sterling. Reprinted and adapted by permission of Praeger Publishers.; 1984 data from *Broadcasting*, 28 Jan. 1985, pp. 45-46.

station or AM/FM combination should be about 2.5 times the station's annual gross revenue, or 7.5 times it annual cash flow (operating revenues less operating expenses). For a stand-alone AM station, the price should be closer to 1.5 times gross revenue or 5 times cash flow; for a television station, 2.5 times gross revenue or 10 times cash flow (Bowles, 9 Nov. 1984).

As shown in Exhibit 10.3, the average price for an operating radio station in 1984 exceeded $1 million. By 1986 the highest price ever paid for a radio station was $44 million, which Noble Broadcasting received from Regency Broadcasting for KJOI-FM in Los Angeles. The record price for a group was Metromedia's 1986 sale of nine of its radio stations and Texas State Networks to an investor

group headed by Carl C. Brazell, Jr., Metromedia radio president, for $285 million.

The average price for a television station (excluding construction permits) in 1984 exceeded $24 million. At one time, independent stations sold for much lower prices than network affiliates. In the mid-1970s, independents began to increase in value, largely because of their improving ability to generate commercially meaningful audiences. KTLA-TV, an independent station in Los Angeles, sold in 1983 for $245 million, at that time the highest price ever paid for any station, affiliate or independent; two years later, Golden West Stations sold it to Tribune Broadcasting for a record-setting $510 million — an increase in value of some $280,000 for each day Golden West had owned the station.

In 1985 publisher Rupert Murdoch announced his intended acquisition of Metromedia's six independent television stations (WNEW-TV, New York; KTTV-TV, Los Angeles; WFLD-TV, Chicago; WTTG-TV, Washington, DC; KNBN-TV, Dallas; and KRIV-TV, Houston) and one network affiliate (WCVB-TV, Boston) for $2 billion. He planned to keep the independents but to resell (*spin-off*) WCVB-TV to the Hearst Corporation for $450 million. Murdoch, who had purchased half ownership of 20th Century-Fox Film Corporation in 1984 for $250 million, acquired the remaining half late in 1985 (after the Metromedia deal) for $325 million. He thus gained complete control over a company with an extensive film library and rights to numerous television series. With this as his programming base, Murdoch in October 1985 announced plans to form a new television network, to be called the Fox Broadcasting Company. With Murdoch's six stations (reaching about 20 percent of all U.S. television households) as its core, the network was to be aimed at younger, more affluent and sophisticated viewers than were being served by ABC, CBS, and NBC.

Television Network Transactions After more than three decades of seemingly impervious continuity of ownership, each of the three major networks found itself the object of a takeover attempt in 1985. ABC was first. Capital Cities Communications* announced that it would acquire American Broadcasting Companies, parent of the ABC network, in a *friendly* deal valued at more than $3.5 billion.

---

*Referred to in the industry as "Cap Cities," its name derives from the fact that the company's first two stations were located in state capitals: Albany, New York, and Raleigh, North Carolina.

The name of the combined organization became Capital Cities/ABC, Inc.

Because Capital Cities was a much smaller operation than ABC, some saw the transaction as "the minnow swallowing the whale." It was the latest in a series of so-called *leveraged buy-outs*, whereby the buyer borrows most of the purchase price and repays the debt out of corporate revenue. The merger created a conglomerate with more than $4.5 billion in annual revenue from 90 radio, television, and cable operations, 200 affiliated television stations, 36 weekly newspapers and shoppers, 10 daily newspapers, and several magazines. It represented the first acquisition of a television and radio network since Leonard H. Goldenson, the current ABC chairman and chief executive officer, had taken over the same network thirty-two years earlier and combined it with United Paramount Theatres. The 1953 American Broadcasting/Paramount Theatres merger had been valued at $25 million.

Capital Cities had earned industry respect as an efficient media operator and applied to ABC the same rigorous cost cutting that had made Cap Cities one of the most profitable owners of newspaper, television, and cable properties. The new company had to divest itself of more than $1 billion worth of communication operations in order to comply with FCC ownership rules. Combined ABC and Cap Cities television stations, for example, would have reached nearly 29 percent of the nation's audience, a violation of the FCC's 25-percent limit. Rules against network ownership of cable systems required Cap Cities, at the time the nation's nineteenth largest MSO, to sell its systems.

Within weeks after the Capital Cities/ABC announcement, Atlanta entrepreneur Ted Turner (see Box, pages 276–277) grabbed the spotlight with his *unfriendly* (or *hostile*) offer to buy CBS in a highly complex deal he valued at

Ted Turner — "Captain Outrageous"

Surely no more colorful a character inhabits and influences the world of electronic mass media than Ted Turner, chairman of the board and president of Turner Broadcasting Systems (TBS). TBS owns and operates Superstation WTBS, Cable News Network, Headline News, Turner Program Services, the Atlanta Braves (baseball) and the Atlanta Hawks (basketball).

Referred to variously as "Terrible Ted," "Captain Outrageous," and "The Mouth of the South," Turner is known for his outspoken opinions, his willingness to challenge the establishment, his aggressive, entrepreneurial spirit (his creed: "Lead, Follow, or Get Out of the Way"), his driving ambition ("My desire to excel borders on the unhealthy," he admits), and his ego (he once told an interviewer, "If I only had a little humility, I'd be perfect"). Physically he is the prototype of the southern gentleman: tall and lanky, with silver-streaked hair and mustache, cigar-smoking, speaking with more than a bit of Georgia drawl. His favorite movie is *Gone With the Wind*. He even named one of his five children Rhett.

Turner attended Brown University, where he was vice president of the Debating Union and commodore of the Brown Yacht Club. The latter experience was later to serve him in good stead when in 1977 he won the premier international sailing trophy, the America's Cup. He was thrown out of college twice and was once dropped from his fraternity for burning down its homecoming display.

Turner began his career as an account executive with his father's advertising company in Savannah, later joining the company's office in Macon, Georgia, as general manager, and in 1963 becoming chief executive officer of the various Turner companies headquartered in Atlanta. His invasion of broadcasting began with his 1970 acquisition of Atlanta's Channel 17, a failing independent UHF television station. There he originated the superstation concept on December 16, 1976. WTBS (then WTCG) began to beam its signal by satellite to cable systems, making its programming available to millions of viewers across the country and beyond.

On June 1, 1980, Turner launched Cable News Network (CNN), the first live, 24-hour-a-day, all-news cable network. Knowledgeable observers predicted its early demise, but by

about $5.2 billion. Turner's offer to CBS stockholders for their CBS shares included no cash. Rather, he offered what security analysts called "junk bonds" (high-risk, high-yield debt securities) plus some stock in his Turner Broadcasting System (TBS). He sought 67 percent of CBS stock to gain control of the corporation.

Even more than the Cap Cities/ABC merger, Turner's proposal represented the minnow trying to swallow the whale. TBS,

with 1,800 employees, had 1984 profits of $10 million on revenues of $282 million; CBS, with 30,000 employees, had 1984 profits of $212 million on revenues of nearly $5 billion.

Twice before, Turner had tried unsuccessfully to realize his ambition of owning a major broadcast network. In 1981 he met with CBS executives to discuss possible relationships with his organization, and in 1983 he proposed a merger with each of the three major networks. As in the past, and as expected this time, CBS

Source: Photo by Kelly Mills/TBS, Inc.

1986 over 8,500 cable systems carried CNN to a potential 33 million homes or more. It is also seen in Europe, Japan, and Australia, and its signal is available even in Communist bloc countries. In 1981, Turner began a second cable news service, CNN-2 (now called Headline News), a continuously updated 30-minute cycle of hard news carried not only by cable systems but also by some television stations. In August 1982 he formed CNN Radio, a 24-hour all-news network with affiliates throughout the nation.

In 1984 Turner formed Cable Music Channel (CMC), a music-video service to compete with Music Television (MTV). He said he needed 10 million subscribers to get under way, but when CMC premiered in October 1984 it claimed only 2.2 million. A week later the number fell to about 350,000, and 36 days later, Cable Music Channel closed down. MTV bought some CMC assets for $1 million plus free advertising on Turner's other cable services.

Turner's biggest battle came in 1985 when he aimed his guns at CBS. Although he lost that one, too, he went down swinging and came up smiling as the new owner of MGM's film library, including his beloved *Gone With the Wind*.

management summarily rejected Turner's bid, calling it "grossly inadequate and detrimental to the interests of CBS and its shareholders." The network embarked on a series of defensive maneuvers designed to defeat Turner's efforts, including the purchase of 21 percent of its own stock for $1 billion. The plan worked, and in late 1985 Turner withdrew his offer. Though victorious, CBS was wounded. To shore up its financial position the network initiated several budget cutbacks, including the layoff of several

hundred employees, and in December 1985 it sold one of its owned-and-operated stations, KMOX-TV in St. Louis, to Viacom International for $122.5 million.*

---

*Early in 1986, CBS declined a "friendly" offer of about $3.7 billion for the network from oilman Marvin Davis, former owner of 20th Century-Fox. Network management seemed relieved when Loews' chairman Laurence Tisch bought 12 percent (later upped to almost 25 percent) of CBS's stock. Later in 1986, Tisch became the network's CEO and William Paley returned as chairman.

The effort cost Turner, too: about $20 million. But Turner did not walk away from the spotlight. No sooner had he abandoned his attempted hostile takeover of CBS than he announced his plan for the friendly acquisition of MGM/UA Entertainment (and the subsequent spin-off of UA), one of Hollywood's motion picture giants, for approximately $1.7 billion. The takeover of MGM, completed early in 1986, gave Turner control over the company's library of 2,200 motion pictures, including *The Wizard of Oz*, *Mutiny on the Bounty*, *Ben Hur*, and *Gone With the Wind*, for use on his superstation WTBS. Ironically, in order to finance this deal, Turner explored the possibility of selling an interest in his Cable News Networks; CBS and NBC were among the prospective buyers.

In December 1985 it was NBC's turn. General Electric (GE), one of the nation's leading industrial giants, announced that it would buy RCA, the oldest and among the largest of broadcasting companies, and parent company of NBC. The deal, valued at $6.28 billion, represented the biggest non-oil acquisition ever made in the United States. It made NBC a part of the nation's second largest industrial corporation (excluding automobile companies), with annual sales of over $40 billion. Unlike the Cap Cities and Turner situations, the buyer was the whale this time: GE was nearly three times the size of RCA.

Two years earlier, GE had sold its eight radio stations and two of its three television stations, saying it wanted to focus on other businesses. Its third station, KCNC-TV in Denver, which NBC had previously attempted to buy, would now become the sixth NBC owned-and-operated television station. With this addition, NBC-owned stations would cover 20.94 percent of the country, behind ABC (24.39 percent) but ahead of CBS (19.45 percent). To conform to FCC rules, NBC would likely have to sell its radio stations

in New York, Chicago, and Washington, where it also owned television stations.*

These network transactions were not without social implications. First, they furthered the trend toward concentration of media control. Media analyst John Morton, commenting on the Cap Cities/ABC merger, suggested, "We're a long way away from the day when a handful of companies will control all of the media, but not far away from the day when a handful will control most of it" (quoted in *New York Times*, 24 Mar. 1985). Second, they raised questions about control of editorial content. As Richard D. Smyser, president of the American Society of Newspaper Editors, observed: "We are a business and would be nothing else, but given our constitutional role and guarantees, we are a special business. The emphasis now seems overweighted on the media as a commodity" (quoted in *New York Times*, 24 Mar. 1985).

Sales of Cable Systems   There are several rules of thumb for measuring the value of a cable system, some more accurate than others. Perhaps the most commonly used measure is dollars-per-subscriber; that is, a dollar value is assigned to each household that subscribes to the system. In the mid-1980s that figure was about $1,000 per subscriber. Thus, for example, a system with 10,000 subscribers would sell for approximately $10 million. As with similar formulas for determining selling prices for radio and television stations, this per-subscriber method yields only very rough

---

*This was not the first association of these companies. In 1919 General Electric had created the Radio Corporation of America as a subsidiary to handle the telegraph business of the newly purchased American Marconi (§2.7). The first NBC radio network, organized in 1926, included RCA, GE, and other station groups. And the first "network" television broadcast, in 1940, linked WNBT-TV (now WNBC-TV) New York with GE's WRGB-TV in Schenectady, New York.

estimates. It ignores such factors as geographical location, number of homes passed by the system (which are therefore potential subscribers), age and channel capacity of the system, amount of construction remaining, number of pay channel subscribers, subscription rates, franchise conditions and expiration date, and so on.

A method of establishing value that does account for some of the above factors involves projecting the cable system's cash flow for the first year of operation following the proposed sale. Recent selling prices have, on the average, been about 8.2 times the first-year projected cash flow (Holman, 5 Nov. 1984). As in radio and television station sales, brokers arrange most cable system sales, taking fees of 2 to 6 percent of the purchase price or, in some cases, accepting part ownership of a system in lieu of cash commission.

By the end of 1986 the largest cable system transaction was Westinghouse Electric's sale of its Group W Cable subsidiary to a consortium of five cable operators: Comcast, Tele-Communications, Daniels & Associates, Century Southwest Communications, and American Television & Communications. The deal included about 135 cable systems serving more than 2 billion subscribers nationwide, and was valued at $2.1 billion, or about $1,050 per subscriber. Westinghouse had assembled much of its cable operation in 1981, when it bought systems with about 1.4 million subscribers from Teleprompter for $646 million plus another $300 million in tax liabilities and debt. The new owners planned to divide the systems among themselves, with each keeping the systems adjacent to those it already owned. Westinghouse would remain active in the cable business, however, through its Group W Satellite Communications, a cable programmer offering The Nashville Network, Home Theatre Network, and a regional sports network, Home Team Sports.

Cable Network Transactions   The cable industry's settling and maturing process in the early and mid-1980s gave rise to a number of sales and mergers of cable networks. Some were designed to enable more effective competition, and others simply made sense from an investment perspective. Still others resulted from a network's inability to survive.

In 1983 Showtime and The Movie Channel merged but continued to operate as separate networks, hoping that the combination would compete more effectively with the leading pay service, HBO, than either had been able to alone. The following year, Showtime/The Movie Channel bought out a competing service, Spotlight, a pay cable network founded by Times Mirror in 1981, and absorbed Spotlight's subscribers. Finally, for the first time since its 1978 beginning, Showtime/The Movie Channel was able in 1984 to show a profit.

The total revenue of ad-supported cable networks in 1984 reached about $500 million, not an impressive amount by broadcast standards (§9.4). More important, advertising dollars proved sufficient to earn profits for only a few cable program services. The results have been mergers and acquisitions. For example, in 1984 Daytime and the Cable Health Network combined to create a new advertiser-supported service called Lifetime. In the same year, ABC, which already owned 15 percent of ESPN, purchased the remaining 85 percent for $202 million, selling 20 percent of the service four months later to Nabisco for $60 million. Also in 1984, HBO acquired a 15-percent interest in BET (Black Entertainment Television), a struggling cable network specializing in programming for minorities, and assumed responsibility for marketing it to cable systems and advertisers.

In 1985, in a complex series of deals valued at $690 million, Viacom (a major MSO, programmer, syndicator, and half-owner of Showtime/The Movie Channel) acquired full ownership of Showtime/TMC and of MTV Networks (operator of three basic cable services: MTV, VH-1, and Nickelodeon). These acquisitions made Viacom the largest cable programmer, the only programmer with significant stakes in both basic and pay cable services, and a candidate as a new DBS operator.

Early cable promoters promised that their new technology, with its many channels, would deliver programming not regularly offered by the commercial television networks, such as cultural programming attractive to select, rather than mass, audiences. Economic reality, however, made it nearly impossible for cable to deliver on that promise. In 1982, after sustaining some $30 million in losses, CBS ceased operating its cultural channel, CBS Cable, for lack of advertiser support. In 1984, hoping to consolidate resources and advertiser dollars, two other cultural programming networks, Arts and The Entertainment Channel, merged to form the new Arts & Entertainment network.

There were others. Like the CBS deal, some of the more controversial cable network transactions were dreamed up by that perennial wheeler-dealer, Ted Turner (see Box, pages 276-277).

10.6 Funding Public Broadcasting

Ask public broadcasters to name their most serious problem, and they invariably answer, insufficient funding. As far back as the 1930s, some advocates proposed nonprofit rather than noncommercial radio, allowing the sale of time sufficient to defray operating costs. But when the FCC was planning television channel assignments, educational interests realized that their only hope for winning congressional approval of channels reserved for public broadcasting lay in complete disassociation from commercialism.

The noncommercial character of public television stations does not, however, preclude crediting commercial donors of program funds (*underwriters*), selling goods at auction, contracting with school systems to receive payment for telecasting classroom instruction, selling production services, and even selling advertising in printed program guides.

Contrast with Commercial Television Exhibit 10.4 compares the finances of commercial and public television. It demonstrates the poverty about which public television officials complain. Public television tries to provide an alternative program service but has only a fraction of commercial television's income. Public television revenue on all levels in 1984 amounted to $3.45 for every man, woman, and child in America, whereas in the same year commercial television received over $85 per person.

Funding Sources   Exhibit 10.5 shows the diversity of public broadcasting's funding sources. Each of these sources brings different obligations with its funding, has different system costs and resultant benefits, and has its own biases. To accommodate the conflicting goals of their numerous and varied contributors, public broadcasters often resort to bland, noncontroversial programs — a notorious weakness of commercial programming. A monopoly source of funding could also be unduly restrictive, of course, but as things stand, public broadcasting executives have to serve too many masters. They spend an inordinate amount of time on fund-raising and are too financially unstable to plan effectively.

Government Role   From the beginning of public radio, state and local governments were

Exhibit 10.4 Comparison of Public and Commercial TV Economics

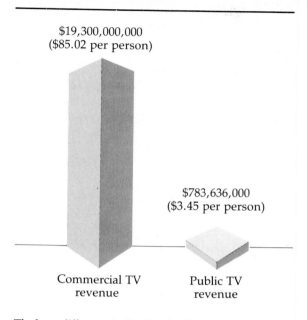

$19,300,000,000
($85.02 per person)

$783,636,000
($3.45 per person)

Commercial TV
revenue

Public TV
revenue

The huge difference in funding levels between public and commercial television is evident in these figures. While the dollar data change each year, the percentages change far more slowly. Radio is not compared here, for the only good statistical information on public radio refers to the CPB-qualified small minority of stations and thus any comparison with commercial radio would be misleading.

Sources: Public television revenue from the Corporation for Public Broadcasting 1984 *Annual Report* (Washington: CPB, 1985), p. 3. Commercial television revenue from Robert J. Coen, McCann-Erickson, Inc., in *Broadcasting Marketing and Technology News* (NAB, Washington, August 1985).

important supporters of the system, at both the station and state-network levels. Government support expanded with television stations. By the mid-1960s, local and state tax funds provided about half of all public broadcasting income. Later, however, the state proportion of support declined, dropping to about 20 percent of total income by the 1980s. Local government (predominantly school-board) support fell to under 5 percent.

Until 1962 the federal government had no financial input into the system. The FCC set up the noncommercial FM and TV educational class of licenses by administrative ruling (§3.6), but public broadcasting received no legislative recognition until the Educational Television Facilities Act of 1962. This amendment to the Communications Act explicitly acknowledged federal responsibility for noncommercial broadcasting. It authorized $32 million to be awarded over a five-year period by the Department of Health, Education and Welfare for the construction (but not operation) of educational television stations. A driving force behind this law was the need to get more educational stations on the air to "protect" the reserved channels against commercial pressures for reclassification.* Limited to a maximum of $1 million for any one state, federal funds for noncommercial broadcasting had to be matched by funds from other sources — one federal dollar for each dollar raised locally. This educational facilities act, extended and revised, continued to assist equipment and facility funding for public broadcasting in the 1980s.

Long-Range Funding   During the late 1960s and early 1970s, Congress, citizen groups, and think tanks considered a number of funding alternatives for public broadcasting. Suggested sources included excise taxes or license fees on television receivers, acceptance of limited advertising on public stations,

---

*Some commercial stations assisted noncommercial stations by donating broadcast equipment and tower space for antennas — not always for altruistic reasons, however, but more often to keep the educational channels from turning into commercial competitors.

Exhibit 10.5   Public Broadcasting Revenue by Source: 1984

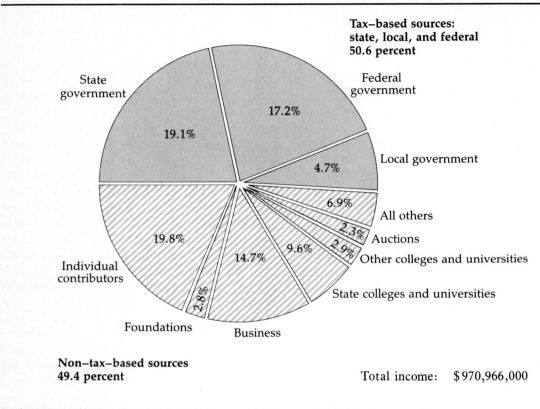

Tax–based sources:
state, local, and federal
50.6 percent

Federal government   17.2%

State government   19.1%

Local government   4.7%

6.9%   All others

2.3%   Auctions

2.9%   Other colleges and universities

9.6%   State colleges and universities

14.7%   Business

2.8%   Foundations

19.8%   Individual contributors

Non–tax–based sources
49.4 percent

Total income: $970,966,000

In the 1980s public broadcasting depended more and more on non-tax-based sources of revenue. In 1979 tax-based sources accounted for more than two-thirds of all revenue; by 1984 they provided only about one-half.

Source: Corporation for Public Broadcasting 1984 *Annual Report* (Washington: CPB, 1985), p. 3.

conversion of public television to pay-TV operation, a tax on commercial broadcasting, earmarking of regular income taxes for public television, leasing access to spectrum space (involving an annual fee for broadcast and other use of the spectrum), and ownership and leasing of a satellite.

Although none of these proposals achieved much support, there was agreement on the following goals: (1) *insulation* of public broadcasting from the political pressures of annual funding; (2) an *adequate level* of funding to allow system growth; (3) year-to-year *stability* of income; and (4) funding over the *long range* (generally defined as five or more years) to allow for more orderly planning, especially of program and technical development. But several attempts at a congressional bill for even two-year funding achieved no success. In 1973, for example, legislation passed only to be vetoed by President Richard M. Nixon. The Public Broadcasting Finance Act of 1975 authorized funds for five years, though it actually appropriated funds for only three. The new act retained the matching principle, with congressional money released at the ratio of $1.00 for each $2.50 raised by the public broadcasting system from other sources.

Three years later Congress approved a follow-up bill, the Public Telecommunications Financing Act of 1978, which carried funding authorizations into the 1980s — but again with strings attached. This time the bill's matching provision called for $1.00 of federal funds for every $2.00 raised. Again, the bill set specific levels of authorized federal spending, but in practice the appropriations (when Congress actually releases the money) were for only three years at a time, and almost always for less than originally authorized.

Public broadcasting's struggle was not eased by the election of Ronald Reagan as President in 1980 and his reelection in 1984. Although supportive of the principle of public broadcasting, Reagan said that the service should look more to the private sector and less to the federal government for funding. A 1984 bill would have set Corporation for Public Broadcasting (§8.3) budgets at $238 million for 1987, $253 million for 1988, and $270 million for 1989. In view of the substantial cuts needed in his administration's overall budget, Reagan vetoed the bill. One month later he vetoed a second bill with slightly lower budgets, again citing the need to reduce federal funding. Later bills authorized $214 million for 1988, $238 million for 1989, and $254 million for 1990, but projected an end to federal funding by 1992.

The NPR Crisis   Meanwhile, National Public Radio was experiencing a severe financial crisis that threatened to put it out of business entirely. NPR faced a 1983 fiscal year multimillion dollar deficit, which was blamed partly on the recession and reduced funding but mostly on poor management. Frank Mankiewicz, who resigned as president of NPR in May 1983, bore the brunt of the blame. Praised for expanding and improving the organization, he was criticized for failing to provide an adequate financial base and for hiring more than eighty people while the fiscal problems were mounting.

Under new leadership, first of interim president Ronald Bornstein and later of its new president Douglas J. Bennet, NPR took steps to recover. Nearly a third of the network's 450 employees were discharged; the fiscal 1984 budget, originally set at nearly $27 million, was trimmed to under $18 million. CPB agreed to a $7 million loan to NPR, guaranteed by its member radio stations.

NPR finished its 1984 fiscal year within its planned operating budget and began to make payments on its debt to CPB. However, faced with a new budget deficit in 1985, NPR requested an additional $1.3 million from CPB. CPB responded with a payment of $921,000 for the two most popular NPR programs, *All Things Considered* and *Morning Edition*.

In 1985, NPR's member stations approved a new financing plan whereby, beginning in 1987, virtually all federal radio dollars would be sent directly to the stations. The plan established a two-fee system of station dues paid to NPR. One fee would cover NPR program representation, development, and legal and engineering services. The other, for stations not interested in purchasing NPR programming, was for station services, as well as for national representation before Congress, the FCC, and other federal agencies.

Program Underwriting   One controversial aspect of public broadcasting fund-raising is a limited form of sponsorship called commercial *underwriting*. A program's producer, in assembling financial backing for a projected or continuing series, secures grants from large business corporations, which become program underwriters. FCC regulations allow companies brief credits in the form of short announcements at the beginning and end of programs. Until 1981, FCC rules even prohibited use of corporate logos, or trademarks. Sometimes several firms share in underwriting a single series. Stations often add local underwriting to cover costs of local acquisition, resulting in long credit "crawls," both national and local, before and after programs.

Underwriters are usually interested in programs that will attract sizable (for public television) audiences; thus some of the more specialized programming that an alternative service should provide fail to gain corporate underwriting. In most cases underwriters will not associate themselves with programs containing highly controversial subject matter, thus making public-affairs programs difficult to fund. It took Boston's public television station WGBH more than six years to find the $5.6 million needed to produce its controversial series, *Vietnam: A Television History*, the highest-rated television documentary of 1983.

Advertising on Public Television   Carrying out-and-out commercials on public television, an idea suggested several times previously, was given a trial when Congress in 1981 created the Temporary Commission on Alternative Financing for Public Telecommunications (TCAF). FCC commissioner James H. Quello served as TCAF chairman; other participants included U.S. senators and members of Congress, as well as public broadcasting representatives. The commission was charged with special authority to test advertising as a funding device.

In January 1982, ten large and small stations volunteered to take part in a fifteen-month experiment with on-air advertising.* Public radio stations did not participate. The legislation authorizing the test stipulated that ads could not interrupt programs, could not exceed two minutes in length, and could not promote political, religious, or other ideological points of view. Station managers also maintained a watchful eye to avoid commercials whose content might be considered inappropriate for a public-service medium. Station WTTW-TV in Chicago earned the most advertising income of all of the participating stations — more than $1 million in the fiscal year ending June 30, 1983, which was nearly 10 percent of the station's entire revenue that year.

Following completion of the test, TCAF reported its findings:

• Limited advertising added significant revenues under conditions where labor unions and copyright holders waived the right to renegotiate existing agreements.
• Advertising produced no negative impact on viewing patterns, numbers of subscribers to public television, or contributions.
• There were no advertising-related effects on programming.

The commission concluded, however, that most public television stations would not carry advertisements because of legal restrictions, local economic considerations, or concerns about advertising's impact on the character of public broadcasting. It added:

---

*Participating stations were WHYY-TV, Wilmington, Delaware; WIPB-TV, Muncie, Indiana; WNET-TV, Newark, New Jersey; WPBT-TV, Miami, Florida; WQED-TV, Pittsburgh, Pennsylvania; WQLN-TV, Erie, Pennsylvania; WKPC-TV, Louisville, Kentucky; WSKG-TV, Binghamton, New York; WTTW-TV, Chicago, Illinois; and WYES-TV, New Orleans, Louisiana. Later, the Louisville station withdrew and was replaced by KCSM-TV, San Mateo, California; the Binghamton station also withdrew but was not replaced.

While the demonstration program allayed the worst concerns about the impact of advertising on other funding sources for public broadcasting, no experiment could show that offsetting reductions of subscriber, underwriter, or legislative support would not result eventually due to the presence of advertising. (TCAF, 1983)

TCAF made no recommendation, leaving Congress to decide whether stations should be permitted to carry advertising on a continuing basis. It did suggest, however, that guidelines for crediting program underwriters on the air should be broadened.

In 1984 the Senate Communications Subcommittee held hearings to examine whether advertising on public broadcasting should be resumed. Several station executives argued for the proposal, but most representatives from CPB opposed the concept (as, indeed, did the president of the National Association of Broadcasters). Following later meetings of public broadcasting associations and individuals, the idea was shelved, at least for the time being.*

In the same year, however, the FCC followed up on the TCAF recommendation to permit "enhanced underwriting." The liberalized rules have resulted in some stations carrying what Bruce Christensen, president of PBS, called "almost commercials" (Smith, 1985). Arguing that the only way to increase donations by corporations is to appeal to them as advertisers rather than as charitable contributors, stations began selling 30-second announcements complete with the mention of specific consumer products — from the Ford Escort to Hilton Hotels. The New Jersey Net-

work of four public television stations, for example, permitted advertisers to talk about products, services, and location, but drew the line at statements about product superiority; in 1985 a commercial scheduled between the *New Jersey Nightly News* and the network's weekly drawing for the state lottery cost $350. Use of this enhanced underwriting increased the network's corporate contributions from $300,000 in 1983 to $900,000 in 1985. New York City's WNET-TV began selling 30-second *general support announcements* (GSAs) at between $1,000 and $1,500 each that could include a company's logo, location, brand and trade names, and a description of a product or service. The station expected to produce over $1 million in annual revenue from these sales.

Even some who advocated this practice of allowing quasi-commercials expressed concern about its possible implications for the character of public broadcasting. Others began pressure anew to permit full-fledged commercials on public stations, now that the door had been opened. Late in 1985 the FCC announced it would investigate complaints that some stations had crossed the line of enhanced underwriting and were, in fact, selling advertising. The commission followed this announcement with a 1986 warning that it would enforce its underwriting rules and would penalize public broadcasters who violate them.

Other Approaches   Individual members of the public contribute about 20 percent of public broadcasting revenue (Exhibit 10.5). Many public television stations, in their constant search for funds, push membership drives to extremes. Several times a year, often over a period of a week to ten days, station staff members and armies of volunteers operate telephone banks while well-known citizens and station personalities sell memberships on the air. They use all the hard-sell

---

*New York City's WNYC-TV is in an unusual position: it holds a commercial license but operated as a noncommercial station and a member of PBS. In 1985 the station announced a plan to begin leasing airtime to commercial broadcasters, mostly foreign-language, to offset reduced federal support.

techniques of commercial television, and then some. Public television polls show great viewer resistance to this means of fundraising, which delays and even interrupts programming, and only one out of ten homes that watch public television ever contributes. Many public broadcasters feel such hard-sell campaigns demean the service. Even more objectionable to some are over-the-air auctions, during which donated articles and services are peddled on the air at length, with all the arts of commercial persuasion. Reacting to criticism, some stations have reduced their on-air campaigns. San Francisco's KQED-TV, for example, canceled sixteen days of such fundraising in 1985 after promising to drop one weekday of on-air appeals for every $50,000 collected by the station, and a Saturday or Sunday for each $100,000 pledged.

In 1980 four community public television stations combined forces to issue a new program guide called *The Dial*. It is not unusual for noncommercial stations to earn income by selling advertising-supported program guides, but *The Dial* not only sold advertising, its stations also used air time to promote the sale of subscriptions. Regional and city magazines affected by this competition complained to the FCC and the courts. Nevertheless, *The Dial* won tax-exempt status, the FCC allowed the stations to continue over-the-air plugs, and the magazine soon attracted additional participating stations. In 1985 *The Dial* published fourteen editions giving program listings and information for fourteen stations and had a circulation of over 1 million.

Some other approaches considered or used to raise funds for public broadcasting include:

1. Selling commercial rights to merchandise associated with public television programs (the Children's Television Workshop obtained a good deal of *Sesame Street's* production funding from such sales).

2. Offering closed-circuit seminars for a fee.

3. Selling programming to commercial pay television for initial showing before release to public television.

4. Renting station facilities to commercial producers.

5. Selling videotapes to viewers.

6. Making commercial tie-ins with noncommercial programming (in 1985 the PBS series *The Sporting Life* carried on-air mention of various companies, which in turn bought newspaper ads stating that purchase of their products would support PBS; all the consumer needed to do was mail in the product's proof-of-purchase stickers, each worth a 25-cent PBS contribution).

7. Exchanging (for a cash payment) a public broadcaster's more desirable VHF channel for a commercial operator's UHF channel in the same market.

Summary

• Most segments of the American broadcasting and cable industries are structured to make a profit.

• The major television networks enjoy healthy profits, as do most radio and television stations. A few pay cable networks and most advertising-supported cable program services are not profitable.

• A large expense incurred by broadcasters and cablecasters involves the acquisition of programming. Program licenses do not confer ownership of the material but rather grant the user the right to show the program a limited number of times over a limited number of years.

- Cable systems rely mostly on subscription fees for their revenue and offer several tiers of program service with a separate charge for each.

- Other media whose revenue comes from subscriptions include multipoint distribution service (MDS), and satellite master antenna (SMATV) systems.

- Capital expenditures in broadcasting and cable range from a few thousand dollars for a small radio station to many millions for cable and satellite operations. A significant portion of the total industry capital investment is made by the consumer through the purchase of radios and television sets.

- Some of the profit in broadcasting and cable comes from the buying and selling of stations and systems. Investors are attracted to the industry because of its typically high profit margin.

- Many factors influence the price of a station or a cable system, but rough estimates are sometimes made based on multiples of projected cash flow.

- Public broadcasting, supported by both government and private entities, operates with resources far below those of commercial radio and television.

- Public television experimented with advertising but dropped the idea as an unacceptable source of income.

- Controversial methods of public broadcast fund-raising include program underwriting and on-air membership drives and auctions.

Prime Time

	9:00	9:30
2	Trapper John	
3	Trapper John	
4	Cheers	Night Court
5	McMillan and Wife (Cont.)	
7	Colbys	
8	Colbys	
9	Movie: The Mad Room	
11	Baseball (Cont.)	
13	Heart of Dragon	
20	Movie (Cont.)	
21	Mystery!	
25	WNYE Presents	

PART 4

Programming

When using or thinking about electronic media, most viewers and listeners consider programming. Critics compare the programming process with the assembly-line manufacture of machine-made products. But as already noted in Part III, and further described here, program decision making involves risks, uncertainties, and problems of supply that are not shared by makers of, say, shoes or cereal. Programming in the electronic media is also, of course, a means to an end, the real business of commercial media being the attraction of audiences for "sale" to advertisers. We begin in Chapter 11 with a general description of the process and practice of programming. Chapter 12 reviews how national networks develop their widely known entertainment, sports, educational, and information programs. The importance of syndication in radio, television, and cable is assessed in Chapter 13, which focuses on nonnetwork programs, including those that are locally produced.

CHAPTER 11

Programming Problems, Processes, and Practices

Broadcasting and cable television programmers share the goal of seeking the largest possible audiences in order to attract advertisers and generate the most revenue. They face two fundamental problems: the shortage of programs and the need to attract the kinds of audiences advertisers want for their advertisements. Solving these problems has led to standardized program production and distribution processes and widely accepted program-scheduling practices throughout the television and cable industries. Radio programmers must also make prudent use of their main resource — recordings — and target narrowly defined audiences in order to appeal to advertisers. All three types of programmers — broadcast television, cable television, and radio — operate within common legal, economic, and technical constraints and use much the same production, distribution, and scheduling strategies for doing so. This chapter discusses programming problems and the strategies used to solve them, looks at the constraints on the program production and distribution processes, examines the typical on-air scheduling practices used by network and local television, radio, and cable, and concludes with a critical appraisal of broadcast and cable programming.

11.1 The Problems: Program Shortage and Advertiser Appeal

Better than a half-century of continuous broadcasting, the growth of cable television, and the availability of home video-playback equipment have combined to create an incredible appetite for programming. The demand for programming far outstrips supply.

The Parsimony Principle To cope with the shortage of programs, and the resulting high cost of those programs produced, programmers resort to a variety of strategies based upon what might be called the *parsimony principle*. This basic rule dictates that program material must be used as sparingly as possible, repeated as often as possible, and shared as widely as possible.

The sharing of program material is achieved by means of recording, networking, and syndication. Without these ways of rising above local limitations, broadcasting would never have developed into such a large indus-try, and cable would have remained viable only in places where broadcast reception was poor. Moreover, the resources for purely local programming would have been quickly ex-hausted, and continuous programming opera-tions would be impossible. Recording stimulates the establishment of centralized production facilities by permitting the delayed use of program materials; networking encour-ages simultaneous use of the same program in different places; and syndication makes possible the resale of programs for later use by other stations, services, and even homes.

At both local and national levels, schedul-ing and formatting strategies ensure sparing and repeated use of programs. Regularly scheduled daily or weekly entertainment pro-grams use standardized openings, closings, and transitions; they present ready-made per-sonalities or characters who build on estab-lished situations or plot lines. Primary examples of the parsimony principle at work in network broadcasting are soap operas and game shows; local television makes heavy use of syndicated reruns; and radio uses standard-ized disc jockey formats. Superstations such as WTBS and cable services such as Showtime originate their own comedy and series pro-grams, copying the frugal practices of the broadcast networks. The frequent reschedul-ing of programs on HBO and other cable serv-ices demonstrates how cable depends on repeated use of every program. The rise of music-video programs shows how television borrows from local radio, just as it once bor-rowed from network radio.

We see the parsimony principle even in the reuse of news stories on later newscasts and in the editing of dramatic action in sports to create instant replays and highlight films of great baseball catches or spectacular football runs. In entertainment, the situation comedy stretches out the same plot gimmick week af-ter week, and weekly dramas reuse the same set of characters year after year.

Targeting and Segmentation   The sec-ond problem faced by broadcasting and cable is, as we have said, the need to appeal to ad-vertisers. Advertisers support commercial television and radio at both network and local levels. The money to pay for the programs (and the profit from operations) comes directly from the sale of commercial time (§9.1). Basic cable also derives some of its support from the sale of advertising (§9.4). To reach the audi-ences that advertisers want, broadcasters have devised the strategy of targeting, or aiming programs at subsets of the mass audience that are most likely to buy the advertisers' prod-ucts. The broadcast networks aim at the larg-est single group of viewers, demographically defined, in every day part. This is predomi-nantly a target audience of women between the ages of 18 and 49. Some cable networks target the same broad audience, and others program for smaller groups. Each service de-fines its audience in terms of *demographics* (age and sex) or *psychographics* (lifestyle and inter-ests). The subgroup must be salable — in other words, acceptable to sufficient numbers of advertisers (and their agencies).

Radio has further refined the process of targeting by using segmentation, or defining extremely narrow subsets of the total radio au-dience. Most radio formats appeal to only one segment of listeners but attempt to attract all the listeners within that narrow group. In any one market, radio stations divide the listening audience by going after different demographic subsets of the total market. Segmentation also involves soliciting advertisers that want to reach the station's listening group and airing advertising and other material appropriate only to that station's format. For example, Coca-Cola ads on rock music stations have rock music backgrounds, whereas the same ads on country or middle-of-the-road stations have background music appropriate for those formats. Contests and games are also selected on the basis of their appropriateness for the targeted audience segment.

Noncommercial broadcasting and pay cable have also adopted the strategy of targeting specific audience groups. They have isolated those groups most likely to offer financial support or to pay regular subscription fees, and schedule programs specifically for those groups. Public television airs large numbers of programs that appeal to middle- and upper-income families; pay cable generally selects movies that target women, or families with children, or young people, and so on. The need to reach large numbers of the people who will pay the bills, whether advertisers or subscribers, has led to strategies of targeting and segmentation in all the electronic media.

11.2 Program Production Processes

Programs are generally obtained in one of three ways: they are locally produced by a station or cable system, produced by a broadcast or cable network and distributed to its affiliated stations or systems, or sold by a syndicator to any station or system that is willing to pay the price. Television stations produce their own local newscasts and some public-affairs programming but little else. The major television networks produce their own early-morning talk and news programs, evening newscasts, and some soap operas and specials, but they obtain most of their programs from the six major Hollywood studios and a dozen big-name independent producers. The Hollywood studios and the top independent producers generate most of the big-name

movies and prime-time situation comedies and dramas. The cable networks go to the same few sources for their programs, which contributes to the general shortage of high-quality programming and the strong similarity among television programs. The major producing studios have their own goals and procedures, and these limit the studios' ability to serve television's needs.

Role of Hollywood Studios in Television

For a short period after World War II, the major motion picture studios attempted to starve the fledgling television industry by withholding their theatrical movies. But Hollywood soon changed direction and became the networks' sole source of movies and main source of prime-time television series. Movies that had completed their theatrical runs were sold to the three networks, enabling them to fill big chunks of airtime with prepromoted popular fare, before being returned for a second round of theatrical exhibition. Program series aired once on the networks and then moved into syndication, the point at which the producing studio made most of their profits. From the late 1950s to the early 1970s, this was the standard pattern.

In the 1970s certain independent producers, not connected with any studio, began creating series such as *All in the Family, The Mary Tyler Moore Show, Laverne & Shirley*, and *Dallas* that ultimately proved to be immensely popular and long-lived on the networks. By the 1980s such independent producers as Lear, Spelling, Goldberg, Lorimar, Tandem, MTM, and Steven J. Cannell dominated prime-time series production, though movies remained largely the province of the Hollywood big six — Twentieth Century-Fox, MGM-UA, Columbia, Paramount, Universal, and Warner Brothers.

Although the Hollywood studios continue to produce some prime-time series (*Benson*

The Big Studios

In the early 1980s, Twentieth Century-Fox showed itself to be one of the most tenacious and financially successful studios in the television business. In addition to financing big box-office hits such as *Star Wars* and its sequels, Fox produced *M*A*S*H* (and *AfterM*A*S*H*) and *Trapper John* for television. Traditionally, Fox tended to prefer buying distribution rights from independent producers to financing its own productions. Murdoch's purchase of Twentieth Century-Fox, however, signals a new role in program production for the 1990s. The movie studio will supply programming for the recently created Fox Broadcasting Company (FBC), that will compete with ABC, CBS, and NBC in some time periods. The network's first production will be *The Late Show Starring Joan Rivers*, to be aired by affiliates at 11:00 or 11:30 P.M.

Warner Brothers and Columbia Pictures Industries, after a slump of several years, surged ahead in the mid-1980s with such enormous box-office successes as *Gremlins* and *Ghostbusters*, but they had few television productions to syndicate. Disney attempted to become the seventh major studio by expanding from children's movies into adult productions, but several failures triggered a decision to produce solely for The Disney Channel, and its library remains mostly G-rated children's fare. All these studios also produce many made-for-TV movies (see §12.2).

Among the major studios, Paramount is one of the biggest success stories in recent years. It has been characterized by long-term commitment to both television and movies, producing prime-time series such as *Happy Days*, *Webster*, and *Cheers*, miniseries such as *Shogun* and *The Winds of War*, and first-run syndication shows such as *Entertainment Tonight* and *Solid Gold*. It was a pioneer in converting from film to videotape, which reduced overhead costs, and in developing its first-run syndication arm (§13.4), which improved profits. Paramount also distributed such box-office hits as *Raiders of the Lost Ark* in 1983 and the sequel, *Indiana Jones and the Temple of Doom*, in 1984.

Source: Photo courtesy of CBS.

and *Cheers*, for example) and much of daytime television, many of the most coveted series come from independent producers. Aaron Spelling, for example, produces *Dynasty*; Lorimar produces *Dallas*; Steven J. Cannell produces *The A-Team*. Several of the big movie studios have turned most of their attention to distributing and syndicating television programs rather than producing prime-time series, because the distribution side of the business generates staggering profit margins. Successful series that remain on a network for five or more years move rapidly into syndication in virtually all of the more than 210 television markets in the United States and in the major foreign markets and can be resold many times in each market over a period of years.

The movie studios are today only the most visible members of complex entertainment conglomerates. Large nonmedia corporations have acquired many studios in recent years, primarily to gain financial control of valuable libraries of old films. For example Coca-Cola purchased Columbia, and Gulf & Western acquired Paramount; Rupert Murdoch, the newspaper media baron, owns Twentieth Century-Fox; and other studios within the industry have swallowed smaller entities (for instance, MGM acquired United Artists, creating MGM-UA, which was purchased in turn and split again by Ted Turner in 1985). Still other studios such as Warner Brothers and Disney are wary of threatened takeovers. Although prohibited by consent decrees of the 1940s from owning theatrical chains, some of these corporations have purchased television stations, as well as other nonmedia businesses, to protect the stability of their revenues.

Today, the movie studios make more money from television, cable, videocassette, and foreign rights than from American theatrical distribution (Exhibit 11.1). In fact, their largest revenues come from syndicating television series (produced either by independents or by themselves), not from making movies. In both television and movie production, a few box-office hits have to carry a large number of failures; but production costs on a rapidly failed television series may run one or two million dollars, whereas costs for movies run in the tens of millions.

It is important to remember, however, that prime-time television production is far from a sure thing. Only a few of many thousands of ideas considered by the networks actually reach pilot production, and most series fail resoundingly. Nearly three-quarters of new prime-time programs are not renewed for a second year, and a short series of episodes has relatively little value in syndication. Moreover, in order to improve a pilot's chances for network acceptance and scheduling, studios and independent producers typically underprice new series and put more production money into them than is economically justifiable, hoping to make sufficient profits on lengthy network runs to cover the actual costs. Major hits may begin to make their producers some profits in the second and subsequent years, but most series continue to accumulate deficits. The high risk of television and the pressure for predictable profits have therefore shifted much of the studios' attention from series production to the distribution business.

Independent Producers   The other major forces in television programming, as we said, are the independent producers. They range in size from large producers such as Spelling and MTM, which have several series in simultaneous production, to very small producers that typically have only a single series under contract at any one time. Their creative ideas influence the networks' production agendas, and their prime-time series compete with those of the big Hollywood movie studios. Be-

Exhibit 11.1   The Movie Distribution Sequence

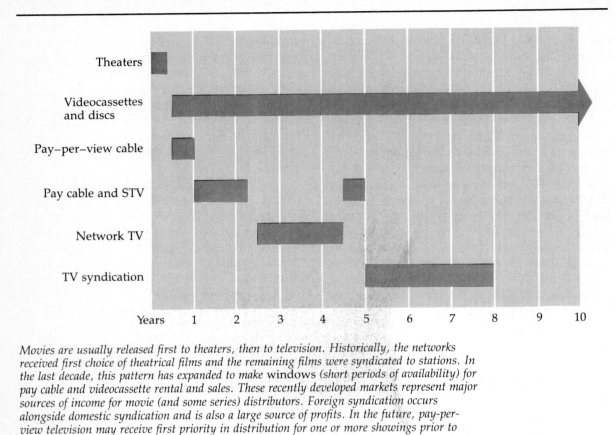

Theaters

Videocassettes and discs

Pay–per–view cable

Pay cable and STV

Network TV

TV syndication

Years   1   2   3   4   5   6   7   8   9   10

Movies are usually released first to theaters, then to television. Historically, the networks received first choice of theatrical films and the remaining films were syndicated to stations. In the last decade, this pattern has expanded to make windows *(short periods of availability) for pay cable and videocassette rental and sales. These recently developed markets represent major sources of income for movie (and some series) distributors. Foreign syndication occurs alongside domestic syndication and is also a large source of profits. In the future, pay-per-view television may receive first priority in distribution for one or more showings prior to theatrical release.*

Source: *Channels' Field Guide to the Electronic Media,* 1985. Copyright Marian Chin, 1985.

cause independent producers often lease production studios, they have marginally lower overhead costs than those paid by the big studios. This lower cost allows independents to offer series to the networks for lower license fees, a distinct advantage in competing for pilot-program selection. At least half the prime-time series shown on television come from the studios of independent producers, who are less constrained than the rest of the movie industry by unwieldy decision-making struc-

tures and corporate demands for quick, high profits. Independent producers usually can concentrate their creative attention and capital on a small number of efforts, which occasionally gives rise to innovative series that are not only popular but attract critical praise as well.

Network News Production   Although the broadcast television networks no longer produce much of their entertainment programming, they have retained tight control of news and public-affairs production. Each commercial network operates a news division, entirely separate from its entertainment functions, that employs about a thousand persons. Cable News Network and Independent News Network operate on a significantly smaller scale.

The broadcast networks seldom accept news footage or documentaries from outside sources, despite criticism from independent producers and the occasional loss of a scoop. The networks argue that in order to function responsibly as news media, they must control the news production process. They contend that the integrity and reliability of network journalism would be jeopardized if their newscasts incorporated material from individuals and organizations that have no allegiance to the networks' journalistic standards. The networks can better justify their editing actions (internally to producers and externally to critics) if they control each stage of news preparation.

On the infrequent occasions when the major networks do air film footage shot by other news organizations (such as other domestic stations, networks, or foreign governments), they carefully label its source — in effect, make a public disclaimer of primary responsibility. For example, footage of events in countries hostile to the United States sometimes comes from non-U.S. sources. And occasionally a citizen or a reporter from another news service will capture unique, on-the-scene footage of an event such as an assassination attempt, a plane crash, or a weather disaster. The network news chiefs recognize that unique film or video footage should not be ignored simply because a nonnetwork camera operator shot it. The competitive pressure on each of the three major networks to give an exclusive slant to their newscasts has resulted in more frequent introduction of "outside" material in recent years, especially on ABC.

CNN's format is not as time- and tradition-constrained, so it uses material from a wider variety of sources.

Local News and ENG   With the advent of electronic news gathering (ENG), local news teams during the 1970s and 1980s could generate enough material to fill longer newscasts. ENG was made possible by the progressive miniaturization of cameras and recorders and the development in 1973 of the time-base corrector (§6.11), which enabled mixing input from small video cameras and videotape recordings with studio and network material. Before ENG, stations depended primarily on 16mm films for on-the-spot coverage of local news events. Such films had to be developed before airing, which was a lengthy process. Even when stations shifted to portable television field cameras, pictures mixing remote and studio sources frequently lost synchronization, causing jumping, rolling, and disintegrating. Time-base correctors eventually eliminated such technical problems.

Mobile equipment was used early in television news production, but it consisted of huge moving vans loaded with heavy, bulky equipment. Modern ENG equipment, however, is eminently portable (Exhibit 6.7): it can be carried in a car, a small panel truck, or a helicopter, and it can be operated by a two- or three-person crew. An ENG unit can travel quickly and economically by car or helicopter to the scene of an event and feed an on-the-spot news story to the studio by means of a microwave or satellite link. Alternatively, the ENG unit can record material that will be edited later at the studio. ENG has caught on rapidly. Whereas only 3 percent of commercial television stations used it in 1973, 90 percent were using it by 1982, three-quarters of them in conjunction with a satellite relay. Moreover, over three-quarters of all television stations expected to have computerized newsrooms and a satellite uplink by the end of 1986 (Yoacam & Cremer, 1985).

Speed, editing flexibility, and mobility have generated more news, greater technical quality, and higher profits. ENG has also influenced station organization, operating procedures, and management practices to an unanticipated degree, since it allows escape from the TV studio and draws the journalist and the electronic technician into an interactive relationship (Yoacam & Cremer, 1985).

ENG has its practical limitations, however. Line-of-sight terrestrial relays are subject to problems of signal blockage, reflection, and excessive distance (§5.6). This problem led to the next major development in local news coverage, news gathering by satellite (NGS). See Exhibit 6.7. Satellite relays make it possible for ENG teams to deliver stories from unlimited distances to their home studios, and their use is growing, but satellite uplinks require more power than many small stations can afford to install in their ENG units. Helicopters are costly and cannot fly in bad weather. And even the fanciest equipment cannot create news where no news exists.

Nonlocal News Sources   Both television and radio affiliates can obtain what amounts to a syndicated television news service from their own networks. Provided by network news divisions, these services feed news items and features over regular network relay facilities during daytime hours when the relays are not tied up with scheduled network programming. Affiliates can record these feeds, selecting items for later insertion in local newscasts after paying their networks a fee for the service. They can also obtain the right to record regular network news programs as sources of stories for later insertion in their local programs.

In 1980 Independent News Network, a syndicated news program service, began relaying a packaged half-hour newscast live via satellite to subscribing independent stations during the hour preceding late-evening newscasts by local network affiliates. Thus, independents could program a half-hour of INN and a half-hour of local news earlier than affiliates could schedule late news. For their local newscasts, independent stations get most of their national and international news and features from UPITN, a combined operation of United Press International (UPI) and Britain's Independent Television News (ITN), which is jointly owned by British television companies. Some stations also subscribe to News Information Weekly Service (NIWS), a national news service. Still another nonlocal syndicated source of news emerged in 1980, when CNN offered to exchange news stories with television stations; in addition, television stations can arrange to air a partial or full schedule of CNN Headline News's five-minute newscasts (§12.6).

11.3 Changes in Entertainment Production Strategies

Movies have traditionally been valued by television networks and stations because they fill large amounts of time and generally hold the interest of an audience from beginning to end. Moreover, movies usually target a young, female audience that appeals to advertisers. In the 1970s, however, the cable industry aggressively acquired a significant portion of the available movies, forcing higher prices and an even greater shortage of programming for broadcasters (§11.2). The demand for more movies on the part of cable networks and local television stations and the rise of a new profitable market in videocassette rental and sales have altered the studios' production and release practices (see Box on facing page).

New Cable Production   The pay cable services pose an inherent challenge to the

Movie Production and Targeting

The total number of movies produced annually in the United States increased in the 1980s, rising from about 120 in the late 1970s to over 250 by 1985. Three trends in the movie business have contributed to Hollywood's recent resurgence: an expanded release period, the popularity of sequels, and a broadening age range for the moviegoing audience.

Peak movie attendance occurs in the summertime, and work schedules create larger audiences on weekends than on weeknights. Consequently, most blockbuster movies have been released on early summer weekends. But because of escalating movie budgets and the resulting greater risk, in the mid-1980s the studios began spreading release dates across the summer, to take more advantage of prepromotion and to give each movie a better chance at capturing an audience. Instead of releasing virtually all films at the same time, the studios now juggle their release dates to avoid opening all their big-budget movies on the same summer weekends. This spreading of major releases over a longer period of time resembles the television networks' spreading of the opening episodes of their new fall programs over several weeks in September and October.

Much-publicized sequels to blockbuster movies also raise the public's general anticipation for new movies, resulting in bigger ticket sales. Sequels have the advantage of being already familiar to the audience and can be counted on to attract most of the audience back to "Part Two" and subsequent spin-offs. Ready familiarity therefore reduces promotional costs and makes ticket sales more predictable.

The third trend is an expanded audience base, the result of attracting more people over age 24 to the movies (Hayes, 1984). Although most major films continue to target the 12-to-24-year-old group (because three out of four moviegoers have been under the age of 40 and most under 30, since television began), even a slight increase in the number of older viewers is an enormous financial bonus. In turn, movies that appeal to this slightly older audience are very valuable to television advertisers.

Moreover, the growth of the videocassette and cable television markets affects the movie business in positive ways. The rental and purchase of movies on cassette and the widespread availability of HBO and other pay cable movie services increase the public's exposure to movies. And viewers of home movies, often older than the traditional theatrical audiences, have begun going out to the movies too, representing part of recent increases in box-office ticket sales. This interaction illustrates the intimate relationship between the theatrical and television audiences for movies.

---

existing financial structure of Hollywood; by distributing movies directly to the home, they by-pass traditional distribution systems. Yet, paradoxically, pay cable has provided an impetus for Hollywood to increase the number of new films produced. HBO alone demands two hundred new movies a year. In 1983, for example, it laid claim to one-third of all films in production, giving it enormous clout with movie producers (because it commands a 60-percent share of the pay-TV market).

In 1977, HBO began financing part of the production costs of movies in order to gain *exclusivity*, the right to show the product first.

Some of these movies, such as *On Golden Pond* and *Sophie's Choice*, were big box-office hits. In 1984, in conjunction with CBS and Columbia, HBO formed a new movie studio, Tri-Star Pictures, which is sufficiently well financed to compete with the major studios. HBO will have exclusive cable rights to all pictures produced by Tri-Star, and these films can later be syndicated to domestic and foreign television markets. Moreover, HBO's parent corporation, Time Inc., was Hollywood's largest financier of movies in the mid-1980s. Time Inc.'s influence derives in part from the American Television and Communications Corporation (ATC), which is its wholly owned, ready-made outlet for HBO and Cinemax and one of the two largest groups of cable systems in the United States.

The shift in the Hollywood power structure represented by these developments promises a profitable future for the pay cable industry. At the same time, it forebodes a reduction in the use of movies by the broadcast networks. Movies have simply become too expensive for the three commercial networks to show, in comparison to the ratings they generate (§12.2). Most movies have already been seen by too much of the television audience, and costs for even the old films are outstripping the local stations' ability to recoup their licensing fees through advertising revenues.

Mini-Network Production   Over the last decade, groups of stations have banded together to share the financing of prime-time specials and miniseries (§13.4). One of the best known of these ad hoc groups, Operation Prime Time, produced and distributed biographies of Golda Meir and Anwar el-Sadat, specials that achieved wide critical acclaim and good ratings. Operation Prime Time also produced several successful miniseries, including *Testimony of Two Men* and *The Bastard*. These were aired simultaneously by nearly a hundred independents and some network affiliates scattered all over the United States. (The term *network* is appropriate to describe such productions because most participating stations, though not permanently affiliated or physically interconnected, scheduled these specials and series to run simultaneously.) The miniseries had the quality of prime-time network programs and could be nationally promoted in the network manner. One key to their success was the promotional ballyhoo that accompanied them. Unlike the usual network arrangement involving station compensation, the stations paid for these programs — an arrangement similar to syndication.

Such ad hoc networks are temporary in nature, generally formed to present only a single miniseries. The use of satellites and receiving dishes have made such temporary relationships easier and cheaper to form than the special telephone-line interconnections that characterized temporary program sharing in the presatellite era.

Other joint production ventures, such as the Program Development Group, have formed to supply prime-time specials and series, but their program output has been limited, resulting in only an hour or two of programming each month. One venture called The New Program Group, however, has attracted national attention with its audience reach and financial clout. Responding to the lack of off-network programs, Gannett Broadcasting Group, Hearst, Metromedia, Storer Broadcasting, and Taft Broadcasting, representing 32 stations, agreed to produce jointly an original situation-comedy series called *Small Wonder*. Together, the stations the group owns (11 independents and 21 network affiliates) reach 45 percent of the viewing public, more than half the audience that ABC, CBS, or NBC commands. The New Program Group has the financial wherewithal to support additional series programming of network quality and may substantially cut into prime-time network audiences.

The new television network (FBC), created out of the Twentieth Century-Fox Studios and the Metromedia stations by Murdoch, is not planned as an ad hoc network. FBC affiliation contracts are for two years and include network compensation payments. Programs will be supplied continuously (in selected time periods) to affiliates, and they will contain network advertising spots.

The Scale of Competition   In contrast to past practices, movie studios and individual station groups are beginning to enter the production and syndication game, even without a guarantee from ABC, CBS, or NBC that a program will air on a network. For example, when NBC canceled the musical series *Fame*, MGM-UA continued to produce twenty-four new episodes, an unusual syndication commitment. Programs from such sources compete directly with the three big networks for the prime-time audience. Still, the amount of programming from all these ad hoc sources adds up to only a fraction of one evening's schedule on one network. An occasional new miniseries and two or three weekly series represent only a few hours of programming per month. As of the mid-1980s, the three major broadcast television networks continued to command most audience and advertiser attention. The trend, however, presages an eventual challenge to the programming dominance of the established broadcast networks.

Program scarcity and audience segmentation have led to the industrywide processes of networking and syndication. These processes occur in broadcast and cable television and in radio, whether the service is commercial or noncommercial. And eventual changes in the sources of programs will likely reinforce these processes, altering only the names of the players.

11.4   Programming Practices

Radio, television, and cable networks, producers, syndicators, affiliated and nonaffiliated stations, and cable systems tend to share a body of strategies. They use a common nomenclature for the various parts of program schedules that is derived primarily from rating practices, and they have two shared goals: to maximize the use of scarce materials and to reach precisely defined audiences that appeal to advertisers.

Dayparting   For scheduling purposes, programmers break air time down into *day parts*. Radio programmers generally divide the day into segments called morning drive, midday, afternoon drive, night, and overnight. Morning and afternoon drives are the periods with the largest audiences for many radio stations, although some music stations have more listeners during the night.

Network television programmers divide the day into segments called prime time (the first hour of which is called access time), fringe time (the hours preceding and following prime time), daytime, and "all other" time. For practical purposes, local TV programmers call the late afternoon reaching up to the news block *early fringe* and call the period after the end of prime time *late fringe*. They often separate access time and the news block from the rest of early fringe and prime time because these are important periods for local programs. The networks lump together all other time for which they do not supply programs. Each day part has its characteristic audience potentialities. Exhibit 11.2 shows how one of the major research companies defines television day parts.

Audience Flow Strategies   Programming strategies center on controlling *audience flow*, the movement of viewers or listeners from one program to another. Occurring mostly at the junction points when one program (or, for radio, one block of songs) ends and another begins, audience flow includes both *flowthrough* on the same station and *outflow* or *inflow* to or from competing stations. Researchers have calculated the amount of television prime-time audience flow. In one study, A. C. Nielsen found that on the average 86 percent of a network's audience flowed through from one half-hour to the next when the same program continued. However, flowthrough dropped to 68 percent when a new program of similar type followed in the next half-hour, and to 50 percent when a program of a different type started in the next half-hour (Nielsen, 1978: 56). Although these precise amounts have been challenged in recent scholarly research as too dependent on the specific samples used by Nielsen and as consequently overestimating the amount of flowthrough, the concepts have become embedded in programming strategy (see Aske, 1980, Headen et al., 1979, and Webster, 1985, for examples).

11.5 Scheduling Strategies

Many media reach consumers in individually packaged physical units — as a film or videocassette, a phonograph record or tape, an edition of a newspaper or a book, or an issue of a magazine. These media reach audiences in single packages, ready for discrete use at the user's convenience. Only broadcasting and cable networks offer the consumer a *continuous* experience. Television and radio programming unfolds, minute by minute, as the day unfolds, providing not merely a succession of information packages but also a coherent program service. For this reason, scheduling plays a major role in the effectiveness of broadcast and cable programming.

Exhibit 11.2   TV Station Dayparts

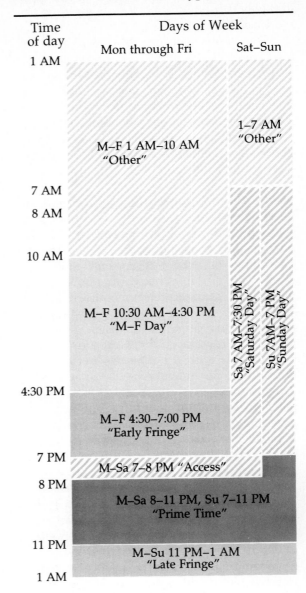

This division of the broadcast days of the week into prime, fringe, day, and "other" day parts is used by the A.C. Nielsen Company in reporting national audience data. It reflects the network outlook on day parts, with the prime-time access half-hour classified as "other". Note that the networks recapture the access half-hour on Sundays, as explained earlier in §8.7.

Source: A.C. Nielsen Company.

When devising schedules, programmers take into account changing audience availability, changing work patterns, and changing needs and interests as the cycles of days, weeks, and seasons progress. They also take into account competition from other program services, using scheduling changes as their primary competitive weapon.

Listed below are some typical scheduling strategies that television, cable, and radio networks, systems, and stations use to exploit audience flow.

1. *Counterprogramming:* seeking to cause audience flow away from the competition and toward one's own station by offering programs different from the competition's. An example would be scheduling light entertainment against the opposing station's news programs.

2. *Block programming:* seeking to maintain audience flowthrough by scheduling programs with similar appeal next to each other. An example would be scheduling an entire evening of comedy programs.

3. *Strong lead-in:* seeking to establish maximum initial audience size by starting a day part with a particularly strong program. An example would be scheduling high-rated local news as a lead-in to network news.

4. *Creating a hammock:* seeking to establish a new program, or to recover the audience for a program already slipping in popularity, by scheduling the program in question in a "hammock" between two strong programs. Flowthrough from the previous (lead-in) program may enhance the initial audience for the hammocked program. Toward the close of the hammocked program, premature inflow from other stations in anticipation of the strong following program may also help to bolster the audience for the hammocked program.

5. *Stunting:* seeking to keep the opposing networks off balance in the short term by such stratagems as making rapid schedule changes, opening a new series with an extra-long episode, and interrupting regular programming frequently with heavily promoted special programs.

Local Television Scheduling After network programs are cleared, a television affiliate has about 35 percent of its time available for syndicated and local programs. The affiliate programmer's most important decision is what to schedule in the early fringe and access periods. Programmers at unaffiliated stations, which make up 20 percent of all stations, have many more scheduling options than those at network affiliates; thus, their chief stratagem, counterprogramming, capitalizes on the network affiliate's inflexibility and targets a different audience. For example, an independent station's scheduling freedom enables it to air sports events at times when affiliated stations are tied up with network shows. Networks can afford to devote prime time to only a few top-rated sports events of national interest. Independents, however, can schedule sports events of purely local interest, such as major league baseball games, even during prime time.

Both affiliates and independent stations schedule virtually all syndicated and local programs to run daily at the same hour, except for programs run on weekends. Monday through Friday *stripping* has three advantages for stations: viewing-habit formation, ease of promotion, and economical package purchasing. Daily scheduling encourages the audience to form regular patterns of viewing, such as a 6:00 P.M. news habit. This strategy borrows from the long-term popularity of non-prime-time programs, such as soap operas, on the networks. In addition, stations can economically advertise their program schedules by using a single promotional spot to describe an entire week's schedule at a given hour. Moreover, the purchase of syndicated programs in large chunks allows for quantity discounts — package deals that reduce the price per unit as the quantity of units goes up.

The practice of stripping off-network reruns, scheduling episodes daily "across the board," has led to an enormous demand for television program series with one hundred or more episodes. Among the best known of these series are *M*A*S*H* and *All in the Family*. Series that remain on network schedules long enough to generate large numbers of episodes command high prices in syndication. Most of these series, however, are getting older and older, and recent series tend not to run long enough on network schedules to build up sufficient episodes. Thus, there is a shortage of long series for stripping.

Blocking is another local television strategy commonly used in the after-school time period and on weekends. Employed concurrently with stripping, it encourages audience flow-through. Blocking of shows with similar appeal is frequently used by independent television stations to capture and hold segments of viewers. Sets of situation-comedy reruns, scheduled one after another, can hold many children, teens, and adults for several hours. On weekends, independent stations commonly counterprogram with large blocks of movies, sports, or religious programs, while affiliates carry the Saturday morning array of network cartoons.

Network Television Scheduling   Each of the three national television networks offers its affiliates approximately a hundred hours of programs per week, filling about 65 to 70 percent of an affiliate's schedule. The main arena of network rivalry is the twenty-two hours of prime time each network fills each week (the three hours from 8:00 P.M. to 11:00 P.M. each night of the week, plus the extra hour from 7:00 P.M. to 8:00 P.M. on Sundays). The profit margin for network daytime programming is greater than that for prime-time programming because of the extraordinarily high cost of prime-time programs. Nevertheless, it is a network's performance in prime time that establishes its prestige and defines its leadership role.

Prime time affords networks access to the largest and most varied audiences and therefore contains the most expensive programming with the broadest appeal. By the same token, prime time invites the keenest competition among broadcast and cable networks and television stations. Because of the high cost of such programming and because networks need scheduling flexibility in order to compete for the audience, prime-time series are normally aired once a week. In other day parts, however, most programming is stripped, Monday through Friday. Network morning programs, soap operas, and evening newscasts, for example, are shown at the same time every day.

Radio and Cable Scheduling   Radio stations use the strategies of counterprogramming, stripping, and blocking even more than television stations. Typically, radio formats are chosen to appeal to groups of people not adequately reached by other stations. Most stations schedule their program elements, whether music or news, in hourly rotations, creating 60-minute content cycles, modified according to day part. Radio stations tend to stick with the same rotation pattern for an entire day part, a form of blocking.

Cable services have also adopted the strategies of counterprogramming, daily stripping, and time-period blocking. Superstations and other broad-appeal basic cable networks, for instance, tend to counterprogram the broadcast networks with sports and older movies, and use daily stripping and blocking strategies. Cable services also use a strategy called *bridging*, or scheduling across the start-times of other programs. For example, pay networks such as Home Box Office and Showtime generally schedule a highly advertised recent movie at 8:00 P.M., so as to span most of an evening's broadcast network programs. This bridges the 9:00 P.M. time period, when the maximum audience is watching television. However, if a movie ends before 10:00 P.M., HBO usually adds filler material to complete the remaining time so as to start a new program when viewers may be hunting for something to watch. Sometimes the pay movie networks try to get the jump on the broadcast networks by starting their movies earlier in the evenings. This strategy works best when broadcast network schedules are already disrupted by late-running sports or political programs.

The pay movie networks recycle their movies as many as a half-dozen to a dozen times a month, typically varying days of the week and non-prime-time start-times to encourage viewing by people with varied lifestyles. The pay networks tend to view their schedules in monthly blocks, because of the monthly publication of most pay cable program guides and the need to encourage the monthly renewal of subscriptions. Local cable access channels, on the other hand, have borrowed a leaf from radio in adopting even more frequent rerunning of their scarce program materials. And basic cable networks such as Cable News Network (CNN) repeat news elements hourly, much like the practice of many radio stations.

11.6 Appraising the Program Services

In this chapter we have discussed specific programming problems from an industry perspective, and we have examined the processes and practices of production and scheduling. What about programming from a critical perspective? What sorts of general issues arise concerning television as a program service?

Has cable made up for broadcast television's limitations? What complaints does the public make about radio? In this section, we will look at these and other questions concerning the quality and usefulness of broadcast and cable programming.

A "Vast Wasteland"? The best-known generalization about television programming was made by Newton Minow, former chairman of the FCC. In his first address to the National Association of Broadcasters back in 1961, Minow challenged station owners and managers to sit down and watch their own programming for a full broadcast day. They would, he assured them, find a "vast wasteland" of violence, repetitive formulas, irritating commercials, and sheer boredom (1964: 52). The "vast wasteland" phrase caught on and became a part of the language of broadcasting.

Fifteen years later, Minow (by then a lawyer in private practice and a PBS executive) told a panel at another NAB convention that he had no regrets; the criticism had jolted broadcasters out of their complacency, at least momentarily. In the intervening years, said Minow, "there has been enormous improvement, particularly in the area of news and information" (Terry, 1976: 5).

In the 1980s, FCC chairman Mark Fowler expressed a very different view about program content in several industry speeches when he referred to television as a "toaster with pictures." The FCC by then had little interest in program content (§17.2) and felt that television should be considered as just another business.

Though few discriminating viewers today watch everything on television, commentators still make sweeping judgments about the medium as a whole. Most concede that television occasionally rises to peaks of excellence, even though — given the nature of things — between the peaks must lie broad valleys (or vast wastelands) of routine programming. How green the valleys depends on the viewer's own tastes and standards.

Network television executives aim to please all sorts of people at all sorts of times of the day and night. No other medium has faced such a demanding task. In attempting it, television makes apparent something that was never before exposed so blatantly: the common denominator of popular taste. As Daniel Boorstin, an authority on American cultural history, explained:

Much of what we hear complained of as the "vulgarity," the emptiness, the sensationalism, the soap-serialism, of television is not a peculiar product of television at all. It is simply the translation of the sub-literature onto the television screen. . . . Never before were the vulgar tastes so conspicuous and so accessible to the prophets of our high culture. Subculture—which is of course the dominant culture of a democratic society—is now probably no worse, and certainly no better, than it has ever been. But it is emphatically more visible. (Boorstin, 1978: 19)

As for radio, while young people listen in ever-increasing numbers, many older people complain about popular music. In general, they express bewilderment at the words and forms of rock music and the bizarre theatricality of recent rock stars. During the last few years, MTV has attracted the pop-music audience to cable television, leaving radio less in the limelight, though ever more prosperous.

However, it makes no sense to measure television or radio with yardsticks different from those used to measure books, plays, symphonies, or paintings. Book reviewers do not make such all-inclusive judgments about "print" or art critics about "paint" as critics do about "television." Countless bad books and bad paintings have not led critics to damn literature and art. Similarly, one cannot rea-

sonably expect to be able to turn on the radio or television set at any time, day or night, and immediately find a program suited to one's particular tastes and needs of the moment. No more would one expect to be satisfied by the first book that came to hand on a library shelf.

Limits on Choice   On the other hand, in a library we can move to another bookcase and keep on browsing until we find the book to suit our needs. It was thought for a time that cable or even newer delivery systems might similarly expand our choices by creating a library of television programming. But no such range of immediate choices exists at this time, for a number of reasons:

1. Most viewers can select only a dozen or two channels or tune in only a few over-the-air stations.
2. At any given moment, several of the available channels are likely to be airing the same program or, at best, the same sort of program.
3. Many unusual options on cable television have failed as commercial ventures (examples include CBS Cable, a high-quality cultural service, and most interactive programs on two-way cable; also, pay-per-view has yet to become a measurable force).
4. Television is a prisoner of time; viewers cannot browse through shelves of past programs to select the one that best serves the needs of the moment. The phenomenal popularity of home VCRs attests to the public's desire to escape this limitation of television. More than half of all homes will have acquired VCRs within a decade, using them primarily for timeshifting and secondarily for the playing back of rented, prerecorded programs, generally films.

Nonetheless, discriminating viewers must have the patience and foresight to plan ahead for viewing those programs that do suit their tastes and interests. Cable television, prerecorded cassettes, and home video recording overcome these limitations on choice to some extent, offering a wider range of immediate choices and the possibility of putting programs on the shelf for later use. But the enlargement of choice they offer is expensive and limited.

In the same way, radio, even in the largest markets, provides a limited range of choices at any given time. Most radio stations adopt the most popular formats, giving interested listeners several choices. But listeners seeking less popular programs and music formats may have only a single option or none at all at a given hour; they must turn instead to records or audio cassettes. Although there are ten times as many radio stations as television stations, most radio stations closely resemble each other, leaving only a few genuine alternatives available to listeners in each market.

Audience Expectations   The preceding discussion is not intended to suggest that the electronic media should be exempt from criticism, but rather that criticism should take into consideration the nature of each medium. Broadcast television, cable, and radio all have their own characteristic limitations and potentialities.

Broadcasting comes directly into the home as an ever-present, ever-ready source of potential pleasure and information. It is federally licensed, which gives it an implied government approval and encourages viewers to feel especially proprietary about it. Cable television has a similar status because it is franchised by local government. Moreover, the public's investment in the purchase, maintenance, and operation of television and radio receivers exceeds by far the entire investment of the industry in the means of production and transmission. Consciously or not, rightly or wrongly, we feel that the electronic media have an obligation to serve our needs.

Summary

• Broadcast and cable programmers face the twin problems of program scarcity and the need to appeal to advertisers. They address these problems by the sparing, repeated, and shared use of programs (the parsimony principle), and also through targeting and segmentation of audiences.

• Hollywood's program production processes limit the number and type of movies and television series that can be produced to fill television program schedules.

• The Big Six studios and the independent producers compete among themselves to have their series programs aired by the three television networks, while cable television and home videocassette recorders offer new markets for Hollywood's movies.

• Networking and syndication are the two industrywide methods of program distribution. Both are ways of solving the problems of program shortage and advertiser appeal. More and more groups of stations have formed mini-networks and, like some cable networks, are entering the production game to fill the remaining programming gap.

• Stations and networks use the practice of dayparting to focus their programs on the maximum number of available viewers or listeners.

• The three main programming strategies used in common by networks, stations, and cable systems are counterprogramming, stripping, and blocking, which are intended to increase or alter audience flow. They also make some use of bridging strategies.

• The broadcast television networks tend to use once-a-week scheduling during prime time. Local affiliates tend to use daily stripping during early fringe and access, the time periods preceding and following local news, whereas local independent stations generally counterprogram affiliates in the same market with entertainment.

• Radio and cable program scheduling follows repetitive cycles that make the most use of their limited program resources and that at-tract the largest possible number of listeners and viewers in specific demographic or psychographic categories.

• Network television faces a demanding task in trying to please the heterogeneous mass audience, and its programs vary from the artistically satisfying to those with lowest-common-denominator appeal. Because of economic and other practical limitations, cable and newer delivery systems have not expanded viewers' choices greatly, although home VCRs have increased the audience's viewing flexibility.

CHAPTER 12

Network Programs

One of the most persistent complaints about television is its lack of diversity — its lack of variety in program genres, in themes and plots within genres, in production styles, and in program sources. This chapter addresses the issue of variety by examining the network selection and scheduling practices for the main types of television and radio programs.

All media content goes through cycles of invention, imitation, and decline. Nowhere is this more immediately apparent than in network prime-time television programs. Types of programs, commonly called *genres*, rise and fall in audience popularity and, perhaps more crucial, vary in their popularity with network programmers. The networks weigh the cost of obtaining and distributing each program in terms of both its prospective dollar return and its less tangible value in building network prestige and positive image. In addition to heeding these ultimately economic concerns, broadcast and cable networks must arrange programs in meaningful arrays, selecting each program according to the needs of the overall schedule.

Within each program genre, the risk of failure is so great that the networks copy a popular program again and again until the next "new" success takes over in popularity.

The networks' homogenizing influence also affects production style; productions from one production company look much like those from another. The big studios and producers dominate network production, effectively closing the door to newcomers with new ideas and new styles. A study of more than 2,000 prime-time programs between 1953 and 1974 revealed not only a narrow range of types but a continuing decline in the number of types over the years (Exhibit 12.1).

Although prime-time network programming lacks diversity, network programmers nevertheless desperately seek novelty. The explanation of this seeming paradox is that they want to be "different" without taking chances. Occasionally, new ideas succeed in surviving the networks' homogenizing influences, sometimes resulting in successes that surprise the programmers. *All in the Family* was one such surprise. Its popularity subsequently made more kinds of irony acceptable to network programming executives. *The Cosby Show* was another surprise, rapidly becoming far more popular than had been predicted.

As used in this chapter, the term *network* encompasses the three broadcast television networks, the noncommercial public broadcasting service, the fifty or so basic-cable and

Exhibit 12.1   Decline in Diversity of Prime-Time Network Programming

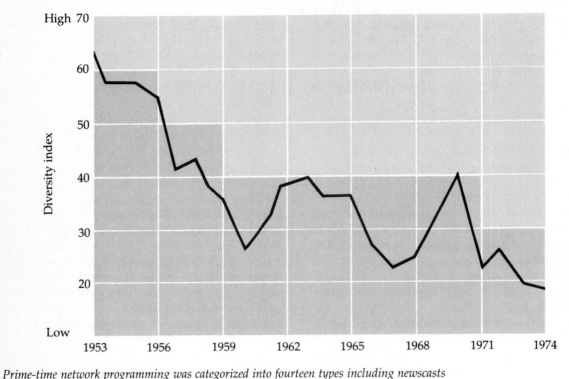

Prime-time network programming was categorized into fourteen types including newscasts and documentaries as separate categories. The chart is based on a "diversity index," which ranges from zero to 79. A score of zero would mean that all of a season's programming consisted of no more than three categories; and a score of 79 would mean that programming that season was divided equally among all fourteen program categories. Unfortunately, no more recent comparable data are available.

Source: Reprinted from "Trends in Network Prime-Time Programming, 1953-74" by Joseph R. Dominick and Millard C. Pearce in the *Journal of Communication*, 26:1 (Winter, 1976) pp. 70-80. Copyright 1976 Annenberg School of Communications.

pay cable networks, and the major radio network services. We consider network entertainment television first, because it dominates public perceptions of all electronic media. Next, we look at network informational television programming, which has recently become more commercially important; these programs show similarities to entertainment programming but also introduce new issues related to journalistic standards. Finally, we examine some of the problems and programs unique to network radio.

12.1 Distribution by Networking

The rapid rise of national networks to dominant positions in both broadcasting and the cable industry is evidence of the parsimony principle at work in both program and advertising distribution. *Networking* began with wired interconnection, which has now been largely replaced by satellite distribution of programming. Networking enables instant sharing of content and is also a means of simultaneous distribution that takes advantage of national program promotion.* In all the electronic media, networking is a means of centrally producing or procuring high-cost program materials and distributing them to many separate users at moderate average cost to each. Advertisers' commercials are distributed simultaneously with the programs (inserted within them) and thus reach the same audiences. In the program industry, the term *networking* also implies that the commercial broadcast networks usually pay stations for carrying their advertising and programs. In cable, however, local systems must usually pay fees to carry basic networks, or pay a percentage of revenues to premium networks.

Structured Commercial Program Service

A broadcasting or ad-supported cable network provides a structured program service to its affiliates that makes optimum use of audience flow strategies, thus maximizing ratings and, in consequence, the rates that can be charged for network, spot, and local advertising time. Such methods of program structuring as dayparting, audience flow, and scheduling were discussed in the previous chapter (§11.4 and §11.5). Here we look at the kinds of choices networks make in program content to structure their program services.

Affiliated stations and cable systems benefit economically from the networks' top-quality programming (at a minimum, network programs have high technical quality). Also,

*The technological aspects of networking were discussed in chapter 7, its structural aspects in chapter 8, and its economic aspects in chapter 10.

network advertisers benefit from getting access to the best stations and cable systems in the nation's major markets in a single transaction. An incidental public benefit is the fact that networks create an instantaneous means of reaching the entire nation with news and information.

On the other hand, commercial network affiliates are dominated by the three big networks and exercise little influence over network practices. ABC, CBS, and NBC program their services to fit their own needs and can change affiliates at the end of their two-year contracts if dissatisfied with local audience size or local management.

Noncommercial Networks   Public broadcasting differs from the commercial services because the stations control the network service (§8.3). Local noncommercial television stations are members of PBS and therefore function as owners and policy makers, rather than as affiliates of some separate entity that sets its own policy.

PBS provides a delivery service for programs produced by others and selected by the affiliated public television stations. Member stations choose to fund programs based on factors such as appeal to local viewers, potential for underwriting, and most important, program costs (each station's share is prorated on the basis of station size and the number of stations voting to help fund the program). PBS acts as a clearing-house, providing a core schedule of prime-time programs, some of which are paid for by underwriters, and "nominating" underfunded programs for stations to "elect." The PBS delivery system has been both praised for increasing democracy within the service and criticized for its emphasis on lowering financial risk. This latter emphasis, some say, has discouraged program innovation, favoring instead the continuation of long-established series and stressing inexpensive shows.

NPR provides only about 20 percent of its members' daily program schedules, and its members are a minority of all noncommercial radio stations on the air. Member stations, which may also contribute programs to the system, are not required to carry any NPR programs. Member stations may also affiliate with other radio networks such as APR.

Commercial and Noncommercial Network Parallels   There are nonetheless many similarities between commercial and noncommercial networks. Like commercial networks, PBS and NPR simultaneously distribute programs to stations across the nation, organizing the programs into a structured service — at least during prime-time hours on PBS and during parts of the day on NPR. Public broadcasting must also deal with program scarcity, but unlike commercial broadcasting, it faces a perpetual shortage of funds for production of new programs.

There are also parallels between public broadcasting and cable practices. Just as popular movies on HBO help local cable systems attract subscribers, so do high-quality programs from PBS and NPR aid member stations in getting local backing. For example, PBS supplies programs with the goal of aiding stations in gaining local support through pledges, contributions, and underwriting. This practice is particularly evident during annual fund drives.

12.2 Prime-Time Entertainment

During the twenty-two hours of prime time each week, the three national broadcast networks vie for huge audiences, the size of which are unprecedented in the history of entertainment. Collectively, the networks captured about 90 percent of the prime-time viewing audience for nearly three decades. In

the 1980s, however, with increasing numbers of cable networks, improved independent station programming, and widespread use of home video recorders, the combined network audience share decreased to less than 75 percent during prime time, and it expected to fall even further in the 1990s. Major news events carried by all three networks, however, can still reach as much as 90 percent of the adult U.S. population. And a few unusually popular episodes of entertainment programs have attracted more than half of all television homes to one network for an hour or so.

Bimodal Appeal   The extraordinarily broad appeal of prime-time television entertainment attracts and holds the attention of tens of millions of people night after night. The most successful programs attain this breadth by appealing to audiences on two or more levels. Paul Klein, a specialist in audience demographics, has called this quality *bimodality* (1971: 22). He cites the example of age bimodality: some programs tend to attract both young and old viewers, but not the age group in between. A graph depicting audience age against program popularity would show a bimodal curve, with two distinct peaks, one at a lower age level and one at a higher age level. Programs such as *The Cosby Show* exhibit age bimodality while appealing to huge numbers of viewers of all ages.

Multidimensional appeals cut across differences that otherwise set people poles apart. *All in the Family* drew large audiences for years because the audience perceived Archie Bunker's prejudices in two different ways: large numbers of viewers agreed with the program's overt antibigotry message; others enthusiastically endorsed what they saw as Bunker's courage in "telling it like it is" (Adler, 1979). Neither group by itself would have been large enough to account for *All in the Family's* high ratings. Working together in unconscious and ironic harmony, this bimodal appeal made the series unbeatable for years.

Series Demographics

Series, the mainstay of prime-time network television, are programs of multiple episodes sharing a common cast, main plot line, and situation. Most new network programs are series, and because most new entries fail to succeed in being renewed, most failed programs are series as well (Eastman, et al., 1985: 125).

Fred Silverman, a legendary programmer of the 1970s, had a powerful impact on series programming (§4.5). Becoming chief of CBS programming in 1970, Silverman participated in what network head William Paley termed "the most drastic overhaul in CBS history" (Paley, 1979: 267). The network scrapped 14 prime-time program series, introduced 8 new ones, and rescheduled 11 others — all to change the network's demographics.

Until the 1970s, CBS's prime-time lead was based on rural comedies such as *The Andy Griffith Show* (1960–1968) and *The Beverly Hillbillies* (1962–1971). Such programs. though popular enough to draw high ratings, had marked bimodal age appeal, attracting the very young and very old age brackets more than the mid-range, "upscale" segment of the audience that accounts for the bulk of consumer spending. CBS's revised programming strategy called for ruthless cancellation of shows with the wrong demographic appeals, no matter how high their ratings. All three networks now favor more contemporary shows that appeal to active, urban, high-consumption audience segments.

As part of a programming revolution rivaling CBS's wholesale changes of 1970, ABC lured Fred Silverman away from CBS in 1975. ABC thereupon concentrated on appealing to teen and very young adult viewers with superficial situation comedies that promoted sex and nostalgia. Its revolution paid off, because

in the 1975–1976 season the unthinkable happened: ABC, after decades of playing third fiddle, moved into the network lead. The next season ABC had seven of the top prime-time programs, including such phenomenal youth-appeal shows as *Happy Days* (1974), its spinoff, *Laverne and Shirley* (1976), and *Charlie's Angels* (1976). ABC was not winning any prizes for quality, but it walked away with all the popularity ratings.

However, ABC's spectacular, and short-lived, success represents only the optimal result of one network's demographic strategy, a strategy that ironically was to lose all three networks some of their mammoth audiences. A programming focus on only one segment of the audience contributed to the first decline in overall network television audience shares by allowing independent and cable to attract both children and older viewers.

In the mid-1980s, after years of running a distant third in network rankings, NBC moved to first position in a close race with CBS. (ABC lost ground and ran in third place.) At least part of NBC's success seems to have come from its chairman, Grant Tinker, and his willingness to let new programs develop their audiences slowly instead of canceling them out of hand if they earned low ratings in their first seasons. For example, programs such as *Hill Street Blues* and *St. Elsewhere* appealed to viewers who would not otherwise watch much network television (as well as to many heavy viewers, of course), and consequently required more than one season to develop their audiences. *Cheers*, another program that attracts a younger audience of light television viewers, took a couple of years to attract a substantial audience for NBC. Although CBS showed some willingness to wait for audiences to build for *All in the Family* and *The Waltons*, its usual strategy was to seek rapid mass audience appeal programs. Going after people who typically watch little network television is a very different strategy from competing head-to-head with the other networks for the same viewers. Grant Tinker's background as a producer and supplier of programs may have strongly influenced his philosophy as NBC's head.

Series Cancellation   In the early 1980s, program expense became the primary criterion for cancellation of broadcast network series. Per-episode costs for new series had more than doubled in a decade. This, combined with an economic recession, forced all three networks to weigh popularity against per-episode profit. No longer could they afford to "carry" one series by counting on profits from another. Nowadays, networks may cancel programs that attract large audiences with the right demographics if another program that can generate similar ratings is available at a lower per-episode cost. The desire of tens of millions of people to continue watching an established favorite is irrelevant if another program in its place would soon draw as many viewers, even if they are different people. This practice annoys many critics and viewers.

The reason for the practice lies in the fixed number of advertising minutes per hour. When program costs rise, advertising rates must rise if profits are to remain constant or improve (and improving profits is the goal of every network executive). However, the already stratospheric network ad rates can only rise slowly, because of advertiser resistance and limited competition during some day parts, so the networks seek other avenues of profit. One of these is reduction of their total of per-episode program costs, sometimes achieved by trading off several high-priced series for one expensive series and several lower-cost ones. Such fiscal pressure has resulted in the cancellation of expensive series such as *Seven Brides for Seven Brothers*, *How the West Was Won*, and *Battlestar Galactica*, and also resulted in a year's hesitation over scheduling *V*, despite its enormously successful pilot.

A related element in program cancellation is program length. Two 30-minute situation comedies used to cost somewhat more than one 60-minute episode in a dramatic series. In consequence, the broadcast networks appeared to be slowly moving away from half-hour programs and toward one-hour programs. At the end of 1983, for example, CBS canceled *One Day at a Time* after nine years, despite only a slight decline in popularity. A great surge in hour-length detective series appeared on all three networks. However, by 1986 the cost picture was again shifting: half-hour situation comedies averaged about $325,000 per episode, whereas most one-hour dramas and action-adventure programs cost $750,000 or more. Once again, the trend in network prime-time program selection reversed.

Series Clones and Spin-offs   Because the cost of failure in entertainment series is so high, the networks avoid the risk of real innovation. This timidity has led to incessant repetition of previously successful program structures (*formats*) and mimicking of already successful series ideas. A *clone* program closely imitates an already popular program, changing only the stars and minor details of plot. Clones are usually created by competing networks. A *spin-off* is a new program starring secondary characters from a previous hit on the same network. Cloning and spinning off have always been evident in the broadcast networks' selection of new programs, but they increased dramatically in the 1980s. For example, successive spin-offs and cloning of *Dallas* (1978–) led to *Knots Landing* (1979–), *Dynasty* (1981–), *Falcon Crest* (1981–), *Paper Dolls* (1984–1985), and *Dynasty II: The Colbys* (1985–). Attempts to copy the success of *Magnum P.I.*, number three in prime-time in the 1983–1984 season, led to *Finder of Lost Loves*, *Hawaiian Heat*, *Hunter*, *Miami Vice*, and *Partners in Crime*, all in the next year.

The networks created the prime-time serial drama, epitomized by the long-successful *Dallas* and its cloned competitors and spin-offs, to capitalize on some of the parsimonious qualities of daytime soap operas. Like daytime soap operas, these hour-long programs command strong viewer loyalty while stretching a complex plot line from week to week with predictably consistent ratings. Most episodes of these prime-time soaps end with a cliffhanger, a suspenseful situation at the program's close that entices viewers into returning a week later for the next installment.

In contrast to the daytime soaps, however, these programs are among the most expensive on prime-time television, running as high as $850,000 per episode on average for *Dallas* and *Dynasty* (with some episodes hitting the million-dollar mark). Their multiple sets, large casts of big stars, and lavish costume budgets create high production costs, but the programs return the outgo in high ratings. Hoping to climb on the bandwagon, NBC's *Berrenger's* joined this high-priced group of elite soaps in 1984, but lasted less than a year. WTBS has also attempted to provide prime-time soap-opera series, generally at much lower than network-sized budgets. How many of these highly involving dramas can be placed in prime time and continue to draw big audiences, and whether these series will function successfully as syndicated reruns on local stations, are merely the latest unanswered questions among programmers.

Situation Comedies Long a staple of prime-time network television, situation comedies (*sitcoms*) are still in high demand for syndication because they are so suitable for daily

stripping. As broadcast network fare, however, they showed signs of ratings slippage in the early 1980s, leading to modified formulas reflecting the changing patterns of U.S. family life. Signaling the loss of broad popularity, *Happy Days*, a hit for eleven years, began to slide in the ratings in the early 1980s and eventually was cancelled. Other sitcoms fell from dominant ratings positions to the worst showings in thirty years. Of the top 10 programs in 1974, seven were sitcoms, but a decade later no sitcoms even made the list. Marvin Mord, vice president of research and marketing for ABC, pointed out, "Performance of all network programs has declined 10 percent, and for sitcoms, it's down 32 percent" (Horowitz, 1984: 23). But by 1985, in another reversal, *The Cosby Show*, *Family Ties*, and *Cheers* dominated the top 10 program listing. Meanwhile, such long-term winners as *The Jeffersons* (1974–1985) had disappeared entirely from the network first-run schedule. By the mid-1980s the total number of network sitcoms was down markedly from the previous decade as a result of ratings slippage for most shows and the use of one-hour series.

The immediate success of *The Cosby Show* and *Kate & Allie* in 1984 illustrates the two new formulas for broadcast situation comedy in the mid-1980s. One formula focuses on a single dominant star in a traditional family; the other features humorous treatment of a nontraditional household situation. *The Cosby Show*, for example, hinges on one outstanding actor who carries a cast of unknowns. The program revolves around a father, mother, and children having predictable but funny domestic problems. This show about a black family succeeds with traditional content and values. *Kate & Allie*, on the other hand, represents the new sitcom social mode. Here, two divorced women with children attempt to make a go of a fatherless, two-mother household situation. In the face of widespread changes in work and

Exhibit 12.2   *Maude*

An example of conspicuous failure to obtain clearance on moral grounds for an entertainment program also involved CBS. Two episodes in the comedy series Maude *dealt with a decision of the title character to have an abortion. The abortion episodes, originally telecast late in 1972, came up for rerun in August 1973. Catholic Church organizations led a campaign to persuade CBS to cancel, or affiliates to refuse clearance for, the reruns of the two episodes. CBS would not back down, but about 20 percent of the affiliates complied by refusing clearance.*

Source: Courtesy of CBS.

family patterns, television series increasingly explore new social relationships and social issues (Exhibit 12.2).

Viewers looking for humorous entertainment in a series format have, in the past, had to watch sitcoms. But recently action-adventure programs have introduced large doses of comedy. Series such as *Magnum, P.I., Moon-*

lighting, and *Remington Steele* now include light-hearted comic scenes and warm-hearted relationships. This broadening of dramatic-series content may have contributed to the overall slide in sitcom popularity.

The reduced numbers of 30-minute situation comedies and the shorter network runs for those that do survive, will have long-term repercussions on the syndication market, where sitcoms are so profitable. The shortage of network sitcoms makes these programs vulnerable on local station schedules because they often lack a cushion of surrounding comedies; blocking of sitcoms (§11.5) helps create a mood that carries over from program to program, reflected in predictable ratings. Some basic cable networks such as WTBS, WGN, and USA have adopted blocking strategies using sitcoms, but those networks also have problems with scarcity in the syndication market.

Police and Detective Dramas

In the mid-1980s, police dramas and detective shows resurfaced as popular prime-time fare, recalling the heydays of *Dragnet* (late 1950s) and *Perry Mason* (1960s). *Hill Street Blues* and *Miami Vice* epitomize two aspects of the recent trend: the former offers the humanizing appeal of personal moral dilemmas in its character-oriented plots, and the latter offers the "new wave" appeal of fast pacing, rapid cutting, neon lights, and macho detecting. *Cagney & Lacey*, CBS's police drama about two women detectives, has similarities to NBC's *Hill Street Blues*, and several detective series have attempted to copy NBC's *Miami Vice* while generally avoiding the seamier sides of crime that characterize it and are part of its appeal.

Theatrical Films, Made-for-TV Movies, and Miniseries

By the 1970s the networks were paying astronomical prices for the right to show outstanding *theatrical films* on television. The movie classic *Gone With the Wind* cost NBC about $5 million for a single showing in 1976, but it captured 65 percent of the television audience. On the other hand, a showing of *Star Wars* in 1983 cost over $10 million but attracted only 35 percent of the audience, finishing second to a made-for-television movie. ABC set a new record in 1984 by paying $15 million for the right to air *Ghostbusters*

in 1986 — this after two years of theatrical and pay cable release. But by 1985 the average movie licensing price had dipped to about $3 million, because the ratings no longer justified extraordinary prices.*

The number of movies declined and film production costs rose in the early 1980s. Because the pay cable networks frequently outbid the broadcast networks for the scarce supply of top quality films, the broadcast networks increasingly turned away from theatrical movies to two other programming sources: *made-for-television movies* and *miniseries*. A network's rental fee for a single showing of a major theatrical feature would more than pay for making a brand-new, modest-budget feature designed for television. Sets, props, and locations need not be lavish because so much detail is lost on small television screens. One well-known star supported by unknowns suffices, because with extravagant promotion the star will command audience attention. And many made-for-television movies have realized audience ratings comparable to those of the most popular theatrical films. In the 1983–1984 season, for example, four of the five top made-for-television movies commanded higher shares of audience than any televised theatrical movie that year.

NBC led the way into made-for-television movies as far back as 1966 with *World Premiere*, a series of two-hour programs costing about $800,000 each, small potatoes compared to the millions budgeted today for even a run-of-the-mill theatrical feature film. Though at first regarded as "a kind of grubby step-child of film" (Whitney, 1974: 21), during the 1970s made-for-television features became a staple

---

*Although costly blockbuster features often cannot earn back their rental fees in advertising revenue, they sometimes can be sound investments for their indirect rewards. Films are especially useful for clobbering the opposition during sweep weeks, periods when ratings services collect viewing data on all the local markets (§14.1).

of network programming. Gradually they increased in scope and ambition, blending into the miniseries format. By 1984, two out of three prime-time movies were made-for-television features. These television movies compete well against cable and independent station movies, and many serve another valuable function as pilot episodes for possible series.

Pay cable networks, especially HBO, responded to the scarcity and high cost of theatrical films by producing their own features for pay cable. These made-for-pay movies offer cable systems *premiere exclusivity*, the right to air the program first. Because the advantage of seeing original material first is a crucial factor in viewers' willingness to renew monthly subscriptions, pay cable networks increasingly seek original programming. They use such original material as new series, musical variety shows, and nightclub comedy to counterprogram the broadcast networks and to differentiate themselves from the broadcast networks and from each other in the audience's mind. Nevertheless, theatrical movies, because of their immense popularity, remain the mainstay of Home Box Office, Showtime, Cinemax, The Movie Channel, American Movie Classics, and Home Theatre Network programming.

Miniseries are highly promoted series that are typically about 8 to 12 hours long and are scheduled over several successive nights in 2- or 3-hour segments. They began appearing on the commercial broadcast networks during rating periods in the late 1970s, accompanied by much promotional ballyhoo. Starting the trend, *Roots,* a 14-hour adaptation of a best seller about the changing roles of blacks in American life, as seen through one family's eyes, drew all-time-high audience shares in 1977. After this, the networks began scheduling miniseries in place of the scarce blockbuster movie. Like the box-office-hit movies, miniseries draw many viewers who do not normally watch television, increasing the total number of households using television. They attract upscale, professional viewers, compete well against cable movies, and can be used to induce sampling of other series by new viewers. Although miniseries can cost a great deal (*Winds of War* in 1983 was said to have cost $38 million for the series and another $25 million for promotion), they bring prestige and high ratings while filling the large chunks of time once taken by blockbuster movies.

Theatrical features, made-for-television movies, and miniseries all impose special scheduling requirements on the broadcast networks. They do best with an 8:00 P.M. or 9:00 P.M. starting time when audiences are largest, and do poorly starting on the half-hour, when many viewers are already committed to watching other television programs. They also need compatible lead-in programs, a difficult requirement to fill because a single movie must match the appeal of an entire series. But the biggest problem with showing theatrical films is that much of the potential audience has already been exposed to them in theaters, on pay cable, and/or on videocassettes, long before their release to the broadcast networks. To attract large audiences, they require lengthy "rests" of as much as two years between air dates in broadcast and cable television. Movies such as *Chariots of Fire* and *Star Wars* had poor network ratings because they had been inadequately rested before their broadcast network showings. Consequently, made-for-TV movies and miniseries look increasingly appealing to the networks.

Public Television   Public television occupies a unique position in a programming game dominated by commercial interests. It serves as a catchall for the cultural and other minority-interest programming that the commercial networks claim they cannot afford to schedule. Intellectually challenging drama and film arts such as ballet and opera appear almost exclusively on public television and on two cable networks, Bravo and the Arts & Entertainment Network.

Public television's outstanding and long-running showcase of culture is *Masterpiece Theatre*, telecast on PBS stations Sunday evenings and repeated later in the week. It gives Americans a glimpse of British video drama at its best. Historical programs, scheduled as miniseries, have characterized *Masterpiece Theatre*, starting with *The First Churchills*, which was followed later by *The Wives of Henry VIII*, *Elizabeth R*, *I, Claudius*, and others. Historical fiction has proved the most popular. The most widely appealing series, *Upstairs, Downstairs*, detailed the doings of an Edwardian family (upstairs) and its servants (downstairs) for four successive seasons. Some critics suggested that this was merely high-class soap opera, but nonetheless *Upstairs, Downstairs* was probably the most popular program on public television, with the possible exception of *Sesame Street* (§12.5). Each episode in the various *Masterpiece Theatre* productions has been introduced by journalist and critic Alistair Cooke. Delivered casually and with great charm, these introductions can be considered social essays in their own right, establishing continuity among the episodes of the most culturally satisfying entertainment series ever to appear on television.

PBS countered the criticism that too much public television fare came from Britain by developing the cultural series *Great Performances*, a showcase for major American artists in plays and musical performances, often taped in actual presentation before theater audiences. These performances help to build American audiences for opera and ballet, turning artists such as Sills, Pavarotti, Sutherland, Horne, Baryshnikov, Nureyev, Makarova, and Kirk-

land into familiar faces in millions of American homes.

Culture on Cable   The cultural cable channels compete for rights to many of the same performance events that PBS seeks. Cultural programming on cable includes dramas, ballet and other dance forms, music, opera, and less frequently the reading of literary works and display of visual art such as sculpture, painting, photography, and design. Because of the shortage of widely appealing drama and fine arts events, Bravo and Arts & Entertainment (A&E) have turned increasingly to movies to fill their schedules. Bravo, a pay cable channel, carries a large number of foreign films, especially classic French, German, and Italian art films of the late 1950s and recent, foreign-made movies. And A&E has begun mixing comedy shows and detective series with its cultural programs to provide broader appeal. These services thus resemble both noncommercial and commercial programming.

12.3 Non-Prime-Time Programs

Although prime time is the main arena of network rivalry, daytime programs yield a higher profit margin for the networks. This is because prime-time programs have extraordinarily high production costs and air a smaller number of commercial minutes.

Outside of prime time, broadcast network programs have traditionally consisted of soap operas, game shows, and talk shows. ABC leavens this mix with reruns of prime-time series and *Nightline*, a late-night news program; CBS once added large blocks of movies, then also turned to series reruns; NBC introduced the comedy/variety series *Saturday Night Live* to late-night television. Music videos and late-night newscasts were introduced on weekends in the 1980s to fill extended network nighttime hours. But soaps, games, and talk still dominate daytime television, just as they once dominated daytime radio.

All three genres have their counterparts on the newer cable television networks. For example, SIN, the only Spanish-language cable and broadcast network, uses a soap-operalike format in several programs (called *telenovelas*) reaching tens of millions of Hispanics in America and Mexico. USA Network carries reruns of game shows such as *The Gong Show* and *Joker's Wild*. Cable News Network (CNN), CBN Cable Network, and Entertainment & Sports Network (ESPN) schedule frequent talk programming. Especially notable is CNN's attention-getting *Crossfire*, which uses a live debate format featuring impassioned interruptions. The format challenges the public's stereotype of television talk programs.

Soap Operas   Among serialized drama formats, the soap opera is the classic case of frugal expenditure of program resources. Soap operas are so called because in radio days soap companies often owned and sponsored them; Procter & Gamble still supplies several on CBS and NBC. Notorious for the snail-like pace of their plots, these daytime serials use every tactic of delay to drag out the action of each episode.

The big growth in the number of broadcast television soaps came in the early 1950s, when the long-running serials that had started on radio in the 1930s switched to television. In the 1970s, the soaps moved toward longer shows to minimize production costs. Because fees for actors, crews, sets, and other production items increase only slightly when soap episodes double in length, 60-minute formats reduce total network costs. *The Guiding Light* (1937–) was the first soap to extend to a full hour (in 1975), but its expansion to 90 minutes in 1978 failed, forcing a retreat to the 60-minute format.

Other recent trends in soap opera series include a tendency to speed up plot development (contemporary viewers apparently have less patience than their parents did), and a willingness to deal with increasingly realistic themes — more evidence of the demand for relevancy that has affected prime-time programming so markedly. Today, topics once considered taboo, such as drugs, social diseases, and family violence, regularly weave in and out of soap opera plot developments. Also, women and minorities appear in a great variety of roles, although the distribution of occupations, races, and sex roles is far from reflecting society's norms.

Increased tolerance for controversial topics and new social roles in soap operas has also resulted from changes in audience composition. Over 10 percent of the soap opera audience now consists of men, and there has also been a spurt of interest on the part of younger, college-aged viewers, especially reflected in the fad for *General Hospital* in the late 1970s and early 1980s. Still, the core of the soap opera audience remains the housewife, an ideal target for manufacturers of household products. Another advertising plus is the extraordinary loyalty of dedicated soap opera viewers, who support several fan magazines, avidly attend shopping center appearances featuring soap opera stars, and buy newspapers that give daily summaries of soap opera plots.

According to NBC's vice president of daytime programs, Brian Frons, "Normally, a viewer has to be dissatisfied with her own soap opera for a good six months before she changes the channel and checks out what you're doing" (1984: 96). The loyalty of soap opera fans creates its own hazards for programmers, however. While millions of Americans watched the 1984 Olympics on ABC (see Box, page 327), other millions stuck to their habitual daytime programs. But ABC's Olympics coverage gave viewers a reason to try out different soaps, and ABC was in danger of losing those who preferred soaps over sports to NBC's and CBS's serials. To offset its vulnerability, ABC retained three of its soaps in shortened, 40-minute versions designed to fit within a special two-hour soap block during Olympic coverage. ABC kept *All My Children*, *One Life to Live*, and *General Hospital*, but canceled *Ryan's Hope*, *The Edge of Night*, and *Loving* to make way for live Olympic events. This strategy was risky. NBC took advantage of ABC's disrupted schedule to premiere *Santa Barbara*, a new, lavishly produced soap, and CBS spiced up its daytime episodes with a viewer contest, cameo appearances by special guests, and heavy promotion, seeking to lure some of ABC's wandering soap opera fans. ABC resorted to cliff-hanger episodes to tide viewers over the two-week 1984 Olympic gap, a strategy that seemed necessary because ABC earns an estimated 25 percent of its revenues and 40 percent of its profits from daytime programming.

The most important afternoon segment on network television is 3:00 P.M. to 4:00 P.M., when viewing reaches its highest daytime levels. The program scheduled at this hour is crucial to network revenues. As of 1984, a gain of a ratings point was worth about $50 million in the daytime (and as much as $65 million in prime time).* Since daytime programs air about seven minutes more commercials than prime-time programs, they require as many as sixteen commercial breaks in each hour to fit

---

*However, these figures refer to a share increase at the expense of the other two networks; otherwise, a share increase may come from an increase in the number of viewers overall and has much less monetary value. (See discussion of shares and ratings in §14.2.)

in all the commercials (§9.7). Constant switching of the plot line from character to character in soap operas (or from story to story in daytime magazine shows) accommodates this large number of interruptions.

The broadly appealing cable networks such as superstation WTBS, USA Network, and CBN have yet to develop daytime soap operas that command the loyalty inspired by their broadcast counterparts. WTBS developed two adult soap operas for prime time but canceled them after disappointing seasons. CBN, a religious cable network, attempted a family-oriented soap opera, but it failed to capture an audience and was soon canceled, perhaps because it lacked the relevance and controversial subject matter essential to successful soaps.

Game Shows   Audience-participation shows, or game shows, are another parsimonious format that became an ingredient of network radio programming a half-century ago. A major advantage game shows have over soap operas is that talent expenses for game shows are limited to the host's salary and, in some cases, fees for a panel of show-business personalities who usually work for minimum union pay. The format capitalizes on the inexhaustible supply of amateurs willing to show off their abilities — or simply make fools of themselves. One of the cheapest of formats, the game show is easy to produce, once a winning formula has been devised.

In the 1980s, television game shows changed hosts and gimmicks with increasing frequency but continued to occupy a substantial portion of daytime network and syndicated television. A few games, such as *The Price Is Right*, have expanded to longer formats; most, however, still run for a half-hour, a length strongly favored by the syndication market because it fits into an access slot (§13.2) and enables more flexible scheduling. Emphasis on real knowledge and the use of seem-

Exhibit 12.3   Parsimony in Game Shows

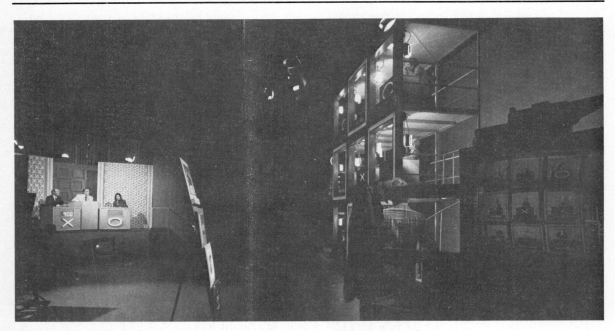

One of the longest-surviving game shows, Hollywood Squares *(1966–), moved from network television to off-network rerun and then, after a brief retirement, continued in first-run syndication. In 1983, it was combined with another game show,* The Match Game, *engendering the awkwardly named* The Match Game/Hollywood Squares Hour, *which uses many of the same contestants in both halves of the hour, a strategy frugal in its use of program resources but limiting in its scheduling flexibility.*

Source: Photo courtesy of National Broadcasting Company.

ingly well-informed participants for the most part went out with the quiz scandals of the 1950s (§3.9). Many modern game shows such as *Family Feud* and *Jeopardy* use frivolous questions, often with risqué overtones. But the current ratings hit, *The Wheel of Fortune*, follows the older pattern of informational questioning.

The predominant genre for first-run stripping in early fringe and access time on network affiliates, game shows require little ongoing promotion and tend to have long lives. A handful of specialists produce most of the successful game shows. Goodson-Todman Productions, for example, grosses about $50 million a year from game shows. Mark Goodson, the surviving member of the team formed in 1946, has pointed out that "soap operas and game shows are the greatest indigenous television forms, and they are alike in one important way. There are no endings. They go on and on and on" (quoted in Buckley, 1979).

Another reason for game shows' profitability is their enhanced commercial content.

The giveaway format justifies adding short plugs for advertisers who donate prizes. Some advertisers even pay cash fees to gain a brief visual and auditory plug for some new product. So active is the television giveaway business that several companies specialize as prize brokers (called "schlockmeisters" in the trade) to handle the collecting, warehousing, and dispatching of game show prize merchandise. The brokers get 40 percent of the retail value of the prizes and are paid by the advertisers.

Basic cable networks such as WTBS and USA Network usually schedule syndicated first-run game shows (or movies) against the broadcast networks' afternoon soaps, and counterprogram the broadcast network game shows with reruns of situation comedies. Their daytime strategy is to attract audiences not being served by the standard broadcast network programming pattern.

TV Talk Shows   In the 1950s, the extension of network television into hitherto unprogrammed early morning and late evening hours was considered extremely radical. "Morning television was available here and there," wrote a chronicler of the *Today* program, "but watching it was a taboo. . . . It was acceptable to listen to morning radio, but like sex and alcohol, television was deemed proper only after sundown" (Metz, 1977: 33). In the 1980s the *Today* show (Exhibit 12.4) shares the 7 A.M.–9 A.M. morning spotlight with the *CBS Morning News* and ABC's *Good Morning America*. Like NBC's program, *Good Morning America* has adopted a variant of the magazine format, using informational talk as a primary ingredient. But *CBS Morning News* counterprograms by sticking closer to hard news in a traditional newscast format.

Although early-morning programs use the talk format and interview celebrities and other guests, the quintessential network talk show is NBC's *Tonight*, a post-prime-time offering called by Les Brown "the premier desk and sofa show" (1982: 430).

Tonight started in 1954 as a showcase for the comic talents of Steve Allen. After a series of other hosts, including Jack Paar, Johnny Carson took over in 1962, becoming the all-time leader in late-night ratings. But in 1979, after seventeen years of monologues and interviews, Carson became restless and threatened to leave the show. Incredible though it may seem, considering that Carson's talent is virtually undefinable and his main previous broadcasting experience had been as emcee of a quiz show, both the NBC network and its parent company, RCA, were shaken by the threatened loss. It was estimated that in 1979 as much as 20 percent of NBC's income came from the 90-minute *Tonight* show; advertisers paid $25,000 for a 30-second announcement to reach Carson's 15-million-plus viewers. At the time, Carson was already the highest-paid performer in television, with a salary reported to be on the order of $3 million a year. In 1980 he signed a new three-year contract, reportedly at $5 million a year; and in 1983 he renewed again, in a contract rumored at twice his previous salary.

NBC placed a second, hour-long, talk show called *Late Night with David Letterman* after Carson, to capitalize on an audience seeking talk. And the new FBC captured Carson's most popular guest host, Joan Rivers, to host a competing late-night talk show.

Although the soap opera is often cited as a format unique to broadcasting, a better candidate might be Carson's type of talk show. The British critic and playwright Kenneth Tynan has pointed out that despite Carson's singular achievement in American television, he is not nearly as well known in other countries as many lesser pop-culture personalities. "The job at which he excels," said Tynan, "is virtually unexportable. . . . Most of what happens on the show would be incomprehensible or

Exhibit 12.4   The *Today* Show

In the 1950s, Today was staged for maximum attention, in full view of passers-by on New York's 49th Street, in a window-front RCA exhibition hall at Radio City. One of the features of the show was the hand-lettered signs people in the crowd on the street would hold up for the cameras, greeting the folks back home in Iowa. Today showcased a series of memorable television personalities, such as Dave Garroway, Hugh Downs, Barbara Walters — and J. Fred Muggs. The latter was an intelligent and mischievous chimpanzee whose antics captured the popular attention, rocketing the show to the top in ratings and making it "the biggest one-year grosser" in broadcasting history in the 1950s (Metz, 1977: 95). Today has continued to serve an audition function for NBC: news stars such as Tom Brokaw, John Chancellor, and Barbara Walters moved up from its ranks.

Source: Photo courtesy of National Broadcasting Company.

irrelevant to foreign audiences, even if they were English-speaking" (1979: 114). Most other countries have yet to develop their own indigenous forms of talk shows.

Cable television also takes advantage of the low production cost and flexibility of talk shows by scheduling these programs within many cable formats. Lifetime, for example, carries a dozen or so talk programs on topics ranging from health to consumer services. CNN regularly schedules shows on money management, as well as news interviews and discussions. The religious networks naturally have religion-oriented talk programs. Even the sport channels contain many sports talk segments and shows.

Video Music   After the rise of rock music and FM radio, television gave little time to popular music until Warner Amex Satellite Entertainment Corporation formed Music Television (MTV), a basic cable network, in 1981. MTV quickly became a 24-hour powerhouse of rock videos. Both broadcast and cable networks followed MTV's lead, NBC with *Friday Night Videos*, ABC with *Rocks*, and USA Network with *Night Flight*, all scheduled only on weekends. These individual network programs reach larger one-time-only audiences than the MTV channel, but each program runs only for a few hours. Cumulatively, MTV attracts enormous teenage audiences.

Videos are even cheaper for networks to run than soaps, games, and talk. Most are provided free of charge and have the added advantage of being reusable. They require minimal program expenditure and allow high scheduling flexibility.

However, video costs are changing. Originally, record companies produced them as promotional tools and gave them gratis to any stations or networks who would play them. Abandoning this industry practice for the first time in 1984, MTV bought exclusive rights to Michael Jackson's first *Thriller* video. To keep ahead of its competition, MTV contracted for exclusive "windows" (periods of availability) for the videos produced by several major record companies, and besides paying for exclusive rights, MTV offered free advertising time to the participating record companies. This strategy renewed the question of royalties for singers, performers, and musicians (§3.2 and §16.5), and demolished the hope that music videos would continue to be a source of free programming. If video pricing trends follow the pattern of other television program genres, costs for the most popular videos will escalate rapidly.

MTV gained much influence with performers and record companies because its 24-hour availability and its tightly controlled song selection and rotation enabled it to achieve precise age targeting. MTV's success has had wide ramifications: prime-time network programs increasingly add musical elements, and there are now several competitors for the cable rock audience. They include WTBS's *Night Tracks*; Dimension Music Cable, a split format of adult contemporary videos in the daytime and hit rock videos at night; Country Music Television (CMTV), a 24-hour network of country videos; and other services. But MTV's biggest competitor for advertising revenue may come from its own sister service, Video Hits 1 (VH-1), which programs a broader range of music videos and targets an older audience, aged 25–49. Both services were purchased by Viacom in 1986.

The popularity of music videos challenges rock radio stations and threatens television's advertising practices. In a 1983 survey, two-thirds of the respondents aged 12–24 reported that they preferred MTV to radio, and one-third of the teen-age respondents said they always turned to MTV during commercial breaks in other television programs (Coleman, quoted in *Broadcasting*, 5 Sept. 1983: 60). The move of young audiences to cable television has contributed to the general reduction in broadcast television ratings and may eventually affect radio ratings.

12.4 The Role of Network Sports

For enthusiasts, sports provide television and radio with ideal subjects: real-life events that occur on predictable schedules but nevertheless are full of dramatic suspense. Fictional drama has wider audience appeal, however; and only a few play-off sporting events such as Super Bowl football and World Series baseball rank among the most popular programs of all time, mostly because these events have elements of pageantry that appeal to a broader audience than year-round sports fans.

Research suggests that more than half of the public watches professional football on television at least occasionally. Next in popularity are professional baseball and basketball, then big-stakes tennis and golf, and after that the number of viewers falls off abruptly, with many fewer watching such sports as auto racing, soccer, and bowling. The main value of sports programs for network television is that they reach the middle-class male audience, a group not reached by most other programs. Sports therefore usually command higher-than-normal advertising rates.

In the 1960s, ABC's search for differentiation led to an all-out emphasis on sports. It pioneered the weekend sports anthology format with its *Wide World of Sports* (1961–). By combining highlights of several sports events into a single program, this format avoids boring audiences with overlong coverage of minor sports; thus even such sports as cliff diving and surfing can be covered. The network's hard-driving and innovative sports chief, Roone Arledge, introduced such novelties as the instant replay, the controversial commentary of Howard Cosell, *Monday Night Football* (1969–), and extensive Olympic coverage.

Sports and Audience Interest   Television spends hundreds of millions of dollars annually on the rights to on-the-spot coverage of sports events. ABC escalated previous contract highs by bidding aggressively for the 1976, 1980, and 1984 Olympics (see Box on facing page) and key play-off games (§10.2).

However, declining ratings for professional and college football gave evidence of a glut in televised football by 1984, signaling a modest decline in network sports interest. Teams had to shift from package deals to individual game contracts, with the ironic result that as the number of games on television proliferated, ratings further declined.

Increasing its overall share of sports programming in 1984, ABC purchased the outstanding shares of ESPN (originally Entertainment and Sports Program Network, the all-sports cable network). ESPN was not financially profitable in its first five years of operation but had become so by 1985. (In 1985 Nabisco bought a part-interest, adding a fresh infusion of money with which to buy television sports rights). The 24-hour cable network supplements ABC's broadcast coverage of sports, and the two networks jointly have even greater bidding power for sports events than they had as competitors. The growth of sports on cable via ESPN, USA Network, WTBS, WGN, WOR, and regional pay sports networks, as well as the formation of a second professional football league, the USFL, have been factors in the decline of the broadcast networks' interest in sports. Audience interest in sports remains high, however, although the many broadcast and cable sports programs must divide a relatively fixed number of viewers.

Scheduling Problems   The seasonal nature of sports events and the limited control stations and networks have over them give rise to scheduling complications. Scheduling football in network prime time was a daring ABC innovation in 1969, because it meant risking a long stretch of extremely valuable time on a single program with only selective audience appeal. Moreover, it meant committing the time for only part of the season. Once football was over, replacement programming

ABC's 1984 Summer Olympics

Cumulatively, more than 90 percent of television households chose to watch some part of the much-promoted 1984 Summer Olympics on ABC. The Los Angeles site permitted extensive live coverage in North American time zones and may have been the key to an unusual surge of viewer loyalty, resulting in high ratings for ABC. The network used an army of 3,500 employees to produce two versions of the 1984 Summer Olympics, one broadcast for American audiences and a "neutral" pictorial record of every event to be excerpted for broadcasts in the rest of the world. Although the network paid a staggering $225 million merely for the right to telecast the Los Angeles Games, and committed an additional $100 million to produce the coverage, it did succeed in attracting about 25 percent of U.S. television households during prime time.

In addition to gaining direct advertising revenues, ABC used the Olympics to showcase its coming fall schedule of prime-time programs, a promotional strategy considered of immense benefit to rating performance. Indeed, ABC's success in winning the number-one position among the networks in the early fall of 1984 has been ascribed to its very early premiere dates and heavy promotional blitz during the Olympics. However, when CBS and NBC later premiered their new fall schedules, the advantage passed to them; apparently, after first sampling ABC's shows, the public turned to the competition. Nonetheless, counting on its strategy succeeding next time, ABC pledged an unprecedented $309 million for the broadcast and cable rights to the 1988 Calgary Winter Olympics.

Source: Wide World Photos

with the same audience appeal had to be found, since much of the nonfootball audience was viewing elsewhere.

Cable networks and independent stations find it easier to handle live sports on a regional and local basis than do broadcast networks and their affiliated stations. A number of ad hoc broadcast and cable networks exist expressly for the purpose of carrying the games of particular colleges, professional teams, and conferences. In 1984, Group W launched a pay cable sports network to transmit different games to cable systems in each of four geographic regions, utilizing the flexibility of satellite delivery to provide games with local appeal. The system of competitive bidding for rights to games, and cable's ability to capitalize on local-audience sports interests, have forced a shift in sports programming. Sporting events are carried less and less by the broadcast networks and more and more by cable, although sports news continues to have a place in local broadcast news. The total number of hours of sporting events on cable now exceeds the number on broadcast outlets, although the events attractive to the largest audiences still remain with the broadcast networks. The possibility of scheduling games on a pay-per-view basis, or on large screen sion ("theater television"), however, has generated considerable attention from sports promoters, which suggests that the most popular sports events may eventually become available only to those who can and will pay. The pay-per-view option, though, awaits the widespread availability of addressable cable technology.

Ethical Issues   Stations and networks are at times tempted to overcome some of the unpredictability of sports events by staging them expressly for television coverage. Few quibble about such obvious entertainment events as *Battle of the Network Stars*, but more subtle ma-

nipulations have raised questions throughout the industry.*

One problematic practice is the creation of commercial time-outs, breaks arbitrarily called by the referees roughly every 10 minutes to accommodate advertising spots within football and, to a lesser extent, basketball games. These breaks can interrupt a team's momentum and introduce an externally controlled factor in pacing that has nothing to do with traditional rules or coaching strategies. Sports historian Benjamin Rader contends that television's need to attract occasional viewers has led to sports rule changes that add continuous excitement at the expense of the traditional balance between offensive and defensive strategies (Rader, 1985).

Another type of sports manipulation affects which games get carried and when. Both those selling the rights and those scheduling games may agree at the last minute to delay the start of a game in order to sign up more stations or cable systems. The financial rewards of larger audience size generate pressure to create last-minute sports windows when large numbers of stations and/or systems can be assembled.† Most commonly, however, game carriage is affected by the blackout rules specifying that games must be sold out in order to appear on local television.

---

*In 1977 the House Subcommittee on Communications held hearings on such abuses, including the manner in which ABC selected fighters for its "U.S. Boxing Championships," and the supposedly deceptive use of the title "Winner Take All" in a tennis play-off sponsored by CBS (House CIFC, 1977).

†In Chapter 11 we described movie windows, short periods of time when new theatrical films are made available to pay television. The term *sports window* has a slightly different meaning. It refers to sporting events not initially scheduled for broadcast or cable showing that become last-minute television fare when a sufficient number of stations and/or systems make time available. This can occur when a particular player has special notoriety, an underdog team has a long winning streak, or a game is sold out at the last minute.

Television stations have been known to buy up the remaining tickets when a game is a couple of thousand short of being sold out, so that the blackout rule will not apply. One Boston television station, for example, did this in 1985 in order to carry a Patriots' game.

Ethical questions also arise because many teams and sports associations insist on having control over the hiring of play-by-play and color announcers. This practice raises the issue of the extent to which sports-events broadcasts should be regarded as news, public relations, or entertainment. Consumer-oriented sports fans assert that broadcasters tend to surrender control over their sports coverage because they need to please the people who govern the sale of coverage rights (Gruenstein, 1978). The FCC once conducted an inquiry into biased sports reporting, reminding broadcasters that they have "a responsibility to refrain from engaging in or permitting others to engage in substantial deception or supression of facts" in sports coverage (48 FCC 2d 237, 1974).

12.5 Network Children's Programs and Other Educational Programs

Children's programming arouses controversy of a different sort. Children have such easy access to television, and it exerts such a powerful hold on their attention, that programs designed to exploit them commercially raise special problems. In addition, the dearth of programs specifically designed for very young children raises other issues concerning appropriateness, violence, role models, and advertising pressure.

Most countries regulate children's programs in considerable detail; some forbid advertising to children altogether. The FCC first singled out children's programming for notice in 1960 when it listed children's programs among those program types that broadcast licensees should pay particular attention to, because of their special public-interest significance.

Dimensions of Children's Television

As of the mid-1980s, each commercial network programmed nix or seven hours of children's television a week, aearly all on Saturday morning. In fact, most programs aimed at children are scheduled on weekend mornings and after school beginning at 4:00 P.M. on affiliates and as early as 3:00 P.M. on independents. The Saturday block is largely cartoons, though old sitcom favorites such as *Gilligan's Island* and *The Lucy Show* occupy some half-hours, and rock music videos are creeping into children's schedules. Independent stations run more child-appeal programming (primarily cartoons) than network affiliates, and much of it in the 6:00 A.M. to 9:00 A.M. time period. The commercial broadcast services, however, usually target children of school age, omitting the preschooler.

Manufacturers of toys, cereals, and candies are the main supporters of commercial children's programs. Although they represent less than 10 percent of television's advertising revenues, children's programs provide good value, because they are scheduled at times not attractive for reaching other audience groups, time periods that might otherwise go unsold.

The very definition of children's programming is open to debate. Programs produced for children are not the only type that attract an audience of children. As a scheduling strategy, local stations frequently place off-network reruns late on weekday afternoons (early fringe time), expecting that a high proportion of people will stay tuned, flowing through to the local news that often follows. The programs that draw these large, very youthful audiences include many older situation comedies such as *Hogan's Heroes* and *I Love Lucy*, as well as cartoonlike adventures such as *Wonder Woman* and *The Hulk*; they also include programs less appropriate for children, such as *Charlie's Angels*. However, the networks and rating companies do not normally list these programs in their "children's" category, even though they are scheduled in times usually reserved for children.

Increasingly, stations find that teen programs gain higher ratings than those for younger children, and they utilize programs such as *Solid Gold* and similar rock and dance shows to provide more opportunities for advertising. Like cartoons, music videos and dance programs can be repeated often and scheduled in a variety of time slots.

Only about 6 percent of the children's programs on the air are locally produced by commercial and noncommercial stations. About half the broadcast children's programs come from syndicated sources, and most of them are cartoons. The three commercial networks account for nearly half of the programs, and independent stations, public television, and cable carry the rest. The Public Broadcasting Service carries six critically admired weekend series, and Nickelodeon, Viacom's cable service for children, has substantially added to the amount of children's programming available. It produces several award-winning series targeting several different age groups. However, at any given hour, Nickelodeon offers only one channel, necessarily attracting only one age group of children, while other age groups may have no programming. Moreover, as of 1985 Nickelodeon reached less than a quarter of U.S. television households.

ACT's Petition

In 1985 congressional leaders spoke out once again about the dismal quality of television for children, but once again took no action. Consumer groups have long complained about exploitative commercials and what they considered to be the limited amount and low quality of children's programming. Traditionally, cartoons and child-oriented situation comedies have been full of sexist and racist stereotypes, laced with violence, and loaded with commercials designed to take every advantage of childish inexperience (Exhibit 12.5). Public complaints were largely ignored until a sophisticated consumer group, Action for Children's Television (ACT), was formed.

In 1971 ACT persuaded the FCC to hold hearings on rules governing several aspects of children's programming. It asked the FCC to require each commercial station to broadcast at least 14 hours of children's programming a week. In addition, ACT stated, these programs should be "age-specific," rather than aimed broadly at children of all ages, which is typical commercial practice. ACT suggested that programs should be tailored to meet the differing needs of at least three separate age groups: preschool (ages 2–5), primary (6–9), and elementary (10–12). Another aspect of ACT's petition asked for advertising reforms discussed in §9.7.

After holding extensive hearings, the commission rejected ACT's rule-making request. Instead, it issued a policy statement in 1974 urging broadcasters to improve children's programming voluntarily along the lines of ACT's proposal. A few years later, a 1979 FCC task force on children's programming found some improvements in advertising practices but little improvement in programming. The FCC reopened the rule-making question, inviting comments on a number of steps that might be taken. However, the trend toward deregulation, along with new appointments to the commission by the Reagan administration, overcame proponents of regulation, and the FCC once again rejected making rules for children's program-

Exhibit 12.5   The Hero Business

One of the most popular Saturday network morning cartoons, generating a profitable sideline in toys, is HE-MAN, whose success has led to several look-alike cartoons featuring superheroes who react physically to most situations. As a further extreme, the cartoon version of the Rambo film series glamorizes war, idealizes combat as male behavior, and implies that war is a fun game. These cartoons raise social questions about the values and stereotypes being conveyed to children.

Source: Copyright Mattel, Inc., 1985. "Masters of the Universe" and associated character names are trademarks of Mattel, Inc., used with permission.

ming, closing the subject in 1984. Yet it remains an open concern in the minds of many parents, educators, and other concerned citizens.

***Sesame Street* and Children's Television Workshop**   There is little disagreement in or out of public broadcasting that one of its major functions is to provide educational material, ranging from in-school (or instructional) programming to more generalized at-home educational programs. Public television stations fill a large portion of their daytime hours with in-school programs (paid for by school districts) and schedule additional special broadcast programs for children early in the morning and again in the afternoon. Public television's most celebrated children's series is *Sesame Street*, which is based on a unique approach to programming for three- to five-year-olds. Ironically all three networks turned down the concept for *Sesame Street* in the late 1960s because they felt commercial sponsors would have little or no interest in a program narrowly focused on such a young age group.

Launched on public television in 1969, *Sesame Street* was developed and produced by an independent, nonprofit corporation, Children's Television Workshop (CTW). Funded initially by foundation and government grants, CTW now earns about half its income from the sale of articles that use the program's name and characters. It is difficult to overstate the impact of *Sesame Street*. The program appeared just as the transition from "educational" to "public" television was taking hold, bringing the first large audiences to the system. Many viewers lived in economically disadvantaged households previously ignored by public television. *Sesame Street* specifically aimed at such viewers, seeking to better prepare inner-city children to read and write. The series made television an educational tool for both home and school. Children who watched this program at home often learned to read more quickly and easily than children who did not watch it. Preschool and primary teachers began to use broadcasts of *Sesame Street* during the school day, recognizing the value of incorporating a popular program in the classroom. Its positive impact on reading skills improved the reputation of television and showed how home viewing could aid education.

Because it was independently funded, CTW could rise above station and PBS quarrels and stick to its own research-backed course. For the first time, the entire technical resources of television were brought to bear on a series directed at children. A wonderfully original set of large-scale puppets called Muppets became the hallmark of the program, providing both entertainment and education. Public television stations repeated episodes, which gave the program wide impact.

No series on either commercial or public television has been given the amount of scheduled air time as has Sesame Street. *Throughout the 1970s, local stations have consistently devoted 29 percent of their weekday school-hour schedule, 14 percent of their weekend daytime schedule, and about 47 percent of their weekday after-school broadcast hours to* Sesame Street. *As the decade came to a close, an average 11.4 percent of the total broadcast hours of each public television station featured* Sesame Street, *with each program aired four times during the year. (Sikes, 1980: 9)*

Some segments of *Sesame Street* were taken out of certain programs and used in others, a kind of interchangeable-parts approach to programming that stretched the series into its second decade and enabled it to serve a fourth or fifth generation of children. Yet the basic aim of the series has remained the same: to lessen the gap between disadvantaged inner-city children and their suburban counterparts in basic reading (letters and numbers) and social skills. Programs are divided into short segments to encourage atten-

tion, with a variety of formats and even "advertisements" (for example, "This segment of *Sesame Street* has been brought to you by the letters *A* and *L* and the numbers 3 and 7 . . ."). Even the entertainment segments, with the Muppets or animated material, serve some educational purpose.

Building on its initial success, CTW branched out with *The Electric Company* for older children, drawing on the methods and research of *Sesame Street* but using more advanced reading concepts. In 1980 CTW began providing a daily science program, *3-2-1 Contact*, in a half-hour format aimed especially at groups that research showed were not interested in science, particularly young females and minorities. As in *Sesame Street*, segments of these series can be pulled apart and reassembled for updated reuse, which stretches the production dollar.

Because of their popularity and their high production quality, CTW's programs create a dilemma for other children's programmers, whose offerings often seem pale by comparison. Few of these programmers have a budget anywhere near that of CTW (largely because of CTW's license revenue from *Sesame Street* characters). And producers of adult programming on public television have been known to wonder why their programs don't become as popular as CTW's (and therefore become as well funded).

Other Children's Programs   In addition to *Sesame Street*, other award-winning noncommercial children's programs include the syndicated *Villa Alegre* and *Carrascolendas*, aimed at Hispanics and available only in cities with large Spanish-speaking audiences. For more than twenty-five years, PBS's *Mr. Rogers' Neighborhood* has taught social skills to preschoolers, making that program second in viewing popularity only to *Sesame Street*. (The Smithsonian's popular-culture exhibit has enshrined Fred Rogers's sweater, commemorating his status with generations of children.) On cable television, Nickelodeon occupies a key place as the only daily all-children's channel. Although begun without advertising, Nickelodeon added a limited number of spot ads in 1984. It schedules programs for preschoolers in the mornings and for older children in the afternoons, including teen-oriented films and concerts. Aside from cartoons on several channels, especially USA Network and WTBS, the only other cable programming for children is provided by The Disney Channel, a pay cable service that reached less than 3 percent of U.S. homes at the start of 1985.

Broadcasts to Classrooms   In addition to programs for the general public, noncommercial broadcasters send instructional programs to classrooms. Experiments and research on instructional, or in-school, radio began in the late 1930s and carried over to television early in the 1950s. Today, instructional programs differ markedly from popular children's fare:

One fundamental characteristic distinguishes instructional programming from general television programming for children. Instructional television . . . is expected to help students achieve identified, specific learning goals under the administration and supervision of professional educators in a formally structured learning environment. ITV [instructional television] requires active, intellectual participation of its viewers. The "success" of a program does not depend on the size of the audience. Rather, the skill of the classroom instructor and the receptivity of the students combine to use television for learning. (Sikes, 1980: 19)

Inherent in this passage is the idea that television is supplemental to regular classroom instruction — that is, is a source of enrichment in an educational program rather than educationally sufficient in itself. It took years of often repetitive experimentation with instruc-

tional programs on both radio and television to establish that broadcasting was not a "hypodermic" educator, capable of injecting knowledge into children and of replacing teachers and classrooms. Time and again instructional television has been found to be neither better nor worse than a classroom teacher; but when used along with a teacher, it can be especially effective.

Nontraditional Educational Television
Television is also a means of reaching nontraditional (older adult) students, and sick and handicapped students who want college credit, as well as adults not interested in credit. Following the example of the British Open University, several American "distant learning" projects now concentrate on the use of television for adult education. The University of Mid-America (UMA), headquartered in Lincoln, Nebraska, has no campus but rather exists as a consortium of eleven midwestern universities that provides over-the-air and for-credit college courses. Students watch the material on a local public television station, pay a registration fee to a local administering college, and thus can learn at home. UMA earns income from the stations showing the program and from the administering colleges, which pay UMA a per-student fee. A similar effort headquartered at the University of Maryland, known as the National University Consortium, was funded by a $150 million grant to the CPB in 1981 by Walter Annenberg, publisher of *TV Guide*. The Annenberg/CPB project has produced such outstanding program series as *The Brain*, which appeals to the general public as well as to a for-credit audience.

Several of the new open-university projects reach students not only through public television but also through direct satellite networking into home or university receiving dishes, or through local cable systems. Such methods have been prompted by the increasing budget pinch that has forced schools and universities to seek new ways to disseminate education while cutting costs. It has become increasingly obvious that closed-circuit systems such as Instructional Television Fixed Services (§7.6), relay networks, home videocassettes, and dedicated cable channels are more suitable for educational programs than broadcasting is, because they can more efficiently target those interested.

12.6 Network Television News

Although entertainment programs make up the largest percentage of network schedules, informational genres are now rapidly increasing their share of total programming. And while the audience for network entertainment has been steadily eroding, audiences for informational programming have grown. As much as one-fifth of viewers may be watching informational programs, broadly defined, at any hour, including prime time (Schonfeld, 1983: 33–38). In the telecommunications industry, the term *information* includes not only regular and special newscasts but also the documentaries, interviews, and panels loosely grouped as "public affairs," and it now incorporates broadly appealing, softer, more popular news as well. Early-morning network talk shows and half-hour syndicated shows such as *Entertainment Tonight* and *PM Magazine* attract part of the mass information audience. Most information, however, comes in the traditional network prime-time newscasts, ABC's late-night *Nightline, 60 Minutes,* and *20/20,* a few scattered documentary programs and special reports such as NBC's *White Papers,* and public television's *MacNeil/Lehrer Newshour.* These programs combine hard news, soft features, and investigative reports. More recently, the networks have added *West 57th*

and *American Almanac* to this list of informational offerings.

Quantity and Popularity   As with entertainment genres, program economics and scheduling considerations constrain the quantity (and perhaps the quality) of news and public-affairs programs on television. Both the broadcast and cable networks weigh the cost of producing newscasts and documentaries against their benefits for network prestige and visibility. In the past, the expenses of maintaining huge news staffs, far-flung facilities, and regular international satellite transmissions generally exceeded the advertising revenues the three broadcast networks earned during their evening news. Public-affairs programs have usually attracted small audiences, and therefore have carried few advertising messages. Traditionally, the networks nevertheless carried some news and public-affairs programs in order to maintain their image and to placate both regulators and the public.

But the recent growth in the popularity of informational programming has now caused the networks to increase their offerings. They have expanded the total number of informational programs on the air, and NBC has plans for an expanded hour of mixed network and local news if its affiliates approve. This would permit NBC to make greater use of the material its news staff gathers and thus improve its news profitability. Cable television's all-news network, CNN, has been able to make money because it programs primarily news and information for the entire day and night, reusing its content while carrying commercial spots throughout the 24-hour period.

Expansion of Network Newscasts   Like radio, television had to struggle to establish its legitimacy as a news medium. CBS launched nightly television network news in 1948 with *Douglas Edwards with the News,* essentially a

Exhibit 12.6   The Anchor as Trusted Source

Walter Cronkite (left) and Dan Rather, his successor in 1981 as anchorman of the CBS Evening News, *along with their colleagues at ABC, NBC, and CNN, are top-rated and trusted sources of news for most Americans. Both Cronkite, who was the CBS anchor for nearly two decades, and Rather began their news careers in Texas.*

Source: Photos courtesy of CBS.

modest 15-minute illustrated radio program (Exhibit 12.7). Fifteen minutes remained the standard newscast length until 1963, when CBS and NBC expanded to a half-hour (actually only about 22 minutes, after time for commercials and opening and closing announcements is subtracted). Despite the fact that the text of an entire half-hour newscast would fill less than a single page of a full-size newspaper, the move to a half-hour format was a major factor in elevating network television to the status of the most widely accepted source of news in the country.

In 1976 the dean of American television journalism, Walter Cronkite, argued strenu-

ously, with widespread support at the networks, for expansion of network evening news to a full hour. All three networks explored the possibility, and CBS went so far as to relay a sample one-hour newscast to its affiliates in hopes of persuading them to accept the change. They nevertheless voted overwhelmingly against the expansion.

The failure to expand network news to an hour-long format was called "a major setback for the forces of responsible broadcasting" (Barrett, 1978: 8). But affiliates wanted to retain the prime-time lead-in slots (6:00 P.M. to 6:30 P.M., usually) for their own highly profitable local newscasts and retain the access hour for revenue-producing syndicated fare. This meant that the networks could expand their news only by invading prime time, the late-evening period, or daytime.

Accordingly, the networks have increased their weekday news schedules at those hours. CBS gradually expanded its morning news, first to a half-hour in 1963, then to full hour in 1969. All three networks now schedule morning news or news magazine programs, as well as short news summaries throughout the day. In 1976 they began inserting one-minute news capsules in breaks between prime-time entertainment programs. These micro-newscasts consist of 42 seconds of news, a 10-second commercial, and 8 seconds of announcements. Because they are aired adjacent to high-rated entertainment, they draw the largest audiences of any regularly scheduled newscasts.

Late in 1979, ABC was surprised to find that sizable audiences tuned to its temporary 11:30 P.M. nightly coverage of the crisis arising from the Iranian seizure of American embassy hostages in Teheran. This led ABC to design a permanent 20-minute late-night network news program, *Nightline*, with each installment concentrating on one or two stories. Briefly, ABC expanded *Nightline* to an hour, but lack of audience-attracting crises forced a cutback to 30 minutes. Charles Kuralt's *Sunday Morning*, on CBS, represents another network news expansion, confined to low ratings by its schedule position but notable as a showcase for Kuralt's folksy style.

In the last decade, traditional broadcast network news has been supplemented by the two 24-hour, all-news cable networks, Cable News Network and CNN Headline News. Ted Turner made the risky decision to pioneer in all-news cable in 1980. Headline News, carried by both cable systems and broadcast stations, provides brief news bulletins every hour for insertion in program breaks. CNN, by contrast, supplies in-depth reportage — much of it live — on more than two-thirds of all cable systems. CNN's successful penetration of cable systems and its popularity with audiences led ABC (with Westinghouse) to attempt an all-news cable service, Satellite News Channel, in 1982. Unable to convince enough cable systems to carry the service, ABC/Westinghouse sold it to Turner a year later.

After an initial struggle, CNN attained equality with the broadcast network news teams in determining rotations for pooled coverages, receiving White House notices, and obtaining major interviews. Without such access, CNN would have been overly dependent on the wire services and relegated to using footage first aired by the broadcast networks. Equal stature as a major news service gives CNN its share of exclusive interviews and its own videotape resources. The latter is especially important, because CNN can take time for in-depth coverage, hour after hour if need be, while the broadcast networks are usually restricted to brief snippets of each story. CNN has expanded into live coverage of ongoing news events, such as court trials, that the broadcast networks cannot cover at length. It matches the best efforts of the broadcast network teams in international and domestic reportage.

In the early 1980s, the broadcast television networks followed CNN's late-night successes by establishing their own middle-of-the-night newscasts: *News Overnight* on NBC, *Nightwatch* on CBS, and two late-night newscasts on ABC. They failed to generate sufficient audience size to justify their expense, however, and by 1985 only CBS's *Nightwatch* remained nightly, at 3:00 A.M., while ABC News scheduled reports on weekends after midnight. The collapse of NBC's *News Overnight* encouraged many of its broadcast affiliates to pick up CNN Headline News for at least one late-night closing broadcast.

Most independent stations draw on INN News (Independent News Network) or CNN Headline News for international and national domestic news stories. These telecasts supplement news stories available from the traditional news agencies, AP and UPI. *The Ten O'Clock News* (*The Nine O'Clock News* during time changes) has been INN's main service, scheduled earlier than local late news to attract viewers not willing to wait up for the 11:00 P.M. or 10:00 P.M. affiliate newscasts. Generally, local independents follow INN with a half-hour of local news. WGN, the Chicago superstation, adopted this pattern with some success, although a few independents schedule their local news in front of INN News using the typical affiliate-network sequence. In the early 1980s, INN also added a 30-minute newscast in the very late hours (scheduled at 2:00 A.M. or 3:00 A.M. daily) and added hourly news bulletins, making independents effective as alternative news sources.

On public television, *The MacNeil/Lehrer Newshour* represents some of television's best in-depth informational programming. The show uses two hosts, one based in Washington, D.C., the other in New York City, who quiz representatives of opposing views on an important news topic. Begun as a half-hour program, *MacNeil/Lehrer* was expanded to an hour in 1983, reflecting the trend toward expansion of news programs to allow greater depth. However, *The MacNeil/Lehrer Newshour* has not achieved widespread success, even by noncommercial standards. Public television stations have trouble finding scheduling positions that do not face competition from commercial newscasts. The *Newshour* gains its largest audience shares when placed against entertainment programs. It also does better in the evening than in early fringe, yet it must then compete for airtime with PBS's core of evening programs. Public television stations frequently vary the program's start-time to fit scheduling of adjacent entertainment shows, which makes it difficult for the *Newshour* to establish a steady viewing audience.

12.7 Public Affairs

Although news and public affairs are usually linked together by stations and networks, the FCC in its licensing forms long distinguished "Public Affairs" as a separate class of programs defined as follows: "local, state, regional, national or international issues or problems, including, but not limited to, talks, commentaries, discussions, speeches, editorials, political programs, documentaries, minidocumentaries, panels, roundtables and vignettes, and extended coverage (whether live or recorded) of public events or proceedings, such as local council meetings, congressional hearings and the like."

Commercial broadcast television networks and most large stations maintain at least one weekly public-affairs discussion series, sometimes a news documentary series, and often minidocumentaries within newscasts. Enthusiasm for documentaries waxes and wanes according to the degree of heat the networks feel from critics and the FCC, as well as the pressure of news events (§15.4). They are expensive to produce, rarely attract large audiences, and often cause a great deal of controversy. CBS's defense of its *60 Minutes* segment about General Westmoreland's actions during the Vietnam War (§15.5 and Exhibit 18.1) cost the network more than $2 million in legal fees. For those reasons and because of their intrinsic informational value, broadcasters regard news documentaries as symbols of achievement, showing that television is capable of being responsible and mature about serious matters when it wants to be.

Influence of Technology   When screened today, early television documentaries still project some of their original fervor, but their style seems stiff and formal. The look of older classics of the 1960s such as *Harvest of Shame* or the 1970s' *Selling of the Pentagon* and *Guns of Autumn* has been supplemented by a new documentary style in the more recent programs such as *Vietnam: A Television History*. CBS newsman Edward R. Murrow's biographer commented on this changed approach to documentary substance and form: "The sharp, shrewd editing of film that enabled a Murrow-Friendly program to make point after point was replaced by a kind of cinéma vérité that substituted impressions for points. The dissecting table became a psychoanalyst's couch. . . . The New Wave offers the viewer a sensory experience rather than balanced judgment" (Kendrick, 1969: 28).

Improvements in the technology of picture making have enabled a less obtrusive use of camera and microphone, abetting the cinéma vérité approach. The physical intrusion of equipment lessened with miniaturization and other technological advances, and production styles changed as it became possible to use concealable microphones, lightweight hand-held cameras, and portable sound recorders with remote synchronization (eliminating the need for a cord between camera and recorder). The use of natural lighting dispenses with the glare of artificial lights and their tangle of cables. Nevertheless, audiences must continue to be tolerant of technically imperfect pictures and sound as the networks and stations chase events that are unusual and difficult to cover. Shots of earth from space, for example, enhanced by computers but still blurred and unstable, heralded a new era of documentary challenge.

60 Minutes   The most striking development in news-related programming since 1980 has been the rise of *60 Minutes*, CBS's magazine-format documentary series, to the very top of the prime-time ratings. In the 1979–1980 season it led all network programs in popularity and since then has generally stayed on the list of the top twenty programs. Its success violated all conventional wisdom about documentary programs, which had previously been considered repellent to audiences. One reason for the failure of documentaries to achieve high ratings, however, may have been the networks' tendency to position them in less favorable time slots and to deny them the luxury of stable scheduling. After years of wandering, for example, *60 Minutes* finally achieved stability at a good hour — specifically because of the prime-time access rule (§13.2), which opened the Sunday 7:00 P.M.–8:00 P.M. time slot for nonentertainment programs (see Box, page 348). Another factor in its success was CBS's counterprogramming strategy; in the 1970s, *60 Minutes* was typically scheduled against children's programming and movies.

Still another reason for the *60 Minutes* success story has been its stellar team of correspondents, notably its original team of Mike Wallace, Harry Reasoner, and Morley Safer (Exhibit 15.1). As a *New York Times* commentator put it:

Their gray or graying hair, their pouched and care-worn countenances, the stigmata of countless jet flights, imminent deadlines and perhaps an occasional relaxing martini, provide a welcome contrast to the Ken and Barbie dolls of television news whose journalistic skills are apt to be exhausted after they have parroted a snippet of wire service copy and asked someone whose home has just been wrecked by an earthquake, "How do you feel?" (Buckley, 1978)

Early on, Dan Rather joined the team; still later, Ed Bradley and Diane Sawyer were added, balancing the program with a black and a female correspondent.

These correspondents, with chief producer Don Hewitt and a staff of some seventy producers, editors, and reporters, develop about 120 segments annually (Stein, 1979). The magazine format allows for scheduling a great variety of subjects and for varying segment length, which adds to the program's popular appeal. Also important is the "confrontation" formula, a Mike Wallace specialty. Confronting his victims on camera with damning evidence of wrongdoing, Wallace grills them unmercifully. Audiences, already in the know, may be fascinated by the victims' evasions, lies, and brazen attempts to bluff their way out of their predicaments. A number of viewers find the means Wallace uses to achieve his ends questionable on ethical grounds, and corporations under scrutiny have found their only defense is "not to talk to Mike Wallace, ever" (Madsen, 1984).

Other Public-Affairs Formats   Each commercial broadcast network also schedules a public-affairs question-and-answer session with newsworthy figures, usually around midday on Sundays. Programs in that time period generally get low ratings, usually about 2 or 3 rating points (§14.3). NBC's *Meet the Press*, dating back to 1947, is the longest-surviving program on network television. CBS launched *Face the Nation* in 1954, and ABC began *Issues and Answers* in 1960, later replacing it with *This Week with David Brinkley*. These programs reach important opinion makers and have far more impact than their low ratings suggest. Every politician of consequence makes appearances, and what is said is frequently reported later on the Sunday and Monday network newscasts.

Public-affairs coverage on cable and broadcast television has been responsible for bringing some of history's most important moments into millions of homes, but the commercial networks' commitment to public affairs, like their commitment to particular entertainment programs, rises and falls with the ratings. The major exception to this practice on cable is the Cable-Satellite Public Affairs Network. C-SPAN has greatly expanded television's capacity for delivering live public-affairs programs (§10.3 and Exhibit 15.4). Using an open-ended, unedited format that reveals some of the pettiness as well as the strengths of day-to-day government, C-SPAN reached nearly 20 million homes nationwide in 1985 with its coverage of the U.S. House of Representatives in session. The story told by the camera (not controlled by C-SPAN operators — see discussion of House coverage rules, §15.5), scanning the empty House during speeches given in the late afternoon, imparts a powerful message to the public. During 1984, C-SPAN incorporated into its schedule two months of nationwide election coverage, originating from fourteen cities around the country. In 1986, C-SPAN II was inaugurated with live coverage of the United States Senate.

The greatest achievements of broadcast news and public-affairs programming take place, like C-SPAN's House and Senate coverage, outside the contrived environment of the studio. The memorable high points of broadcasting have been the actual events it has covered live. The qualities of immediacy and unpredictability lend them special fascination, whether they be Olympic games, dramatic congressional hearings, the first steps on the moon, the pageantry of great events of state, or disasters and tragedies.

Public Affairs on Public Television

Some public broadcasters feel that extended public affairs programming is the key advantage PBS offers as an alternative to commercial programming. Critics say the commercial networks devote too little time to news, dilute it with too much entertainment, and evade real controversy. Public and commercial broadcasters share one problem, however; getting support for such programming. PBS underwriters have no more appetite for controversial programs than do advertisers on the commercial networks.

Public television has provided a steady diet of public affairs over the years. Its current schedule includes award-winning fare such as *Washington Week in Review* and *Nightly Business Report*. In the past it has carried outstanding programs such as *The Advocates* and *Black Perspective on the News*. In the 1984 election year, public television introduced a 13-week series called *The Constitution: That Delicate Balance*. This unusual program used role-playing by distinguished American politicians, attorneys, and public officials, in debates over questions of government and constitutionality. It attracted such participants as former presidents, secretaries of state and of defense, presidents of large corporations, and luminaries of the judicial world. The debate format placed these figures at loggerheads over public-affairs issues, exposing contradictions and intricacies in the internal workings of contemporary American government. This live program combined entertainment, sometimes startling wit, and educational value. It could be taken for college credit through the Annenberg/CPB Project, the program's funders (§12.5).

As a regular nightly program, CNN carries *Crossfire*. Using the debate format, two hosts, representing conservative and liberal positions on domestic and international issues, take on two guests of opposing convictions on some current event. The usual outcome is a free-wheeling argument, full of interruptions and passionately expressed ultimatums that both entertain and inform on issues of widespread interest. These examples suggest the extraordinary formats that could be part of television's informational repertoire.

12.8 Radio Networks

News and public affairs form the primary content of broadcast network radio. In the 1950s, network radio news dwindled to five-minute hourly newcasts and seemed destined to shrink even further as radio programming became increasingly dominated by recorded music. Any important future role for radio networks then seemed problematic.

News Specialization   In 1968, however, ABC began an imaginative response to the demands of formula radio. Recognizing the central role of audience segmentation in program specialization, ABC designed four network services, each with a different type of audience in mind. Each service consisted of five-minute selections of network news and features, with a style of presentation adjusted to suit specific age groups and calculated to fit smoothly into the most popular radio formats. The success of this approach eventually encouraged ABC to increase its number of services to seven (one all-talk) and modify them more tightly to fit particular music formats. For example, ABC's Rock Radio complements the style of rock stations targeting 18- to 24-year-olds with one-minute newscasts covering the entertainment world; the Contemporary network also carries one-minute summaries of news, but these cover a wider range of topics. Another service, FM, is designed for stereo rock stations aiming at a broader-range audience, 12-to-34-year-olds. And ABC's Information service provides five-minute newscasts for middle-of-the-road music formats.

ABC spaces its short news feeds to its several sets of news affiliates throughout each hour, using the intervening time to feed sports and features on a closed-circuit basis for later playback by the stations. Before satellite

Exhibit 12.7 Radio Networks: News

Since the 1960s, network radio has consisted largely of short newscasts, sports play-by-plays, and occasional specials. Radio stations affiliate with a network to get timely national and international news delivered by such distinguished journalists as CBS' Douglas Edwards (left), and NBC's Cameron Swayze (right). Cameron Swayze is the son of John Cameron Swayze, NBC's pioneer television news anchor from 1948 to 1956. Douglas Edwards, who in the 1980s anchored CBS radio news, was the first CBS television anchor (until 1962).

Sources: Edwards, courtesy of CBS; Swayze, courtesy of National Broadcasting Company.

distribution became prevalent, this plan maximized use of the single ABC network circuit available. Nearly twenty years passed before affiliate pressure persuaded CBS and NBC to copy ABC's innovative programming.

Network radio also broadcasts commentaries by television news anchors and such well-known figures as Paul Harvey. Starfleet Blair and Satellite Music Network are music services that call themselves networks because they distribute national advertising within their programming, but they do not distribute their own newscasts.

Radio Talk   Another radio network adaptation capitalizes on the local station all-talk format. Reversing the accepted wisdom that network radio segments must be short and punchy, the Mutual Radio Network offers the all-night Larry King talk show, lasting from midnight to 5:30 A.M. Listeners from all over the nation and from Canada and the Caribbean as well find the blend of interviews, two-way telephone talk, and badinage by host Larry King so fascinating that they are willing to pay for long-distance calls, sometimes waiting for hours to get through to the Mutual studio in Arlington, Virginia. Guests on the show are stimulated by the experience of receiving calls in quick succession from knowledgeable listeners scattered across dozens of states.

Mutual's demonstration of a substantial audience for talk led both NBC, in 1981, and ABC, in 1982, to offer all-talk services. However, NBC avoids direct competition with the enormously successful King and ABC's overnight hosts by scheduling its *Talknet* for six evening hours; and ABC programs the daytime as well as the overnight time period with talk shows for stations affiliated with various of its network news services. The movement of radio networks into talk programming is part of a larger trend toward nationally distributed radio programming of all types. This trend is evident in both the commercial and noncommercial components of the radio industry.

Networking vs. Syndication in Radio

Networking and syndication may sometimes appear to be similar processes in commercial radio, but each has its own typical content, formats, advertising procedures, and payment practices. Networks normally supply news, sports, and specials; syndicators typically supply music programs and music-related features. Network materials tend to be brief (5-minute headline news, for instance), whereas syndicators generally supply 24-hour music. Network programs come with network commercials already inserted in them, whereas syndicated material usually lacks advertising but provides breaks within programs for local sale. The networks provide their programs gratis to their affiliates, even paying compensation to some stations in the larger

markets. Syndicators, on the other hand, normally charge for their programs. However, services such as Mutual, which call themselves networks, function more like syndicators with regard to specific programs such as *The Larry King Show*. Many radio stations that affiliate with other networks for news also pay a fee to carry *The Larry King Show*. Some syndicators distribute barter programs that resemble network sports and entertainment features and contain national advertising. On occasion, some syndicators will even pay stations in large markets to carry a particular program, in order to reach an audience large enough to attract enough advertisers to justify producing the program. Changes in radio have led to the appearance and growth of more than two dozen radio networks for (example, U.S. Radio I and II, CNN Radio Network, Associated Press Network, and Sheridan) and several hundred syndicators.

Public Radio Services   Altogether, public radio stations exhibit a dizzying variety of formats and specializations. The larger, CPB-qualified stations (§8.3), those on which the most information is available, generally allocate more than three-fifths of their time to stereo music, usually classical, sometimes jazz or popular. About one-fifth of their airtime goes to news and public affairs and another one-fifth to cultural programming. Fully 60 percent of public radio station programming originates locally (most of it recorded music); about 20 percent comes from NPR, and the rest is supplied by national noncommercial syndicators.

Public radio experiments more than either the commercial radio networks or public television. NPR has developed a distinctive image, characterized by the late-afternoon news show *All Things Considered*, which has been showered with awards since its beginning in 1971. This Monday–Friday program consists of 90 minutes of news reports, interviews, comment on news events, and other features, about one-third of which come from member stations. It tackles stories ignored by commercial stations, makes greater use of foreign sources, and treats significant events in depth. The result is a program that approaches cult status among its listeners, partly because it differs so sharply from the commercial headline-news services. In 1980 *All Things Considered* spun off *Morning Edition*, which provides a similar approach in the early-morning day part. NPR also distributes concerts and coverage of public events. Much of the tape-recorded NPR music programming comes from the BBC and from Dutch, German, and other foreign sources, reducing somewhat the parochialism of U.S. radio. Local stations often record this material and broadcast it at hours of their own choosing, making audience size and program impact nearly impossible to assess.

Summary

• Network programs are distributed to affiliates by the three major broadcast television networks, the fifty or so cable networks, and about two dozen radio networks.

• Networking is the sharing of programs simultaneously among several outlets and has benefits for both the network and the affiliates. Networks usually pay their affiliates for carrying network programs and the commercials within them.

• Commercial television networks provide affiliates with structured program services that include popular and technically superior programs, arranged to make optimum use of audience flow strategies and designed to bring in top advertising rates.

• Noncommercial stations that are members of PBS or NPR participate in program decision making. Underwriters and member stations pay the costs of noncommercial program production.

• Cable systems usually pay basic cable networks for the right to include the networks in their program packages, and divide subscriber revenues with the pay cable networks.

• The main arena of broadcast network competition is prime-time television. Some of the most successful prime-time programs have bimodal appeal and attract enormous audiences. The networks generally select programs designed to reach an "ideal" demographic group (women 18 to 49 years of age).

• Program cost is one major criterion for cancellation of prime-time series, because the amount of per-program revenue depends on the rates that can be charged for the fixed number of commercials run each hour. Because of advertiser resistance, rates cannot be raised enough to pay the production costs of some programs, so networks may replace them with cheaper programs that will achieve the same ratings.

• Prime-time programs tend toward contemporary relevancy in subject matter and toward longer formats, reflecting a diminished audience for traditional situation comedies and the economic advantages of 60-minute programs. At the same time, the networks demand novelty without radical change. Clones and spin-offs from past successes entail less programming risk than do programs based on new ideas.

• Situation comedies slipped in the ratings during the early 1980s, leading to changes in the traditional sitcom formula to reflect contemporary lifestyles. Cancellation of substantial numbers of network sitcoms after only short network runs threatens the syndication market.

• The networks have replaced most, contemporary theatrical movies with made-for-television movies and miniseries for reasons of cost, scarcity, and scheduling flexibility.

• Public television and cultural channels on cable television are the primary showcase of cultural entertainment, much of which comes from Britain.

• Non-prime-time network television entertainment, consisting mostly of soap operas and game shows, bolstered by talk and music videos, is profitable because it is popular and economical to produce. Its programs are among those most characteristic of American electronic media.

• Sports programming has a natural affinity for television because of the public's interest in live events. Because sports schedules are not always compatible with broadcast network needs, programming opportunities abound for cable television networks such as ESPN. Recent increases in costs for televising major games have made sports less economical than other types of programs for the broadcast networks. Also, sports on television gives rise to ethical questions regarding manipulation, staging, and biased reporting.

• Programming for children, most of which consists of network and syndicated cartoons, raises the issues of violence, role models, advertising, and targeting. ACT has criticized the quantity and quality of children's programming.

• Children's Television Workshop, a non-profit corporation, produces *Sesame Street* and other celebrated children's series for public television. This program has special historical importance because it made television an educational tool for both home and school.

• Educational television includes both in-school instructional and adult at-home programs. Some are broadcast, but many are delivered by ITFS, cable, and videocassette.

• News programming has great importance both because of its social desirability and because of the income and prestige it generates for networks and their affiliates. The commercial networks increasingly seek ways to make news operations more profitable. News occupies only a small percentage of network television time, but the trend is toward longer and more frequent news programs. Cable networks have expanded the availability of television news. Informational programming has also become much more popular with audiences.

• Public-affairs programming has become more visible as a result of the success of documentary magazine shows such as *60 Minutes*. Single-topic news documentaries make an important television contribution to public understanding, but often create controversy. This has led to an increased emphasis on the magazine approach rather than on single programs treating only one topic in depth.

• Public broadcasting has shown a long-term commitment to producing informative public-affairs programs in both the talk and documentary formats. Public-affairs coverage on public radio shows a history of experimentation and special impact.

• Network radio news has changed from a monolithic headline service into multiple, demographically targeted newscasts accompanied by similarly targeted feature programs. It has also added large blocks of talk programming. Differences in content, format, advertising, and payment generally distinguish radio networks from radio syndicators.

CHAPTER 13

Nonnetwork Programs

Nonnetwork programs consist of the local or syndicated materials produced by or licensed to stations and cable systems. They are used to fill nonnetwork station time or local cable channel time. In this chapter, we examine the types of television programs produced locally by individual stations and cable systems and the programs available in syndication. We also analyze the special role of religious programs and review the mix of locally produced and syndicated material used in radio formats.

13.1 Local Program Content

Locally produced programs take up very little time in the schedules of affiliated and independent stations, accounting on the average for less than 10 percent of all television programming. Most of that consists of local news and public affairs; locally produced entertainment programming amounts to less than 1 percent of the total. The evening news, by all odds the most important locally produced program because of the revenues and prestige it generates for stations, is central to local program production for affiliates. During the rest of the day, scheduling for affiliates is largely a matter of filling in the blanks between network day parts and local news with nonnetwork material.

Independent stations usually place their most popular programs, such as syndicated reruns or movies, in time periods not programmed by the networks, such as in access and against early-evening affiliate news, although they often counterprogram the networks with regional or local sporting events during prime time. Only a small number of independents devote resources to local news or other local production.

13.2 Distribution by Syndication

The development of recording contributed significantly to the growth of the broadcasting industry, because it made syndication possible. Syndication is by nature a worldwide phenomenon, because wherever broadcasting or cablecasting exist, the demand for programs exceeds the local supply. Only by means of program resale and networking can the limitations of local production be overcome. Therefore, popular programs are continuously resold, or syndicated, to the various television markets throughout the United States. In addition, overseas sales of syndicated series are an important market for U.S. programming.

The FCC has defined a syndicated program as "any program sold, licensed, distributed, or offered to television stations in more than one market within the United States for noninterconnected [that is, nonnetwork] television broadcast exhibition, but not including live presentations" (47 CFR 76.5p). Syndication is fundamental to the television industry. Nonnetwork hours on affiliates and all hours on independents must be filled with programming; since local production costs exceed the advertising sales value of most programs' spot time, stations use popular series reruns or old movies to fill their most salable time. The successful programs target the audiences that local advertisers (and national spot advertisers) want to reach. Series that had long runs on the networks before being syndicated (*off-network syndication*) are the most popular with affiliates because they command high ratings and can be stripped. Old episodes of long-running programs such as *Magnum, P.I.* can be syndicated to stations while new episodes are still being produced for their original network run. Even game shows such as *Wheel of Fortune* appear in syndication while still being produced for initial network broadcast.

Station programming demand has also created a specialized business called *first-run syndication*, which is the sale of programs produced especially for multiple resale to stations; these programs never appear on the national networks. *Entertainment Tonight* and *People's Court* are two of the best-known first-run syndication programs.

How TV Syndication Works   Distributors of television programs, the syndication companies, obtain the distribution rights to programs from their producers and offer them, on tape or film or by satellite, to individual stations or to groups of commonly owned stations. The station or station group leases the right to a stipulated number of "runs" over a fixed period of time, after which the rights to the program revert to the syndicator. Such rights are normally awarded to the buyer exclusively within the buyer's own market. However, because satellite distribution of programming to widely scattered cable systems tends to obliterate traditional market boundaries, complete *exclusivity* is in practice difficult to maintain. In consequence, regulation of exclusivity clauses in contracts has become a highly controversial subject.

Syndicators obtain most of their programs from Hollywood studios and independent and foreign producers. The distributors showcase their new products at annual meetings of the National Association of Television Program Executives (NATPE) and other national and international trade groups. The two major rating services, Arbitron and Nielsen, document the track records of syndicated programs already on the market, issuing special reports on the size and composition of the audience attracted by existing syndicated series. The most popular off-network series, such as *M*A*S*H*, are sold in as many as two hundred U.S. markets and so rival the market coverage of network programs. The majority of first-run programs, however, reach fewer than a hundred markets at a time.

Some syndicated series have been running for over 20 years, replayed scores of times. *Little Rascals*, a series edited from *Our Gang* film comedies of the 1920s, started in television syndication in 1955 and can still be seen on independents. *I Love Lucy* (1951–1956), the quintessential off-network syndicated series, dates back to before color television and has been syndicated in virtually every country in the world. At times there have been as many as five *Lucy* episodes on the air on the same day in a single U.S. market. More recently, six different episodes of *The Odd Couple* could be seen in one day in cabled homes in the Johnstown-Altoona (Pennsylvania) market.

After a prime-time network series has accumulated a sufficient backlog of episodes, it normally goes into syndication as an off-network series.* Formerly the networks syndicated their own programs through subsidiary companies, but as of 1973 they were forced by the FCC to divest themselves of their domestic syndication operations. Producing studios or independent producers (or their subsidiaries) now command all the syndication rights. The networks began petitioning the FCC in the late 1970s to restore to them at least partial syndication rights, but by the mid-1980s the rules remained intact, and the rights remained with the Hollywood program producers (§17.2). Despite cable's inroads, Congress felt that the broadcast networks were still so strong as to require continuation of this FCC-imposed handicap.

Prime-Time Access Rule   Before 1971, the three commercial television networks filled nearly all the best evening hours of their affiliates' schedules, leaving little opportunity for producers to sell programs aimed at the national market but not good enough (or lucky enough) to be selected by the networks. The only times left open on affiliated stations for first-run or other syndicated material were the fringe hours (those hours immediately

preceding and following prime time). Prime time was available on independent stations, but these were generally the outlets least able to pay high prices for programs.

In part to widen the market for first-run syndicated program production and in part to diminish the hold of the three commercial networks on the best audience hours, the FCC adopted the prime-time access rule (PTAR), effective in 1971 (see Box, page 348). PTAR confines network entertainment programming to a maximum of three of the four prime-time hours. Prime time is the segment of the television broadcast day when the maximum audience is available, and hence the time when maximum program costs are justified. The FCC defines it as the four evening hours between 7:00 P.M. and 11:00 P.M. Eastern and Pacific time (one hour earlier in the Central and Mountain time zones).

In practice, the networks had already abandoned the 7:00 P.M. to 7:30 P.M. slot by the 1970s, so PTAR in effect gave the affiliates the additional half-hour between 7:30 P.M. and 8:00 P.M.; this whole hour between 7:00 and 8:00 is now known as *access time*. Stations can fill it with either locally produced programs or nationally syndicated nonnetwork programs. But PTAR also prohibits affiliates in the top fifty markets from airing off-network syndicated reruns during access time. This leaves all independents and affiliates in the 150-odd smaller markets free to use off-network material during access time if they choose. Since network reruns are generally most popular and most competitive, they do so choose when they can afford to.

Because most locally produced shows draw small audiences, stations usually consider access time too valuable to expend on them. Therefore, the great majority of access-time programming consists of syndicated material, stripped at 7:00 P.M. and 7:30 P.M., Monday through Friday. As mentioned, in the

*The prices stations pay for syndicated programming vary widely according to market size, extent of competition among stations in a market, age of the programs, and bargaining skills of program buyers. A newly available, top-rated network series can bring $100,000 or more per episode in a major market (for example, *Magnum, P.I.* brought $120,000 per title for six runs over a period of four-and-a-half years). Millions of dollars can be involved in a single buy. At the other extreme, a much-played old-timer might go for merely $100 an episode in a small market (Eastman et al., 1985).

PTAR Fallacies, Exemptions, and Exceptions

The prime-time access rule was not, as many people suppose, designed by the FCC to force stations into producing only *local* programs during access periods. This would be an economically unrealistic goal. The aim of PTAR, as the FCC put it, is "to make available for competition among existing and potential program producers, *both at the local and national levels*, an arena of more adequate competition for the custom and favor of broadcasters and advertisers" (25 FCC 2d 326, 1970, emphasis added). In practice, as was to be expected, the great majority of access time is filled with national-level syndicated programming.

Since PTAR aims at curbing the networks' control over prime-time *entertainment*, the rule also bars stations from scheduling off-network syndicated shows in access time, the period preceding the three hours of prime time — in practice, 7:00 to 8:00 P.M. East and West Coast time zones and 6:00 to 7:00 P.M. Central and Mountain zones. By the same token the FCC did not want to discourage the networks from scheduling *nonentertainment* programs. PTAR therefore exempts from the ban network programs for young children (age 2 through 12) as well as public affairs and documentary programs, except on Saturday nights. The FCC wanted to keep Saturday free of encumbrance by exemptions so as to encourage locally produced access programs at least once a week (Saturday being the traditionally favored time-slot for locally produced programs). Networks tend to schedule their major public affairs and documentary programs on Sundays; therefore the networks usually take advantage of the exemptions to use Sunday access time. For example, because of PTAR, CBS moved *60 Minutes*, its prestigious news/documentary series, to the Sunday 7:00 to 8:00 P.M. time slot in 1975.

The rule also makes exceptions for news specials dealing with currently breaking events, on-the-spot news coverage, broadcasts by and for political candidates, regular network newscasts when preceded by a full hour of locally produced news or public affairs programming, runovers of live afternoon sports events, and special sports events such as the Olympic Games.

It must be borne in mind that the PTAR restrictions apply only to *affiliates* (including O&O stations) in the *top fifty markets*. This leaves independents in all markets and affiliates in the 150-odd smaller markets free to use off-network material during access time if they choose.

top fifty markets these must be first-run, not off-network, syndicated programs.

Regularly scheduled network newscasts are not considered part of the three prime-time hours that the networks are allowed to supply, as long as they are preceded by a local half-hour newscast in the 6:30-to-7:00 P.M. time slot. Also, because of other PTAR exemptions and exceptions, the networks still program Sunday access time (Exhibit 11.2). (For many stations, Saturday access time is the period most often chosen for presenting locally produced programs, because it is available and typically attracts small audiences.)

One half-hour may not seem like much for the networks to surrender. However, when that half-hour of access time is multiplied by the 260 weekdays in the year and by the 150 network affiliates in the top fifty markets, PTAR yields an annual large-audience market of 39,000 half-hours on major stations. This time was not available before 1971 to syndicators or local producers except at the price of preempting network shows. PTAR has therefore given a significant new incentive to producers of nonnetwork programming.

Programming produced for the access-time market necessarily has a considerably smaller budget than network prime-time programming, for two reasons. First, early prime time is less valuable in terms of advertising revenue than is prime time from 8:00 P.M. onward. Second, the many sellers of syndicated material (which is composed mostly of game shows and magazine shows) must scramble to place their programs in access time, usually on relatively short lists of stations. Each network, on the other hand, is assured of placement on most of its 200-odd affiliates during the most valuable segments of prime time.

13.3 Off-Network Syndication

Most off-network syndicated reruns are series programs. Half-hour series are the most desired, because they permit scheduling flexibility. During the important late-afternoon period, as the audience of working adults builds up, successive half-hour shows gain bigger audiences. Hour-long programs, on the other hand, fail to attract many new viewers during their second 30 minutes.

Affiliates schedule off-network series in the time period preceding local news (early fringe, the period from 4:00 P.M. to 6:00 P.M.) and after the late news. Smaller market affiliates and independents can schedule off-network series at any time, though they usually save them for large-audience periods. Independents often position them against network and local newscasts. When affiliates

preempt some portion of prime time, as they occasionally do, they can then schedule off-network reruns during access time, because the total of network programming still falls within the three-hour limit. But because off-network programs are normally sold in sets of many episodes, affiliates rarely fill a single available hour or half-hour with material normally prohibited during prime time.

In syndicated rerun, a series program typically earns a rating about 10 points lower than it earned in its first network appearance. The programs that do best on the networks usually also excel in syndicated rerun. When scheduled in the half-hour immediately preceding local news, for example, programs such as M*A*S*H and Barney Miller have generated large audiences with desirable demographics. Moreover, these audiences often stay tuned for the ensuing affiliate newscasts.

13.4 First-Run Syndication

The best first-run syndicated programming is hardly distinguishable from network programming. For example, a 30-minute daily syndicated variety show such as Entertainment Tonight (see Box, page 350) has much in common with such network magazine series as ABC's 20/20. Indeed, programs discarded by the networks often turn up in first-run syndication. A recent well-known example of this sort of program is Fame, canceled by ABC when its ratings declined. When reintroduced in syndication as a first-run series, some off-network episodes were included in its package. Too Close for Comfort, also canceled by ABC, followed the same pattern.

Low-cost first-run syndicated game shows such as Family Feud, Joker's Wild, Tic Tac Dough, and Jeopardy have been mainstays of access time. Magazine shows are the other major type of access program. This group in-

Entertainment Tonight

Entertainment Tonight (and *Entertainment This Week*) revolutionized the syndication business by proving that expensive, original, non-network programs could be profitable for stations as well as for producers and syndicators. Until *Entertainment Tonight*'s success, programmers thought that first-run access programs had to be cheaply produced to make money for all participants. Game shows had set the pattern of production cost, licensing price, and advertising rates in access time.

Although it was introduced in the late 1970s, *Entertainment Tonight* did not take off until its distributors began delivering it by satellite in the 1980s ("bicycling," mail or truck delivery of videotapes, was too slow for the topical, up-to-date essence of the daily program). The distributors' second innovation was programming the sixth day with a weekend wrap-up called *Entertainment This Week*. Typically, stations strip series for five days, Monday through Friday, but the magazine-style format and popular subject matter of *Entertainment Tonight* permitted the producers to create a wrap-up of the best of the week's content for a sixth day. This sixth show costs relatively little to produce, since it is composed mostly of rerun segments with new introductions, but it provides an extra day's advertising revenues.

An oddity in the ratings calculations of advertising agencies and stations permits this small addition of a day to greatly increase the series's value: stations can take the average rating for five days (Monday through Friday) and add on the Saturday (or Sunday) show rating. For example, if *Entertainment Tonight* averaged a 10 rating Monday through Friday and earned a 5 rating for the extra show on Saturday, it would be sold to advertisers as a 15 rating — which makes both its national and its local sales potential skyrocket. Although this strategy is occasionally imitated by local magazine shows, *Entertainment Tonight* occupies a unique position among first-run syndicated access programs and became an all-time success story.

Like most game shows, however, *Entertainment Tonight* has the disadvantage of being unsuitable for rerun in subsequent years. Because its topical nature gives each episode a very brief period of audience appeal, original shows must be produced continuously. Initially, it capitalized on a revived trend toward gossip, personality, and show-biz fluff in all the media. But the producers later tried to overcome the program's lightweight image by introducing brief think-pieces, some hard news reporting, and wider scope for most stories. More recently, in an attempt to revive sagging ratings, the producers have dropped many segments about the media itself (the "insider" gossip) in favor of content with broader appeal. One of *Entertainment Tonight*'s selling points has been its strong coverage of rock music and the video scene.

Source: Photo from Paramount Pictures Corporation.

cludes *Entertainment Tonight, PM Magazine, Hour Magazine,* and the popular courtroom series *People's Court.* All of these programs cost relatively little to produce, have a virtually unlimited life expectancy, and have succeeded in attracting sizable audiences in access time. Most of these programs appear in markets with four or more stations (the top fifty) during access time.

Barter Syndication   In the 1970s barter syndication began to play a role in access-time programming (§10.2). Usually, syndicators obtain the rights to a series and then sell the program to a station, which fills the advertising slots with local and national spot ads. Barter syndicators, on the other hand, presell some of the advertising slots inside the episodes in the national market before licensing the program to stations. In other words, instead of buying national-spot time outright, *barter syndicators* offer stations programs containing ads in exchange for their program and advertising time. In many cases only a portion of the advertising time is presold, so the station retains some spot availabilities within the program. Perhaps the best-known example of barter syndication is *Memories with Lawrence Welk,* a new version of *The Lawrence Welk Show.* Through barter syndication, advertisers who specialize in products designed for "the Geritol generation" reach viewers who are passionately loyal to Welk's schmaltzy music. Other well-known barter series are *Solid Gold* and *Dance Fever.*

Alternatively, a national advertiser or ad agency sometimes obtains the rights to a program, either by purchasing it from a syndicator or by underwriting a new production. The advertiser then fills the show with its own ads and syndicates it to stations. Advertisers thus gain station time with assurance that their commercials will appear in program settings of their own choosing. *Wild Kingdom* is a well-known example of an advertiser-produced barter program (from Mutual of Omaha).

Barter deals come in several other variations. A hybrid *cash-plus-barter* arrangement requires the station to pay a fee for a program in which only a portion of the advertising slots has been presold; the remaining spots can be sold locally to produce revenue for the station. *Wheel of Fortune* is syndicated in this fashion. *Time-bank* syndication refers to barter deals in which advertisers exchange programs for spots to be scheduled in other programs, usually at a later time.

Less than one-fifth of daily first-run syndicated programming and very few off-network series are offered for barter. However, up to 85 percent of weekly syndicated first-run shows were bartered in 1984. Once-a-week programs that lack a ready-made following are difficult to sell to stations because the ratings of such shows are unpredictable; producers must sell most of the advertising themselves and offer the programs cheaply, sometimes even gratis, to stations. On the other hand, daily programs, even new ones, develop track records quickly. The demand for successful strippable shows is high. Although it takes a great deal of capital to produce a daily program, once one becomes successful the producer can then require cash payment for program licenses and avoid barter deals.

Prime-Time Syndication   The prestigious prime-time mini-network syndicated programming that evolved in the late 1970s has been misleadingly referred to in the trade press as the beginning of a possible fourth network. Among these syndication groups were Operation Prime Time, the Program Development Group, and the Mobil Showcase Network. These joint ventures produced new network-quality prime-time miniseries and specials for simultaneous presentation on stations in major markets (§11.3). In many instances, network affiliates preempted their own network's offering in order to make room for these syndicated specials. Mobil Corporation chose to sponsor several of these syndicated shows rather than network series because it wanted to use issue-oriented commercials of a type the networks would not accept (§9.7).

Quality and Opportunity in Syndicated TV   Networklike programming of the type just described is atypical of the great bulk of first-run syndicated material. Syndicated television concentrates on low-budget formats such as quizzes, game shows, rock music videos, semidocumentary wildlife programs, and voice-over travelogues. Stations, as well as critics and audiences, complain of the lack of high-quality syndicated programming and the consequent dreariness of nonnetwork programming.

The prime-time access rule has created opportunities that did not exist before 1971 for producers outside the elite group of companies that turn out the prime-time network series. For example, all the networks rejected *The Muppet Show* (1976–1981) as a regular series, but because PTAR made access time available nationwide, Jim Henson, its creator, was able to get large television audiences on 160 stations.

Because early-fringe audiences generally do not watch television every day, syndicators typically supply series with discrete episodes (such as *Star Trek* and *M*A*S*H*) for late-afternoon viewing. Until recently, serial programs such as the prime-time soap operas were considered unsuitable for syndication, because it seemed necessary for viewers to tune in daily in order to follow the plot. In the mid-1980s, however, syndicators began testing prime-time soaps such as *Dynasty, Dallas,* and *Falcon Crest* to see whether a substantial audience exists for serial programs in early fringe time. The initial audiences for *Dynasty* reruns were

promising in several markets, suggesting the existence of a heretofore unexploited reservoir of programming. *Dallas* was not as successful, however.

Another recent change in the syndication market occurred when the Hollywood film studios began releasing large batches of previously untelevised theatrical films. These were films that the studios had hoped to sell to the television networks, but network movie cutbacks eliminated that option (§12.2). These films thus became available for syndication to stations and cable television networks. Developments such as these have created more important roles for syndicators, connecting them with production and film distribution more closely than in the past.

13.5 Local News

News has been called television's "noblest service, the major source of its prestige" (Brown, 1977: 303). News has played a lesser role in radio, generally functioning as a headline service on talk and music stations except during national emergencies and wartime (§2.5 and §3.4). But the FCC has historically regarded news as a key ingredient in broadcast schedules. In fact, at one time the commission went so far as to cite the news function as the main justification for allocating spectrum space to broadcasting in the first place:

One of the most vital questions of mass communication in a democracy is the development of an informed public opinion through public dissemination of news and ideas concerning the vital public issues of the day. Basically, it is in recognition of the great contribution which radio can make in the advancement of this purpose that portions of the radio spectrum are allocated to . . . radio broadcasting. (13 FCC 1249, 1949)

Scholars examine three basic areas of concern about news. They look (1) at how news is produced, scheduled, and marketed; (2) at what the news content is; and (3) at what effects news has on society. The broadcast industry uses frequent audience surveys. They report that the public likes the news pretty much as it is and trusts television news very much. One problem with asking the public (in surveys, for example) what kind of news it wants and how news should be produced is that the public knows only what it is used to. Eric Barnouw has said:

The public is caught in a . . . self-regenerative circuit. The more that people rely on the tube for their idea of world events, the less they can know what may be missing. So their trust begets more trust. (Barnouw, 1978, p. 2)

As audiences for newscasts grew, stations began investing heavily in news operations. Million-dollar budgets became commonplace for local news departments in large markets, enabling stations to purchase or lease helicopters, portable electronic news-gathering equipment, microwave relays, satellite uplinks, computerized newsrooms, and other high-tech facilities for news gathering. Large stations developed their own investigative reporting and documentary units. By 1980 many had even begun dispatching news teams to distant places to get local angles on national news events, sending stories back to home base via satellite. So important had local news become, for network affiliates at least, that being number one in local news usually meant being number one in the market.

By the 1970s, some local newscast lengths were extended to two or two-and-a-half hours, especially in the Los Angeles, New York, and Washington, D.C., markets. Because 24-hour news and news/talk radio had captured substantial audiences, television tried to emulate radio. All-news formats proved unviable for broadcast television stations, but in the 1980s CNN stepped into this void, supplying news buffs in cable markets with 24-hour all-news programming on televi-sion. Lower production and staff costs combined with revenues from advertising to a large national audience allowed cable all-news formats to succeed where over-the-air television could not.

Local News Controversies The influence of show business on news has continued to surface, particularly in the controversy over "happy talk." This term refers to the jazzing up of local news presentations with informal banter among members of the on-air news team: usually two news anchors, a sports reporter, a weather reporter, and various other on-camera reporters. Their calculated diversions create, as one critic put it, "an aura of exaggerated joviality and elbow-jabbing comradeship" (Powers, 1977: 35). A second element in the controversy is the deliberate addition of "happy news," stories that lack news value but that afford viewers a feeling that something good happened in the world that day. This type of story relieves the steady diet of war horrors, natural disasters, lurid crimes, and other violence that has generated criticism of newscasts.

In part, at least, happy talk and happy news resulted from the advice of news consultants, marketing specialists who rose to prominence in the 1970s. A survey of the one hundred top television markets in 1979 indicated that half the stations had used consultants, and seven out of ten news directors said they would not reject their advice (American University, 1979). Among the hundreds of these consulting firms, two of the best known are Frank N. Magid Associates and McHugh-Hoffman. The former started as a market researcher, the latter as an entertainment program consultant. As news consultants, their role is to jack up the ratings of news programs.

Under contract to station management, news consultants move in with a battery of audience surveys and focus groups to analyze public perceptions of a station's news content and news personnel. They also examine the organizational relationships within the station. Their advice can range from wholesale replacement of news personnel to the adoption of an on-the-air dress code. Conscientious television journalists complain that consultants tinker with the news itself, though consultants vehemently disclaim any interference with professional journalistic judgments. In a book highly critical of news consultants, Ron Powers concluded:

When local stations create and choreograph entire programs along the guidelines supplied by researchers — toward the end of gratifying the audiences' surface whims, not supplying its deeper informational needs — an insidious and corrosive hoax is being perpetrated on American viewers. . . . The hoax is made more insidious by the fact that very few TV newswatchers are aware of what information is left out of a newscast in order to make room for the audience-building gimmicks and pleasant repartee. (1977: 234)

Another on-going news controversy concerns the concept of "action news." When television journalism concentrates on action, say critics of news consultants, it aggravates two of its own natural limitations: its brevity and its dependence on pictures. Action news favors events that lend themselves to photography, such as fires and accidents, and makes stories as short and "punchy" as possible. The fact is, television has not been adapted to deal at great length with hard news stories, nor can conventional photography add anything to stories that lack intrinsic visual content. Imaginative graphic displays help clarify stories, but television still cannot communicate "actionless" news as well as newspapers can. News stories on the economy and the energy crisis, for example, do not usually lend themselves to action-oriented visuals; consequently, news anchors dispose of them in a few lines of copy read over meaningless stock slides, racing on to the fire or football footage.

Nevertheless, television's very brevity has done its part in creating an expanding interest in information, and viewers who want more depth can always turn to other sources.

13.6 Cable Access Programming

Few of the more than 6,000 cable systems in the United States produce their own newscasts. Some generate many hours of programming by covering public meetings and community events, but only about 10 percent of larger cable systems offer locally-originated programs of any kind (Agostino and Eastman, in Eastman et al., 1985: 284). The local programs that are offered range from community-affairs calendars (often merely event listings) to high-school sports, though the latter are seldom cablecast. About half of cable's local programming consists of informational public affairs, typically community meetings and discussion programs on local political, environmental, and educational issues. The other half is a mix of entertainment and religion, increasingly with commercial sponsorship.

Public meetings are the type of event cable television can produce more economically and effectively than broadcast television can. To be profitable, broadcast programs must fit within predetermined 30- and 60-minute schedules and be appealing to advertisers, whereas many cable systems have public access and local origination channels that use low-cost equipment and are not supported by advertising. Cable systems can thus afford to attract smaller audiences than broadcast stations can. Public-affairs interview and panel programs on cable are becoming important outlets for politicians; national, state, and local candidates for public office often use local cable systems as a forum for political discussion. At election times, candidates for the House and

Senate and state and local offices fill large parts of the cable programming day in major markets. Even at nonelection times, local cable access programs serve a role in local democracy by enabling taxpayers to see and hear local officials in action at the vital, if sometimes interminable, public meetings of school boards, local councils, and the like.

Cable also gives many local musicians, dancers, video artists, and craftspeople their only means of reaching an audience. As yet largely unstructured and amorphous, this type of specialized cultural programming serves social goals that mass-audience commercial broadcasting cannot meet.

13.7 Syndicated Religious Programming

Contemporary religious programming plays an unusual role on commercial stations. At one time, it would have seemed contradictory to include a section on religious broadcasting in discussions devoted to commercial television and cable. But since the mid-1970s, a highly commercialized approach to religious broadcasting, the so-called electronic church, has become an active and controversial element in commercial programming.

Move from Television to Cable   Preachers and religious organizations were among the first to recognize the potentials of radio broadcasting. The first preacher to win a prime-time slot on national network television, Catholic bishop Fulton J. Sheen, outdrew the best that entertainment television of the 1950s had to offer. Broadcasters welcomed Bishop Sheen's sermons not only because he drew large audiences but also because he stuck to religion. They had been sensitized to the danger of getting embroiled in controversial issues not of

their own choosing by the right-wing crusade of Father Coughlin on radio back in the 1930s (§3.1).

As a result of that experience, the more conservative stations and networks had adopted a general policy of refusing to sell time to promoters of any ideological viewpoint (Brown, 1980). However, the distinction between the sale of ideas and the sale of goods and services has become difficult to maintain. When applied to religion, the concept of selling ideas heats emotions among both adherents and opponents.

Until the 1970s, most *large* stations and networks gave free time to religious groups, mainly to the large, mainstream Catholic, Jewish, and Protestant coalitions. An alternative solution was to refuse to give free time to any religious group. For *small* stations, the reaction of the manager of a CBS affiliate in the Southwest was different: he told a reporter in the early 1970s, "We only sell time for religion. If you give time to the Baptists, then you have to give time to Christian Scientists and the Presbyterians and the Catholics and the Methodists, and you've got an impossible situation" (Bagdikian, 1973). Since none of the mainstream religious groups would buy time, small stations with audiences that would watch religious programs began selling time to evangelical preachers. Nowadays, at least one independent in each of the larger markets usually carries a great deal of religious programming, and affiliates and independents in conservative communities may carry many hours of religious programs if cable has not already saturated the market with them. Most of this time is purchased by the religious organization.

As the stations upped the ante for religious broadcasters, many electronic pastors turned their attention to cable television, a far less expensive medium. The CBN Cable Network built up a cable network that supple-

work that supplemented its three owned television stations as an outlet for its originally produced programs. TBN (Trinity Broadcasting Network) and PTL (Praise The Lord) followed suit, creating part-time cable networks that each featured a single dominant personality with a religious message. Other well-known figures such as Oral Roberts and Jerry Falwell, however, continue to appear regularly on commercial broadcast stations.

Origins of TV Evangelism

Televised religion arose as a natural outgrowth of the tent shows and mass rallies of fundamentalist revivalism, a long-standing American tradition. For example, Oral Roberts, famous as an itinerant faith healer since the early 1950s, carried on his revival meetings in what he called his Canvas Cathedral. As television developed, though, he found it harder and harder to fill his tent (said to have been the world's largest): " 'People were no longer attracted by its novelty,' he said. Television cut into the entertainment value of an evening of singing and preaching. Moreover, his own constituency was becoming better educated and more sophisticated in its taste" (Fiske, 1973: 17).

Roberts realized that through television he could transform the whole country into a vast electronic tent. He finally folded away his canvas cathedral for good in 1967, concentrating his energies instead on Oral Roberts University. He is credited with having been the first of the major evangelists to exploit the full resources of television. His idol, Billy Graham, also used television, but originally more as a news medium, a way of reporting on "crusades" staged for auditorium and stadium audiences. Roberts capitalized more fully on the medium's show-business techniques, using lights, costumes, music, cameras, scenery, and video effects to create programs expressly designed to capture the attention of home viewers.

If Oral Roberts represents the metamorphosis from tent to tube, M. G. "Pat" Robertson represents the new, television-bred generation of evangelists. The contrast between Roberts and Robertson is vivid. Robertson is the son of a U.S. senator and a graduate of Yale Law School. Now president of the Christian Broadcasting Network (CBN) and star of its principal syndicated series, *The 700 Club*, his skillful, low-key interviews with celebrated born-again Christians on the daily 90-minute talk/variety program inevitably remind his critics of the format of the *Tonight Show* — with a generous dollop of news from "a Christian perspective." In fact, Robertson is frequently referred to as the Johnny Carson of the electronic church. In 1986 he began campaigning for president of the United States after testing the strength of his personal following developed on *The 700 Club*.

Syndicated to many broadcast stations (with time paid for by CBN), including four CBN owned-and-operated UHFs and six FM stations, and fed to over 3,500 cable systems, *The 700 Club* is only the most visible part of the Robertson communications empire. CBN finances and produces several family-oriented programs for its 24-hour cable network and sells commercial spot time in them. It also supports CBN University, which has a large communications school.

Dimensions of Religious Broadcasting

During the 1970s, commercialized religious broadcasting became one of the most rapidly expanding sources of industry income. Presently, at least 80 percent of television stations sell time for religious programs, mostly in mid-sized and small markets. Estimates of the regular viewing audience for religious television programs range from over 13 million people to twice that amount. A two-year study of religious programs by the Annenberg School of Communications and the Gallop Organiza-

Exhibit 13.1 Televised Religion

Among the charismatic leaders of conservative religious (and sometimes social and political) forces making extensive use of television are Baptist minister Jerry Falwell, head of the Moral Majority coalition, and Pat Robertson (right), founder of the Christian Broadcasting Network and its widely-viewed 700 Club. These figures rely on massive audience donations to support their purchase of television time.

Sources: (A) UPI/Bettmann; (B) AP/Wide World.

tion found that viewers of religious television tend to be more frequently female, nonwhite, older, less educated, and have lower incomes than the general television audience (Gerbner et al., 1984). Members of fundamentalist and evangelic denominations and people who hold strong evangelical beliefs most commonly view religious programs. Although there are nearly two dozen UHF stations and over five hundred radio outlets that program predominantly religious material, the larger impact of religious broadcasting comes from the purchase of time from hundreds of other stations not predominantly religious in format, and from the presence of at least one religious network on most cable systems.

Evangelists and religious groups spend millions of dollars annually buying time for sponsored religious program series. These are referred to as syndicated programs, although the usual syndication transaction, in which the station pays the syndicator for the use of a program, is reversed. In the case of sponsored religious shows, the syndicators pay the station commercial rates for the use of time. So universal is this practice that SRDS, the publisher of station rate card listings (§9.5), routinely reports whether paid religious programs are accepted on each of more than 11,000 broadcast stations.

Religious programs survive in this commercial market primarily by means of small voluntary donations from viewers and the sale of publications and merchandise. According to the Annenberg study, many religious viewers contribute regularly to three or more programs. Income is also realized from the commercial operation of some religious broadcasting stations and from paid spot advertising on religious cable services. Some evangelists spend much of their program time imploring viewers to send in "love offerings" to assist in expanding their "television ministries." The FCC rule against program-length commercials (which was dropped in the early 1980s) did not apply to this sort of appeal, though it did apply to sales pitches for specific objects, religious or otherwise. A Catholic critic pointed out that only two kinds of advertisers had "the option of producing 15- or 30- or 60-minute commercials: politicians and preachers" (Clancy, 1979: 272).

Issues in Politics and Religion   With so many millions of dollars passing through the mails, questions about the fiscal responsibility of religious broadcasters inevitably arise, especially because churches are tax-exempt. Many religious organizations resent inquiries into their financial operations, seeing such questioning as an invasion of constitutionally guaranteed freedom of religion. Jim Bakker, star of *The PTL Club*, a syndicated religious talk/variety clone of *The 700 Club*, flatly refused to give the FCC information about the disposition of funds solicited on the program (71 FCC

2d 324, 1979). Bakker claimed, among other things, that the inquiry violated "First Amendment guarantees of the free exercise of religion and freedom of speech" (p. 328). He used *The PTL Club* program freely as a forum for attacking the FCC and urged viewers to protest its interference with the group's activities.

Radio was long a favorite vehicle for extreme right-wing fundamentalists, but a similar blend of preaching and politics did not emerge as a noticeable trend in television until the 1970s. Typical of the issues on which syndicated television preachers have advocated conservative views are abortion, homosexual rights, the equal rights amendment, the Supreme Court ruling against prayer in public schools, children's sex education, and medical treatment of severely handicapped infants. Television evangelists and their followers exploited such issues during the 1980 national elections, succeeding in bringing down several liberal candidates they had targeted for defeat. By the 1984 elections, religious figures from the more moderate, established churches began to make the front pages of newspapers with pronouncements about candidates' views on abortion and other topics.

Fundamentalist preachers have attempted national boycott campaigns against television programs that they regard as morally objectionable. They are vocally opposed by such prominent television figures as producer Norman Lear — an ironic confrontation, considering both sides are struggling to influence the development of a medium that created them both.

It would, however, be easy to overstate the significance of the electronic church. Its television program boycotts have had only minimal, short-term effects. The electronic church has been widely publicized because of its colorful and controversial aspects, but its actual audience is small — according to the

Annenberg study, less than 7 percent of the total television audience. Not a united movement, it encounters opposition from within the evangelical camp, as well as from mainstream churches. Its apparent political successes reflected the influence of a broad social trend, not the narrow sectarianism of individual television preachers. They neither created nor control the groundswell of conservatism in the 1980s, which was generated more by economic than by theological forces.

13.8 Other Types of TV Syndication

Many of the 50 or so national cable services fill large portions of their schedules with syndicated programs. Services such as USA Network and WTBS fill 24 hours daily with off-network series and barter specials, as well as movies. Necessarily, many programs are repeated often. The national cable market has also stimulated the first-run syndication business by providing another level of sales for every program.

In local cable, however, syndication plays a rather small role. Local systems may purchase the rights to old movies or series just as television stations do, though usually for much lower rates, since their audiences are likely to be tiny. Cable television reached only half the total television households by the mid-1980s, and even in homes with cable service, viewing is divided among many channels. Only the tiniest fraction of the audience typically watches locally programmed cable channels. Moreover, to date very few local systems have had budgets large enough to purchase any substantial amount of syndicated material.

Instructional and educational programming for children and adults is available through dozens of noncommercial syndicators. Among the best known are Agency for Instructional Television (AIT) in Bloomington, Indiana; the Great Plains National Instructional Television Library (GPNITL) in Nebraska; and the Annenberg/CPB project, producers of several prime-time adult learning series (§12.5). These nonprofit agencies license program series for inclusion on public television and radio station schedules. Were commercial stations or cable systems to purchase the material, they would have to edit it drastically, since it includes no slots for commercials. However, the rights are generally available only to noncommercial users. Many of the programs target children or offer cultural and educational material for adults. Two well-known noncommercial series are *Thinkabout* (AIT) and *Anyone for Tennyson* (GPNITL). *The Ascent of Man*, an adult-learning series featuring Dr. Jacob Bronowski, was made available to commercial stations and carried by WTBS. As much as 15 percent of local public television station schedules consist of in-school instructional programs (§12.5), such as whole courses intended to teach beginning Spanish or basic science, supplied by noncommercial syndicators. In addition, many religious organizations and government agencies offer free programs to any station or system that cares to schedule them.

13.9 Radio Syndication

In radio, syndication plays a commanding role in the total programming picture. It is the solution to two problems: the shortage of broadcast material and the need to attract audiences that advertisers want. Syndicators supply entire 24-hour program schedules in prespecified formats, as well as the short features and specials that supplement locally originated DJ programs, distributing these materials on tape and live by satellite. As postage and delivery costs rise, and satellite time charges for audio signals fall, more and more syndicators are shifting to satellite distribution to reap both economic and promotional advantages. By the mid-1980s, nearly half of U.S. radio syndicators made their material available by satellite. The use of live satellite transmission has advantages for both station and producer, allowing program originators to alter record sequences and feature elements in quick response to the public's whims.

Audience Definition   Format radio aims highly selective programming at well-defined audience segments (§11.1), creating loyal if limited followings. The definition of target segments is made easier by the fact that demographics — age, sex, and particularly, rural versus urban residence — have strong statistical relationships to musical tastes. For example, twice as many people of age 64 and over prefer middle-of-the-road (MOR) stations as do people between the ages of 18 and 24. Similarly, three times as many rural as urban listeners prefer country stations. On the other hand, the transitory nature of musical trends makes it impossible for a station to rest once it develops a successful formula. Stations constantly change formulas as fads come and go; the rapid shift from disco music in the late 1970s to punk rock in the early 1980s is an example. Some stations, however, scrap their existing formulas to jump on a new bandwagon, only to find the fad waning, sometimes within months.

Station Automation   Over half of radio stations, and most television stations, use some degree of automation, most commonly to handle routine time logging of program details and billing of advertisers. Much of the work in the program, production, and business departments of radio stations is highly repetitive and so lends itself readily to automation. The daily program log, for example, normally requires only minor updating from day to day. Most of the items such as commercials, public-service announcements, promotional spots, and station identification announcements remain in place over a period of time. Automated systems provide for deleting old material and adding new without altering the rest.

More sophisticated automation systems can carry out most programming, production, traffic, and engineering functions. For example, automated transmitter systems (ATS), first authorized by the FCC in 1977, provide for the automatic adjustment of power and modulation levels. If a malfunction develops, the system shuts itself down and sends an alarm signal to an engineer.

Automated systems make an ideal marriage with syndicated music formats, which demand precise controls over content and timing. Modern radio automation uses microprocessors and digital memories, keyboards on which instructions can be typed in plain English, video screens that give the keyboard operator instructions and information on the status of the system, and hard-copy printers that deliver information for the record, such as program logs. Recent developments in electronic automation, however, have resulted in the breaking down of the traditional distinction between local and nonlocal programming. Although formats are selected locally and may use live DJ assistance, the control of automated formats essentially resides with their producers. Radio critics are often more concerned about program standardization than network or syndicator dominance, but it is clear that choice in programming has been relinquished by many stations. By using specialists in music programming rather than local programmers, stations maximize their demographic targeting and, in many cases, save on costs as well.

Exhibit 13.2 Radio Program Automation

This example of an installation at KYYX (FM) in Seattle shows three modes of tape playback: conventional reel-to-reel machines (left), banks of individual cartridge players called Instacarts (center), and oval lazy Susans called Gocarts that revolve to move cartridges into position for playback (right). The three different playback modes allow efficient integration of varied program elements such as music, commercials, promos, PSAs, and IDs, which are automatically switched on and off in sequence according to the program log.

Source: IGM Communications, Inc.

In a new twist that combines the advantages of syndicated formatting and the advantages of a live radio personality, a single on-the-air disc jockey may speak for two or three dozen stations while playing one music tape interspersed with commercials, weather, and community announcements local to each community served by a participating station. By means of microprocessors operated at a distance by two-way interconnection, one orchestrator can command prerecorded tape cassettes of local advertisements and regional weather to play at each of dozens of station headends, occasionally interrupting with a chatty line or two heard only by that station's audience, to establish the presence of "your local, live DJ." This practice hardly differs from the concept of networking, although in radio, the big national networks supply mostly news and sports. Automation, then, is a partial solution to the problem of program shortage and the need for precise targeting to specific audiences. It has the additional advantage of encouraging management efficiency.

Format Syndicators   So exacting has the art of music-program design and execution become that many radio stations now employ the services of firms called *format syndicators*. Like networks, these provide the actual program material and a wide range of advisory services. In contrast to most radio networks, however, format syndicators typically supply a full 24-hour schedule of music. Most radio networks, as we said, supply only short blocks of programming, such as news headlines or a sportscast or special feature, that must be surrounded by local programming or by other syndicated material.

Format syndicators distribute full schedules of programming tailored to particular formats. About a dozen major companies operate as format syndicators, each supplying as many as six or more targeted formats. Bill Drake, of Drake-Chenault Enterprises, is one of the most influential programmers in the field of radio today. His company, founded in 1963, is the oldest and probably the largest format syndicator. Its eight formats include Contempo-300, appealing to the 18- to 44-year-old age group, and XT-40, appealing to the 18- to 34-year-old age group.

Another popular format syndication firm, Bonneville Productions, offers a beautiful-music service designed especially for automated stereo FM stations. Its basic library consists of over 100 tapes, each of which holds four quarter-hour segments (minus time for local insertions). Each quarter-hour is programmed to fit into a particular hour of the 24-hour broadcast day and is carefully calculated to match audiences available in each of eight different day parts. In addition, the formula reflects changes between spring and summer ("happier, more up-tempo") and fall and winter ("more romantic"). The client station receives a manual of instructions along with the tapes, additional services such as a promotional kit, and ongoing advice based on monitoring of the station's output. Bonneville's bland and unobtrusive sound is aimed primarily at females of age 18 to 49, on the theory that women usually control the choice of station even when men in this age group are also listening.

Feature Syndicators   Another type of radio syndicator, the *feature syndicator*, supplies ready-made program items packaged to fit within particular formats. Feature syndicators supply stand-alone programs both in series and for use as specials, to be interwoven with a locally or distantly produced DJ format. These range from sets of religious sermons to series of baseball games, and may be distributed on tape or by satellite. Such features add glitter and variety to otherwise predictable replays of fixed sets of recordings. Popular-music stations, for example, seek out short interviews with nationally known performers to spice up all-music formats; AM stations typically carry many sports and informational features. Syndicated radio features and musical specials generally cost more to produce than a single station could pay, but because the same series (for example, Dick Clark's *Top 40 Countdown* or Casey Kasem's *American Top 40*) can be sold to many stations, the cost is shared.

Feature syndicators may be large companies that supply several syndicated formats or may be small outfits with only a few specials or a series to market. Brought about by developments in sound technology, the nationwide distribution of the elements of radio programming — records, features, and perhaps DJ voices — signals the approaching end of the traditional regulatory distinctions between local, syndicated, and network origination. At present, rapid mixing of video sources cannot be achieved with the same ease as audio mixing, so radio continues to lead television in evolving new distribution processes.

13.10 Radio Formats

Radio is often characterized as a local rather than national medium, especially in comparison to television. Although this characterization is generally accurate as a description of the two media's advertising bases, it does not take into account the national scope of music recordings. Records are a syndicated medium, since the same record is sold all over the country simultaneously; music promoters send free copies of virtually every recording to every appropriate station, as a promotional strategy. Increasingly, radio uses syndicated formats and feature materials, assembled in a mix of syndicated recordings, network and syndicated features, and live talk.

The majority of radio stations employ music formulas, but there is also great variation among the 8,000-plus commercial stations on the air. Some stations broaden their appeal by block programming — the use of several formats, each suited to a different day part. For example, some schedule all-news programming during drive times, shifting to middle-of-the-road music at other times. Some promote disc jockey personalities, others suppress them. Some abide by rigid formulas, some favor free-form programming. Even the old-fashioned general-interest-program philosophy still claims some followers, especially in very small towns.

Most parsimonious of all broadcast formats, the disc jockey show fully exploits the availability of recorded music. It also reduces production costs to the lowest possible level. Whatever the musical genre, the DJ format represents a form of expression that was once unique to radio but is now much copied by video jockeys (on MTV, *Night Flight*, *Night Tracks*, and elsewhere). The DJ format allows for the exploitation of personal idiosyncrasies and for the interaction of a radio personality with the rapidly changing popular music scene.

Music Formats   Of all radio formats, rock is by far the most popular. More fine distinctions among rock formats exist than within any other format. Variations include adult contemporary (AC), contemporary hit radio (CHR), album-oriented rock (AOR), Top-40, teeny bopper rock, soft rock, heavy metal, and so on. Of these, adult contemporary is by far the most common format for successful stations in the top fifty U.S. markets. Like rock, country music has several subvarieties, such as urban and rural. It draws high ratings equivalent to those of rock in the South and Midwest. Country is the second most popular radio format (Exhibit 13.3).

Easy listening, a broad-appeal format combining orchestrated music and popular songs, has adherents in most radio markets and is especially common in doctors' and dentists' offices, elevators, department stores, and so on. Several syndicated music services, such as Muzak, supply easy listening instrumental formats without commercial advertising for public places and offices. These syndicated subscriber services are carried on a subcarrier that requires specialized decoders for reception (§6.4). Listeners to the main broadcast signal cannot tell when a subcarrier is being used, and standard radios cannot decode subcarrier signals.

Exhibit 13.3   Radio Formats: 1985

| Format type | Percentage of stations with format: | | |
	AM	FM	All stations
Top 40 (CHR, AC)	2%	26%	18%
Soft and oldies	9	20	16
Country	12	11	11
Beautiful/background	1	14	10
Album-oriented rock	1	16	11
Black/urban	8	9	9
News/talk	26	*	9
Middle-of-road/variety	21	*	7
Nostalgia	11	*	4
Hispanic	6	1	2
Religion/gospel	4	1	2
Classical	*	2	1
Unknown/others	1	*	*

*Less than 1 percent

This table lists format percentages for 1,378 AM stations and 1,487 FM stations. The third column lists overall percentages for the AM and FM stations combined (2,865 stations). There is clearly as much specialization among FM as among AM stations; but note that most talk and news has remained on AM, whereas popular music formats make use of FM's better sound. Figures may not total 100% due to rounding.

Source: James Duncan, Jr., *American Radio*, Spring 1985, p. A-19. Reprinted by permission.

Other commercial music formats widely recognized across the United States include beautiful music, nostalgia, urban contemporary, gospel, religious, and, occasionally, classical music and jazz. Beautiful music differs from easy listening largely because the latter contains some vocals. Most nostalgia formats are syndicated by satellite, permitting the local station to concentrate on selling advertising spots. Urban contemporary typically appears only in large cities, gospel generally in the South and Midwest. Religious music, generally fitting the gospel classification, appears as a stand-alone format in many markets and dominates Sunday mornings on many stations. Classical music appears on commercial stations in the largest markets, but in smaller markets on public radio only. The jazz format, although much beloved by its listeners, has not proved very successful commercially.

Information Formats   Radio also uses information programming, within music formats, as a stand-alone format, and combined with talk. Within music programming, news may consist of as little as one-minute network news headlines. For "information stations," however, the format may include local and network news headlines and in-depth newscasts, interviews, feature materials, and telephone conversations with public figures and listeners. In addition, a new information format, farm news, has been developed in recent years. Most information stations have news/talk formats. A variant, the all-news station, programs news 24 hours a day.

Representing only about 2 percent of all radio formats, all-talk stations typically combine drive-time news programming with daytime and late-night in-studio and telephone interviews using two-way telephone calls from listeners. The best known of the network radio talk hosts, Larry King, employs his caustic wit in the overnight hours, providing participatory radio for those who work nights or cannot sleep. The two-way telephone format attracts an older and generally conservative class of listeners — people who have both the time and the inclination to engage in polemics with talk-show hosts. Program directors must take care lest a small but highly vocal group of repeat callers, often advocates of extremist views, dominate the talk and kill advertiser interest.

Even less widespread than the news/talk format, the all-news format, a particularly striking example of the parsimony principle at work, emerged in the 1960s. In a sense, the name is a misnomer, because there is never enough fresh, relevant news available to fill every single hour of programming. So-called all-news stations actually devote only a quarter or less of their time to hard news and repeat even that small segment frequently. Many kinds of non-news informational and service features fill the rest of the time. All-news stations count on holding the attention of listeners for only about 20 minutes at a time, long enough for listeners to arm themselves with the time of day, the latest news headlines, weather tips, and advice about driving conditions. To succeed, this revolving-door programming must have a large audience reservoir to draw upon. All-news stations thus occur only in the largest markets. Moreover, because news is expensive to program, most news-oriented stations fill in around the major news blocks with audience call-in and interview shows. Less than 10 percent of radio stations have information formats, and only a very few of those are strictly all news.

About 3 percent of midwestern stations have evolved a specialized format called *farm news*. These stations usually schedule farm information in early mornings and at noon, repeating vital information during breaks in music or variety programming.

Radio farm news is essential to modern farming. Office and factory workers may find weather reports a convenience, whereas they are crucial to planting, fertilizing, harvesting, and the other outdoor activities of agricultural life. Like hard news of other types, farm news requires timeliness and has a special urgency for its listeners. For example, information on new fertilizer products approved for sale by a federal agency has an immediate impact during certain seasons. Market prices for commodities shift hourly in the midwestern exchanges, sometimes affecting the entire annual income of those with grain, hogs, or other products to harvest and sell.

The U.S. Department of Agriculture now distributes background information and taped radio and television series by satellite in order to keep farmers current on federal policy and plans. The government's radio series called *Agritape Farm Program Report* is aimed at the farmer and the agribusiness sector. In addition, the Department of Agriculture responds to a hundred or more telephone calls on a daily call-in news service distributed to many farm-oriented radio stations.

The more than 275 farm broadcasters have a strong interest in helping their audiences with economic information, because their advertising revenues are closely tied to the overall farm picture. For example, the manufacturers of heavy agricultural equipment such as tractors and combines buy few ads when farmers have little capital to spend. Seed and chemical advertisers, on the other hand, continue to buy ads in the appropriate seasons irrespective of the farm economy.

One issue in news broadcasting is the degree to which farm broadcasters become advocates of the farmer rather than news journalists. Farm reporters have a tendency to identify with farmers and their financial problems, especially on local issues. In addition, the sponsorship relationship is of special concern, because so many farm broadcasts have regular sponsors rather than varied spot advertisers. Most stations deal with this problem by placing news stories about farming and agribusiness in regular newscasts and reserving farm broadcasts for timely information that aids farmers.

Exhibit 13.4   Farm News

More than 275 farm broadcasters provide an essential service to American farmers with regular crop reports, market analyses, and updated farm news and methods. Shown here is veteran broadcaster Kelly Lenz of Wichita, Kansas.

Source: WIBW Farm News.

Religious Radio Formats   Broadcasting has attracted religious organizations and charismatic figures since its earliest days. Over fifty religious organizations held station licenses in the 1920s, but like the educational licensees, most of them later gave up their grants. Only a dozen of these pioneer AM stations survive, but more recently FM has encouraged a resurgence of religious radio stations (§13.7).

The practice of selling time to promoters of religious programming, one of the most striking features of modern radio, has always been controversial, and some stations still oppose it. Nevertheless, such sales amount to a multimillion-dollar business that even nurtures its own specialized advertising agencies. Much religious radio consists of old-fashioned back-to-the-Bible fundamentalist preaching,

Pacifica Radio

Particularly influential in the public radio movement was a small group of stations sometimes labeled "free-form noninstitutional radio." The original inspiration came from Lew Hill, an idealist who initiated the movement when he founded KPFA (FM) in Berkeley, California, in 1949, under the umbrella of his Pacifica Foundation, so named because of Hill's lifelong devotion to pacifism (Trufelman, 1979). Four more stations were later added to the group, in Houston, Los Angeles, New York City, and Washington, D.C. Pacifica stations operate noncommercially, depending on listeners and foundations for financial support and supplemented by income from a news bureau and a tape syndication service.

Pacifica stations have scheduled such unusual features as the news read in Mandarin Chinese, a reading of all the Nixon Watergate tapes of the early 1970s, recitations of lengthy novels such as Tolstoy's *War and Peace* and Joyce's *Ulysses* in their entirety, and a two-hour opera improvised on the air by phone-in singers. Absurd though some Pacifica programs have been, limited though their audiences have remained, they have played a useful role in shaking up established radio. Hundreds of stations have benefited, if only indirectly, from Pacifica's challenge to the safe, the conventional, and the routine (Post, 1974). And thousands of listeners, including influential figures on the political left, have sought out the best that Pacifica stations offer. On the other hand, Pacifica's Houston station was bombed off the air twice in the 1970s as a protest over its programming. This was one of very few terrorist acts against an American broadcast station since broadcasting began.

supplemented with church and even country musical background, but there are also recognized religious musical formulas: traditional gospel, contemporary Christian, and Christian rock (Routt et al., 1978: 211).

Community Radio   In the 1960s, as a reaction to rigidly formatted radio and as an expression of dissent from established values, some small stations began what was called underground or free-form radio. These were mostly noncommercial FM stations that were willing and able to risk experimentation, partly because they were free from the constraint of having to appeal to advertisers. "Some great things were done," recalls one observer. "Tough, creative, unpolished, kinky scenes, but great. FM radio was a world full of surprises, like the world of early television" (Pichaske, 1979: 151). Stations using antiestablishment formats have come and gone in great numbers, but a small group called the Pacifica stations have survived because of the overall quality of their programming, their major market locations, and their financial base in the Pacifica Foundation (see Box, above). The Pacifica stations have been constantly embroiled in legal challenges, internal disputes, and outrageous programming experiments. The Pacifica name is attached to the only Supreme Court decision on broadcast indecency, the "seven dirty words" case (§18.2).

Another form of community radio is the public radio station (§12.8), which is affiliated with NPR and/or with networks such as American Public Radio and U.S. Audio. Despite network affiliation, most noncommercial stations must supply the bulk of their programming locally or purchase it from syndicated sources. Two approaches common on noncommercial radio are the classical and jazz formats, neither of which can support commercial operation except in the very largest cities. Classical music and jazz have special appeal for public radio broadcasters not only because they represent alternatives to common commercial formats but also because they uphold a positive cultural tradition, attracting an upscale audience. Listeners to classical radio tend to subscribe to support the station, whereas, interestingly, jazz listeners tend not to subscribe. Local public radio normally operates with small, low-salaried staffs supplemented by volunteers, enabling it to present formats that would not be commercially viable.

Cable radio services, unlicensed audio services available only as supplements to cable television services, have copied both commercial and noncommercial practices. Several companies supply 24-hour music channels to cable systems, for a fee, for inclusion on cable radio, and sound much like commercially syndicated music formats. A few services, however, hark back to the days of underground FM, supplying eclectic mixes of music and talk in nonstandard, unformatted sequences intended to attract counter-cultural audiences.

Summary

• Syndication means selling and reselling the same program on a station-by-station basis. This enables many stations to use the same program sequentially while also sharing it simultaneously among many markets.

• At the local level, broadcast and cable stations either license syndicated programs or produce their own programs. Most nonnetwork programs are syndicated rather than locally produced.

• Television syndication has been much expanded as a result of the prime-time access rule. The two kinds of syndicated programs are off-network and first-run. Off-network syndicated programs are reruns of network series. First-run syndicated shows are new programs that never aired on the networks.

• Syndicated shows may be licensed for cash, bartered, or licensed for cash-plus-barter.

• Programs produced by mini-networks for prime-time syndication are designed to run opposite network prime-time programs and compete effectively with them.

• Local television news consumes most of affiliates' production energies. Newscasts play an important role in creating an informed democracy and are also profitable for local stations. "Happy talk" and the absence of in-depth reporting on nonvisual news topics are two controversial issues in local news.

• Local cable programs supply local public-affairs coverage and provide an audience for politicians, religious figures, artists, and other community members.

• Syndicated religious programming has become highly visible on television and radio. Evangelical fundamentalists purchase large amounts of commercial time on affiliated and independent stations and also operate several cable networks. The electronic church uses television, cable, and radio programs to raise money and to promote its political views, as well as to teach and exemplify religion.

• Radio makes use of mixes of network and syndicated material and live talk to create the typical DJ music programming and informational formats. The radio networks distribute mostly news and sports, whereas format syndicators supply 24-hour schedules of music, often by satellite. Combining a syndicated format with automated playback keeps station costs low.

• Rock and country music formats are the most common types of radio programming, but news/talk and all-news formats also exist in large markets. Farm news is a relatively new format used especially on midwestern stations.

• Noncommercial radio is exemplified by formats such as jazz and classical music that are not usually commercially viable. Cable-only radio has become the new underground medium in some communities.

PART 5

Effects

So far, we have examined what makes broadcasting and other electronic media in America the way they are. We have reviewed the world development of broadcasting, its history and technology, the economics of American electronic media today, and the programming carried on an increasing variety of delivery systems. Now we will reverse our perspective and look at electronic media as *cause* rather than effect. In order to do so, we must learn how we find out about the impact of electronic media and the roles they play in American society.

This inquiry gives significance to all we have discussed thus far. That is to say, radio, television, cable, and related services merit serious attention only *because they have consequences*. People buy receivers, advertisers purchase time, donors give to noncommercial broadcasting — all in expectation of getting something of value in return. As we will see in Part 5, Congress passes laws, the FCC makes regulations, other public and private forces seek to exert control over these media — all on the assumption that they produce results, some good and some bad. Seen in this perspective, everything we have examined up to this point about the development and role of the electronic media in America culminates in the study of what we know and what we infer about their effects.

CHAPTER 14

Audience Measurement and Testing

In Parts 3 and 4 we discussed such audience-centered topics as dayparting, audience flow, program scheduling strategies, ratings, station and network economics, and advertising rates. All of these topics presuppose knowledge about audience size and composition. How that knowledge is obtained is the subject of this chapter.

Broadcasters need feedback that is free of their own personal biases and those of their social surroundings. They need objectivity, consistency, and completeness, to the extent that these ideals can be obtained in an imperfect world. For these reasons, most day-to-day audience research is conducted by independent commercial companies, using scientific methods for probing into human behavior and attitudes.* Over fifty such companies operate at the national level, many more at the local level. They use a variety of testing methods, first to assist in the preparation of programs and advertising messages, later to assess their outcomes in terms of such effects as purchas-

ing, brand recognition, and the "image" projected by performers, stations, networks, and programs. We hear more, however, about *ratings* — reports on the sheer numbers of people exposed to broadcasts.

We hear so much about ratings because of the inherent drama in reports from the broadcasting battle front, telling which programs, stations, and networks claim to be ahead in the endless struggle for survival and supremacy. Because ratings play such a decisive role in the selection of the programs we see and hear, they merit special study. For that reason most of this chapter is devoted to that one area of audience study — the theory and practice of ratings research.

14.1 The Ratings Business

Media Comparisons   Although broadcast ratings are widely publicized, we seldom if ever hear about magazine or newspaper ratings. No national newspaper or magazine readership surveys are regularly issued. Magazine and newspaper readership is reported

---

*This is *applied* research. Theoretically oriented audience research is also conducted, mostly at universities and think-tank institutions (§14.8, §15.2, and §15.7).

once a year by the Audit Bureau of Circulation, which has aided advertisers by compiling the paid circulations of both since 1914. Several other agencies also do specialized print media research. But whereas few people are aware of this print research, practically everyone has heard of the Nielsen television ratings. In the network battle for ratings dominance, the rise and fall of prime-time programs is news in itself.

Again we are reminded of the unique nature of broadcasting. Other media can measure their audiences inferentially by counting the number of copies or admission tickets sold. But broadcasting and cable have no readily countable physical output. Programs are "published" in a continuous process, with audiences flowing at will from one program to another.

Arbitron and Nielsen   Two ratings firms, Arbitron and Nielsen, stand out because their reports are the usual sources of measurements in the electronic media and advertising communities. These two companies have been locked in methodological and commercial competition for years. Though there have been other competitors, most have lasted only a few years (Beville, 1985).

The two services' revenues come mainly from subscriptions by individual radio and television stations and advertising agencies. About 90 percent of all television stations subscribe to at least one of these two firms' reports, and those in the middle and largest markets usually subscribe to both. Station subscription rates vary according to station revenue, ranging from an average of about $350,000 a year for metered markets down to about $5,000 for diary towns (§14.2). Major advertising agencies pay somewhat less, since they need to subscribe to both network and local-station ratings reports, sometimes spending more than $500,000 a year. Other purchasers of ratings reports include the networks, national sales rep firms, program suppliers, and syndicators. Most advertisers rely on their advertising agencies' subscriptions.

The Arbitron Ratings Company is a subsidiary of Control Data Corporation, a large conglomerate. A. C. Nielsen Company, the largest market research firm in the world, became a subsidiary of Dun & Bradstreet in 1984, and has operations in a score of foreign countries as well as in the United States. Broadcast ratings are a highly visible but fairly small portion of its market research activities, which mainly consist of food and drug marketing.

Local Ratings   Ratings data are gathered and published for each broadcast market — some 214 television and 260 radio markets. These local reports reflect the relative position of each station among its competitors, and estimate the size of the local audience for network, syndicated, and locally produced programs.

Data for local television ratings are not collected continuously, as the cost of such an effort would be too high. Instead, data are gathered in short spurts known as *ratings periods*. The number of these periods per year varies according to market size and station demand, with more scheduled for larger cities. In addition, ratings firms survey all (or nearly all) local radio markets at the same time twice a year, and all local television markets four times annually. These surveys, called *sweeps*, allow comparisons on a national scale, an important factor in the sale of national spot advertising, as discussed in §9.6.

Local ratings reports are the primary tools stations use in selling their time to advertisers, and in evaluating their own programming and that of their competition. Sweeps also supply an in-depth picture of network audiences, based on simultaneous individual market samples. This information supplements the

Exhibit 14.1   Local Market Radio Ratings Report

MONDAY–FRIDAY
6.00AM–10.00AM

STATION CALL LETTERS	TOT. PERS. 12+ %	MEN					WOMEN					TNS. 12-17 %
		18-24 %	25-34 %	35-44 %	45-54 %	55-64 %	18-24 %	25-34 %	35-44 %	45-54 %	55-64 %	
WDAE	6.0			4.2	7.5	15.2		1.4	2.3	5.9	14.4	1.3
WFLA	5.0	2.8	5.7	8.1	5.5	3.6	1.0	2.1	4.4	8.1	7.6	.8
WFLA FM	3.1	1.2	4.5	6.4	.9	1.2	2.8	7.3	3.4	2.3	3.5	.6
WFNN	.4			1.0								
*WGUL	1.3			1.3		2.1			1.0		.8	
WGUL FM	2.0			3.2	2.4	2.7		.6		2.3	3.0	
TOTAL	2.9			3.2	2.4	4.8		.6	1.0	2.3	3.8	
WIQI	6.5	1.2	11.1	13.2	8.6	4.0	11.5	14.4	13.8	9.8	1.8	1.3
*WLFW	2.2				1.9	6.4			3.6	2.2	4.8	
WMGG	4.4	5.2	12.1	9.3	.9		4.2	12.3	7.0	3.0	.8	2.3
WPLP	4.1	1.2	.9	1.9	3.4	8.6		2.1	.8	4.4	7.4	
WQYK	10.3	5.9	9.9	19.6	27.5	5.8	9.6	8.7	20.0	20.6	10.3	4.5
WRBQ	4.5	6.8	5.5	6.1	3.2	2.1	7.8	10.9	5.1	5.4	2.1	6.5
WRBQ FM	16.8	26.4	34.1	24.5	9.0	3.1	32.3	33.8	21.0	8.4	6.6	33.5
TOTAL	19.8	31.9	36.3	27.4	11.4	5.3	40.2	38.5	23.1	13.1	8.7	37.8

Shown is a small portion of one page from an Arbitron report for the Tampa–St. Petersburg, Florida, radio market in the spring of 1984. It covers weekday morning drive time and shows cumes (ratings based on estimated total numbers of listeners in each group over a 90-day survey period) for different audience demographic breaks. Stations are listed alphabetically (only some are shown here), with audiences for co-owned AM and FM stations shown both separately and combined.

Source: © 1984 Arbitron Ratings Company.

more frequent but less extensive network ratings reports based on national metered samples (§14.2).

The principal sources of market ratings reports (Exhibit 14.1) include the following:

• *Arbitron radio markets.* Arbitron covers 260 local radio markets in the twelve-week spring sweep and 130 again in the fall, and surveys a few markets in larger cities in summer and winter.

• *Arbitron television markets.* Arbitron covers 214 local television markets four times per year and larger markets three additional times.

• *Arbitron metered markets.* In eleven large cities Arbitron combines electronic meter and diary methods of research for overnight reports on television viewing.

• *Nielsen Station Index.* Nielsen surveys 205 local television markets, nearly all four times a year, the largest seven times.

- *Nielsen metered markets.* Nielsen covers television viewing in twelve major cities by overnight measurement, with daily on-line reports and weekly printed reports.
- *Birch Radio.* This is the newest national firm doing local ratings, having begun in 1978. It covers 125 radio markets, issuing monthly reports and quarterly summaries.

Network Ratings   Network ratings present a much different problem for research firms than do local ratings, because networks demand much faster and more frequent reporting than do local stations. But in two ways network ratings are easier to obtain: (1) there is no need to survey every market in order to get a reliable national picture of network audiences; and (2) there are far fewer competing networks at any one time than there are competing stations.

Nielsen supplies the only continuous television network ratings, issuing them every two weeks (Exhibit 14.2). Its customers can receive rough approximations of audience size from "overnights," daily ratings reports based upon data from a few key cities. Nielsen's regular network reports are based on a national sample of metered homes (§14.2). The ratings reported in newspapers and trade magazines are nearly always from this national metered sample.

The only national radio network ratings service is RADAR (Radio's All-Dimension Audience Research). It is financed by the networks, which contract with Statistical Research, Inc., an independent firm, to conduct the surveys regularly. RADAR issues reports twice a year, each covering a sample week, based on continuous surveys of six thousand respondents.

Rating the New Services   The development of new means of delivering programming has raised questions about the size and characteristics of the audience for these media. To what extent, for example, do cable viewers differ demographically from broadcast television viewers? How much do the various channels cut into each other's audiences? And how do remote channel-switching devices and home recorders change viewing habits? As advertisers move to cable and other media, they demand the same sort of audience research they refer to when considering radio and television advertising.

A. C. Nielsen has established a new division, the Nielsen HomeVideo Index (NHI), to develop means of measuring audiences of the new services. Four times a year it issues *Pay Cable Report*, which covers all television activity in a sample of homes subscribing to pay cable. It provides national audience data on about 10 of the larger national cable networks.

A number of the newer services do not raise major audience research issues, however. SMATV, MMDS, and DBS, regardless of their eventual degree of marketplace success, "are readily adaptable to present-day measurement techniques (including meters and diaries)." They provide fewer channels than cable, and therefore it is likely "that programming schedules would be more structured and more widely promoted than cable" (Beville, 1985: 288).

Special Studies   Both Arbitron and Nielsen publish many supplementary reports, based upon data they gather in preparing their regular subscription reports. These supplements include reports devoted exclusively to market-by-market analyses of syndicated programming (§13.4), analyses of minority-audience preferences, and analyses of trends in ratings of particular program types. In addition, clients can order special reports tailored to their needs. For example, a local station can commission a study to determine how a new local program is doing against the competition, or a study to find out how much it appeals to specific audience subgroups.

Exhibit 14.2 Nielsen's National Network Ratings

A-20

Nielsen NATIONAL TV AUDIENCE ESTIMATES — DAY MON.–FRI. FEB.11–15, 1985

| TIME | 7:00 | 7:15 | 7:30 | 7:45 | 8:00 | 8:15 | 8:30 | 8:45 | 9:00 | 9:15 | 9:30 | 9:45 | 10:00 | 10:15 | 10:30 | 10:45 |

WEEK 1

ABC TV
- TOTAL AUDIENCE (Households (000) & %): 5,350 / 6.3 — GOOD MORNING, AMERICA-730 (CO-OP) (PARTICIPATING) → 5,860 / 6.9 — GOOD MORNING, AMERICA-830 (CO-OP) (PARTICIPATING)
- AVERAGE AUDIENCE (Households (000) & %): 4,160 / 4.9 ; 5,010 / 5.9
- SHARE OF AUDIENCE %: 21 ; 22
- AVG. AUD. BY ¼ HR. %: 4.8 4.9 ; 5.8 6.0

CBS TV
- TOTAL AUDIENCE: 3,910 / 4.6 — CBS MORNING NEWS 1 ; 4,330 / 5.1 — CBS MORNING NEWS 2 ; 6,200 / 7.3 $25,000 PYRAMID ; 5,690 / 6.7 PRESS YOUR LUCK
- AVERAGE AUDIENCE: 3,060 / 3.6 ; 3,570 / 4.2 ; 5,260 / 6.2 ; 4,920 / 5.8
- SHARE OF AUDIENCE %: 16 ; 16 ; 23 ; 21
- AVG. AUD. BY ¼ HR. %: 3.5 3.8 ; 4.1 4.2 ; 5.9 6.5 ; 5.6 5.9

NBC TV
- TOTAL AUDIENCE: 5,350 / 6.3 — TODAY SHOW-7.30AM (CO-OP) (PARTICIPATING) ; 5,010 / 5.9 — TODAY SHOW-8.30AM (CO-OP) (PARTICIPATING) ; 3,400 / 4.0 TIME MACHINE ; 5,260 / 6.2 SALE OF THE CENTURY
- AVERAGE AUDIENCE: 4,160 / 4.9 ; 4,330 / 5.1 ; 2,720 / 3.2 ; 4,410 / 5.2
- SHARE OF AUDIENCE %: 21 ; 19 ; 12 ; 19
- AVG. AUD. BY ¼ HR. %: 4.8 5.0 ; 5.1 5.1 ; 3.1 3.3 ; 4.9 5.4

WEEK 2

ABC TV
- TOTAL AUDIENCE: 18,170 / 21.4 [REAGAN NEWS CONF.-ABC (8:00-8:37PM) (SUS)(-OP)] — ABC THURSDAY NIGHT MOVIE DEADLY MESSAGES (8:37-10:37PM)(OP)(-OP)(SD) — 18,930 / 22.3 ; 20/20 (10:37-11:37PM)(OP)(-OP)
- AVERAGE AUDIENCE: 9,680 ; 13,160
- SHARE OF AUDIENCE %: 11.4 9.3* 10.1* 11.3* 13.7* 15.5 17.1*
- AVG. AUD. BY ¼ HR. %: 17 14* 14* 16* 21* 27 28* ; 9.3 9.3 9.9 10.2 11.0 11.6 13.3 14.2 17.0 17.2

CBS TV
- TOTAL AUDIENCE: 20,800 / 24.5 [REAGAN NEWS CONF.-CBS (8:00-8:35PM)(SUS)(-OP)] MAGNUM, P.I. (8:35-9:35PM)(OP)(-OP)(SD) — 23,940 / 28.2 SIMON & SIMON (9:35-10:35PM)(OP)(-OP)(SD) — 18,930 / 22.3 KNOTS LANDING (10:35-11:35PM)(OP)(-OP)
- AVERAGE AUDIENCE: 16,050 ; 19,020 ; 15,960
- SHARE OF AUDIENCE %: 18.9 16.7* 20.3* 22.4 21.4* 23.3* 18.8 19.1*
- AVG. AUD. BY ¼ HR. %: 27 24* 29* 33 31* 35* 33 32* ; 16.0 17.2 19.5 21.2 21.6 23.0 23.6 19.0 19.1

NBC TV
- TOTAL AUDIENCE: 23,940 / 28.2 [REAGAN NEWS CONF.-NBC (8:00-8:35PM)(SUS)(-OP)] BILL COSBY SHOW (8:35-9:05PM)(OP)(-OP) ; 22,330 / 26.3 FAMILY TIES (9:05-9:35PM)(OP)(-OP)(SD) ; 20,970 / 24.7 CHEERS (9:35-10:05PM)(OP)(-OP) ; 17,910 / 21.1 NIGHT COURT (10:05-10:35PM)(OP)(-OP) ; 17,150 / 20.2 HILL STREET BLUES (10:35-11:35PM)(OP)(-OP)
- AVERAGE AUDIENCE: 21,310 ; 20,720 ; 19,020 ; 15,880 ; 13,580
- SHARE OF AUDIENCE %: 25.1 24.4 22.4 18.7 16.0 16.5*
- AVG. AUD. BY ¼ HR. %: 36 35 33 28 28 27* ; 22.5 26.1 24.0 24.8 22.3 22.4 19.0 18.9 16.7 16.4

| TV HOUSEHOLDS USING TV (See Def. 1) | WK. 1 | 60.4 | 61.7 | 62.5 | 64.2 | 66.2 | 68.0 | 68.3 | 68.0 | 66.6 | 67.0 | 66.7 | 65.9 | 62.1 | 61.1 | 59.4 | 56.3 |
| | WK. 2 | 61.2 | 62.0 | 63.0 | 64.7 | 66.1 | 69.7 | 67.7 | 69.0 | 69.7 | 70.0 | 68.4 | 67.4 | 65.5 | 64.7 | 60.8 | 58.6 |

U.S. TV Households: 84,900,000 — For explanation of symbols, See page A.

Above is a weekday daytime report, showing a comparison of the three morning network news shows. Below it is an evening prime-time schedule showing a presidential news conference that has pushed normal network shows back about 35 minutes from their normal starting time. Week numbers refer to the fact that each report contains ratings for two consecutive weeks. (Abbreviations: OP = other short program items that occur in this time segment and are rated elsewhere in the report; SUS = sustaining or nonsponsored program; SD = short duration.)

Source: A. C. Nielsen Co., *Nielsen National TV Ratings*, February 11–24, 1985. Used with permission.

14.2   Collecting Set-Use Data

Whatever the electronic medium, the three main means of collecting data on which to base ratings are diaries, meters, and telephone calls. Several other approaches and combinations are also used. Each has its own advantages and disadvantages, although none is completely satisfactory.

Diaries   Arbitron and Nielsen researchers using the *diary* method for gathering data persuade listeners or viewers in local market sample homes to keep a daily record of their set use by filling out printed forms. To gather radio data, Arbitron sends a separate diary to each *person* over 12 years of age in every sample household. The diary keepers are asked to write down their listening times and the stations they tune to, keeping track of away-from-home as well as in-home listening for one week (Exhibit 14.3).

To gather television data, Arbitron assigns a separate diary to each television *set* in each sample home. Diary keepers are asked to write down viewing and demographic information about all viewers, including any visitors, again for an entire week. Arbitron draws a different sample of homes for each survey week. Nielsen, too, uses diaries, but only for its NSI local market ratings outside of the largest cities.

Meters   The Nielsen metering device (Exhibit 14.4) attached to a television set automatically records complete and precise information about television use. In eliminating the factor of human subjectivity, however, the unaided meter also eliminates information on audience composition; it cannot even indicate whether anyone was present in the room while the receiver was in operation.

As the chief developer and proponent of meters, the A. C. Nielsen Company has evolved a sophisticated system of "instantane-ous" meter reporting. For its Nielsen Television Index (the network ratings report), Nielsen connects all receivers in each sample home to a small on-site computer. This *Storage Instantaneous Audimeter*, as Nielsen calls it, stores data on the use of all sets in the home. It makes an exact record of tuning from channel to channel as well as of on-off times. On cue, each home storage device in each metered home sends its data by telephone line to a central processing facility in Dunedin, Florida.

To make up for the lack of information about audience composition, Nielsen supplements the data it gathers from metered homes with information from a separate sample of homes using diaries called *Audilogs*. Devices the company calls *Recordimeters* are attached to sets in diary homes to give viewers audible and visual reminders to fill out their diaries every half-hour while the set is on. Recordimeters also keep a simple on-off record of receiver use. Data from Recordimeter homes, which are entirely separate from the diary homes Nielsen uses for local market measurements, serve only to supplement and confirm the data derived from the national Audimeter sample of 1,700 metered homes used for network ratings. Nielsen activates about seven hundred of the diary home samples a week, reporting audience-composition data about thirty times a year.

This elaborate combination of methods would be far too expensive to employ on a market-by-market basis throughout the country. Nielsen uses meters only for its network ratings and for obtaining overnight local ratings in the largest cities.*

---

*By 1985 Nielsen provided daily and weekly reports for New York, Los Angeles, Chicago, San Francisco/Oakland, Philadelphia, Detroit, Washington, D.C., Boston, Dallas/Fort Worth, Houston, Miami/Fort Lauderdale, and Denver.

Exhibit 14.3   Local Market Diaries

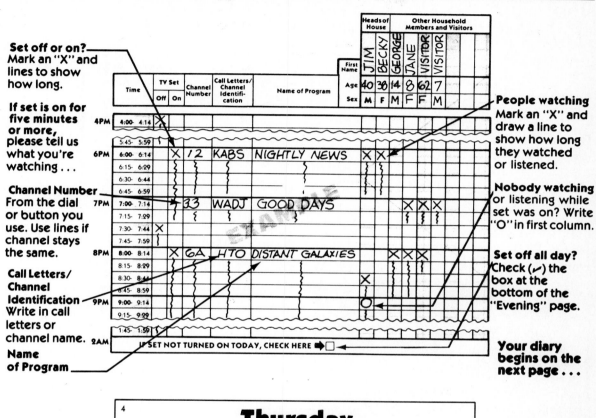

This sample page from a television diary (top) demonstrates the information sought from Arbitron sample families. A portion of a radio diary shows that the two are similar in approach, although where listening takes place is an important factor in radio listening research.

Source: © 1984 Arbitron Ratings Company.

Exhibit 14.4A   The Ratings Gathering Systems: Nielsen

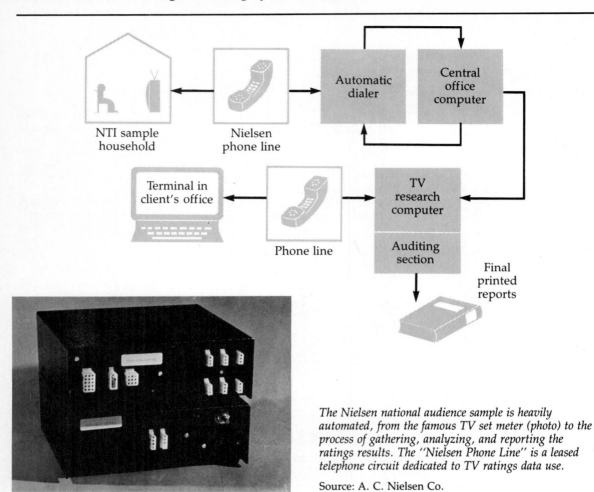

The Nielsen national audience sample is heavily automated, from the famous TV set meter (photo) to the process of gathering, analyzing, and reporting the ratings results. The "Nielsen Phone Line" is a leased telephone circuit dedicated to TV ratings data use.

Source: A. C. Nielsen Co.

Coincidental Telephone Calls   The *coincidental telephone* method is the oldest and, many feel, the most accurate means of obtaining audience-size information.* The method is called coincidental because respondents are asked what they are listening to or watching during (that is, *coincidental* with) the time of the call. The factor of memory is thus entirely eliminated, and the possibility of faking greatly reduced. The researcher asks whether a set is on at that moment, and if so what program, station, or channel the set is tuned to, plus a few questions about the number, sex, and age of those watching.

*The first experiments with telephone audience research came in the late 1920s and were the basis of the first ratings. The Cooperative Analysis of Broadcasting of 1930–1946 and the 1934–1950 Hooper ratings for network and local radio (the Nielsen ratings of their time) relied on this approach (Beville, 1985).

Exhibit 14.4B   The Ratings Gathering Systems: Arbitron

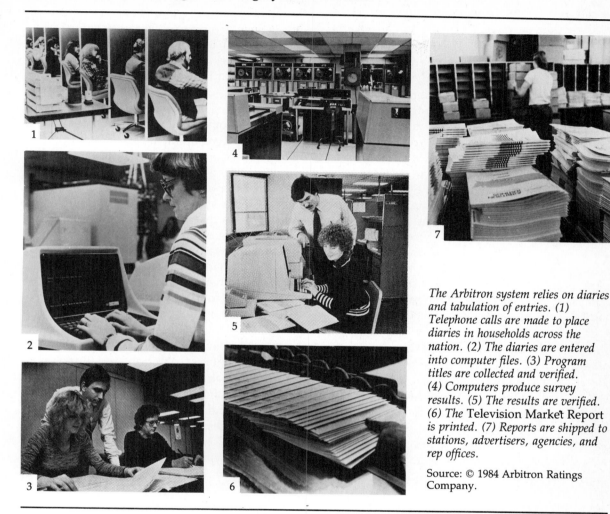

The Arbitron system relies on diaries and tabulation of entries. (1) Telephone calls are made to place diaries in households across the nation. (2) The diaries are entered into computer files. (3) Program titles are collected and verified. (4) Computers produce survey results. (5) The results are verified. (6) The Television Market Report is printed. (7) Reports are shipped to stations, advertisers, agencies, and rep offices.

Source: © 1984 Arbitron Ratings Company.

Because this method provides only *momentary* data from each respondent ("What are you listening to or watching *now*?"), it requires a large number of calls, spaced out to cover each period of the day, in order to build up a complete profile of listening or viewing. Properly conducted, the coincidental call method is expensive, because it requires large batteries of trained callers. Another disadvantage is that it is not feasible to call people after 10:30 P.M. or before 8:00 A.M.; for information about these hours, researchers must ask respondents to recall the programs they listened to or viewed.

Coincidental telephone surveys are widely used, but none of the major ratings companies presently uses this method for regular reports, primarily because it is too expensive for continuing or wide-ranging research. Nielsen does, however, offer a special coincidental service for customers who require quick answers to specific questions.

Telephone Recall

Tricks of memory make the *telephone recall* method less reliable than the coincidental method, though also marginally less expensive, since more data can be gathered per call. However, the problem of unreliability has been minimized by modifications developed in a major comparative study of radio research methods (ARMS, 1966). RADAR, the only source of radio network ratings, uses telephone recall. The main feature of the RADAR approach is the use of *daily* calls by prearrangement over a period of seven days, thus attaining a week's coverage while minimizing errors of memory. RADAR employs *random digit dialing*, a technique for generating telephone numbers at random by computer, to design a national sample of individuals (not households, in this case).

People Meters

In the 1980s, audience analysis began to focus more on individual viewing and listening habits. Advertiser interest and computer capability have prompted the development of *people meters*. As with Nielsen's Audimeters, these electronic devices keep a record of when the set is on and to which channel it is tuned. But when people meters are used, each viewer must also "check in" whenever he or she begins to view television by pushing a special handset button (there are several visitor buttons as well). The set and viewer information travels by phone line to a central computer, which contains household demographic data gathered when the people meter was installed in the home.

Several people-meter variations were being tested by A. C. Nielsen, Arbitron, and AGB, a British firm, in the mid-1980s. Nielsen uses a box with lights that flash red when the set is turned on. Viewers press their assigned buttons (which turn green) to indicate which household members are watching (Exhibit 14.5). The box reports data to a central computer once a minute. Nielsen began a three-year national test of the system late in 1983 and projected full-scale operation, replacing the traditional household meter, by the fall of 1987.

AGB tested a variation of this approach in 400 Boston homes, and announced plans for a $60 million investment in a thousand-person nationwide sample using people meters that would compete directly with Nielsen. In Denver, Arbitron and Burke Marketing Services have tested a system called ScanAmerica that not only records viewing but also allows electronic reading of product codes. Viewers pass a portable "wand" over each new purchase they have made. The wand stores product data, and when it is inserted back into the main system unit, it sends the product information to a central computer, allowing correlation of viewing and buying behavior. Because this system requires a greater effort from respondents, Arbitron and Burke paid each participating household about $400 per year. Questions about viewer response rates over time, and the cost and acceptability of such measures to broadcasters and advertisers, were to be answered at least tentatively in tests involving two hundred homes. Initial test results in 1986 encouraged expansion of the test to more Denver homes.

If successful, as appeared likely in 1986, people meters could replace both diaries and traditional meters in television audience measurement. They eliminate the need to fill in diaries, yet provide the demographic information missing with traditional meter measurements. Indeed, even those unable to speak or write English can be measured with people meters, which goes some way toward correcting the undermeasurement of some minorities (§14.7). People meters can also better measure the audiences for cable and other me-

Exhibit 14.5   The People Meter

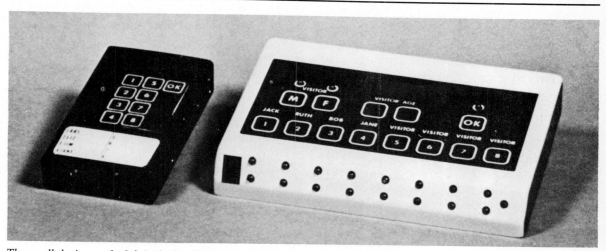

The small device on the left is the hand-held unit used to record actual viewing. The larger base unit on the right is the central recorder for all sets (and hand-held units) in a given household.

Source: A. C. Nielsen Co.

dia, since a computer can keep track of which receiver input (cable, VCR, and so forth) is on the screen (§14.6).

Personal Interview   The use of in-person, door-to-door surveys based on probability samples has declined in recent years because of the hazards of knocking on strange doors on strange streets. However, personal interviews, or *convenience* samples (also called *judgment* or *purposive* samples) are often used in studies other than ratings research that need not be based on probability. Typically, interviewers question people on busy streets or in shopping centers, or, for car radio listening, at stoplights. Data gathered in these ways have limited significance because the results are not projectable to the general population. If taken to be statistically significant, such data can be very misleading.

Combinations   Of course, if cost is no object, the most reliable and valid method of audience research is some combination of the methods detailed above. Combinations of meters and diaries, or telephone calls with diaries or meters, help to provide added information while allowing checks on, and comparisons with, findings derived by different methods. People meters combine methods efficiently, provided respondents are willing to cooperate fully (§14.4).

14.3 Ratings Concepts

Market Delineation   The first step in current audience measurement is to define geographically the local market covered by a cluster of stations. Determining a national system of clearly defined markets is essential to the broadcast advertising business. The expansion of cable systems has complicated this process, since many cable markets include nonadjacent geographical areas. To be useful for cable and broadcast network and national spot sales planning, any market system must avoid overlaps, so that markets can be grouped regionally or nationally without counting the same people more than once.

The most widely accepted system for defining television markets is Arbitron's *Area of Dominant Influence* (ADI), though Nielsen has its own version, called *Designated Market Area* (DMA). An ADI is made up of one or more surrounding counties in which the dominant share of viewing is concentrated on stations located in a central town or city. ADIs are usually smaller in the East and larger in the West, where markets are farther apart. Arbitron assigns each of the more than three thousand counties in the United States to only one ADI, updating the assignments annually, though conditions change only slightly from one year to the next. ADIs range from No. 1 (New York City, with over 6.7 million television households) to No. 214 (tiny Glendive, Montana, with but 5,200).*

Units of Measure   Another preliminary step in rating research is to define what will comprise a single entity when counting an au-

dience. In drawing a sample, researchers refer to this as the *elementary sampling unit*. In broadcasting, it is usually defined in terms of either persons or households.

Households (defined as any housing units, including houses, apartments, and single rooms) are the most convenient unit of measure to use. They are easier to count than individual people, because they stay in one place and are fewer in number (though households today can represent traditional family groups of two or more persons, or multiadult households). The fact that television viewing has traditionally been a family activity makes the household a logical unit of measure, even though a majority of households now have two or more television sets. A single diary can be used to record the viewing or listening of all members, or a different diary can be used to cover each set. Ratings reports based on household counts thus also report more or less accurately the individual viewing or listening of all people in that household, *if* diaries or meters cover each receiver in the home.

But such an approach fails to account for viewing in hotels, dormitories, barracks, and institutions. Counting by persons rather than by households is preferred for radio audience measures because (1) radio listening is clearly more of an individual activity, and (2) much radio listening takes place outside the home, in cars and workplaces. In the sections that follow, however, we will assume that the household is the elementary sampling unit unless otherwise noted.

Derivation of Ratings   A rating is a *comparative estimate* of set tuning in any given market (or combination of markets, for network ratings) at any given time.* The word *comparative* is used because a rating compares the

---

*Arbitron uses two other terms to describe slightly different market definitions. The *home* county is a smaller area than the ADI, usually restricted to the county in which a station is specifically licensed. Also, Arbitron refers to some markets as *metros*, meaning the metropolitan statistical area (MSA), a geographical region defined for census and other statistical purposes by the U.S. Department of Commerce and usually containing several counties around a central city core. Both the home and metro measures are smaller in geographical and audience size than the ADI. On the other hand, the *total service area* (TSA) is the largest local region reported. It includes 98 percent of a market's viewing or listening audience, thus including counties outside the ADI. Every published rating book includes a map of the area reported on, showing the differences between all of these measures.

---

*Definitions in this chapter conform to the National Association of Broadcasters' *Standard Definition of Broadcast Research Terms* (1973).

actual estimated audience with the *total possible* audience. A rating is an *estimate* because it is based on the sets used by only a sample of the audience, and samples can never yield absolute measurements, only approximations (§14.4). A rating of 100 would mean that all (100 percent) of the households in a market were tuned in to a particular station. But this never happens, for some people are not at home, others have broken receivers, and still others are doing something else.

The most successful broadcast entertainment program of all time, an episode of *Dallas* in 1980, had a Nielsen rating of 53.3. Prime-time television programs average a 17 rating; daytime programs average about 6. HBO averages a 2 prime-time rating across all television homes and an 8 rating in homes equipped with pay cable. Radio ratings are usually too low to be meaningful — often less than 1, and rarely more than 2 or 3. Radio therefore relies more on *cumulative* measures, discussed later in this section, under "Cumes."

The calculation of ratings is simplicity itself. A rating is a measure found by dividing the number of households tuned to a given program by the total television households in the market. Thus, if in a sample of 400 households, 100 are tuned to a given program, the program's rating is found by dividing 100 by 400 (the 400 figure represents the full sample, and the 100 is derived from diary reports for a specific hour). The solution to this equation is 0.25, but the decimal point is dropped to result in a rating of 25. The concept is illustrated in Exhibit 14.6.

A properly derived rating is *projectable*. That is, expressed as a percentage, it can be applied to the total population represented by the sample. Continuing with the example above, assume a total population of 100,000, derived from census data. Multiply this by the rating with the decimal restored (0.25), and we have an estimated total audience of 25,000 households.

HUTs and Shares   As mentioned, a rating gives an estimate of the percentage of the total possible audience that is tuned to a program. A station's share of the audience, on the other hand, is calculated on the basis of the percentage of *households using television* (HUT). A HUT of 55 indicates that in a given time period an estimated 55 percent of all television households are actually tuned in to *some* station receivable in that market. In other words, HUT measurements refer to viewing in the market as a whole, not to any individual station or program receivable in that market. HUTs vary with day part, averaging nationally about 25 for daytime hours and about 60 for prime-time hours.

Shares are derived from HUT data. Each station's estimated viewing audience (in thousands) is divided by the number of homes using television at that time to figure a proportion that is usually stated as a percentage, as shown in Exhibit 14.6. A station's share percentage for a given time period is always *larger* than its rating. For example, whereas top network prime-time programs usually earn ratings of just over 20, their corresponding shares are about 30.

Share percentages are usually preferred as programming tools, and ratings act as advertising sales tools. This is because share percentages give programmers a more immediate estimate of their competitive position within one medium, whereas ratings more readily allow comparison of advertiser "reach" across media. Audience size is essentially a matter of time of day. The availability of listeners within given day parts varies little from day to day unless extraordinary events cause people to change their normal habits. But changes in program appeal can cause audience flow (§11.4 and §14.5), thereby increasing or decreasing the audience share obtained by any particular program, even though the total audience for that time period remains about the same.

Exhibit 14.6   Rating Concepts

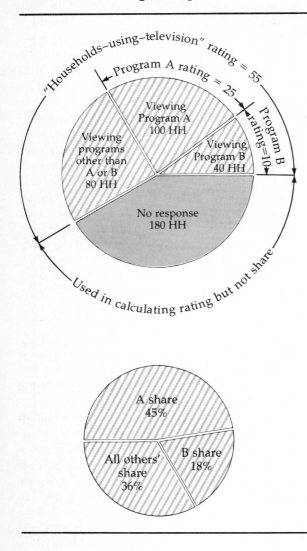

The pie shows television set-use information gathered from a sample of 400 households, representing a hypothetical market of 100,000 households.

Note that program ratings are percentages based on the entire sample (including the "no response" households). Thus Program A, with 100 households, represents a quarter (25 percent) of the total sample of 400. The rating is expressed as 25, without the percentage symbol. The formula is 100 ÷ 400 = .25, the decimal being dropped when the number is expressed as a rating.

Projected to the entire population, this rating of 25 would mean an estimated audience of 25,000 households. The formula is .25 (the rating with the decimal restored) × 100,000 = 25,000.

The smaller pie, 55 percent as large as the bigger pie, represents only the households using television, in this case 80 + 100 + 40 households, or a total of 220 (expressed as a households-using-television or HUT rating of 55 as shown in the larger pie). Shares are computed on the basis of treating the total number of households using television, in this case 220, as 100 percent. Thus program A's 100 households divided by 220 equals about .445, expressed in rounded figures as a share of 45.

Cumes   Because radio ratings are so low, advertising agencies use the larger share-percentage figures to determine market size. But even more significant for radio are *cumulative audience* (cume) figures. A radio signal reaches a relatively small number of people in a given quarter-hour; but over a period of many hours, or during the same period over a number of days, radio reaches a surprisingly large number of *different* listeners when all are added together, or cumulated. A *cume rating,* is simply the number of persons tuning a station, expressed as a percentage of all potential radio listeners in a particular market. For example, a person who, during the two or four weeks that typically make up a rating period, listened several times to a particular station for at least five minutes at a time, on different days, would be counted only once in constructing a cume figure. A person listening only once during that period would also be counted once, because the purpose of a cume is to show how many different people tuned the station during a given period of time. *Reach* and *circulation* are other terms indicating cume audience measurements.

Demographics   Rating books report on audience composition in terms of gender and age. These *demographic breaks*, or simply *demographics*, divide overall ratings into subgroup ratings for men, women, teens (age 12–17), and children. The adult audience is further divided into age-group categories, typically composed of decade units (such as men 35–44) for radio, and larger units for television (for example, women 18–34 or 25–49), though a category simply called "adults 12 +" is also used (Exhibit 14.8).

In advertising's stereotyped world (see Chapter 9), most products are seen as appealing mainly to specific groups (horror movies for teens, beer for men, denture products for the elderly, and so forth). Thus advertising agencies usually "buy" demographics rather than generalized audiences. Most advertisers would rather have a moderate audience with exactly the right demographics for their product than a huge audience with too many of the wrong demographics.

14.4 Sampling

No matter which research method is used, around-the-clock monitoring of the private listening and viewing behavior of millions of people tuning to thousands of stations and scores of cable channels in more than two hundred markets presents a formidable challenge. The task would be impossible without drastic simplification by means of *samples*.

Sampling to Simplify   The *sampling* process is applied to simplify research in three aspects of ratings: behavior, time, and number of people.

1. *Behavioral sampling.* Individual response to programs can vary over an almost endless range of observable human behavior. Researchers decided years ago that the minimum universal behavioral response that is easiest to measure accurately for ratings is the process of turning on a receiver, selecting a station, and later turning the set off. Each ratings company has adopted an arbitrary span of time (ranging from three to six minutes per quarter-hour) that the set must be turned on to count as being "in use" by an audience member.

This simple *set-use test* leaves out of consideration much that we would like to know about broadcast audiences. It tells us nothing about whether listeners liked a program, whether they understood what they heard or saw, whether they chose the program after considering alternatives or merely passively accepted it because it came on the channel already tuned in, whether some family members imposed their choice on others, and so on. Indeed, the set-use test cannot tell us if anyone is watching at all, let alone paying attention. Receivers are often left on after users leave the room. It is important to realize that most ratings are based on this set-use test, seldom on more revealing assessments of audience behavior.

2. *Time sampling.* The second simplification used in ratings relies on the repetitive daily and weekly cycles of broadcast and cable programming. A sample taken every few weeks or months from this continuous stream suffices for most purposes. As we have seen, only network audiences and a few major-city audiences are sampled daily (§14.2).

3. *Number of people sampled*. The most controversial ratings simplification is the use of only a few hundred people to represent the program choices of thousands or millions of others. To those unfamiliar with sampling, it seems unreasonable to claim that set meters that record tuning in 1,700 homes could be used to assess the tuning behavior of over 234 million people in some 84 million households. Typical sample sizes for three of the major surveys are given below.

• *Arbitron radio market surveys* (diaries placed in each of 214 markets): from about 200 to 3,500 households per market, depending on market size.
• *RADAR national radio network surveys* (telephone calls throughout the country): 6,000 persons.
• *Nielsen national television network surveys* (meters placed in households across the country): 1,700 households.

Random Samples   Sampling works because when members of a population are *randomly* selected to serve as part of a sample, the laws of chance, or *probability*, predict that a relatively small number of people will be representative of the entire population. Major characteristics of the population as a whole will appear in such a sample in about the same proportion as they are distributed throughout the entire population. Audience research is but one of many areas of human study in which a complete census would be impossible, and in which the use of samples thus makes practical and economic sense.

Choosing at random is not as easy as it sounds. The "random" choice of passers-by for street or shopping-center opinion interviews by news reporters is anything but random. For, oddly enough, a high degree of systematic planning has to go into the making of random choices. This is because random selection means that ideally *every* member of the entire population to be surveyed must have an *equal* chance to be selected. This condition is most often met in lotteries in which drawing of numbers is a case of pure *probability sampling*. But sampling from general human populations always involves compromises on ideal randomness.

Sample Frames   For example, drawing a sample randomly from a large human population requires some way of identifying each member of the population by name, number, location, or some other unique distinguishing label. In practice this usually means using either lists of people's names or maps of housing unit locations. Such listings are called *sample frames*. Ratings companies use either updated telephone directories or census tracts (maps showing the location of dwellings) as frames. But such frames never cover literally everybody; besides, they go out of date even before they can be printed.

Nielsen's national sample of metered television households is drawn from U.S. census maps by a method known as *multistage area probability sampling*. This method ensures that the number of sample members chosen from each geographic area will be proportionate to the total population of that area. "Multistage" refers to the fact that, in the process of random selection, areas are successively narrowed down in several steps, starting with counties and ending with individual housing units (Exhibit 14.7). For its market-by-market ratings of stations, however, Nielsen uses special updated telephone directories, as do Arbitron and most other firms engaged in ratings research.

About 97 percent of U.S. households have telephones, making telephone directories the most readily available sampling frames. Directories have drawbacks, however: many listed numbers represent businesses rather than households, and not every residential telephone is listed in a directory. Random digit di-

Exhibit 14.7   Sampling in Practice

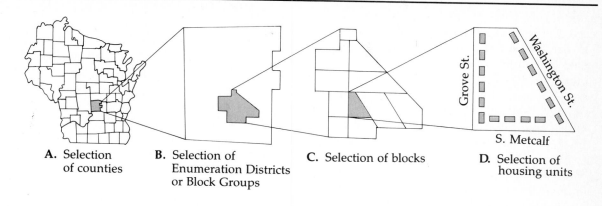

A. Selection
of counties

B. Selection of
Enumeration Districts
or Block Groups

C. Selection of blocks

D. Selection of
housing units

*The four steps shown here demonstrate (a) the selection of the county-size area to be sampled,
(b) the selection of specific districts or blocks within the county from which the sample will be
drawn, (c) the selection of specific city blocks, and (d) the selection of actual housing units
within each block. Basic demographic information in each case is based on official Census
Bureau data.*

Source: A. C. Nielsen Co.

aling can solve the problem of reaching
unlisted and newly installed telephones,
which in a large city amount to between
25 and 40 percent of all telephone-equipped
households.

Sample Turnover   Ideally, each time a
survey is made, a brand-new sample is drawn
so that imperfections in any one sample will
not have a permanent effect. On the other
hand, if the sampling and data-gathering
methods are expensive, it costs too much to
discard each sample after only one use. Nielsen tries to retain each meter household in its
national sample for five years. The company
staggers its contracts with householders, replacing a fifth of the total each year. Thus the
sample constitutes a relatively stable panel of
viewers without becoming completely static.

Choice of Sample Size   The researcher's
next task is to decide how large a sample to

choose. In general, the larger the sample the
higher its reliability. But reliability increases
approximately in relation to the squaring of
sample size (the sample size multiplied by itself). For example, to double reliability requires a fourfold increase in size. Thus a point
of diminishing returns is soon reached, after
which an increase in sample size yields such
small gains in reliability it is not worth the
added cost.

Researchers and their clients therefore
have to balance the degree of certainty desired
against the level of expense involved. At best
sampling yields only estimates, never absolute
certainty. The issue becomes how much uncertainty can be tolerated in a given sampling
situation.

Sampling Error   The built-in uncertainty
of all measurements based on samples arises
from *sampling error*. This term refers not to
mistakes made in gathering data, which are

*non*sampling errors, but to the laws of probability. These laws state that any given sample-based measurement could be equally correct if increased or decreased by a certain known amount. Putting it another way, repeated sample-measurements would vary among themselves, but the chances are that *most*, but probably not all, of the measurements would be *near* the real amount. The *probable* amount of statistical uncertainty in ratings (that is, the amount of sampling error to be expected) can be calculated in advance ("probable" because there is uncertainty even about uncertainty!).

Nonsampling errors arise from a legion of mistakes, both intentional and inadvertent, that produce *bias* in the results. Bias can come from deliberate misrepresentation by respondents as well as from honest mistakes. Researchers may be consciously or unconsciously prejudiced. Both avoidable and unavoidable failures to fulfill sampling designs may occur. The wording of questionnaires may be misleading, and mistakes may occur in recording data and calculating results. Some degree of bias arising from nonsampling error is inevitable when researchers sample large human populations.

Response Rate   Samples are sometimes reported as the number of people (or households) the researcher contacted, but the key question should be how many actually *participated*. The value of a sample is directly related to the number of sample members who actually take part or respond. In practice, a *response rate* of 100 percent is never achieved.

Ratings companies make special efforts to encourage participation of the preselected sample members and to ensure that those who agree to participate actually carry out their assigned tasks. Arbitron, for example, first writes a letter to prospective diary keepers, follows up with a telephone call before and again during the sample week, and offers a small cash payment to encourage sample members to mail in complete diaries. Nielsen makes special efforts to encourage cooperation because the initial cost of recruiting households and installing and maintaining meters is so great. Nielsen encourages long-term cooperation by agreeing to pay half of any receiver repair costs and a small monthly cash payment. Throughout their five-year contracts, "Nielsen families" receive frequent mailings and personal visits from field representatives.

Despite such efforts, nonresponse remains a serious limitation on ratings accuracy. For some age groups, for example, the return rate for radio diaries is very low, and those who do return them may not be representative of the vast majority who do not. One or two diaries can make a crucial difference in final market ratings and shares, both overall and within some age groups, especially in smaller markets. Overall, diary and meter methods yield a usable response rate of about 40 percent, the telephone method close to 75 percent. The number of such usable responses is termed the *in-tab sample*, because they are *in*cluded in the actual *tab*ulations used to produce a given ratings report.

Typical kinds of nonresponse in the chief methods of data collection include:

• *Diaries:* refusal to accept diaries; failure to complete accepted diaries; unreadable and self-contradictory diary entries; drop-off in entries as the week progresses ("diary fatigue"); and failure to mail in completed diaries.
• *Meters:* refusal to allow installation; breakdown of receivers, meters, and associated equipment; telephone-line failures.
• *Telephone calls:* busy signals; no answers; disconnected telephones; refusals to talk; inability to communicate with respondents who speak foreign languages.

Compensations for Sampling Deficiencies   Ratings books contain supplements acknowledging the multiple limitations involved in sampling. Arbitron, for example, lists fourteen limitations in a page-long discussion of criteria for reporting station audiences. The fact is, no company attempts pure probability sampling. Instead, researchers take advantage of the fact that nonrandom sampling can be justified if the degrees and sources of nonrandomness can be identified and controlled. For example, *stratified sampling* ensures that sample members are drawn in such a way as to represent known characteristics of the population in correct proportions. This procedure is possible because prior research, especially the work of the U.S. Census Bureau, has developed considerable national, regional, and local information about populations. Both Nielsen and Arbitron use stratified sampling to match the size of subsamples to the known population of areas being sampled.

A similar corrective is often applied to data after collection. Known biases can be minimized by *weighting* the data — giving extra numerical weight to the information received from certain sample members, corresponding to their known weight in the total population. All ratings services use weighting in an effort to improve the representativeness of their data. But research that uses weighting assumes that what is being weighted is representative of the population being measured. If the data suffer from a high degree of nonresponse, as with some radio diaries in smaller markets, weighting can compound the bias caused by an unrepresentative sample.

14.5 Broadcast Audiences

The cumulative result of years of intensive ratings research is a vast storehouse of knowledge about broadcast listening and viewing habits — surely the most analyzed mass media activity in history. After we have examined broadcast audiences in this section, we will take up cable and newer media audiences in §14.6.

Size Potential   The most fundamental statistic about radio and television audiences is set *penetration* or *saturation*, expressed as the percentage of all homes that have broadcast receivers. This measurement defines the ultimate potentiality of broadcast audience size. In the United States, the penetration of both radio and television has long since peaked at between 98 and 99 percent. Indeed, most homes have several radios and more than one television. In short, for practical purposes it can be said that the broadcast audience *potential* is the entire U.S. population of over 84 million households.

Actual Size   Of course, not all households have their sets turned on at the same time. HUT measurements (§14.3) give an estimate of the percentage of television households in which sets are in actual use. Television viewing climbs throughout the day from a low in winter of about 12 percent of households at 7:00 A.M. to a high of about 70 percent in the top prime-time hour of 9:00 P.M. to 10:00 P.M. Though the advent of cable has not altered these proportions, home video can interrupt both broadcast and cable viewing, making audience measurement more difficult.

Radio listening has a flatter profile, with the highest peak in the morning drive-time hours. Audience levels for television change predictably with the seasons: viewing is highest in January–February and lowest in April–June, reflecting the influence of weather on the choice of indoor versus outdoor activities and hence on audience availability.

In the early years of broadcast television, many observers predicted that as the medium matured and its novelty wore off, the levels of set use would decline. Instead, HUT levels continued to climb. The first hints that the growth curve might have flattened out, or even begun a downward trend, came in the late 1970s. In 1976 a drop in Nielsen network ratings caused a temporary panic, but the drop was not confirmed by other research and in the end was attributed to aberrations in data collection (Hickey, 1976). In 1978 another momentary drop in ratings shook the industry, but again it was explained as more apparent than real.

Nevertheless, audiences are steadily gaining more viewing options. No one seriously doubts that audiences for traditional over-the-air television will be increasingly affected by the growing competition from cable and home video, and possibly other services (§14.6).

Size Stability   "The single most important thing to know about the American television audience," wrote network programming expert Paul Klein, "is its amazingly constant size" (1971: 20). Long-term trends aside, in any particular season of the year people tend to turn on their television sets day by day in the same overall numbers, with no apparent regard to the particular programs that may be scheduled. Expressed in terms made famous by Marshall McLuhan, what matters is the medium, not the message.*

Paul Klein proposed a different terminology, the theory of the Least Objectionable Program (LOP). Half-jokingly, he theorized that people stay with the same station until driven

away by an objectionable program. But even if they find *all* programs objectionable, according to the LOP theory, they will stay tuned in to the *least objectionable* one rather than turning off the set entirely.

This accounts, wrote Klein, for the steady 90 percent of the prime-time audience gathered in by the broadcast networks and the struggle among them, until about 1980, for a 30-percent share or better.* It also explains why seemingly excellent programs sometimes fail (because they are put up against even better programs) and seemingly mediocre programs sometimes succeed (because they oppose even more objectionable mediocrities).

Whatever the reasons, ratings data seemed to confirm that audiences maintained an overall size stability, varying mostly because of changing day parts and seasons, until recently. This constancy of the audience pool forced each network to focus its programming efforts on prying audiences loose from the other two major networks by means of counterprogramming strategies. It was a rare program that forged ahead by virtue of enlarging the total sets-in-use figure; most succeeded only by diverting existing audience members from rival programs.

By the 1980s, however, this static scene had begun to change dramatically. Competition from independent stations, cable channels, and newer services created a more complicated and volatile situation for programmers and audience researchers, especially in prime time.

Tuning Inertia   A corollary of LOP is *tuning inertia*. Whether because of viewer loyalty to a station or network, or more likely because

---

*Canadian communications theorist H. Marshall McLuhan (1911–1980), a cult figure in the 1960s, wrote a series of iconoclastic books about the impact of media on society. The most important statement of his thinking is in *Understanding Media* (1964). There he explained his view that the nature and proliferation of media said more about society than any content carried by those media.

---

*Klein wrote the article in 1971. By the mid-1980s, as discussed in more detail in §14.6, competition from cable and home video recording had eroded the broadcast networks' combined share to less than 80 percent.

of sheer inertia, sets, once turned on, tend to remain tuned to the same station. Usually the proportion of flowthrough viewers (those staying tuned to the same station) is larger than the proportion that flows away to different stations (§11.4). However, remote-control devices and the large number of cable channels have altered this pattern in the 1980s (§14.6).

Tuning inertia characterizes radio, too; in large markets with as many as 40 stations to choose among, listeners confine their tuning on the average to only two or three favorite stations.

Time Spent   Another measure of broadcasting's audience impact is the total amount of time people devote to listening and viewing. This is perhaps the statistic that arouses the most concern among critics of the media as social institutions. Any activity that takes up more time than sleeping, working, or going to school, they reason, surely has profound social implications.

Weekly average viewing per household was over fifty hours in the 1980s — on the order of seven hours a day. Of course, this total represents the sum of viewing by all members of households. As a group, women are the heaviest viewers, followed by children aged 2 to 11. Teen-agers and college students are the lightest viewers. But on the average, all age groups view close to the same number of hours per week; the differences between groups depend more on the accessibility of receivers than on deliberate choice.

Demographic Influences   Averages, however, conceal differences of detail. Demographic influences profoundly influence audience set-use behavior. The following demographic variables, listed here along with examples of generalizations audience research has made (Exhibit 14.8), hold the most interest for broadcasters:

1. *Age.* Among adults, viewing increases with age.
2. *Education.* Viewing decreases with education.
3. *Ethnic origin.* Blacks view more than whites.
4. *Family size.* Large families view more than small families.
5. *Occupation.* Blue-collar workers view more than professionals.
6. *Place of residence.* Urbanites view more than rural dwellers.
7. *Sex.* Women view more than men.

Radio formats, for example, are highly selective in terms of age (§13.10). Contemporary music formats appeal most strongly to people in their late teens and twenties; classical, country, and MOR formats to people in their thirties and forties; and old-time music, news, and talk formats to people in their fifties and older. Interest in radio news and talk formats increases markedly with age.

Among television viewers, more women than men tune to the *Today* show, but more men than women watch the early fringe television news shows. For most sports events, male viewers outnumber female viewers, but nearly as many women as men watch horse racing and tennis. Teen-agers do not care much for sports on television, but NCAA championship basketball games attract a much larger percentage of teen-agers than other sports events.

Demographic differences such as these could of course be predicted without benefit of research, but ratings data help by giving advertisers fairly precise measurements of their actual impact. Advertisers are willing to pay higher prices to reach specific audiences that

Exhibit 14.8   Demographics in the TV Audience

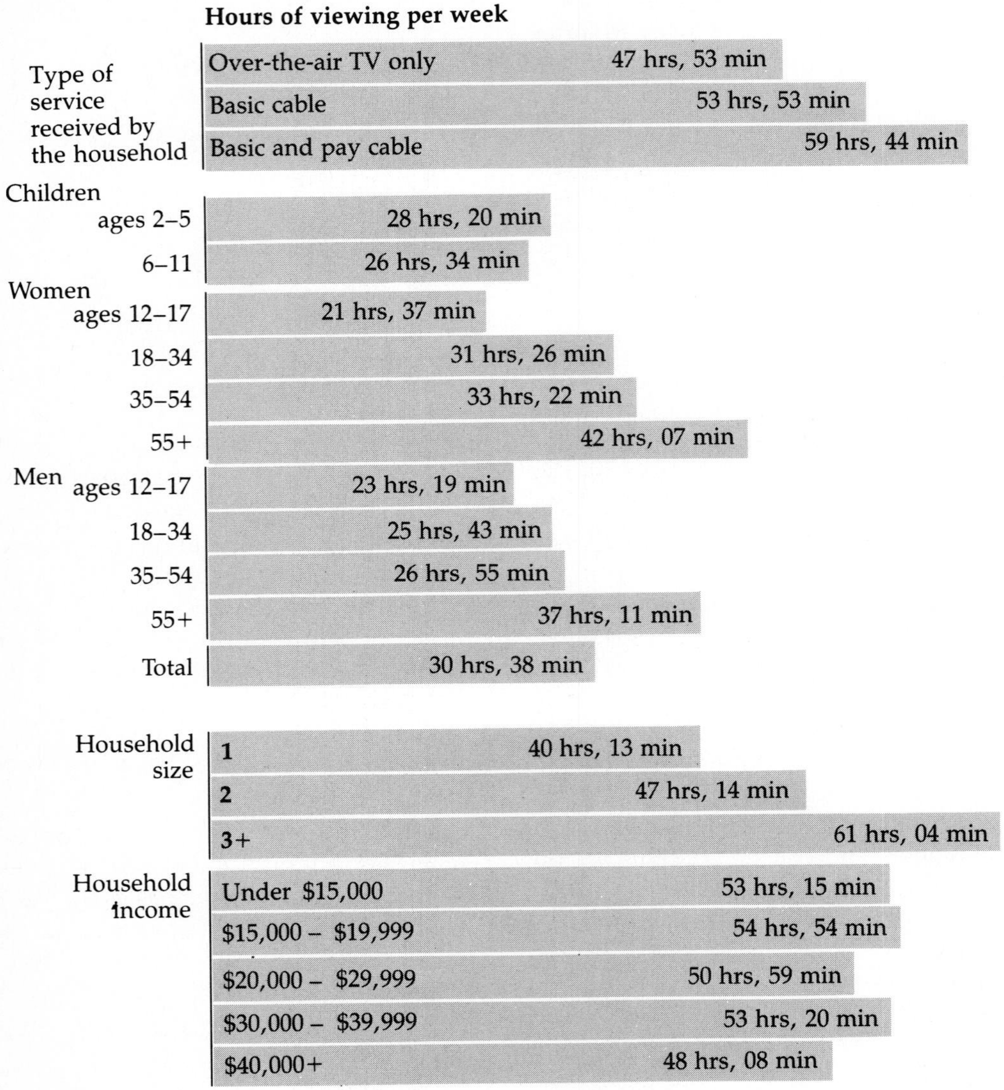

Hours of viewing per week

Type of service received by the household		
Over-the-air TV only	47 hrs, 53 min	
Basic cable	53 hrs, 53 min	
Basic and pay cable	59 hrs, 44 min	

Children ages 2–5	28 hrs, 20 min	
6–11	26 hrs, 34 min	
Women ages 12–17	21 hrs, 37 min	
18–34	31 hrs, 26 min	
35–54	33 hrs, 22 min	
55+	42 hrs, 07 min	
Men ages 12–17	23 hrs, 19 min	
18–34	25 hrs, 43 min	
35–54	26 hrs, 55 min	
55+	37 hrs, 11 min	
Total	30 hrs, 38 min	

Household size		
1	40 hrs, 13 min	
2	47 hrs, 14 min	
3+	61 hrs, 04 min	

Household income		
Under $15,000	53 hrs, 15 min	
$15,000 – $19,999	54 hrs, 54 min	
$20,000 – $29,999	50 hrs, 59 min	
$30,000 – $39,999	53 hrs, 20 min	
$40,000+	48 hrs, 08 min	

Many things affect how much television is watched in the average week, and several are shown here. Note that weekly viewing hours increase with presence of children in home, lower income, pay cable, and age of viewer.

Source: A. C. Nielsen Co.

are measurably more useful to them than undifferentiated audiences. The cost differentials are reflected in CPM (cost per thousand) data (§9.5). The more precisely the target audience demographics are defined, the higher the cost of reaching that audience.

14.6 Audiences for Cable and Newer Media

The development since the early 1970s of additional ways of delivering programming to the home (§4.8) has considerably complicated the researcher's task. Researching cable television audiences is less difficult than studying users of those media that have barely penetrated the market, such as DBS, MMDS, and the various teletext and videotex offerings. The rapid growth of videocassette recorders in American homes may represent the biggest research problem of all.

It is much easier to measure the audience for broadcasting than for these newer electronic media services because:

1. There are a known and limited number of broadcast stations per given market area.
2. Audiences for radio and broadcast television tend to tune in only one or two stations in the course of several hours of attention.
3. Virtually all broadcast research methods now used have been under development for decades and have been fairly well debugged by firms long-established in the field.
4. The financial support for such research — from stations and advertisers — is consistent.

The Research Problem The electronic media vary greatly in terms of audience penetration and appeal. The basic problem for the audience researcher is how to measure the audiences for these newer services fairly and adequately, in such a way that several conflicting needs are met. Among the questions awaiting answers are these:

1. Do audiences for cable differ from those of broadcasting? If so, how?
2. Since cable at any given time offers more choices (channels) than previously, does this larger menu result in more diverse viewing habits?
3. What effect do remote control of channel selection and use of VCRs have on patterns of viewing?
4. Do people devote a fixed block of time to electronic media as a whole, or has the addition of services expanded the time spent? Are the newer services diverting audiences from the old?
5. Can broadcast research techniques be used to measure cable and the newer services, or must new research techniques be devised? If some new method is developed, how then can comparisons be drawn between the new and old services?
6. What standard for cable and VCR audiences can be developed and agreed upon to match the broadcasting standard of HUT?
7. How can such research be supported? Do the recent attempts to measure cable audiences that have foundered for lack of lasting support indicate future failure? Will enough advertisers begin to use cable and the newer services to fund continuing research?

These are merely some of the initial questions facing researchers as they deal with an ever-expanding universe of services to be measured. The answers are readily determined for some aspects of cable viewing. Cable companies know how many households are on the cable (except for signal pirates), and the newer addressable systems can provide automatic measures of how many viewers

Exhibit 14.9   Sources of Household Viewing: 1985

Type of home	Prime-time weekly average ratings*				
	Network-affiliate stations	Other off-air (Public, Independent)	Basic cable	Pay cable	Total weekly TV use†
All TV homes	51	13	4	4	65
Homes with off-air only	53	12	0	0	61
Homes with basic cable	51	14	8	0	68
Homes with basic and pay cable	47	13	8	12	71

*Ratings are for Monday through Sunday, 8-11 P.M.
†Because of simultaneous viewing, totals may be less than the sum of reception sources.

TV viewing is highest in homes with both basic and pay cable service; but network television remains the major viewing element in all TV homes. The networks' shares of household viewing (not shown above) range from 66 percent in pay cable households to 87 percent in homes lacking cable service.

Source: A. C. Nielsen, *Television: 1986 Nielsen Report*, page 14. Figures are rounded.

(though not specifically who) are watching each channel at any given time. But as cable systems grow larger, the problem of evaluating audiences spread across sixty or more channels becomes more complex.

Measures of Penetration   The first steps in measuring any new service are to examine how available it is to consumers and how fast it is developing. Of the newer electronic services, cable has been around since 1948 but is just now reaching half of all homes in the country, though penetration is some markets is naturally much higher. Cable penetration is expected to reach 55 percent by 1990. Compared to broadcasting's potential audience of 84 million households, cable reached about 35 million in 1985.

No other new service even comes close to cable's penetration, nationally or locally; and small penetrations mean small potential audi-

ences and thus limited or selective impact. It seems likely that a number of the so-called new technologies will never become more than that — undeveloped technologies not adopted for lack of consumer interest or response. The failures of DBS and videodiscs in the home market are but two recent examples (§4.8). To be useful, audience research must focus on marketplace success — that is, where the audience is. And for the foreseeable future, the main concern of audience research on new services will be the measurement of basic cable (since many cable channels are advertiser-supported and thus need audience data) and videocassettes.

Timeshifting   The videocassette recorder, a relatively recent consumer product, has had considerable impact. By 1986, VCRs were in 30 percent of all homes in the country. The primary appeal of the VCR is that it

Exhibit 14.10 Use of VCRs

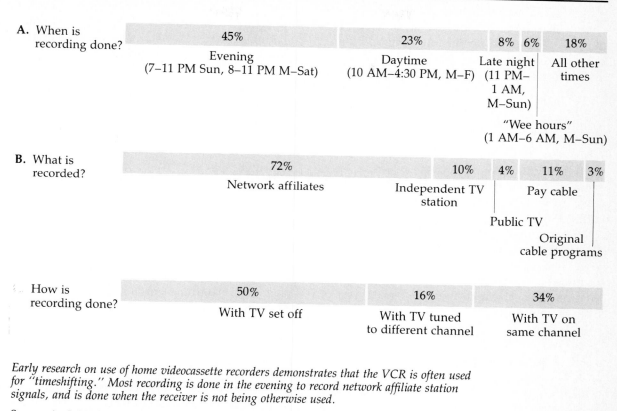

A. When is recording done?

45%	23%	8%	6%	18%
Evening (7–11 PM Sun, 8–11 PM M–Sat)	Daytime (10 AM–4:30 PM, M–F)	Late night (11 PM–1 AM, M–Sun)	"Wee hours" (1 AM–6 AM, M–Sun)	All other times

B. What is recorded?

72%	10%	4%	11%	3%
Network affiliates	Independent TV station	Public TV	Pay cable	Original cable programs

How is recording done?

50%	16%	34%
With TV set off	With TV tuned to different channel	With TV on same channel

Early research on use of home videocassette recorders demonstrates that the VCR is often used for "timeshifting." Most recording is done in the evening to record network affiliate station signals, and is done when the receiver is not being otherwise used.

Source: A. C. Nielsen, *Television: 1986 Nielsen Report*, pp. 12, 14.

enables viewers to control the time at which they watch programs. VCRs are also used for playing rented cassettes and building libraries of cassettes; but timeshifting is their chief use (§4.7).

Nielsen research is summarized in Exhibit 14.10. Since research also indicates that most viewers cut out or "zap" commercials while recording, researchers have a hard time judging not only program impact on the audience but also commercial impact. On the one hand, once a program has been recorded, it may be seen more than one time and by several different viewers; but, on the other, advertisements may be seen only once, if at all.

The problem of measuring audience use of timeshifted material is extremely complex. For example, what kind of audience composition should be credited to a program recorded when no one is at home? How should replays that occur weeks later be counted? And how should multiple replays be handled? These are some of the questions audience researchers must answer (Beville, 1985: 287).

Competition　Of most immediate concern to those in the media industry is the degree to which electronic media services become interchangeable — the use of one substituting for another. Broadcast television network audiences, overall, declined from a high point of about 90 percent of total prime-time viewership in 1975 to less than 80 percent in 1985. Most of the loss is ascribed to audience diversion to independent television stations and basic and pay cable services. Despite the fascination they hold for many, home computers are only a small part of this scene; they figure in only about 12 percent of homes, and their growth pattern appeared to be leveling off by 1985.

Does it make any difference to viewers by which channel their entertainment and news arrive? As a rule, no. Indeed, surveys have shown that many in the audience are not sure whether the channel they are watching is over-the-air, basic cable, or some other mode.

14.7 Use and Abuse of Ratings

Ratings Investigation　Complaints about the reliability of ratings mounted to such a pitch in the early 1960s that Congress launched an investigation: the House commerce committee commissioned a study of the statistical methods used in ratings research. Issued in 1961, the Madow Report stated that critics of ratings were putting too much emphasis on sample size and that more emphasis should be put on improving research methods and determining the significance of nonresponse (House CIFC, 1961, 1963–1965). While Congress conducted its hearings, the Federal Trade Commission made its own investigation. The FTC ordered the ratings companies to account for noncooperation in sampling, to cease making misleading claims about sampling, to cease mixing data from incompatible sources, and to cease using arbitrary and often

unspecified "adjustments" on research findings. One unexpected result of all this government activity was that in 1964 Nielsen stopped measuring radio audiences; most of the complaints had concerned the radio sample, which was already a money loser.

Industry Self-Policing　One industry response to the barrage of criticism was to set up the Broadcast Rating Council in 1964 — which in 1982 became the Electronic Media Rating Council, or EMRC — as an independent auditing agency representing ratings users. The EMRC accredits specific ratings services that meet its standards and submit to annual auditing. EMRC also ensures full disclosure of methods in ratings reports (Beville, 1981, 1985). Nowadays, the ratings services withhold from public scrutiny only some details of the way they edit the raw data they collect from diaries and meters.

But this does not mean that criticism has ceased. Today's complaints focus on such problems as the persistent failure of stations and networks to acknowledge the factor of sampling error, the tendency to underrepresent segments of society most difficult to sample, and the station practice of trying to inflate ratings during sweep weeks by means of program-scheduling tricks.

Reliability of Ratings　Perhaps the major misunderstanding about ratings is the tendency to think of them as precise measurements, rather than merely *estimates*. Users of ratings tend to act as though differences of even fractions of a rating point have crucial significance, when in fact sampling error makes such precision impossible. Even repeated measurements of programs over time can only slightly reduce sampling error, not eliminate it.

It is important to keep in mind that ratings by their very nature can give us only limited information about audiences — and give it with only limited certainty. Hugh M. Beville, Jr., a former head of the Broadcast Rating Council, gives four warnings that every ratings user should heed (Beville, 1985):

1. Ratings are approximations.
2. All ratings are not equally dependable.
3. Ratings measure quantity, not quality.
4. Ratings measure [set use], not opinion.

Validity of Ratings   *Validity* in research refers to the degree to which research data actually measure what they purport to measure. Ratings purport to measure the *entire* broadcast audience, but in practice they can only account for the broad middle-range majority of that audience. People at ethnic, economic, and geographic extremes are less likely to be solicited by, or cooperate with, ratings services than people in the middle range. Thus ratings tend to underrepresent the very rich, the very poor, and ethnic minorities. In recent years, both Arbitron and Nielsen have made special efforts to persuade minority respondents in their samples to participate fully.

The fact that television ratings are based on households rather than individuals also affects validity. About a quarter of today's households are occupied by lone individuals with lifestyle (and therefore, broadcast use) patterns that quite often differ from those of multiperson households. And the viewing habits of households with small children are quite different from those of all-adult households. Also, residents of group quarters such as college dormitories are omitted from household samples altogether, much to the distress of stations in college towns.

Tampering and Hypoing   The ratings system is vulnerable to tampering, because if the viewing habits of even a few sample households are influenced, there can be a substantial impact on the resulting ratings. Thus, the identity of sample households is a closely held secret. Still, there have been a few cases of outright manipulation of viewers, causing ratings services to junk reports for some programs, and even entire station or market reports for a given ratings period.

A far more widespread industry practice known as *hypoing* also skews ratings. Hypoing is the deliberate and overt attempt by stations or networks to influence ratings by scheduling extraordinary programming and promotional efforts during ratings sweeps (§14.1). Although both the FTC and the FCC have investigated hypoing, little can be done about it. In fact, the effects may balance out, since most stations do it. Television hypoing involves jamming attractive programs and movies into prime time during ratings sweeps. Radio stations hypo with listener contests. Stations feel compelled to play the hypoing game because their competitors do. No one can afford a bad drop in ratings levels, even if it is artificially induced.

Qualitative Ratings   Ever since the need for high ratings began to dominate programming strategies, critics have argued that the present ratings system encourages mediocrity by emphasizing sheer size, to the exclusion of *qualitative* aspects of programs. Time and again, programs seemingly of above-average quality receive enthusiastic reviews and substantial audience followings but fail to meet the rigid minimum-share requirements for commercial survival. Critics question whether a program that is merely tolerated by a very large audience should automatically win out over a program that attracts a smaller, but intensely interested, audience. Yet this is what the quantitative ratings approach decrees: the system favors the "least objectionable" programs over the best possible programs.

In Britain and some other countries, broadcasters are required to conduct research on qualitative aspects of their programs and to take audience preferences into consideration in program decision-making (§1.9). That may be one reason so many Americans find British television programming more appealing. For a number of years, U.S. public broadcasters have worked to establish a qualitative ratings system. Noncommercial broadcasting must, by virtue of its very nature as an alternative system, find evidence to support the need for its tax-supported services, which have strong appeal to a limited number of people. But thus far, U.S. commercial broadcasters have shown interest in only a very limited type of qualitative ratings research, aimed at measuring the likeability of performers.*

There seems to be little prospect that the rule of numbers as determined by household set-tuning will be soon replaced as the primary force controlling the choice of commercial programming. Generating continuous ratings is an extremely costly business; the stations and users that invest in the ratings system demand answers that are as simple, as clear-cut, and as nearly irrefutable as possible.

14.8   Nonrating Research

Definition   Nonrating research probes into the subjective reasons behind predicted as well as past audience behavior. It tries to find out what people like and dislike, what interests and bores them, what they recognize and remember, and what they overlook and forget. For this subjective approach, investiga-

---

*Market Evaluations, Inc., regularly estimates ratings for images projected by major performers, based on national samples of a thousand families. From mail questionnaires, the firm constructs both familiarity and likeability ratings (the two do not necessarily coincide). The same company conducts the better-known TvQ (or TV Quotient) research on popularity of specific programs. This qualitative rather than quantitative research uses questionnaires to determine the level of program appeal to different demographic groups.

tors usually use *attitudinal* research methods, which reveal not so much people's actions (in this case, set use) as their *reactions* — their *reasons* for action, as revealed in their attitudes toward programming.

Commercial attitudinal research often makes no attempt to construct probability samples, because its purpose is usually not to make quantitative estimates of behavior projectable to entire populations. Instead, investigators choose respondents informally, assembling small panels of *focus groups* from which to gain insights about people's motivations.

Concept Research   Program *concept* research, for example, tries out ideas for programs. A small group's reactions to a one-page program description can help programmers decide whether to develop an idea further, change some of its details, or drop it entirely. Concepts for commercials are often tested early on, before final commitments to full production costs are made. These tests may simply involve presentation of graphic storyboards, or they may employ *photomatics*, videotaped versions of the original storyboards with camera effects and sound added to make them look and sound something like full-scale commercials (Arlen, 1979).

Program Analysis   To test new or changed programs, and to foresee their probable impact, researchers show characterizations and potential casts in pilot versions to small sample audiences. People watch, give their reactions, and sometimes discuss the reasons for their attitudes with a session director. These discussions are frequently videotaped so writers and others can study the reactions further.

Minute-by-minute reactions to a program can be processed by a *program analyzer*, a device first developed in the 1940s that enables test-group members to express favorable, neutral, or unfavorable reactions by pushing one of several buttons at regular intervals on cue. The machine automatically sums up the reactions of the entire test group, furnishing a graphic profile. A follow-up discussion can then probe for explanations of changes in audience interest at given moments in a script.

Theater vs. In-Home Testing   The motion picture industry has long used theater previews to gauge audience response. Several firms specialize in staging similar theater previews of television programs and commercials. Tests of advertisements are usually disguised as tests of programs, the commercials seeming to be only incidental. Viewer reactions are gathered by questionnaire or discussion.

All such staged previews have the disadvantage of being conducted in an environment quite different from the home. Cable television has introduced a testing method that allows a more realistic approach, enabling researchers to test viewers in their normal surroundings, using their own receivers. One research firm owns several small cable systems that it uses for research on commercials. One group of subscribers receives one version of test materials, while a second group gets a different version. The company asks the subscribers to keep diaries of their purchasing, thus giving concrete evidence of the influence commercials have on actual buying behavior.

Physiological Testing   Most methods so far described depend on self-analysis by panel members. In an attempt to eliminate this element of subjectivity and to monitor responses more subtly, researchers have identified a number of involuntary physical reactions that are clues to audience response. Among the reactions that have been measured for this purpose are changes in brain waves, eye movements, pupil dilation, breathing, pulse rate, voice quality, perspiration, and sitting position (the "squirm test").

For example, a number of researchers have capitalized on the well-known fact that the human brain is two-sided. Each side has its own specialized functions and reacts to different stimuli. For example, reasoning ability seems to be centered in the brain's left side and emotions in the right. It follows that commercials for products whose appeal is primarily emotional should, if correctly oriented, stimulate the right side of the brain more than commercials whose appeal is based mainly on logical considerations. Commercials shown to viewers wired for brain-wave recording can be tested to find out if they elicit the desired brain-wave responses.*

Test Markets   Test markets are realistic devices for appraising the effectiveness of advertising, but their use is complicated. Researchers select two or more markets, distant from each other but well matched demographically. Each market then views a different version of a proposed national advertising campaign carried either on a broadcast television station or a cable channel. Researchers judge the effectiveness of each local version by its influence on actual product sales. They measure sales by keeping track of the physical movement of goods in the market or (more easily) by using direct marketing in which the product is offered only through broadcast or

---

*In the 1950s, there was a flurry of interest in so-called *subliminal* advertising. Such ads were simple messages of a word or two flashed on the screen so briefly as to be unnoticed consciously. But these subliminal messages were shown to have an unconscious impact when theater audiences began to buy greater quantities of popcorn or other foods mentioned in the messages. Fear of widespread use of this means of advertising—a type of thought control—on unsuspecting audiences led to pressure against the strategy, and the FCC ruled against it.

cable advertising and only in response to mail or telephone orders.

Research on Children   Several companies specialize in analyzing children's likes and dislikes and how they influence adult purchasing decisions. It is well known among marketers that children can have an impact on what brands or products adults will buy. One research firm gains insight into children's preferences and motivations by turning a group of kids lose in a miniature supermarket. As the children go on a shopping spree, researchers secretly observe and record their behavior. This kind of research is not widely publicized, both to keep the results confidential and to avoid criticism for taking what some would term unfair advantage of children (Chagall, 1977).

Audience Response   Although broadcasting is generally a one-way medium, every telephone call or letter to a station, network, or advertiser about programs or commercials provides additional audience response, or information, to the medium. Indeed, voluntary mail from listeners was the first source of audience information back in the 1920s. But people who write or call a station are not statistically representative of the entire audience, and can thus give very misleading impressions. Research has shown that letter writers differ significantly from the general population in terms of race, education, income, type of job, age, and marital status — all differences important to advertisers and programmers (McGuire and LeRoy, 1977). Further, it is all too easy to motivate letter-writing campaigns for or against a given point of view or service.

For these reasons, stations do not take telephone calls as seriously as the more systematically gathered ratings. But a few strong letters of complaint, especially if they differ from one another and are not merely copies of a sample provided to the writers, do get attention, since broadcasters and advertisers know that a few complaints of a focused kind probably represent a sizable number of dissatisfied listeners.

Summary

• There are two kinds of applied audience research: studies that generate program ratings and studies that pre- and post-test programs or advertising.

• Audience research methods for electronic media differ from research methods for print media circulation, because electronic audiences are much more difficult to count than print media readership.

• Ratings measure audience size in both local and national markets. The most commonly used market delineation is the Area of Dominant Influence.

• Arbitron and Nielsen are the two important national ratings research companies. Arbitron performs only local market surveys for both radio and television, and Nielsen performs national and local market surveys for television only.

• Data for ratings are usually gathered by written diaries, meters attached to sets, telephone calls, or a combination of these. A new method that may largely replace the older approaches is the use of people meters. Each method has its particular strengths and weaknesses.

• Ratings are percentages that estimate the proportion of the total possible audience tuned to a particular program. These data help in developing HUT (households using television) and audience-share statistics. When audiences are small, as in the case of radio, cumulative data can be used to show the aggregate reach of a program over a period of days or weeks.

• In addition to showing audience size, ratings can supply information on audience composition in terms of sex, age, and other demographic characteristics.

• Ratings make use of three kinds of sampling: behavioral sampling (usually set tuning), time sampling (most measures are made periodically, not continuously), and number of people sampled (all ratings are based on relatively small, representative cross-sections of populations).

• Accurate sampling requires the use of sample frames, the systematic random selection of sample members for representativeness, the fulfillment of sample design (sufficient response rate), and the avoidance of bias. Because sampling inevitably falls short of this ideal, there is a probable range of error in the results.

• Within given time frames, the size of the broadcast audience is remarkably stable, with audience members tuning from station to station or channel to channel rather than turning sets on and off.

• Ratings provide a reasonably accurate picture of broadcast audiences as long as the rather severe limitations on their accuracy and significance are kept in mind.

• Although there is little commercial demand for them thus far, qualitative ratings that measure the degree to which people like programming would be a desirable supplement to the present quantitative ratings system.

• The development of audience research for cable and new electronic media is still in its early stages. Among the problems this kind of research faces are the large number of channels available, the rising use of nonbroadcast material on home VCRs, and multiple channels using the same material.

• Nonrating research is widely used to test commercials, programs, and the popularity of performers both during program planning and after production. Such research generally relies on small focus groups, probing the reactions of test subjects for personal motives and attitudes.

• One major problem in nonrating research is artificiality in the test environment; cable television can provide researchers with an ideal setting in the home in which to conduct certain kinds of subjective research.

CHAPTER 15

Social Consequences

The consequences of the media for individuals and society are only beginning to be understood in the 1980s, and considerable controversy surrounds what is known. In this chapter we examine a selected inventory of electronic media consequences,* those that are generally regarded as both significant and relatively verifiable. Electronic media have such varied and widespread impacts that a complete survey would be endless. Moreover, such a survey would be complicated by the impossibility of isolating the contribution of any one medium from other influences.

Media are imbedded in the fabric of our society. Communication, like housing, food, clothes, and transportation, is essential to our lives. To study media, we must artificially extract them from their imbedded state within society, and then construct notions such as

content, exposure, and effects to evaluate them. These give us a way of seeing what is otherwise invisible. Most of the media consequences discussed in the sections that follow have many contributing causes that interact in complex and sometimes hidden ways within the broader social process.

Research on the impact of media has usually focused on the medium of greatest importance at the time the research was done. There is thus a good deal of audience research on film and radio from the period between 1930 and 1950. Television has dominated the research agenda in the decades since, but although a great deal has been published on the "effects" of television, much of it has repeated work done on earlier media. We begin here with a brief discussion of the theoretical underpinnings of that television research, and follow with a selective inventory of findings.

15.1 Approaches to Research

Analysis of the role of electronic media in society has involved a constant search both for the "right" methods and a framework within which to place the results. The lack of agree-

---

*Observers speaking of the consequences or impact of media often talk about their *effects*. The term *effect* indicates a fairly specific relationship between two things or events. The term also suggests *cause*, but, as we shall see, little media research can pinpoint media as the sole and specific cause of societal or individual behavior. In this chapter we will use all of these terms, just as the research does. But we do not thereby imply cause-and-effect relationships unless specifically noted.

ment on either point has contributed to constant ferment among researchers and constant rethinking of what we think we know.

Need for Unifying Theory   Traditionally, a science develops general laws that support an overarching *theory* of the phenomena in that field. Some fields in the social sciences are working toward similar explanatory theories. But although many theories have been put forth to describe the process and effects of communications, thus far no universally recognized unifying theory of mass communication has emerged to give systematic coordination to investigations or to account for the impact media have on individuals and society. Despite this, research on these phenomena goes on at an accelerating pace.

Research about media has tended to cluster around certain ways of looking at the *process* of communicating. Media researchers increasingly feel that emphasis on process, rather than a search for laws, may yield the most useful results. In the 1980s, a number of *models* of how mass communication works have received close attention. A model is essentially a diagram that expresses the phenomena or elements of interest, the roles they are assumed to play, and the nature of their relationships. We will examine three quite different models — the effects model, the uses-and-gratifications model, and the accommodation model — as examples of the extensive theoretical work now going on that seeks to provide the all-important context for research on media consequences.* The point is not that one of these models is right and the others wrong. Rather, all theory has a purpose and must be understood from the perspective of that purpose. Theories, and their support-

ing models, are used to describe processes from an expressed viewpoint, or with a focused purpose in mind. Taken together, the different approaches provide varied ways of assessing the same phenomena.

Effects Model   In fairly traditional media *effects* research, the model is quite direct.

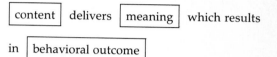

Much is assumed here, however. Perhaps most important is the notion that media content acts in isolation from other societal influences. In addition, the model appears to indicate that content has a direct causal relationship to end behavioral results.

Joseph Klapper summarized the status of effects theories in his book *The Effects of Mass Communication*, after studying the findings of more than a thousand research reports done up to 1960. He concluded that ordinarily communication "does not serve as a necessary and sufficient cause of audience effects, but rather functions among and through a nexus of mediating factors and influences" (1960: 8). Up to that time, research had failed to support popular beliefs about the effects of mass communication. The media could persuade people to buy products, the research indicated, but not to change their political allegiances, or to adopt a new religion.

Media managers welcomed this conservative conclusion, called the "law of minimal effects," because it gave apparent scientific sanction to the industry's rejection of consumer arguments that programs could be blamed for causing antisocial behavior.*

---

*The authors are indebted to Dr. James Anderson of the University of Utah for suggesting this approach to us, and for his advice throughout this first section.

*In fact, CBS was so pleased that it hired Klapper to conduct social research for the network, which he did — in a quite neutral scientific fashion — until his death in 1984.

During the 1970s, the opinion of many researchers began to shift away from the minimal-effects concept, largely because of intensive research conducted on the effects of violence in media (§15.7). As the authors of a 1981 review of research put it, the 1970s "witnessed a revival of the view that the mass media exert powerful influences on the way people perceive, think about, and ultimately act in their world" (*Annual Review of Psychology*, 1981: 308).

But this shift in opinion did not mean a return to the primitive hypodermic-injection effects model of the 1920s. Contemporary researchers tend to avoid talking about effects as such, for the very word implies an oversimplification of what is now understood to be an extremely complex process. Researchers prefer to speak in terms of associating certain inputs with certain outputs. They avoid going so far as to imply the simple, straightforward cause-and-effect relationship indicated by the effects model. One authoritative research team summed up the current view on effects in typically cautious language:

Science cannot tell us conclusively whether television violence contributes to serious crime because its methods are too imperfect. It can empirically test hypotheses whose confirmation or disconfirmation alters the probability that such a proposition is true and verify the consistency of observed fact with such a proposition. Conclusions of a grander sort depend on judgments about the acceptability of various assumptions and the risk of error that is tolerable. Consequently, the argument that there is no conclusive scientific evidence on this and other broad causal relationships is not impressive. The wrong question is being asked. (Comstock et al., 1978: 3)

Uses-and-Gratifications Model   In recent years, some researchers have focused on the *uses-and-gratifications* research approach. Note that in this model the emphasis is more on process than on content.

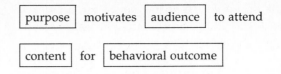

Here we are concerned more with how individual audience members use media content — specifically, what their purpose is in viewing or listening to media. The consequences or impact of media are assessed in terms of what media do *for* audiences rather than what they do *to* audiences. According to the uses-and-gratifications model, people use the media in different contexts, and thus researchers need to understand the process of media use as well as the varied functions of people–media interactions.

To contrast the effects and uses-and-gratifications approaches, consider the changing behavior of politicians, as discussed further in §15.5. Politicians no longer criss-cross the country by train, making speeches to small crowds at every whistle stop. They now reach massive audiences across huge distances, all at once, by using electronic media. The speech style of pretelevision politics was apparently too long-winded and boring to make effective use of the medium. So campaigns and political conventions appear to have been totally reshaped to meet the needs of the all-important microphone and camera. Did television's capacity to deliver mass audiences change political campaigns (the effects approach), or did politicians decide that reaching mass audiences instantaneously was a better campaign strategy, thus bringing about changes in the mode of audience contact as a side effect (the uses-and-gratifications approach)?

The chief gratifications audiences get from electronic media are entertainment and escape, of course, although these are complex notions. One of the landmark analyses of television audience attitudes found that most of the people surveyed were more satisfied with television as a *medium* than with specific programs. Remarkably, respondents agreed that the medium is relaxing but is also a waste of time (Steiner, 1963: 411). The same conflicting attitudes prevailed two decades later (Bower, 1985). Television fulfills different roles for different users. At various times and for various groups, it serves as an information source, medium of relaxation and entertainment, topic of conversation, means of socialization, prime way of defining the rhythm of the day and week, and companion. Each of these uses helps to define the impact the medium has in a given circumstance.

Early researchers failed to give adequate attention to the role of entertainment, the major element in media content and thus in audience time (§15.6). This led one critic to comment: "Ironically the concept of entertainment and its functions seems to have no place in empirical media research and was relegated to the critics and analysts of popular culture" (Katz et al., 1974: 13). One reason for this failure to recognize the full importance of media's entertainment function (and hence for serious underestimation of the role of broadcasting) was the influence of government funding for studies concerned with how media affected opinion formation in the political realm. Thus research focused on *news* programming almost exclusively. Another reason was that few researchers adopted the broad stance of media specialists who had an interest in the entire range of media content, effects, and processes. In recent years, this neglect of a major aspect of electronic media content has been rectified somewhat, especially because of greater interest in the effects of violence, stereotyping, and advertising on children.

For the mass audience, electronic media answer the compelling question of what to do to fill what might otherwise be an unendurable void. Boredom is neither an exceptional

nor an inconsequential state of mind in modern culture. It is a by-product of the economic and social changes that have freed much of mankind from the bondage of the personal struggle for the bare necessities of life. What to do with surplus time has become a major preoccupation of our culture. The media give people a way of occupying their leisure time.

Accommodation Model   A third theoretical model describing the role of media in society takes what some call an *accommodation* approach. More than the first two models, this one places the communication process in a broad context.

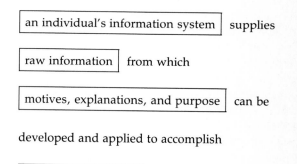

an individual's information system   supplies

raw information   from which

motives, explanations, and purpose   can be

developed and applied to accomplish

behavioral outcomes

This is a more complicated model than the effects and uses-and-gratifications models, but it is also far more realistic. The media are seen here as but part of an individual's information system — one among many factors that interact to bring about specific behavioral outcomes. Note the importance of what the individual brings to the process of using electronic media. The individual's information system consists of, among other things, his or her own experience, interpersonal contacts, and content material presented in the media. Experience and interpersonal contacts heavily color the way all of us learn from and make use of media.

15.2 Methods of Studying Consequences

The People Problem   In designing research projects to study media effects, investigators face the frustrating problem of accurately describing how people react to media, and why. Many effects consist of *subjective responses* beyond the reach of direct observation and measuring instruments, such as human attention, understanding, learning, likes and dislikes, and opinion formation. Some of these effects do produce observable physical clues — for instance, brain waves and other involuntary signals (§14.8) can be detected — but these signals usually reveal little about subjective experiences in human terms.

Even when media effects emerge as overt, observable responses, a subjective link is nevertheless still involved. In tracing the sequence of events from media cause to behavioral effect, researchers lose the trail when it disappears into the subjective consciousness of the people being studied. What goes on inside the human brain certainly influences the final outcome, but it cannot yet be directly studied by the researcher.

For these reasons, most research on effects depends in whole or in part on questioning people about their subjective experiences rather than observing their reactions. Self-reporting, however, is not altogether reliable. People may be unwilling or unable to tell the truth about their inner experiences; or they may be willing but forgetful, or unaware of their own subconscious motivations. Furthermore, listening and viewing are usually private acts, occurring in all sorts of situations in which the intrusion of an outside observer is not feasible. Consequently, data gathering, whether based on self-reporting or direct observations, almost always introduces an element of artificiality, referred to in the research literature as *intrusiveness*.

Investigators account for the problem of subjective response by using four major strategies in effects research: sample surveys, content analysis, laboratory experiments, and field studies. There are many variations of these, such as field experiments, plus some lesser-used strategies. Analysis of a sample of studies published in major communications journals shows that sample surveys were used in 55 percent of the studies, content analysis in 13 percent, laboratory experiments in 10 percent, and field studies or field experiments in another 10 percent (Lowry, 1979). Qualitative research using ethnographic methods accounts for less than one percent, but this is a growing area, especially for studies of new technologies. Each of the strategies varies in terms of the extent of its reliance on human subjects, its degree of intrusiveness on those subjects, and its cost.

Sample Surveys   The research strategy most familiar to the general public is the sample survey, used in opinion polls and audience rating reports. We noted earlier (§14.4) how such surveys can estimate characteristics of entire populations through use of very small random samples. An additional advantage, as with ratings, is that data are gathered in the settings in which listening or viewing normally takes place. As pointed out in §14.4, commercial rating services use sample surveys to measure behavioral effects of the most basic and objective kind: set tuning, without reference to the effects of actual listening or viewing that may ensue after the set is on. Sample surveys thus tell us nothing about the *causes* of tuning. This is the major weakness of the survey strategy generally: "causal inferences typically are not permitted" (Comstock et al., 1978: 493).

Content Analysis   Researchers using content analysis examine and summarize the content of communication materials (programs, commercials, films, and so forth), describing and quantifying whatever features particularly interest them. Television programming is so bewilderingly massive and varied that the mind boggles at even talking about it without the help of summarizing categories. When we speak of public affairs, news, soap operas, situation comedies, and so on, we are using the broad categories of content analysis as descriptive shorthand.

We also are interested in content details that reveal what electronic media are saying or implying about various subjects. Are minorities portrayed in predominantly inferior roles? How much and what kinds of violence occur in entertainment shows? Who are the victims and the aggressors? Do such content dimensions as these change significantly over time? We are concerned about these kinds of details because we at least suspect that their presence in the media has consequences.

Conducting a content analysis may seem a fairly easy matter of carefully defining the content items to be counted, drawing a representative sample, and finally counting the occurrences of the designated content items in the sample. But in practice it is by no means easy to agree on how to define the relevant content items; and interpretation of the results is even more controversial.

The "Violence Profile" developed by George Gerbner and his associates provides one practical example of these problems of definition and interpretation (§15.7 and Exhibit 15.6). The profile is based upon annual analyses of violent content in samples of network entertainment series. CBS challenged the Gerbner data on several grounds (Blank, 1977). For example, CBS objected to putting comic violence, accidents, and natural disasters in the same category as intentional human violence enacted in a serious context. But the Gerbner team responded that comedy can be used to convey serious lessons and that violence in different contexts is still violence (Gerbner et al., 1977). The disagreement went much further, touching virtually every aspect of definition and analysis, with neither side convincing the other.

Another problem is deciding where the content categories to be studied and compared should come from. Traditionally, researchers have applied their own ideas of meaning to television programming, personal conversations, and other communications. This means that researchers are interpreting the message, when in fact they may misunderstand, or, more commonly, fail to perceive, the entire content that comes from context — the private history and set of circumstances experienced by a viewer that no researcher can see.

Laboratory Experiments   Regarded as the classic strategy for conducting behavioral research, laboratory experiments enable investigators to control various experimental factors precisely and to exclude extraneous events and influences. Both subjectively reported and objectively observed data can be derived from such experiments.

For decades, the most popular experimental variable used in studying communication was *attitude change*. Briefly, the method works as follows: a group of people is tested for current attitudes on a given topic. The experimenter then exposes them (either in a face-to-face talk or via a recording) to a persuasive message on that subject. A second test then determines if any change in attitude has occurred.

One trouble with this approach is that attitudes measured in a laboratory situation do not always govern real-life actions. People often say one thing but then do another. This discrepancy has been noted in differences between expressed television program preferences and actual television viewing.

Moreover, lab experiments put people in artificial situations that bear little resemblance to the complex situations in which they actually experience the mass media.

Field Studies   Research projects done in more naturalistic settings, known as *field studies*, attempt to observe behavior in the real world without intruding into the situation or influencing the participants. In studying the impact of violent programming, for example, field-study researchers observe children in their normal home or school environment rather than moving them into a lab setting.

A pioneering field study of television impact was held in Chicago in 1951, after President Truman had recalled General Douglas MacArthur from his command in the Korean War. The general returned to a series of welcomes in cities across the country. Researchers selected a "MacArthur Day" parade in Chicago for their study, and compared reactions of live viewers on the street with those of a group of television watchers. The differences were striking: the event appeared far more crowded, dramatic, and emotional as portrayed on television than when seen live on the scene. The contrast between the on-the-scene version and the television version showed how television affects the apparent nature of reality, an inevitable result of the production process. Television conveyed a more unified version of the Chicago parade, laden with added meanings often missed on the spot. "The selectivity of the camera and the emphases of the commentary gave the televised event a *personal* dimension, nonexistent for the participant in the crowd" (Lang and Lang, 1984: 45).

Some researchers believe that only by long-term participation in a situation can they come to understand the behavioral consequences of the media in particular situations. For them, the real meaning of, say, a violent scene on television has to do with how a particular viewer uses what he or she sees, not with what the producer and director thought they were saying, or what critics interpreted the scene to mean, or what researchers perceived the scene to have communicated. Children adapt television to their fantasy play; adults selectively borrow phrases from television to use in arguments; teens copy from music videos with little regard for a song's words. According to this viewpoint, meaning resides in the user's interpretation of television and other media, and thus there are countless variations of "impact," depending on each person's private context. Such field studies attempt to uncover some of these layers of meaning in order to understand more fully the complexity of human behavior.

Field Experiments   A compromise between the tight controls and artificial context of the laboratory experiment and the unstructured naturalism of the field study can be achieved in *field experiments*. Here, researchers set up situations for testing in field, or real-life, situations. However, these experiments cost a great deal in time and effort to arrange, and some of their methods can be just as questionable as those used in laboratories. Thus they are comparatively rare. An unusual study funded by CBS illustrates the problems inherent in field experiments.

At the request of researchers, CBS produced three different endings for an episode of a prime-time dramatic series called *Medical Center*. One version showed a theft of money followed by punishment of the offender; the second version showed the same act without punishment; and the third (or control) version showed no criminal behavior. In each of three test cities, the audience saw one of the three versions at the series' regularly scheduled time. To test whether the versions showing criminal behavior had any effect in terms of causing similar behavior, a sample of audience members in each city were recruited by means of an offer of a free radio they were said to have "won." Winners were asked to come to a certain address to pick up their radios. There, they were briefly left alone in a room with a conspicuously full charity donation box similar to the one shown in the television episode. Some of the respondents in each group stole money; but the researchers found no significant differences between the groups. About as many thefts were committed by those who had not seen the crime on television as by those who had. CBS spent half a million dollars to pay for the experiment, which seemed to show only that crime on television had little perceptible effect, as there were so many people *already* disposed to commit crimes.

15.3 Consequences of Advertising

No consequence of broadcasting and cable, the two advertiser-supported electronic media, is more subject to measurement and manipulation than the immediate effects of advertising. Advertisers demand results. But our concern here is with the broader, long-range social consequence of advertising rather than with its immediate business applications as discussed in Chapter 14.

Advertising as Subsidy   It is often noted that advertising plays a useful social role by reducing the direct costs of media to the public. In the case of electronic media, for example, advertising appears to pay the entire cost of the service (except for pay cable and other viewer-supported services). This view is misleading, however. Consumers eventually pay the full cost of media, because advertising expenses are included in the final prices of con-

sumer goods and services.* In addition, as noted earlier (§10.1), audience members have to purchase, operate, and maintain radio and television sets. This public investment, combined with the fact that broadcasting uses the publicly "owned" frequency spectrum (§16.1), gives the consumer more equity in radio and television than in other media. Cable exacts a triple price, adding a subscriber fee to advertising and receiver costs.

Synthesizing Wants   Does advertising impose a penalty on consumers by generating a desire for unnecessary purchases — what economist John Kenneth Galbraith terms the *synthesizing of wants*? Clearly, electronic media advertising can stimulate widespread demand for goods and services for which consumers had no prior need. Advertising can build overnight markets for often useless products or "new and improved" versions of old products. For example, automobiles change little from year to year, but advertising stimulates consumers to replace cars only a few years old with flashier new models.

Power of Advertising   Critics often assume that advertising can overcome almost any defense a consumer can muster. Advertising practitioners find themselves wishing it were only so. The failure of a high proportion of new products each year hardly supports the assumption that advertising is all-powerful. Examples of advertising failures are the Edsel car of the 1950s, Corfam (synthetic leather) shoes of the 1960s, and possibly the "new"

---

*Although this hidden subsidy is distributed widely and weighs lightly in any individual purchase, its cost per person over a number of years is substantial. In this sense, advertising is a more equitable way of charging the public for a broadcast service than the set-use license fee widely used abroad (§1.7). In countries with license fees, many set users evade paying fees, unfairly increasing the burden on those who do pay.

Coca-Cola drink formula of the 1980s. All these products were supported by intensive research and marketing tests, were backed by established firms (Ford, DuPont, and Coca-Cola, respectively), and were pushed by massive advertising campaigns.

Not only do many products fail to catch on, but leading products often give way to competitors, despite intensive advertising support. The transfer of *brand loyalty* is a well-recognized marketing problem — and opportunity. In fact, much television and radio advertising is designed simply to keep brand names visible and viable in the marketplace.

Advertising to Children   All we have said so far about advertising assumes that its targets are rational adults. Commercials in children's programs raise special issues of fairness and equity (§9.7 and §12.5). Children start watching television before age four, and they find commercials just as fascinating as programs. In fact, one of the major concerns of Action for Children's Television and other such consumer organizations is that commercials take unfair advantage of young children not yet able to recognize the purpose of advertising, or indeed that advertisements are not part of programs themselves.

Another major issue is that most commercials aimed at children urge them to consume sugared foods and beverages. One study quoted by the FTC staff examining the issue in the 1970s counted over 7,500 network food commercials aired during daytime weekend children's programs throughout the first nine months of 1976 (excluding ads for fast-food outlets). Of these ads, half promoted breakfast cereals and a third pushed candy, gum, cookies, and crackers. The staff concluded that the FTC had ample authority to ban such advertising. But the recommendation galvanized industry lobbyists and eventually precipitated a Congressional crackdown on the FCC, which

quickly gave up the idea of banning children's television advertising.

Other studies were conducted at about the same time by the FCC's Children's Television Task Force (FCC, 1979) and by a panel of experts funded by the National Science Foundation (Adler et al., 1980). The five-volume study by the FCC group reported that some progress had been made during the 1970s in eliminating selling by program hosts and in cutting back on commercial time in children's programs. The task force recommended encouraging alternative nonbroadcast sources of entertainment for children. This recommendation was in keeping with the emerging deregulatory trend; instead of forcing the industry to change its practices by regulation, the FCC began to rely instead on the pressure of competition to achieve policy goals.

The National Science Foundation (NSF) panel analyzed twenty-one existing research studies and concluded that still more study of children's television habits was needed. More specifically, it found that parents generally overstate the degree of control they have over what and how much their children view, and also overestimate their children's understanding of commercials. In addition, the NSF found no evidence linking televised food commercials to children's food consumption.

15.4 News Impact

Since most people in the United States are known to depend primarily on television for news (Roper Organization, 1985: 3), it seems safe to assume that this category of programming has important effects. Presumably, most of us perceive the world beyond our neighborhoods pretty much the way the electronic and print media present it to us.

Gatekeeping Only a tiny fraction of the events that occur in the world on any given day end up on our plate as "the news of the day." On its way to becoming the neatly packaged tidbits of the evening news, the raw material of events passes through the hands of many *gatekeepers*. Some open and close gates deliberately, deciding which events to cover in which places and how stories should be written, edited, and positioned in the news presentation. Some gatekeeping is inadvertent, the result of the accessibility of news events and the availability of transportation or relay facilities. Some is institutional and some ideological. Network news, for example, has been described as being:

shaped and constrained by certain structures imposed from without, such as government regulation of broadcasting and the economic realities of networks; certain uniform procedures for filtering and evaluating information and reaching decisions; and certain practices of recruiting newsmen and producers who hold, or accept, values that are consistent with organizational needs, and respect others. (Epstein, 1973a, 43)

Thus media profoundly affect the material they transmit, both deliberately and inadvertently, in the very process of transmission.

An example of involuntary gatekeeping is the elementary fact that television demands pictures. This tends to bias the medium toward covering events that have intrinsic visual content, despite the fact that much news is not inherently pictorial. Effects of visual bias in television news include (1) a preference for airing stories that have good pictures and (2) a forced effort to illustrate nonvisual stories with essentially irrelevant stock shots, as when scenes of bidding on the floor of the stock exchange are used to illustrate a story on financial trends. However, computer-based graphics have enabled video news to visualize nonpictorial stories more easily. Animated symbols, charts, and other "visuals" can be

Exhibit 15.1   60 Minutes

The top-rated CBS Sunday evening news magazine program stars journalists (clockwise from front): Diane Sawyer, Ed Bradley, Mike Wallace, Harry Reasoner, and Morley Safer. Stories on 60 Minutes *have considerable impact simply because of the program's popularity and its role as an agenda setter.*

Source: Courtesy of CBS.

counted on to illustrate stories lacking visual impact of their own.

Agenda Setting One example of the filtering and shaping process of gatekeeping is the control exerted over which subjects will be presented to audiences. Gatekeeping focuses our attention temporarily on specific events, persons, and issues temporarily in the news. The list changes frequently as old items drop out and new ones claim attention. This overall process of selection and ranking, termed *agenda setting*, is regarded as one of the primary ways media affect our perception of the world.

A related effect is *prestige conferral*. The very fact that an event appears on the current news agenda gives it an aura of importance. Well-known anchors and correspondents lend glamour and significance to the events and persons they cover. Commenting on how television coverage has exaggerated the importance of the state primary elections that come earliest in national political campaigns, former presidential news secretary Ron Nessen pointed out that television acts as a kind of giant megaphone, capable of greatly amplifying the significance of some events (Nessen, 1980). If the story were not important, would Dan Rather, Tom Brokaw, and Peter Jennings be covering it?

In 1984 and 1985, television helped focus U.S. and world attention on starvation in Africa. The drought-caused human disaster had been building for two years before a BBC film team's report appeared on a November 1984 NBC *Nightly News*. The grim scenes of Ethiopian refugees, soon repeated on other television news programs, created a public outcry that vastly increased the aid effort. In mid-1985, "Live Aid," an unprecedented satellite-fed marathon of sixteen hours of rock music from England and Philadelphia, seen in more than eighty countries, led to promised contributions of some $75 million dollars. In both cases, television opened the gate and set the agenda for expanded aid efforts.

Media News Staging   Television's need for images creates an ever-present temptation to enhance the pictorial content of news stories artificially. Even when news crews make no move to provoke reactions, the very presence of cameras in tense situations tends to escalate ongoing action. After their experience covering the urban riots of the 1960s, networks and many stations adopted written guidelines for their news personnel that aimed at minimizing the effects of cameras at scenes of public unrest. Even so, legitimate exercise of news judgment in the process of editing can raise awkward problems for conscientious broadcasters. News documentaries are prone to charges of bias and of tampering with the facts. Selective editing has been described as deliberate misinterpretation; encouraging people to express opinions has been construed as sensationalism; and selecting cases to illustrate a theme has been called deception (F. Smith, 1974).

As a practical matter, a certain amount of artifice is accepted as permissible in news coverage. In televised interviews, for example, cameras generally focus on the interviewee the entire time. Shots of the interviewer are taken afterward and spliced into the interview, to provide a visual give-and-take. This allows a single camera and a smaller crew to cover interviews. The FCC recognized the need for this kind of latitude in rejecting claims that the networks had staged fake news stories at the riot-plagued 1968 Democratic national convention in Chicago:

In a sense, every television press conference may be said to be "staged" to some extent; depictions of scenes in a television documentary — on how the poor live on a typical day in the ghetto, for example — also necessarily involve camera direction, lights, action instructions, etc. . . . Few would question the professional propriety of asking public officials to smile again or to repeat handshakes while the cameras are focused upon them. (16 FCC 2d 656, 1969).

Pseudoevents Staged by News Subjects
Outright staging of events by the *subjects* of news occurs when press agents and public re-

lations counselors seek to "plant" information in the media or to create happenings designed to attract media coverage. Daniel Boorstin (1964) coined the term *pseudoevent* to describe these contrived happenings, analyzing the many forms they take, such as press conferences, trial balloons, photo opportunities, news leaks of supposedly confidential information, and background briefings (in which information is released anonymously, "not for attribution"). But not all preplanned events deserve condemnation. When a newsworthy figure such as a president is involved, a certain amount of ceremonial event-making is expected. The events that deserve the term pseudoevent are deliberate attempts to disguise fabricated nonevents as genuine news. Organizations interested in maintaining a favorable public image constantly churn out self-serving material in the guise of news. Government departments no less than private organizations exploit pseudoevents.

Conscientious broadcast news departments avoid using self-serving news handouts. But free *news clips* are a tempting money saver for stations short on photographic material. These short items supplied by business and government public relations departments contain pictorially interesting material in which the real message is unobtrusively buried. For example, a dramatic sequence of helicopter shots showing offshore oil drilling that could be used to illustrate an energy story might just incidentally name the company engaged in the drilling. Or a film about high-school training in auto mechanics might happen to feature students working on a particular make of car (Kiester, 1974). Use of such free clips is widespread at smaller stations, though it is widely criticized.

Publicity Crimes   News staging for self-publicity took a vicious turn when terrorist organizations began committing crimes for the purpose of gaining coverage in the news. Ever more common in the 1980s, these events of seemingly random violence against often innocent third parties are acts usually perpetrated by small and desperate political or religious groups seeking world attention. Such *publicity crimes* are paradoxical blends of pseudoevents and real events. Bombings of airport terminals, hijackings, and kidnappings, the most common kinds of terrorist stories, pose difficult ethical dilemmas for the news media. The very act of reporting a publicity crime transforms the media into accomplices in the crime; and the avidity with which the public awaits the latest news about it makes members of the public accomplices as well.

Publicity crimes reached bizarre new heights with the taking of American hostages in the Middle East — American embassy personnel in Iran in 1979, and TWA airline passengers in Beirut in 1985. The Iranian episode lasted 444 days and contributed to the demise of the Carter administration. American broadcasters had never before faced such a news dilemma. Every time they showed footage of street rallies with Iranian marchers burning American flags, or of hostages paraded before cameras to mumble transparently grudging "praise" for their captors, the American networks gave the terrorists priceless publicity.

But the pressure to air every scrap of footage and information about the hostages in both cases was almost irresistible. In the seventeen-day standoff in Beirut six years later, newscasts developed every possible angle of the story, including seemingly intrusive interviews with hostage families. Intense network competition for viewers led to heavy emphasis on the crisis. Even before it finally ended, a hue and cry went up that television's unselective coverage encouraged future terrorist action by providing an unedited forum for terrorist views. The media appeared captive to terrorist manipulation of the story. Airing of options and military planning in the Beirut case led some to argue that television was making a difficult situation worse by providing the terrorists with advance knowledge of what the United States might do in response to their actions.*

Effects on Subjects of News Coverage

Media coverage of the celebration over the return of the Iranian hostages in 1981 and of those from Beirut in 1985 raised questions about the effects of media coverage on those returning. Some critics even speculated that the overwhelming barrage of media attention might cause more psychological trauma than the imprisonment itself.

In less unusual situations, media coverage undoubtedly does affect news subjects. For example, many people featured in *60 Minutes* reports have ended up paying fines or going to jail after on-camera exposure by reporters such as Mike Wallace (Kowet, 1979). Though in these cases the coverage itself did not cause the penalties, the cameras and reporters did call attention to the subjects' earlier actions in compelling fashion. In other news events, people appear to be playing to the cameras by acting more for television than for the event television is covering (Exhibit 15.1).

More widespread but also more ambiguous effects may occur when people become the subjects of other types of coverage. For example, for years cameras and microphones were banned in virtually all courtrooms (§18.2). The ban was based on the assumption that (1) broadcast coverage would affect the

behavior of witnesses, lawyers, and defendants, and that (2) these effects would be detrimental to the judicial process. Experience has suggested, however, that the effect is minimal, especially after the novelty of the coverage has worn off.

Three factors account for this minimal effect. Equipment is smaller and less obtrusive than when the ban was established in the 1930s. Broadcast crews are more professional and more sensitive to the need to avoid disruption. And society has become more tolerant, even expectant, of broadcast access to official activities. Increased public access has been specifically mandated by *sunshine laws* (which require many official bodies to meet in public) and the *Freedom of Information Act* (which mandates access to many types of government information formerly withheld from public scrutiny).

These changes suggest that although coverage has effects, the effects may not be as unfavorable as at first supposed. There is reason to believe that with long exposure, camera subjects eventually accept the equipment and crew as a normal part of their environment.

15.5 Consequences for Political Life

Crisis Management   In times of crisis, open communication allays panic and eases the stress of transition. The electronic media, with their immediacy and instant national scope, can play a vital role in managing crisis situations.

The first great test of television's role in such a crisis came in November 1963 when President John F. Kennedy was assassinated in Dallas. Canceling commercials and commercial programs for "the most massive and the most concentrated broadcasting coverage in history," the networks won praise for com-

---

*Later, the news media revealed that they had in fact shown restraint in not disclosing certain U.S. countermoves, but criticism centered largely on the indiscriminate relaying of news conferences staged and controlled by the terrorists.

petence, sensitivity, and dignity in handling the crisis (*Broadcasting*, 2 Dec. 1963).

Since then, the media have risen to the occasion of other national crises with equal distinction. For example, the broadcast networks covered the historic House Judiciary Committee hearings on impeachment charges against President Richard Nixon in full in the summer of 1974. For 54 days, they rotated the assignment day by day. It was the first time the House had permitted television coverage of any of its committee hearings, and the experience helped pave the way for full television coverage of House activity, as discussed later in this section.

Election Campaigns   Almost from its beginning, broadcasting has exerted a powerful influence on political campaigning. Radio speeches by Calvin Coolidge, whose low-key delivery suited the microphone, were believed to have been one factor in his 1924 reelection. Radio became especially important to Democratic candidates because it gave them a chance to appeal directly to voters, going over the heads of the newspapers, most of which were controlled by Republicans. Franklin Roosevelt used radio masterfully in his four presidential campaigns.

Television brought Madison Avenue sales techniques to the presidential campaign of 1952, when a specialist in the hard-sell commercial, Rosser Reeves, designed spots for Dwight Eisenhower. The commercialization of political campaigns has increased ever since. By 1968, when Richard Nixon won the presidential election, television had become the most important factor in political campaigning.

Since 1968, national party conventions have been completely restaged to make them more effective as television programs. Timing is now worked out to the second, with a certain number of minutes allowed for so-called spontaneous demonstrations for specific candidates. Little is left to chance; it has been years since there was much doubt about who would be nominated in a national convention.

In recent years, televised debates between presidential candidates have stolen the spotlight from the conventions as campaign highlights. This tradition began with the confrontation between candidates Kennedy and Nixon in 1960, made possible by a special act of Congress that exempted their televised appearance from the equal-time law (§18.6). Often called the "Great Debates" (though they were, in fact, neither), these contests may have decided that close race. Exhaustive research suggests that Kennedy came across to viewers as more precise and visually crisp than Nixon (Rubin, 1967). After the Kennedy–Nixon debates, presidential debates lapsed for sixteen years, mainly because the incumbent president usually would not agree to face his opponent. Then, in 1976, President Gerald Ford faced Georgia governor Jimmy Carter, and the challenger won the election. A pattern seemed to be established four years later when President Jimmy Carter agreed to debate Ronald Reagan, and once again the incumbent lost. But the pattern changed in 1984, when President Reagan faced Walter Mondale and went on to win a landslide reelection. The debates themselves, of course, did not work alone to these ends. In 1984 it was widely believed that Reagan lost the first debate with Mondale but came back much stronger in the second, recovering the momentum of his campaign.

Given the undoubted power of television to influence the outcome of campaigns, it might seem a foregone conclusion that candidates with the most money to buy the most time and the best media consultants would inevitably win elections. But elections have shown that the candidate with the greatest access to television does not always win. One reason may be that television provides cover-

Exhibit 15.2   Televised Election Debates

Nationally-televised presidential debates have become common features of campaigns. Top, Kennedy debates Nixon in one of four confrontations in 1960, with Howard K. Smith as moderator. The next debate came 16 years later when Carter debated Ford. Middle, Carter debates Reagan in 1980. Bottom, Mondale debates Reagan in the first debate of 1984. The format has changed over a quarter century, but not as much as one might expect.

Sources: CBS News photo; World Wide Photos, Inc.; UPI/Bettmann Newsphotos.

age of two different kinds, that of advertising and public relations, and that of news and public affairs. Bona fide news and public-affairs programs about candidates have a credibility that can never be attained by 30-second advertising spots and candidate-controlled appearances.

The impact of television coverage of presidential campaigns is perhaps most controversial on the evening of national election days. For two decades the debate has gone back and forth as to whether early television reports of voting trends have an adverse impact on voters in states where polls are still open. Does a presidential candidate's concession of defeat early in the evening (eastern standard time), or victory projections broadcast on national television before polls close in western states, keep people who live on the West Coast from bothering to vote? Many members of Congress have felt this is the case, despite the lack of definitive research findings either way (Tannenbaum, 1984). Though the networks have been defensive on this point, citing lack of any consistent research that supports this stand, they agreed in 1985 not to air predictions of a state's results until after the polls in that state had closed.

Presidential Television   After the campaign is over, the elected American president enjoys almost insurmountable advantages over political opponents in exploiting the media. Other branches of government and members of opposing parties can apparently do little to counterbalance the influences of *presidential television*. Presidents have endless opportunities for manufacturing pseudoevents to support their policies or to divert attention from their failures. No matter how clearly news editors sense that the president or the president's staff is exploiting them, they dare not ignore presidential events, for virtually everything the head of state says or does has inherent news value.

One familiar presidential diversionary tactic is to make a foreign trip to visit other heads of state. President Kennedy is said to have been the first to capitalize on this ploy: "The farther he was from Washington, the less he was seen as a partisan political figure and the more he was viewed as being President of all the people" (Halberstam, 1979: 316). President Nixon's several overseas trips at the height of his domestic Watergate troubles were clearly an attempt to achieve the same status. But the approach can backfire. When President Reagan went to Europe in 1985 for the 40th anniversary celebration of the end of World War II, his visit to a German war cemetery created huge controversy. The overall purpose of his trip was obscured by public reaction to the cemetery visit.

The single most powerful weapon an incumbent chief executive has is the option to call upon all the networks to provide simultaneous national coverage of a presidential address (Exhibit 15.3). Development of cable news networks has added to a president's impact, since they add yet another means of delivering the message. Such an event gives the president a gigantic captive audience — a virtual monopoly of access to perhaps 80 percent of the potential viewers. Moreover, opinion surveys suggest that such exposure usually pays off in increased acceptance of presidential policies (Rutkus, 1976: 18).

Nothing requires the networks to defer to such presidential requests for time, and indeed it was not even customary for the networks to do so until President Lyndon Johnson's administration. During the 1966–1975 period, presidents experienced only a single refusal in forty-five requests for simultaneous television time. Thereafter, perhaps because of the Nixon administration's Watergate troubles, network news divisions began to evaluate such requests more critically. In 1975, only ABC carried an address by President Ford on the economy; and in 1978, CBS turned

Exhibit 15.3   Presidential Television

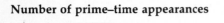

Number of prime–time appearances

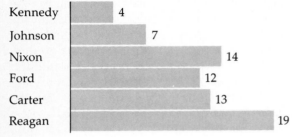

Kennedy	4
Johnson	7
Nixon	14
Ford	12
Carter	13
Reagan	19

Hours of prime–time airtime

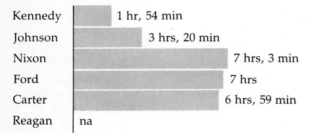

Kennedy	1 hr, 54 min
Johnson	3 hrs, 20 min
Nixon	7 hrs, 3 min
Ford	7 hrs
Carter	6 hrs, 59 min
Reagan	na

The rising importance of television access is evident in these figures (which cover the first 19 months in office for Kennedy, Johnson, and Nixon; the first 15 months for Ford; and the first 25 months for Carter and Reagan). These include both news conferences and other appearances.

Source: Christopher H. Sterling, *Electronic Media: A Guide to Trends in Broadcasting and Newer Technologies, 1920-1983.* New York: Praeger, 1984, p. 177.

down coverage of an address by President Carter on the Panama Canal treaties.

Ronald Reagan, perhaps the most effective user of preplanned broadcasts since Franklin Roosevelt in the 1930s, has made notably effective use of broadcast time to gain public (and thus congressional) support for his policies. In the 1980s, Reagan continued his long-established use of radio, recording a

weekly address for Saturday airing, the content of which was often widely reported in other media.*

At the same time, Reagan's staff has increasingly isolated the White House from probing reporters. All recent presidents have been accused of hiding behind their staffs and venturing out only in controlled media-covered affairs, such as White House "photo opportunities" for still and television cameras, at which questions are not allowed. By using network television effectively for set speeches and limiting access by reporters (who might ask probing questions) the Reagan administration has strengthened presidential television.

Congressional Television   The failure of Congress to take full advantage of television can be explained in terms of personalities and the effects of the generation gap. During the years when television was developing, Congress was dominated by older men such as House Speaker Sam Rayburn. Rayburn had no love for the press. When handed a petition from journalists asking that radio and television be allowed more access to cover the House, Rayburn simply muttered an obscenity and tore up the paper. The lack of television coverage diminished the impact of the House. Congress was televised only when the president came to address a joint session: "Then the congressmen could be seen dutifully applauding, their roles in effect written in by the President's speech writers" (Halberstam, 1979: 250).

The Senate, unlike the House, allowed television coverage of its committee hearings (subject to committee chair approval) in the early 1950s, leading to some notable television

---

*In keeping with the Fairness Doctrine (§18.4), stations airing the president's weekly radio addresses gave equivalent time to representatives of the Democratic party to reply. Symptomatic of the incumbent's advantage, Reagan's talks received much more notice than those of his opponents.

coverage.* The first coverage of a House committee came only in 1974, when the Judiciary Committee debated the Nixon impeachment resolution. But for decades neither house allowed broadcast coverage of its general sessions.

In 1966 Congress began to use television to challenge the president's advantage. That year, Senator William Fulbright, chairman of the prestigious Foreign Relations Committee, boldly began to question White House policy on the Vietnam War in televised hearings before his committee:

Television in the beginning had trivialized both the debate and the forces involved in Vietnam. It had confirmed the legitimacy of the President, made his case seem stronger than it was, and made the opposition appear to be outcasts, frustrated, angry, and rather beyond the pale. The Fulbright hearings gradually changed this balance. Like the Ervin [Watergate] hearings some seven years later, they were the beginning of a slow but massive educational process, a turning of the tide against the President's will and his awesome propaganda machinery. . . . From that time on, dissent was steadily more respectable and centrist. (Halberstam, 1979: 506)

Although the Senate led the House in opening committees to live broadcast coverage, the reverse was true when it came to allowing coverage of actual sessions of Congress. Bills to authorize radio coverage of House debates had appeared since 1941. Approval for radio and television coverage finally came in 1979, but the House refused to let outsiders run the show. It established its own closed-circuit television system, run by House employees, inviting broadcasters to plug into the system at will. Unenthusiastic about coverage they do not themselves control, commercial broadcasters use only occasional excerpts of House debates. Cable subscribers, however, can see gavel-to-gavel coverage on the C-SPAN cable network.

House coverage became briefly controversial in 1984 when television cameras began to pan the House floor during speeches when theretofore they had focused only on the podium (§12.7). This was a political ploy ordered by the Democratic House leadership to embarrass Republican speechmakers delivering addresses for home consumption — to a virtually empty House chamber. The flap that ensued showed both the importance of the coverage and the danger of allowing politics to enter into decisions on who and what to cover. Despite such episodes, which set back efforts to gain television access to Senate proceedings, the overall favorable record of House television encouraged the Senate to allow full-time coverage. In 1978 it experimented with live radio coverage, when National Public Radio carried some 300 hours of debate on the Panama Canal treaties. Only in 1986 did the Senate first experiment with, and then finally approve, regular television coverage of all floor sessions. Congress has finally achieved a degree of video parity with the White House.

Television's First War   Radio broadcasting played a highly supportive role in helping to build both civilian and military morale during World War II (§3.4). Television's first experience of war came with the Vietnam conflict (the Korean War occurred early in the 1950s, when television news was in its formative years). The impact of television on this "living room war," as it was dubbed by *New Yorker* critic Michael Arlen, was far from entirely supportive. It considerably influenced national morale and government policy, though the

---

*The 1951 televised crime hearings catapulted Senator Estes Kefauver onto the Democratic ticket in the following year's presidential campaign. The 1954 Army–McCarthy televised hearings led to the censure of the Wisconsin senator by his colleagues and to the end of McCarthyism. Investigation of Teamster Union officials began with Senate hearings in 1956–1957, showing in a very active role a young government attorney named Robert Kennedy.

Exhibit 15.4   C-SPAN

(Left) Then Speaker of the House Thomas "Tip" O'Neill opens another session of U.S. House of Representatives floor debate as carried live by the public affairs network of the cable industry. Cameras are controlled by the House, but the full-time coverage is available to all. (Right) In 1986, C-SPAN opened a second channel to cover the U.S. Senate — though the chamber was often nearly empty during debates.

Source: Nan M. Gibson/C-SPAN

ultimate dimensions of its impact have yet to be clearly defined.

David Halberstam, who won a Pulitzer Prize for his work as a war correspondent in Vietnam, supports the thesis that television had a decisive impact on the course of the war: "The war played in American homes and it played too long" (Halberstam, 1979: 507). In total, this longest war in United States history played in living rooms for fifteen years. CBS sent its first combat news team to Vietnam in 1961, and news photography of the final evacuation of Saigon, showing desperate pro-American Vietnamese being beaten back as helicopters lifted off the landing pad atop the U.S. embassy, came in 1975. During the height of the war, each network maintained its own news bureau in the field, with each

bureau sending back two or three photographic stories and eight or ten radio tapes daily. In addition, many individual stations assigned reporters to the scene.

During the earlier years of the Vietnam War, coverage tended to be "sanitized," stressing U.S. efficiency and might and playing down the gore and suffering of actual combat. Little military censorship had been imposed, as it had in all previous wars, but public relations was uppermost in the minds of the generals, who went to great lengths to obtain the kind of optimistic coverage expected by the administration back home.

A new, more violent phase of news coverage came as a result of the 1968 Tet offensive, which brought fighting to the very doors of the Saigon hotels where correspondents were staying. At that point, broadcast news coverage turned to the realities of war. Vietnam became a real war in American living rooms, not the sanitized war of military public relations. Analyzing the contradictory images of war projected by television news, critic Edward Epstein wrote in *TV Guide:*

It is no doubt true that television was to a large extent responsible for the disillusionment with the war, as those in the media take relish in pointing out. But it is also true that television must take responsibility for creating — or at least, reinforcing — the illusion of American military omnipotence on which much of the early support of the war was based. (13 Oct. 1973: 54)

During the Tet offensive by the North Vietnamese, several events combined to strengthen U.S. opinion against the war. For one thing, Walter Cronkite of CBS reported negatively on the war after a visit to Vietnam (David Halberstam reported that it was the first time a war had been declared over by an anchorman.) Loss of Cronkite's support for the war solidified President Lyndon Johnson's decision not to run for reelection. At about the same time, two especially vivid photographic images from the battlefields became icons of American disillusionment. Correspondent Morley Safer was responsible for one, a film showing an American Marine holding a Zippo lighter to the straw of a Vietnamese hut, starting a fire that leveled 150 homes in the village of Cam Ne. The second image was that of a South Vietnamese general calmly shooting a suspected Vietcong sympathizer in the head, during the 1968 Tet offensive. (Exhibit 15.5).*

---

*Controversy over the war and its coverage was revived a decade later when General William Westmoreland, once U.S. commander in Vietnam, brought suit against CBS for a *60 Minutes* report alleging a cover-up in reports of enemy troop strength (Exhibit 18.1). After a prolonged and heavily reported libel trial, the general dropped the case. By not pursuing his charge to the end, Westmoreland lost his after-the-fact battle for public opinion (§18.2).

Exhibit 15.5   Televised War

While some film coverage of Korea and other conflicts was carried on American television, the war in Vietnam was televised nightly for more than a decade. Development of television and satellite technology made live coverage possible by the early 1970s. Two famous visual images of the war stand out years later — both taken from televised stories carried on evening network newscasts.

Sources: Courtesy of CBS; Wide World Photos.

More Wars   Broadcasting's role in the Vietnam conflict raised troublesome questions about what part it should play should the United States again become involved in overseas fighting. Could the military afford to allow television to bring home, night after night, the horror of war? The 1983 terrorist bombing of a U.S. Marine barracks in Beirut raised this issue. After U.S. television covered the aftermath of the bombing, which had killed some 240 Americans, the continued "peacekeeping" role of the Marines in Lebanon lost domestic support and became politically untenable. The United States pulled out of the area shortly thereafter.

On the other hand, if the military imposed tight censorship on television coverage, as did not happen in Vietnam, would the U.S. public blindly support a war it was prevented from seeing? The U.S. invasion of the Caribbean island of Grenada in 1984 suggested not. Military authorities enforced a tight news blackout for two days after U.S. forces hit the beach and mopped up what little resistance they encountered. Press reports and public opinion about the affair were decidedly mixed. The Grenada experience led the Department of Defense to set up plans for a news pool arrangement to allow for coverage of future military actions.

The Reagan administration's opposition to the Sandinista regime in Nicaragua, and the guerrilla fighting in several Central American countries, served as a testing ground for television's journalistic maturity in the 1980s. Considerable controversy surrounded coverage of these conflicts. New Right politicians claimed that television was weakening the effort to gain U.S. support for "freedom fighters"; others, remembering Vietnam, said that television's coverage might serve to keep the country out of another prolonged, undeclared conflict.

15.6 Entertainment

Entertainment, as well as news and public-affairs programming, tends to play an agenda-setting role. It is safe to predict that any big news story that holds the headlines for any length of time will soon turn up as the subject of a special program or miniseries and will influence future episodes of established entertainment series. Docudramas (§12.2) are especially striking evidence of this tendency. Moreover, to the extent that docudramas change the facts around to suit the needs of drama, they add still more distortions to the already simplified version of reality perceived by broadcast audiences.

Stereotypes   Fiction influences audience perceptions by reinforcing *stereotypes*, which are versions of reality deliberately oversimplifed to fit in with preconceived images. Examples of stereotypes are the stock characters of popular drama: the Italian gangster, the inscrutable Oriental, the mad scientist, the bespectacled librarian.

Even authors capable of more individualized and realistic character portrayals resort to stereotypes when writing for television, in order to save time — both their own and that of the medium. Stories must be told with the utmost efficiency to fit them into the confines of half-hour and hour-long formats (minus time-outs for commercials, of course):

Television dramas have little time to develop situations or characters, necessitating the use of widely accepted notions of good and evil. Since the emphasis is on resolving the conflict or the problem at hand, there is little time to project the complexities of a character's thoughts or feelings or for dialogues which explore human relationships. To move the action along rapidly, the characters must be portrayed in ways which quickly identify them. Thus the character's physical appearance, environment, and behavior conform to widely accepted notions of the types of people they represent. (U.S. Commission on Civil Rights, 1977:27)

Stereotypical images on television help to establish and perpetuate those same images in the minds of viewers. As the U.S. Commission on Civil Rights put it, "To the extent that viewers' beliefs, attitudes, and behavior are affected by what they see on television, relations between the races and the sexes may be affected by television's limited and often stereotyped portrayals." The commission was careful not to state flatly that such effects always occur, but it called for research to assess the extent to which they do occur.

World of Fiction   When researchers take a census of the characters in a body of television plays, they find that demographic characteristics of the fictional population invariably differ markedly from the characteristics of people in the real world. Compared to life, the world of fiction has far more men than women, for example. Most of them are young adults, with few very young or elderly persons. Many have no visible means of support, but those who do work have interesting, exciting, action-filled types of jobs. Fiction therefore contains an unrealistically higher proportion of detectives, criminals, doctors, scientists, business executives, and adventurers than does the real world, where most jobs are unglamorous, dull, and repetitive. Most people in the real world solve their personal problems undramatically, even anticlimatically or incompletely, using socially approved methods. Fictional characters are much more likely to solve their problems with decisive, highly visible acts, often entailing violence.

All of this is to be expected, of course. Fact may be stranger than fiction, but fact does not occur in neatly packaged half-hour episodes, with periodic commercial interruptions.

Socialization   Nevertheless, the make-believe world of radio and television serves as a model of reality for countless people, especially for children at the very time when they are eagerly reaching out to learn what the world is all about. Those too young to read, those who never learned to read or to acquire the habit of reading, and those who have little access to printed sources of information and entertainment all depend heavily on radio and television to inform them of the world outside their own immediate surroundings.

Dramatic fare is especially influential, because viewers and listeners identify with heroes, participating vicariously in their adventures. Research indicates that young children are especially vulnerable. They tend to believe what they see on television, making no distinction between fact, fiction, and advertising. The proportion of believers is higher among disadvantaged children than among those whose lives contain more opportunities. It is also higher among black children than white.

Given the enormous amount of time most children spend watching television, this means that broadcasting has become a major agent of *socialization* — that all-important process which turns a squalling infant into a functioning member of a society. Socialization is enormously complicated and is a lifelong process, but much of it occurs in the first few years of life when a child begins to learn the language, the meticulously detailed rules of behavior, and the value system of his or her culture.

In the past, socialization has always been the jealously guarded prerogative of family and religion, formalized by education and extended by peer-group experiences. The intrusion of a new, external agent of socialization represents a profound change. Of course, broadcasting is part of national culture, too, but it comes from beyond the immediate circle of the family and its community-linked supports. It imports ideas, language, images, and practices that may be alien to the local culture.

Just what effects the intrusion of broadcasting into socialization has or might have is the subject of much research and much debate. The effects could of course be both good (*prosocial*) and bad (*antisocial*). Such programs as *Sesame Street* and *Fat Albert and the Cosby Kids* were researched and designed with prosocial effects in mind. Follow-up research indicates that such programs do in fact succeed in achieving prosocial results. Much more effort, however, has gone into research to prove the existence of antisocial effects of television program content, most of it focused on the effects of violence.*

Significance of Time Spent   One cannot help feeling that any activity that takes up as much of people's time as radio and television do must have profound effects. At the very least, time spent on broadcasting could have been spent in some other way — perhaps on some useful, constructive activity. Some critics take it for granted that *anything* active would be more beneficial than passive absorption. This criticism seems to imply a moral judgment, the unstated feeling that it is wrong for people to waste their time staring like zombies at the television tube. Long ago one of the pioneers of social research on broadcasting, Paul Lazarsfeld, noted this tone of moral criticism. He pointed out that intellectuals who had

fought for shorter hours and other labor reforms unconsciously resented the fact that the masses failed to take constructive advantage of their hard-won leisure. Instead they wasted it in passive enjoyment of broadcasting (Lazarsfeld and Kendall, 1948:85). But it has not been demonstrated that listening and watching necessarily displace more useful and active forms of recreation. In the absence of broadcasting, people would do other things with their time, of course, but not necessarily better or more beneficial things. And in fact, many people have their radios or televisions turned on while doing other things.

In any event, all those hours of passive listening and watching may be far less significant than they seem. Subjectively, time is relative, dragging on interminably in some circumstances, passing all too quickly in others. Each clock-hour has exactly the same value; not so each hour of human experience. It follows that the huge amount of time that audiences devote to broadcasting may have far less psychological significance than the sheer number of hours suggests.

15.7 Impact of Violence

Concern that the portrayal of violence and crime might have antisocial effects dates back to well before television. The first systematic research on the effects of media violence was undertaken in the 1930s, when a foundation underwrote a series of studies on the impact of feature films (Jowett, 1976:220). Concern about the potential effects of violence shifted to radio and comic books in the 1950s, and later to television and rock videos. Along the way there occurred a shift in emphasis toward buttressing conclusions about effects with scientific evidence, rather than merely taking effects for granted.

---

*The closely related topic of the effects of pornography has also been studied intensively. This research is not discussed here because pornography, as legally defined, has so far been effectively excluded from broadcasting, though it plays a role in pay cable. The moralistic campaigns against sex in broadcast television that erupt periodically are aimed at programs that do not remotely approach legally preventable pornography (§18.2).

Direct Imitation Real-life cases of violence modeled on similar actions in films or television programs occasionally surface in news reports. Many have long assumed that such imitation is direct evidence that televised violence can *cause* violent behavior on the part of at least some viewers. But as with so much else about people, the answer is not that simple. Exhaustive research from many quarters has demonstrated that television or film viewing is at most a *contributing factor* in any subsequent violent activity; in other words, that the act of viewing is merely one of a string of background events and individual characteristics that, taken together, may, in some circumstances, lead to antisocial behavior. (see discussion of the accommodation model, §15.1).

A particularly repellent instance of such imitation led to an unprecedented lawsuit. In 1974 NBC broadcast a made-for-television film called *Born Innocent*, in which inmates of a detention home for young delinquents "raped" a young girl with a mop handle. Four days after the telecast, a nine-year-old California girl was subjected to a similar ordeal by four older children using a bottle. Parents of the child sued NBC, asking $11 million in damages for negligence in showing the film scene, which, they alleged, had directly incited the attack on their daughter. The case raised a major question for broadcasters: could they be held legally responsible for the reactions of audience members to their programs? Network attorneys persuaded the trial judge to define the issue as a First Amendment question, rather than as one of negligence. The case collapsed when it thus become impossible to show that NBC had surrendered its First Amendment protection by *deliberately inciting* the children to attack their victim.

Generalized Effects However, public concern about media violence is based primarily on its possible generalized effects rather than on the risk of occasional direct imitations. Adverse social effects are assumed to be far more widespread and pervasive than isolated instances of imitation. This point of view emerged in another much-publicized court case in 1977.

A 16-year-old Florida boy, Ronnie Zamora, was charged with murdering an elderly neighbor during an attempted robbery. The boy's attorney tried to build his defense on the argument that Zamora was a television addict, "intoxicated" by the thousands of murders he had seen enacted on the screen, and therefore not responsible for his violent behavior. The trial judge rejected this argument, and the boy was convicted of murder. Though ill-considered, this attempt to blame television for the crime was inspired by the findings of research on the generalized adverse effects of televised violence that had accumulated rapidly during the 1970s.

The Surgeon General's Scientific Advisory Committee on Television and Social Behavior sponsored a large group of studies in 1969. Congress allotted $1 million for the research, which resulted in five volumes of reports and papers. The final conclusion of all this work was expressed ambiguously, but when questioned by a Senate Committee, the Surgeon General said flatly:

The broadcasters should be put on notice. The overwhelming consensus and the unanimous Scientific Advisory Committee's report indicates that televised violence, indeed, does have an adverse effect on certain members of our society. . . . [I]t is clear to me that the causal relationship between televised violence and antisocial behavior is sufficient to warrant appropriate and immediate remedial action. (Senate CC, 1972: 26)

A comprehensive analysis of the research literature, commissioned by the committee, established that, of all the types of television effects that had been studied, television's linkage to aggression had been the most intensively analyzed. The fact that every research method available had been employed in the study of televised violence made the cumulative evidence of its effects especially persuasive. The researchers later summarized their findings in these words:

The evidence is that television may increase aggression by teaching viewers previously unfamiliar hostile acts, by generally encouraging in various ways the use of aggression, and by triggering aggressive behavior both imitative and different in kind from what has been viewed. Effects are never certain because real-life aggression is strongly influenced by situational factors, and this strong role for situational factors means that the absence of an immediate effect does not rule out a delayed impact when the behavior in question may be more propitious. (Comstock et al., 1978: 13)

As a result of this work, and other studies done in the years since (including a revisit a decade later by some of the same researchers involved in the 1972 report), Congress and various private groups have pressured the FCC to act to limit televised violence. But for various reasons, chiefly the First Amendment and the trend to deregulation, no lasting governmental role has been forthcoming (§18.1).

Violence and Perceptions of Reality

During the 1967–1968 television season, George Gerbner and his associates at the University of Pennsylvania began conducting annual analyses of television violence. From these data they constructed "The Violence Profile," based on a content analysis that enumerated every violent act in a sample week of prime-time and weekend morning network entertainment programs (Exhibit 15.6). In this way they tracked changes in the level of violence from year to year according to network and program type. The Gerbner data indicated, for example, that animated cartoons depict a higher percentage of violent acts than

any other program category (the coding system counted comic, as well as serious, acts of violence).

Gerbner theorized that violence in programs creates anxiety in viewers, because they tend to perceive the real world in terms of the television world. Viewers identify with victims of violence in fiction who are like themselves. Gerbner found that the elderly, the poor, and blacks have high "risk ratios," or expectations of becoming victims. This anxiety effect, he said, may be a much more important by-product of violence than the imitation effect.

Desensitization   The Gerbner risk ratio hypothesis reverses an older hypothesis that predicts that people exposed to fictional violence will become *desensitized*. According to the latter view, when the experience of violence in fiction becomes routine, people grow indifferent to real-life violence. The many instances that can be cited of callousness in the face of urban violence lend color to this hypothesis. For example, in 1979, eleven young people were crushed to death in a scramble to get into an arena to hear a rock concert. Appalled observers reported later that the fans, in their rush to enter the hall, trampled with complete indifference over the bodies of those who had fallen to the floor.

A related hypothesis holds that viewers become indifferent to violence because it is depicted so unrealistically on television, having been deliberately sanitized. The consequences of violence are made to seem neat and clean compared to what happens when real people are hurt. The revolting, bloodly aftermath, the screams of agony, are never seen or heard. Joseph Wambaugh, a one-time police officer who became a writer of police stories, withdrew from a television series based on his writings because the producers treated violence so unrealistically. He was quoted in the

Exhibit 15.6   Trends in Television Violence, 1967-1983

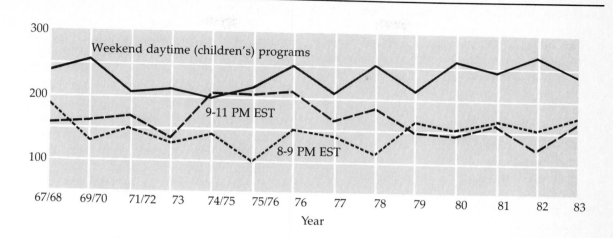

The scale on the left refers to the Gerbner "violence index," a measurement of the level of violence in programs that combines values for three variables: " the extent to which violence occurs at all in the program sampled, the frequency and rate of violent episodes, and the number of roles calling for characterization as violents, victims, or both." The dip in the 8-9 P.M. index in 1975 reflects the introduction of the family viewing hour restraints in that year. Notice that the index level for children's programs is generally much higher than that for adult programs.

Sources: From "The Mainstreaming of America: Violence Profile No. 11," by George Gerbner, Larry Gross, Michael Morgan, and Nancy Signorielli in *Journal of Communication*, (Summer 1980), p. 13, and an unpublished paper by G. Gerbner for National Council of Churches, Sept. 1984.

press as saying, "If they had a cop kill someone on TV, you never saw the blood. You never saw the face shot away. And you never saw the cop throwing up afterwards." Wambaugh put his finger on a seemingly insoluble dilemma: such graphic consequences should perhaps be seen, but the public would never tolerate the showing of them.

In Defense of Violence   Given the range and depth of research evidence showing the antisocial effects of television violence, the television industry has found it increasingly difficult to defend its use. Yet if television is expected to serve as a medium for serious ar-

tistic expression for adult viewers, it is relevant to ask how far the industry should be expected to go in banning violence, which is, after all, integral to all literature. The stage is littered with bodies when the curtain falls on some of Shakespeare's tragedies. Popular entertainment and sports have always featured violence.

Writers would face a difficult challenge if they had to create sufficient plays for the needs of television without resorting to violent clashes between opposing forces. A study made of the attitudes and opinions of those responsible for network entertainment — the writers, producers, network executives, and program standards chiefs — supports this position (Baldwin & Lewis, 1972). The problem, as most of them saw it, was well expressed by a playwright who pointed out that authors of dramas have at their disposal four basic types of conflicts around which to build their plots. Only one of the four is well adapted to the limitations imposed by television, and that happens to be the one most likely to involve personal violence.

1. *Man against nature:* "This is usually too expensive for television."
2. *Man against God:* "Too intellectual for television."
3. *Man against himself:* "Too psychological, and doesn't leave enough room for action."
4. *Man against man:* "This is what you usually end up with."

Defenders of current practice argue that violence in television merely reflects violence in real life. To ignore it or to pretend that it does not exist would restrict writers unreasonably. Curiously enough, however, comparison of American culture with other cultures does not seem to bear out the assumption of a positive correlation between real and fictional violence:

If television were the sole determinant of violent behavior, it would be difficult to explain the disparity in aggravated assault rates (almost 8 to 1) between Boston and Montreal, since these cities are both saturated with the same and similar television programs. This does not mean that there is no relationship between television violence and actual violence; it simply means that such a relationship cannot be defined explicitly at present. (Kutash, 1978: 118)

Japan offers an interesting example in this connection. Crime statistics in Japan indicate a much lower level of social violence than that of the United States. Yet Japanese television regularly imports the most violent of U.S. action dramas, whose violence is mild compared to the ferocity seen in homegrown Japanese television plays (Barnard, 1978).

Another justification of violence in programming holds that the witnessing of staged violence has a positive role in defusing people's aggressive instincts. The ancient Greek theory of *catharsis*, as propounded by Aristotle, held that stage tragedy cleanses the emotions of the viewer through pity and fear. The analogous modern argument is that television viewers' feelings of aggression will be drained off in harmless fantasies as a result of watching fictional violence. Experimental studies have not always supported this assumption. In fact, most studies suggest that seeing violence in fiction arouses viewers' aggressive feelings rather than purging them (Comstock et al., 1978: 237).

•   •   •

Claims about the impact of the electronic media vary from the grand generalizations made by media theorist Marshall McLuhan (§14.5 footnote) to the complaints of business executives about the way they are depicted in television dramas. Virtually everybody has an ax to grind when it comes to controlling the real or imagined effects of electronic media. Critics want either to prevent effects they believe unfavorable to their interests or to encourage effects they hope will promote their goals. These perceived consequences of the media are a prime factor in media regulation, as discussed in chapters 16–18.

Summary

• The mere fact that electronic media produce consequences justifies serious study of those media. The impact of media in different circumstances is a matter of considerable research and even more controversy.

• There is no overall unifying theory in mass-communication effects research. Several research perspectives focus on one or more aspects of the communication process. Among the models useful in explaining the role of media are the effects model, the uses-and-gratifications model, and the more complicated but realistic accommodation model.

• The four principal strategies used in studying mass communication are survey research, content analysis, laboratory experiments, and field studies or experiments. Several modifications and other approaches have been developed in recent years.

• As a medium of advertising, television can have a powerful impact on consumers, especially children. But as business failures demonstrate, advertising alone cannot create demand.

• Electronic media journalists largely define our sense of what is happening around us, by a combination of gatekeeping and agenda setting. Media coverage can confer prestige on subjects but at the same time can be exploited by those who stage pseudoevents. Terrorists, who often commit publicity crimes in order to gain world attention, present the media with the special dilemma of playing a role in making news simply by covering terrorist activities.

• Broadcasting has long exerted a strong influence on U.S. election campaigns. For many reasons, American presidents have made more effective use of the medium than has Congress.

• Years of television coverage of the Vietnam War showed the impact of a long and frustrating war on the U.S. public and demonstrated how deeply broadcasting can affect public opinion. More recent war coverage has had a direct impact on the making of foreign policy.

• Television entertainment, which draws much of the electronic media audience, can reinforce stereotypes and often gives a false impression of everyday life and work. Nevertheless, television can play a positive role in the socialization of children, and provides many viewers with a gratifying means of spending leisure time.

• Whether television contributes to violent behavior is a matter of controversy. It appears that the medium can be a contributing factor to violent action on the part of some people. It may also serve to desensitize people to violence. Further, television violence can reinforce the self-image that members of some groups have of themselves as victims.

PART 6

Controls

We have explored the electronic media's historical development, physical limitations, economic support and structure, programming, audience measurement techniques, and impact on audiences. We turn now to the constraints society places on these media, especially traditional broadcasting, to ensure that they will generally reflect the nation's sense of social welfare, political responsibility, and cultural identity.

Chapter 16 looks at the formal legal controls that govern the electronic media and, in addition, examines the social control exerted by the nation's general political climate, public opinion, the educational system, industry self-regulation, and organized pressure groups. In Chapter 17 we focus on FCC administrative controls. Chapter 18 reviews some of the controversial constitutional issues concerning the nature of electronic media content that arise when such controls are put into effect.

CHAPTER 16

Agencies of Control

In this chapter, we begin with the statutory or legislative basis for electronic media regulation and the underlying organic law, analyzing electronic media law's place in the constitutional scheme and its component parts. We then explore the major agencies of control, both governmental and private, that attempt to regulate the electronic media today.

16.1 Constitutional Context

As we saw in §2.11, the Radio Act of 1927 brought to an end a period of chaotic development that dramatized the need for federal regulation. The 1927 act was the first U.S. legislation to concern itself explicitly with broadcasting.

Scarcity Factor   This intrusion by government upon the freedom of American citizens to communicate by whatever means they choose would ordinarily be forbidden by the Constitution, whose First Amendment explicitly prohibits Congress from making laws abridging freedom of speech (see Box, page 503). One reason for adopting the First Amendment had been to prevent government

licensing of newspapers. Yet in 1927, Congress instituted a comprehensive system for licensing broadcasters, certainly a break with constitutional traditions.

A major justification for this unusual abridgement was the *scarcity of channels*. Not everyone who wanted a station could be granted a channel, because too many channels on the air caused intolerable interference, as had occurred before passage of the 1927 radio act. Because channels were scarce, the government, as represented by the Federal Radio Commission (later the FCC), had to make choices between applicants. When applications were "mutually exclusive," either because they made claims on the same channel or on adjacent channels whose activation would cause interference with existing stations, only one license could be granted. Thus the freedom of the rest was abridged.

Today the scarcity factor as a justification for regulation is being challenged as never before. Opponents of traditional regulation point to the increase in the number of stations since the 1927 act was written — from about six hundred to over ten thousand. They argue that, even though there is still a demand for more channels in densely populated areas, cable television makes available unlimited numbers of supplementary channels, converting scarcity into abundance. Some suggest that all media should be counted, and in that sense electronic media scarcity — if any — is offset by the diversity of nonelectronic information sources available. Thus less, not more, regulation is called for.

We will analyze the validity of this argument against regulation based on scarcity later. In the meantime, however, it should be understood that Congress and the courts relied on the scarcity factor as a major justification for government regulation throughout the evolution of broadcast law.

Broadcasting as Commerce   Before Congress could act to regulate broadcasting, however, it had to determine whether or not it had the right to, given the limits placed on its power by the Constitution. The specific constitutional justification for Congress to step in and take control of radio comes from Article I, Section 8(3), which gives Congress the power "to regulate commerce with foreign nations, and among the several States." This is the well-known *commerce clause*, which has played a vital role in U.S. economic development, preventing individual states from undermining unity of the nation by erecting internal trade barriers. Although not "commerce" in the original sense of the exchange of tangible goods, the exchange of information by mail and wire had long been accepted as a form of commerce under the Constitution. Seen in this light, a statute governing radio could be regarded as one link in a chain of responsibility that extends from the Constitution to the people, as shown in Exhibit 16.1.

The commerce clause gives Congress jurisdiction over *interstate and foreign* commerce, but not over commerce within individual states. However, electromagnetic waves are regarded as *inherently interstate* in nature. Even when a radio service is designed to cover only a limited area within a state, as in the case of a radio-operated taxi-dispatching service, for example, its signals cannot be cut off at state boundaries. Zones of radio interference extend unpredictably far beyond zones of service. Wire communication, on the other hand, can be cut off precisely at the city line or at any other geographic boundary.*

FCC's Relation to Congress   It would be impossible for Congress itself to attend to the endless details of regulation in the communications field. It therefore created the Federal Radio Commission and, in 1934, its successor, the Federal Communications Commission, to act on its behalf under what is called "delegated authority." Although the president appoints FCC commissioners, with the advice and consent of the Senate, the FCC remains a "creature of Congress." Congress defined the FCC's role in the Communications Act of 1934, and only Congress can change that role by amending the act. The FCC is constantly monitored by the House and Senate subcommittees on communications and must come back to Congress annually for budget appropriations.†

---

*Telephone and related common-carrier services are subject either to state or federal regulation, depending on whether a given service crosses state lines. For example, states have their own utility commissions that approve changes in telephone rates for in-state systems. Systems that cross state lines, however, need FCC approval for changes in rates. In the 1980s the FCC seemed increasingly likely to preempt or otherwise limit state regulation as it strove for a deregulated marketplace.

†Indeed, after 1983 the FCC was no longer a permanent agency of government but had to be reauthorized every two years. This change in status grew out of congressional displeasure with the strong regulatory role of the Federal Trade Commission during the Carter administration, and a feeling that government agencies needed to toe the congressional line a bit more closely. Thus far, the practical effect of this change on FCC activity has been limited, although Congress can more readily tack changes onto the communications act and can apply added doses of pressure on the FCC.

Exhibit 16.1 Chain of Legal Authority over Electronic Media

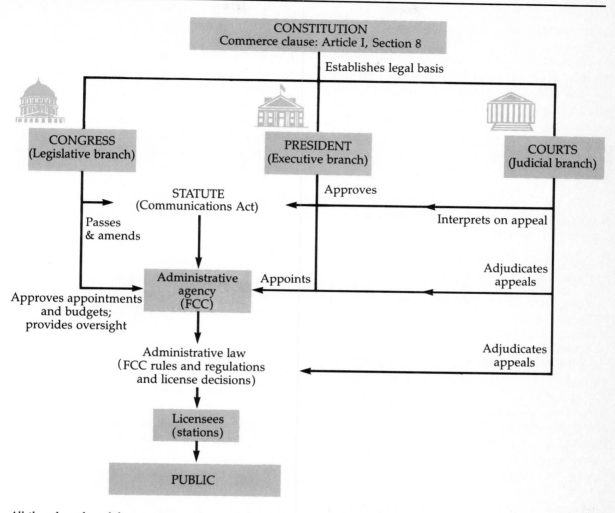

All three branches of the government play a role in controlling electronic media under the general umbrella of the Constitution.

Congress's delegation of authority gave the FCC the power to adopt, modify, and repeal rules and regulations concerning interstate electronic media. These rules carry the force of federal law, deriving their power from the Communications Act of 1934. Although the FCC has a good deal of freedom to use its own discretion, this freedom has its limits, which are spelled out in the act. Any FCC rule not fully justified by the act can be overthrown by congressional action or by appeal to the courts.

Constitutional Challenges   All actions of Congress and the FCC of course, must comply with the Constitution. The Radio Act of 1927 had scarcely been signed when the first challenges to its constitutionality began. Here are three examples of fundamental constitutional questions addressed to the courts in the first few years of the act's existence:

• *Is broadcasting in fact interstate commerce?* In reply to this question, put by the American Bond and Mortgage Company in 1929 when its license was deleted because of interference, the appeals court said firmly:

It does not seem to be open to question that radio transmission and reception among the states are interstate commerce. To be sure it is a new species of commerce. Nothing visible and tangible is transported. . . . But that result is the transmission of intelligence, ideas, and entertainment. It is intercourse, and that intercourse is commerce. (31 F 2d 448, at 454, 1929)*

• *Does deleting a license deprive a person of property without due process of law, in violation of the Fifth Amendment?* When this question was asked by a radio preacher who lost his license because of program excesses (§3.1), the appeals court replied:

One who applies for and obtains a grant or permit from a state, or the United States, to make use of a medium of interstate commerce, under the control and subject to the dominant power of the government, takes such a grant or right subject to the exercise of the power of the government, in the public interest, to withdraw it without compensation. (62 F 2d 850, at 854, 1932)

---

*The full names of the cases mentioned in the text, together with their sources, are given in the citation list at the end of the book.

• *Does deleting a license deprive a person of freedom of speech or press, in violation of the First Amendment?* In the same case the court, after reviewing the ways in which the preacher had misused his station, said that to take away the license "is neither censorship nor previous restraint, nor is it a whittling away of the rights guaranteed by the First Amendment, or an impairment of their free exercise." He was free to say whatever he liked, said the court, "but he may not, as we think, demand, of right, the continued use of an instrumentality of commerce for such purposes . . . except in subordination to all reasonable rules and regulations Congress, acting through the Commission, may prescribe" (62 F 2d 850, at 853, 1932).

Basic constitutional questions were laid to rest by such cases as these in the early years of regulation. The underlying constitutionality of the act has thus long since been settled in the courts, but specific interpretations of the act by the FCC continue to provoke litigation.

16.2 Communications Act Basics

Passage   The Radio Act of 1927 (§2.11) imposed some order on broadcasting, but it left control of some aspects of radio and of all interstate and foreign *wire* communication still scattered among several federal agencies. To introduce a more centralized approach, the Communications Act of 1934 went beyond radio, bringing wire as well as wireless communication under unified control. The effect of this new act on broadcasting was minimal, however, because Congress simply reenacted the broadcasting provisions of the 1927 law as part of the 1934 act. This means that the framework of broadcasting law in the 1980s was established some six decades ago, during the early development of radio. Although the act has been amended many times, its underlying concepts remain unchanged.

The very first paragraph of the 1934 act sets forth the underlying reasons for creating the FCC and for repealing the preceding 1927 act. These actions were taken:

for the purpose of regulating interstate and foreign commerce in communication by wire and radio so as to make available, so far as possible, to all the people of the United States a rapid, efficient, Nation-wide, and world-wide wire and radio communication service with adequate facilities at reasonable charges, for the purpose of the national defense, for the purpose of promoting safety of life and property through the use of wire and radio communication, and for the purpose of securing a more effective execution of this policy by centralizing authority heretofore granted by law to several agencies and by granting additional authority with respect to interstate and foreign commerce in wire and radio communication.

Organization

The Communications Act of 1934 consists of seven major chapters, called *titles*.* They cover roughly the following subjects:

I. Definition of terms, provision for setting up and operating the FCC.
II. Common carriers.
III. Broadcast licensing, general powers of the FCC, limited program and advertising controls, and public broadcasting.
IV. Hearings on and appeals from FCC decisions.
V. Penal provisions.
VI. Cable communications (§17.6).
VII. War emergency powers of the president, and other general provisions.

---

*Until late 1984, the act had six titles. When Congress passed the Cable Communications Policy Act of 1984, it became a new Title VI, making the existing Title VI a new Title VII. References to Title VI issued before 1985 refer to what we now know as Title VII.

Definition of Broadcasting

As we have seen, in the early 1920s American Telephone & Telegraph at first tried to treat broadcasting as a common carrier (§2.9).

Common carriers supply communication services to all comers without concern for what is communicated over their facilities. Telephone companies are the most familiar examples of common carriers, but the field has become diversified as more and more uses are found for satellites, microwave, optical fiber, and other high-technology devices for getting information from point A to point B. Another characteristic of common carriers is that their rates have historically been subject to government approval (by the FCC, in the case of interstate operations), although in recent years, rate regulation has been reduced.

If broadcasting were to be classed as a common carrier, programming would be entirely at the discretion of those who bought time on stations and networks, which in turn would be obliged to charge fixed prices in accordance with an FCC-approved tariff (rate) scale. As we pointed out in §2.11, this concept of broadcasting was rejected in practice in the 1920s. The communications act formalized the distinction in Section 3:

"Common carrier" or "carrier" means any person engaged as a common carrier for hire, in interstate or foreign communication by wire or radio or in interstate or foreign radio transmission of energy . . . but a person engaged in radio broadcasting shall not, insofar as such person is so engaged, be deemed a common carrier.

The same section defines the term *broadcasting* as "the dissemination of radio communications intended to be received by the public, directly or by intermediary of relay stations."

The key phrase "intended to be received of the public" excludes from the definition of broadcasting any private radio communication services aimed at individuals or specific groups of individuals. Yet radio communications not intended for the general public can be *received* by anyone who has the right kind of receiver. People can tune in to police, ship-to-shore, satellite, and other nonbroadcast transmissions for their own entertainment. But these messages are not *intended* for the general public, and the communications act's Section 705(a) on "unauthorized publication or use" forbids the disclosure of nonbroadcast messages to people for whom they are not intended. In recent years, Congress, the courts, and the FCC have made it illegal for people to intercept for their own use nonbroadcast signals such as pay television. Nor may people use broadcasting to send private messages not intended for the general public (§16.5). Thus it is technically illegal for athletes, for example, to greet their families over the air during interviews at sporting events.

Finally, Section 3 of the act defines *radio communication* as "transmission by radio of writing, signs, signals, pictures, and sounds of all kinds, including all instrumentalities, facilities, apparatus, and services . . . incidental to such transmission." By giving the word *radio* such a broad definition, Congress made it possible for the radio provisions of the act to be applied without alteration to television when it became a licensed service nearly fifteen years after the 1927 act was adopted.

For a long time the legal status of cable television under the communications act was uncertain, and hence the FCC's jurisdiction over cable was questioned. Much cable programming comes from television stations, linking cable closely to broadcasting; yet cable systems deliver programs by wire over closed circuits, not by radio waves, and can thus arguably be described as interstate commerce. Cable systems are usually limited to intrastate coverage and hence are not subject to federal wire communications law; yet cable television uses interstate satellite networks to obtain much of its program material, and some systems rely on interstate microwave relays to pick up distant television stations. Cable operators sometimes act like neutral common carriers, as when they offer local access and leased commercial channels; yet they strongly assert their First Amendment rights as originators of programs.

The 1984 cable amendment to the communications act (§17.6) finally clarified cable's role: it is neither a common carrier nor a broadcaster; the FCC has some responsibilities for cable, but they are far less extensive than its responsibilities either for broadcasting or for interstate wire systems. States also have some authority, but Congress has strictly limited their ability to regulate cable programming or subscriber rates.

Provisions for the FCC   The president appoints the five FCC members, with the advice and consent of the Senate. No more than three of the five commissioners may be of the same political party. Congress thus sought to minimize economic and political bias on the part of the commission. Terms run for five years, although many commissioners leave before the end of their terms. When that happens, those appointed to replace resigned members are appointed only for the unexpired period of the term. Reappointment is fairly common. Some commissioners have served for decades; the record is held by Robert E. Lee, who served for twenty-eight years.

The term of five years, contrasted with the presidential term of four years, makes it theoretically impossible for an incoming president to change the commissioners all at once (the terms of the commissioners are staggered so that no more than one expires each year). On the other hand, the act gives an incoming president a chance to have immediate impact on the commission by allowing the president to appoint one of its members as chairman, and to select new members during the first term.

Section 4 of the act gives the commission broad power to "perform any and all acts, make such rules and regulations, and issue such orders . . . as may be necessary in the execution of its functions." In a few instances Congress tied the commission's hands with hard-and-fast requirements, such as the original upper limit of three years on the terms of broadcasting licenses and the requirement that licensees be U.S. citizens. But most provisions of the act give the commission wide latitude in applying its own experience and (presumably) expert judgment to the particular sets of facts presented by each case.

Congress knew, however, that the new law would meet the same fate as the Radio Act of 1912 if the commission were given *unlimited* discretionary latitude. It was precisely such an undefined grant of licensing power that had caused urgent demand for new legislation in the 1920s (§2.11). What was needed was a highly flexible yet legally recognized standard by which to limit the commission's discretion every time it made a decision not dictated by specific requirements of the act. Congress chose for this purpose a phrase familiar since the 1850s in the public utility field — "public interest, convenience, and [sometimes "or"] necessity."

Origins of Public-Interest Standard

The idea that radio communication must serve the public interest emerged during the earliest days of maritime radio, when it became obvious that selfish interests and commercial profit could not be allowed to stand in the way when lives were at stake in emergencies at sea (§2.11).

When broadcasting emerged, it too was recognized as carrying an obligation to serve the public interest. As Secretary of Commerce Hoover said at a congressional hearing in 1924, "Radio communication is not to be considered as merely a business carried on for private gain, for private advertisement, or for entertainment of the curious."

At the Fourth Radio Conference, in 1925, the National Association of Broadcasters presented a resolution recommending that a law be enacted making "public convenience and necessity" the basis of choice among competing applications. At that conference, Hoover remarked, "We can surely agree that no one can raise a cry of deprivation of free speech if he is compelled to prove that there is something more than naked commercial selfishness in his purpose."

The legislative history of the Radio Act of 1927 shows that Congress adopted essentially this point of view. In answer to the NAB's later contention that the commission was created merely to regulate technical aspects of broadcasting, Senator Burton K. Wheeler replied, "I went through all those hearings at that time, sat as a member of the committee, and it was not the intention of the committee, nor of the Senate, just to regulate these physical things" (Senate CIC, 1944: 238).

Whenever Congress intended to give the FCC maximum latitude to use its own judgment, it used the "public interest" phrase. The phrase occurs in the key sections of the broadcasting parts of the communications act. For example, Section 303 begins: "Except as otherwise provided in this Act, the Commission from time to time, as public convenience, interest, or necessity requires shall. . . ." The section goes on to list nineteen functions, ranging from the power to classify radio stations to the power to make whatever rules and regulations the FCC needs to carry out the provisions of the act. The public-interest phrase similarly occurs in the crucial sections dealing with granting, renewal, and transfer of broadcast licenses.

Definition of Public Interest   Most people think of the public-interest clause as being aimed directly at broadcasters, forcing them to operate "in the public interest." In turn broadcasters tend to picture themselves as constantly faced with excruciating dilemmas as to what the public interest requires.

Actually, nowhere does the communications act address the public interest phrase directly to licensees. It invariably tells the *commission* to decide what the public interest requires.

Of course the ultimate aim is to ensure that broadcast licensees operate in the public interest, but the act does not leave them adrift in a sea of doubt as to how to interpret the phrase. That is the job of the commission. As an appeals court put it:

The only way that broadcasters can operate in the "public interest" is by broadcasting programs that meet somebody's view of what is in the "public interest." That can scarcely be determined by the broadcaster himself, for he is in an obvious conflict of interest. . . . Since the public cannot through a million stifled yawns convey that their television fare, as a whole, is not in their interest, the Congress has made the F.C.C. the guardian of that public interest. (516 F 2d 526, at 536, 1975)

This does not mean that the FCC entirely preempts the obligation of broadcast licensees to judge what would be in the public interest for their particular publics. Only the licensee can make informed judgments on local matters. One pattern that has emerged is for the FCC to set general requirements that broadcast licensees perform certain functions, without specifying exactly how to carry out those requirements. If what a licensee does is challenged, the FCC then decides whether or not what was done was "reasonable." If it was, the FCC will uphold the licensee.

Since many different ways of doing things can be judged to be reasonable, such an approach allows licensee implementation of FCC policies to vary to meet local circumstances. The commission says, for example, that it is in the public interest for stations to carry *some* programs touching on *some* local community issues. But it remains for the licensees to identify important issues and then decide what kinds of programs, and how many such programs, to devote to this aspect of their public-service obligation.

Because the very purpose of the public-interest standard was to give the FCC maximum flexibility in meeting new and unforeseeable situations, it is unavoidably open to the charge of vagueness. But as an appeals court judge pointed out, "It would be difficult, if not impossible, to formulate a precise and comprehensive definition of the term 'public interest, convenience, or necessity,' and it has been said often and properly by the courts that the facts of each case must be examined and must govern its determination" (153 F 2d 623, at 628, 1946).

In sharp contrast, the major recent amendment to the communications act, the Title VI cable provisions, nowhere uses the phrase "public interest." The 22-page amendment gives the FCC discretionary powers that might well have been made subject to the public-interest test. On the whole, though, the FCC has far less latitude in dealing with cable than with broadcasting (§17.6). Perhaps the most basic reason for this is that the framers of the amendment had little confidence in the FCC's reading of the public interest as a regulatory standard.

16.3 Communications Act Issues

Favorable View   It can be argued that Congress devised a remarkably sound piece of legislation when it wrote the Radio Act of

1927. Congress found no reason to change the substance of the broadcasting statute in 1934 when it adopted the communications act. And the law survived in the 1934 version, though much amended, into the 1980s.

Written at a time when broadcasting consisted of only about six hundred AM stations and two networks, the act managed to survive the development of FM radio, VHF and UHF television, use of satellite relay services, cable television, and many other innovations. It now presides over a dozen national networks (counting radio and television separately) and scores of regional and ad hoc networks, while the number of stations on the air has increased to more than ten thousand.

Amendments   Framers of the original 1927 legislation could not have anticipated in detail every new problem that would arise, but they ensured flexibility in the law by giving the FCC wide discretionary powers. In addition, subsequent Congresses made many changes in the act by amendment. Not counting amendments to the original 1927 law prior to adoption of the 1934 act, by 1985 the statute had been amended more than a hundred times. These changes never altered the underlying philosophy of the act as outlined in preceding sections of this chapter, indicating substantial continuing support for the basic approaches of the 1920s and 1930s.

Amendments sought (1) to correct unforeseen weaknesses, (2) to adapt to new conditions or to introduce new subjects of regulation, and (3) to curb certain actions that the FCC had taken under the broad grant of discretionary powers conferred upon it by the act. Below are examples of each type of amendment:

• *Type 1:* The unforeseen effect of the equal-time provision for political candidates on news coverage of candidates (§18.6) led to amend-ment of Section 315 in 1959 to exempt bona fide news programs in which candidates appear.

• *Type 2:* To encourage UHF television, Congress in 1962 gave the FCC power to force the manufacture of all-channel television receivers. Since then, amendments have required the FCC to encourage new technologies.

• *Type 3:* Objecting to the way the FCC used its discretionary powers to curb trafficking in licenses, Congress in 1952 adopted an amendment forbidding the FCC from interfering with the selection of station buyers.

Contrary View   Despite its longevity, the act has not lacked critics. For example, historian Erik Barnouw wrote that the act was "based on a premise that had been obsolete in 1927 and by 1934 was totally invalid: that American broadcasting was a local responsibility exercised by independent station licensees" (1968: 33). Barnouw was referring to the fact that national syndication, especially in the form of networks, preempted most local program production, despite the act's emphasis on the localism ideal.

In addition, many First Amendment scholars objected that imposing any limits at all on the licensee's freedom of choice in programming violated a basic constitutional guarantee. Broadcasters themselves complained about these limitations and also about the shortness of the license period and the uncertainty of license renewal.

These and other rumblings of discontent gained strength from a general sense of disillusionment with government overregulation that emerged in the 1970s. For the first time, serious attempts were made in Washington to scrap the 1934 act in favor of entirely new legislation. Although called "rewrites," these legislative proposals went far beyond the kinds of patching-up done by earlier amendments to the act.

Rewrites   The House Subcommittee on Communications began working up a major communications act "rewrite" in 1977, proposing a new philosophy of regulation and sweeping changes in the method of administering the statute.

The draft bill (H.R. 13015, "The Communications Act of 1978") received a great deal of publicity, much of it favorable at first. After weeks of hearings, however, it became evident that the necessary votes for passage in the House could not be mustered, and the bill died in committee.

During the next two years, three more new bills were introduced: two competing "partial rewrites" in the Senate and a House "rewrite of the rewrite." But with broadcasting, cable television, and common-carrier issues competing for attention, no single bill was able to resolve simultaneously all the conflicting industry, consumer, and government interests.

Despite their failure, the 1977–1981 rewrite efforts are worth studying because they brought into focus the chief criticisms of the 1934 act, affected FCC policies, and illustrate the range of policy alternatives under consideration. Examples of major broadcasting issues addressed in the bills follow:

• *Public-interest standard.* The first attempted rewrite eliminated the public-interest standard. Because the proposed new commission would no longer have the broad mandate of the FCC, there was no need to set limits on its discretionary powers. Instead, market competition was counted on to ensure that licensees would serve the public interest. Regulation was to be used only when market forces proved deficient. Later rewrites restored the public-interest standard but reduced somewhat the commission's powers under the 1934 act.

• *Localism.* The first rewrite eliminated the fairness doctrine (§18.4) and then-current FCC rules for ascertaining local needs (§17.2). Nevertheless, it allowed the commission to require television stations to broadcast "some" news, public affairs, and locally produced programs and to treat controversial issues fairly. It also required channels to be allocated so as to ensure "the maximum" full-time services in every community. Some of the proposed bills encouraged establishment of more local stations by changing spectrum policies and by encouraging new types of service.

• *Spectrum use fees.* The provision of the first rewrite that drew the most energetic protests from existing commercial broadcasters would have exacted substantial fees for use of the spectrum. These were not merely filing fees but use fees, based upon the economic value of each channel, as indicated by station income. Revenue from fees was to be used to pay the expenses of running the commission, to help support public broadcasting, to encourage minority ownership, and to develop rural telecommunications. The commercial broadcasters' protests appeared to be effective, for the use-fee concept disappeared as further rewrite bills evolved.

• *License term.* As one of many attempted tradeoffs, the rewrites assured broadcasters indefinite licensing in place of the renewable three-year licenses of the 1934 act. Consumer groups opposed this provision because it deprived them of the leverage they gained from having the right to oppose renewals of broadcasters they thought were not serving them well. Strong support from industry and government witnesses prevailed, however, and most rewrite proposals retained this provision — which would have gone into effect immediately for radio, and after a decade for television.*

---

*So intense was the pressure for extending the license term that the first communications act amendment passed by the Ninety-seventh Congress in 1981 lengthened licenses to seven years for radio, five for television. Quick adoption was obtained by attaching the amendment as a rider on unrelated budget legislation.

• *Competing applications.* The rewrites agreed on the need to eliminate the cumbersome hearing procedures used under the 1934 act to choose among applicants competing for new facilities (§17.3). Instead they proposed deciding the winner by lot, completely eliminating the commission's discretionary role in choosing among applicants.

• *Role of cable.* Though not strictly one of the rewrites, the Cable Communication Policy Act of 1984, now Title VI of the communications act (§17.6), came as a logical consequence of the deregulatory philosophy of the 1980s. This act tried to settle power struggles between broadcasting and cable and between cable operators and city governments in ways that would maximize competition and minimize regulation.

Marketplace-Based Alternatives   Congress's failure to adopt comprehensive rewrites of the 1934 act left the existing public-interest framework in place. In the 1970s and especially in the 1980s, new interpretations of the 1934 act began to be promoted by the FCC and accepted by the courts. These new interpretations emphasized that, in many areas of telecommunication, it would be best if the FCC did not regulate but rather assumed that competition or the workings of the marketplace would be just as effective as government regulation and less contrary to U.S. traditions of minimal media regulation.

The problem, of course, was how to make such marketplace-based approaches compatible with the 1934 act. The solution to this problem was to argue that what the marketplace produced was by definition "in the public interest," since the marketplace catered to public acceptance and popularity (Fowler and Brenner, 1982). Following this approach, the FCC sharply reduced its oversight of broadcast programming. In support of its actions, the commission successfully argued in court, on appeal, that extensive regulation of pro-

gramming was no longer necessary because competition among stations and other media would produce programming in the public interest. Marketplace-based theories also led the FCC to authorize such new services as low-power television and direct-broadcast satellites (§17.2) with minimal regulation, its reasoning being that freedom to compete with little government supervision would further the public interest.

Broadcaster support for judicial acceptance of marketplace-based approaches to defining the public interest demonstrate the enduring flexibility of the public-interest standard. Relying on marketplace competitive forces is certainly different from relying on detailed FCC oversight regulation; but the courts have found both approaches consistent with the 1934 act. The comprehensive rewrites of the act had been shown to be politically unworkable, but deregulation made them less necessary.

16.4 Telecommunication Policy

As federally regulated enterprises under the communication act, broadcasting and cable television must be considered in the larger context of national telecommunication policy. *Telecommunication policy* refers to the theory and process the government employs when selecting among alternative ways of regulating and overseeing domestic and international common carrier and electronic media services. All users of electromagnetic energy share the same spectrum, and, as we have seen, there are many links between spectrum-using and non-spectrum-using forms of electronic media. Technological convergence has driven the formerly quite separate fields of electronic mass media and telecommunication closer together. Such convergence requires comprehensive approaches to policy that sometimes exceed FCC responsibilities.

NTIA   In 1970 the Nixon administration established the Office of Telecommunications Policy (OTP) as part of the executive office of the president. The OTP staff of several hundred lawyers, engineers, and economists developed considerable expertise on spectrum, media, and common-carrier policy questions just as technology was bringing about major changes in those fields. The OTP's job was to examine long-range concerns, as opposed to the day-to-day operational focus of the FCC. The OTP played a strong role in several media controversies, expressing concern, for example, about network news bias. But any program associated with Richard Nixon became a political liability after the Watergate crisis of 1973–1974. Thus OTP coasted under an acting director during the Ford years, and early in 1978 it was abolished by the Carter administration to make way for a new agency.

The *National Telecommunications and Information Administration* (NTIA) was set up in 1978 as part of the Department of Commerce. It acts as the president's chief adviser on telecommunication and information policy questions and as administration spokesperson for those topics. The NTIA often appears before Congress to represent the administration and files briefs in many FCC proceedings. It also helps to further new technological developments, conducting research in the telecommunication sciences, and helps to coordinate federal spectrum allocations. Finally, NTIA is the government's disbursement agent for facility grants in support of expanding public telecommunication systems — a role that by the late 1980s was costing twice as much to fulfill as the rest of the agency's operations combined.

Federal Spectrum Users   The communications act makes the president of the United States responsible for federal government agency use of the spectrum. The president delegates this coordination role to NTIA (and to the Office of Management and Budget, which acts to oversee the entire executive branch). Federal spectrum users are about equally divided between military and civilian units, the latter including such agencies as the Coast Guard, the Forestry Service, and the Voice of America. Under the act, the FCC regulates only private, state, and local government users.

A special coordinating body within the NTIA, the *Interdepartmental Radio Advisory Committee* (IRAC), brings together representatives of all major federal agencies concerned with access to the spectrum. The FCC participates as liaison for nonfederal, private commercial, and private noncommercial users and also represents Congress, just as the NTIA speaks for the executive branch (Exhibit 16.2). The NTIA supplies the chairperson and administrative support for IRAC, the oldest continuing government telecommunication entity (it was begun in 1922). IRAC helps determine priorities among conflicting agency demands for spectrum access and otherwise coordinates federal spectrum usage.

Policy Trends   During the 1970s, telecommunication policy became a lively topic of discussion for federal agencies and the private sector. Computers and communication were assuming a primary role in society, and the impact of telecommunication on labor, trade, education, and the home gave rise to questions that no single agency could answer. The attempted rewrites of the communication act noted earlier were one major forum for these discussions. Later, breakup of the AT&T telephone monopoly (footnote, page 42) complicated the scene. Meanwhile, a political trend (backed by considerable economic evidence) suggesting that the marketplace, rather than government, should define the direction of telecommunication widened the debate.

The overall result was a relaxing of government regulation. The communications act

Exhibit 16.2   Spectrum Management

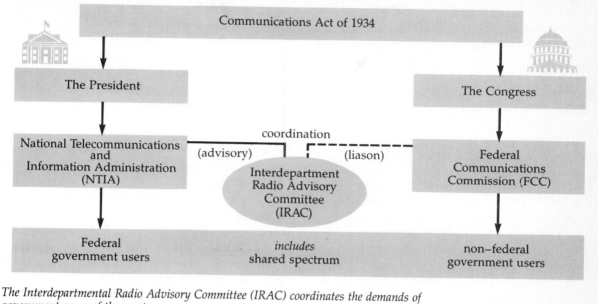

The Interdepartmental Radio Advisory Committee (IRAC) coordinates the demands of government users of the spectrum.

Source: International Telecommunication Union, *Telecommunication Journal*, June 1980.

and the FCC had grown out of President Franklin D. Roosevelt's New Deal, during a time in which views of government's role vis-à-vis business were much more regulation-oriented than they are a half-century later. In the 1980s, FCC Chairman Mark Fowler referred regularly to the FCC as a "New Deal dinosaur." Rather than favoring relatively tight FCC control in support of a general public-interest standard, both business and government now seek what some call a "level regulatory playing field," where media services can compete on equal terms. This theory suggests that the competition resulting from marketplace pressures will serve the public by providing a greater diversity in electronic media services than regulatory fiat would.

The results for electronic media are already evident. As discussed in more detail in §17.6, cable television has been substantially deregulated. The FCC has decided not to regulate several newer services and has begun to dismantle decades of regulatory structure controlling radio and television. The short-term result of these moves is a very uneven playing field, with broadcasting still regulated far more than other media. But further congressional and FCC deregulation of radio and television appears likely.*

---

*Some efforts have been made to apply these deregulatory theories internationally, but implementation has been difficult, because most other nations hold more limited views of the benefits of competition in communication. Nevertheless, in the 1980s the United States has tried to authorize new private competitors in the international cable and satellite arena, which had been dominated by various government-backed monopolies.

16.5 Copyright

As we have seen, the Communications Act of 1934, as amended, is the basic federal statutory framework for regulating broadcasting, cable, and other electronic media. But laws and policies affecting print and other media also have impact on the electronic media. Of fundamental and controversial importance is copyright law, our subject here. Other laws affecting the electronic media, such as press and business law, are covered in §16.6.

Basics   The U.S. Constitution recognized the fundamental importance of encouraging people to be creative for the benefit of the new nation. Section 8, the same passage that gave Congress the right to regulate interstate commerce, also called on it to "promote the progress of science and the useful arts, by securing for limited times to authors and inventors the exclusive right to their respective writings and discoveries." This provision resulted in the patent and copyright laws (both aspects of what is termed *intellectual property*) that enable inventors and other creative people to profit from their achievements but that also assures reasonable public access to those achievements.

When radio broadcasting began, authors and composers had to rely on the Copyright Law of 1909, which dealt primarily with *printed* works and *live* performances. This law could not anticipate the numerous recording, duplication, distribution, and reproduction technologies that later emerged. Congress amended the 1909 law from time to time during the following sixty-seven years, but it remained fundamentally out of date. After two decades of study and debate, Congress finally passed the Copyright Act of 1976, effective for works published in 1978 and later. The task took so long because it was complicated by the need to balance conflicting interests. An ideal copyright law would promote creativity without stifling the development of new technologies; it would prevent plagiarism and piracy without denying the public the benefits either of using those technologies or of enjoying the creative output of the country's citizens.

The 1976 act is administered by the Copyright Office, which is part of the Library of Congress. Relevant key provisions of the act can be summarized as follows:

- *Purpose*. The Constitution gives Congress the power to enable authors to make a profit from their works. Copyright holders *license* others to use their works in exchange for payment of *royalties*. "Use" consists of making public by publishing, performing, displaying, and the like.
- *Copyrightable works*. In addition to traditionally copyrightable works such as books, musical compositions, motion pictures, and broadcast programs, such works as sculptures, choreographic notations, and computer programs can also be copyrighted. Among the things *not* copyrightable are ideas, slogans, brand names, news events, and titles.
- *Length of copyright*. In general, a copyright is good for the life of the creator of the work, plus fifty more years. After that a work enters the *public domain* and can be used without securing permission or paying royalties.
- *Compulsory licensing*. In some cases it is expedient to *compel* copyright owners to license their works on a fixed-royalty basis. The 1976 law mandated compulsory licensing to cable systems, for example. Owners of copyrighted material who license television stations to use their works must grant *retransmission rights* to cable systems that lawfully pick up such programs off the air and deliver them to subscribers. Cable systems, however, must pay for these uses.
- *Fair use*. Absolutely rigid enforcement of copyright restrictions would defeat the object

of copyright law — the promotion of new creative activities. It would prevent, for example, a student from photocopying a magazine article, or a scholar from quoting other writers without securing permission. The new act retained the traditional concept of *fair use,* which permits some limited uses of copyrighted works, without payment or permission, for certain specific purposes that are critical or creative in nature (such as reviews of books and musical works).

Each of these provisions proved controversial, with electronic media often struggling among themselves as well as with copyright owners for favorable interpretation.

Broadcast Music Licensing   Radio and television stations continue to obtain rights to play recorded music by reaching agreements with ASCAP, BMI (§3.2), and SESAC. Most stations hold *blanket licenses* from these licensing agencies, which allow use of any music in their catalogs in return for payment of an annual percentage of each station's gross income. Though some radio stations (especially those with talk formats) pay on a per-use basis, most radio and all television stations and networks hold blanket licenses. Over the years, payment rates and billing systems have been the subjects of court battles between broadcasters and the performing-rights societies. Stations as a group hire "all-industry" negotiating groups that annually negotiate rates with ASCAP, BMI, and SESAC. The resulting deadlocks usually end in court proceedings and result in higher rates each year, though not as much as the licensing agencies originally request. Early in 1985 the Supreme Court let stand an appeals court ruling that the blanket license was not in violation of antitrust laws, as television broadcasters had contended in a six-year legal battle (744 F 2d 217, 1984). Television networks had earlier lost the same battle.

Cable Issues   The 1976 copyright act set up a complicated royalty system by which cable television systems were to pay owners of copyrighted material. This system represented a tradeoff on the parts of broadcasters and copyright-holder interests (mainly the Hollywood film studios). Both assumed that in return for their agreement to the royalty plan, the FCC would sharply limit cable system use of TV signals. Given limited use, they were willing to accept a system under which cable paid for a compulsory license to use "distant-signal" imported broadcast material. When the FCC in 1980 removed the rules limiting cable system use of imported television signals (§17.2), the copyright compromise was placed in jeopardy, because cable systems were then allowed to import whatever distant signals they wanted. This led to a great increase in the retransmission of copyrighted programming.*

The vehicle the copyright act established for determining the rates and payment process of the royalty system is the Copyright Royalty Tribunal (CRT). In the case of cable television, the CRT has two major tasks: to establish the rates cable is to pay for use of copyrighted material (defined as imported distant television broadcast signals), and to divide the pooled royalty money among the copyright holders. The process of apportioning payments has been snarled in legal proceedings from the day the CRT was created. Barely meeting the initial deadline set by Congress for a decision on how to divide the first royalties (for 1978), the CRT finally managed to make everybody unhappy. Broadcasters were to get just over 3 percent of the royalty

---

*Broadcast programming imported by cable systems (in other words, from other than local stations in the cable system coverage area) is doubly licensed. Copyright holders are paid by (1) the initial carrier (the network or, in the case of syndicated programs, the station) and (2) by the cable system as a retransmitter.

Exhibit 16.3   The Copyright System

A. Music Licensing System

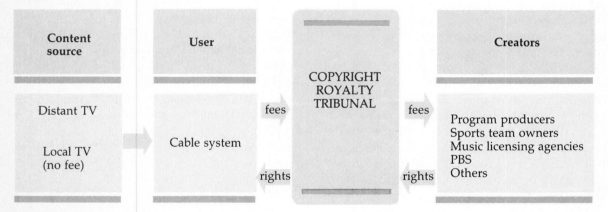

B. Cable TV compulsory license system

Above, the music licensing system has not changed substantially in more than a half century. Broadcasters and other users pay fees to the music licensing entities ASCAP, BMI, and SESAC, which pass on those fees to the actual creators and publishers of the music. In turn, users receive rights to use the music paid for. The more complicated compulsory license system for cable television, below, is based on provisions of the 1976 copyright act. Cable systems are assessed fees based on their overall revenue and the number of distant signals imported. The Copyright Royalty Tribunal, an agency of government separate from the Copyright Office, collects the fees and decides which portion of the total should go to the many different creators of programming.

money (to be distributed through a quasi-independent committee set up by the NAB), program syndicators the lion's share of 75 percent, sports team interests 12 percent, PBS just over 5 percent, and music licensing agencies nearly 5 percent. Appeals filed by many of these parties delayed the payment process. Over the next four years, the portion allotted to commercial television increased to 4.5 percent, but broadcasters and other aggrieved parties tied up the proceedings in further court appeals.

Similarly controversial was CRT's approach to its other mandate, to fix the rate of copyright royalty that cable systems were to pay for use of distant television station material. Copyright holders and broadcasters complained about extremely low levels of payment, some as low as a few hundred dollars per year. In 1981 the CRT raised the rates to meet complaints and inflation. To compensate for this rate increase, most large cable systems importing distant signals must now pay 3.75 percent of their gross revenues to the CRT every six months.* In 1985 cable and broadcast interests agreed ahead of time to a further rate increase and presented the compromise to the CRT.

Throughout its short history, the CRT has lacked sufficient staff and expertise to resolve the contentious issues assigned it. In 1982 the agency's chairperson told Congress he felt that the whole process was unworkable and unfair and that Congress should reconsider the treatment of cable in the copyright act. A successor repeated the same charge in 1985. By late 1985 the CRT was down to only two

members (a full complement is five), and one CRT chairperson had been forced to resign because of earlier writings alleged to be racist. Bills introduced in Congress in 1985 advocated substantial revision in, or replacement of, the CRT and modification or elimination of cable's compulsory license system.

Domestic Piracy   The 1976 copyright act allows limited use of copyright materials under the fair-use principle. But interpretation of what is fair is open to considerable controversy. Two major fair-use problems are receipt of cable television or satellite material without payment of required fees, and unauthorized recording of broadcast and other media material.

Until the mid-1980s the chief *signal piracy* problem was direct illicit hookup into cable television feeder lines, which allowed people to receive cable reception without paying monthly subscriber fees. As pay cable developed, the use of "black boxes" even made possible the illegal reception of scrambled signals. The cable industry estimated that at least 10 percent of cable homes had illegal hookups, with the proportion rising to perhaps 25 percent in urban areas. Over-the-air subscription television suffered the same problem.

Until 1985 such reception appeared to violate section 605 of the communications act, since the signals were *intended* for reception only by subscribers paying to use special unscrambling devices. Cable systems prosecuted violators under the provisions of Section 605 and widely publicized the resulting felony convictions, which entailed fines of up to $10,000 and jail terms of as much as one year. Over half the states passed antipiracy laws prohibiting the manufacture, sale, or use of unauthorized decoders or antennas (NAB, 1985: 372). The cable industry found technical solutions to the problem of direct theft of pay cable services by switching from easily circum-

---

*Because Ted Turner's WTBS superstation is technically a distant signal, according to the CRT decision, it would cost those systems picking it up 3.75 percent of their gross revenues. Turner has appealed this ruling, given that his station is designed as a cable network. Cable networks, like broadcast networks, provide programming with copyright fees prepaid before local system or station use.

vented "traps" for pay channels to "addressable" converter systems, which are much harder to defeat.

The problem expanded when the prices of television receive-only earth stations began to fall. By 1986 more than a million TVROs were in service, with thousands being added monthly. Nearly all were used to receive basic cable and pay networks directly from satellites. Pay cable operators began to scramble satellite signals to protect their investments from pirates. The cable industry and pay system operators challenged the fast-growing home receiver antenna industry (and their users) in hearings before Congress. As a result, Congress modified (and renumbered) Section 605 as a part of the 1984 cable act (§17.6).

The new Section 705 allows any individual to pick up satellite cable programming *if* it is not scrambled and *if* the cable programmer does not market to individuals (or, if it does, the individual has obtained authorization, usually for a fee). The authorization applies only to satellite programming intended for personal use, not resale. Part of the cable industry's problem, of course, is how to market economically to such a scattered potential audience, about which there is no central information source.

The second major fair-use problem concerns home video recording of material off the air, off cable, or from rented cassettes. In 1976 a number of program producers brought suit against Sony, the pioneering manufacturer of home video recorders, for indirect copyright infringement.* A district court found in favor of Sony, concluding that home recording fell within the fair-use provision of the new copyright law, so long as such recordings were not resold or shown for profit. An appeals court

overturned the ruling and held that such recording *was* an infringement, a kind of piracy. Finally, the U.S. Supreme Court, after a highly unusual two-step set of oral arguments on the case, decided 5–4 that the original decision in favor of Sony had been correct (464 US 417, 1984). The high court agreed with audience research that most home recording of broadcast signals was for timeshifting purposes only (§14.6), and that "Sony's sale of such equipment to the general public does not constitute contributory infringement of respondent's copyrights."

Unresolved, however, was the legality of recording cable or pay programming, because the Sony case covered only over-the-air, or "free," broadcast material. Also not clarified was the legal status of showing a taped copy of a copyrighted film or program to a group outside the home (Ferris et al., 1983: 23A–22), a problem exacerbated by the growth of the video rental business. Hollywood producers began to apply pressure on Congress to modify the copyright act to provide for some system of extracting royalty payments from those engaging in home recording, perhaps in the form of a surcharge on recorders or tapes at the time of purchase or rental fees paid by customers to video rental stores.

The Sony case, the unexpected proliferation of TVROs, and the growth of the video rental business all illustrate the problem of keeping laws in step with technology. It is extremely difficult to reconcile conflicting demands of copyright holders and users, especially when mass usage means that great sums of money ride on the outcome, and it is likely that Congress will amend the copyright laws further, just as, when necessary, it has amended the Communications Act of 1934.

International Piracy   With the growth of cable and satellite television in foreign countries, international copyright agreements have

---

*"Indirect" because Sony was sued as the first provider of the *means* of infringement — the machines that made such "contributory infringement" of copyright possible.

become increasingly important. The United States enters into treaties with other program-producing and program-using countries in an attempt to suppress the rising tide of international program piracy. Third World countries, which typically have no substantial commercial markets for their own cultural products, depend heavily on foreign sources. They therefore usually lack effective copyright laws for protection of foreign material. (The same was once true of the United States, which in the nineteenth century was notorious for its piracy of European literature.) The International Federation of Phonogram and Videograph Producers estimated in 1985 that pirates market a quarter of all discs and tapes sold in the world, which amounts to a loss of $1.2 billion by authorized producers. Satellite-distributed programs of U.S. television stations and cable channels are routinely pirated by Caribbean stations and cable systems. The U.S. government uses the threat of general trade restrictions to dissuade other governments from engaging in such piracy, but these measures often fail to control operators of private distribution systems.

16.6 Other Laws Affecting Electronic Media

In addition to copyright, other laws that have impact on electronic media include a number of international treaties, the law of the press, advertising law, antitrust regulation, laws regarding obscenity and lotteries, and labor law, including affirmative action and equal employment opportunity. Also, broadcasters and cable system operators are subject to many narrowly focused state and local laws.

International Treaties   Agreements between the United States and other nations concerning radio and wire communications

have the status of treaties, which means that after endorsement by the U.S. Senate they have the force of federal law. Section 303 of the communications act gives the FCC the task of carrying out such treaties.

Separate regional treaties governing AM, FM, and television broadcasting have been entered into by the United States and its neighbors. AM agreements cover the widest territory, because long-distance sky-wave propagation affects the scattered islands of the Caribbean as well as the two common-border nations, Canada and Mexico. Agreements on FM and television have been reached with Canada and Mexico.

On a broader scale, treaties and agreements have been reached governing the allocation of spectrum and orbital positions for satellite communications — a truly international issue, since all geosynchronous satellites orbit over the equator. Also, as a member of the International Telecommunication Union, the United States is involved in a number of worldwide agreements (§1.5). The increased number and importance of ITU meetings has encouraged the U.S. Department of State to heighten its concern with international telecommunication policy. Thus what was once a minor office has been enlarged to the bureau (assistant secretary) level. During the 1980s, major conflicts arose from time to time over whether NTIA or the State Department had authority to set international telecommunication policy.

Law of the Press   Electronic media share with print media a miscellaneous body of laws, precedents, and privileges known as the law of the press. Press law relies heavily on common-law traditions, case-law precedents, and constitutional theories built up over many generations. Broadcasting law, in contrast, is based mostly on statute and has a relatively short history.

Nevertheless, much of press law also affects electronic media owners and programmers. Typical areas of common concern are libel, obscenity, fair trial, freedom of access to information, right of privacy, labor laws, advertising laws, copyright, and reporter's privileges. The last includes the asserted right of news personnel to withhold the identity of news sources and to refuse to surrender personal notes (including audio and video "outtakes," in the case of recorded news and news documentaries). Many of these concerns — libel, fair trial, privacy, access, and reporter's privilege — are influenced by state law and can vary considerably.

Advertising Regulation   Like the communications act, the Federal Trade Commission act created a regulatory agency to oversee an aspect of interstate commerce. Similarity between the two acts stops at about that point. The communications act set out to regulate a new technology with little legal precedent. The FTC act, however, applies to a field that has a long tradition in the common law, which greatly complicates its regulatory activity.

The FTC act as originally conceived in 1914 was intended to protect businesses from unfair competition, not consumers from unfair business practices. Consumers were expected to look out for themselves — the doctrine of *caveat emptor*, or "let the buyer beware." Not until the 1930s was it legally recognized that "the rule of *caveat emptor* should not be relied upon to reward fraud and deception" (302 US 112, 1937).

The FTC act was amended in 1938, making it unlawful to use "unfair methods of competition in commerce, and unfair or deceptive acts or practices in commerce" (15 USC 45). The amendment gave the Federal Trade Commission the basis for attacking deceptive broadcast advertising even if no harm to a competitor could be shown. This was a needed weapon, in that the communications act gives the FCC no such authority over advertising, except insofar as a licensee's character qualifications may be brought into question as a result of actions by the FTC.

In general, the FCC does not regulate the content of broadcast advertising. That is left to the FTC, which can take action against ads it finds to be false or deceptive. In the past, the FTC has also acted against misleading advertising, though generally it has not asserted that authority in the 1980s. The FCC expects broadcasters and cable operators to cooperate with the FTC and to drop any ad campaigns the FTC finds unlawful.

Antitrust Laws   The Sherman Act of 1890, the first of the two major U.S. antitrust statutes, reflected the same philosophy of protecting businesses from each other as the later FTC act. In 1914, the year the FTC act was passed, Congress complemented the Sherman Act with the Clayton Act. Together, the two antitrust acts are intended to prevent the creation of monopolies and are the basis for government actions such as the 1984 breakup of AT&T (footnote, page 42).

Courts have long held that, despite the First Amendment, generic business laws such as these antitrust statutes apply to the media. Indeed, antitrust laws are held to promote the First Amendment notion of protecting competing ideas. To some degree, antitrust law in the 1980s has become a substitute for communications policy, and its importance to the communications industries may well increase as a consequence of marketplace-based deregulation.

Lottery and Obscenity Laws   Statutes directed specifically against broadcasting of lotteries and obscenity are found not in the communications act but in the U.S. Criminal Code. The latter theoretically allows for more severe penalties than the FCC could impose for violations in these areas. The FCC, however, has retained its own rules and regulations against both.

1. *Lotteries.* The broadcast of advertising or information promoting lotteries is subject to a fine of $1,000 and/or a year's imprisonment for each day's offense (18 USC 1304). The FCC's rules usually result in more modest fines. This law created a dilemma for broadcasters when individual states began legalizing their own state lottery operations. Congress therefore amended the law to permit licensees to carry lottery information and advertising, but only within their own and adjacent states. The exemption applies only to state-operated lotteries.

The antilottery statute has a wider effect on broadcasters because of the frequent use of *contests*, both by advertisers and promotional campaigns. Care must be taken that such contests do not qualify as lotteries in the legal sense. This happens when three elements are present: a *chance* for a *prize* for a *price*. A contest that requires participants to pay any kind of entrance fee ("price" or "consideration") in which the winner is chosen by lot ("chance") and which awards the contestant something of value ("prize") is a lottery and can get a station into serious trouble.

Efforts have been made in Congress to liberalize the antilottery statute, and it seems possible that advertising of charitable and nonprofit lotteries may eventually be permitted.

2. *Obscenity.* "Whoever utters any obscene, indecent, or profane language by means of radio communication shall be fined not more than $10,000 or imprisoned for not more than two years, or both" (18 USC 1464). The FCC requested Congress to amend this law so as to explicitly broaden it to cover not only language but also visual presentations. No legis-lative action was forthcoming, however. Cases arising from this potentially significant source of program control are discussed in §18.2.

Equal Employment Opportunities
Broadcasting, once rated as one of the most discriminatory fields of employment, substantially improved its record during the 1970s as a result of the Civil Rights Act of 1964, which prohibits discrimination in employment practices by any firm with fifteen or more employees. In 1969 the FCC incorporated federal Equal Employment Opportunities (EEO) requirements in its own rules, becoming the first federal administrative agency to take such action (§17.4). Later, the addition of a new Title VI to the 1934 communications act reinforced the FCC's obligation to enforce EEO requirements in cable.

State and Local Regulation   Under the Constitution, federal laws prevail over state laws in areas designated as federal matters. This means that a state law cannot rise above the communications act; but state laws nevertheless govern many broadcaster activities that are not covered by the act.

The most notable instance of federal-state conflict in broadcasting arose between the laws of *libel* (which are a state matter) and Section 315 of the communications act, which prohibited licensees from censoring political candidates. Broadcasters were thus caught in a dilemma: they could be sued for libel as a result of broadcasting material over which they had no control. The matter was settled by the Supreme Court in 1959 when it ruled that broadcasters were exempt from state libel laws under such circumstances (360 US 525).

A study of state laws that affect broadcasting found that they touch upon no less than 89 different aspects of the medium (Sadowski, 1974). The areas most frequently affected by state laws are: (1) individual rights (libel, for example); (2) advertising (laws controlling advertising of specific products and services, for example); (3) educational broadcasting (many states have commissions to coordinate statewide public broadcasting activities); and (4) business operations (state taxes, for example).

Many state statutes govern cable television as well. Most were adopted in the 1970s, and the vast majority deal with franchise or cable right-of-way regulations, theft of service, and laws that regulate the attachment of cable lines to telephone poles. The pace of state activity in cable regulation declined in the late 1970s, however (Sterling, 1984: 308). Municipalities, too, have enacted many local regulations on cable franchising. State and local authority over cable, however, has been much limited by the addition of Title VI to the 1934 communications act (§17.6). Pending the inevitable court challenges, franchising authorities do have the power to require cable systems to provide channels for public, educational, and government access uses.

16.7 Informal Controls

Many forces outside the formal regulatory structure also influence the conduct of electronic media owners. Some of these forces operate indirectly by influencing the formal process through lobbying and participating in hearings and court cases. Others operate directly on broadcasters and cable system operators, using social and economic pressures to force changes in their conduct (Exhibit 16.4).

We have seen how all three branches of government (executive, legislative, and judicial) have input in the formal regulatory process. The FCC's divided allegiances put it under constant and often conflicting pressures — from Congress, the White House, the courts, the industries it regulates, the lobbyists who represent various special interests,

and the general public, the ultimate consumers of broadcasting and cable services. As three scholars of FCC practice noted, "To achieve its goals in a changing and dynamic milieu, the Commission must often try to gain or sustain political support against opposition" (Krasnow et al., 1982: 10).

Congressional Intervention   Although Congress gave the FCC a mandate in the Communications Act of 1934 to act on its behalf, it continually brings the commission up short if it wanders too far afield. In addition to the Senate's approval of nominations to the FCC and congressional control of the all-important budget process (§17.1), Congress conducts frequent hearings on the commission's performance and plans. In fact, it tends to second-guess the FCC on virtually every major regulatory issue that arises. This oversight is effective because the commission is extremely sensitive to congressional criticism. As a result of the rapid changes in telecommunications in the 1980s, Congress has become more active in trying to shape policy in this field. After the FCC announced plans to change the rules limiting broadcast station ownership, for example, Congress held hearings and effectively postponed the change, then persuaded the commission to modify its approach (§17.7). Given the importance of electronic media in communicating news and images of Congress to voters, lawmakers give a sympathetic hearing to licensees' and franchise holders' views on upcoming legislation; but Congress has also been particularly anxious to protect its own interests, through laws governing access to broadcasting. (§18.6).

Executive Branch Intervention   The White House has found ways to express its concerns about broadcasting ever since the 1920s, usually by indirect means. Franklin D. Roosevelt occasionally asked the FCC to pass on to the radio networks his dissatisfaction

Exhibit 16.4   Regulatory Players

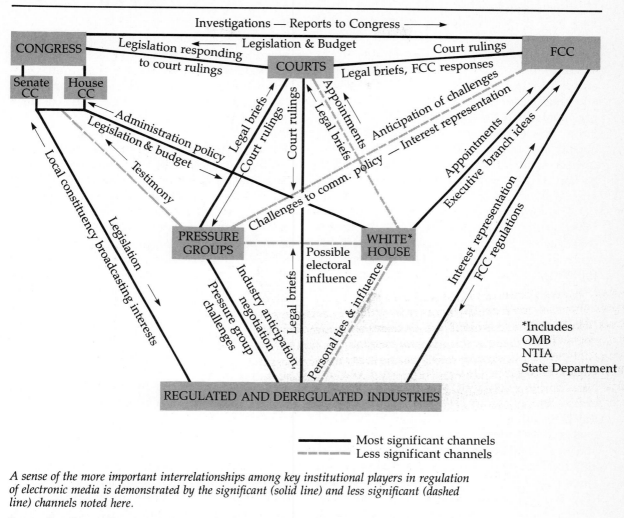

A sense of the more important interrelationships among key institutional players in regulation of electronic media is demonstrated by the significant (solid line) and less significant (dashed line) channels noted here.

Source: Based upon Krasnow, Erwin, et. al., *Politics of Broadcast Regulation* (New York: St. Martin's Press, 1982, 3rd. ed.), page 136.

with the way they handled news stories. This process reached its height with Richard Nixon's Office of Telecommunications Policy (§16.4), which seemed to devote much of its time to obtaining sympathetic news treatment of administration activities and goals. OTP director Tom "Clay" Whitehead warned net-work affiliates that it was their job to set the record straight when the networks provided "ideological plugola" or "elitist gossip." If they did not, he suggested, they might be held responsible at license renewal time. It was a shrewd attempt to drive a wedge between networks and their affiliates.

More recently, the White House played a role in a complicated economic proceeding. The FCC was considering dropping some rules that restricted network activity in the program production and distribution field. Concerned, the Hollywood production community applied pressure on Ronald Reagan, who has close ties with that industry. The president, in turn, called the FCC chairman Mark Fowler for an "informational" talk. Shortly thereafter, under pressure from concerned members of Congress as well, the FCC backed off the proposed deregulation of program production. (§17.2).

The long-term effectiveness of these and other White House maneuvers to influence broadcasting by nonregulatory means is hard to gauge. Most such efforts take place behind the scenes and are difficult to document. Broadcasters sometimes publicize such pressures widely as one means of protecting their position while also seeking support from other media.

Court Review   Those unhappy with FCC decisions or even legislation passed by Congress often take their disputes to court. Under the U.S. political system (Exhibit 16.1), however, courts are essentially passive institutions that react to disputes brought before them by others. They play two important communications policy roles. First, although this is rare, they have the power to declare that some action of government is unconstitutional. This is known as constitutional review. In 1984, Supreme Court ruled that the limits Congress had placed on editorializing by public broadcasters violated the First Amendment rights of those licensees (484 US _____).

More often, the courts review implementation of a statute or regulation. Most FCC decisions that are appealed involve such statutory review. Here the courts' role is to decide whether the activity being questioned is a fair interpretation of congressional intent in drawing up the statute. Courts themselves do not make policy doing this; rather they review the agency's *process* of making policy and the resulting policy decision reached. Courts usually do not tell administrative agencies such as the FCC what they must do; they more often tell agencies that they can *not* do something they have done, or that they ought to do it differently.

Citizen Action   The most effective route ordinary citizens can take in trying to influence the behavior of broadcasters is the *boycott*. This usually involves the threat of refusing to buy advertised products. In a pluralistic society, it is difficult for boycotters to achieve sufficient consensus and discipline to do substantial economic damage. Were it not for the fact that advertisers and broadcasters often surrender without attempting to call the boycotters' bluff, boycotts would rarely have any discernible success.

Although broadcasting and cable boycotts often have worthwhile goals, the technique is negative and can be counterproductive. Boycotts seek to impose by coercive means the values of one group of people on all other groups. Not only do they rarely accomplish anything of lasting value, they run the risk of alienating prospective supporters who value freedom of expression. Even those who may agree philosophically with boycott objectives may refuse to cooperate because they dislike being told by self-appointed judges what they may see and hear.

Economic boycotts have the regressive tendency of forcing advertisers to intrude further into program decision making. Direct advertiser control over programs, as was common until the early 1960s, inevitably invites conflicts between commercial expediency and the broader public interest. In fact, advertiser control over programs is expressly forbidden in the broadcasting laws of most countries other than the United States.

Boycotts usually arise because programs, or even proposed programs, offend (1) church groups, (2) ethnic groups, or (3) single-issue groups. Following are examples of each:

1. *Church groups.* A widely publicized attack on immorality in television emerged in 1981, spurred by the success of fundamentalist religious broadcasters in the 1980 political campaign. The Coalition for Better Television, a joint venture by several fundamental groups (including the Moral Majority movement, spearheaded by the Reverend Jerry Falwell), threatened to boycott advertisers whose commercials appeared in programs judged to be immoral. The coalition set up a national panel of monitors to evaluate levels of sex, profanity, and violence in television. It kept the identity of its monitors secret and revealed no data on the validity of the methods used or the reliability of the findings.

Unlike most previous boycott campaigns, this one aimed at programming in general, not simply at a few especially provocative programs. The networks vigorously denounced the coalition's goal of forcing its views on the rest of the public, but the advertising community, as usual, reacted less militantly. Procter & Gamble, the biggest television advertiser, announced it had withdrawn advertising from fifty program episodes found to be morally objectionable; other advertisers showed concern by consulting with coalition leaders. With the exception of this advertiser capitulation, which was remarkably similar in pattern to what had happened in the blacklisting episodes of the 1950s (§3.9), the impact of the coalition on program content was minimal.

2. *Ethnic groups.* Ethnic awareness and separatism increased markedly during the 1970s; members of minority groups are now quite sensitive to the images of them projected in broadcast fiction. Common stereotypes of American Indians, Chinese, Irish, Italians,

Japanese, Jews, Mexicans, and Poles have all come under attack. Old films are now routinely edited for television to remove the gross ethnic slurs they often contain.

Ethnic groups are also much more outspoken about station hiring practices than they once were. A recent ethnic-group boycott occurred in 1986 when CBS-owned-and-operated WBBM-TV in Chicago was picketed for weeks after a black newscaster with low ratings was demoted. The issue grew into a broader-based controversy about the role a television station should play in a market that has a substantial minority population. Although CBS appointed a black general manager for the station, demands for minority-hiring quotas and training programs continued unabated. As this book goes to press, the issues had not been resolved.

3. *Single-issue groups.* Months before CBS showed a 1975 television documentary called "The Guns of Autumn," the National Rifle Association and similar organizations began a boycott of companies that intended to buy advertising time on the program. As a result, when the 90-minute program about hunting went on the air, fourteen of its sixteen commercial spots remained unsold. CBS reported that it received nineteen thousand letters of complaint, its largest mail count since Edward R. Murrow's famous *See It Now* program on McCarthy (§3.9).

In view of such a high level of interest, CBS followed with a second program called "Echoes of the Guns of Autumn," in which both opponents and producers of the program had a chance to argue their case face-to-face. CBS could find only one advertiser willing to risk being identified with the show.

Even public broadcasting, ostensibly freer to present a variety of points of view without concern for advertisers, has been the target of citizen action. In 1984, PBS presented a highly acclaimed thirteen-part series on the Vietnam War, produced in cooperation with British and

French firms. Even a decade after the war's conclusion, however, the role of the United States, and thus the series' depiction of that role, was highly controversial. A conservative media watchdog group, Accuracy in Media (AIM), produced a 50-minute documentary "reply" to the PBS series, attacking details and the overall tone of the program. PBS aired the AIM attack in mid-1985, following it with a 45-minute discussion between producers and researchers of both programs. This latter program brought more complaints against PBS for having "given in" to its critics.

Consumerism   A distinction can be made between boycotts and *consumer activism*, or *consumerism*. The differences are often blurred, but fundamentally consumerism represents a more constructive, positive approach to social control than does the boycott. Consumer goals are often broader in scope and less wedded to special interests than are organized boycotts. Even when the basic goals are the same, the methods of consumerism are likely to result in more beneficial and longer-lasting results than will come from merely persuading advertisers to withdraw a commercial commitment or network affiliates to turn down a particular program. Consumerism activities might include, for example, the encouragement of new programs that portray ethnic minorities fairly rather than the suppression of existing programs that treat them unfairly.

During the 1960s, several factors converged to strengthen the consumer movement, chiefly civil rights activism and opposition to the Vietnam War. Consumer-oriented activities flourished in this era, and among them was heightened interest in broadcast reform, especially in the quality of programming. The single most important event that crystallized this interest in broadcast reform was a forceful direct intervention by a federal court of appeals in the license-renewal case of television station WLBT.

Consumer Standing and the WLBT Case
In 1955 a group of citizens made the first of a series of complaints to the FCC about the conduct of WLBT, a VHF station in Jackson, Mississippi. Although 45 percent of the station's potential audience was black, the station blatantly discriminated against blacks in program content and hiring practices. The FCC dismissed the complaints, saying that the local citizens had no legal right to participate in a licensing decision. When WLBT's license came up again for renewal in 1964, local groups obtained legal assistance from the Office of Communications of the United Church of Christ (UCC), in New York.

The UCC petitioned the FCC on behalf of the local groups for permission to intervene in the WLBT renewal application, but the FCC again rejected the petition, saying that citizens had no legal *standing* to intervene. At that time, the commission recognized only signal interference and economic injury as reasons to give other parties the right to demand a hearing in renewal cases. This meant, in effect, that only other licensees had standing to challenge existing licensees. The fact that the 45 percent of the Jackson population that was black had made a substantial investment in receiver purchase and repair had not, in the FCC's view, given it a sufficient economic stake in the station's operation.

The UCC appealed to federal court, claiming that the FCC had no right to broadly bar representatives of the viewing public from intervening in renewals, or to award a renewal without a hearing in the face of substantial public opposition. The court agreed, noting that there was ample precedent in nonbroadcast areas for allowing consumers public standing to challenge administrative actions.

Accordingly, the court directed the FCC to hold hearings on WLBT's renewal and to give standing to some representatives of the public to participate (359 F 2d 994, 1966). The FCC dragged its feet, fearful (along with the broadcasting industry) of a flood of petitions swamping commission hearing rooms. Finally, the FCC held a hearing and grudgingly permitted UCC to participate. The outcome, however, was yet another renewal for the operators of WLBT.

Frustrated with this treatment by the FCC, the UCC again went to court. In 1969 the exasperated court reconsidered the case — fourteen years after the first complaints had been recorded. The court rebuked the FCC for "scandalous delay" and a continued reluctance to allow public intervention. In view of the commission's record and its treatment of intervening citizens, the court ordered the WLBT license canceled and an interim operator assigned while a proceeding to select a new licensee was underway (425 F 2d 543, 1969). But ten more years were to pass before a new permanent licensee was selected. Altogether, the case stretched over a quarter-century of delays.

The WLBT case had far-reaching impact. In the short term, the case triggered many more petitions to deny renewal, just as the FCC had feared. However, this "reign of terror," as a trade magazine called it, resulted in few actual hearings and still fewer denials. Of the 342 challenges in 1971–1973, only 16 resulted in license-renewal denials.

An exacting standard of evidence set up by the FCC and approved by the court was responsible for this high rate of petition failure. The communications act, said the FCC and the courts, called for overwhelmingly convincing evidence that a hearing was needed to decide whether a renewal would be in the public interest, before renewal could be delayed. Only after an opponent presented such evidence was the FCC obliged to schedule a license-renewal application for hearing (466 F 2d 316, 1972). This meant that challengers who opposed license renewals had to gather highly relevant, concrete, and legally convincing evidence simply to force the FCC to hold a hearing.

To make this exacting process easier, the FCC in 1971 mandated that stations keep license-renewal applications and other important documents in a station public file (§17.4), readily available for public inspection. In 1974 the commission issued a *Broadcast Procedure Manual* providing details on what intervening parties should do to construct sound legal cases. The manual, though badly dated in parts, is still legally required to be in every station's public file. It explains how the FCC handles complaints and how citizens can participate in its proceedings (39 FR 32288, 1974). In 1976 the FCC established an office of consumer assistance to provide further guidance, but by the 1980s, budget cuts and changes in administration philosophy had substantially reduced the office's activities.

Consumerism in Decline   Later deregulatory activity by the FCC made citizen intervention much harder (§17.2). The FCC lifted requirements that licensees keep detailed logs and complicated renewal forms with a wealth of programming data, past and proposed, in their public files. The commission's actions paralleled a general political and economic trend to lessen government's regulation of business. In broadcasting, the effect of this trend was to reduce the leverage intervening citizens could bring to bear on both licensees and the commission.

A good example of this was the rapid rise and subsequent decline in importance of *negotiated settlements*. The fact that the FCC had to consider consumer challenges radically changed licensee attitudes toward consumer groups in the 1970s. Even weak challenges could cause a great deal of trouble, obliging licensees to prepare expensive legal cases for possible hearings and putting routine renewal in jeopardy. Licensees learned to take steps to prevent complaints from growing into full-scale petitions to deny. One approach was to negotiate a settlement of differences in return for withdrawal of a threat to petition the FCC.

Settlement by agreement proved particularly effective in situations involving proposed changes of ownership. An offer to buy is good only for a stipulated period of time. Citizen group opposition to a sale can make would-be buyers especially anxious to come to terms before the seller's offer expires. Thus several group sales (§17.8) were expedited when buyers made agreements with ethnic and racial groups about training for minorities and modifications in programming. In 1975 the FCC adopted a policy statement giving guidelines for such agreements (57 FCC 2d 42). Taking a cautious approach, the commission said it would neither approve nor disapprove of lawful agreements, but that licensees had to retain ultimate responsibility for all programming and hiring decisions. Also, the FCC held that a negotiated settlement between a licensee and an intervening group did not preclude the group from filing a petition to deny renewal. The FCC further required that written agreements be kept available in a station's public file.

An indication of the declining effectiveness of consumerism was the outcome of controversy over *format changes*. Listener groups sometimes opposed changes in radio programming from classical to popular music, or jazz to talk, or all-news to music, especially when the changes came about because of new ownership. Although such opposition affected relatively few radio stations in the 1970s, a fundamental question was raised: Should marketplace competition be the only control over diversity of broadcast programming? The FCC said yes, but its decision was overturned by an appeals court in the *WEFM* case (506 F 2d 246, 1974). In that case, a citizens' group had protested a Chicago FM station's switch from a classical-music format to a rock format, after having had a classical-music policy for thirty-six years. In a later decision, the same court held that since the marketplace did not always work perfectly, the commission might well have to intervene to preserve a viable format unique to a market. The commission appealed, and in 1981 the Supreme Court upheld the FCC, agreeing that the commission, not courts, should set policy and that the FCC's view that programming decisions are best left to the interplay of market forces should stand (101 S. Ct. 1266, 1981). The decision came as a significant affirmation of the FCC's growing reluctance to regulate and an indication of diminished powers of courts to overturn FCC decisions with which they disagreed (Krasnow et al., 1982: 145).

In the 1980s consumerism in general faced the most hostile political climate in 30 years. A reaction had set in against what many voters regarded as excessive government solicitude for consumer interests in areas such as the environment, occupational safety, and public health. Some consumer groups did manage to present effectively argued points of view before the FCC and Congress concerning laws, rules, and policies, and certainly consumer group pressure was important in the retention and even expansion of EEO policies for electronic media. But consumer-interest activities suffered when budgets were cut at federal agencies such as the FCC and the FTC. Many once-active consumer groups closed up shop, and those that remained seemed shrill anachronisms on the sidelines of a fast-changing field. The same thing happened on the local level; consumer groups that promoted the public-service aspects of cable faded when municipal governments and cable operators largely ignored them.

Industry Codes   Many large industries adopt voluntary codes of conduct to cultivate favorable public relations and forestall abuses that might otherwise bring about government regulation. But codes can also be used to limit competition. For this reason, enforceable private-industry codes that affect the freedom to compete are unlawful under antitrust laws.

The National Association of Broadcasters developed a code for radio programming and advertising practice in 1939, following it up with a parallel television code in 1952. These codes were necessarily voluntary, using broad generalizations and lots of "shoulds" and "should nots" but leaving decisions to the discretion of station management. Nonetheless, the codes established generally observed standards, especially regarding the amount of time that television stations could devote to advertising during different times of the day.

Despite the precautions the NAB had taken to avoid any hint of coercion in the language and administration of the codes, the Department of Justice brought suit against it in 1979. The suit alleged that the advertising time standards in the television code "artificially curtailed" advertising, repressing price competition and depriving advertisers of "the benefits of free and open competition." The move was surprising, since the FCC had tacitly accepted the NAB's recommended standards as a reasonable norm, although without adopting them officially. Late in 1982 a federal district court approved a consent decree between the NAB and the Justice Department that put an end to the NAB codes (NAB, 1985: 138).

The demise of industrywide NAB codes has seemed to have little effect, however, as the networks and many stations continue to follow their own internal standards, some of which are tougher than the NAB codes. Marketplace competitive pressures also apparently keep in check the amount of time devoted to advertising. But critics argue that the amount and intrusiveness of advertising has increased. Thus far, there is little solid research to support either point of view.

As the use of industrywide codes has declined, networks' program standards departments, which evaluate commercials and programs at various stages of development, have become much more important. Network standards officials therefore exercise multilayered control over television programs, from basic program concepts to the specific words and scenes in final productions. Most theatrical films are "edited for television," not only for length but to meet the fairly conservative standards of the television networks.

Cable television has much more relaxed standards than does broadcast television, and even major independent stations tend to be more liberal than the networks in what they will accept and show. Pay cable's regular showing of films with uncut violence, profanity, and nudity has raised questions of taste, but to nowhere near the degree such material on over-the-air television would. Still, perceptions of obscenity in cable programming have raised local objections and spurred several court cases (§18.2). Cable's looser approach, and audience appeal, applies pressure on the networks to loosen their standards as well.

Professional Self-regulation   Broadcasting is often referred to as a profession, a term that implies both self-regulation and self-denial. "A rough-and-ready way to decide whether you have a profession," wrote Harold Lasswell, "is to find out if people will turn down jobs" (1952: 160). He felt that principle should outweigh income.

By this test, probably not many practicing broadcasters would qualify as professionals. There is not much evidence of broadcast employees (as distinguished from owners and managers) turning down jobs on the grounds that to accept them would violate their own personal codes of ethics or be contrary to the public interest. Aside from engineers, probably the broadcast employees that come closest to meeting the test of professionalism are those represented by the Radio Television News Directors Association (RTNDA). Members subscribe to a "Code of Broadcast News Ethics." They support a code that gives accurate and comprehensive presentation of broadcast news precedence over all other motives. Article Six of the code appears to mandate refusal to distort the news to suit the whims of owners and managers:

Broadcast journalists shall seek actively to present all news the knowledge of which will serve the public interest, no matter what selfish, uninformed or corrupt efforts attempt to color it, withhold it, or prevent its presentation.

Instances of news personnel denouncing attempts of owners to control the news occasionally surface, but not very often. It appears that ethical journalists are more likely to leave a station when this happens than to make it a public issue.

Press Criticism   Coverage of broadcasting, cable, and related services in the trade and popular press not only informs others of industry developments but often has considerable effect on the making of policy. Congress, the White House, the FCC, and other agencies closely follow stories on the activities of the electronic media, thereby judging to some extent the impact and success of their policies. Certain writers and trade newsletters are especially important in this respect, for how a new policy or rule "plays" in the trade press is an indication of how it is likely to be received by the industry itself. Indeed, many policymakers first learn of important initiatives by other agencies (and sometimes their own!) in press reports. Nominations to the FCC are conspicuously displayed on pages of the trade press long before names officially are sent to the Senate.

As for programming criticism, writers in major newspapers and magazines probably have more impact on news and public-affairs programming than on mass entertainment. Moreover, they influence producers of such programs more than they do the general audience. Their agenda-setting role, however, can sometimes focus government and industry attention on areas of controversy such as violence, advertising of certain products, and copyright matters.

The most serious attempt at organized self-criticism of the news media, the National News Council, failed after a ten-year struggle for recognition. An independent, grant-funded watchdog agency organized in 1973 to deal with complaints of unfairness in print and broadcast news, the council was made up of a mixture of journalists and people from other fields, with newspeople in the minority. In its short life, it reviewed thousands of complaints, finding sometimes for the complainer and sometimes for the medium, but in each case making an extensive investigation. Although the council's members and methods were beyond reproach, even by its critics, and though it lacked any enforcement powers, many in the media were greatly disturbed by the idea of an organization that seemingly took upon itself the duty of deciding what was right or wrong about news stories. A number of major newspapers therefore refused to cover the council's findings, and this lack of coverage led to the dissolution of the council in 1984.

Summary

• Constitutionally, electronic media come under the control of Congress because of the commerce clause. Through the Communications Act of 1934, Congress delegates supervisory responsibility to the FCC, using the broad guideline of "public interest, convenience, and necessity" to define the commission's discretionary powers.

• Though many attempts have been made to rewrite or replace the 1934 communications act, most notably the rewrite efforts in 1977–1981, amendments have been remarkably few for an act so old and a field subject to such rapid change. Cable communication was the subject of a new Title VI added to the act in 1984.

• The most important regulatory trend in the late 1970s and the 1980s has been toward a general *deregulation* of electronic media (§17.2). This trend helped defuse pressure for replacement of the 1934 communications act.

• The National Telecommunications and Information Administration (NTIA) develops telecommunication policy for the executive branch of the federal government. Among its tasks is spectrum allocation to federal agency users of radio communications.

• Copyright regulation is based on the 1976 copyright act, which took effect in 1978. This act provides for a means of apportioning payments to copyright holders, and allows limited fair use of copyrighted material without payment.

• Copyright is a controversial area of law, especially when comparing the rights of cable owners and broadcasters. Some issues, such as music-licensing payments and performer royalties, are longstanding, whereas others, including piracy of signals from satellite networks, are recent developments from fast-changing technology.

• The electronic media are also subject to many other laws: international treaties, the law of the press, advertising regulation, antitrust laws, bans on lotteries and obscene material, equal employment opportunity requirements, and (especially for cable) state and local regulation.

• Informal controls on broadcasting and cable include intervention by the executive and legislative branches in FCC actions, court reviews of FCC and congressional decisions, citizen group actions (now in decline), network and station codes of conduct, professional self-regulation (especially by engineers and newsmen), coverage by the trade press, and general public criticism of electronic media.

CHAPTER 17

FCC Administration of the Law

In the last chapter we surveyed the statutory basis of federal electronic media law. Congress left to the Federal Communications Commission, as the expert administrative agency, most of the details of implementing this law with specific rules and regulations. This chapter explores the way the FCC has used the authority granted it by the communications act to carry out the practical day-to-day licensing and regulation of electronic media. Our discussion covers FCC policy as of mid-1986 — a point we wish to emphasize, since electronic media regulation is in the midst of rapid change in the 1980s.

17.1 FCC Basics

Regulatory Agencies　Starting with the Interstate Commerce Commission in 1887, Congress set up a series of independent regulatory agencies to supervise federal aspects of private activities in commerce, power, transportation, labor, and finance. The growth of such agencies accelerated tremendously before and after World War II, to the extent that there are now over eighty. What to do about this runaway bureaucratic growth, with the countless intrusions by federal agencies into practically every aspect of national life, emerged as a major political issue after 1975.

Federal agencies play a unique role in Washington, D.C., blurring the lines separating legislative, executive, and judicial branches of government. As a "creature of Congress," the FCC acts on behalf of the policymaking legislative branch, and when it makes rules and regulations, it acts in a quasi-legislative capacity. Operationally, it also functions as an executive agency, putting the will of Congress into effect. And when the FCC interprets the 1934 communications act, conducts hearings, or decides disputes, it takes on a judicial role.

Budget and Organization　In fiscal year 1985, Congress appropriated over $95 million for operation of the FCC. Part of this budget pays the five commissioners and their staff of just under nineteen hundred. The Field Operations Bureau, Common Carrier Bureau, and Mass Media Bureau are the three largest operation units, each with about four hundred staff members.

The unit of most interest here is the Mass Media Bureau. It has four divisions, the duties of which are as follows:

1. *Audio services.* Directs the processing of applications for construction permits (§17.3), licenses, and license renewals for radio stations and auxiliary operations.

2. *Video services.* Directs the processing of applications for construction permits, licenses, and license renewals for television stations and related auxiliary operations. Maintains a small staff for the FCC's few remaining cable television responsibilities.

3. *Policy and rules.* Handles FCC proceedings that produce new rules and conducts economic studies needed for policymaking decisions.

4. *Enforcement.* Processes complaints, ensures compliance with statutes and rules, issues interpretations of rules, represents the Mass Media Bureau in hearings within the commission.

The managing director of the FCC, who reports to the chairman, supervises the FCC's financial and operational aspects. A number of offices provide general services for all FCC operational bureaus. The Office of Plans and Policy is largely an economic research unit. The Office of Chief Engineer includes much of the engineering expertise of the FCC and runs the FCC Laboratory, which grants *type acceptance* of broadcast transmitters and other equipment (indicating that a given electronic device will not cause interference with other services, and may thus be used). The Office of General Counsel represents the FCC before other agencies and the courts, and provides internal legal advice for the commission.

Commissioners As we have seen, the president nominates FCC commissioners, but the nominations are subject to approval by the Senate. The five members* serve five-year

terms and may be reappointed. Commissioners must be citizens, may not have a financial interest in any type of communications business, and must devote full time to the job. The commission chairman, designated as such by the president, is the chief spokesperson for the agency. Either in person or through designated subordinates, the chairman represents the FCC at congressional hearings and in other formal government contacts. The five commissioners meet as a decision-making group several times each month, in meetings open to the public.

Commissioners generally do not originate commission policy. Generation of FCC policy is a staff function, though commissioners are active in shaping, and sometimes rejecting or altering, proposed staff drafts of commission orders. Each commissioner has two or three staff assistants who help analyze the flood of complex issues presented at each meeting. Commissioners (often referred to collectively as "the Eighth Floor" for their location in the FCC headquarters building on M Street Northwest in Washington) are in many ways creatures of their own staffs.

Staff Roles References to "the commission" usually signify not only the five commissioners but also the senior staff of the FCC's various divisions. Most applications, inquiries, and complaints are handled by staff members and do not come to any commissioner's personal attention. The staff handles thousands of letters from the public, as well as applications and forms from the industries it regulates. Over twenty-five forms affect broadcast stations alone, ranging from initial applications for construction permits to reports on employment statistics. Deregulation, however, has reduced the paperwork burden (§17.2). Except for the very top administrators (who are appointees of the chairman), the staff is a part of the federal civil service, and many members

---

*Until 1982, the FCC had seven members. In authorizing the commission's budget for that year, Congress reduced the number to five. One major cause of the streamlining was a political battle over appointments to the agency, although there was considerable agreement even within the commission that the change would not affect FCC actions and would save funds.

Exhibit 17.1   Organization of the FCC

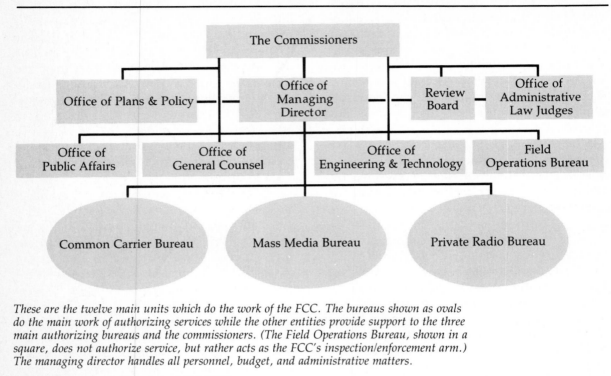

These are the twelve main units which do the work of the FCC. The bureaus shown as ovals do the main work of authorizing services while the other entities provide support to the three main authorizing bureaus and the commissioners. (The Field Operations Bureau, shown in a square, does not authorize service, but rather acts as the FCC's inspection/enforcement arm.) The managing director handles all personnel, budget, and administrative matters.

Source: *Telecommunications Journal* 47-6 (1980).

serve for years, developing in-depth expertise on which commissioners depend.

Staff decisions, based upon formally delegated authority from the commissioners, are guided by *processing rules.* These spell out which decisions may be settled at the staff level and which need to be put on a meeting agenda for consideration by the five commissioners.

Staff recommendations accompany items forwarded for formal commission consideration. The staff thus exerts a pervasive influence, not only on day-to-day operations but on long-term policy. Barry Cole, who spent several years closely observing the commis-

sion, noted that "staff members who are accomplished politicians and wily empire builders may find themselves with greater power than any single commission member . . . key staff members have the power to decide what information to bring to the commission's attention and in what form" (Cole and Oettinger, 1978: 11).

Rule Making   The function of rule making generates the large body of administrative law called FCC *rules and regulations.** When the

---

*The phrase "rules and regulations" is traditional, though in practice a rule does not differ from a regulation.

commission receives a petition to undertake a certain action, or acts on its own, it may issue a *notice of inquiry* (for a subject that needs preliminary comment and research), a *notice of proposed rule making* (for a subject on which specific new rules are offered for public comment), or a combination of both. These notices invite comment from interested parties, most of whom are attorneys who represent affected individuals, stations, companies, or whole industries. A few public-interest groups participate as well (§16.7). Parties often submit extensive research studies to buttress their arguments for or against the FCC's intended action. On rare occasions, proposed rule changes of special significance or controversial nature may be scheduled for oral argument on "the Eighth Floor."

After digesting these outside comments, the staff prepares a proposed decision for the commissioners, usually in the form of a recommended *report and order* announcing the new rule with some background discussion. Once the FCC acts, adopting or modifying the proposed report and order, its actions are subject to petitions for reconsideration by the commission and/or by appeal to the U.S. Court of Appeals for the District of Columbia (Exhibit 17.2). Indeed in controversial matters, some party or another appeals nearly every so-called final FCC decision, thus delaying implementation by months or years.

In some situations, rule making would be too cumbersome, too restrictive, or simply too difficult to defend. In such cases the FCC may resort to *policymaking* instead — that is, summarizing past actions and laying down general directives instead of hard-and-fast rules. An example of this process is the FCC's response to a petition from Action for Children's Television for rule making on children's television programs. Instead of adopting rules as proposed by ACT, the commission issued a state-

Exhibit 17.2 Rule-Making Process

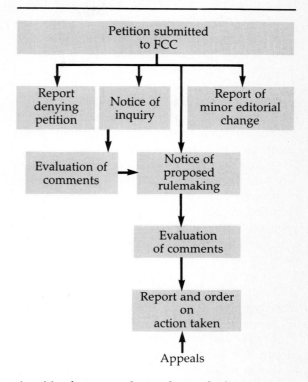

A petition for a new rule or a change of rules can come from the general public, from any branch of the federal government, or from a unit within the FCC itself. A denial or an adoption may be appealed for reconsideration. Each step of the process must be documented in the Federal Register *so that all interested parties can keep themselves informed of rule-making actions.*

ment of general policy that outlined what it expected of licensees (§18.3).

Adjudication   The second major class of FCC decision making is *adjudication*. This procedure settles specific disputes, whether between outside parties (rival applicants for a television channel, for example) or between the FCC and an outside party (the Mass Media Bureau and a broadcast owner who is resisting imposition of a fine, for example). The simplest disputes may be settled summarily at the staff level, but many become the subjects of *hearings* or further sanctions (§17.8).

Informal Regulation   In addition to formal rule making and adjudication, the FCC can influence licensee conduct through public statements in meetings, speeches, and articles, and through personal contacts with licensees or their attorneys. This indirect, "raised eyebrow" approach to regulation conveys an implied threat: "If you don't take it upon yourselves to put your own house in order, the government may step in and do it for you."

Carried a bit further, the raised eyebrow technique of regulation turns into general *jawboning*. In the mid-1970s, for example, the FCC found itself under intense pressure from Congress and public groups to do something about the exposure of children to increasing levels of televised violence and sex. Knowing that a direct assault on the problem would certainly collide with First Amendment protections (see Box, page 503), the commission jawboned the networks and the NAB, which then had a code of self-regulation (§16.7), into "voluntarily" adopting *family viewing time* standards of program content. The industry representatives agreed in 1975 not to schedule "entertainment programming inappropriate for viewing by a general family audience" until after the first two hours of prime time; in cases where postponements were not feasible, they agreed to flash advisories on the screen to alert viewers that family standards might be violated. A number of writers and directors took the FCC–industry agreement to court as a violation of the First Amendment. In 1979 a federal district court judge held that the policy indeed violated the First Amendment, be-

cause the government had clearly coerced the industry into agreement (423 F Sup 1134, 1976). An appeals court overturned the decision (609 F 2d 355, 1979), and the case was eventually settled out of court in 1984 (*Broadcasting*, 7 Jan 1985). By that time, however, the FCC's whole approach to electronic media had changed radically.

17.2 Deregulation

During the 1970s, many responsible critics both outside and within the FCC agreed that the commission had failed to practice what it preached. It had set up elaborate standards to govern renewal, choice among competing applicants, public service programming, ownership diversification, and other matters. But when it came to deciding actual cases, the commission often ignored its own high-sounding standards. The FCC needed to bring its professed standards into closer harmony with actual practice. Many felt that if the rules could not, or should not, be enforced, they should be changed. The practical and economic theory underlying this attitude moved to the forefront as deregulation fever struck Washington in the 1970s, starting under Gerald Ford, continuing under Jimmy Carter, and accelerating under Ronald Reagan. Whereas the Democrats seemed concerned about this pragmatic cleaning out of "regulatory underbrush," the Republicans took an ideological approach, pursuing with considerable zeal what they termed regulatory overkill. Commission chairman Mark Fowler referred to the benefits of "unregulation." Deregulation affected not only the FCC but other federal administrative agencies as well. It is the administrative counterpart of the legislative rewrites discussed in §16.3.

Deregulation came about as most policymakers became convinced that government regulations often cost far more to administer than they paid back in public benefits. According to the increasingly prevalent economic and political thinking, marketplace competition could better achieve the goals of much regulation. As noted in §16.4, deregulation became part and parcel of national telecommunication policy in the 1980s.

Radio Deregulation   At the FCC in the mid-1970s, a move known somewhat confusingly as "reregulation" developed to do away with many minor regulations. But few important or controversial requirements were dropped until the 1980s, when the FCC focused first on commercial radio, with proposals to reverse the trend of regulation.

In 1981, after an inquiry initiated four years earlier, the commission deleted four of its longstanding constraints on radio licensees. It abandoned requirements or guidelines for (1) following the formal and complicated process of ascertainment of local community needs as a background to programming decisions (a requirement for general knowledge of the community of license was retained); (2) keeping specifically formatted program logs; (3) setting a minimum level of nonentertainment programming; and (4) setting a maximum level of advertising time on the air (84 FCC 2d 968).*

To justify its decision, hotly controversial at the time (partially because some thought

the commission had always had formal rules on programming and advertising and because others feared deregulation might mean the end of religion on the air), the FCC relied on economic theory, arguing that the public interest can best be served by curbing government regulations and unleashing competitive forces in their stead:

Producers (providers) of goods and services must be responsive to consumers' desires in order to compete successfully with rival producers. Consumers, by their choice of purchases, determine which producers (providers) will succeed. Moreover, not only does the competition among producers for consumers lead to the production of the goods and services that consumers want most, the same competitive process forces producers continually to seek less costly ways of providing those goods and services. As a result, parties operating freely in a competitive market environment will determine and fulfill consumer wants, and do so efficiently. (73 FCC 2d 457, at 492, 1979)

According to deregulatory theory, the FCC should abandon most regulation of *behavior* (requiring licensees to go through the ascertainment procedure to determine local needs, for example). Instead it should rely on *structural* regulation, which affects the number of competitors able to offer services to the public (rules on the number of stations under single ownership, crossownership between broadcast stations and other types of media outlets, and the ease with which new competitors can enter a market, for example). The FCC would pursue a hands-off policy on licensee behavior except in cases of market failure.

TV and Network Deregulation   Having paved the way with commercial radio deregulation, the FCC followed by deregulating educational radio and television (98 FCC 2d 746, 1984) and then commercial television (98 FCC 2d 1076, 1984). In each case, the commission lifted requirements for the ascertainment of·

---

*Items 3 and 4 of this list are examples of the commissioners' delegation of authority, noted in §17.1. The FCC, contrary to general opinion, never had *rules* mandating specific amounts of nonentertainment programming or maximum amounts of advertising time. Instead, it had set up *guidelines* that allowed staff processing of applications unless those guidelines were exceeded, in which case the application had to go before the full commission. The practical effect, of course, was that the guidelines became virtual quotas as applicants sought to avoid the close scrutiny and the delay that would result if the staff kicked a decision "upstairs" to the commissioners.

community needs and for program logs, and for commercial television lifted the programming and advertising guidelines parallel to those for radio.

But in one important sense, as Commissioner Mimi Dawson argued (*Broadcasting*, 15 Aug. 1983), abandonment of these rules represented *re*regulation. In other words, although the FCC eliminated guidelines calling for a minimum amount of nonentertainment programming, it put something else in their place. Partly because of congressional and court pressure, the commission now required all stations to place in their public files (§17.5) quarterly statements of problems and issues and a list of programming measures the licensees had taken to meet or deal with those problems (96 FCC 2d 930, 1984). The FCC also instituted a nebulous general requirement that licensees attempt to address (somehow) the major issues in their communities.

Television networks, a more difficult deregulatory target, were the subject of an intensive FCC special inquiry in 1979–1980 (§4.5). A special staff undertook exhaustive research on the potential for new broadcast networks, the jurisdiction of the FCC in network regulation,* questions of broadcast station and cable system ownership (§17.7), the impact of existing FCC network regulations, and the degree to which cable and newer media had broadened competition. The staff reported that prior network regulation had utterly failed to bring about its stated goals of fostering increased diversity of programming; rather, it had stifled competition, often by protecting the networks from the competition of new technologies. It

concluded that the commission should undo most of its existing network rules (FCC, 1980: 491).*

When the commission tried to follow the special-inquiry recommendations, industry lobbyists fought the effort to a standstill. Program syndicators strongly supported the prime-time access rule (§13.2), which the special staff report opposed. Syndicators have thrived on the PTAR, though it does little to curb network domination of evening television time, as originally intended. Even more contentious was the attempt to lift two related rules governing financial interest and syndication. These rules restrict network ownership and distribution of programs once programs complete their network runs. After the FCC voted to issue a Notice of Proposed Rule Making (NPRM) to drop the rules, lobbyists pressured Congress into holding hearings to get the FCC to postpone implementation. In an unprecedented action, President Reagan directed the NTIA, and pressured the FCC, to change their plans to deregulate in this area (§16.7).

Cable Deregulation   In the development of new media services, however, the FCC has substantially streamlined procedures and requirements. As discussed in §4.2, the development of cable was initially delayed by the heavy hand of FCC regulation in the 1965–1975 period. As the first nonbroadcast mass electronic medium to develop, cable took the brunt of the FCC's usual policy of that period: protect the status quo, regulate first, and check the impact later. The commission sought especially to protect UHF television de-

---

*Bear in mind that the communications act gives the FCC no explicit power to regulate the networks. Section 303(i) gives the commission the right to "make special regulations applicable to radio *stations* engaged in chain broadcasting" (emphasis added) but not to networks directly. The commission regulates network policies indirectly by regulation of licensees that are affiliates or O&Os.

---

*Impossible to undo, however, was the chief reason for the three-network broadcast television system: the FCC's original 1952 television-channel allotment plan (§3.6), which made it impossible for a fourth network to recruit enough VHF affiliates to compete directly and effectively on a national basis with the established "big three."

Exhibit 17.3   Deregulation of Cable

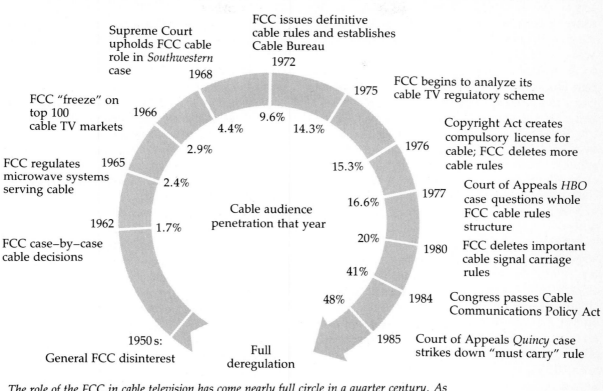

The role of the FCC in cable television has come nearly full circle in a quarter century. As cable expanded, so did broadcaster fear of the service. But since 1975, regulation of cable has steadily diminished for reasons discussed in the text, culminating in the strongly deregulatory cable act of 1984 which limited state and local regulators as well as the FCC.

velopment, which it thought rapid cable expansion would endanger. A series of court reverses, followed by the economic rethinking noted above, resulted in the FCC's dropping most of its cable regulation by 1980 (Exhibit 17.3).

By 1985, the most controversial FCC restriction on cable still in place was the *must-carry* rule, which called for cable systems to carry the signals of all "significantly viewed" television stations within the system's cover-

age areas. Cable-specific program services thus had to compete for carriage with stations that had assured channel space. The rule was intended to protect broadcasters from discriminatory treatment by cable operators and to help stations with weak signals, usually nonnetwork UHF and public stations, by equalizing the strength of all stations' signals.

The must-carry rule, however, penalized cable systems, especially those with small numbers of channels, by filling up their available channels with broadcast signals, leaving few options for cable-specific programs. Systems whose service areas straddled two or more broadcast markets sometimes had to carry two or more affiliates of the same networks, stations that duplicated all but a few local programs. Systems in communities near San Francisco, for example, sometimes had to carry three signals from the same network because of overlapping markets.

Ted Turner, as an operator of satellite-delivered program services, along with a small cable system owner the FCC had charged with violating the must-carry rule, challenged the rule in court. They claimed it not only deprived subscribers of program options but also violated the First Amendment rights of cable operators. In 1985 an appeals court agreed that the rule, as written, violated the Constitution (768 F 2d 1434, 1985). This meant that, subject to possible reversal by the Supreme Court, cable operators could thereafter pick and choose among television stations in filling their channels. In mid-1986, under pressure from broadcasters and Congress, the FCC required cable systems to carry all local broadcast signals for five years, until 1991 (*New York Times*, 8 Aug. 1986: C13).

Technical Standards   Though the electronic media industry agreed with most aspects of radio and television *behavioral* deregulation, it was uneasy when the FCC re-examined its role as technology regulator. This issue came to the fore in proceedings to select a technical standard for AM stereo. What happened demonstrates how the commission's approach to its regulatory role can change in a short space of time. The final decision has become an often-used but sometimes ignored precedent for further FCC technical deregulatory moves.

When the FCC approved FM stereo in 1961 (§3.8), it turned down a parallel proposal for AM stereo, in order to allow FM to get a strong start. Less than two decades later, AM stations, feeling the competitive pinch, sought to implement their own stereo system. As had happened with FM (and television standards before that), the industry made comparative tests as a basis for determining a standard to recommend to the FCC. However, the five AM stereo systems that emerged, though quite different from one another in technical design, offered little basis for picking one over the others. The industry could not make up its mind, nor, apparently, could the FCC.

In early 1980 the commission finally chose one of the systems, but industry engineers immediately attacked its technical quality and reliability. The FCC therefore withdrew its decision. Of the seven commissioners in 1980, only two voted against choosing a standard. But by March 1982, after a change in membership and with a quite different view of government's regulatory role in ascendance, the commission voted 6 to 1 to leave the choice to the marketplace, setting only minimal standards to prevent interference (51 RR 2d 1, 1982). The 1982 commission determined that the industry itself should decide which of the systems to adopt — if, indeed, AM stations did not in the end decide to use several of the systems.

This instance of a hands-off approach to technical, as well as behavioral, regulation set a precedent. The AM stereo decision was the first of a string of FCC decisions allowing the marketplace to set specific technical standards. Similar decisions for DBS, teletext, television stereo, and other services soon followed, indicating that economists had superseded engineers in commission policymaking, even in largely technical matters. The "marketplace" in each case consisted, of course, not of consumers but of station owners, operators, and major equipment manufacturers or purchasers. Broadcasters would have to make a decision on which transmission standard to use, hoping that set makers would eventually gear up to supply receivers to consumers.

New Services   The commission's current approach to technical standards indicates a receptivity to developing technologies. Such was not always the case, however. For decades the commission zealously protected its broadcast licensees, tightly regulating competition and delaying the entry of new services. Examples of FCC discouragement of new services include its experiment with cable rules (§4.2) and its even longer history of holding up over-the-air pay television (§4.4). Since 1980, however, the FCC has avoided regulating newer services, trusting in competitive marketplace pressures to aid or hinder technical development. The idea has been to make available as many services to as many people as possible, letting competition decide which services will survive.

An example of this trend was the FCC's decision on DBS service (§4.8). Although economic reality appeared to have killed off American DBS by the mid-1980s, the commission earlier had taken a stand in favor of DBS and had pushed that policy through in a remarkably short time to final decisions authorizing spectrum assignments and satellite authorizations. From the first filing for a DBS system in 1980, to final detailed authorization of minimal standards in 1982, the FCC moved with unaccustomed speed to authorize this brand new service touted as a boon to rural areas. Moreover, the agency moved ahead despite strong opposition from a broadcast industry fearful of potential competition.

In another case, the commission moved too fast and created a huge processing problem. The idea for low-power television (LPTV, §7.6) was so appealing that late in 1980 the FCC allowed applicants to file for the new service even before final technical and operational rules had been worked out. Inundated with an avalanche of applications, most of which were mutually exclusive, the commission had to put a freeze on new applications. Even so, by the time the first LPTV outlets took to the air in 1983, some twelve thousand applications had piled up. Computerized processing and a change in the communications act by Congress, which permitted the FCC to select "winners" through a lottery system, helped move the process along, but the FCC's premature acceptance of LPTV applications delayed LPTV's emergence.

The FCC's permissive approach to newer technologies has led to a very uneven playing field among the services. Broadcasting, despite the deregulation already discussed, remains the most heavily regulated of all mass media. Cable, once pervasively controlled, is now under very little regulation. And though subscription television emerged long before cable, its development was so retarded by regulation that by the time restrictions were lifted, economic pressures from pay cable had killed it. Some newer services, on the other hand, have not been regulated as mass media at all. Multichannel multipoint distribution systems, for example, are still regulated as common carriers (although that anomaly is likely to soon change, when the FCC gathers all these media services under a single regulatory approach and bureau).

17.3 Licensing

The FCC's most important function is to authorize services. Thus the licensing of radio and television stations is central to the role of government in regulating electronic media. Like other aspects of the FCC, the licensing process has undergone considerable deregulation.

"Ownership" of Channels   It is generally recognized internationally that the electromagnetic spectrum cannot be literally "owned," either by persons or by nations (§1.2). In the early days of radio, however, some broadcasters claimed they had acquired perpetual squatter's rights to the channels they already occupied. Conscious of this potential problem for the success of broadcast regulation, Congress went to special lengths to prevent claims of channel ownership. One of the aims of the communications act, said Congress in Section 301 of the act, is

to maintain the control of the United States over all the channels of interstate and foreign radio transmission; and to provide for the use of such channels, but not the ownership thereof, by persons for limited periods of time, under licenses granted by Federal authority, and no such license shall be construed to create any right beyond the terms, conditions, and periods of the license.

Congress stressed the point still further by requiring in Section 304 that each licensee sign a waiver "of any claim to the use of any particular frequency or of the ether as against the regulatory power of the United States because of the previous use of the same." Furthermore, although the FCC may determine the form of station licenses it issues, Section 309 stipulates that every license *must* include the condition that it "shall not vest in the licensee any right to operate the station nor any right in the use of the frequencies designated in the license beyond the term thereof nor in any other manner than authorized therein."

Finding a Channel   A would-be licensee must apply for specific facilities (channel, power, antenna pattern, time of operation, and so on). Because the FCC has allotted all FM and television channels to communities in advance, the applicant consults the allotment tables to find a vacant channel. Alternatively it is possible to petition for a change in the allotment tables. In the case of AM channels, how-

ever, there are no such tables. Applicants must employ engineering consultants to search out locations where AM channels could be activated without causing interference.

The most desirable commercial channels have long since been licensed, so that the would-be licensee of today nearly always seeks to buy an existing station (§10.5). Rarely are new broadcast assignments made available. A notable exception was the FCC's creation of nearly seven-hundred new FM assignments in the mid-1980s, made possible because of improved technology that limits interference with stations already on the air. Another exception, LPTV, is intended to fit among existing allocations, but always on a secondary basis.

Permits and Applications   Congress was concerned that because of limited engineering experience with broadcasting at the time the communications act was passed in 1934, licensees might take advantage of the unpredictability of radio propagation patterns. To make sure transmitters behaved exactly as planned and authorized, the act requires would-be licensees to apply first for a *construction permit* (CP). Only after a facility is built and after satisfactory transmitter "proof of performance" testing may the holder of a CP apply for a regular license to broadcast.

A basic FCC application called Form 301 is used to seek a construction permit and must be filled out for any change in ownership (Form 340 is used for noncommercial operations). If granted, the permit allows the applicant to construct a new commercial station or to make changes in an existing station, such as relocation of a transmitter or main studio. Form 301 requires details on the financial, technical, and character qualifications of applicants (discussed in the following sections) as well as other technical information. Deregulation in the 1980s largely eliminated questions on programming and detailed financial information.

A CP gives its holder a limited time (usually 18 months for television and 12 months for radio) to construct and test the station. The CP holder then uses Form 302 (Form 341 for noncommercial stations) to apply for a full license. This form is basically a record of technical testing. With FCC permission, a licensee may begin on-air program testing while the Form 302 application is pending.

Licensee Qualifications   In some ways, Congress was quite specific in enumerating licensee qualifications. Section 308 of the communications act requires that licenses be granted only to *U.S. citizens*, who qualify as to *character, financial resources,* and *technical ability.* But although Congress set up these basic tests, it left the FCC substantial discretion in implementing and interpreting them.

1. *Character.* Applicants are expected to have personal histories free of evidence that suggests defects in character sufficient to cast doubt on their ability to operate in the public interest. Criminal records and violations of antitrust laws are examples of such evidence. Any previous history of misrepresentation to the FCC is considered a defect nearly fatal to an application. Close scrutiny of corporate licensees could endanger scores of existing licenses, as few large corporations have survived commercial wars without blemish.* In

1981 the commission instituted a wide-ranging inquiry into its interpretation of the character qualification, especially the consideration of nonbroadcast activity of applicants, licensees, and parent corporations. One aim of this inquiry, still in progress in 1986, is to do away with much of this aspect of licensee qualification.

2. *Financial resources.* Form 301 once required detailed disclosure of financial resources showing that the applicant had sufficient funds to operate without depending on station income for at least 90 days. Now applicants merely have to certify that they have "sufficient" financial resources; there are no precise FCC guidelines defining what this means.

3. *Technical ability.* Most applicants hire engineering consultants to prepare their technical applications. Such consultants specialize in showing how a proposed station will get maximum physical coverage without causing objectionable interference to existing stations. Engineering plans must also show expertise in meeting FCC engineering standards.

Usually, all competing applicants meet these minimum statutory qualifications for licenses. The FCC therefore resorts to its right under the communications act to specify "other qualifications," such as the extent to which ownership is localized and the role of minorities in station management. These criteria become crucial when the FCC has to

---

*This became evident in 1980 when the FCC, in a surprise move, refused to renew the licenses of three major market television stations licensed to RKO General, Inc., in Boston, Los Angeles, and New York. Among the FCC's reasons for the harsh action was the fact that RKO's parent corporation, General Tire and Rubber Company, had admitted to the Securities and Exchange Commission to illegal contributions and possible bribery of foreign officials (78 FCC 2d 1, 1980). RKO owns 13 radio stations, all of which were designated for hearing in 1984, along with 149 mutually exclusive applications from others for the sta-

tions. Although a court ruling in 1981 overturned parts of the FCC decision, including the denial of the Los Angeles and New York renewals, it let stand the Boston denial (670 F 2d 215, 1981) and kept open the possibility that other licenses would be lost. The New York station became part of a complicated political tradeoff. New Jersey had long lacked its own commercial VHF outlet. Legislation paved the way for RKO to retain its license if it agreed to relocate its facilities in New Jersey, increasing its coverage of that state. This RKO readily agreed to as the action freed their license of past problems.

choose among several competing applicants, as is usually the case.

Mutually Exclusive Applications   In the days before all the desirable channels had been licensed (and even today, when desirable channels become available because of deletions of existing licensees or changes in channel allocation rules), several applicants might compete to obtain a license for the same channel in the same market. Such competitors are called *mutually exclusive* applicants, and the FCC makes a choice among them after conducting *comparative hearings*. These are usually long-drawn-out and costly proceedings that take place at FCC headquarters.

A notorious example of delay because of such proceedings involved Channel 9 in Orlando, Florida. The original application dated back to 1953, when the commission granted a license to applicant Mid-Florida TV. Competing applicants challenged this award, and three times in succession the appeals court overturned FCC decisions favoring Mid-Florida. In 1969, pending still further hearings, the commission allowed the five competing applicants to operate the station jointly on an interim basis. After twenty-eight years of uncertainty, the channel finally became a fully licensed operation when the interim joint venture became permanent. Another interim operation kept the lucrative AM radio station KRLA in Pasadena, California, on the air for eighteen years while twenty applicants fought for the license. The nonprofit interim operator turned station income over to public broadcasting in the area until the case was finally settled in 1980, when a coalition of five applicants won the license.

Lotteries   The huge build-up of applications for LPTV service (§17.2) led the FCC to pressure Congress for the right to select new (*not* renewal) LPTV license applicants by means of a *lottery* system rather than by the time-consuming process of comparative hearings. The FCC insisted this would save time and money and thus speed new service to consumers. The commission admitted that the comparative process was imperfect and that it did not necessarily produce the best licensees. In 1981–1982, Congress amended the communications act to allow selection by lottery (Section 309[i]).

The current system allows the FCC to check an electronic media applicant's qualifications to hold a license only after the applicant has been chosen by lottery. (The FCC argued that to check the qualifications of all applicants before any lottery had been held would defeat much of the purpose of having a lottery in the first place.) As a result of the 1981–1982 amendment, applicants more than 50 percent controlled by minorities and applicants with no other media ownership interests were given a two-to-one preference in lotteries. These minority and diversity preferences, which could be combined, were intended to diversify television programming through the LPTV service. In mid-1985, the FCC decided that the statute did not offer it the option of giving preference to women. The commission also said it would use lotteries for regular broadcasting applications only when comparative hearings resulted in ties.

The need for a congressionally mandated scheme of *preferences* for certain groups delayed lottery implementation. The first lottery, held in September 1983, resulted in twenty-three license grants for LPTV service, eight of these to minority interests. In late 1985 the FCC held the first lottery to choose among the thousands of applications for multichannel multipoint distribution systems.

It became clear, however, that by implementing lotteries the FCC had inadvertently created a paperwork monster:

Lotteries were not ideal because with them the FCC had less reason to ask the many questions previously included on application forms. The new forms were so easy to file that application "mills" cranked out tens of thousands of bids for entry into new communications technologies. There were 5,000 applications to operate cellular telephone systems, 16,000 to operate the new MMDS multichannel "wireless cable" systems, and 20,000 to run low-power television stations. The sheer volume of paper descending on the FCC thwarted the basic aim of issuing licenses speedily. (Tannenwald, 1985: 42)

Licensing of Auxiliary Services   The procedure for authorizing auxiliary services is much simpler than even the lottery approach. Radio stations that use their carrier waves for auxiliary services (§10.3) not related to broadcasting and not received on regular radio sets need no longer apply for special licenses for these services. Neither do television stations that use vertical blanking intervals for teletext and related services (§6.11) need to be specially licensed. This easing of licensing requirements is another part of the FCC's deregulation program intended to encourage new and different services with a minimum of regulatory red tape.

Cable Franchising   Cable licensing, or *franchising*, follows a totally different pattern from broadcast licensing. Physically, installation of cable systems is a local affair, using streets and other public property subject to municipal jurisdictions (§17.6). The granting of permits to operate cable systems, in the form of franchises, is therefore a local rather than federal function. The federal role in cable regulation is limited to broader subjects such as crossownership, equal employment opportunities, obscenity in programming, and universal technical standards.

17.4 Operating Under License

After an applicant completes construction and finally receives a license, several operational rules come into play.

Nondelegable Responsibility   It would be pointless from a regulatory viewpoint for the licensee to go through the licensing procedure only to turn over actual operation to some other party that had not met the same tests. To prevent this from happening, the FCC places considerable emphasis on the licensee's *nondelegable responsibility* to maintain control over the station's operation, especially its programming. Ignorance is no excuse. Licensees cannot plead that a program was in a foreign language, that offensive material was buried in an otherwise inoffensive program, or that a speaker made an unauthorized comment. Legally, licensees are responsible for all content they air. They cannot, in theory, delegate program decision making to networks (although in practice this occurs all the time). And licensees cannot enter into agreements with citizen groups (§16.7) that delegate program decisions to anyone other than the licensee.

Nondelegable responsibility has also been debated in terms of popular-music formats. In the early 1970s the FCC issued rules later upheld by a court of appeals decision that required radio stations to be aware of the lyrics of rock music so as to avoid airing songs that promote drug use or illicit sex (478 F 2d 594, 1973). The same issue arose again in 1985, with music distributors this time being asked by the broadcasting industry (not the FCC) to provide copies of lyrics for all songs provided for broadcast use.

Employment Policies and Practices
Applicants for new CPs that propose to have five or more full-time employees must set up a "positive, continuing program of practices to assure equal employment opportunities." These EEO requirements refer to women in all cases, and to minority groups in cases where minorities form 5 percent or more of the work force in a station's or cable system's service area. Guidelines in the Form 301 CP applica-

tion show how to set up EEO programs and call for statements about plans or practices with regard to:

- general EEO policy.
- the officer responsible for implementing the EEO policy.
- methods of publicizing the policy.
- methods of recruitment and training to be used.
- an analysis of the racial composition of the population in the station's or cable system's service area (usually obtained from census records).
- promotion policies.

Operating stations and cable systems with five or more full-time employees must submit annual employment reports to the FCC. These reports must be kept in the station's public file. The FCC pays strict attention to a licensee's recent EEO record when considering its application for license renewal. To help pin down what EEO policy is, the commission has established detailed guidelines (Exhibit 17.4).

In the early 1980s, controversy arose over the role of the FCC in equal employment opportunity. Conservatives opposed quotas and guidelines in employment practices. Yet in the cable act of 1984 (§17.6), Congress extended the FCC's broadcast EEO requirements to cable systems, calling for the same employment ratios for cable. At the same time, however, the Reagan-appointed members of the U.S. Commission on Civil Rights questioned the need for FCC enforcement of EEO standards.

Public File   As noted in Chapter 16, the FCC requires that every station maintain a public file at its main studio. The file is a collection of documents that applicants and licensees must assemble and keep ready to show during business hours to any member of the public on request. Its purpose is to assist con-

Exhibit 17.4   EEO Guidelines

Number of full-time employees	EEO requirements
1 to 4*	Need not file an EEO plan.
5 to 10	Stations will have their EEO programs reviewed by the FCC unless minorities and/or women are employed on a basis of half of their local labor force representation. In other words, if a market's labor force, as defined by the Census Bureau, is half black, at least a quarter of a licensee's employees in that market should be from that minority group. In the top job categories (officers and managers, professionals, technicians, and salespersons), the stations should have a minority employee ratio of at least one-quarter of that minority's market labor force representation. In the example used above, where half the labor force is black, the top four station job categories should be at least 12.5 percent black.
11 or more	Should employ at least half as many minorities and/or women as are represented in the local labor force overall *and* in the top four job categories (officers and managers, professionals, technicians, and salespersons).
50 or more†	Same as for stations with 11 or more employees; but in addition, EEO programs are regularly reviewed.

*This category includes many radio stations.

†Most of these are television operations.

sumers in assessing the station's performance, and if need be, in gathering data to challenge license renewal.

Requirements for the file's contents, as of 1986, are essentially the same for all stations, commercial and non-commercial, radio and television. Among major items to be included are the construction permit or license application (if filed within the past seven years), the two latest license renewal applications, ownership reports and annual employment reports for the past seven years, the two latest EEO model programs (if required — see Exhibit 17.4), the now badly out-of-date work entitled "The Public and Broadcasting — A Procedural Manual" that was issued by the FCC in 1974, a record of any political broadcasting time requests from the past two years, and a quarterly listing of programs the licensee feels provided the most significant treatment of community issues.

Recent deregulatory decisions such as the abandonment of community ascertainment requirements, the adoption of postcard renewal (§17.5), and the deletion of programming guidelines have reduced the amount of material kept in the file. Many critics (not to mention broadcasters) feel that the file is a waste of time, since the public, for whom it is intended, rarely uses it.

Dealing with the FCC   While keeping one eye on the store, the licensee must direct the other toward Washington to keep up with the new FCC regulations and new interpretations of old ones. These tasks would amount to an overwhelming load of administrative paperwork, for a station of any size and stature, were it not for the help that comes from numerous trade organizations, their publications, and a corps of communications attorneys in Washington.

Lawyers who represent stations in FCC dealings belong to the Federal Communications Bar Association (FCBA), which had about fifteen hundred members in 1985 (members handle both common-carrier and broadcasting matters). Most stations of any size keep an FCBA lawyer on retainer as a precautionary measure:

Like dentists, the communications lawyers can tell their clients to come to them before they have trouble — or later when it will hurt worse. Lawyers point out that the FCC lacks clear guidelines on many important policies and procedures, that it sometimes enforces its rules in an arbitrary fashion, and that the FCC has traditionally preferred a "case-by-case" or "let's-wing-it" approach to making decisions. (Cole and Oettinger, 1978: 30)

Because of such ambiguities and because of the FCC's ultimate power to put them out of business, broadcasters used to have exaggerated fears about confrontations with the commission — fears that communications lawyers at times tend to encourage. Nevertheless, proximity to the commission and personal contacts with FCC staff members enable Washington lawyers to get things done faster than distant licensees unfamiliar with federal bureaucratic labyrinths.

Most of the routine work of communications lawyers is simply a matter of keeping their clients alert and properly informed. Very few of all the thousands of applications, petitions, and other matters the FCC handles ever reach the point of being "designated for hearing," when formal legal representation becomes indispensable. Most lawyers mail out information regularly to their clients, reminding them of filing dates, informing them of new regulations, and interpreting recent decisions. Legal clinics are a common feature of trade association meetings, such as those of the National Association of Broadcasters. The NAB also publishes special primers on how to handle political candidates, how to comply with EEO guidelines, and how to avoid violating the antilottery law (see page 455).

Appraisal of Licensee Performance   In the course of normal operations, a conscientious broadcaster experiences little official supervision or monitoring. The FCC actively inspects only technical aspects of operation through its engineering field offices. Questions about programming and commercial practices, if they arise at all, are usually brought to FCC attention by the general public, consumer groups, other licensees, and competing applicants at renewal time.

The Mass Media Bureau's Complaints and Investigations Branch receives more public comments than any federal agency other than those dealing with environmental protection and consumer product safety. This office came into being in 1960 in the aftermath of quiz and payola scandals (§3.9). Originally planned as an active monitoring arm of the FCC, it settled into the more passive role of disposing of the thousands of cards and letters sent to the FCC each year by the general public.

Few people seem to realize the FCC's legal limitations. Most letters of complaint have to be discarded simply because they ask the commission to censor material the writers personally dislike. The leading topics vary only slightly from year to year, often influenced by organized letter-writing campaigns as well as by program trends. The most persistent letter-writing campaign started in 1975 in reaction to a petition for rule making. The petition came from two somewhat unconventional but deeply committed believers in listener-supported radio, Jeremy Lansman and Lorenzo Milam.

The Lansman/Milam petition asked the FCC to stop exempting noncommercial educational FM and television stations from the multiple ownership rules. It also asked for a freeze on licensing of such stations to government and religious groups, pending an investigation of the extent to which they complied with the fairness doctrine and fulfilled the educational purposes of the noncommercial channel allocations. The FCC turned down the petition in August 1975, less than a year after it had been submitted.

That should have closed the episode, because Lansman and Milam did not ask for reconsideration. But the dismissal of the petition had no effect whatever on the flood of mail opposing it from letter writers who had been misled into believing that the petition asked for a flat ban on religious programs. By 1985 over 16 million complaints had been received. There was a double irony in this mindless outpouring of thousands of letters per week: not only had the petition long since been denied, but the writers were even misinformed as to what it would have done if accepted by the FCC.

With so many groundless complaints pouring in, the complaints staff has difficulty sorting out those that might have substance and merit. One observer who described the complaints procedures at the FCC in detail noted that cases clearly needing investigation tended to be thrown out along with the "junk mail." He concluded that the commission had been unable to find "a middle ground on which frivolous public objections would be turned aside politely and serious derelictions of broadcasters' public trusteeship would be investigated and corrected" (Cole and Oettinger, 1978: 120).

17.5 License Renewal

One of the most controversial areas of FCC action is the renewal of broadcast station licenses. Even though 98 percent or more of licenses are renewed, broadcasters have traditionally feared this process that might remove their right to operate (normally seven years for radio and five years for television). From both the licensee's and the FCC's point of view, a contested renewal can become a very expensive and time-consuming process.

Renewal Application Routes   The communications act stipulates in Section 3.09(a) that licenses shall be renewed *if public interest, convenience, and necessity would be served* by renewal. The process is now easier than ever

Exhibit 17.5 Renewal Deregulation

One deregulatory benefit for broadcasters is demonstrated by the difference between the more than sixteen pound filing for renewal of four stations in Nebraska in 1971, and the short stack of paper sufficient to renew the same stations in 1983. Seven staff members spent time developing the material in 1971. A key document in the change is the FCC's postcard renewal form.
Sources: *Broadcasting*; FCC.

before. In 1981 the FCC adopted as a deregulatory move a simple post-card-sized renewal form (Exhibit 17.5) for commercial radio, and in 1984 it extended the form's use to commercial television and noncommercial broadcasting. A station files the card four months prior to the expiration of its current license. Any problems that surface are followed up by FCC computer-generated forms, or by mail or telephone inquiry.

In making its renewal decision, the FCC uses any information that may have accumulated in its file on a licensee as a result of complaints or penalties during the license period. Whether or not renewal decisions make any use of this evidence depends on the route the renewal application takes through the FCC bureaucracy. As shown in Exhibit 17.6, renewal applications take one of three basic routes: the uncontested route, the petition-to-deny route, or the mutually exclusive application route.

1. For the great majority of stations, renewals present no problem because they are *uncontested*. If there have been no serious complaints lodged against a station, no major penalties inflicted on it during the preceding license period, and no opposition filed, the FCC staff uses its delegated authority to renew its license almost automatically. In fact, one of the major complaints of consumer advocates is that the FCC's Mass Media Bureau merely rubber-stamps uncontested applications, no matter how mediocre a station's previous performance may have been. Some 98 percent of all renewals fall into this category.

2. Petitions to *deny renewal*, though rare nowadays, come from citizen groups or other parties that oppose incumbent licensees without themselves wanting to take over the license. Such groups claim that incumbents have failed to meet public-interest standards and therefore should not be allowed to retain their licenses.

3. *Mutually exclusive* applications (§17.3) arise when would-be licensees try to displace incumbents, claiming that they can do a better job in serving the public interest.

Contested Renewals   Contested renewals present the FCC with very difficult decisions and considerable controversy. The commission is torn between two desirable but opposite goals: (1) giving incumbent licensees "legitimate renewal expectations," but at the same time (2) ensuring that incumbents nevertheless feel a "competitive spur" to keep on striving to serve the public interest. On the one hand, incumbent licensees need a reasonable assurance of continuity to justify investments in equipment, personnel, and programming. Without a strong assurance of renewal at the end of a license period, no prudent investor (commercial or non-commercial) would be willing to build a station.

On the other hand, if incumbent licensees feel assured of automatic renewal no matter how poor their program performance, they may be tempted to take the low road, wringing maximum profit out of their stations and giving no serious consideration to the public interest other than providing what ratings indicate the audience wants. Assured renewal would in effect give existing licensees a monopoly on channels, freezing out worthy competitors. And though the philosophy of the Communications Act of 1934 plainly rejects this solution, stating that renewals must serve the public interest, not merely the private interest of the licensee, the deregulatory trend of the 1980s has had the practical effect of merging private and public interests and creating permanent incumbent licensees.

In deciding between incumbents and competing applicants, the FCC faces the dilemma of comparing apples and oranges — an incumbent's *actual* past service with a competitor's *proposed* future service. What sort of performance

Exhibit 17.6   License Renewal Routes

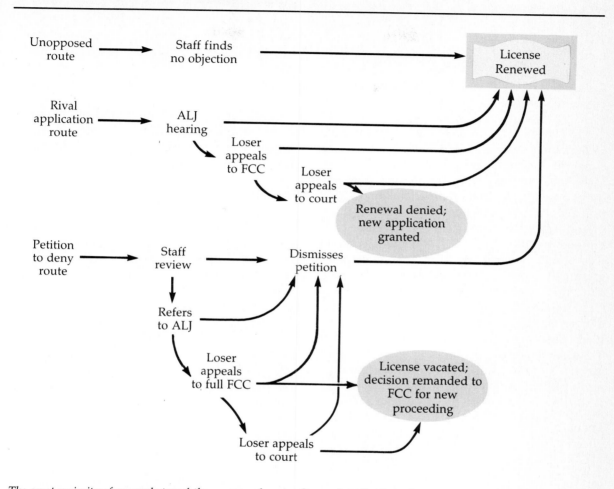

The great majority of renewals travel the unopposed route. Opposed applications, however, sometimes travel a long and rocky road before renewal or denial becomes final.

by an incumbent licensee should the FCC accept in preference to a would-be licensee's glowing promises to do even better if given a chance? Should merely average past performance assure renewal? Better than average performance? Superior performance? What evidence should the FCC weigh in grading past performance to decide whether an incumbent deserves a superior, passing, or failing grade? It is significant that all

of these questions concern programming, the crucial licensee role the FCC is most reluctant to appraise.

FCC attempts in 1970 to ease out of such comparisons were rebuffed in court (447 F 2d 1215, 1971), which forced the commission to fall back on criteria it had established in 1965 to be weighed in comparative renewal decisions (1 FCC 2d 393). According to the several criteria, choices were to be made in the interest of diversification of media ownership and localism in management and programming. The inevitable tendency to favor the incumbent licensee over challengers remained. But ironically, in the well-known case of Simon Geller, the FCC's decision not to renew an incumbent licensee's application was overturned by an appeals court.

In 1982 the FCC initially denied renewal to Geller, the owner and sole staff member of a classical-music FM station in Gloucester, Massachusetts. Instead, the commission granted the competing application of Grandbanke Corporation, a group owner that promised programming much more in the public interest as defined by the 1965 FCC statement. Geller was a folk hero in his local area who programmed opera and classical music and virtually no news or public-affairs material. Grandbanke, on the other hand, promised to devote nearly 29 percent of its overall schedule to news and public affairs and thus to offer a more balanced programming service to the residents of the fishing and resort community north of Boston. The administrative law judge who first heard the case for the FCC favored Geller's renewal, but the commission found Geller not entitled to the renewal, despite his strong listener support. The court of appeals, however, remanded the case to the FCC for further work, telling the commission it had been inconsistent in the application of ownership diversity (§17.7) benefits for Geller. Throughout the long proceeding, Geller kept at his 13 hours per day of classical music. Finally, late in 1985, the FCC reversed itself and renewed Geller's license (102 FCC 2d 1443).

Dilemma: Renewal Criteria   A number of court reversals of FCC decisions in renewal cases seemed to call for one of two solutions: either (1) the statute should be changed so that the FCC is not put in the position of having to conduct comparative hearings on re-

newals; or (2) the FCC should establish clear-cut objective criteria for measuring the relative "substantiality" of past performance by incumbent licensees against proposals of challengers. The FCC preferred the first approach, and legislative initiatives of 1977–1981 proposed eliminating the need for renewal proceedings by having the FCC first pass on renewal for those seeking it, and receive competing applications only if the incumbent licensee failed to meet the renewal standard. But none of the changes was enacted.

If the FCC were to opt for evaluating licensee performance more rigorously, it would need to clarify what kind of service merits renewal. The following criteria have been suggested at various times as elements of a quantitative test for measuring licensee performance (it seems unlikely that, given the present deregulatory mood, any would be seriously considered today):

• the percentages of time devoted to nonentertainment and locally produced programs (the now-defunct processing guidelines on programming [§17.2] were a step in this direction).
• the number, placement, and variety of public-service announcements (a proposal specifically rejected by the FCC in 1980).
• the number, types, and scheduling of children's programs free of commercial exploitation (urged repeatedly by Action for Children's Television (§18.3) and as often rejected by the FCC).
• the number and intrusiveness of commercials (the FCC advertising guidelines now dropped approached this standard).
• the extent to which licensees reinvest profits in improved programming services (though the FCC stopped collecting industry financial data after 1980).

But gathering and applying such data for program performance (not to mention qualitative evaluations) seems to require a level of government intrusion that would violate the First Amendment and would certainly be politically unacceptable. Moreover, the FCC would need an expanded staff in a time of shrinking budgets. Thus, whereas program standards seem only logical and reasonable from a consumer perspective, from the industry and political perspective they seem unattainable. The dilemma remains.

Cable Franchise Renewal   Under Title VI, Section 626 of the communications act, the local franchising authority, not the FCC, handles cable license renewals. The local authority is not required to find that renewal will serve the public interest but may simply renew a license without ceremony. If, however, the local authority wants to deny renewal, it must hold a hearing that, in effect, raises public-interest issues by deciding whether the incumbent operator has (1) complied with the law; (2) provided a quality of service "reasonable in light of the community needs"; (3) maintained the financial, legal, and technical ability to operate; and (4) prepared a renewal proposal that "is reasonable to meet the future cable-related community needs and interests." Section 626 makes no mention of considering proposals from competing would-be franchisees during the course of renewal grants or renewal hearings.

17.6 The Cable Policy Act

For two decades, local governments, Congress, the FCC, and cable operators debated cable television policy without benefit of explicit guidance from the Communications Act of 1934. The FCC and the courts improvised control of the new medium by extrapolating from words written fifteen or more years

before the invention of cable television. This statutory void was filled by the Cable Communications Policy Act of 1984 (47 USC 601). The wide-ranging act severely limits both federal and local controls on cable operators. The legislation was a compromise among three parties: the National Cable Television Association, the National League of Cities, and the National Council of Mayors. As is often the case, Congress felt it could not act until the key players had agreed among themselves on the general outline of what had to be done. Following the establishment of this limiting legislation, the FCC's must-carry rules were suspended (§17.2); thus, few federal barriers to the cable industry remained.

Cable Rules   The resulting policy statement on cable television became the new Title VI in the communications act and codified a strongly deregulatory approach to the medium. Among the important provisions of the new title are the following:

- Cable is defined as a one-way video programming medium; two-way services are not included in the cable policy act (Sec. 602).
- Public, educational, and governmental access (PEG) channels may be required by local franchise authorities (Sec. 611), although some critics doubt the constitutionality of this requirement in view of the First Amendment (see §18.2).
- Cable systems with more than 36 channels must set aside 10 percent to 15 percent of those channels for *leased access*, to be used by someone other than the cable owner, who sets the rates for leasing the channels but has no editorial control (Sec. 612).
- Cable companies are banned from owning overlapping local television stations or telephone companies (except in rural areas for the latter), thus codifying an existing FCC ownership rule (§17.7). The FCC may set up other crossownership rules with regard to cable if it

choses (Sec. 613). FCC bans on network ownership of cable systems, and co-ownership of telephone companies and cable systems, are not mentioned in the act but continue to apply.

• Local franchise authorities may charge franchise fees of no more than 5 percent of gross cable revenues (Sec. 622).

• Federal or state regulation of rates that cable systems charge subscribers for basic cable service is prohibited. The statute codifies the existing FCC ban on any regulation of pay cable rates (Sec. 623).

• Cable signal piracy is subject to fines and imprisonment (Sec. 633).

• The FCC's equal employment opportunity reporting guidelines for broadcasting (§17.4) apply to cable systems as well (Sec. 634).

• Cable system transmission of "any matter which is obscene or otherwise unprotected by the Constitution" (§18.2) is subject to fines (Sec. 639).

Local Authorities   The cable act does not do away with the primary regulatory role played by local authorities, but it does limit their freedom of action.* The most important local regulation arises from the franchise process, by which a cable system obtains its initial legal authority to build a facility in a given political jurisdiction: a city, a town, or a portion of a larger metropolitan area.† Such a franchise is necessary because lines may have to cross, or be built under, such public facilities as streets and parks.* In addition, cable systems are generally monopolies in their service areas, and as such they fall under utility regulatory policies in most communities.

The franchise process begins when a mayor, city council, or other local governing body decides cable service should be provided locally. As a rule, this governing group first develops an *ordinance*, a formal legal document describing the conditions under which a cable system will be allowed to operate. Drawn up in many cases with the advice of outside experts, the ordinance typically provides for (1) the term of the franchise (usually 10 to 15 years); (2) the specific quality of service to be provided; (3) technical standards (such as minimum number of channels and interconnection with other systems); and (4) the franchise fee.

Franchises are awarded in a competitive process. Interested companies bid on the basis of a proposed system design and timetable, usually outlined in the franchise authority's *request for proposals* (RFP). Although franchisers usually grant franchises to only one bidder, multiple awards are possible. Some cable operators have argued in court that cities should grant multiple franchises so long as there is space on poles or in conduits for the system's cable and equipment. In the 1980s, controversy arose over unduly optimistic promises made by successful bidders and later not fulfilled. A few communities have avoided such problems by opting to operate cable systems themselves (§10.5).

Title VI of the communications act gives local authorities several specific rights, including the following:

---

*Eleven states regulate cable, but they have had little overall effect on the development of the medium. State laws usually assign responsibility to existing public utilities commissions.

†These "portions" are sometimes totally separate jurisdictions, as in the Greater Los Angeles area, which has many political divisions. In other cases, single jurisdictions may divide large city populations into subareas, each franchised to a different firm. Chicago, Philadelphia, and New York City are examples of large cities apportioned in this way.

---

*Cable systems (really SMATV systems) that can manage to avoid use of public rights of way — for example, those that only service large apartment complexes entirely on private property — are not subject to the act and are generally unregulated by state or federal authorities.

- Cities may require upgrading of cable facilities and channel capacity when the system franchise is renewed.
- Cable must be made available to the entire franchise area, on a schedule to be worked out between the system operator and the franchise authority.
- Franchise authorities may require a specific number of PEG channels in a new RFP or when a system applies for franchise renewal.
- A franchise authority may grant one or more franchises in its territory, as it sees fit.

17.7 Mass Media Ownership Regulation

Diversification   First Amendment theory (§18.1) stresses the value of maintaining a marketplace in which ideas, information, and opinions from many diverse and antagonistic sources can compete for acceptance. Under modern conditions, however, unregulated competition may soon lead to one entity gaining a monopoly. Government can play a positive First Amendment role by means of devising regulations to prevent media monopolies; *diversification* of ownership and control therefore becomes a major goal of FCC regulation. This is *structural* regulation, to use the term employed by deregulation theorists (§17.2), as contrasted with the *behavioral* regulation discussed in Chapter 18.

Examples of structural regulation include rules on (1) the number and kinds of stations licensed to any one owner; (2) concentration of control over program production and distribution; (3) *cross-media* ownership (stations, systems, and other media under common ownership); and (4) equal employment opportunities (§17.4).

Multiple Ownership   Every broadcast station is a kind of monopoly, since it is licensed to have exclusive use of a given chan-

nel in a particular market. The FCC prevents this form of monopoly from getting out of hand by imposing signal-power limitations on each class of station and by regulating station ownership in national and local markets.

Because of the monopolistic nature of even a single station, the FCC has considered it necessary to place limits on multiple station ownership. On a national scale, the *12-12-12 rule* limits single owners to ownership of no more than twelve stations in each broadcast service; AM, FM, and television (§8.1).* For television stations, the total potential national audience reached by any owner may not exceed 25 percent of television households, with UHF stations counting for only half of their market potential because of their reduced coverage.

In the 1980s the FCC eliminated a number of other limitations on ownership, including the "trafficking" rule, which required that a station be held at least three years before being sold; the rule that a single entity could own only one VHF station in the top fifty markets (a rule never enforced while on the books); the limitation on regional concentration of ownership; and fairly tight rules that defined minor financial holdings in broadcast companies as "ownership." All of these changes reflected the FCC's policy of relying on marketplace competition rather than structural regulation to safeguard the public. Still, many financial analysts saw adoption of the more liberal 12-12-12 station limit in 1985 as one reason for the exploding demand for

---

*The 12-12-12 rule was instituted in 1985. For 32 years the FCC had limited multiple ownership to no more than seven stations of each type. The commission, basing its action on the vast increase in stations during the preceding three decades, initially wanted to abolish the limitation rule entirely by 1990, but pressure from Congress and the motion picture industry (which was concerned about network ownership of more stations) led to the 12-12-12 compromise. Under certain circumstances, combinations of stations controlled by members of minority groups can go as high as 14-14-14.

broadcast and cable properties that sparked a media merger mania beginning in 1985 (§10.5).

On the individual market level, the *duopoly* rule established by the FCC in 1940 holds that no single owner can have more than one station of the same type (for instance, AM) in the same market. Originally one owner could have a single-market AM-FM-television combination, but in 1970 the FCC banned such combinations under one owner in the same market, limiting licensees to either radio (AM and FM) or television stations. Exceptions were often made to allow radio and UHF television station combinations, however.

Most of the broadcast ownership rules are softened by *grandfathering* (exempting present owners) and by the right to request waivers. Furthermore, noncommercial stations are not limited by any of these rules. Thus, restructuring of local ownership will take place over time, as grandfathered groups are broken up when sold and as new licenses are issued on more of a one-to-a-customer basis.

None of this regulatory complexity concerning ownership exists for competing electronic media. There are no FCC limits on multiple ownership of cable systems (§8.4) or other electronic media. For example, even though LPTV stations constitute a broadcast service, they are not subject to formal ownership limits (although in the 1980s the FCC has established application processing limits of no more than 15 LPTV stations per owner).

Cross-Media Ties   Every broadcast license or cable franchise granted to a newspaper publisher automatically reduces diversification of media ownership. This reduction in alternative public sources of information (sometimes called media "voices," as opposed to actual outlets such as stations or systems) is especially undesirable in small communities in which the only newspaper might own the only broadcasting stations or cable system.

For decades the FCC struggled to find a politically acceptable solution to the problem of newspaper-broadcasting crossownership in the same market. The commission issued rules banning such ownership in 1975, avoiding a confrontation with the most powerful newspaper interests by grandfathering all but a very few existing combinations, and was upheld by the Supreme Court (436 US 775, 1978). On the other hand, although the FCC and Congress have considered a newspaper-cable crossownership limit on several occasions, none has been adopted.

The FCC does not allow broadcast networks to own cable systems anywhere in the country (although one experimental exemption was granted to CBS for a brief time). Nor can local television stations own cable systems that fall in their primary coverage areas. Furthermore, local telephone companies cannot operate cable systems in their telephone service areas. All these crossownership limitations date from 1970, and an FCC concern that the older services might control programming decisions of the newer medium. As noted earlier, Title VI, Section 613 of the communications act codifies all these limits except the one banning network ownership of cable systems. There are no limits on broadcast crossownership with services other than cable or newspapers.

The merger mania of the 1980s raised an unexpected cross-media problem. A number of the takeovers and mergers created commonly owned collections of broadcast stations that were too large (more than thirty-six stations in all, or more than twelve of a particular type of service) and situations in which the new companies owned stations and cable systems or newspapers in the same market. Virtually all of the companies affected applied for waivers of up to two years to sell some of the properties, and the FCC granted them. The industry argued that if the commission moved to force short-term sales, financial values could be vitally affected.

In addition to FCC rules, of course, antitrust regulations (§16.6) play a potential role in media ownership regulation. FCC approval of a jointly owned combination of stations or other media does not necessarily mean that the resulting entity is immune from prosecution under the antitrust statutes.

Ownership by Minorities   Initially the FCC did not consider the minority status of owners as an aspect of the diversification of media control. A series of court reversals in the 1960s and early 1970s, however, caused it to reexamine this position (Meeske, 1976).

In the Orlando Channel 9 case mentioned earlier (§17.3), the commission had refused to give much weight to the fact that one of the competing applicants had two black stockholders, despite the fact that about one-quarter of Orlando's population was black. The communications act was, in the words of the FCC, "color blind." The appeals court rejected this view, pointing out that it was consistent with the diversification principle "to afford favorable consideration to an applicant who, not as a mere token, but in good faith as broadening community representation, gives a local minority group media entrepreneurship" (495 F 2d 937, 1973). As a result of this and other cases, the FCC began to give more consideration to minority applicants.

In 1978, spurred on by Carter administration policies on aid to minorities, the FCC took two steps that further enhanced the opportunities for members of minority groups to become licensees.

1. After prodding by the NAB, the FCC agreed to issue *tax certificates* to licensees proposing to sell stations to minority interests. These certificates encourage such sales by allowing the sellers to defer paying capital-gains taxes on their profits, and to avoid the taxes altogether if they purchase another station within two years.

2. The FCC also agreed to allow *distress sales* to minority groups. Normally, the commission will not permit an owner whose license is in serious danger of nonrenewal to sell anything other than the station's physical assets. But to encourage sales to minority applicants, the FCC will make an exception, permitting the endangered licensee to gain some, but not all, of the total value of both tangible and intangible assets. For example, the FCC agreed in 1979 to drop fraudulent billing charges against a small AM station in Connecticut when the incumbent offered to sell the property to a minority group for 75 percent of its appraised value. The 75-percent figure thus became a standard in distress sales.

In late 1982 the commission expanded the use of tax certificates and distress sales by allowing them when a racial minority held as little as 20 percent of licensee equity but had a strong voice in management. At the same time, cable system sales became eligible for tax certificate consideration. Use of lotteries for LPTV and MMDS services also encouraged minority ownership (§17.3). Although minority ownership of stations increased sharply after the late 1970s (to 18 television and 178 radio outlets by 1982), the National Black Media Coalition reported that to achieve ownership of stations by minorities in proportion to their actual numbers in society, 1,224 broadcast stations would have to be owned by blacks and 436 owned by Hispanics. Clearly, the industry has a long way to go.

Network Ownership   As the chief producers, procurers, and distributors of broadcast programming, the television networks have long been the target of FCC structural controls.

Network ownership of local outlets (stations and other media) has been a specific subject of policy concern. Networks, like all other group owners of broadcast stations, fall under the 12-12-12 rule. But they may not, as we have seen, own cable systems, as do other group owners. And although the networks have cross-media interests in cable networks and programming, the steady development of cable networks (§8.4) since the late 1970s has reduced FCC concern over the three-network bottleneck in national program distribution. Nevertheless, several behavioral rules for television networks remain, held in place by support from elements of the broadcast and motion picture industries. The prime-time access rule (§13.2) and the syndication/financial-interest rules (§17.2) are examples. Designed originally to increase diversity by maintaining the programming independence of network affiliate stations, these rules have served to build up independent television stations and their suppliers. Those elements of the business have put pressure on Congress to retain the rules, and Congress in turn pressures the FCC to preserve the status quo — another example of informal regulatory controls (§16.7).

17.8 Enforcement

At first, Congress relied on the threat of license loss as the means of enforcing the communications act. The act gives the FCC two procedures for taking away a license, refusal to renew and outright revocation. In practice, however, penalties of such finality seemed too extreme for the types of infractions that most often occurred. Accordingly, Congress has amended the act to allow for milder penalties such as fines and shorter license terms, as discussed below.

Appeals and Hearings   A fundamental safeguard of individual liberties under the Constitution is the *due process* clause of the Fifth Amendment. It guarantees that government may not deprive a person of "life, liberty, or property without due process of law." Among many other things, this means that the FCC (as "government," in this case) may not use its powers arbitrarily. Fairness, the goal of due process, requires that applicants and petitioners have ample opportunity to present their cases for adjudication under nondiscriminatory conditions; and it stipulates that parties adversely affected by decisions must have the right to appeal for rehearings and for review by higher authorities than the ones that made the initial decisions. Many due process rights are protected by the Administrative Procedure Act. Adopted by Congress in 1946, this act specifies how administrative agencies, including the FCC, must conduct their proceedings to preserve fairness and due process for all parties participating.

When an issue arises that requires presentation of opposing arguments, an FCC *hearing* may be held to settle the dispute. Senior FCC staff attorneys called *administrative law judges* (ALJs) preside over initial FCC hearings. They conduct the proceedings like courtroom trials, with sworn witnesses, testimony, evidence, counsels for each side, and so on. Initial decisions of ALJs can be reviewed by the FCC Review Board, and then by the commissioners themselves. When opposing sides exploit all the possibilities for reviews and appeals, final decisions can take a long time. In extreme cases, there may be years of delay and millions of dollars in legal costs before settlement.*

---

*The longest-running case in FCC annals began in 1941, when the agency was six years old. Among other things, it entailed an argument over nighttime use of the 770-kHz AM radio channel used by KOB in Albuquerque and WABC in New York. After years of appeals, the FCC in 1977 again confirmed WABC's primary status on the

Procedural rules head off frivolous interventions and intentional delays by carefully defining the circumstances that justify hearings and the qualifications of those parties entitled to standing (§16.7). This means that procedural rules, tedious though they seem, are important to anyone trying to lodge a complaint. Here are three examples of such rules:

• Section 309 of the act requires the commission to advise license applicants of its reasons for rejecting an application. The applicant may reply, and if the commission still decides against the applicant it must then set the matter for hearing, "specifying the particular matter and things at issue."

• On the other hand, if the commission grants a license application *without* a hearing, for the next thirty days the grant remains open to protest from "any party in interest"; if the FCC finds that the protesting parties raise pertinent issues, the commission must then postpone the effective date of the grant and hold a hearing.

• If the commission wishes to fine a licensee, Sections 312 and 503 require the FCC to invite the licensee to "show cause" why such action should not be taken.

Court Appeals   Even after all the safeguards of FCC hearings and rehearings have been exhausted, the communications act gives people who are adversely affected by FCC actions a further recourse. Section 402 provides that appeals concerning station licenses must go to the U.S. Court of Appeals for the District of Columbia Circuit, in Washington, D.C. This court consists of nine judges, but most cases are heard by panels of only three. The court

may confirm or overturn commission actions, in part or in whole. It may also *remand* a case, sending it back to the commission for further consideration in keeping with the court's interpretation of the communications act and other law. Appeals from FCC decisions in cases not involving licenses may be initiated in any of the twelve other U.S. Courts of Appeals, each serving a specific region called a "circuit," hence they are called circuit courts of appeals.

From any one of the federal circuit courts, final appeals may be taken to the Supreme Court of the United States. The request for consideration by the Supreme Court, called a *writ of certiorari*, may be turned down ("*cert. den.*"). If that happens, the appeal process can go no further. Refusal to hear a case does not mean that the Supreme Court necessarily agrees with the lower court's finding, but the earlier decision stands nonetheless.

Losses of License   In the half-century from the FCC's creation through 1984, only 149 stations lost their licenses. Most of these losses were due to nonrenewal; revocations being very rare. The average rate of involuntary deletions amounted to a mere three stations per year. That is remarkably few, given the thousands of stations and the tens of thousands of renewals granted during that time. In short, though an ever-present background threat, loss of license hardly ever becomes a reality.

Nonrenewal of broadcast licenses occurs more frequently than revocation because the burden of proof for showing that the renewal would be in the public interest falls on the licensee. In contrast, revocation, the canceling of a license before its normal term expires, puts the burden of proof on the FCC. Exhibit 17.7 lists reasons given by the FCC for taking away licenses during the 1934–1978 period. The frequency with which the various types of violations were cited makes a striking com-

channel. KOB's "final" objections appeared quashed by a 1980 appeals court affirmation of the FCC order that the Supreme Court refused to review. In 1981, however, KOB's irrepressible owner filed a new petition asking the FCC to reclassify the channel, giving him yet another avenue of appeal.

ment on the FCC's regulatory outlook. Program infractions such as news slanting and overcommercialization figure only rarely as reasons for taking a station off the air. In the great majority of cases, the FCC cited nonprogram violations related to the character standard, such as misrepresentation, concealment of ownership, technical violations, and fraudulent billing of advertisers. This reflects the fact that the FCC is on much safer constitutional ground when it exacts the maximum penalty for nonprogram violations.

In most cases of license revocation or nonrenewal, loss of license climaxed a sorry history of willful misconduct by a station. Most deleted stations have been obscure radio outlets guilty of long lists of misdemeanors and lacking in any redeeming qualities. Misrepresentation heads the list of reasons for loss of license, because the FCC is most severe when licensees compound their violations with lies and evasions. The FCC is often extraordinarily lenient with transgressions, as long as licensees are candid in admitting error and contrite enough to promise reform.

We have already alluded to some key cases of loss of license: the stations deleted for program excesses in the 1930s (§3.1), and television station WLBT's loss of license for failing to serve the black population in its area (§16.7). We noted RKO's loss of a television license because of bad business practices by its management, and long delay in renewal of its other licenses (§17.3). The following cases show the types of behavior the FCC has found severe enough to warrant the rare penalty of license deletion:

• *Fraudulent billing.* The appeals court upheld the FCC's 1978 denial of renewal to a Berlin, New Hampshire, AM radio station charged with double billing (§9.7). The station collected over $22,000 in overcharges to national advertisers. Claiming that the two other

stations and the newspaper in his market did the same thing, the owner pleaded "business necessity" — an interestingly candid acknowledgment that so-called market forces do not always operate in the public interest! The court was especially severe in its condemnation, pointing out that double billing probably also violates the mail fraud statute. Said the court, "It appears to us that the Commission has not been giving sufficient consideration to the fraudulent conduct implicit in double billing as the serious *criminal* violation it constitutes" (626 F 2d 869). The FCC ultimately refused to renew *all three* of the stations in Berlin. Early in 1986, the FCC deleted its rules in this area relying instead on competing stations keeping one another in line.

• *Failure to serve minorities.* In 1970 the FCC refused to renew the licenses of eight stations of the Alabama Educational Television Commission. This case was unique for the number of stations involved and for the severity of punishment given a noncommercial licensee.

• *Character defects.* In denying renewal to five commercial radio outlets licensed to Star Stations of Indiana, the FCC said "The record reflects a reprehensible course of conduct involving the basic character qualities of the licensee" (51 FCC 2d 95, 1975). Don Burden, the owner, claimed the FCC's action cost him $20 million. The long list of transgressions charged against Burden included the use of fake audience research data, fraudulent billing, fraudulent contests, illegal political donations, and slanting of news. Climaxing a long-drawn-out legal battle, the Supreme Court declined to review the FCC's decision.

• *Staging of news.* The FCC denied the renewal application of a Tucson, Arizona, AM station in 1980 because of an irresponsible promotional stunt. When a recently employed DJ temporarily left town on personal business, the station management concocted a story that he had been kidnapped. The station broadcast

Exhibit 17.7   Reasons for FCC Sanctions against Broadcasters

A. Major Reasons for FCC Deletion of Station Licenses (1934–1978, N=142 reasons)

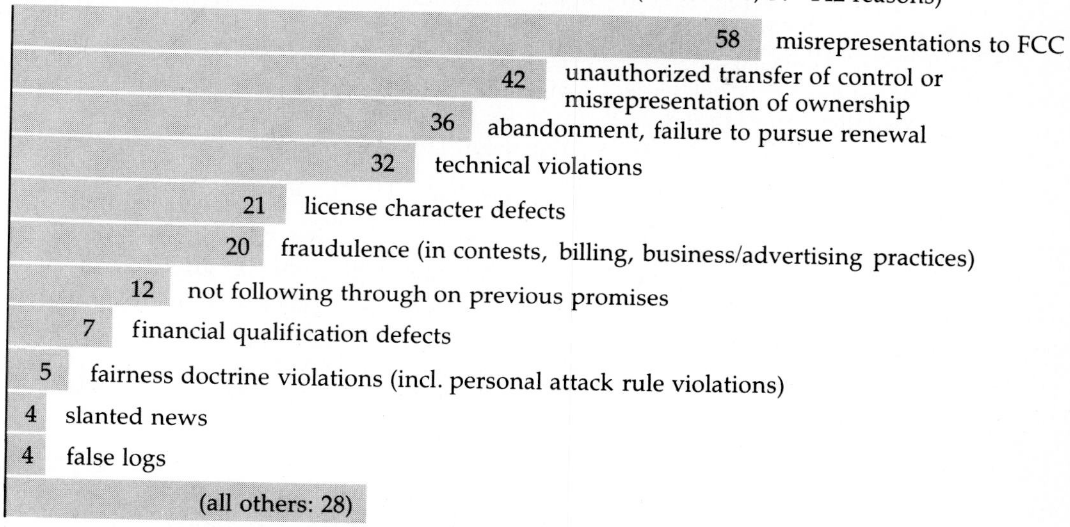

58	misrepresentations to FCC
42	unauthorized transfer of control or misrepresentation of ownership
36	abandonment, failure to pursue renewal
32	technical violations
21	license character defects
20	fraudulence (in contests, billing, business/advertising practices)
12	not following through on previous promises
7	financial qualification defects
5	fairness doctrine violations (incl. personal attack rule violations)
4	slanted news
4	false logs
(all others: 28)	

B. Major Reasons for FCC Fines Against Licensees (1961–1978, N=2,005 forfeiture notices; 2,540 reasons)

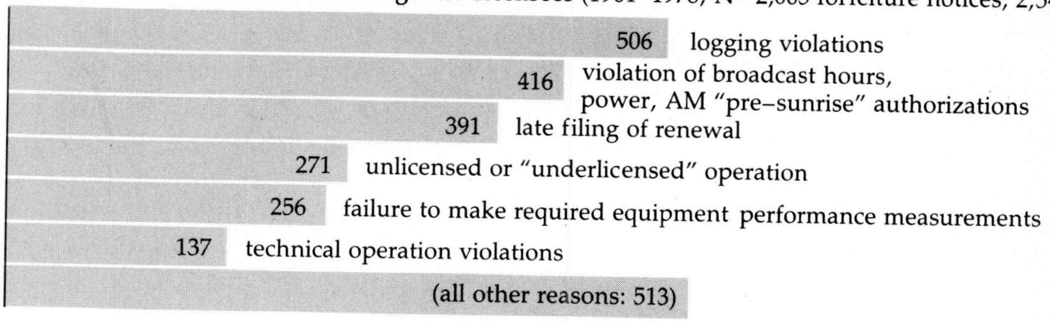

506	logging violations
416	violation of broadcast hours, power, AM "pre–sunrise" authorizations
391	late filing of renewal
271	unlicensed or "underlicensed" operation
256	failure to make required equipment performance measurements
137	technical operation violations
(all other reasons: 513)	

C. Major Reasons for FCC Short–Term Renewals (1960–1981, N=269 stations)

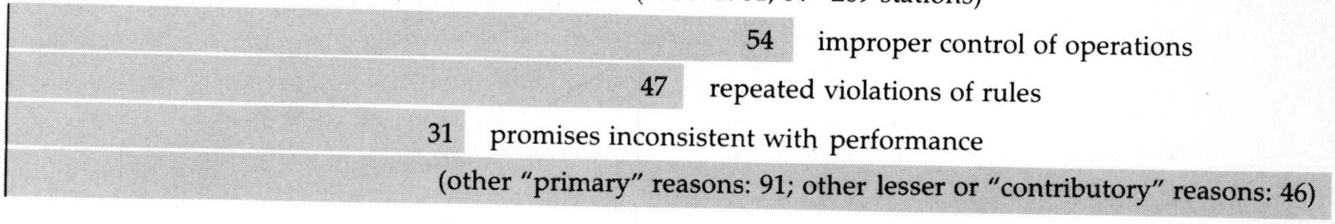

54	improper control of operations
47	repeated violations of rules
31	promises inconsistent with performance
(other "primary" reasons: 91; other lesser or "contributory" reasons: 46)	

Most stations that are deleted, fined, or given short-term renewals have violated several rules.

Source: Christopher H. Sterling, *Electronic Media: A Guide to Trends in Broadcasting and Newer Technologies, 1920-1983* (New York: Praeger, 1984), pp. 289, 301, 302.

"news" of the kidnapping over a period of five days, even faking a police interview. Listeners that were taken in by the hoax flooded the Tucson police lines with calls. The deception was finally exposed by a local television station. The FCC would not allow the absentee owner to shift responsibility: "A licensee cannot expect to be insulated from the irresponsible conduct of a vice-president and director" (78 FCC 2d 865, 1980).

• *Misrepresentation.* An FM station was denied renewal after the majority stockholder unlawfully transferred control, made misrepresentations to the FCC, willfully violated technical rules, and lacked candor (87 FCC 2d 87, 1981).

Aftermath of Deletion   When a station is deleted, the licensee is not the only loser. The public loses a broadcasting service. Even if the station's service was substandard, the FCC may question whether it is in the public interest to deprive a community of its only local broadcast service. This consideration may account for some cases in which the FCC has seemed excessively lenient.

When hearings delay renewals, licenses remain in effect until the case is settled. If a station loses its last appeals, the FCC gives it a grace period to wind up its affairs. During this interim period a new applicant may well arrive on the scene to pick up the pieces and make a fresh start, or the commission may appoint an interim operator.

Lesser Penalties   Not all offenses, of course, warrant the capital punishment of license loss. For lesser offenses, the FCC inflicts the milder sanctions of short-term renewals, conditional renewals, or forfeitures (fines).

Short-term renewal (usually for only a year instead of the standard renewal term) puts the licensee on probation, so to speak, pending the correction of general deficiencies evident during the preceding license period. *Conditional renewal* might also be granted, pending correction of some specific fault.

The FCC can also impose penalties for day-to-day infractions of the rules without waiting for the end of the license period. These take the form of *forfeitures* ranging in amount from $25 to a maximum of $20,000 (the FCC has asked Congress to increase the maximum to $100,000, but no action has resulted). A study of forfeitures imposed from 1961 to 1978 revealed that the FCC levied an average of only a little more than a hundred fines per year (Clift et al., 1980). Most of them were penalties for violations of technical operating rules. There have been few fines for program violations. When contrasted with the large number of stations on the air, the low number of forfeitures reflects the FCC's generally lenient treatment of licensee wrongdoing. Commissioners tend to sympathize with marginal radio stations struggling to survive, which are the ones that commit the great majority of punishable infractions.

17.9   FCC Issues

Over the years, the FCC has been among the most frequently analyzed and scathingly criticized of the federal regulatory agencies. Official investigations and private studies of the commission and its methods have reached negative conclusions with monotonous regularity. A few of the recurrent criticisms have been the following:

• The politically controlled process for choosing commissioners often fails to come up with suitably qualified people.

• As a consequence, commissioners tend to lack the expertise and sometimes the dedication assumed by the communications act.

• Fraternizing by commissioners with the regulated broadcast industries, as well as commissioners' hopes for future jobs with those industries, undermines concern for the public interest.

• Commission policies have had the effect of encouraging, rather than preventing, a quasi-monopoly situation in network television.

• Taken as a whole, the regulatory process long had an air of make-believe, setting up high-sounding goals that neither the industry nor the commission seriously tried to achieve.

• More recently, deregulatory ideology has outpaced concern for the larger public interest.

Commissioner Appointments Despite the power the FCC wields over vital aspects of national life, appointments to the commission do not carry high rank in the Washington political pecking order. The president uses regulatory commission appointments primarily to pay off minor political debts. The degree of personal involvement varies with each president, of course, but most are far too busy with higher-level appointments to take much interest in the FCC.

Despite the fact that the commission is supposed to represent the public interest, few appointees have been primarily identified with consumer interests. The majority have come from other federal government jobs, usually with training as lawyers. Appointees with relevant experience in engineering, professional media or common-carrier careers, or academic specialties have been rare. Nor do many stay in office long enough to attain great expertise; the more ambitious and well qualified soon move on to something else, often to a much higher-paying job in private communications law practice.

Appointments can become political footballs. For example, an argument between the White House and Congress in 1982 led directly to a reduction in the number of commissioners from seven to five. The White House

had submitted a nomination (the FCC's general counsel, Steven Sharp), but several senators who perceived a past commitment by the White House had another appointment in mind. The appointment of Sharp was first delayed, then approved, but only after the reduction to five commissioners went through, limiting Sharp to less than a year's service as a commissioner.

The first woman commissioner, Frieda Hennock, served from 1948 to 1955. The next woman was not appointed until 1971, but since 1979 at least one commissioner has been a woman. The first black commissioner was Benjamin Hooks (1972–1977), a Memphis lawyer and county judge. He was succeeded by another black and then by the FCC's first Hispanic member, Henry Rivera of New Mexico (1981–1985).

Ex Parte Contacts Once in place, commissioners spend a great deal of time speaking before industry groups and are ardently courted by industry representatives and pressure groups. The constant interaction between commissioners and the people they regulate creates the possibility for *ex parte* contacts. This is the legal term for private meetings between judges (or people acting in a judicial capacity, including commissioners) and individual litigants that may give unfair advantage to one side over another. All parties in interest should be present at such meetings, but representatives of the public are usually conspicuously absent when commissioners attend private functions staged by members of electronic media industries. Many such contacts are legitimate (the FCC now has strict rules on recording the substance of such contacts in the public record).

FCC meetings were once held behind closed doors, as was the practice with all regulatory commissions. In the 1970s, however, Congress passed "sunshine" legislation, opening up commission meetings to the public, except for a limited number of issues that justified closed meetings (personnel matters, items of adjudication, and the like). Furthermore, the commissioners themselves may not meet in groups larger than three except in such open public forums.

Regulation as Myth   In the years before deregulation fervor dominated the FCC, the commission was often accused of not enforcing its own regulations. Commentators, critics, scholars, and commissioners all made remarkably similar comments suggesting that the FCC went through an elaborate charade in granting licenses and renewals. Only the most egregious cases came up for hearing, and even fewer licensees failed to gain renewal.

The FCC's attitude — if not its actions — changed to a degree in the late 1970s. As the FCC lifted many regulations, it made clear its intention to enforce the remaining rules firmly. But the resulting sanctions were usually light — letters or small fines, with few deletions or revocations of license. Still, it was apparent that the commission's actions (or lack of action) and its stated goals were growing more consistent. It became government's role to license services or otherwise make them available with minimum fuss, and then get out of the way.

Certainly the most vocal architect of the FCC's changing role was Mark Fowler, appointed commission chairman by Ronald Reagan in 1981 and reappointed in 1986. In often humorous speeches, Fowler made clear that he felt television was simply a "toaster with pictures" and should be regulated like any other appliance (§11.6). Again and again, he pounded home the message that commercial broadcasting should be governed by "market forces rather than trustee duties," where stations act under close government supervision (Fowler and Brenner, 1982: 259). With a majority of commissioners supporting most of his initiatives, if not his ideological zeal, Fowler transformed the FCC into a more efficient processor of applications, a sympathetic patron of new services, and an active deregulator of existing media.

The move to deregulation can be seen as a huge, risky experiment (§19.5). Only time will tell whether the FCC's lower regulatory profile will have a positive or a negative effect — or any effect at all — on the electronic media's service to the public.

Summary

• The Federal Communications Commission consists of five presidentially appointed commissioners and a professional staff of about 1,900. It operates under provisions of the Communications Act of 1934 and is primarily accountable to Congress for overall policy direction and budget.

• The commission is organized into operating bureaus and offices. The Mass Media Bureau was created in 1983 out of the old Broadcast and Cable Television Bureaus. Nearly all licensing and regulation of electronic media is based here.

• The FCC imposes regulation through formally adopted rules, processing standards, adjudicatory decisions, and informal "raised eyebrow" and "jawboning" activities.

• In the 1980s the FCC took a strongly deregulatory stance, abolishing long-existing rules and guidelines governing broadcasting, cable, and technical standards generally. New services were introduced without heavy regulation.

• The FCC controls broadcasting through its licensing power. License applicants must be U.S. citizens and qualify in terms of financial resources, technical ability, and character.

Cable television, however, is licensed by municipal franchise authorities, not by the FCC.

• In 1982 the FCC received authorization from Congress to begin using a lottery system to award initial licenses in such new services as LPTV and MMDS.

• Broadcast licensees still have nondelegable responsibilities to enforce equal opportunity employment programs, to maintain a public file that includes listings of community problems and programs, and to keep up with FCC rules changes.

• Most broadcast license renewals are uncontested and are therefore awarded almost automatically. Contested renewals usually arise because of rival applications. In deciding how to handle a contested renewal, the FCC must strike a balance between offering incumbents reasonable renewal expectancy and giving new applicants a chance to improve existing service. Cable renewals lack this complication.

• The 1984 cable act (Title VI of the communications act) largely deregulated cable. Local communities acting as franchise authorities exercise limited control over cable system operators.

• FCC control of electronic media ownership is a major means of structural regulation, which limits the number of broadcast stations any one owner can control, restricts cross-ownership, encourages minority ownership, and occasionally reviews network control of programming development and syndication. Under the cable act, cable ownership by local television stations and common carriers is also prohibited.

• The threat of license loss is the FCC's strongest weapon. However, the commission actually deletes few licenses through nonrenewal and fewer still through outright revocation. Lesser penalties include short-term renewals, conditional renewals, and forfeitures or fines. Few stations suffer any of these sanctions.

• FCC commissioners are appointed by a political process that sometimes leads to appointees with little experience in the field. Consumers and minorities are not heavily represented among commission members. Commissioners often serve for short periods and then move on to lucrative positions in the media industries.

CHAPTER 18

Freedom and Fairness

We turn now from our discussion of the practical day-to-day regulation of electronic media, most of which comes from the FCC, to considering the broader question of the constitutional limits on such regulation. The First Amendment prohibits federal regulation of speech — yet the communications act indeed imposes federal regulation. This paradox is not unique to the treatment of electronic media. There are many occasions in which the welfare of society calls for a balance between ideal freedom and the practical need to limit speech that might harm individuals or society as a whole. Defining the point of compromise between these contradictory goals is the essence of the First Amendment issues discussed in this chapter.

18.1 First Amendment Basics

In staking their future on the Bill of Rights as a constitutional shield against government tyranny, the framers of the first ten amendments to the U.S. Constitution knew they were embarking on a risky experiment. They counted on people to rule themselves; and crucial to that function is unhampered access to information, ideas, and opinions.

Theory   A robust and wide-open *marketplace of ideas* is the goal of freedom of speech and freedom of the press. Theory suggests that in such a marketplace, concepts and opinions from various sources will compete for acceptance. As the Supreme Court noted in a major electronic media decision, for example, "it is the purpose of the First Amendment to preserve an uninhibited marketplace of ideas in which truth will ultimately prevail, rather than to countenance monopolization of the market" (395 US 390, 1969). Although freedom of expression occupies only a part of one amendment among the ten that make up the Bill of Rights, it has had a pivotal role in the success of the U.S. political system (see Box, page 503). In the words of the late Supreme Court Justice William O. Douglas, the First Amendment "has been the safeguard of every religious, political, philosophical, economic and racial group amongst us" (341 US 494, at 584, 1951).

"No Such Thing as a False Idea"   Many critics and governments have argued that freedom should be allowed only when used "constructively," "responsibly," or "truthfully." But such provisos subvert the central meaning of the First Amendment, which makes no prior assumptions. "Under the First Amendment," said the Supreme Court, "there is no such thing as a false idea. However pernicious an opinion may seem, we depend for its correction not on the conscience of judges and juries, but on the competition of other ideas" (418 US 323, at 339, 1974) — again, the marketplace metaphor.

A fundamental goal of the First Amendment is to encourage disagreement. "A function of free speech under our system of government is to invite dispute," wrote Justice William O. Douglas. "It may indeed best serve its highest purpose when it induces a condition of unrest, creates dissatisfaction with conditions as they are, or even stirs people to anger" (337 US 1, at 4, 1949).

Anger was clearly one reaction to broadcasts from Dodge City, Kansas, in the 1980s. Station KTTL (FM) broadcast daily hour-long sermons by two fundamentalist ministers attacking Jews, blacks, and other groups. They urged listeners to ignore police officers and attack such groups at will. The invective poured forth in such abundance that several local groups protested to the FCC that the station's license should not be renewed (it expired in June 1983), because the station was inciting listeners to violate the law.

A huge media uproar resulted, with a congressional subcommittee hearing in August 1983 and extensive press coverage of the station owner's extremist conservative views favoring local armed vigilante groups. In mid-1985, the FCC designated the license for a comparative hearing with another applicant for the same facility (§17.5), while at the same time imposing a forfeiture, or fine, on the station for several rule violations (§17.8). But in a controversial conclusion, the FCC decided that the First Amendment protected the broadcasts, offensive though they might be to many listeners (FCC, 14 Aug 1985). The commission found that because the material did not present a *clear and present danger* to the public, a test long established by the U.S. Supreme Court, it did not qualify as an unprotected kind of speech (249 US 47, at 52, 1919). In other words, the actual inciting of listeners to take illegal or dangerous actions did not "rise far above public inconvenience, annoyance, or unrest" (36 FCC 2d 635, at 637, 1972).

Private vs. State Censorship   Many people assume that the First Amendment affords protection from *private* censorship. But the amendment aims at protecting people from *government*, not from each other. Station, system, and network officials who edit, cut, bleep, delete, revise, and otherwise mangle programs may be guilty of bad judgment, timidity, and other faults, but they are not violating the First Amendment. They may even go so far as to break FCC rules and federal laws without violating the amendment. Only if private censorship takes place because of *state action* — as in the family viewing situation in the 1970s, where the FCC attempted to reduce television violence by informal pressure — is it unconstitutional (§17.1).

Freedom of Religion   Another First Amendment clause of particular interest to electronic media is the guarantee of religious freedom. In addition to assuring the "free exercise" of religion, the amendment explicitly rules out the designation of any particular creed as the official state religion. Although the likelihood of that happening today is remote, the Supreme Court has held that even the smallest step in that direction violates the First Amendment. The overt intrusion of television evangelists into the national election campaigns of 1980 and 1984, with the aim of electing officials conforming to one particular set of religious convictions, disturbed many people sensitive to First Amendment rights. Of course, that same amendment protected the right of the evangelists to have their say.

Doubly protected by the freedom of speech and the freedom of religion clauses of the First Amendment, some religious broadcasters have been emboldened to treat FCC regulation with extraordinary highhandedness. On many occasions, religious organizations holding FCC licenses have claimed near-immunity from commission requirements, simply because of their perceived right of absolute religious freedom.

Uniqueness of Electronic Media   Just as some types of speech lack First Amendment protection (§18.2), some means (or media) of expression are less protected than others. Although this country has a strong tradition of press freedom, court findings have consistently held that broadcasting has a somewhat different First Amendment status than other media. Broadcasting and some of the other electronic media, it is argued, have unique features that justify imposing regulations on them that would be considered violations of the First Amendment if imposed on print media.

The most striking evidence of this traditional distinction was shown in the opposing Supreme Court conclusions in the *Tornillo* and *Red Lion* cases. The *Tornillo* decision overthrew a Florida law that gave political candidates the right to reply to attacks against them printed in newspapers (418 US 241, 1974). But five years previously, the same court had taken exactly the opposite view with regard to broadcasting. In *Red Lion* it upheld the FCC's rule that entitled persons attacked on broadcast stations a right of reply (§18.4).

The basis of this traditional distinction between the two media has been that publishers have the right to print what they choose by virtue of owning the publishing organizations, and often the printing facilities. Broadcasters, however, cannot fully own their "publishing" facilities. They are temporary licensees, bor-

rowing access to segments of the publicly owned electromagnetic spectrum, which has no counterpart in print publishing. Because the spectrum is a limited resource, broadcasters obtain licenses with the understanding that they will use their part of the spectrum to serve the public interest under FCC oversight. Such reliance on the concept of spectrum scarcity has come under legal attack, however, especially after the Supreme Court commented, in a widely quoted footnote to its 1984 decision allowing public broadcasting stations to editorialize:

The prevailing rationale for broadcast regulation based on spectrum scarcity has come under increasing criticism in recent years. Critics, including the incumbent Chairman of the FCC, charge that with the advent of cable and satellite television technology, communities now have access to such a wide variety of stations that the scarcity doctrine is obsolete. . . . We are not prepared, however to reconsider our long-standing approach without some signal from Congress or the FCC that technological developments have advanced so far that some revision of the system of broadcast regulation may be required. (484 US ____, footnote 11, 1984)

"Composition of the Traffic"   Government licensing or franchising does not, in and of itself, represent a significant loss of freedom. First Amendment theory accepts the practical need for *traffic management* of various forms of communication by government: "Rules to effect this purpose are entirely manageable and, if they are non-discriminatory, either promote, or at least do not seriously impair, the system of free expression" (Emerson, 1972: 168). In an important early Supreme Court case on broadcasting, the industry argued that the FCC had the right to regulate only technical aspects of broadcasting and claimed that any further regulation would violate the First Amendment. But the Court emphatically rejected this argument, saying:

We are asked to regard the Commission as a kind of traffic officer, policing the wave lengths to prevent stations from interfering with each other. But the Act does not restrict the Commission merely to supervision of the traffic. It puts upon the Commission the burden of determining the composition of that traffic. (319 US 190, at 215, 1943)

By "composition of that traffic" the Court meant the choice of stations arrived at through the licensing process. But deciding which licensees will best serve the public interest necessarily takes program services into account. The courts have since frequently cited the composition-of-the-traffic rationale of this landmark decision as legal precedent for approving limited control of programming. Whereas specific program rulings by the FCC prior to broadcast would certainly violate the First Amendment, rulings that come after broadcasters have violated commission program rules or legislative statutes in their *broadcasts* have usually been upheld by the courts.

18.2 Unprotected Speech

Despite the uncompromising command "Congress shall make no law . . . ," U.S. legislative bodies do in fact make laws that punish *unprotected* speech. This is speech or publication that is defamatory or obscene, or speech that plagiarizes, invades privacy, or incites insurrection. Such punishable types of speech are called unprotected because they are regarded as falling outside the First Amendment's shield warding off government interference. It is assumed that such speech contributes nothing to the marketplace of ideas.

Chilling Effect   To be sure, laws against defamation and the like do not normally impose prior restraint. They punish only after the event. Nevertheless, the very fact that

---

The First Amendment

The First Amendment protects four fundamental citizen rights that governments in all ages have had the most reason to fear and the greatest inclination to violate: freedom to believe, to speak, to gather together, and to ask rulers to correct injustices. The amendment conveys all of this in but forty-five words, of which only a few guarantee freedom of expression:

Congress shall make no law respecting an establishment of religion, or prohibiting the free exercise thereof; or abridging the freedom of speech, or of the press: or the right of the people peaceably to assemble, and to petition the Government for a redress of grievances.

Congress, the courts, and the executive branch, as well as state and local governments, are all bound by those words. The FCC is also restricted by the wording of Section 326 of the communications act:

Sec. 326. Nothing in this Act shall be understood or construed to give the Commission the power of censorship over the radio communications or signals transmitted by any radio station, and no regulation or condition shall be promulgated or fixed by the Commission which shall interfere with the right of free speech by means of radio communication.

---

punishment may follow a given course of action tends to inhibit freedom to take that action.

This threat of future punishment is said to have a *chilling effect*. It cools down argumentative ardor and willingness to make facts and ideas public. Self-censorship can, for all practical purposes, have the same repressive effect as external prior restraint. For this reason any government action that potentially has a broad and indiscriminate chilling effect can be held to violate the First Amendment, even if the action is aimed only at preventing unprotected speech. Arguments that FCC rules have this potential have generally been rejected by the courts.

Libel   The law of libel affords the best example of how the chilling effect of prospective punishment can undermine First Amendment goals.*

Criticism of those in power triggers a significant test as to whether a society enjoys true freedom of expression. Democratic societies count on tenacious news reporting to uncover official wrongdoing, sloth, or incompetence, even at the highest political levels. Vigorous investigative reporting cannot flourish, however, in a society in which harsh, easily invoked libel laws threaten journalists with ruinous fines or imprisonment when they dare to criticize public officials.

Libel laws thus involve conflicting social interests. On the one hand, defamation should be punishable because society has an interest in protecting the welfare and dignity of the individual citizen. On the other hand, society also has an interest in exposing official corruption and incompetence. The chilling effect of harassing libel suits can serve as a screen to protect crooked politicians.

A dictator's first act upon seizing power is to suppress the freedom of the media to criticize the new regime — ironically, even when one of the complaints against the old regime

was the lack of freedom to criticize. In the United States, however, not only politicians but all public figures must be prepared to face harsh, sometimes even unfair and ill-founded, criticism from the media without being able to retaliate easily with libel suits.

The leading case establishing the relative protection of the news media from easily won libel suits occurred during the civil rights protests of the 1960s. By chance it involved an instance of "editorial advertising" (§18.4), not investigative reporting.

Supporters of the Montgomery, Alabama, bus boycott protesting segregation bought space in the *New York Times* for a full-page advertisement that criticized Montgomery officials. Some of the statements in the advertisement were false, though apparently not deliberate lies. One of the officials in question, a man named Sullivan, sued for libel in an Alabama court (since libel laws are under the jurisdiction of the states, all libel suits have to be initiated at the state level). The court's award of half a million dollars in damages was affirmed by the Alabama Supreme Court. On appeal to the U.S. Supreme Court, however, the *New York Times* won a reversal. Criticism of public officials, said the Court, had broad First Amendment protection. Even though some of the allegations against Sullivan were untrue, they did not constitute libel.

Argument over public issues, said the Court, should be "uninhibited, robust, and wide-open." It is likely to include "vehement, caustic, and sometimes unpleasantly sharp attacks on government and public officials." Such freewheeling debate is discouraged if, in the heat of debate, the critic must pause to weigh every unfavorable word:

The constitutional guarantees require, we think, a federal rule that prohibits a public official from recovering damages for a defamatory falsehood relating to his official conduct unless he proves that the statement was

---

*Libel is defamation by published words tending to bring upon its victim public hatred, shame, and disgrace. Spoken defamation is called *slander,* but because broadcasting spreads spoken words far and wide, broadcast defamation is treated as libel. If defamation can be proved, victims can sue for damages. Juries often award very large sums in libel suits, as happened in the *Faulk* case (§3.9).

made with "actual malice" — that is, with knowledge that it was false or with reckless disregard of whether it was false or not. (376 US 254, at 279, 1964)

Subsequent libel cases broadened the term "public officials" to include anyone who, because of notoriety, could be classed as a *public figure*. People so classified had little chance of bringing a successful libel suit against the media. Even if stories about public figures could be proved false, deliberate malice on the part of a news medium was exceedingly difficult to prove.

In 1979, and again six years later, libel cases arising from television coverage of the Vietnam War focused on the issue of malice toward well-known people. The first suit concerned a highly decorated officer, and the second the senior American military commander in Vietnam (Exhibit 18.1). Ironically, both suits grew out of interviews conducted by CBS reporter Mike Wallace.

In 1970, Colonel Anthony Herbert had accused the Army of covering up atrocities committed by American troops during the Vietnam war. CBS reporter Mike Wallace's interview of Herbert on *60 Minutes* was based on investigations of Herbert's claims by program producer Barry Lando. Herbert, alleging that the program depicted him as a liar, sued Lando for libel. He surprised media officials when, in order to find evidence of malice, he sought to determine Lando's "state of mind" while the program was being prepared. Herbert claimed that he needed to find out if Lando was personally convinced he was lying, and had used the program to make that point (which would have constituted actual malice). Lando refused to answer such questions, claiming a *journalist's privilege* to keep news sources and editorial processes confidential. But on appeal, the Supreme Court upheld Herbert's claim, saying that "according an absolute privi-

lege to the editorial process of a media defendant in a libel case is not required, authorized or presaged by our prior cases, and would substantially enhance the burden of proving actual malice, contrary to the expectations of *New York Times*" (441 US 153, at 169, 1979).

This decision presented broadcast and other journalists with a severe setback in defending libel suits. Complainants could now rummage through tape archives, correspondence files, and program outtakes to determine the state of mind of reporters and editors. The ruling was soon extended to other cases, making "journalists nearly as vulnerable for what they did *not* say as for what they did" (*Time*, 4 Mar 85: 94).

The Herbert decision contributed to the already evident rise in the number of libel cases filed against the media by public figures. These suits often seek huge financial awards, but even when such awards are granted, they are often overturned or reduced on appeal. Although the media have usually won such cases, defending against a libel suit is expensive,* and, more to the point, has a chilling effect on investigative reporting efforts. That is, in fact, exactly what some lawsuits seek — a more "responsible" reporting of news and public affairs. Other critics feel that most media libel cases should go to arbitrators rather than courts, resulting in corrections if stories are in error, and more reasonable monetary awards. This procedure would consume far less time than libel suits and their appeals.

With the Supreme Court decision about questioning Lando in hand, Herbert pressed on for a trial on the substance of his case — the statements made in the CBS program that

---

*Many media owners now have libel insurance. Typically, broadcast stations are willing to absorb some of the legal expenses and monetary judgment losses as "deductibles" in libel policies, thereby reducing premiums.

he felt libeled his reputation. Finally, early in 1986, a federal appeals court ruled that Herbert had no grounds for bringing the libel suit in the first place, and the case was closed. The *Lando* precedent remained, however.

The second case never reached a jury, but had far wider press coverage. On January 23, 1982, the CBS television network presented an hour-long documentary entitled "The Uncounted Enemy: A Vietnam Deception" that alleged a military cover-up of enemy troop strength during the height of the Vietnam War in the late 1960s. Prominent in that program were interviews reporter Mike Wallace conducted with the top American military commander in the war, General William Westmoreland (Exhibit 18.1).

In May, *TV Guide* published a lengthy article accusing CBS news of breaking reportorial norms, including its own policies, to "get" Westmoreland (*TV Guide*, 29 May 82). CBS responded with an intensive internal investigation (Benjamin, 1984). It found that several network rules had indeed been violated in producing the program, although there was support for the overall program conclusion of a cover-up. Finally, in September, General Westmoreland filed a $120 million libel suit against the network, saying that his reputation had been ruined by the program and its aftermath. Conservative foundations and individuals underwrote most of the $3 million cost of the five-month trial, which began in October 1984.

Late in February 1985, after a preponderance of testimony supporting the CBS program, Westmoreland abruptly withdrew his suit. Apparently his backers, sensing that the verdict would go against the general, decided to cut their losses and accept an equivocal statement from the network.

Westmoreland had sought three things: (1) an apology from CBS, (2) a retraction of its charges, and (3) millions of dollars in dam-

Exhibit 18.1   The General vs. Television

As discussed in the text, General William Westmoreland, commander of American forces in Vietnam, claimed he had been libeled in a 1982 CBS documentary in which he was interviewed by 60 Minutes reporter Mike Wallace.

Source: Photo courtesy of UPI/Bettmann Newsphotos.

ages. He won none of these, although he regarded a short and generalized CBS disclaimer as an apology. The libel principle established by the *Sullivan* case, that malicious intent must be proved, survived the Westmoreland case, as did CBS's journalistic credibility; but defending the suit cost CBS millions.

Invasion of Privacy   Closely related to libel is the changing legal concept of *invasion of* *privacy*, which varies from state to state (there is no federal law on privacy). Privacy laws generally hold that an individual is entitled to the following: a right of physical solitude; protection of the details of one's private life; protection from being presented in a false light (for example, from being said to be in support of something one is actually against); and protection from unauthorized use of one's name or image for commercial gain. Investigative reports by local stations that seek to televise pictures of a kitchen of a restaurant found in violation of local cleanliness standards, for instance, may run up against the right of that establishment to control access to private property. Taken together, the personal protections of libel and privacy laws represent a limit on media access. Although courts have held that public officials, performers, or anybody involved in news events have lesser right to privacy claims because of legitimate public interest in those persons or events, privacy laws still serve to limit media by supporting individual rights.

Evolution of Obscenity Law   Prior to the 1930s, obscenity in literature and art could be arbitrarily suppressed at the whim of officials and censorship boards. The successful defense in 1933 of James Joyce's literary masterpiece *Ulysses* initiated a series of court decisions that have set up complex legal barriers against heavy-handed suppression by zealous moral watchdogs.

Current obscenity law is based on the 1973 *Miller* case, in which the Supreme Court ruled on the constitutionality of a California state obscenity law. The decision emphasized that *community standards* vary from place to place: "It is neither realistic nor constitutionally sound to read the First Amendment as requiring that the people of Maine or Mississippi accept public depiction of conduct found tolerable in Las Vegas or New York City."

Nevertheless, warned the Court, state laws must be carefully defined because of the dangers inherent in government regulation of any type of speech. In summary:

We now confine the permissible scope of such regulation to works which depict or describe sexual conduct. That conduct must be specifically defined by the applicable state law. . . . A state offense must also be limited to works which, taken as a whole, appeal to the prurient interest in sex, which portray sexual conduct in a patently offensive way, and which, taken as a whole, do not have serious literary, artistic, political, or scientific value. (413 US 15, at 24, 1973)

The practical result of the *Miller* case, along with some later cases that added minor modifications, was to restrict censorship for obscenity to hard-core pornography. All that remained was for the states to define hard-core pornography, a task that is exceedingly difficult to fulfill to everyone's satisfaction. In any event, the law rules out abuses of power that were freely committed by censors in the past. For example, the First Amendment now prevents censors from taking such arbitrary action as follows:

• condemning an entire work because of a few isolated obscene words;
• using outdated standards no longer common to the local community;
• applying as a standard the opinions of hypersensitive persons who are untypical of the general public;
• ignoring serious artistic or scientific purpose in judging a work.

In other words, the *context* of the supposedly obscene material is pertinent to a legal decision. Generally speaking, the law requires the courts to consider the average person when applying contemporary community standards in assessing potentially obscene material. Of course, those standards will be stricter for the most people when the material is available to children. There is general agreement that material possibly acceptable for interested and consenting adults is not acceptable for children under the age of fifteen or sixteen.

Obscenity in Broadcasting   Section 1464 of the U.S. Criminal Code makes punishable the utterance of "any obscene, indecent, or profane language by means of radio communication," but the FCC long remained in doubt as to its powers to enforce the law. Because of broadcasting's ready availability in the home, especially to children, material acceptable on other media might be regarded as obscene, indecent, or profane by many in the broadcast audience. Furthermore, because broadcast and cable network services are national, they confront a great variety of local standards.

Broadcasting's traditional conservatism delayed its response to the liberal social climate of the 1960s, but the liberalization of standards in other media inevitably had its effect. In the early 1970s a "topless radio" fad triggered thousands of complaints to the FCC. The format invited women to call in and talk on the air about intimate details of their sex lives. Such talk shows are commonplace today, but at that time the FCC received a flood of complaints about one blatant example. The FCC imposed a $2,000 fine on an Illinois station, WGLD-FM, in accordance with the forfeiture clause of Section 502 of the communications act, which explicitly authorizes fines for obscenity violations (41 FCC 2d 919, 1973). The FCC had actually hoped the station would contest the fine, thus precipitating a test case, but the station dutifully filled out a check instead.

In 1973 the FCC finally got its test. A noncommercial station, WBAI-FM in New York, included in a discussion of social attitudes about language a recording by comedian George Carlin. Called "Filthy Words," the monologue satirized society's hang-ups about seven sexually oriented words not likely to be heard on the air. This time, though, they were — 106 times in 12 minutes. A single complaint was voiced by a man who, as it later turned out, was associated with a group called Morality in Media. He happened to hear the early-afternoon broadcast while driving in his car with his teen-age son. The fact that the youth was exposed to Carlin's language became a key element in the case.

On the rather flimsy basis of that lone complaint, the FCC wrote to the station advising that the broadcast was indecent and in violation of the obscenity statute. The FCC defined "indecent content" as content that, in a potentially offensive fashion, according to contemporary community standards for broadcasting, depicted sexual or excretory activities or organs when children were likely to be in the audience. The licensee, Pacifica, (see Box, page 367), challenged the ruling as a matter of First Amendment principle. After an initial setback in appeals court, the FCC won Supreme Court approval of its reasoning. Focusing its argument on the Carlin monologue as indecent rather than obscene (it could hardly have been found obscene, according to the Supreme Court's definition of the term), the FCC stressed the fact that the broadcast came at a time when children would normally be in the audience.

Children, said the commission, are entitled to be protected from indecency, which the FCC defined as material that fails to conform to "accepted standards of morality." In referring to the court-approved "community standards" test, the commission slipped in a significant qualifier of its own, making it read "community standards *for broadcast media.*"

Instead of meeting the First Amendment head on by flatly banning such material as the

Carlin monologue, however, the FCC said it should be *channeled* to a part of the day when children are least likely to be in the audience.* The channeling concept had a precedent in nuisance law, which recognizes that something acceptable in one setting could be an illegal nuisance in other settings.

The Supreme Court agreed with the nuisance law rationale. Recalling that a judge had once said that a nuisance "may be merely a right thing in a wrong place — like a pig in the parlor instead of the barnyard," the Court added that if the FCC "finds a pig has entered the parlor, the exercise of regulatory power does not depend on proof that the pig is obscene." The Court also tacitly accepted the FCC's redefinition of community standards by adding the words "for broadcasting," saying, "We have long recognized that each medium of expression presents special First Amendment problems. . . . And of all forms of communication, it is broadcasting that has received the most limited First Amendment protection" (438 US 726, at 748, 1978).

Cable Obscenity Issues

Because it is regulated by states as well as by the federal government, cable obscenity issues have caused conflicts of jurisdiction as well as of substance. At issue are state laws that attempt to apply the findings of the Supreme Court's *Miller* and *Pacifica* cases to cable television content.

By mid-1985, decisions in four cases, three of them brought in Utah, had found state cable obscenity and indecency legislation in violation of the First Amendment. Courts threw out laws limiting indecent programming, finding them too broad in scope. Because cable does not use the open spectrum, the scarcity argument (§16.1) that had supported obscenity limitations on broadcasting could not be applied. Since cable was paid for, the courts reasoned, it was not as "uniquely intrusive" as broadcasting, and for similar reason it was considered not as available to children. The judge in one case suggested that the real responsibility for preventing children from seeing such programming rested with parents (11 MLR 2217).

The Cable Communications Policy Act of 1984 (§17.6) seems to provide a nationally applicable strategy for keeping obscenity off cable. Section 639 provides for fines of $10,000 or up to two years' imprisonment for anyone who "transmits over any cable system any matter which is obscene or otherwise unprotected by the Constitution." How this rule will square with the limits on broadcast obscenity remains to be seen.

In 1986 the Supreme Court ruled unanimously that cable television is protected by the First Amendment. But the high court also held that protection must be balanced against what it called "competing social interests," without specifying how that might be done (Slip Opinion, 1986:6).

Free Press vs. Fair Trial

Sometimes protecting the constitutional rights of individuals challenges the First Amendment rights of the press. Persons accused of crimes are assured fair play by the due process clause of the Fifth Amendment; some of the elements of due process are also spelled out in the Sixth Amendment, among them the right to a public trial. Ordinarily, the press is therefore free to cover trials; but press coverage can subject defendants to such intense publicity that a fair trial becomes impossible. In this *free press vs. fair trial* confrontation, the constitutional

---

*In assessing the channeling rationale it should be borne in mind that the notion of most children being present in audiences only at certain hours of the day may be an illusion. It appears from ratings research data that nearly as many children watch television in late prime time as in the traditional children's enclave, the Saturday morning hours.

rights of the press sometimes give way to the constitutional rights of defendants. Electronic media become deeply involved in this thorny issue when they attempt to air on-the-spot coverage of highly publicized trials or pretrial proceedings.

For several decades, there was virtually no live or recorded radio or television coverage of trials. The American Bar Association (ABA) had recommended that radio, television, and photographic coverage should be discouraged because they tended "to detract from the essential dignity of the proceedings, degrade the court and create misconceptions with respect thereto in the mind of the public." The 1960s trial of convicted swindler Billie Sol Estes in Texas (for a time one of only two states that did not follow the no-camera rule) seemed to support this stand; an appeals court reversed Estes's guilty verdict because of the circus atmosphere created by twelve cameras and attendant lights and crews (this was in the days before ENG equipment). The U.S. Supreme Court upheld the appeals court decision (381 US 532, 1965).

But in the 1970s, with improved equipment and less need for high-intensity lights, and with changing social standards and more mature broadcast journalism practices, the ban against live coverage of trials began to seem less urgent. Accordingly, the ABA recommended that judges be given wide latitude in allowing photo and video coverage of trials. In 1981 the U.S. Supreme Court noted the improved technology and held that "the risk of juror prejudice . . . does not warrant an absolute constitutional ban on all broadcast coverage" (449 US 560). Today, more than half the states have either allowed cameras in their courtrooms or have conducted experiments to that end. But federal courts remain off-limits to such coverage in the 1980s, despite several media attempts to breach that barrier (Exhibit 18.2).

18.3 Control over Programs

The communications act is surprisingly unexplicit about programming content, although of course the public-interest concept speaks volumes. As noted in the Box on page 503, Congress recognized the First Amendment with the censorship disclaimer in Section 326 of the communications act. But despite this, the FCC has over the years attempted to force broadcasters to pay attention to local programming, which the commission has regarded as essential to meeting the public-service criterion of the communications act.

Localism   The FCC's localism principle has two aspects; the widespread distribution of stations and the airing of locally produced programming on those stations. By promoting localism, the FCC encourages broadcasters to reflect local community needs and to serve community interests.

Section 307 of the communications act gives the FCC a guideline for acting on applications for new broadcast stations: "The Commission shall make such distribution of licenses, frequencies, hours of operation, and of power among the several States and communities as to provide a fair, efficient, and equitable distribution of radio service to each of the same." Despite this policy of localizing station distribution, people in major American cities can choose from forty or more stations, whereas people in many rural areas have little or no choice. Localism in station distribution, when governed by the economic marketplace, inevitably leads to maldistribution — too many stations where the money is, and not enough where stations cannot operate at a profit.

As cable penetration in the United States increases (by 1986 serving nearly half the homes in the country) it evens up the choices available in urban and suburban areas. How-

Exhibit 18.2   Trial by Television

Broadcast coverage of trials began with the 1925 Scopes trial but reached a nadir of overkill with (top left) the 1935 trial of Bruno Hauptman for the kidnap and murder of Charles Lindbergh's son. Reaction to that overcoverage by radio and film led to the ABA's "Canon 35" banning trial coverage for decades. An early experiment with television coverage (top right) took place in Texas in Billie Sol Estes' trial for fraud. The Supreme Court later overturned the Estes' conviction due to interference of television coverage in the courtroom. More recently, (bottom), the Watergate hearings of 1973 demonstrated the power of television in covering a Senate investigation.

Sources: Top left and bottom, AP/Wide World Photos; top right, UPI/Bettmann Newsphotos.

ever, cable, too, suffers financial problems in rural areas; moreover, it depends increasingly on its own network services, which usually will not promote local programming.

On the other hand, many countries had opted for a policy of equitable *service*, at the price of equitable *local* service. This kind of national service relies on fewer, larger, more powerful stations, strategically positioned to serve the widest possible areas. Big cities have fewer choices, but rural areas have far more — almost as many as do metropolitan areas. The aim of such a policy is to cover entire populations using the fewest possible transmitters (in fairness, it must be added, most countries implementing this policy have much smaller land masses than that of the United States to cover).

But as we have suggested, localism means not only promoting the growth of local stations but expanding local access to stations. Ideally it affords opportunities for local public-service agencies to communicate their objectives, for partisans in local controversies to air their points of view, for local governments and political candidates to inform the electorate, for local educational and cultural institutions to broaden their community service, for local firms to advertise, for local talent to have an outlet, and so on. A station offering such programming thus serves its area by affording a means of community self-expression, giving it a broadcast voice as well as a broadcast ear. A press parallel is the local weekly newspaper that reports on local developments and through letters and op-ed pages provides a means of local self-expression.

Localism in this sense draws on the deep-rooted American political tradition of community autonomy. Idealists in the early days of radio looked to the new service to revive the fading spirit of the traditional New England town meeting. They hoped that, given local radio voices, communities would find new opportunities for grass-roots citizen participation in local affairs. Radio, they thought, might bring a new sense of community togetherness and awareness. Influenced by such thinking, the FCC pushed localism heavily in pretelevision days. The 1946 FCC report *Public Service Responsibilities of Broadcast Licensees*, known by its cover as the "Blue Book," represented the high-water mark of FCC attempts to assure local production and programming roles for broadcasters. The Blue Book philosophy was echoed in the commission's 1960 program statement (44 FCC 2303), which listed categories of programming each licensee should strive to include during a given week.

Such hopes were sadly doomed to failure. The irresistible forces of networking (Chapter 12) and syndication (Chapter 13) swept away most local production. This does not mean that localism has been totally abandoned, however. Licensing and renewal policies continue to hold it up as a formal, though increasingly hollow, goal. For example, local residence is a point in favor of an applicant for a new station as against an absentee owner (§17.3 and §17.5). And as late as 1980, program guidelines for radio and television required that information on local news, public affairs, and other nonentertainment programming be entered on applications (§17.2). By then, however, the FCC's localism concerns were more procedural than substantive in nature.

Broadcasters often hold up the need to preserve localism when threatened by a newer service — especially cable and, in the 1980s, direct-broadcast satellites. They argue that the new delivery channels are based almost entirely on national program services, whereas broadcasters still preserve station-based localism — this despite the pervasive national syndication in radio and the network domination of television.

Programs for Needy Groups   The most persistent advocates of localism and public-service programming are those who speak for children, minority groups, and the elderly. Most controversial is the push for educational and cultural programs for young children on commercial TV, to supplement the limited amount of material on public stations (§12.5).

At the heart of these arguments, most of which have taken place in congressional hearings and FCC proceedings, is the issue of whether government can or should force a privately owned industry in the midst of deregulation to produce certain program types or formats. The trend is clearly away from any kind of program controls, including mandated programs for specific audiences. Proponents of controls argue that the marketplace mechanism does not, by its very nature, work for groups such as children, nor for elderly people and ethnic minorities, who may not be worthwhile targets for advertisers. In the 1970s and 1980s, at least one FCC commissioner spoke out for the needs of such groups, and some members of Congress from urban districts often argued for the same needs, while providing a forum for others to be heard. But the industry, most FCC officials, and much of Congress leaned the other way. Despite initiatives by spokespersons for each of these underserved groups, little regulatory action took place or seemed likely. The FCC nebulously requires that all broadcast stations provide at least some "issue-responsive," though not necessarily local, programming, and has stated that television licensees must not ignore the needs of children; but these are hardly forceful policies.

18.4   Regulated Fairness

Perhaps the most controversial government intrusions into broadcast licensees' use of their facilities are rules seeking to ensure *fair play* in the discussion of controversial issues. When government regulates fairness to enhance the public good arising from broadcasting, it plays the role of ally rather than enemy of First Amendment values. But most licensees complain vehemently about the chilling impact of such government intrusion into editorial decisions.

Access to Means of Expression   In order to enjoy First Amendment privileges, citizens need to be able to listen to diverse voices in the marketplace, but they also need to have voices of their own. The notion of *access* thus has reciprocal meanings — access both to what is expressed and to the means of expression.

Not every person who wants to express ideas over the air can own a broadcasting station; nor is it feasible to give everyone access to broadcasting stations owned by others. The FCC chose to deal with this problem by assuring access to broadcasting for *ideas* rather than for specific *people*. But even access for ideas has to be qualified. It would be impracticable to force stations to give time for literally every idea that might be put forward. The FCC mandates access only for ideas about *controversial issues of public importance*, thus stressing another First Amendment value.

The FCC's solution for the access problem has two advantages: (1) it allows licensees to retain general responsibility for programming, leaving to their discretion, for example, decisions about which issues have public importance and who should speak for them; and (2) it obligates licensees, though in a relatively unstructured way, to allow access to some ideas other than their own. Thus licensee First Amendment rights are generally preserved along with those of the public at large.

Eventually the FCC elaborated its access concept into a formalized set of procedures called the *fairness doctrine*. In the pages that follow, we will discuss the development and the rationale of this doctrine in terms of First Amendment goals.

Evolution of Fairness Doctrine   Implicit in broadcast regulation from the outset was the notion that fairness played a central role in the *fiduciary responsibility* of licensees — that is, in their role as holders of broadcast channels *in trust* for the benefit of the general public. However, the fairness requirement as a set of formal precepts did not emerge until 1949, with the issuance of an FCC report on editorializing by licensees.

In an earlier ruling, known as the *Mayflower* decision, the FCC had said that licensees took an unfair advantage when they used their facilities for expressing their own points of view in the form of editorials. The 1949 policy statement reversed that ruling. It would be fairer to all concerned, the FCC concluded, to encourage licensees to introduce controversial issues by means of editorials, provided that they also gave outsiders access to their facilities to express opposing points of view.* In announcing this fairness concept the FCC said:

It is the right of the public to be informed, rather than any right on the part of the Government, any broadcast licensee or any individual member of the public to broadcast his own particular views on any matter,

which is the foundation stone of the American system of broadcasting.

This affirmative responsibility on the part of broadcast licensees to provide a reasonable amount of time for the presentation over their facilities of programs devoted to the discussion and consideration of public issues has been reaffirmed by the commission in a long series of decisions. (13 FCC 1249, 1949)

In effect, the FCC was saying that it is a kind of unfairness for a licensee to program nothing but bland entertainment, avoiding all serious or provocative program matter. That policy would deprive the public of an important First Amendment benefit that it had a right to expect from broadcasting.

Although the fairness doctrine began as an FCC administrative interpretation of the general public interest mandate of the communications act, Congress in 1959 lent statutory endorsement to the concept in an incidental way when it amended Section 315 to exempt bona fide news programs about political candidates from equal-time requirements (§18.6). After enumerating four types of exempt news programs (newscasts, interviews, documentaries, on-the-spot coverage) the amendment continued (emphasis added):

Nothing in the foregoing sentence shall be construed as relieving broadcasters, in connection with [the exempt news programs], from the obligation imposed upon them under this Act to operate in the public interest and to afford reasonable opportunity for the discussion of conflicting views on issues of public importance.

The phrase "in connection with" seems to limit such discussions to news-related issues. Nevertheless, the FCC and the courts have treated this statement as congressional endorsement of the fairness doctrine generally.

Attacks and Editorials   Doubt still lingered as to whether the FCC could enforce the fairness doctrine without violating the First Amendment. Two additional fairness re-

---

*Only in 1984 was the right to editorialize extended to public broadcasters. The 1967 public broadcasting amendments to the communications act had included in Section 399 a prohibition on editorializing by any station that received grants from the Corporation for Public Broadcasting (whose funds came from Congress). Furthermore, no noncommercial station could support or oppose any political candidate. The limitation, intended to further insulate public broadcasting from government programming interference, was appealed by the Pacifica Foundation and the League of Women Voters. A federal district court found the ban to be unconstitutional, as a violation of the First Amendment. The U.S. Supreme Court, in a 5–4 vote, upheld the lower court, and the ban was lifted, giving equal rights to stations of all kinds (484 US, _____, 1984).

quirements, the *personal attack* rule and the *political editorializing* rule, both adopted in 1967, caused special concern to opponents of FCC interference. Both of these requirements were issued as formal rules and both required that those affected by specific broadcasts be given copies of the relevant material within specified time limits.

The personal attack rule provided that stations had a duty to inform individuals or groups of personal attacks on their "honesty, character, integrity or like personal qualities" that occurred in the course of discussions of controversial public issues. Within a week of the offending broadcast, licensees must inform those attacked of both the nature of the attack and how replies could be made.

The political editorial rule stipulated that a candidate must be given a chance to respond when a licensee endorsed his or her opponent. A station must inform the opposing candidate(s) within twenty-four hours of any editorial endorsement. The rule did *not* apply to use of a station's facilities by opposing candidates, for that was covered under the political rules (§18.6).

Judicial Affirmation: *Red Lion* Objections to these 1967 rules led to a crucial Supreme Court test of the fairness doctrine's constitutionality in 1969. The Court heard two separate appeals simultaneously, issuing a single opinion. The lower courts had ruled favorably to the FCC in one case, unfavorably in the other. Most of the Supreme Court's attention was focused on the first, the *Red Lion* case, which was an appeal by a licensee from a personal attack violation ruling by the FCC (see Box, pages 516–517).*

---

*The other case challenged the political editorial and the personal attack rules as such. It was initiated by the Radio and Television News Directors Association, which argued that the station's personal attack case might not be strong enough to afford a definitive test of the First Amendment issue.

By unanimously supporting the FCC in the *Red Lion* case, the Supreme Court generally affirmed the fairness doctrine concept in an opinion written by Justice Byron White (395 US 367, 1969). It was notable for his trenchant commentary on several of broadcasting's recurrent First Amendment issues. Following is a sampling:

- *On the uniqueness of broadcasting:* "It is idle to posit an unabridgeable First Amendment right to broadcast comparable to the right of every individual to speak, write, or publish."
- *On the fiduciary principle:* "There is nothing in the First Amendment which prevents the Government from requiring a licensee to share his frequency with others and to conduct himself as a proxy or fiduciary."
- *On the public interest:* "It is the right of the viewers and listeners, not the right of the broadcasters, which is paramount."
- *On the scarcity factor:* "Nothing in this record, or in our own researches, convinces us that the [spectrum] resource is no longer one for which there are more immediate and potential uses than can be accommodated, and for which wise planning is essential."

With the *Red Lion* case, the fairness doctrine achieved emphatic if not absolute legal endorsement from the highest court. Although Justice White rejected broadcaster arguments that the fairness doctrine had unconstitutional chilling effects, he did limit the decision to the facts of the case and suggest that if the facts were different, the constitutionality of the doctrine might be questioned. In a footnote to a 1984 decision (484 US, _____, 1984), the Court noted Justice White's comment about *Red Lion* and seemed to imply that it would be receptive to a new case to review the fairness doctrine's applicability in an era of expanding technological options. In the meantime, however, legal appeals concerned not the doctrine itself but its applicability in given cases. Not surpris-

A Place and a Case Called *Red Lion*

An unlikely small-town station, a long-time syndicated religious broadcaster, a writer, and a major political party combined to create the basis for one of the most important Supreme Court decisions on the electronic media. During the 1960s, right-wing radio preachers inundated radio with syndicated political commentaries. Backed by conservative multimillionaries such as H. L. Hunt through tax-exempt foundations, these program series provided much-needed radio income in one-station markets that became local outlets for extremist views.

syndicated programs, carried by the station, had attacked author Fred Cook. Cook had criticized defeated Republican presidental candidate Barry Goldwater and had written an article on what he termed the "hate clubs of the air," one of which

HARGIS   COOK

The landmark case was initiated in 1964 on WGCB, a southeastern Pennsylvania AM/FM outlet licensed to John M. Norris, a conservative minister, under the name Red Lion Broadcasting. In 1964, one of Reverend Billy James Hargis's

was the Hargis series, *Christian Crusade*. Hargis had charged Cook with having communist affiliations and with attacking the FBI and the CIA — the usual litany of accusations he routinely made against liberals in his broadcasts.

Cook accused the station of violating the fairness doctrine by failing to inform him of a personal attack, and wrote to the station asking for time to reply to the attack on his integrity. The station responded with a rate card and invited him to buy time like anyone else. Cook appealed to the FCC, which agreed that he was entitled to

ingly, considering the latitude licensees have in responding to fairness doctrine complaints, disputes about that applicability continued to arise.

Summary of Fairness Doctrine Obligations

As we have noted, the FCC has long held that to serve the public interest, each licensee should devote some time to the discussion of public issues. Such discussions invoke the fairness doctrine, obligating stations to schedule time for expression of opposing viewpoints on issues of public importance. This obligation means that licensees should

free air time in which to reply to the attack, and ordered WGCB to comply. It would have been easy for the licensee to grant Cook a few minutes of time, but it refused on First Amendment and other grounds, and appealed the commission decision. The FCC was upheld by the Court of Appeals, but WGCB took the case to the Supreme Court, despite concern by many broadcasters that this was not a sufficiently strong case to test the constitutionality of the fairness doctrine. As related in the text, the fairness doctrine was upheld in the 1969 *Red Lion* decision.

Several years later, Fred Friendly, a CBS news executive, began looking into the background of this case for a book he was writing about the fairness doctrine (Friendly, 1976). He discovered that Cook had been subsidized writer for the Democratic National Committee and that his fairness doctrine complaint was, if not inspired by, at least linked to, a systematic campaign mounted by the Democratic party to discredit right-wing extremists such as Hargis. According to Friendly, the Democrats set out to exploit the fairness doctrine as a means of harassing stations that sold time for the airing of the ultraconservative political programs. Cook had mimeographed his letter of complaint against the Hargis program and mailed it to some 50 stations. Friendly concluded that Cook had been part of a campaign to pervert the fairness doctrine into "an instrument of politics and ambition."

Cook and others from the Democratic National Committee held that Friendly had misinterpreted their activities. They maintained that Cook had acted as a private individual, not as an agent of the Democrats, in bringing his complaints against the Hargis program. WGCB had invited retaliation, they claimed, when it refused to supply reply time, as required under the FCC's personal attack rules.

FRIENDLY

First Amendment absolutists (§18.7) regard the *Red Lion* case as yet another area in which the amendment has been weakened for electronic media. The broadcast industry, which had been understandably concerned about the case when it went before the Supreme Court, now had to live with the resulting strong judicial decision upholding both the 1959 legislative statement and the FCC's developing case-law approach to applying the fairness doctrine.

Source: Photos courtesy *New York Times* Pictures

continously monitor their own programming to make sure that if anyone introduces controversial issues, fair opportunities for reply are offered to opposing interests. If licensees themselves introduce controversial issues in the form of station editorials, they must offer time for the expression of opposing views.

Licensees make their own decisions under the fairness doctrine on such questions as:

• whether or not a subject qualifies as an issue of public importance.
• how much time should be devoted to replies.

• when replies should be scheduled.

• what format replies should employ.

• who should speak for opposing view-points (except, of course, for those replying to personal attack).

In practice, however, stations afraid of controversy ignore the first requirement with little risk of FCC objection. Only once has the FCC reprimanded a station for failing to *initiate* a controversy. This occurred in 1976 when a congresswoman and others complained that WHAR, a small AM radio station in West Virginia, refused to air a tape she had sent. The congresswoman had circulated the tape to a number of stations, in order to counteract arguments against a strip-mining bill that had already been circulated on tape by the U.S. Chamber of Commerce. Having neither aired the chamber tape nor raised the issue of the strip-mining bill locally on its own, WHAR claimed it had no obligation to air a reply. However, the FCC agreed with the congresswoman. It was, said the FCC, a violation of the fairness doctrine to *fail to bring up* an issue of great local importance (59 FCC 2d 987, 1976).

It is no mystery why stations ordinarily ignore with impunity their fairness doctrine obligation to initiate discussion about controversial subjects. The FCC sits back and waits for third parties to bring station misbehavior to its attention, rather than conducting its own monitoring to seek out violations (§17.4). In the nature of things, the most frequent and urgent fairness doctrine complaints are *reactive*. They come from people reacting to ideas that have already been discussed on the air, rather than from people who want to initiate discussions of new issues.

The FCC gives licensees wide latitude. For example, a homosexual-rights organization alleged that a station was unfair in the way it granted replies to attacks on homosexuals that occurred in the syndicated fundamentalist religious series *PTL Club*. The attacks occurred during eight hours of the program over a four-month period. The "reasonable opportunity" for reply offered by the station consisted of a single program repeated nine times during a four-day period. Despite the discrepancy between attack and reply opportunities, the FCC decided the licensee had used reasonable discretion (68 FCC 2d 1500, 1978).

Given such latitude, conscientious broadcasters normally have no reason to fear that fairness doctrine obligations will impose undue demands on station time. Not all broadcasters, however, are willing to act in good faith by complying with the fairness doctrine. Some use their stations to promote extreme positions on controversial issues, oblivious of the fact that as licensees they have an obligation to offer opportunities for rebuttal.

One of the most publicized instances of licensee one-sidedness occurred when WXUR, a Media, Pennsylvania, AM/FM radio station, lost its license for defying the fairness doctrine and lying about its intent to comply with the doctrine. WXUR was licensed to an organization headed by Carl McIntire, a cantankerous right-wing fundamentalist preacher. Despite opposition from citizen groups in the community, he had acquired WXUR when stations in nearby Philadelphia refused to carry his *Twentieth Century Reformation Hour*, a syndicated radio series noted for its intemperate attacks on opponents of McIntire's ultraconservative philosophy.

From the moment the station went on the air in 1965, citizen groups began bombarding the FCC with complaints about WXUR's "hate clubs of the air." In 1970 the FCC finally refused to renew the license, alleging not only fairness doctrine violations but also failure to fulfill program promises and to ascertain local needs. An appeals court upheld the FCC's action, making WXUR the first station to lose its license because of fairness doctrine violations. The court of appeals used unusually strong language in condemning McIntire's stewardship. "With more bravado than brains," said the court, his station ". . . went on an independent frolic, broadcasting what it chose, abusing those who dared to differ from its viewpoints" (473 F 2d 16, at 48, 1972).

Few fairness complaints have such drastic consequences. Of the thousands that arrive at the FCC each year, most complaints tend to come from zealous partisans with strong views on such emotional issues as gun control, abortion, women's rights, gay liberation, environmental protection, prayers in schools, and nuclear power. Most complaints are dismissed out of hand by the FCC. Either the complainants cite no legally definable controversial issue or they fail to show that the overall programming of accused stations has in fact denied reasonable opportunities for opposing sides to be argued.

Fairness in Advertising   Only one commercial product has ever been the subject of a fairness doctrine complaint — cigarettes. In 1968 the FCC decided, in ruling on a complaint brought against WCBS-TV in New York for refusing to give time for antismoking spot announcements, that because of the Surgeon General's report on the dangers of smoking, and Congress's 1965 labeling act (requiring a warning on cigarette packages and printed advertising), cigarette advertising presented a unique fairness doctrine issue. The commission was upheld on appeal on the ground that the ruling, far from limiting freedom of speech, actually added information for the public (405 F 2d 1082, 1968). The surge of antismoking spots that followed subsided after Congress banned broadcast advertising of cigarettes in 1972, thus removing the fairness doctrine obligation to carry the counteradvertising spots. As part of the 1968 ruling, the

FCC said that the cigarette case would not be a precedent for applying the fairness doctrine to other commercial products, although there have been flurries of concern every few years about the advertising of beer and wine on television.*

Editorial advertising, or "advertorials," however, pose a different kind of problem. Traditionally, the electronic media have opposed advertising addressed to controversial issues, arguing that (1) serious issues cannot be adequately discussed within the confines of spot announcements; and (2) selling larger blocks of time for editorializing by outsiders involves surrender of editorial responsibility. Also present in this mix is the less high-minded, play-it-safe motive of avoiding controversy.

Several controversial attempts at issue advertising developed in the 1960s, and two cases progressed simultaneously to the Supreme Court. Business owners opposed to the American role in the Vietnam War had unsuccessfully attempted to purchase time for spots arguing against the war and countering Army recruiting campaigns. At the same time, the Democratic National Committee had been turned down when it attempted to buy time to put Democratic views on national television networks. Had these plaintiffs prevailed, the cases might have created a new right of access to the airwaves. Instead, the Court, joining the two cases, upheld the principle of licensee journalistic discretion:

Since it is physically impossible to provide time for all viewpoints . . . the right to exercise editorial judgment

---

*Hard-liquor advertisements, though not legally banned by the act or any FCC rule, have seldom been carried on broadcast stations because of the threat of a congressional ban if such advertising did appear. Liquor ads were for years disallowed by the NAB radio and television codes (§16.7). The overall effect, of course, is the same: liquor advertising does not, as a rule, run on American radio and television.

was granted to the broadcaster. The broadcaster, therefore, is allowed significant journalistic discretion in deciding how best to fulfill the Fairness Doctrine obligations, although that discretion is bounded by rules designed to assure that the public interest in fairness is furthered. (412 US 94, at 111, 1973)

But the question refuses to subside. Controversies persist between potential advertisers and broadcasters. In several cases, ads turned down for television have appeared in print or on cable television, with pointed comment about the refusal of broadcasters to allow the airing of paid points of view. The networks and their owned-and-operated stations remain, as a matter of policy, the principal holdouts against selling time for issue advertising. A 1980 Television Advertising Bureau survey indicated that about 90 percent of all other television stations were willing to at least consider accepting such advertising on a case-by-case basis.*

Future of the Fairness Doctrine   By the 1980s, several trends supported diluting or abolishing the fairness doctrine. Late in 1985 the FCC itself came out against the doctrine, although it concluded that it could not unilaterally abolish it because of the reference to it in the communications act.

For years, critics of the doctrine (not all of them licensees) have pointed out developments that weakened the doctrine's aims and impact. In the first place, the many new delivery services have lessened the uniqueness of broadcast stations, providing more channels

---

*Late in 1984, for the first time since Mark Fowler became chairman, the FCC found a station guilty of a fairness doctrine violation. The station had carried a series of ads supporting construction of a nuclear power plant, and the FCC ruled that the station had "failed to afford a reasonable opportunity for the presentation of viewpoints contrasting to those presented in the advertisements" (NAB, 1985: 16).

of information; no longer does the spectrum scarcity argument or bottleneck factor (§16.1) carry as much weight. Also, journalists have long complained that the doctrine has a chilling effect on investigative reporting and public-affairs programs in general, because of the constant need to consider that those with opposing views may demand time to reply. But former NBC newsman Ford Rowan summed up existing research when he noted that hard statistical evidence about the alleged chilling effect of the fairness doctrine is inconclusive, partially because the very revelation of specific cases might open up stations to fairness doctrine complaints (1984: 123).

In view of these criticisms, and after a lengthy investigation, a marketplace-oriented FCC in mid-1985 recommended scrapping the fairness doctrine altogether. The commission concluded:

On the basis of the voluminous record compiled in this proceeding, our experience in administering the doctrine and our general expertise in broadcast regulation, we no longer believe that the fairness doctrine, as a matter of policy, serves the public interest. . . . Furthermore, we find that the fairness doctrine, in operation, actually inhibits the presentation of controversial issues of public importance to the detriment of the public and in degradation of the editorial prerogatives of broadcast journalists. (102 FCC 2d 143, 1985)

The commission sent Congress its evidence that the scarcity rationale no longer justified the doctrine and urged Congress to consider amending the act to eliminate it. The commission also encouraged broadcasters to initiate a test case and then use the FCC's report as anti-fairness doctrine ammunition in a court appeal.

Nonetheless, elimination by Congress seemed unlikely. For as former FCC chairman Newton Minow put it when the FCC released its condemnation of the doctrine:

Scarcity still exists when channels are not available to all. And as long as scarcity exists, the need for some measure of regulation will exist. Most Americans get most of their news and information from radio and television. . . . The Fairness Doctrine stops no one from speaking; it simply encourages that all sides be heard. How can this policy harm the public? (Minow, 1985: A23)

On the other hand, a number of critics argue that the fairness doctrine is actually a defensive shield for timid broadcasters who don't want to deal with controversy, and thus run the risk of alienating audience and advertisers. According to these critics, the claim that the doctrine has a chilling effect on coverage of controversy conveniently shifts any onus from station or network decision-makers to the government.

18.5 Fairness and News

Perhaps nowhere is the fairness doctrine or even a general sense of being fair more controversial than when applied to electronic media news and documentary programs. News clearly deals with controversial topics. Yet if every reference to a controversial issue in the day's news opened the electronic media to imminent threat of fairness doctrine complaints, the media might soft-pedal or avoid stories touching on such issues. Therefore, bona fide news programs, while formally subject to fairness doctrine requirements, have to a considerable degree enjoyed FCC and court support in fairness doctrine cases. Government officials generally defer to journalists' editorial discretion. The practical result is that regular news programs are "protected" from constant litigation in a fashion somewhat parallel to their formal legal exemption from political broadcast equal-time rules (§18.6).

The FCC's rules requiring licensees to allow on-the-air responses to broadcasts of personal attacks could also cause electronic media journalists difficulties when airing news that shows individuals in an unfavorable light. Again the FCC comes to the rescue, exempting bona fide news stories from the personal attack rules. Specifically exempted from the right of reply are on-the-air attacks made against foreigners, those made by political candidates and their spokespersons during campaigns, and those occurring in news interviews, on-the-spot news coverage, and news commentaries (47 CFR 73.1920).

Role of Editorial Discretion   In fairness cases, FCC officials and the courts generally assume that reporters and editors use *editorial discretion*, which calls for fair and considered news treatment of events, people, and controversies. No one believes that journalists always use the best judgment, or that they are without bias or prejudice. The First Amendment holds, however, that it is better to tolerate journalists' mistakes and even incompetencies than to set up some government agency as an arbiter of truth.

The Supreme Court has reaffirmed this reliance on journalistic judgment. In confirming the FCC's decision rejecting a fairness complaint, the court remarked:

For better or for worse, editing is what editors are for; and editing is selection and choice of material. That editors — newspaper or broadcast — can and do abuse this power is beyond doubt, but that is not reason to deny the discretion Congress provided. Calculated risks of abuse are taken in order to preserve higher values. (412 US 94, at 124, 1973)

Reliance on journalistic discretion, however, does not mean that the FCC should ignore *deliberate* slanting, distortion, or withholding of news, although the commission normally leans over backward to avoid conflict with the First Amendment by giving journalists the benefit of the doubt. As the commission put it in a detailed 1974 statement on the role of the fairness doctrine, "We do not believe that it would be either useful or appropriate for us to investigate charges of news misrepresentations in the absence of extrinsic evidence or documents that on their face reflect deliberate distortion" (48 FCC 2d 21). Such evidence is difficult to come by, and therefore few authentic instances of calculated misuse of broadcast news have come to light.*

News Bias   Critics sometimes accuse the electronic media, and especially television network news departments, of a more pervasive kind of journalistic unfairness, overall *news bias.* Typically such charges come from political conservatives, who tend to believe that the news media and their personnel are generally too liberal in outlook. They argue not so much that specific news stories are false but that the cumulative effect over time tends to build up one-sided perceptions of issues.

In response to a 1972 complaint by the American Security Council Educational Foundation (ASCEF) that CBS was "soft" on national security coverage and should thus offer time for opposing viewpoints, the FCC noted that the conservative foundation bringing the complaint had failed to single out a specific controversial issue as required by fairness doctrine procedures. On appeal, a court of appeals agreed, saying that to grant the complaint

would create a precedent that might well have a serious effect on daily news programming, by inducing broadcasters to forego programming on controversial issues or by disrupting the normal exercise of journalistic judgment in such programming that is aired. . . . In attempting to comply with the fairness doctrine as interpreted by ASCEF, an editor's news judgment would be severely altered. An editor preparing an evening newscast would be required to decide whether any of the day's newsworthy events is tied, even tangentially, to events covered in the past, and whether a report on today's lead story, in some remote way, balances yesterday's, last week's or last year's. (607 F 2d 438, at 451, 1979)

Research studies, usually some variety of program content analysis, have appeared supporting both sides of the bias question — and thus the debate continues.

Partially because it has often scheduled more hard-hitting documentary programs than other networks, CBS has been the target of such complaints from the political right more often than ABC, NBC, or Ted Turner's Cable News Network. In the mid-1980s, critics took a new tack when conservative minister Jerry Falwell and others advised their followers to buy CBS stock, so as to become news anchor Dan Rather's "boss." In 1985, conservatively oriented media maverick Ted Turner attempted, unsuccessfully, to take over CBS (§10.5).

Documentaries   Carrying investigative documentaries is a highly effective means of meeting the public-interest requirements for broadcasting and cable, and building a prestigious news image (§12.7). But programs that take a point of view on news events almost inevitably provoke controversy. Because they also draw small audiences, it is usually hard to find advertisers willing to help cover their costs. Thus, the overall number of network documentaries declined in the 1980s.

---

*In one of the rare cases of prosecution for news manipulation, the FCC deleted five radio stations owned by Star Stations of Indiana, partly because the licensee had ordered news personnel to give favored treatment to political candidates he preferred (§17.8 and 51 FCC 2d 95, 1975).

In preparing documentaries, producers often resort to techniques that could be regarded as the staging or rigging of news events. They have been charged with helping to stage the invasion of a foreign country (planned, but not carried out), mislabeling pictures offered as evidence, organizing a pot-smoking party at a university for a program about the topic, and using interview replies out of context and thus giving a misleading impression. Such charges triggered both FCC and congressional investigations on several occasions in the 1970s, but they uncovered no evidence of deliberate dishonesty on the part of broadcast management. Individual employees, however, were sometimes guilty of indiscretion and bad judgment, if not of outright deception.

One case of alleged misrepresentation in a news documentary caused a dramatic confrontation between a network president and Congress. In 1971, CBS aired "The Selling of the Pentagon," a documentary criticizing the huge sums spent for propaganda directed at American citizens to drum up support for higher military budgets. Critics attacked details of editing that suggested biased interpretations. For example, postprogram research by others showed that replies of military spokespersons in recorded interviews were sometimes taken out of context, giving a false impression of what was actually said.

The defense lobby created such a furor that a House committee held hearings and subpoenaed material CBS had edited out of the program. Appearing as a witness, Frank Stanton, the president of CBS at the time, declined to turn over the film outtakes. To do so, he said, would have an unconstitutional chilling effect on the freedom of journalists to produce news programs. He testified that "the First Amendment would bar this subpena [sic] if directed at the editing of a newspaper report, a book, or a magazine article" (House CIFC, 1971: 73).

Angered at Stanton's defiance, the committee recommended that the full House find him in contempt of Congress. The House failed to act, however, averting a showdown between the federal government and electronic media journalists. When asked by the committee what it planned to do, the FCC replied that it regretted any misrepresentations that might occur, in news programs, but steadfastly maintained its position that newscasters, not the FCC, should use editorial judgment. The FCC should not, it said, "dictate the particular response to thousands of journalistic circumstances" (30 FCC 2d 150, at 153, 1971).

Two years later, the commission seemed to reverse course over objections to an NBC documentary on the failures of private industrial pension plans. A conservative media-watchdog organization complained to the FCC that NBC had shown only one side of the issue. Congress was then considering legislation to tighten pension laws, so this time the FCC felt impelled to substitute its judgment for that of journalists. It ordered NBC to advise how it proposed to make time available for a pro-industry reply. Although it would have been expedient for the network to give a few minutes to an industry spokesperson, NBC felt a principle was at stake and took the commission to court. NBC was vindicated when the appeals court agreed that the FCC had been inconsistent in applying its own fairness doctrine principles:

The Commission's error of law is that it failed adequately to apply the message of applicable decisions that the editorial judgments of the licensee must not be disturbed if reasonable and in good faith. The licensee . . . has wide discretion and latitude that must be respected even though, under the same facts, the [FCC] would reach a contrary conclusion. (516 F 2d 1101, at 1118, 1974)

The editorial discretion of electronic media journalists was thus upheld, and the chance of fairness doctrine harassment lessened. But the court of appeals had based its decision on faulty FCC procedures, not First Amendment grounds.

18.6 Political Broadcasts

The most substantial explicit program requirement of the communications act is the well-known equal-time provision for political candidates. A cynic might conclude that the politicians who originally wrote the statute only too naturally took their own welfare as their first concern. The fact is, however, that incumbent members of Congress were sufficiently public-spirited to ensure that their well-funded rivals would have equal opportunities to oppose them on the radio in the next election.

"Equal Opportunities" for Candidates
Congress correctly foresaw in 1927 that broadcasting would one day exert a major influence on voters. If the party in power could monopolize broadcasting (as of course it now does under authoritarian regimes elsewhere in the world), candidates of opposing parties would stand little if any chance of winning elections. In order to equalize the political benefits of broadcasting as nearly as it could, Congress adopted the equal-time provision (which actually refers to "equal opportunities"), now Section 315 of the act:

If any licensee shall permit any person who is a legally qualified candidate for any public office to use a broadcasting station, he shall afford equal opportunities to all other such candidates for that office in the use of such broadcasting station: Provided, That such licensee shall have no power of censorship over the material broadcast under the provisions of this section. No obligation is imposed under this subsection upon any li-censee to allow the use of its station by any such candidate.

Originally, the "no obligation" clause in the last sentence at least gave licensees a chance to avoid being subjected to demands for equal time. This option was summarily removed as far as candidates for federal offices were concerned by a series of amendments adopted to bring the communications act in line with the Federal Election Campaign·Act of 1971. One of the 1971 amendments mandated letting federal candidates have time, by adding to Section 312 a new basis for license revocation:

willful or repeated failure to allow reasonable access to or to permit purchase of reasonable amounts of time for the use of a broadcasting station by a legally qualified candidate for Federal elective office on behalf of his candidacy.

Other changes mandated by the Federal Election Campaign Act of 1971 were incorporated in a new subsection of Section 315 itself, limiting stations to their "lowest unit charge" for candidates (federal and nonfederal) in the weeks just before elections.

Candidates in the News   Section 315's
original equal-time mandate had the potential for interfering with news coverage of candidates. This problem lay dormant for over thirty years because, according to the prevailing FCC interpretation, Section 315 left licensees free to make their customary judgments as to newsworthiness, to distinguish between self-promotion and bona fide news in covering candidates' activities.*

---

*That newsworthiness is an acceptable guide in distinguishing self-promotion from news is well recognized. For example, an appeals court pointed out that in situations in which to publish routine information about a lottery would be illegal, it would nevertheless be legal to treat the reactions of a big winner in a lottery as a news story (414 F 2d 990. 1969).

In 1959, however, the FCC surprisingly reversed its interpretation, ruling in the *Lar Daly* case that even a bona fide news-related broadcast involving a candidate was a political "use" of broadcasting that triggered equal-time obligations (26 FCC 715, 1959).

This unexpected ruling came in response to a petition from a colorful eccentric named Lar Daly. He qualified technically as a legal candidate for the office of mayor of Chicago, opposing the incumbent mayor, the famed political boss Richard Daley, who was running for reelection. Every time Mayor Daley was personally involved in a broadcast news story about the mayor's office, Lar Daly claimed equal opportunities under Section 315.

The irony of the FCC ruling was that Lar Daly, though legally qualified, was never a serious contender. Campaigning in a red, white, and blue Uncle Sam costume, he was a perpetual candidate who ran with absolutely no success for president, governor, senator, and lesser offices.

Lar Daly had, of course, a perfect right to run for office, no matter how eccentric his causes or how hopeless his case. Indeed, Section 315 is predicated on the very principle that all candidates are entitled to equal opportunities, regardless of party or platform. But the ruling in Daly's favor meant, in practical terms, a blackout of in-person news broadcast involving Chicago's mayor. Broadcasters were not prepared to give Lar Daly equal time to advance his doomed candidacy every time they covered the mayor opening a new children's playground.

This was indeed a strange subversion of congressional intent. While ensuring equal treatment of all candidates, Section 315 unintentionally also denied the public the right to receive political news of possible consequence. At the same time it prevented licensees from using their right to make responsible judgments as to what qualifies as news. This affront to First Amendment principles caused a furor, galvanizing Congress into action with unaccustomed speed.

Though he failed to win political office, Daly won a small niche in broadcasting history as the gadfly who drove Congress to amend Section 315 of the communications act. The amendment adopted in 1959 added to the opening of Section 315 the following four exemptions:

Appearance by a legally qualified candidate on any —
(1) bona fide newscast,
(2) bona fide news interview,
(3) bona fide news documentary (if the appearance of the candidate is incidental to the presentation of the subject or subjects covered by the news documentary), or
(4) on-the-spot coverage of bona fide news events (including but not limited to political conventions and activities incidental thereto),
shall not be deemed to be use of a broadcasting station within the meaning of this subsection.

The amendment liberated political news coverage from equal-time harassments by future Lar Dalys, but it also left many knotty problems of interpretation to the FCC and the courts.

Political Rules in Practice   Some of these problems of interpretation arise from confusion between the two kinds of access to station time: access protected by the fairness doctrine, and access covered by the equal-time rules governing political candidates. As shown in Exhibit 18.3, the fairness doctrine allows for access for ideas and offers only reasonable opportunities to opposing points of view. The political rules, on the other hand, based on Sections 315 and 312 of the communications act, concern specific categories of persons (candidates) and require equal opportunities for persons in the same categories (candidates for the same office). People speaking on behalf

Exhibit 18.3   Fairness Doctrine and Equal Time Law Compared

Basis of comparison	Fairness doctrine	Equal time law
Legal status based on:	FCC policy Clause in Section 315 Rules for personal attack and political editorials	Section 315, supplemented by Section 312 of communications act
Access for:	Controversial *issues* of public importance	Political *candidates* in person
When invoked?	Any time	During political campaigns only
Right of access initiated by:	Introduction of an issue	"Use" by another candidate for same office (but Section 312 does require access for federal candidates)
Speakers chosen by:	Licensee	Candidate — all other candidates automatically eligible
Amount of access time required:	*"Reasonable* opportunity" to reply	Equal opportunity
Permissible time charges, if any:	None if speaker unable to pay (exception: spokespersons for political candidates)	"Lowest unit charge" (but depends on stage of campaign)
Types of programs affected:	All (see text for discussion of news)	Any except four types of bona fide news programs listed in Section 315
Format chosen by:	Licensee	Candidate
Licensee editing allowed?	Yes	No (if appearance is based on Section 315 obligation)
Special features:	Notification by licensee within specified times in case of personal attacks and political editorials	Candidates must be legally qualified and request time within a week of "use" by rival candidate

It is called the fairness doctrine because most of it takes the form of policy rather than explicit rules. Equal opportunities, on the other hand, are mandated as a matter of law in the communications act.

of candidates cannot make Section 315 claims; only candidates themselves can.

Here are a few examples of the kinds of questions that have arisen in the application of these rules and that have caused the FCC to change its mind:

• *Which candidates are covered?* The equal-time rules apply both to candidates for party nomination in a primary election and to nomi-nees in a general election. Equal opportunities can be claimed only by candidates for each specific office. For example, if the candidate for Congress in a specific district purchases time, all candidates in the same district for the same post are entitled to purchase equivalent time, but candidates for other districts or other offices are not.

• *Are presidential news conferences bona fide news programs?* Although the FCC originally felt the answer to this question was no, in recent years it has held that when such news conferences are covered as bona fide news events, they are exempt from claims under Section 312 or 315.

• *Are presidential candidate debates news?* Here again, the rules have changed. Until 1975, political debates did not count as bona fide exceptions to Section 315. After 1975, the FCC held that presidential debates qualified as bona fide news events as long as third parties with no personal interest in the outcome controlled the event. Thus in 1976 and 1980 the League of Women Voters, a nonpartisan group, sponsored the debates. In 1983, however, the FCC ruled (and an appeals court upheld) that the electronic media could sponsor, as well as cover, such debates. The television networks themselves presented the two 1984 campaign debates between President Ronald Reagan and former vice president Walter Mondale, as well as the vice-presidential debate between George Bush and Geraldine Ferraro.

• *Are interview and talk programs exempt from equal-time requests?* Talk and interview programs are now exempt, after still another FCC reversal of opinion. Whereas in 1980 the FCC held *Donahue* not to be a bona fide news interview program, the commission in 1984 changed its mind on the grounds that the program had been long-running, was carefully controlled, and could in no way be "stacked" in favor of a given candidate. On the basis of that ruling, the FCC gave similar exemption to Larry King's evening radio talk show on the Mutual network. Magazine programs such as NBC's *Today* and ABC's *Good Morning America*, and traditional news interview programs such as *Meet the Press*, have long qualified for exemption.

• *How much time provides "reasonable access?"* Some stations tried to limit candidates to one- or five-minute political spots because of formats that didn't lend themselves to extended

political speeches. But the FCC held that this violated the reasonable access provisions of Section 312.

• *May live news appearances be recorded for later playback and still be exempt?* For some time, the FCC held that a broadcast held within 24 hours of a news event would be considered on-the-spot coverage, and thus exempt. In 1983 this limit was lifted, and interpretation is now a matter of licensee judgment: any "reasonably recent event" recorded and presented to inform and not to favor a given candidate is exempt, no matter how delayed in presentation.

• *What constitutes a station's "lowest unit charge?"* This phrase in Section 315 defines the maximum rates licensees may charge candidates (federal, state, or local) who buy time for political purposes shortly before elections (45 days in the case of a primary, sixty days for a general election). Whereas a commercial advertiser might have to buy several hundred spots to qualify for the maximum quantity discount (§9.5), a political candidate benefits from the maximum discount even when buying only a single spot announcement. When one station proposed charging a candidate for a five-minute program more than five times its rate for a one-minute spot, on the grounds that program rates differ from spot rates, the FCC ruled that the lowest-unit-charge provision would allow a rate no more than five times the one-minute spot.

• *How does the FCC deal with PACs?* In the past few years, the monetary role of PACs (political action committees) in campaigns has become more important. FCC concern arises when PACs purchase time in favor of a given candidate without acting directly on behalf of the candidate. PACs are by nature independent of given campaigns: they are interested in political issues rather than specific candidates and support anyone backing their views. Do they still fall under Sections 315 and 312? The FCC, citing its *Zapple* decision, holds that they do, but only during campaign periods.* Thus, if a PAC for a particular candidate buys time during a campaign, the candidate's opponent may demand equal time, but must, of course, pay equally for it. In other than campaign periods, the FCC holds that PACs may request time for reply to opposing points of view only under the fairness doctrine.

• *May a candidate demand whatever time he or she wants?* Candidates do not have the privilege of decreeing when their ads will run. Though the FCC has held that banning all political advertising in prime time is a violation of Section 312's requirement of "reasonable access," keeping political spots out of a particular program is within licensee discretion. A licensee may also select the nonfederal races it will sell time for.

• *May a candidate use obscene material?* Even though Section 315 forbids censorship of a candidate's speech, this rule does not oblige a station to broadcast obscenity. When in 1984 *Hustler* publisher Larry Flynt threatened to use arguably obscene material in a possible campaign for the presidency, licensees were alarmed and asked the FCC for policy guidance. The commission held that the U.S. Criminal Code ban on obscenity (§18.2) overrode the "no censorship" provision of Section 315.

• *May electronic media endorse political candidates in editorials?* Electronic media may endorse candidates, but if they do, they must notify opposing candidates and offer reply time (this rule was under consideration for change by the FCC in 1985).

• *Are cable systems held to the same regulations of political broadcasting as broadcasting stations?* Regulations apply only for channels on which the cable operator originates programming. Cable systems are not responsible for political program decisions made by stations or services they carry but do not originate.

• *May a licensee ignore political broadcasting problems by banning any political advertising?* Section 312(a)(7) of the communications act requires broadcasters to provide "reasonable access" for candidates for federal office (House, Senate, president, vice president). Any licensee not allowing access by such candidates risks its license.

18.7 Issues in Content Regulation

Can the marketplace concept for controlling the electronic media work in place of the many past regulations? Should regulation of the content of electronic media differ from that of other media? Is the fairness doctrine a workable solution to the problem of access to broadcasting? These are enduring issues for the electronic media.

Relevance of Marketplace Concept
Newspaper publishers of the eighteenth century entered the marketplace of ideas as small traders, competing on relatively equal terms. A *self-righting* process was expected to occur. Given time and diverse input of printed ideas, people were expected to be able to explore many options and to draw their own conclusions.

Now, however, entry into the mass marketplace of ideas is prohibitively expensive, as made clear by the wave of media mergers occuring in the mid-1980s (§10.5). Giant media conglomerates now distribute ideas instantaneously throughout the world. A few national media can saturate the entire country with an

---

*In 1970, in response to a query from Nicholas Zapple, a senior staff member of the Senate communications subcommittee, the FCC held that if broadcasters gave or sold time to *supporters* of a candidate during a campaign, the fairness doctrine required them to treat supporters of opposing candidates equally — give them the same amount of time, the same rate, and so forth. Such instances are referred to as "quasi-equal opportunities" (23 FCC 2d 707, 1970).

idea overnight, which calls into doubt whether the self-righting process has enough time to take effect.

One response to this trend of consolidation is enforced ownership diversification, discussed in §17.7. However, research has thus far failed to demonstrate conclusively that diversification of broadcast station ownership actually produces the predicted beneficial results. In fact, marginal stations or systems are less likely to behave responsibly than are large, group-owned stations or systems. The manager of a failing enterprise, worried about meeting next week's payroll, may look less critically at questionable programming practices that managers in sounder financial condition would refuse to consider. Integrity is a luxury that marginal operations often cannot afford.

Thus, diversification of media ownership as a means of promoting First Amendment values remains somewhat hypothetical. Nevertheless, most First Amendment theorists remain convinced that freedom of ideas is best promoted in the long run if the maximum number of voices can get a hearing in the marketplace of ideas.

Access as a Right   Another response to the contemporary distortions of the marketplace is to assert *right of access* as a new First Amendment right. As we indicated in §1.6, the notion of access as a fundamental human right is part of recent worldwide communication theory. In the United States, however, the FCC and courts seem to be moving away from acknowledging a formal right of access, as demonstrated by the commission's attempts to have the fairness doctrine repealed, and the series of court cases in the 1960s and 1970s that denied a right of access to media. On the other hand, Congress's 1984 cable legislation calls for public and leased access channels to be made available (§17.6). Arguments that favor retention of the fairness doctrine often refer to the need to provide a means of public access to electronic media.

Is the Fairness Doctrine Fair?   The FCC's fairness doctrine, as supported by legislation and court tests (§18.4), attempts to solve the dilemma of too many potential demands for personal access by shifting the emphasis from persons to issues. Most electronic media owners oppose the doctrine, claiming that it has a chilling effect, causes a lack of parity with print journalism competitors, who face no such requirements, and is not needed now that there are a rising number of new delivery systems. As Exhibit 18.3 suggests, the doctrine is also open to political exploitation.

Yet even in the 1980s, with far more broadcast and newer media services available to many Americans than was the case when the doctrine was developed (1949), endorsed by Congress (1959), and upheld by the Supreme Court (1969), critics argue forcefully for its retention. Noting the trend toward conglomerate media ownership, as well as the reliance of most Americans on television for their news and public-affairs information, these critics feel that the fairness doctrine, limited though it is, helps provide a means of access for opposing ideas.

Parity Across Services   As we have mentioned, the unique characteristics of broadcasting — such as its intrusion into the home, its accessibility to children and continuous availability, its use of a scarce public resource, and its dependence on consumer investment in receivers — have long set it apart from print media. Again and again, one or more of these characteristics have been cited by the FCC and the courts as justification for treating broadcasting differently from print media in regard to First Amendment restraints on government regulation.

First Amendment absolutists, however, reject the concept of one law for broadcasting and another for press or motion pictures. They argue for First Amendment *parity*, equal treatment of all media. They interpret the words "Congress shall make no law" literally, rejecting any infringement on freedom of expression.

The issue has gained more urgency with the development of cable and other new services. Broadcasting is far more tightly controlled than any of these similar services, which creates a paradoxical lack of parity even within the electronic media. As a result of economic research, new technical options, and changing political ideology, the FCC and Congress have taken a generally *nonregulatory* approach to the new services while pursuing a *deregulatory* trend in broadcasting. As discussed further in §19.5, however, it appears that regulation will continue to be more stringent for radio and television than for other media in the near future.

If a future Supreme Court were to endorse First Amendment parity across all media, the decision would have considerable impact on programming in the electronic media services. Despite complaints by moral watchdogs about indecency, broadcasters still follow much more restrained standards than other media. Magazines, motion pictures, and pay cable use material that would still never be considered for broadcast. First Amendment parity that would put broadcasting on a par with *Hustler* magazine continues to seem a long way off.

Summary

• Regulation can be seen as both limiting the First Amendment rights of electronic media owners and furthering First Amendment goals for viewers and listeners. The constitutional guarantee of free expression is embodied in the metaphor of a marketplace in which ideas compete for acceptance. The First Amendment protects even inflammatory, hateful, and false ideas from government interference, but does not prevent private censorship unless it is carried out on behalf of the government.

• Unprotected forms of speech such as libel, invasion of privacy, and obscenity are punishable after the fact, but punishment must not be so easily imposed as to have a chilling effect on the freedom of speech in general.

• Former restrictions on cameras in courtrooms are giving way in the face of less intrusive technology, but electronic media are still not allowed in federal courts.

• For decades the regulation of broadcast content was heavily influenced by an FCC policy of emphasizing service to local community needs. Stations and cable systems are licensed to local communities, but their programming is mostly national in origin.

• The fairness doctrine had its roots in earlier decisions but was formalized in a 1949 decision allowing broadcast editorializing. It was codified by legislation in 1959 and upheld by the *Red Lion* Supreme Court decision of 1969. In 1985 the FCC urged Congress and the courts to rescind the doctrine, claiming it was no longer needed.

• The fairness doctrine has two requirements: electronic media journalists should cover controversial issues of local importance; and when they do, they should provide opportunities for differing points of view to be heard.

• Only one commercial product — cigarettes — has ever been subject to provisions of the fairness doctrine. (This occurred before cigarette ads were banned from radio and television in 1972.)

• Few stations or systems will accept payment for "advertorials," or issue advertising.

When they do, however, the fairness doctrine comes into play only if commercials deal explicitly with controversial issues of public importance.

• When deciding questions of fairness in news and public-affairs programs, the FCC and the courts give heavy emphasis to broadcast journalists' editorial discretion.

• Section 315 of the communications act provides for equal opportunities in use of broadcast and cable facilities for opposing candidates for the same office. Bona fide news and public-affairs programs are exempted from equal-time provisions. These laws continue to give the FCC many difficult problems of interpretation.

• Attempts to diversify station ownership in order to diversify programming appear to have had limited impact. On the other hand, the general public has failed to achieve a guaranteed right of access to privately owned media facilities.

• First Amendment absolutists call for regulatory parity, arguing against treating electronic media differently from print, or one electronic medium differently from another.

EPILOGUE

Future of
Electronic Media

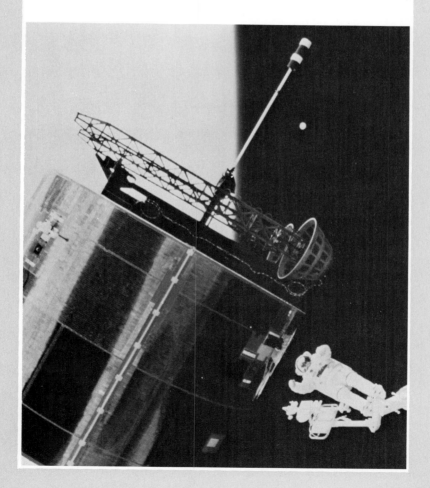

CHAPTER 19

Future Prospects

In this concluding chapter we look at what is likely to occur in the electronic media in the coming five to ten years. Only the most audacious futurists venture to guess what may occur in the longer term. In the following sections, frankly speculative in nature, we play devil's advocate, adopting a skeptical view to counteract what we suspect are unrealistic promises — some the outcome of legitimate research but many the product of mere opportunism.

19.1 Views of the Future

Radical View The new technologies inspire enthusiasts for radical change to predict the end of traditional broadcasting in the near future. They foresee the established networks and stations shrivelling away. In their zeal for the new, these enthusiasts predict varied combinations of computer, satellite, and fiber-optic providers that will store and deliver unlimited varieties of information, entertainment, and other services. According to this point of view, instead of passively viewing conventional receivers, subscribers will actively use home and office communication centers equipped with two-way channels for sending as well as receiving.

Much more than conventional information, entertainment, and education will be provided. Subscribers will use their home centers to plug into services not previously associated with broadcasting, services such as shopping, banking, mail delivery, utility meter reading, and security surveillance. If broadcasting in its traditional form survives at all, we are told, it will be merely one rather minor service among a wide range of options.

True believers among social planners and research-and-development innovators envision the day when communications technology now on the market or projected for the near future will coalesce into a single, multipurpose home communications center. In contrast to the earlier trend toward miniaturized, personalized, and highly portable units, the home center would be an elaborate and permanent installation. An entire room would be dedicated to reception, recording, storage, playback, and initiation of communication. The video screen, glowing like a queen bee in the center of an electronic hive, would be fed by an army of working inputs: disc and tape recorders and players, cable and over-the-air

535

program suppliers, videotex reception capable of making hard-copy print-outs, direct-broadcast satellite relays picked up by rooftop antennas, two-way communication circuits, and so on.

Conservative View

Undeniably, the technical resources do exist to make all the wonders predicted above come true. Less certain is the economic support, including the institutional framework, sufficient mass-consumer participation and expenditure, and creative reserves for filling all the prospective new communication channels. Although changes in traditional broadcasting patterns have occurred and will continue to occur, we suspect that they will neither come as fast nor go so far as the enthusiasts for the new technologies have been predicting.

True, radio in the 1920s and modern television in the late 1940s swept the country and the world. With unprecedented speed they became household necessities, more prized (and more widely owned) than refrigerators or indoor plumbing. The newer technologies promise no such fundamentally different service, only variations on and combinations of existing themes. Thus far, their success has been in terms of novel methods of delivery, with little difference in the content delivered.

The need to reach and retain enough viewers to support the newer services leads directly to popular broadcast-type programming. Advertisers "buy" the large audiences reached by popular station and network programs, just as people buy (subscribe to) popular cable channels and other services. In each case, *popular* describes programming of broad appeal rather than for specialized groups.

The unanswered question is whether the mass of consumers, as distinguished from the minority eager to keep abreast of any new trend, will come to regard these improved delivery methods and their content as necessities

regardless of cost. And in calculating those costs, one must remember that newer technologies rely on consumers to make the initial investment and pay the ongoing expense of operating television receivers. The costs of basic and pay cable, videocassette machines, and the rest are piled on top of that minimum consumer investment.

It seems increasingly evident that consumers are not always willing to make the investment needed for new services. Several innovations have failed to achieve sufficient public support to survive. For example, videodiscs faded as a consumer product in the face of price drops for the more versatile videocassette reorders. Single-channel pay systems could not retain viewers when multichannel options were offered at close to the same monthly price. Audiences reacted with a yawn to quadraphonic, or four-channel sound, FM broadcasting and recordings, since the product was not sufficiently different from two-channel stereo. Direct-broadcast satellite, first announced with great fanfare in 1979, had disappeared from the United States communications scene six years later; the huge investment needed to design and launch a satellite, the lack of any unique programming to be offered, and the rapid growth of cable and home video systems made the exotic DBS delivery system redundant. Home computers, the rage of the 1977–1984 period, still had not reached 15 percent of all U.S. homes by 1986. Growth in computer sales for home use all but stopped. A dramatic shakeup among hardware and software firms caused massive layoffs in the fabled Silicon Valley.

Even for the new-technology winners — especially pay cable and to a lesser degree videocassette recorders — growth had slowed down by the late 1980s. Indeed, these media seemed to feed more on each other than on broadcast television. As the percentage of homes equipped with videocassettes surged past 30 percent, the pay cable networks HBO and Showtime appeared to level out in number of subscribers, and continue to grow only at a very slow pace. Viewers opted for home video on videocassettes, with its greater freedom of timing and content choice, just as they had opted for the benefits of pay cable over older broadcast television. Despite the increasing convenience, however, home video offered limited change in, or increased variety of, content.

Overall, broadcasters experienced much potential competition but remarkably little outright displacement of their central role. Not only were broadcast company investments in the newer technologies on the increase, but the audiences for traditional radio and television were also growing. After all, once consumers own receivers, broadcast radio and television exact no further direct payments — which is not the case with most of the newer delivery systems.

19.2 The Technological Future

The most remarkable physical fact about broadcasting has always been its wirelessness. The unique ability of radio to reach any receiver was once highly prized as an invaluable achievement. Now, ironically, many dismiss wirelessness as being old-fashioned, preferring instead improved forms of the major nineteenth-century mode, wire communication.

Cable and Optical Fiber   Undeniably, the cable and optical fiber methods of delivery offer great advantages: an enclosed, interference-free environment not constrained by spectrum crowding, far more channels per community than is possible with over-the-air service, and the potential for two-way communication, among other things. But these advantages exact the penalty of added expense.

Stringing cables on poles or burying cable or fiber underground is very costly. A separate physical link has to be installed at every individual delivery point. Cable and optical fiber tie users to fixed locations.

Transoceanic fiber-optic links should be in service by the late 1980s, providing the first cost-effective threat to satellites. If at least some point-to-point spectrum-using services are transferred to fiber in the 1990s, spectrum crowding may be eased, allowing the development of applications that require use of the spectrum.

On the other hand, wireless can reach unlimited numbers of listeners within a transmitter's service area at no additional cost, and receivers can be moved with ease. These features, combined with the continuing widespread appeal of radio and television programs suggest that the popularity of broadcasting is unlikely to change substantially even by the turn of the century.

Direct Satellite Reception   Millions of backyard TVRO antennas were installed in the 1980s, with thousands more added every month. TVRO-equipped homes can directly tune in satellite services, intercepting programs intended for delivery by broadcast stations or cable systems. However, as the scrambling of satellite signals (to protect carrier and programmer investments from unauthorized viewers) increases in the late 1980s, the growth in use of private home TVROs is slowing down.*

Improved Broadcast Transmission
High-definition and stereo television afford far

---

*Virtually all cable systems and most broadcast stations also now use TVROs, though usually of a larger and more complicated nature than home antennas. Ironically, satellite services help to strengthen broadcast stations by making them less dependent on their networks, as we will see in §19.4.

more satisfaction than present-day service, but it will be difficult to make them commercially viable. FCC approval of stereo transmission in 1984 did stimulate new interest in the sound of home television in general. But in the absence of a low-cost means of band compression, broadcast HDTV will not be feasible before the end of the century. Instead, HDTV will appear first in theaters, where its need for very wide channels and special receivers will not be a limiting factor, since the electromagnetic spectrum is not used in distribution.

19.3 The Future of Mass Appeal

The ability of broadcasting to reach a national audience simultaneously has long been considered praiseworthy. Ironically, some observers in recent years felt that this was a limitation, as the kind of national unity symbolized by the melting pot image receded in a rush to ethnic and regional diversity. Most recently, however, the pendulum may have swung back again; it is no longer fashionable to be culturally nonconformist in America. Traditional broadcasting, with its *massification* of people into undifferentiated national audiences, appears to be riding this new mood with considerable success. It favors cultural conformity rather than cultural pluralism. Its target is the majority, not the many separate minorities making up that majority.

Cable's Promise   Cable television was acclaimed as a wonderful corrective to this massification tendency. Its many channels have the potential to segment the audience into specialized groups, each served by appropriately specialized programs. Optimistic observers predicted that systems that had channels to spare would give even the smallest, most untypical groups access to express themselves

and their ideas. In his book *The Third Wave*, futurist Alvin Toffler predicted the assumed demassification of media by alternative technologies, concluding: ''All these different developments have one thing in common: they slice the mass television public into segments, and each slice not only increases our cultural diversity, it cuts deeply into the power of the networks that have until now so completely dominated our imagery'' (1980: 180).

Cable's Reality   In theory, audience segmentation and corresponding specialization in programming on cable television should become economically viable, because satellites make it possible to aggregate many very small local cable audiences into a national audience that is large enough to justify the cost of specialized programming. There is no guarantee, however, that commercial ventures that succeed in this sort of enterprise will not eventually behave as other commercial ventures usually do — that is, will try and generate still more money out of a good thing. Cable program providers tempted to broaden the appeal of dedicated channels tend to return to the situation they were supposed to rescue us from, showing mass appeal programs aimed at the largest possible audiences. This trend is evident in multiple system operations, which combine scores of local cable systems under centralized control; in the massive appeal of the top pay syndicators such as HBO, which provide identical programs from coast to coast; and in the increasing intrusion of advertising into cable services, which encourages programs attracting the largest possible audience.

Thus, in reality, cable itself has adopted a kind of massification policy. Audience segmentation survives in only a few dedicated channels, continuous program services of specific interest to such large target groups as children, women, rock fans, weather watchers, and sports enthusiasts.* Several attempts to develop channels focused on arts and culture programming failed in the 1980s for lack of a sufficient audience willing to pay the price.

Viewers vs. Subscribers   Traditional broadcasting relies on the fact that once a home owner installs a receiving set, the appeal of the medium and the absence of use restraints (further payments) usually guarantee regular and frequent tuning in. Broadcast listenership and viewership therefore have proved to be relatively stable and predictable. A certain amount of audience flow does occur, pushing first one and then another program, network, or station into the lead; but the sets-in-use ratings vary primarily according to time of day and season. It seems likely that this pattern will continue for the forseeable future.

The growth of cable subscribership was so spectacular in the 1970s that its enthusiasts can be forgiven for thinking the entire nation would soon be cabled. But by 1986, cable subscribership had leveled off at about 50 percent of all American homes — a huge audience, but only half the universal penetration of broadcasting. Although more than 75 percent of American homes now have the opportunity to hook into passing cables, it appears that subscribership to basic cable may not exceed 60 percent by 1995. About half the basic cable

subscribers take at least one tier of pay service, but rising competition from videocassette recorders suggests that pay cable penetration may grow only slowly in the future.

Cable subscribership is much more volatile than broadcast viewership, because cable introduces new variables — the ability and the willingness of consumers to pay for the service. Subscribers are constantly dropping out, either voluntarily or involuntarily, because of failure to pay their monthly fees. At the same time, cable companies carry on vigorous recruiting campaigns to replace dropouts and, if possible, to increase the percentage of subscribing homes among the houses their cables pass. Thus a certain amount of the subscribership is always moving in and out of the cable audience, not merely flowing from one channel to another. The cable industry is secretive about the extent of this turnover, but it is believed to be considerable, especially in newly cabled areas where many subscribers try the service for novelty, only to find the expense greater than the reward. This pattern of constant change is also likely to continue.

Estimates of cable viewing levels must also take into account the fact that, at any one time, a cable system's audience is divided among its many channels. A cable system claiming three thousand subscribers, a typical size, might average about 150 viewers per channel for a twelve-channel system in prime time (it is unlikely, of course, that all channels would attract viewers equally).

Broadcast audiences are also divided among competing signals. But the average number of homes per station is still relatively large, for two reasons: (1) the potential audience, virtually all homes in range of a transmitter, is larger to start with, and (2) the number of competing over-the-air television stations is almost always less than the number of competing cable channels.

---

*Like cable, VCRs promised to be all things to all people, offering tapes for any and all subject interests. But as the software market moved from a sale to a rental base, the same desire to maximize return led VCR programmers to follow their broadcast and cable forebears into concentrating on tapes with the broadest possible audience appeal. With the exception of adult movies, all home videos have counterparts in broadcasting and cable. Massification is taking hold in even the most individually chosen of the electronic media.

Localism as Demassification By definition, localized programming counters massification. But cable operators have little incentive to produce effective local programs. The cable operator whose local offerings are dull and ineffectual can be secure in the knowledge that subscribers who tune them out will simply switch to another channel of the same cable system. But the broadcaster who drives audience members away sends them to competitors. Broadcasters therefore usually have a stronger sense of commitment to their local program efforts, especially in the area of news. Newer delivery services such as MMDS and SMATV, on the other hand, provide almost no news programming, local or otherwise, relying exclusively on entertainment.

19.4 The Economic Future

The rise of alternative delivery channels in the 1970s has increased the analysis and prediction of economic factors in electronic media. These concerns focus on ownership of media units and the role of advertising in the newer services.

Mergers Multimedia mergers characterized the 1980s, with firms expanding both horizontally (incorporating many units of the same type, such as stations) and vertically (integrating program production and distribution levels). The merger frenzy suggested that investors regard electronic mass media systems as interchangeable. Common ownership of different systems protects investment in programming used by all.

Reduction of government regulatory (including antitrust) restraints in favor of marketplace rule encourages mergers. Many people have questioned whether such concentration of media power in the hands of fewer large corporations is in the public interest. But the cost of developing media delivery systems and programming in the 1980s is so high that entrepreneurs often have a hard time surviving, if indeed they are able to raise the kind of capital needed to start up.

Future of TV Networks By the mid-1980s, the traditional audience share of commercial network television, 90 percent or more in prime time, had begun to shrink. Industry experts expected it to drop to about 80 percent by the end of the decade, for several reasons. For one thing, independent television stations had begun to attract larger audiences. Also, the sameness of programming shaped by the frantic network ratings wars was blamed for driving away some viewers. And of course the diversion created by both basic and pay cable was growing by the mid-1980s, as was the diversion from broadcasting by home VCRs.

Although attaining only an 80-percent share of the audience would hardly put the networks out of business, all three television networks expanded their operations into other electronic media, especially cable programming services, capitalizing on their programming expertise. For example, CBS cooperates with HBO to produce original motion pictures to be shown first on the pay service, and later on the broadcast network. This kind of venture will likely increase as competing firms look for commonality of interests.

The commercial networks, following the lead of public broadcasters, have switched from landlines to satellites for distributing their programming to affiliates. Now that most affiliate stations have their own TVRO antennas, however, they can more easily and cheaply pick up program feeds from suppliers other than their own networks. An affiliate may be tempted to skip low-rated network programs to carry more popular programs from other sources. With affiliates able to shop around for programs from a variety of sources, networks may have more trouble maintaining stable station line-ups for advertisers.

The effect of all this on public-service programming could be devastating. The mass audience is notoriously unreceptive to even the most significant and engrossing public-affairs programs that are not prepackaged for entertainment value. Will affiliates be willing to devote hours to the network's coverage of an important congressional hearing, for example, if they can easily substitute popular entertainment programming, more attractive to advertisers and audiences alike?

Role of Advertising   The question posed above is but one example of the continuing and pervasive pressure that the need to sell advertising exerts on the electronic media. One selling point for pay cable is its lack of advertising clutter. If the customer pays directly, interruptions for advertisements seem unfair. Nevertheless, the pressure on cable services to seek advertising rose in the late 1980s, and a number of advertising-free pay networks failed, only to be reconstituted as advertiser-supported services. It was even rumored that several of the pay networks were considering a combination approach: holding down increases in subscriber rates, but adding "tastefully inserted" advertising.* However, although many predicted in the early 1980s that cable would become a major advertising medium, at a time when it served 30 percent of the nation's homes, advertiser interest was barely evident even as cable

reached half the nation's television homes in 1986.

Cable competes with itself as well as with well-established television stations and networks. Not only is a cable system's subscribership divided among many channels but a number of those channels consist of broadcast programming already loaded with commercials that the cable operator is unable to delete. Furthermore, cable increasingly pursues the same mass audience that established television does, rather than the specialized audiences once thought to be its target. There is thus small danger that cable will cause a stampede of advertisers away from television similar to the kind that occurred in the early 1950s when television devastated radio.

Advertisers also expressed interest in another forum. Public television's chronic need for funds, combined with advertiser desire to reach that system's upscale audience, pushed hitherto noncommercial television toward increasing use of advertising support in the 1980s. Declining federal support will further that dependence on advertising.

19.5 The Regulatory Future

For years the FCC protected radio and television broadcasting from competitors, notably from over-the-air pay television in the 1950s and from cable in the early 1970s. But according to current Washington doctrine, each service must stand or fall on its own, with minimal government interference.

A Level Playing Field?   For the electronic media, the current deregulatory philosophy raises the specific question of whether like services should be regulated in like fashion. Broadcasting, as the oldest service, the one most dependent on substantial spectrum allocation and most readily available to the public,

---

*There is an interesting parallel in print media. In the mid-1950s, the *Reader's Digest*, which had never carried advertising, asked its readers to choose between accepting advertising or raising the cover price. Readers chose the ads, but the cover price continued to rise even as ad space continued to expand. Media firms in general experience pressure from investors to maximize financial returns, no matter what the cost in quality of service.

is still the most tightly regulated, despite considerable 1980s deregulation. Cable was first ignored, next limited, then pervasively regulated for a short period, and finally progressively deregulated after 1975. The newer services have been from the outset largely free of regulation. One of them, MMDS, is still regulated as a common carrier, and DBS, should it ever come to fruition, may be regulated as a common carrier/broadcasting hybrid.

Both history and strongly held beliefs on the part of the public favor continued imbalanced treatment of the media. Legislative or administrative tampering with broadcasting involves serious political risk. Most deregulation will be supported by the industry but fought by many consumer groups and media competitors. The notion that operation in the public interest relies on government oversight dies very slowly.

It is much easier not to regulate a new service than to deregulate an old one. As one network president put it, the new technologies with no history to give evidence of their ultimate appeal and impact are treated as "neutral and harmless" and therefore entitled to go unregulated; in the meantime, broadcasting is still governed by the FCC. For example, cable companies have no legal obligation to provide local programming, whereas broadcasting does; cable companies may combine into expanding multiple system operations, whereas broadcast companies are allowed to own relatively few stations; and cable companies nearly always enjoy monopolies in their franchise areas, whereas broadcast stations have to compete with other stations as well as with cable.

In the 1980s under Chairman Mark Fowler, the FCC, building on deregulation begun in the 1970s by Chairman Charles Ferris, is rapidly abandoning whole domains of formerly regulated territory. Congress reinforced the trend in 1984 with the strongly deregulatory cable additions to the communications act — the first legislative recognition of any of the new media. Those who speak of regulatory pendulum swings have a feeling that the pendulum will be stuck in an extreme no-regulation position for years to come.

Does Scarcity Exist?   There seems to be increasing agreement that the spectrum scarcity argument has less relevance. In debates over retention of the fairness doctrine in the mid-1980s, critics cited the fourfold increase in the number of radio stations alone since the doctrine was established. There is no more justification for a fairness doctrine in broadcasting, they say, than there is for one in print media. But proponents rejoin by noting that the multiple applicants for almost every broadcast channel for sale, and the ever-higher prices being paid for stations, suggest that scarcity still exists. The huge backlog of applications for low-power television stations early in the 1980s, most of them mutually exclusive, demonstrates the continuing need to make choices among applicants for the same channels.

In the next few years, the scarcity argument may be resolved into a question of free services versus subscriber services — in other words, of services that reach virtually all users who have purchased receivers and that use the electromagnetic spectrum (scarce) versus services that exact subscription fees and often do not use the spectrum (and thus are not scarce). Relying on marketplace forces alone, the newer services, including cable, will probably reach no more than half the nation's population, even by the end of the century. On the other hand, the scarcity factor for the universally available broadcasting service seems likely to continue in the near future.

Scarcity of channels must also be viewed in terms of a medium's accessibility to users. Despite its many channels, cable television has thus far not eliminated scarcity of *access*, nor have still newer services. The courts have held that none of the electronic media is required to provide access to any given person or point of view, with the single exception that political candidates must have access to broadcast stations and to cable local-origination channels. Thus the public is denied any assured access to the spectrum, despite the theory that the spectrum belongs to all as a common resource. Even the fairness doctrine gives access to conflicting ideas rather than to specific proponents of those ideas. Nevertheless, it, too, may someday be swept aside by deregulation.

Uncertain Technological Standards In the 1980s the FCC embarked on an important and risky experiment in technological deregulation. With its 1982 decision to let the marketplace determine the standard for AM stereo, the commission initiated a very different approach than the one that had long guided technical development of broadcasting. Similar hands-off decisions on standards for teletext, DBS, and television stereo transmission followed. How well this marketplace approach to establishing technical standards will work is not yet clear. Some critics argue that a lack of government leadership will delay technical innovation, because consumers and manufacturers alike will be unwilling to risk investment in telecommunication that may become obsolete because of rapid changes in technology.

19.6 Conclusion

In this book we have attempted to describe the attributes of broadcasting and its electronic contributors and competitors. We have discussed radio and television as unique among competitors in public communications. To review some of its main attributes, broadcasting:

• uses a scarce public resource, the electromagnetic spectrum.

• is expected to operate in the public interest in view of its dependence on that public resource.

• can reach recipients without physical interconnection, and can thus reach few or many within a service area at the same cost.

• is subject to interference, and therefore must be technically regulated.

• is regulated on a national rather than local basis, since its coverage and impact, because of its wirelessness, cannot be confined within fixed geographical boundaries.

• has a major advantage over other electronic media because it is available in virtually all homes.

• can instantaneously shift focus from a local to a regional or national scope.

• has a special responsibility to consumers because of their investment in receiver purchase and repair.

• depends for its effectiveness on various forms of syndication, of which networks are the most characteristic type.

No single rival electronic medium achieves this combination of attributes that makes broadcasting unique. Broadcasting's most important rival, cable television:

• requires a physical connection to each and every receiver, so that every additional receiver adds to a system's cost, and some homes remain beyond reach.

• is regulated locally by franchise authorities within the framework of a generally deregulatory national policy, as expressed in the 1984 additions to the communications act.

• is free of most government controls over both basic and pay channel programming, as well as ownership and finances.

• provides a simultaneous choice of services on from twelve to over a hundred channels, depending on the particular system.

• delivers ready-made program services from external sources with little or no local origination.

• requires audiences to pay for service through subscriber fees, as do most other new electronic media.

• reaches only about half the nation's homes.

The limitations of the newer services can best be summarized in terms of three characteristics:

• They deliver content identical to that found in broadcasting or cable.

• They are supported directly by subscribers (the end audience), not advertisers.

• They serve only a small minority of the nation's population.

It is for the reader to decide whether broadcasting's continuing unique status should be preserved. Would it be in the public interest to allow cable and other subscription media to so dominate programming that audiences would be forced to pay fees merely to obtain the same material they once enjoyed free from broadcasting? Would it be in the public interest to abandon the goal of a varied or pluralistic system, leaving broadcasting entirely to marketplace economic controls without regard to the aspects of public interest that cannot be measured solely in terms of profit and loss?

Summary

• Enthusiasts of newer technologies see traditional broadcasting being replaced within a very few years. More likely is a continuing evolution of all services, with broadcasting retaining its major importance as the most efficient means for delivering mass entertainment, information, and education.

• Marketplace competition had already created some new technology "losers" by the mid-1980s: single-channel pay systems, videodiscs for the home market, and DBS were prime examples. None of the new services will reach a majority of the nation's population. Cable, by far the largest new service, reaches half the country's households.

• Major technological developments in the 1980s will include expansion of cable and optical-fiber links. With the exception of DBS, satellite services will continue to expand. High-definition and stereo television show promise for the future, but HDTV will appear first in theaters, not on home receivers.

• Broadcasting will continue to be the single most effective means of reaching a broad national audience. But despite newer services' more limited penetration, they will increasingly follow the massification example of radio and television in their broad rather than specialized audience appeal. Cable proponents had seen cable as a medium encouraging specialized channels, but economic reality will continue to force cable to stress mass appeal.

• A fundamental difference between broadcasting and cable and other newer delivery options is the means by which each is supported. Broadcasting's viewers watch free once they have receivers. The newer services require some kind of direct subscription payment in addition to receiver ownership. No change is likely in this regard.

• Whereas local programming is not of major importance in broadcasting, it will continue to be nonexistent in the newer services.

• Broadcast networks will continue to decline in importance, and may eventually change to news and information services. Affiliate stations will have an increasing ability to pick and choose among many satellite-delivered services.

• Advertising, with its promise of substantial revenue, is likely to creep into the newer electronic media in the next several years. Listeners, however, will continue to pay subscriber fees.

• A level regulatory playing field is unlikely in the near future; broadcasting will continue to carry more regulation because of its wider availability and continued scarcity of channels.

• The trend toward deregulation will continue as the nation expands its experiment (one that many see as permanent) in business self-direction and control.

Further Reading

A Selective Guide to the Literature on Electronic Media

Christopher H. Sterling

This guide, organized by the chapter and section headings of the text, gives suggestions for further reading on each topic. Limited space allows for only representative selections from the rapidly growing literature of the field. We include examples of the most significant book-length publications that should be readily available and are of current interest as of mid-1986. Following the chapter-by-chapter guide are an annotated discussion of relevant periodicals and a brief bibliography of bibliographies. Although many of the books mentioned here are cited in the text, this guide independently assesses each title. Every work cited below and within the text is listed in full detail in the bibliography.

Chapter 1:   Global Context

1.1 Convergence   A handsome coffee-table book with a historical approach but a lot of current information is Antébi, *The Electronic Epoch* (1983). A valuable overview by a long-time student of communication is Pool, *Technologies of Freedom* (1983), which focuses on free speech in an electronic age.

1.2 Common Grounds   The starting point for a broad-based philosophical discussion of broadcasting in different societies is Head, *World Broadcasting Systems: A Comparative Analysis* (1985). Earlier works still of value include the discussion of British, American, Japanese, Canadian, and several European systems found in Smith, *The Shadow in the Cave: The Broadcaster, His Audience, and the State* (1973); and the broad surveys of television in both developed and developing lands in Green, *The Universal Eye* (1972), and Dizard, *Television: A World View* (1966). Rogers and Balle, *The Media Revolution in America & Western Europe* (1985), offers 17 research papers on all aspects of the topic. Emery, *National and International Systems of Broadcasting* (1969), includes both foreign and regional material while stressing broadcasting in Europe. Two multi-volume paperback series detail specific countries from all regions of the world: IIC, *Broadcasting in . . .*; and UNESCO, *Communication Policies in . . .* Finally, Martin and Chardhau, *Comparative Mass Media Systems* (1983), compares the West, Communist nations, and the Third World on seven topical subjects.

1.3 Political Philosophies   Material on American broadcasting is detailed under later chapters. A useful comparative study of eight developed nations is Kuhn, *The Politics of Broadcasting* (1985). See also Head, and Smith, under §1.2. The development of British radio and television is well told in Briggs, *The BBC: The First Fifty Years* (1985), and Sendall, *Independent Television in Britain* (1982–1983). For more on Soviet and related systems see Paulu, *Radio and Television Broadcasting in Eastern Europe* (1974), and Mickiewicz, *Media and the Russian Public* (1981).

1.4 Pluralistic Trend   In addition to the titles under §1.3, see Tunstall, *The Media in Britain* (1984), for the broad context of pluralism, and Paulu, *Television and Radio in the United Kingdom* (1981), for specific details on broadcasting.

1.5 Legal Foundations   For material on American media law, see notes under chapters 16–18; for British material see §1.3. The ITU is detailed in Codding and Rutkowski, *The International Telecommunication Union in a*

Changing World (1982). A collection of important documents from world agencies is gathered and annotated in Ploman, *International Law Governing Communications and Information* (1982).

1.6 Access to the Air   The best comparative analysis is found in Berrigan, *Access: Some Western Models of Community Media* (1977). See also Head, under §1.2.

1.7–1.8 Economics and Geography   The standard annual of information on broadcasting systems and programming is Frost, *World Radio-TV Handbook*. Also issued annually, but with a descriptive rather than directory approach, is Paterson, *TV and Video International Guide*. A standard handbook of information on all media in most countries is UNESCO, *World Communications* (1975), revised about every 10 years and statistically updated in UNESCO, *Statistics on Radio and Television, 1960–1976* (1979), and UNESCO, *Statistical Yearbook*, annual. A good analysis of the development of three conflicting systems of color television is in Crane, *The Politics of International Standards* (1979). The many European and British "pirate" broadcasters are detailed in Harris, *Broadcasting from the High Seas* (1977).

1.9 Programs and Schedules   See Frost, under §1.7, and the titles under §1.3. Katz and Wedell, *Broadcasting in the Third World* (1977), is the best overview on that topic. See also Head, *Broadcasting in Africa* (1974); Lent, *Broadcasting in Asia and the Pacific* (1978); Boyd, *Broadcasting in the Arab World* (1982); and Alisky, *Latin American Media* (1981), for detailed regional analyses.

1.10 Transborder Broadcasting   There is a large body of literature on propaganda, much of it based on World War II experiences. A good starting point on the current role of radio is Browne, *International Radio Broadcasting* (1982), which covers major countries and stresses recent developments. Soviet activity is reviewed in the last two titles under §1.3 and in Shultz and Godson, *Dezinformatsia: Active Measures in Soviet Strategy* (1984). RFE and RL activities are detailed in the annual reports of the Board for International Broadcasting. The rationale for beginning a transborder service, in this case Radio Martí into Cuba from the United States, is found in the *Final Report* of the Presidential Commission on Broadcasting to Cuba (1982). A useful discussion of program exchanges is in Eugster, *Television Programming Across National Boundaries: The EBU and OIRT Experience* (1983).

1.11 U.S. Dominance   A good deal of the literature on this cross-cultural debate is highly polemical. The best international statement of the free-flow versus balanced-flow issue is found in UNESCO's McBride Commission, *Many Voices, One World* (1980). Nordenstreng, *The Mass Media Declaration of UNESCO* (1984), reviews that agency's increasing activity in this area. A similarly strong argument is presented in Smith, *The Geopolitics of Information: How Western Culture Dominates the World* (1980). A good discussion of the four Western world news agencies is in Fenby, *The International News Services* (1986). Western points of view are found in Tunstall, *The Media Are American* (1977), and a Twentieth Century Fund Task Force on the International Flow of News, *A Free and Balanced Flow* (1979). A counter-argument, suggesting to Third World nations that they not let themselves be overwhelmed by Western media, is offered by Hamelink, *Cultural Autonomy in Global Communications* (1983).

Chapter 2:   The Rise of Radio

2.1 Precedents   Tebbel, *The Media in America* (1975), is a good print-oriented survey of media development; Csida and Csida, *American Entertainment* (1978), provides a text and picture scrapbook approach to popular culture as taken from the pages of *Billboard*; and Toll, *The Entertainment Machine* (1982), is a very useful general tracing of American show business, including vaudeville, in this century. A handbook of historical statistics and trends in all the media is found in Sterling and Haight, *The Mass Media* (1978), partially updated in Sterling, *Electronic Media* (1984). Emery and Emery, *The Press and America* (1984), is the best overall history of newspapers and magazines. Advertising's development is covered in Fox, *The Mirror Makers* (1984), and Pope, *The Making of Modern Advertising* (1983). The two standard histories of the phonograph are Gelatt, *The Fabulous Phonograph* (1977), and the more detailed and equipment-oriented Read and Welsh, *From Tin Foil to Stereo* (1976). Two useful histories of American film are Jowett, *Film* (1976), and Balio, *The American Film Industry* (1985). A highly insightful analysis of the telegraph, motion picture, and radio and their impact on America is given in Czitrom, *Media and the American Mind from Morse to McLuhan* (1982).

2.2 Wire Communication   An old but useful survey of electrical communication history is found in Harlow, *Old Wires and New Waves* (1936), including telegraph, telephone, and radio. Davis, *Electrical and Electronic Technologies* (1981–1985, three volumes), provides a technical chronology by year and by topic. Thompson, *Wiring a Continent* (1947), is the definitive history of the telegraph to the formation of the Western Union monopoly in 1866.

Coates & Finn, *A Retrospective Technology Assessment: Submarine Telegraphy* (1979), is a fascinating analysis of the impact of the 1866 trans-Atlantic cable. Brooks, *Telephone* (1976), is an informal history of AT&T; and Pool, *The Social Impact of the Telephone* (1977), shows how that impact has varied with time. Kleinfield, *The Biggest Company on Earth* (1981), looks at AT&T on the eve of its breakup. Development of telecommunication industry and policy is related in Brock, *The Telecommunications Industry* (1981); and Shooshan, *Disconnecting Bell: The Impact of the AT&T Divestiture* (1984), and Irwin, *Telecommunications America* (1984), provide early assessments of the dramatic changes of the mid-1980s.

2.3 Big Business and Patents   The premier study of patents in radio is Maclaurin, *Invention and Innovation in the Radio Industry* (1949), which carries the story to early television. The FTC, *Report on the Radio Industry* (1924), focuses on patents in the rise of RCA. The rise of GE and Westinghouse is found in Passer, *The Electrical Manufacturers: 1875–1900* (1953), and in Bright, *The Electric-Lamp Industry: Technological Change and Economic Development from 1800 to 1947* (1949).

2.4 Invention of Wireless   In addition to Maclaurin (see §2.3), the definitive treatment on this subject is the two-volume work by Aitken, *Syntony and Spark: The Origins of Radio* (1976), which relates the work of Hertz and Marconi, and *The Continuous Wave* (1985), which continues the story to 1932. Leinwoll, *From Spark to Satellite* (1979), is a brief survey of radio development. Dunlap, *Radio's 100 Men of Science* (1944), provides brief biographies on inventors discussed in the text. Jolly, *Marconi* (1972), is the most recent biography of the key inventor. One of the few really good company histories in this field is Baker, *A History of the Marconi Company* (1971). Tyne, *Saga of the Vacuum Tube* (1977), is a very detailed study of the subject to about 1930. Lacking modesty but providing human-interest detail is de Forest, *Father of Radio* (1950). Compare it to Lessing, *Man of High Fidelity* (1956), a biography of Edwin Armstrong.

2.5 Initial Development of Wireless Services Because of the predominant role of the U.S. Navy in the period, Howeth's *History of Communications-Electronics in the United States Navy* (1963) is essential to an understanding of nonmilitary events and international and domestic regulation, as well as of the cover topic. For the general role of shipboard radio, see Hancock, *Wireless at Sea* (1950), a Marconi company history of technical applications. Radio's role in the *Titanic* disaster is best told in Marcus, *The Maiden Voyage* (1969). The second part of

Schubert, *The Electric Word* (1928), provides a useful account of radio in World War I on land and sea.

2.6 Experiments with Radiotelephony
Fessenden, *Fessenden* (1940), is a good biography of the inventor by his wife. See also de Forest's autobiography, and the discussion in Aitken (1985) under §2.4.

2.7 Government Monopoly: The Road Not Taken
See Howeth, under §2.5; the FTC report, under §2.3; and the Archer histories discussed under §2.9, all of which detail the formation of RCA and the patent pool. For the final government ownership debate see House CMMF, 1919.

2.8 The "First" Broadcast Station   The inception of amateur radio is related in De Soto, *Two Hundred Meters and Down* (1936). The major histories of American broadcasting include Barnouw, *A History of Broadcasting in the United States* (1966–1970, three volumes); Sterling and Kittross, *Stay Tuned: A Concise History of American Broadcasting* (1978); and the anthology edited by Lichty and Topping, *American Broadcasting* (1975). All three cover both radio and television, beginning with technical developments and continuing into the 1970s, though each is arranged differently. Best analysis of "Broadcasting's Oldest Station" is the article of that name by Baudino & Kittross (1977).

2.9 Radio Broadcasting vs. Radiotelephony
Ponderous and not clearly organized, but still important for its detailed view of the "radio group" side of the debate, is the two-volume history by Archer, *History of Radio to 1926* (1938) and *Big Business and Radio* (1939), both biased toward RCA's point of view. For a balancing telephone-company view see Banning, *Commercial Broadcasting Pioneer* (1946), which is the story of WEAF to 1926. The most objective contemporary telling of these events is in Schubert, under §2.5.

2.10 Evolution of Radio   See the discussion of the early years of NBC and CBS in the Archer histories, under §2.9, and also Bergreen, *Look Now, Pay Later: The Rise of Network Broadcasting* (1980). For biographies of the key leaders see Dreher, *Sarnoff* (1977), and Paley, *As It Happened* (1979). Best analysis of the development of radio advertising is Hettinger, *A Decade of Radio Advertising* (1933), which includes data and documents found nowhere else. The first books written about how to advertise with the new medium were Felix, *Using Radio in Sales Promotion* (1927), and Dunlap, *Advertising by Radio* (1929), both filled with fascinating detail about early network and station operations.

2.11 Government Regulation   An overview of the period is Rosen, *The Modern Stentors: Radio Broadcasters and the Federal Government 1920–1934* (1980). Howeth, under §2.5, covers the 1910 and 1912 acts. Best study of the 1927 act is Davis, *The Law of Radio* (1927). See also House CIFC, *Regulation of Broadcasting* (1958). Kittross, *Administration of American Telecommunications Policy* (1980), collects reports of the radio conferences among other key documents.

Chapter 3:   From Radio to Television

3.1–3.2 Radio During the Great Depression and Radio Controversies   For a year-by-year retrospective see Broadcasting Publications, *The First 50 Years of Broadcasting* (1981). See the general titles listed under §2.8 as well as MacDonald, *Don't Touch That Dial!* (1979), and Settel, *A Pictorial History of Radio* (1967), both of which stress network programming, as does Slide, *Great Radio Personalities in Historic Photographs* (1982). Codel, *Radio and Its Future* (1930), is an anthology suggesting the likely direction of the industry. Late in the 1930s a whole literature criticizing that direction began to appear: Frost, *Is American Radio Democratic?* (1937), and Brindze, *Not to Be Broadcast: The Truth About Radio* (1937), are examples. Hettinger and Neff, *Practical Radio Advertising* (1938), reflects organization and practices in the industry in the 1930s. The most detailed narrative of radio's ASCAP and AFM troubles is found in chapters 12–14 of Warner, *Radio and Television Rights* (1953). For reference and specific data see U.S. Bureau of the Census, *Radio Broadcasting* (1935), the first-indepth national government survey; and *Broadcasting Yearbook*, an annual beginning in 1935.

3.3 Television and FM Radio   The best history of television's technology is Abramson, *Electronic Motion Pictures* (1955), and "A Short History of Television Recording," (1955, 1973). The rise of the industry through 1941 is related in Udelson, *The Great Television Race* (1982). For a life of Farnsworth see Everson, *The Story of Television* (1949). Goldmark and Lee, *Maverick Inventor* (1973), suggests the crucial but changing role of an inventor in a large corporation, in this case CBS. For FM's development see Lessing, under §2.4, and Siepmann, *Radio's Second Chance* (1946). For material on the rise of LP recordings see the works on the phonograph under §2.1.

3.4 Broadcasting at War (1938–1946)   A fascinating analysis of early radio news and comment impact is found in Culbert, *News for Everyman* (1976); a more popular treatment is Fang, *Those Radio Commentators!* (1977). Individual biographies abound: the best of the lot is Kendrick, *Prime Time: The Life of Edward R. Murrow* (1969). For television developments see Abramson, under §3.3.

3.5 Radio Networks: Development and Decline
Several works detail radio's structure at its pretelevision peak: Rose, *National Policy for Radio Broadcasting* (1940), is the best early analysis of structural and regulatory problems; White, *The American Radio* (1947), is a critical analysis pleading for more public-service and education applications; and Landry, *This Fascinating Radio Business* (1946), describes network radio development and the peak years. Early college texts on the structure of the industry include Siepmann, *Radio, Television, and Society* (1950), focusing on impact of the media; Wolfe, *Modern Radio Advertising* (1949); and Midgley, *The Advertising and Business Side of Radio* (1948). The definitive official analysis of radio network structure and operations is FCC, *Report on Chain Broadcasting* (1941), which is analyzed in Robinson, *Radio Networks and the Federal Government* (1943). See also the early chapters of Bergreen, under §2.10. Network radio programming is described in Dunning, *Tune in Yesterday* (1976), an alphabetical guide to most program series; Stedman, *The Serials* (1977), dealing with the genre on radio, films, and television; and Wertheim, *Radio Comedy* (1979).

3.6 Television at Last   A solid analysis of television allocation to the late 1950s is found in House CIFC, *Network Broadcasting* (1958). The famous "Sixth Report and Order," which ended the Freeze, is found in its entirety in *FCC Reports*, Vol. 41. That same volume includes the 1950 and final 1953 color decisions.

3.7 The TV Age Begins   Two good general surveys of television development are Barnouw, *Tube of Plenty* (1975), and Greenfield, *Television: The First Fifty Years* (1977), a coffee-table illustrated program history with an intelligent text. Shulman and Youman, *How Sweet It Was* (1966), is the best picture treatment of the first 15 years of network TV programming. An overall picture approach is in Settel, *A Pictorial History of Television* (1983). For network developments see House CIFC, under §3.6; Paley, under §2.10; Metz, *CBS* (1975); Quinlan, *Inside ABC* (1979); and Campbell, *The Golden Years of Broadcasting* (1976), about NBC. O'Conner, *American History/American Television: Interpreting the Video Past* (1983), reviews specific programs and events in television history. For directories of network program series see titles under §12.2.

3.8 Radio Responds to Television General surveys of music and radio developments are Eberly, *Music in the Air: America's Changing Tastes in Popular Music, 1920–1980* (1982), and Passman, *The Deejays* (1971), both informal narratives dealing with personalities and musical trends on radio. Later radio music programming is detailed in Sklar, *Rocking America: How the All-Hit Radio Stations Took Over* (1984). The changing structure of the industry under television is evident in three contemporary texts or professional books: Head, *Broadcasting in America* (1956), the first edition of this textbook; Seehafer and Laemmar, *Successful Television and Radio Advertising* (1959); and Reinch and Ellis, *Radio Station Management* (1960).

3.9 Ethical Crises A definitive treatment of the quiz scandals is found in Anderson, *Television Fraud* (1978), which includes transcripts of several programs. Blacklisting is a topic now widely discussed: see Vaughn, *Only Victims: A Study of Show Business Blacklisting* (1972), for a good survey. Important contemporary books include the original broadcast blacklist, *Counterattack, Red Channels* (1950); Cogley's *Report on Blacklisting II: Radio Television* (1956); and Faulk's telling of his own case in a suspenseful narrative, *Fear on Trial* (1964).

Chapter 4: Era of Electronic Media

Reference statistics on trends in broadcasting and cable are found in Sterling, *Electronic Media* (1984). A useful broad background on the topics in this chapter is offered in Compaine, *Understanding New Media (1984); Gross, The New Television Technologies* (1986); and Singleton, *Telecommunications in the Information Age* (1986).

4.1 The Limits of Television Criticism of television grew in the 1960s and 1970s, leading to books recommending changes in the medium. An example of the genre is the practical guide by a FCC commissioner of the time: Johnson, *How to Talk Back to Your Television Set* (1970).

4.2 Rise of Cable Television Any book on cable prior to the early 1980s is useful today only as a history. Land Associates, *Television and the Wired City* (1968), is one early view of cable's potential. Among books designed as history, the most useful is Le Duc, *Cable Television and the FCC* (1973), which carries the story through the 1972 rules. A good sense of those rules and of the beginning of their demise is in Rivkin, *A New Guide to Federal Cable Telvision Regulations* (1978). Hollowell, *Cable Handbook* (1975), shows

the thinking on cable's role on the eve of pay cable's appearance.

4.3 The Cable Establishment The important policy decisions leading to approval of domestic satellites are reviewed in Magnant, *Domestic Satellite* (1977). There is as yet no overall history of pay television or even of pay cable. Ted Turner is profiled in Williams, *Lead, Follow, or Get Out of the Way* (1981). Most of the literature on interactive cable is in the form of research reports, but see Bretz, *Media for Interactive Communication* (1983), for a sense of the technical basics and applications, and *The Interactive Cable TV Handbook* (1984) for industry development. Whiteside's "Cable" (1985) is an excellent narrative of the development of cable television. Survey overviews of most aspects of cable are found in Roman, *Cablemania* (1983), and Baldwin and McVoy, *Cable Communications* (1983). Early experiments and hopes for cable are evident in Gillespie, *Public Access Cable Television in the United States and Canada* (1975).

4.4 Pay Television The best study of STV is Howard and Carroll, *Subscription Television* (1980). For background on pay cable development see Scott, *Bringing Premium Entertainment into the Home via Pay-Cable TV* (1977), and Technology & Economics, Inc., *The Emergence of Pay Cable Television* (1980). For the multiple-channel services see Frank, *Multichannel MDS* (1984).

4.5 Traditional Broadcasting The FCC network investigation is in FCC (Network Inquiry Special Staff), *New Television Networks* (1980, two volumes), which gives a great deal of economic information on television network structure and operations today. Useful analysis of the modern radio business appears in Fornatale and Mills, *Radio in the Television Age* (1980); see also the books listed under §3.8.

4.6 Public Broadcasting The broadest survey of public broadcasting development and operation is Wood and Wylie, *Educational Telecommunications* (1977). Gibson, *Public Broadcasting: The Role of the Federal Government, 1912–1976* (1977), shows the growing federal financial support function; and Blakely, *To Serve the Public Interest* (1979), provides an overall historical picture. The two Carnegie reports are CCET, *Public Television* (1967), and CCFPB, *A Public Trust* (1979).

4.7 Home Video Center There is a growing literature on the development of computers and microelectronics. A good survey is Augarten, *Bit by Bit: An Illustrated History of Computers* (1984). The development of video recording is detailed in Abramson, "A Short History of Television Recording" (1955, 1973). Economic and political assessments of home video are found in Noam, *Video Media Competition: Regulation, Economics, and Technology* (1985). A valuable annual assessment is *Channels of Communications* magazine's *Field Guide* to the new technologies with short articles on each. EIA, *Consumer Electronics* (annual), is a free booklet of statistics and text showing trends in electronic media components.

4.8 Developments to Come   There is a large amount of literature on teletext and videotex. A comprehensive assessment is in Tydeman et al., *Teletext and Videotex in the United States* (1982), and the technical basics are best detailed in Martin, *Viewdata and the Information Society* (1982). A substantial number of reports appeared during the short heyday of DBS; of them, the best are Taylor, *Direct-to-Home Satellite Broadcasting* (1980); and NTIA, *Direct Broadcast Satellites: Policies, Prospects, and Potential Competition* (1981). Material on HDTV and stereo television is limited to current periodicals.

Chapter 5:   Basic Physical Concepts

A dictionary of electronics may be useful as a resource for chapters 5–7. A good one is Graham, *The Facts on File Dictionary of Telecommunications* (1983). See also Langley, *Telecommunications Primer* (1983), which has very clear diagrams and text; Meadows, *Dictionary of New Information Technology* (1982); Martin, *Future Developments in Telecommunications* (1977), which though dated has very clear material on signal distribution; and Pierce, *Signals: The Telephone and Beyond* (1981), which details technical basics and assumes no prior knowledge. An in-depth background on all topics discussed in this and the next chapter is found in Crutchfield, *NAB Engineering Handbook* (1985), which does assume a technical background on the part of readers. The *McGraw-Hill Encyclopedia of Electronics and Computers* (1983) is a good technical reference.

5.1 Electromagnetic Spectrum   Levin, *The Invisible Resource: Use and Regulation of the Radio Spectrum* (1971), remains the definitive study, dealing equally with technical, economic, and political aspects of the topic. A political scientist and an engineer's point of view are combined in McGillam and McLauchlan, *Hermes Bound: The Policy and Technology of Telecommunications* (1978).

5.2–5.6 Waves, Modulation, and Propagation   A fascinating discussion of the kinds and impact of sound is found in Schaefer, *The Tuning of the World* (1977). Truax,

Acoustic Communication (1985), deals with all aspects of sound. A good diagram-illustrated discussion of sound modulation is presented in Beck, *Words and Waves* (1967).

5.7 Antennas   See Crutchfield under the general chapter 5 note.

5.8 Spectrum Conversation   See titles under §5.1. The official detailed record of frequency use and management in the United States is NTIA, *Manual of Regulations and Procedures for Federal Radio Frequency Management* (regularly updated). Glatzer, *Who Owns the Rainbow?* (1984), is a simplified discussion of spectrum-use trade-offs. *Radiofrequency Use and Management* (1982) compares U.S. and ITU spectrum decisions.

Chapter 6:   Technology of Traditional Broadcasting

6.1 Gaining Access to the Spectrum   For information on the ITU, see titles under §1.5.

6.2–6.4 Interference, AM, and FM   Details on current broadcast practice are in Crutchfield, under general chapter 5 note.

6.5 Short-Wave Stations   The standard annually revised source book for all radio "hams" is the American Radio Relay League, *The Radio Amateur's Handbook*. In addition to Frost, under 1.7–1.8, see Fallon, *Shortwave Listener's Handbook* (1976), for details on the hows, whens, and wheres of SW listening.

6.6–6.9 Television   There is a substantial technical literature about television. One of the best introductions remains Fink and Lutyens, *The Physics of Television* (1960), which is directed at the layperson. Details and diagrams are found in Spottiswoode, *The Focal Encyclopedia of Film and Television Techniques* (1969), and in Marsh, *Independent Video* (1974). See also Crutchfield, under general chapter 5 note.

6.10 TV Transmission and Reception   An engineering text of value here is Freeman, *Telecommunications Transmission Handbook* (1981). See Crutchfield, under general chapter 5 note.

6.11 Technical Innovations   Periodical articles are important here, one of the best sources being the *Journal of the SMPTE*. For ENG equipment, see Yoakam and

Cremer, *ENG: Television News and the New Technology* (1985).

Chapter 7: Delivery, Distribution, and Storage

7.1 Basic Concepts   A dated but interesting approach to topics considered in this chapter is found in Bretz, *A Taxonomy of Communication Media* (1970), which compares transmission and recorded technologies and their applications and interrelationships.

7.2–7.3 Sound and Picture Recording   Alten, *Audio in Media* (1981), is a detailed how-to guide to this topic. A good diagram-illustrated guide is Overman, *Understanding Sound, Video & Film Recording* (1978).

7.4 Terrestrial Relays   See Crutchfield, under general chapter 5 note, and Freeman, under §6.10.

7.5 Space Relays   Though dated, good diagrams, photos, and a clear text highlight Polcyn, *An Educator's Guide to Communication Satellites* (1973). Alper and Pelton, *The Intelsat Global Satellite System* (1984), contains a wealth of understandable technical information. The annual reports of NASA, Comsat, and Intelsat are good current data sources.

7.6 Over-the-Air Hybrids   Arnall, *Instructional Television Fixed Service* (1984), reviews ITFS potential and problems. Biel, *Low Power Television: Development and Current Status of the LPTV Industry* (1985), discusses translators and low power.

7.7–7.8 Cable Television   See chapters 1-5 in Baldwin and McVoy, *Cable Communication* (1983); Grant, *Cable Television* (1983); and Harrell, *The Cable Television Technical Handbook* (1985).

Chapter 8: Stations, Systems, and Networks

8.1 The Commercial Broadcast Station   Surprisingly, the book literature on management and organization of radio and television stations is not large. Most recent are McCavitt and Pringle, *Electronic Media Management* (1986), and the more specific Keith and Krause, *The Radio Station* (1986). Quaal and Brown, *Broadcast Management* (1975), is still the most substantial overview of both radio and television stations. A recent study of successful

radio station management is offered in NAB, *Radio in Search of Excellence* (1985). Johnson and Jones, *Modern Radio Station Practices* (1978), also profiles many actual operations. Kirkley, *Station Policy and Procedures: A Guide for Radio* (1985), provides advice on internal station guidelines. Dessart, *Television in the Real World* (1978), provides a case study of getting a commercial TV station on the air. For books on station ownership, see titles under §10.5. *Independent Thinking: An Overview of the Independent Television Industry* (1986) covers non-network stations.

8.2 Commercial Broadcast Networks and Affiliates   The definitive analysis is the FCC Network Inquiry Special Staff, *New Television Networks* (1980). The economic and political lessons of that two-year study are clearly brought out in Besen et al., *Misregulating Television: Network Dominance and the FCC* (1984), and Botein & Rice, *Network Television and the Public Interest* (1981), adds some research analyses to the debate over the role of networks. See also the titles noted under chapter 12.

8.3 Noncommercial Broadcasting   Most useful and current are the many statistical reports issued by the Corporation for Public Broadcasting (1111 16th St. N.W., Washington, D.C. 20036), especially the *Status Report on Public Broadcasting*, which is revised every three or four years, and the CPB *Annual Report*, which details spending and the overall shape of public radio and television. The most detailed discussion of public radio is found in NAPTS' *Public Television and Radio and State Governments* (1984, two volumes). The debate behind the national organizations is discussed in Avery & Pepper, *The Politics of Interconnection* (1979). For material on funding, see titles under §10.6.

8.4 Cable Systems and Networks   The standard annual reference directories to systems, networks, and owners are the *Broadcasting Yearbook* and the *Television Factbook*, each of which includes a large cable section and some statistics. Background data are given in Sterling, under the general chapter 4 note.

8.5 Employment   A useful descriptive guide to career options is found in Reed and Reed, *Career Opportunities in Television and Video* (1982). See also *Opportunities in Broadcasting* (1983), *Opportunities in Cable Television* (1984), and *Opportunities in Telecommunications* (1984). Until 1981 the FCC collected and reported annual broadcast and cable television employment information. The role of minority employment, as well as content in programming, is detailed in the U.S. Commission on Civil Rights, *Window Dressing on the Set* (1977, 1979). The only book on broadcasting unions is Koenig, *Broadcasting and Bargaining* (1970).

Chapter 9:   Broadcast and Cable Advertising

Readers may find a general advertising text a useful supplement to this chapter. The *Advertising Age Yearbook* is a good source for general trends in the field. A good systems approach with unique diagrams is DeLozier, *The Marketing Communications Process* (1976). Barnouw, *The Sponsor* (1978), is a critical essay on the development of the advertiser's role in radio and television. Heighton and Cunningham, *Advertising in the Broadcast and Cable Media* (1984), and Ziegler and Howard, *Broadcast Advertising* (1984), cover all aspects of the topic. Murphy, *Handbook of Radio Advertising* (1980), is the only recent book on the topic. Poltrack, *Television Marketing: Network, Local, and Cable* (1983), is a valuable guide to the buying and selling of video time. The content of television advertising is assessed in Geis, *The Language of Television Advertising* (1982), and less formally in Hall, *Mighty Minutes: An Illustrated History of Television's Best Commercials* (1984). Busch & Landeck, *The Making of a Television Commercial* (1981), shows the complex process in detail.

9.1–9.3 Advantages-Disadvantages-Scheduling of Broadcast Advertising
See the discussions in Heighton and Cunningham and in Poltrack, noted above. Promotion in broadcasting is assessed and described in Eastman and Klein, *Strategies for Broadcast and Cable Promotion* (1982), and Bergendorff, *Broadcast Advertising and Promotion* (1983).

9.4 Cable Advertising
See Poltrack, under general chapter 9 note, and Kaatz, *Cable: An Advertiser's Guide to the New Electronic Media* (1982), for general discussions of cable's advantages and disadvantages. More recent is Jones, et. al. *Cable Advertising: New Ways to New Business* (1986). See also Roman, and Baldwin and McVoy, under §4.3.

9.5–9.7 Advertising Rates, Sales, and Standards
Heighton and Cunningham, under general chapter 9 note, is most useful here. Regular issues of *Standard Rate and Data Service* reprint radio, television, and cable rate cards for all markets. Warner's *Broadcast and Cable Selling* (1986) is a comprehensive guide. Children's television advertising was most comprehensively reviewed in the Federal Trade Commission, *Staff Report on Television Advertising to Children* (1978), which, even though nothing came of it, makes a strong case for government as parent.

Chapter 10:   Other Economic Aspects of Electronic Media

10.1 Financial Framework
Useful context on media structure in the United States is found in Turow, *The Media Industries* (1984). Dated, but providing context and comparisons across media is Owen, *Economics and Freedom of Expression* (1975).

10.2 Program Economics
The best discussion of network program economics is found in the FCC Network Inquiry report, under §4.5. Included are documents and analysis of network-affiliate contracts, compensation schemes, program procurement, etc. Though dated, much of the overall view in Owen et al, *Television Economics* (1974), remains valid.

10.3 Subscription and Other Supports
Webb, *The Economics of Cable Television* (1983) reviews issues and the structure of both basic and pay cable.

10.4 Capital Investment
About the only general information on this topic is contained in the NAB's *Radio Financial Report* and *Television Financial Report*, issued annually. These detail expenses and investment for different sizes of stations in different size markets, based on an annual national survey. For material on satellites, see titles under §4.5 and §4.7.

10.5 Buying and Selling Properties
Each year in a January issue, *Broadcasting* reviews major sales and transfers of broadcast licenses in the previous year. A very clear and detailed guide to the process is Krasnow and Bentley, *Buying or Building a Broadcast Station* (1983). Industry structure and FCC rules are discussed in Besen and Johnson, *An Assessment of the Federal Communication Commission's Group Ownership Rules* (1984), and by Sterling, in Compaine, *Who Owns the Media?* (1982). A strong attack on what is described as an overly concentrated media ownership is presented in Bagdikian, *The Media Monopoly* (1983). *The Knowledge Industry 200* (1983), gives a detailed breakout of holdings of the major media firms in the early 1980s, along with some sense of corporate structure and operation.

10.6 Funding Public Broadcasting
For current information see the most recent hearings before the House Committee on Energy and Commerce on the budget request of the Corporation for Public Broadcasting, and the CPB *Annual Report*.

Chapter 11:   Programming Problems, Processes, and Practices

There are a number of books useful for this chapter and the two that follow. Among them, Eastman et al., *Broadcast/Cable Programming* (1985), is the most inclusive assessment dealing with strategies for all types of stations and systems. Brown, *Les Brown's Encyclopedia of Television* (1982), is a very good reference, with entries on all aspects of programming.

11.1–11.3 Program Problems, Processes and Strategies
Several books describe the seasonal programming process in television, among them Christensen and Stauth, *The Sweeps: Behind the Scenes in Network TV* (1984); Gitlin, *Inside Prime Time* (1984); Levinson and Link, *Stay Tuned* (1981); and Cantor, *Prime-Time Television* (1980). All of them deal with the institutions and major players in program decision making. Bedell's *Up the Tube: Prime-Time Television and the Silverman Years* (1981), reviews trends through the career of the only man to hold high positions in all three networks.

11.4–11.5 Programming Practices and Scheduling Strategies
For more on the strategies discussed here see Eastman et al., under general chapter 11 note.

11.6 Appraising the Program Services
Newcomb's *Television: The Critical View* (1983) is a respected collection of articles assessing television programs. Smith, *Beyond the Wasteland: The Criticism of Broadcasting* (1980), discusses the difficulty a critic faces in dealing with a transitory medium. Two works by Himmelstein, *On the Small Screen: New Approaches in Television and Video Criticism* (1981) and *Television Myth and the American Mind* (1985), both review programming, the first by studies of selected critics, and the second in a unified essay. Adler's *Understanding Television: Essays on Television as a Social and Cultural Force* (1981) offers original essays on programs and programming. Mander's *Four Arguments for the Elimination of Television* (1978) is highly critical.

Chapter 12:   Network Programs

12.1 Distribution by Networking
Books on the process of programming are listed under chapter 11. Books on networks per se appear under chapter 8. Here we include titles on specific program types or formats — just an indication of a substantial body of literature.

12.2 Prime-Time Entertainment
As one might expect, there is a massive amount of literature on this topic, with at least one book for any popular series. An excellent guide to TV program types is Rose, *TV Genres* (1985). For series program reference, see Brooks & Marsh, *The Complete Directory to Prime Time Network TV Shows* (1985); for details of specific episodes see the four-volume Gianakos, *Television Drama Series Programming* (1978–1983), and Eisner and Krinsky, *Television Comedy Series: An Episode Guide to 153 TV Sitcoms in Syndication* (1984). Case studies of comedy programs are found in Adler, *All in the Family* (1979), which includes three scripts from the pioneering series of social satire, and in Feuer et al., *MTM 'Quality Television'* (1984), which dissects a number of successful programs from one production house. A content analysis of drama program portrayals is found in Greenberg, *Life on Television* (1980). For a directory to all the made-for-TV movies and miniseries see Marill, *Movies Made for Television* (1984). Eliot, *Televisions: One Season in American Television* (1983), provides a cross-section of the industry through programs of the 1981–1982 season. The potential for culture on cable is reviewed in detail in Beck, *Cultivating the Wasteland* (1983). Rose, *Television and the Performing Arts* (1986) details dance, classical music, opera, and theater on network broadcasts. See also titles under §11.1–11.3.

12.3 Non-Prime-Time Programs
Aside from the huge amount of fan literature on soap operas, several scholarly studies shed light on this enduring format. Stedman, under §3.5, is a history of serials in films and broadcasting; Cantor and Pingree's *The Soap Opera* (1983), discusses the development, content, audience, and impact of such programs; Cassata and Skill's *Life on Daytime Television: Tuning-In American Serial Drama* (1983), offers a collection of content analyses; Allen's *Speaking of Soap Operas* (1985), reviews the production and consumption of the genre; and Intintolli's *Taking Soaps Seriously: The World of Guiding Light* (1984), is a detailed examination of a long-running program. Fabe, *TV Game Shows* (1979), is dated but remains the best survey of that format. The longest-running daytime network talk show is informally detailed in Metz, *The Today Show* (1977).

12.4 Role of Network Sports
The first book on sports television programming was Johnson, *Super Spectator and the Electronic Lilliputians* (1971), based on a series of articles in *Sports Illustrated*. The early days of the most successful network sports coverage is related in Sugar, *"The Thrill of Victory:" The Inside Story of ABC Sports* (1978). Rader, *In Its Own Image: How Television Has Transformed Sports* (1984), is a critical commentary on what has been lost to

sports because of TV coverage. Powers, *Supertube: The Rise of Television Sports* (1984), is a history of three decades of development in sports coverage.

12.5 Network Children's Programs and Other Educational Programs

A massive study of how much programming was provided for young children is given in FCC, *Television Programming for Children* (1979), which found little to cheer about. The historical research for that study appears in expanded form in Turow, *Entertainment, Education and the Hard Sell: Three Decades of Network Children's Television* (1981). A more popular view is found in Fischer, *Kids' TV: The First 25 Years* (1983), and the definitive directory is Woolery's two-volume *Children's Television: The First Thirty-Five Years, 1946–1981* (1983–1984). Of the many guides for parents, Charren and Sandler, *Changing Channels: Living (Sensibly) with Television* (1983), is by far the best.

12.6 Network Television News

Here again, the literature is extensive and growing; some is descriptive, some scholarly, and much highly critical. The standard review of both network and station-level journalism has been the biennial Barrett, *The Alfred I. duPont-Columbia University Survey of Broadcast Journalism* (1969–1982), issued in connection with annual awards for quality programs. Matusow, *The Evening Stars* (1983), is a very readable narrative on development of the network news anchor. Gates, *Air Time: The Inside Story of CBS News* (1978), is the only book that tells the story of the leading news network. A content analysis of international news content in the 1972–1981 period appears in Larson, *Television's Window on the World* (1984). See also titles under §15.4.

12.7 Public Affairs

See all titles under §12.6, §15.4, and §15.5. The development of television documentary is described in Bluem, *Documentary in American Television* (1965), and, for the 1965–1975 period, in Hammond, *The Image Decade* (1981). Madsen, *60 Minutes: The Power and Politics of America's Most Popular TV News Show* (1984), traces the CBS program's development and current operations.

12.8 Radio Networks

See titles under §3.8 and §4.5.

Chapter 13:   Nonnetwork Programs

13.1–13.4 Syndication

There is no book-length material on syndication per se. See Eastman, under general chapter 11 note.

13.5 Local News

A scathing attack on the news programs of local stations is presented in Powers, *The Newscasters* (1977).

13.6 Cable Access Programming

Shaffer and Wheelwright, *Creating Original Programming for Cable TV* (1983), includes access programming.

13.7 Syndicated Religious Programming

Hadden and Swann, *Prime Time Preachers* (1981), suggests that conservative programs have nowhere near the audience they claim. Horsfield's *Religious Television: The American Experience* (1984) is the definitive study of the genre to date, with close analysis of the dramatic changes in religious programming over the past 15 years.

13.8 Other Types of TV Syndication

See under chapter 11.

13.9–13.10 Radio Syndication and Formats

See Eberly and Sklar, under §3.8. Every two years a detailed content analysis of the major public radio stations appears in CPB, *Public Radio Programming Content*.

Chapter 14:   Audience Measurement and Testing

The long-standing dearth of current books on this topic has finally been rectified with publication of a number of useful studies.

14.1–14.3, 14.7 The Ratings Business and Process

The single most important book to supplement this chapter is the definitive work by a long-time ratings researcher: Beville, *Audience Ratings: Radio, Television, Cable* (1985). He reviews the major ratings firms and their development, the rating methods used, problem areas, and likely directions. For terminology see NAB, *Standard Definitions of Broadcast Research Terms* (1973). A practical station workbook in how to use ratings is found in Fletcher, *Squeezing Profits Out of Ratings: A Manual for Radio Managers, Sales Managers and Programmers* (1985). Each of the main ratings firms will provide booklets on their methods on request.

14.4 Sampling

There is no book devoted to sampling in broadcasting. See Beville, under 14.1, and chapter 6 of Madow, under 14.7.

14.5–14.6 Audiences

Changes in television audience make-up and preferences can be traced through Steiner, *The People Look at Television* (1963); Bower, *Televi-*

sion and the Public (1973); and Bower, *The Changing Television Audience in America* (1985), which report, respectively, on parallel national surveys taken in 1960, 1970, and 1980. For radio and other audience data see the tables of section 6 in Sterling (1984), under 2.1. The definitive assessment of research on the television audience is Comstock's *Television and Human Behavior* (1978). Frank and Greenberg's two volumes of research based on a national survey are *The Public's Use of Television* (1980), which covers commercial stations and networks, and *Audiences for Public Television* (1982).

14.7 Use and Abuse of Ratings   Criticism of ratings company data and methods are reviewed in Beville, under 14.1. For the ratings investigation, see House CIFC, *Broadcast Ratings* (1963, 1964) and Madow, *Evaluation of Statistical Methods Used in Obtaining Broadcast Ratings* (1961).

14.8 Nonrating Research   Four recent works add greatly to our knowledge of research methods in mass communication. Dominick and Fletcher, *Broadcasting Research Methods* (1985), collects 20 original articles on all aspects of electronic media research, both scholarly and business-oriented. Broader instruction in methods across all media is found in Stempel and Westley, *Research Methods in Mass Communication* (1981), and in Wimmer and Dominick, *Mass Media Research: An Introduction* (1983). Fletcher, *Handbook of Radio-TV Broadcasting: Research Procedures in Audience, Program, and Revenues* (1981), is a guide for station managers.

Chapter 15:   Social Consequences

15.1 Approaches to Research   A dated but still useful overview is Klapper, *The Effects of Mass Communication* (1960), updated to some degree by the reviews that appear every three or four years or so in *Annual Review of Psychology*. An introductory survey to all this is found in Davis and Baran's *Mass Communication and Everyday Life: A Perspective on Theory and Effects* (1981). About every 18 months, another volume in the series edited by Dervin and Voigt, *Progress in Communication Sciences* (1979–1986), provides insightful essays on various aspects of media impact. Meyrowitz's *No Sense of Place: The Impact of Electronic Media on Social Behavior* (1985) is a very useful statement of recent work, covering all aspects of TV's role. A good introduction to communication theory is DeFleur and Ball-Rokeach, *Theories of Mass Communication* (1982); Blake and Haroldson, *A Taxonomy of Concepts in Communication* (1975), introduces the major terms and ideas. For current

views see McQuail, *Mass Communication Theory* (1983), and the graphic approach in McQuail and Windahl, *Communication Models for the Study of Mass Communications* (1981). Two books take a historical look at audience research developments: Lerner and Nelson's *Communication Research — A Half Century Appraisal* (1977), and Lowery and DeFleur's *Milestones in Mass Communication Research* (1983).

15.2 Methods of Studying Consequences   See titles under §14.8. Also useful in Alreck and Settle, *The Survey Research Handbook* (1985).

15.3 Consequences of Advertising   Any good survey of advertising can provide a current overview of research results. A recent critical survey is Shudson's *Advertising, The Uneasy Persuasion: Its Dubious Impact on American Society* (1984). For the impact of children's advertising see Adler, *The Effects of Television Advertising on Children* (1980).

15.4 News Impact   There is a huge and growing literature on all aspects of television news impact. The classic pseudo-event study is Boorstin, *The Image* (1964), and a useful agenda-setting study is McCombs and Shaw, *The Emergence of American Political Issues* (1977). Lesher's *Media Unbound: The Impact of Television Journalism on the Public* (1982) is based on the author's experience and interviews with news officials.

15.5 Consequences for Political Life   The best survey of work to 1975 is Kraus and Davis, *The Effects of Mass Communication on Political Behavior* (1976). Greenberg and Parker, *The Kennedy Assassination and the American Public* (1965), is a classic analysis of media in a national crisis. More recent crises are reviewed in Nimmo and Combs, *Nightly Horrors: Crisis Coverage in Television Network News* (1985). Lang and Lang, *Politics and Television Re-Viewed* (1984), collects insightful research reports from MacArthur's 1951 return through the Watergate events of the 1970s. The same authors' analysis of television impact during Watergate is *The Battle for Public Opinion: The President, the Press, and the Polls During Watergate* (1983), but see Lashner, *The Chilling Effect in TV News* (1984), for a detailed content analysis comparing print and television news coverage. The combination of Jamieson, *Packaging the Presidency: A History and Criticism of Presidential Campaign Advertising* (1984), and Tebbel and Watts, *The Press and the Presidency* (1985), which assesses noncampaign relationships, provides a full historical account. Diamond and Bates, *The Spot: The Rise of Political Advertising on Television* (1984), focuses on television's role. An example of the large amount of literature devoted to media in specific campaigns is Robinson and Sheehan's *Over the Wire and on TV: CBS and UPI in Campaign '80* (1983). Swerdlow, *Beyond Debate: A Paper on Televised Presidential Debates* (1984), summarizes what has been learned and how the process might be changed. The most comprehensive study of the struggle for television coverage of Congress is Garay, *Congressional Television: A Legislative History* (1984). Many works deal with the American experience in Vietnam, but three stand out for this study of media impact: Braestrup's *Big Story: How the American Press and Television Reported and Interpreted the Crisis of Tet 1968 in Vietnam and Washington* (1977) dissects the turning point in the war and American support for it; MacDonald's *Television and the Red Menace: The Video Road to Vietnam* (1985) assesses TV news coverage in the years before that war; and Hallin, *The "Uncensored War"* (1986) compares print and television coverage.

15.6 Entertainment
Two interesting studies of minorities and the media are MacDonald, *Blacks and White TV: Afro-Americans in Television since 1948* (1983), and Greenberg, *Mexican-Americans and the Mass Media* (1983). Marc's *Demographic Vistas: Television in American Culture* (1984) reviews the general impact of television entertainment programming. Winn's *The Plug-In Drug: Television, Children, and the Family* (1985) is sometimes overwrought, but suggests that parental control of "kidvid" is crucial. Scholarly research on children's use of television is reviewed by Liebert et al. , *The Early Window: The Effects of Television on Children and Youth* (1982).

15.7 Impact of Violence
The definitive study of how scholarly research can have an impact on policy is Rowland's *The Politics of TV Violence: Policy Uses of Communication Research* (1983), which focuses on the first Surgeon General's committee. That committee's work is found in Surgeon General, *Television and Growing Up* (1972). The second such committee reported its work in National Institute of Mental Health, *Television and Behavior: Ten Years of Scientific Progress and Implications for the Eighties* (1983).

Chapter 16:   Agencies of Control

A. General Background   Several books are of background value for chapters 16–18. For the history of early broadcast regulation see titles under §2.11. In addition, two 2-volume works are excellent for tracing broadcast policy development: Socolow, *The Law of Radio Broadcasting* (1939), and Warner, *Radio and Television Law* (1948) and *Radio and Television Rights* (1953). A chronological collection of the most important legal cases and other docu-

ments is given in Kahn, *Documents of American Broadcasting* (1984). Ferrall, *Yearbook of Broadcasting Articles* (1980), shows in a collection of law journal articles the increasing complexity of broadcast regulation from 1959 to 1978. Two more recent case books on broadcast and cable regulation that include extensive excerpts from FCC and court decisions as well as congressional actions are Ginsburg, *Regulation of Broadcasting* (1979), and Jones, *Cases and Materials on Electronic Mass Media* (1979). Even more recent, but terse, is Bensman, *Broadcast Regulation: Selected Cases and Decisions* (1985). An excellent primer to all the subjects discussed below is Krasnow et al., *The Politics of Broadcast Regulation* (1982). Two important economic critiques of regulatory trends are Noll et al., *Economic Aspects of Television Regulation* (1973), and Levin, *Fact and Fancy in Television Regulation* (1980), both of which are wide-ranging and show the changes brought about by initial deregulation. For some background on general media law see the following, all regularly updated: Gillmor and Barron, *Mass Communication Law: Cases and Comment* (1984); Zuckman and Gaynes, *Mass Communication Law in a Nutshell* (1983), an inexpensive paperback; and Carter, *The First Amendment and the Fourth Estate* (1985). For a more journalistic orientation see Pember, *Mass Media Law* (1984).

B. Staying Current   The documentation of administrative agencies, the courts, and Congress may seem forbidding reading to the uninitiated, but here are some tips on staying current. A dated but still useful introduction is Le Duc's "Broadcast Legal Documentation" (1973). The definitive but unofficial source for keeping up with electronic media regulation is Pike and Fischer, *Radio Regulation*, a loose-leaf reporter service that is updated weekly and carefully indexed. Instructions on its use appear in the "Current Service" volume. In 1986, the FCC announced that due to budget constraints, it would no longer publish all of its own decisions in either the *Federal Register* or *FCC Reports* — making the Pike and Fischer publication even more crucial for researchers. Decisions for the U.S. Court of Appeals for any circuit appear officially in the *Federal Reporter*, and Supreme Court decisions are reported officially in *United States Reports*. *Media Law Reporter* is another loose-leaf commercial service that rapidly reports matters of journalism law, including electronic media. The annual PLI, *Communications Law*, provides a compendium of cases, decisions, and analyses of media issues over the previous year. The *NAB Legal Guide to FCC Broadcast Regulations* (1984) is a single-volume desk reference aimed at station managers. The NAB's *Broadcasting and Government*, updated twice yearly, and *Broadcasting* magazine's "Where Things Stand," which appears at the beginning of each quarter, briefly summarize current status of major issues.

16.1 Constitutional Context

Good treatments of First Amendment issues are found in Barron & Dienes, *Handbook of Free Speech and Free Press* (1979), and in Tedford, *Freedom of Speech in the United States* (1985). Chamberlin and Brown, *The First Amendment Reconsidered: New Perspectives on the Meaning of Freedom of Speech and Press* (1982), discusses the impact of changing technology. In-depth analysis of early thinking is given in Chafee, *Government and Mass Communications* (1947).

16.2 Communications Act Basics

The official chronological compilation of all U.S. laws (legislation) on telecommunication from the 1910 act to date is in U.S. Congress, House of Representatives, *Radio Laws of the United States,* which is revised by the addition of material every several years. For an annotated printing of the act as it currently stands, see FCC, *The Communications Act of 1934, As Amended* (1983), which is issued in loose-leaf form with updated parts as needed, usually every couple of years. The compilation includes the 1962 Communications Satellite Act, which created Comsat; the 1967 Public Broadcasting Act (part of Title III of the 1934 act), and the 1984 cable act (new Title VI of the 1934 act). Of considerable historical interest is Dill, *Radio Law* (1938), written by the senator most responsible for the 1934 act.

16.3 Communications Act Issues

The multivolume hearing transcripts on the various rewrite attempts, though voluminous, are very useful for a broad view of issues on telecommunication and broadcasting. The process began with publication of House CIFC, *Options Papers* (1977), a very broad survey of possible courses of action for Congress and the FCC. This led to seemingly endless hearings through 1981, and a detailed record of changing industry and interest-group positions. For the major hearings see House CIFC, *The Communications Act of 1978: Hearings on H.R. 13015* (1979); House CIFC, *The Communications Act of 1979: Hearings on H.R. 3333* (1980), for the first and most comprehensive rewrite attempts; and Senate CCST, *Amendments to the Communications Act of 1934* (1980), which marked the Senate's first serious interest in the subject.

16.4 Telecommunication Policy

For a good overview of the players and process see "Telecommunications in the United States," a special issue of *Telecommunication Journal* (1980). Though NTIA does not issue formal annual reports, the IRAC issues brief summary reports twice a year that review federal spectrum use.

16.5 Copyright

This is a complicated and changing field, so these resources are for general background rather than current specifics. Johnston, *Copyright Handbook* (1982), provides an excellent survey of the copyright act and its provisions, as well as some of the early case law. Strong, *The Copyright Book: A Practical Guide* (1984), is just that.

16.6 Other Laws

For international treaties see §1.5. Press law is covered in the general texts discussed under Note A, above. A practical approach to current EEO rules is found in Aird, *A Broadcaster's Guide to Designing and Implementing an Effective EEO Program* (1980), and the NAB legal guide, under Note B.

16.7 Informal Controls

Cole & Oettinger, *Reluctant Regulators: The FCC and the Broadcast Audience* (1978), is a very insightful view of the policymaking process and the general Washington environment. Specific case studies of the process are given in Krasnow et al., *The Politics of Broadcast Regulation* (1982). Assessments of the most active years of citizen-group action are found in Grundfest, *Citizen Participation in Broadcast Licensing Before the FCC* (1976), and in Guimary, *Citizen's Groups and Broadcasting* (1975). One good study of the limitations of self-regulation is Brogan, *Spiked: The Short Life and Death of the National News Council* (1985). A case study of the interaction of government and industry self-regulation is discussed in Cowan's *See No Evil* (1979), on the "family viewing" case. Of the many books on media ethics and self-regulation, the best overview is Rivers et al., *Responsibility in Mass Communication* (1980).

Chapter 17:   FCC Administration of the Law

17.1 FCC Basics

A fascinating account of the development of the regulatory agency idea, told through the lives of four key individuals, is in McGraw's *Prophets of Regulation* (1984). Kittross, *Administration of American Telecommunications Policy* (1980), collects important documents on development and criticism of the FCC. A key document for study is the FCC *Annual Report.* FCC rules and regulations are annually revised in the CFR (*Code of Federal Regulations*), *Title 47: Telecommunication.* Of the four volumes, the first covers FCC organization and procedures, the second common carriers, the third broadcasting, and the fourth cable and emergency procedures. Most proposed and final rules of the FCC appear in the daily issues of the FR (*Federal Register*) and are gathered chronologically in FCC and FCC 2d (*Federal Communications Commission Reports*, 1st and 2nd series), now accumulating at the rate of four to six fat volumes each year. See also Pike and Fischer, under Chapter 16 Note B.

17.2 Deregulation   As yet, no book-length studies devoted to electronic media deregulation have appeared. See the FCC annual report for its own report of yearly actions.

17.3–17.5 Licensing, Operating, and Renewal The titles listed under Chapter 16 Note B include material on the licensing process, the NAB legal guide being most specific. The *CTIC Cable Books* (1982) offer a detailed guide to local cable television policy, especially franchising. Rice, *Cable TV Renewals and Refranchising* (1983), detail that sometimes-complicated process.

17.6 The Cable Policy Act   PLI, *The New Era in CATV: The Cable Franchise Policy and Communications Act of 1984* (1985), collects the act, legal commentary on the act, and the legislative report urging its passage into a kind of handbook. The definitive legal work on cable is the three-volume Ferris et al., *Cable Television Law* (1983), which is regularly updated.

17.7 Mass Media Ownership Regulation   See titles under §10.5. On the role of networks, see titles under §8.2.

17.8 Enforcement   See works on the FCC under §17.1, DeVol, *Mass Media and the Supreme Court* (1982), collects major decisions and commentary.

17.9 FCC Issues   The appointment of FCC and FTC commissioners over a 25-year period is the subject of Graham and Kramer, *Appointments to the Regulatory Agencies* (1976). A number of works on deregulation are appearing; one that comments specifically on telecommunication is Derthick and Quirk, *The Politics of Deregulation* (1985).

Chapter 18:   Freedom and Fairness

18.1 First Amendment Basics   See titles under §16.1.

18.2 Unprotected Speech   See titles under Chapter 16 Note A. For examples of the chilling effect see the titles on Watergate, under §15.5. Detailed analysis of changes in libel law is found in Sack, *Libel, Slander and Related Problems* (1980) and Smolla, *Suing the Press* (1986). The Westmoreland case is analyzed in Kowet, *A Matter of Honor: General William C. Westmoreland versus CBS* (1984).

For the question of reporter privilege see van Gerpen, *Privileged Communication and the Press* (1979).

18.3 Control over Programs   For material on children's programs, see §12.5.

18.4–18.5 Fairness   A reasoned argument by an author with a background in both law and network reporting is Rowan, *Broadcast Fairness: Doctrine, Practice, Prospects* (1984), which contends that the fairness doctrine has outlived whatever usefulness it had. A solid history of the development of the fairness doctrine is found in Simmons, *The Fairness Doctrine and the Media* (1978). Two earlier works argue strongly for a public right of access to media: Schmidt, *Freedom of the Press vs Public Access* (1976); and Barron, *Freedom of the Press for Whom?* (1973), which is the key work promoting access. Friendly, *The Good Guys, The Bad Guys, and the First Amendment* (1976), reads like a novel and tells the entire story of the Red Lion case.

18.6 Political Broadcasts   The NAB regularly revises booklets that guide station managers in how to best treat the problem of providing access to political candidates.

18.7 Issues in Content Regulation   For Mark Fowler's own assessment of his goals for the FCC see Fowler and Brenner, "A Marketplace Approach to Broadcast Regulation" (1982). Titles on access and the fairness doctrine are noted under §18.5.

Chapter 19:   Future Prospects

(Note: Book material on the future of electronic media is beginning to appear. What there is thus far tends to meld across subject lines covered in this chapter, so rather than dividing along chapter sub-sections, the reading suggestions here appear in a single essay.) The most well-known popularizer of futuristic thinking is Toffler whose *The Third Wave* (1980) touches on telecommunications among many other topics. Naisbett, *Megatrends: Ten New Directions Changing Our Lives* (1982) was a best-seller for months — the first "direction" discussed is communication. Haigh et al., *Communications in the Twenty-First Century* (1981), and Singh, *Telecommunications in the Year 2000: National and International Perspectives* (1983), both take broad perspectives which include but are not limited to media. Didsbury, *Communications and the Future* (1982), focuses on the applications of changing technology in all aspects of life. Taking a more specific focus on broadcasting are three British works assessing where radio and television may be heading in coming years: Hoggart and Morgan, *The Future of Broadcasting* (1982); Wenham, *The Third Age of Broadcasting* (1982); and Murphy, *The World Wired Up: Unscrambling the New Communications Puzzle* (1983). An increasing number of books try to sort out the many newer electronic media delivery systems, comparing and contrasting their development and prospects. Among them are three straightforward textbook treatments, regularly updated: Gross, *The New Television Technologies* (1986); Singleton, *Telecommunications in the Information Age* (1986); and Dizard, *The Coming Information Age: An Overview of Technology, Economics and Technology* (1985), the latter taking a more analytic approach. Two very insightful anthologies of the writing of several researchers and scholars going over some of the same ground — how changing technology is remaking the structure and impact of electronic media — are Compaine, *Understanding New Media: Trends and Issues in Electronic Distribution of Information* (1984), which assembles a number of good papers from a Harvard think tank, and Greenberger, *Electronic Publishing Plus: Media for a Technological Future* (1985), made up of scholarly papers for a conference. A tour de force of assessment, and the final book by a renowned scholar of communications, is Pool, *Technologies of Freedom* (1983), which raises many questions that are of concern to policymakers and media users alike.

Bibliographies

This brief selected list includes the most useful media bibliographies for research or further reading on American electronic media. Libraries should have most of them. Full citations are in the bibliography. In addition, readers should check library availability of electronic data bases for more efficient literature searches.

Blum, *Basic Books in the Mass Media* (1980). Standard overall annotated guide, divided by medium, and including foreign as well as domestic citations.

Brightbill, *Communications and the United States Congress: A Selectively Annotated Bibliography of Committee Hearings, 1870–1976* (1978). Unique, covering all matters on media and common-carrier communications.

Cassata and Skill, *Television: A Guide to the Literature* (1985). Provides an intelligent assessment of books on the topic, well divided by subject categories.

Comstock et al., *Television and Human Behavior* (1975). A three-volume bibliography of the research literature: a main list, 50 key studies with detailed annotations, and work in progress at the time, along with an integrative review.

Cooper, *Bibliography on Educational Broadcasting* (1942). Far more inclusive than the title suggests—it's the best annotated survey of pre-World War II literature on domestic broadcasting.

Friedman, *Sex Role Stereotyping in the Mass Media* (1977). The best annotated guide to this topic, with a great deal on television programming.

Gordon and Verna, *Mass Communication Effects and Processes: A Comprehensive Bibliography, 1950–1975* (1978). Not annotated but covers a lot of ground, providing some context for the electronic media studies.

Hill and Davis, *Religious Broadcasting: An Annotated Bibliography* (1984). Details the increasing descriptive and research writing on this topic.

Johnson, *TV Guide 25 Year Index* (1979). An index that covers the period 1953–1977.

"Mass Communication" (title varies), in *Annual Review of Psychology*. Appears every several years with a review article and appended list of research studies for the period covered. See Vol. 13 (1962): 251–184, for writings up to 1960; Vol. 19 (1968); 351–386, for research published in 1961–1966; Vol. 22 (1971): 309–336, for the 1967–1970 period; Vol. 28 (1977): 141–173, for 1970–1976 research; and Vol. 32 (1981): 307–356, covering 1976–1979 work.

McCoy, *Freedom of the Press* (1968 and 1979). Wide-ranging, with excellent annotations covering two centuries.

Matlon, *Index to Journals in Communication Studies Through 1979* (1980). Includes chronological tables of contents and subject-author indexes for 15 journals, including those of the Speech Communication Association, *Journalism Quarterly*, and *Journal of Broadcasting*. The latter issued its own 25-year index in 1982.

Meringhoff, *Children and Advertising: An Annotated Bibliography* (1980). One of the more complete guides to the topic.

NAB, *Broadcasting Bibliography* (1984). An invaluable booklet of subject-divided listings, plus current periodicals listing.

Performing Arts Books: 1876–1981 (1981). A massive card catalog that also has an index of serial publications.

Shearer and Huxford, *Communications and Society: A Bibliography on Communications Technologies and Their Social Impact* (1983). Emphasizes various kinds of impact of the electronic media.

Shiers and Shiers, *Bibliography of the History of Electronics* (1972). Offers detailed annotations on the history of telegraph, telephone, radio, television, and related services.

Signorielli et al., *Role Portrayal and Stereotyping on Television* (1985). Covers studies on women, minorities, aging, sexual behavior, health, and handicaps.

Smith, *U.S. Television Network News: A Guide to Sources in English* (1984). The most inclusive guide to the topic.

Broadcast-Related Periodicals

The following brief list includes the more important and/or useful electronic media-related periodicals, most of which should be in any good library. Given the rate of change in this field, these are the best sources for current developments.

Advertising Age (1929, weekly). The main trade paper for the industry, with details of new accounts and agency doings and periodic statistical summaries.

Broadcasting (1931, weekly). The single most important trade paper for the business; although it usually takes a strong pro-industry stance, it is indispensable for understanding current events, especially those concerning management and relations with government. *Broadcasting Yearbook* (1935) is a directory of stations, systems, and support industries.

CableVision (1975, biweekly). Provides the best coverage of all aspects of cable.

Channels of Communications (1981, bimonthly). Offers criticism and analysis on all electronic media including the annual *Field Guide* summary of media status.

Columbia Journalism Review (1962, bimonthly). Specializes in critiques of print and electronic journalism.

Critical Studies in Mass Communications (1984, quarterly). Focuses on content studies and criticism across all media.

Electronic Media (1981, weekly). Colorful tabloid on U.S. and overseas television, radio, and cable trends.

Federal Communications Law Journal (1946, triannual). Specializes in detailed legal analysis of current concerns in regulation of electronic media by the FCC.

InterMedia (1970, bimonthly). Reviews worldwide communication trends and issues in brief news pieces and longer essays, concentrating on Western Europe.

Journal of the SMPTE (1916, monthly). Technical publication of the Society of Motion Picture and Television Engineers with articles on TV development and systems.

Journalism Quarterly (1924, quarterly). Made up of academic research on print and broadcast media, with excellent book-review sections.

Journal of Broadcasting and Electronic Media (1956, quarterly). Provides scholarly research on all electronic media.

Journal of Communication (1951, quarterly). Has focused since 1974 on mass communication with research, opinion, and reviews.

Media Law Reporter (1974, loose-leaf). Texts of recent court decisions, stressing journalism.

Pike and Fischer, *Radio Regulation* (1948, loose-leaf). Main source for FCC rules, regulations, reports, and related court cases.

Public Opinion Quarterly (1937, quarterly). A respected source of research on polls, media, opinion measurement, etc.

Telecommunications Policy (1976, quarterly). Offers scholarly work on media and broader telecommunication concerns, emphasizing United States and foreign policy development.

Television Digest (1945, weekly). Industry and regulatory trends in video media plus material on consumer electronics.

Television Factbook (1945). Has in recent years become a massive, two-volume annual directory of broadcast television, cable, and related services.

Television News Index and Abstracts (1972, monthly). Lists the exact content of network evening newscasts, indexed by topic with an annual index.

Television/Radio Age (1953, biweekly). The trade journal stressing advertising, with in-depth special articles on news, FCC affairs, foreign developments, etc. Once a month includes *Cable Age*.

Topicator (1965, monthly). Indexes broadcast and advertising periodicals with an annual index.

TV Guide (1953, weekly). The standard guide to programs, with many excellent articles and an annual Fall Preview issue.

Variety (1905, weekly). The major trade paper for show business: stage, screen, music, television, and foreign developments.

Bibliography

The following lists both textual citations and the works annotated by Sterling in the guide to further reading.

ABC *Nightline* (1984), December 21.

Abel, John A., et al. 1970. "Station License Revocations and Denials of Renewal 1934–1969," *Journal of Broadcasting* 14 (Fall): 411–421.

Abramson, Albert, 1955. *Electronic Motion Pictures: A History of the Television Camera.* U. of California Press, Berkeley.

———. 1955, 1973. "A Short History of Television Recording," *Journal of the SMPTE* 64 (February): 72–76; and 82 (March): 188–195.

AD (Appellate Division, New York Supreme Court). 1963. *John H. Faulk* v. *AWARE, Inc., et al.* 19 AD 2d 464.

Adams, William, & Schreibman, Fay. 1978. *Television Network News: Issues in Content Research.* George Washington U., Washington, DC.

Adler, Richard P., ed. 1979. *All in the Family: A Critical Appraisal.* Praeger, New York.

———. 1980. *The Effects of Television Advertising on Children: Review and Recommendations.* Lexington Books, Lexington, MA.

———. 1981. *Understanding Television: Essays on Television as a Social and Cultural Force.* Praeger, New York.

Advertising Age Yearbook. Annual. Chicago: Crain.

Agostino, Don. 1980. "New Technologies: Problem or Solution," *Journal of Communication* 30 (Summer): 198–206.

———, and Eastman, Susan. 1985. "Local Originated Cable Programming," in Eastman et al.

Aird, Enola. 1980. *A Broadcaster's Guide to Designing and Implementing an Effective EEO Program.* National Association of Broadcasting, Washington, DC.

Aitken, Hugh G. 1976. *Syntony and Spark: The Origins of Radio.* Wiley, New York.

———. 1985. *The Continuous Wave: Technology and American Radio, 1900–1932.* Princeton U. Press, Princeton, NJ.

Alisky, Marvin. 1981. *Latin American Media: Guidance and Censorship.* Iowa State U. Press, Ames.

Allen, Robert C. 1985. *Speaking of Soap Operas.* U. of North Carolina Press, Chapel Hill.

Alper, Joel, and Pelton, Joseph. 1984. *The Intelsat Global Satellite System.* American Institute of Astronautics and Aeronautics, New York.

Alreck, Pamela, and Settle, Robert. 1985. *The Survey Research Handbook.* Dow Jones-Irwin, Homewood, IL.

Alten, Stanley R. 1986. *Audio in Media.* 2d ed. Wadsworth, Belmont, CA.

American Radio Relay League. Annual. *The Radio Amateur's Handbook.* A.R.R.L., Newington, CT.

American University School of Communications. Dec. 1979. "Broadcast News Doctors: The Patient Is Buying the Cure." AUSC, Washington, DC.

Anderson, Kent. 1978. *Television Fraud: The History and Implications of the Quiz Show Scandals.* Greenwood Press, Westport, CT.

Annual Review of Psychology. Annual. Annual Reviews, Inc., Palo Alto, CA.

Antébi, Elizabeth. 1983. *The Electronic Epoch.* Van Nostrand Reinhold, New York.

Archer, Gleason, L. 1938. *History of Radio to 1926.* American Historical Society, New York.

———. 1939. *Big Business and Radio.* American Historical Company, New York.

Arendt, Hannah. 1964. "Society and Culture," in Jacobs, Norman. 1964. *Culture for the Millions? Mass Media in*

Modern Society. Beacon Press, Boston: 43–52.

Arlen, Michael J. 1969. *Living-Room War*. Viking, New York.

ARMS (All-Radio Methodological Study). 1966. *ARMS: What It Shows, How It Has Changed Radio Measurement*. National Association of Broadcasters, Washington, DC.

Arnall, Gail. 1984. *Instructional Television Fixed Service*. Corporation for Public Broadcasting, Washington, DC.

Aske Research Ltd. 1980. *The Effort of Switching Channels: Report Prepared for the Independent Broadcasting Authority*. Aske Research Ltd., London.

Astrachan, Anthony. 1975. "Life Can Be Beautiful/Relevant," *New York Times Magazine* (March 23): 12.

Augarten, Stan. 1984. *Bit By Bit: An Illustrated History of Computers*. Ticknor & Fields, New York.

Avery, Robert K., & Pepper, Robert. 1979. *The Politics of Interconnection: A History of Public Television at the National Level*. National Association of Educational Broadcasters, Washington, DC.

Avery, Robert K., et al. 1980. *Research Index for NAEB Journals, 1957–1979*. National Association of Educational Broadcasters, Washington, DC.

Baer, Walter S. 1973. *Cable Television: A Handbook for Decision Making*. Rand Corporation, Santa Monica, CA.

Bagdikian, Ben H. 1971. *The Information Machines: Their Impact on Men and Media*. Harper & Row, New York.

———. 1973. "Out of the Can and into the Bank," *New York Times Magazine* (Oct 21): 31.

———. 1983. *The Media Monopoly*. Beacon Press, Boston.

Baker, W. J. 1971. *A History of the Marconi Company*. St. Martin's Press, New York.

Baldwin, Thomas F., & Lewis, Colby. 1972. "Violence in Television: The Industry Looks at Itself," in Comstock, George, & Rubinstein, E., eds., *Television and Social Behavior: Media Content and Control*. Vol. 1. Government Printing Office, Washington, DC: 290–365.

Baldwin, Thomas F., and McVoy, D. Stevens. 1983. *Cable Communications*. Prentice-Hall, Englewood Cliffs, NJ.

Balio, Tino. 1985. *The American Film Industry*. 2d ed. U. of Wisconsin Press, Madison.

Bandura, A. D., et al. 1963. "Imitation of Film-Mediated Aggressive Models," *Journal of Abnormal and Social Psychology* 66: 3–11.

Banning, William P. 1946. *Commercial Broadcasting Pioneer: The WEAF Experiment, 1922–1926*. Harvard U. Press, Cambridge, MA.

Barnard, Charles N. 1978. "An Oriental Mystery," *TV Guide* (Jan. 28): 2.

Barnouw, Erik. 1966. *A Tower in Babel: A History of Broadcasting in the United States to 1933*. Oxford U. Press, New York.

———. 1968. *The Golden Web: A History of Broadcasting in the United States, 1933–1953*. Oxford U. Press, New York.

———. 1970. *The Image Empire: A History of Broadcasting in the United States since 1953*. Oxford U. Press, New York.

———. 1975. *Tube of Plenty: The Development of American Television*. Oxford U. Press, New York.

———. 1978. *The Sponsor: Notes on a Modern Potentate*. Oxford U. Press, New York.

Barrett, Marvin, ed. 1969–1982. *The Alfred I. duPont-Columbia University Survey of Broadcast Journalism* (title varies). 8 vols. Publisher has varied: Grosset and Dunlap, Crowell, and Everest House, all of New York.

Barron, Jerome A. 1973. *Freedom of the Press for Whom? The Right of Access to Mass Media*. Indiana U. Press, Bloomington.

———, & Dienes, C. Thomas. 1979. *Handbook of Free Speech and Free Press*. Little, Brown, Boston.

Barthel, Joan. 1975. "Boston Mothers Against Kidvid," *New York Times Magazine* (Jan. 5): 15.

Baudino, Joseph E., & Kittross, John M. 1977. "Broadcasting's Oldest Station: An Examination of Four Claimants," *Journal of Broadcasting* 21 (Winter): 61–83.

BBC (British Broadcasting Corporation). Annual, from 1928. *BBC Handbook* (title varies). BBC, London.

———, International Broadcasting Audience Research. 1983. "World Radio and Television Receivers" (June). BBC, London.

BBDO (Batten, Barton, Durstine & Osborn). Annual. *BBDO Audience Coverage and Cost Guide*. BBDO, New York.

Beck, A. H. 1967. *Words and Waves: An Introduction to Electrical Communication*. McGraw-Hill, New York.

Beck, Kirsten. 1983. *Cultivating the Wasteland: Can Cable Put the Vision Back in TV?* American Council for the Arts, New York.

Bedell, Sally. 1981. *Up the Tube: Prime-Time TV and the Silverman Years*. Viking, New York.

Bendiner, Robert. 1957. "FCC: Who Will Regulate the Regulators?" *The Reporter* (Sept.): 26.

Benjamin, Burton. 1984. *The CBS Benjamin Report*. The Media Institute, Washington, DC.

Bennett, Robert M. 1981. "The Television Station's Future Identity." Keynote Address to National Association of Television Program Executives Annual Convention, March 16, New York.

Bensman, Marvin R. 1985. *Broadcast Regulation: Selected Cases and Decisions*. U. Press of America, Lanham, MD.

Bergendorff, Fred, et. al., 1983. *Broadcast Advertising and Promotion*. Hastings House, New York.

Bergreen, Laurence. 1979. "What's Edward VII Doing in 'The Incredible Hulk's' Time Slot?" *TV Guide* (Feb. 24): 25.

————. 1980. *Look Now, Pay Later: The Rise of Network Broadcasting*. Doubleday, New York.

Berrigan, Frances J., ed. 1977. *Access: Some Western Models of Community Media*. UNESCO, Paris.

Besen, S.M. 1973. "The Value of Television Time and Prospects for New Stations." Rand Corporation, Santa Monica, CA.

————, et al. 1984. *Misregulating Television: Network Dominance and the FCC*. U. of Chicago Press, Chicago.

————, and Johnson, Leland. 1984. *An Assessment of the Federal Communication Commission's Group Ownership Rules*. Rand Corporation, Santa Monica, CA.

Beville, H. M., Jr. 1981. "Understanding Broadcast Ratings," 3rd ed. Broadcast Ratings Council, New York.

————. 1985. *Audience Ratings: Radio, Television, Cable*. Lawrence Erlbaum Associates, Hillsdale, NJ.

Biel, Jacqueline. 1985. *Low Power Television: Development and Current Status of the LPTV Industry*. National Association of Broadcasters, Washington, DC.

Bitting, Robert C., Jr. 1965. "Creating an Industry," *Journal of the SMPTE* (November): 1015–1023.

Blake, Reed H., & Haroldson, Edwin O. 1975. *A Taxonomy of Concepts in Communication*. Hastings House, New York.

Blakely, Robert J. 1979. *To Serve the Public Interest: Educational Broadcasting in the United States*. Syracuse U. Press, Syracuse, NY.

Blank, David M. 1977. "The Gerbner Violence Profile," *Journal of Broadcasting*. 21 (Summer): 273–279.

Bluem, A. William. 1965. *Documentary in American Television; Form, Function, Method*. Hastings House, New York.

Blum, Eleanor. 1980. *Basic Books in the Mass Media: An Annotated, Selected Booklist*. 2d ed. U. of Illinois Press, Urbana.

Blumler, Jay G., & Katz, Elihu. 1975. *The Uses of Mass Communications: Current Prospectives on Gratification Research*. Sage Publications, Beverly Hills, CA.

Board for International Broadcasting. Annual. *Annual Report*. Government Printing Office, Washington, DC.

Boorstin, Daniel J. 1964. *The Image: A Guide to Pseudo-Events in America*. Harper & Row, New York.

————. 1978. "The Significance of Broadcasting in Human History," in Hoso-Bunka Foundation. *Symposium on the Cultural Role of Broadcasting, October 3–5, 1978*. Summary Report. Hoso-Bunka Foundation, Tokyo: 9–23.

Booz, Allen & Hamilton, Inc. 1978. *Feasibility of a New Local Television Audience Measurement Service: Phase I Final Report*. Television Bureau of Advertising, New York.

Botein, Michael, & Rice, David M., eds. 1981. *Network Television and the Public Interest: A Preliminary Inquiry*. Lexington Books, Lexington, MA.

Bower, Robert T. 1973. *Television and the Public*. Holt, Rinehart & Winston, New York.

————. 1985. *The Changing Television Audience in America*. Columbia U. Press, New York.

Bowles, Jay. 1984 Telephone Interview, Blackburn & Co., Atlanta, GA. Nov. 9.

Boyd, Douglas, ed. 1982. *Broadcasting in the Arab World*. Temple University Press, Philadelphia.

Braestrup, Peter. 1977. *Big Story: How the American Press and Television Reported and Interpreted the Crisis of Tet 1968 in Vietnam and Washington*. 2 vols. Westview Press, Boulder, CO.

Bretz, Rudy. 1970. *A Taxonomy of Communication Media*. Educational Technology, Englewood Cliffs, NJ.

————. 1983. *Media For Interactive Communication*. White Plains, NY: Knowledge Industry Publications.

Briggs, Asa A. 1965. *The Golden Age of Wireless: The History of Broadcasting in the United Kingdom*, Vol. 2. Oxford U. Press, London.

————. 1985. *The BBC: The First Fifty Years*. Oxford U. Press, London.

Bright, Arthur A., Jr. 1949. *The Electric-Lamp Industry: Technological Change and Economic Development from 1800 to 1947*. Macmillan, New York.

Brightbill, George D. 1978. *Communications and the United States Congress: A Selectively Annotated Bibliography of Committee Hearings, 1870–1976*. Broadcast Education Association, Washington, DC.

Brindze, Ruth. 1937. *Not to Be Broadcast: The Truth about Radio*. Vanguard, New York.

Broadcasting. (Note: the only articles listed here are lengthy special reports. Other specific article citations are found only in the text.)

1963. "A World Listened and Watched." Special Report. (Dec. 2): 36.

1970. "A Play-by-Play Retrospective." Special Report. (Nov. 2): 74.

1977. "CBS: The First Five Decades." (Sep. 19): 45.

1979. "Minorities in Broadcasting: The Exception Is No Longer the Rule." Special Report. (Oct. 15): 27.

1979. "Children's Programming." Special Report. (Oct. 29): 39.

1980. "The Top 100 Companies in Electronic Communications." (Jan. 7): 35.

1980. "The Washington Lawyer: Power Behind the Powers That Be." Special Report. (Jun. 16): 32.

1981. "Faint Victory." Editorial. (Jan. 12): 106.

1983. "The Congressman and the Achilles Heel [Rep. Timothy Wirth]." Special Report. (Oct. 17): 43.

1984 "State of the Art: Technology." (Oct. 8): 54.

1984 "The New Order Passeth." (Dec. 10): 43.

1984 "Perspectives 1985." (Dec. 31): 72.

1985. "Broadcasting: Top 50 Advertising Agencies." Special Report. (Feb. 4): 40.

Broadcasting Publications, Inc., Annual. *Broadcasting/Cablecasting Yearbook*. Broadcasting Publications, Washington, DC.

———. 1981. *The First 50 Years of Broadcasting*. Broadcasting Publications, Washington, DC.

Brock, Gerald W. 1981. *The Telecommunications Industry: The Dynamics of Market Structure*. Harvard U. Press, Cambridge, MA.

Broder, Mitch. 1976. "The Late Show Clocks 25 Years," *New York Times* (Feb. 22): D-29.

Brogan, Patrick. 1985. *Spiked: The Short Life and Death of the National News Council*. Twentieth Century Fund, New York.

Brooks, John. 1976. *Telephone: The First Hundred Years*. Harper & Row, New York.

Brooks, Tim, & Marsh, Earle. 1985. *The Complete Directory to Prime Time Network TV Shows: 1946–Present*. 3rd ed. Ballantine Books, New York.

Brown, James A. 1980. "Selling Air Time for Controversy: NAB Self-Regulation and Father Coughlin," *Journal of Broadcasting* 24 (Spring): 199–224.

Brown, Les. 1971. *Televi$ion: The Business Behind the Box*. Harcourt Brace Jovanovich, New York.

———. 1977. *New York Times Encyclopedia of Television*. Times Books, New York.

———. 1982. *Les Brown's Encyclopedia of Television*. New York Zeotrope, New York.

Browne, Donald. 1982. *International Radio Broadcasting: The Limits of the Limitless Medium*. Praeger, New York.

Buckley, Tom. 1978. "Popularity of '60 Minutes' Based on Wide-Ranging Reports," *New York Times* (Dec. 17): 99.

———. 1979. "Game Shows—TV's Glittering Gold Mine," *New York Times Magazine* (Nov. 18): 49.

Busch, H. Ted., & Landeck, Terry. 1981. *The Making of a Television Commercial*. Macmillan, New York.

Cable TV Financial Databook. 1984. Paul Kagan Associates Inc., Carmel, CA.

Campbell, Robert. 1976. *The Golden Years of Broadcasting: A Celebration of the First 50 Years of Radio and Television on NBC*. Scribners, New York.

Cantor, Muriel G. 1980. *Prime-Time Television: Content and*

Control. Sage Publications, Beverly Hills, CA.

———, and Pingree, Susanne. 1983. *The Soap Opera*. Sage Publications, Beverly Hills, CA.

Carey, William L. 1967. *Politics and the Regulatory Agencies*. McGraw-Hill, New York.

CCET (Carnegie Commission on Educational Television). 1967. *Public Television: A Program for Action*. Harper & Row, New York.

CCFPB (Carnegie Commission on the Future of Public Broadcasting). 1979. *A Public Trust*. Bantam Books, New York.

Carroll, Raymond L. 1980. "The 1948 Truman Campaign: The Threshold of the Modern Era," *Journal of Broadcasting* 24 (Spring): 173–188.

Carter, T. Barton, et al. 1985. *The First Amendment and the Fourth Estate*. 3rd ed. Foundation Press, Mineola, NY

Cassata, Mary, and Skill, Thomas, 1983. *Life on Daytime Television: Tuning-In American Serial Drama*. Ablex, Norwood, NJ.

———. 1985. *Television: A Guide to the Literature*. Oryx Press, Phoenix, AZ.

Cater, Douglass, & Nyhan, Michael. 1976. *The Future of Public Broadcasting*. Praeger, New York.

Chamberlin, Bill, and Brown, Charlene J. 1982. *The First Amendment Reconsidered: New Perspectives on the Meaning of Freedom of Speech and Press*. Longman, New York.

Charren, Peggy, and Sandler, Martin W. 1983. *Changing Channels: Living (Sensibly) with Television*. Addison-Wesley, Reading, MA.

CFR (*Code of Federal Regulations*). Annual. 47 *CFR* 0.1 ff. *Telecommunication*. 4 vols. Government Printing Office, Washington, DC.

Chafee, Zechariah, Jr. 1947. *Government and Mass Communications*. U. of Chicago Press, Chicago.

Chagall, David. 1977. "The Child Probers," *TV Guide* (Oct. 8): 8.

———. 1978. "Can You Believe the Ratings?" *TV Guide* (June 24): 2; (July 1): 20.

Channels, Editors of. Annual. *Field Guide to the Electronic Media* (title varies). New York.

Christensen, Mark, and Smith, Cameron. 1984. *The Sweeps: Behind the Scenes in Network TV*. Morrow, New York.

Chu, Goodwin, & Schramm, Wilbur. 1967. *Learning from Television: What the Research Says*. National Association of Educational Broadcasters, Washington, DC.

Clancy, Thomas H. 1979. "Nine and a Half Theses on Religious Broadcasting," *America* (Apr. 7): 271—275.

Clift, Charles, III, et al. 1980. "Forfeitures and the Federal Communications Commission: An Update," *Journal of Broadcasting* 24 (Summer): 301–310.

Coates, Vary T., & Finn, Bernard. 1979. *A Retrospective Technology Assessment: Submarine Telegraphy—The Transatlantic Cable of 1866*. San Francisco Press, San Francisco.

Codding, George, and Rutkowski, Anthony. 1982. *The International Telecommunication Union in a Changing World*. Artech House, Dedham, MA.

Codel, Martin, ed. 1930. *Radio and Its Future*. Harper, New York.

Coen, Robert J. 1984. "U.S. Advertising Volume," *Advertising Age* (May 14): 63.

Cogley, John. 1956. *Report on Blacklisting II: Radio-Television*. Fund for the Republic, New York.

Cole, Barry, & Oettinger, Mal. 1978. *Reluctant Regulators: The FCC and the Broadcast Audience*. Addison-Wesley, Reading, MA.

Compaine, Benjamin M., et al. 1982. *Who Owns the Media? Concentration of Ownership in the Mass Communications Industry*. 2d ed. Knowledge Industry Publications, White Plains, NY.

———, ed. 1984. *Understanding New Media: Trends and Issues in Electronic Distribution of Information*. Ballinger, Cambridge, MA.

Comstock, George, et al. 1975. *Television and Human Behavior*. 3 vols. Rand Corporation, Santa Monica, CA.

———. 1978. *Television and Human Behavior*. Columbia U. Press, New York.

Coolidge, Calvin. 1926. *Message to Congress*, 68 *Congressional Record* 32.

Cooper, Isabella. 1942. *Bibliography on Educational Broadcasting*, U. of Chicago Press, Chicago.

CPB (Corporation for Public Broadcasting).
   Annual. *Annual Report*.
   Annual. *Summary Statistical Report of CPB Qualified Public Radio Stations*. (Title varies).
   Annual. *Summary Statistical Report of Public Television Licensees*. (Title varies).
   Biennial. *Public Radio Programming Content by Category*.
   Biennial. *Public Television Programming Content by Category*.
   1981. *Status Report on Public Broadcasting*. (earlier editions: 1973, and 1977).

Counterattack. 1950. *Red Channels: The Report of Communists in Radio and Television*. Counterattack, New York.

Cowan, Geoffrey. 1979. *See No Evil: The Backstage Battle Over Sex and Violence on Television*. Simon & Schuster, New York.

Crane, Rhonda J. 1979. *The Politics of International Standards: France and the Color TV War*. Ablex Publishing, Norwood, NJ.

Crutchfield, E. B. 1985. *NAB Engineering Handbook*. 7th ed. National Association of Broadcasters, Washington, DC.

Csida, Joseph, & Csida, June Bundy. 1978. *American Entertainment: A Unique History of Popular Show Business*. Billboard Books, New York.

C-SPAN. 1985. "Something Personal," (Apr. 1): 1.

CTIC Cable Books. 1982. *The Community Medium*, and *A Guide For Local Policy*. Cable Television Information Center, Arlington, VA, (two vols.).

Culbert, David H. 1976. *News for Everyman: Radio and Foreign Affairs in Thirties America*. Greenwood Press, Westport, CT.

Czitrom, Daniel. 1982. *Media and the American Mind from Morse to McLuhan*. U. of North Carolina Press, Chapel Hill.

Danielian, N. R. 1939. *AT&T: The Story of Industrial Conquest*. Vanguard, New York.

Davidowitz, Paul. 1972. *Communication*. Holt, Rinehart, & Winston, New York.

Davis, Dennis and Baran, Stanley. 1981. *Mass Communication and Everyday Life: A Perspective on Theory and Effects*. Wadsworth, Belmont, CA.

Davis, Henry B. O. 1981–1985. *Electrical and Electronic Technologies: A Chronology of Events and Inventors*. 3 vols. Scarecrow Press, Metuchen, NJ.

Davis, Stephen. 1927. *The Law of Radio*. McGraw-Hill, New York.

DeFleur, Melvin, and Ball-Rokeach, Sandra. 1982. *Theories of Mass Communication*. 4th ed. Longman, New York.

de Forest, Lee. 1950. *Father of Radio*. Wilcox & Follett, Chicago.

DeLozier, M. Wayne. 1976. *The Marketing Communications Process*. McGraw-Hill, New York.

Department of Commerce, 1922. "Minutes of Open Meeting of Department of Commerce on Radio Telephony." Mimeo.

———. 1924. *Recommendations for Regulation of Radio*. Government Printing Office, Washington, DC.

Derthick, Martha, and Quirk, Paul J. 1985. *The Politics of Deregulation*. Brookings Institution, Washington, DC.

Dervin, Brenda, and Voigt, Melvin., eds. 1979–1986. *Progress in Communication Sciences*. 7 vols. Ablex, Norwood, NJ.

De Soto, Clinton. 1936. *Two Hundred Meters and Down: The Story of Amateur Radio*. A.R.R.L., West Hartford, CT.

Dessart, George. 1978. *Television in the Real World: A Case Study in Broadcast Management*. Hastings House, New York.

DeVol, Kenneth, ed. 1982. *Mass Media and the Supreme Court: The Legacy of the Warren Years*. 3rd ed. Hastings House, New York.

Diamond, Edwin, and Bates, Stephen. 1984. *The Spot: The Rise of Political Advertising on Television.* MIT Press, Cambridge, MA.

Didsbury, Howard F. Jr., ed. 1982. *Communications and the Future: Prospects, Promises, and Problems.* World Future Society, Bethesda, MD.

Dill, Clarence C. 1938. *Radio Law: Practice and Procedure.* National Law Book Co., Washington, D.C.

Dizard, Wilson P. 1966. *Television: A World View.* Syracuse U. Press, Syracuse, NY.

_____. 1985. *The Coming Information Age: An Overview of Technology, Economics, and Politics.* 2d ed. Longman, NY.

Dominick, Joseph R. and Fletcher, James E. 1985. *Broadcasting Research Methods.* Allyn & Bacon, Boston.

Drake-Chenault Enterprises Inc. 1978. "History of Rock and Roll." Drake-Chenault, Canoga Park, CA.

Dreher, Carl. 1977. *Sarnoff: An American Success.* Quadrangle/New York Times Book Co., New York.

Duncan, James. Semiannual. *American Radio.* Duncan Media Enterprises, Kalamazoo, MI.

Dunlap, Orrin E. Jr. 1929. *Advertising By Radio.* Ronald Press, New York.

_____. 1944. *Radio's 100 Men of Science* Harper, New York.

Dunning, John. 1976. *Tune in Yesterday: The Ultimate Encyclopedia of Old-Time Radio, 1925–1976.* Prentice-Hall, Englewood Cliffs, NJ.

Eastman, Susan Tyler, and Klein, Robert. 1982. *Strategies for Broadcast and Cable Promotion.* Wadsworth, Belmont, CA.

Eastman, Susan Tyler, et al. 1985. *Broadcast/Cable Programming: Strategies and Practices,* 2d ed. Wadsworth, Belmont, CA.

Eberly, Philip K. 1982. *Music in the Air: America's Changing Tastes in Popular Music, 1920–1980.* Hastings House, New York.

EIA (Electronic Industries Association). Annual. *Consumer Electronics.* EIA, Washington, DC.

Eisner, Joel, and Krinsky, David. 1984. *Television Comedy Series: An Episode Guide to 153 TV Sitcoms in Syndication.* McFarland & Co., Jefferson, NC.

Eliot, Marc. 1983. *Televisions: One Season in American Television.* St. Martin's Press, New York.

Ellis, Elmo, 1960. *Radio Station Management.* 2d ed. Harper, New York.

Emerson, Thomas I. 1972. "Communication and Freedom of Expession," *Scientific American* (September) 163–172.

Emery, Edwin, and Emery, Michael. 1984, *The Press and America: An Interpretive History of the Mass Media.* 5th ed. Prentice-Hall, Englewood Cliffs, NJ.

Emery, Walter B. 1969. *National and International Systems of Broadcasting: Their History, Operation and Control.* Michigan State U. Press, East Lansing.

Ennes, Harold E. 1953. *Principles and Practices of Telecasting Operations.* Howard W. Sams, Indianapolis.

Epstein, Edward J. 1973a. *News From Nowhere: Television and the News.* Random House, New York.

_____. 1973b. "What Happened vs. What We Saw," *TV Guide* (Sep. 29, Oct. 6, Oct. 13): 7, 20, 19.

Ettema, James S., and Whitney, D. Charles, eds. 1982. *Individuals in Mass Media Organizations: Creativity and Constraint.* Sage Publications, Beverly Hills, CA.

Eugster, Ernest. 1983. *Television Programming Across National Boundaries: The EBU and OIRT Experience.* Artech House, Dedham, MA.

Everson, George. 1949. *The Story of Television: The Life of Philo T. Farnsworth.* Norton, New York.

F (*Federal Reporter,* 2d Series)
1926 *U.S.* v. *Zenith Radio Corp.,* 12 F 2d 614.
1929 *U.S.* v. *American Bond & Mortgage,* 31 F 2d 448.
1931 *KFKB* v. *FRC,* 47 F 2d 670.
1932 *Trinity Methodist Church, South* v. *FRC,* 62 F 2d 850.
1946 *WOKO* v. *FCC,* 153 F 2d 623.
1948 *Simmons* v. *FCC,* 169 F 2d 670.
1962 *Suburban Broadcasters* v. *FCC,* 302 F 2d 191.
1966 *Office of Communication* v. *FCC,* 359 F 2d 994.
1968 *Banzhaf* v. *FCC,* 405 F 2d 1082.
1969 *N.Y. State Broadcasters Assn.* v. *U.S.,* 414 F 2d 990.
1969 *Kilby* v. *Noyce,* 416 F 2d 1391.
1969 *Nat. Assn. of Theater Owners* v. *FCC,* 420 F 2d 194.
1969 *Office of Communication* v. *FCC,* 425 F 2d 543.
1971 *Citizens Communications Center* v. *FCC,* 447 F 2d 1201.
1971 *Friends of the Earth* v. *FCC,* 449 F 2d 1164.
1972 *Stone et al.* v. *FCC,* 466 F 2d 316.
1972 *Brandywine-Maine Line Radio* v. *FCC,* 473 F 2d 16.
1973 *Yale Broadcasting Company* v. *FCC,* 478 F 2d 594.
1973 *TV 9* v. *FCC,* 495 F 2d 929.
1974 *Citizens Committee to Save WEFM* v. *FCC,* 506 F 2d 246.
1974 *NBC* v. *FCC,* 516 F 2d 1101.
1975 *Nat. Assn. of Independent TV Distributors* v. *FCC,* 516 F 2d 526.
1975 *Polish American Congress* v. *FCC,* 520 F 2d 1248.
1975 *Public Interest Research Group* v. *FCC,* 522 F 2d 1060.

1976 *Chisolm et al* v. *FCC*, 538 F 2d 349.

1977 *Warner-Lambert Co.* v. *FTC*, 562 F 2d 749.

1977 *ACT* v. *FCC*, 564 F 2d 458.

1977 *Kuczo* v. *Western Connecticut Broadcasting Co.*, 566 F 2d 384.

1977 *Home Box Office* v. *FCC*, 567 F 2d 9.

1978 *Office of Communications* v. *FCC*, 590 F 2d 1062.

1978 *Central Florida Enterprises* v. *FCC*, 598 F 2d 37.

1979 *American Security Council Education Foundation* v. *FCC*, 607 F 2d 438.

1979 *Writers Guild* v. *ABC*, 609 F 2d 355.

1979 *WNCN Listeners Guild* v. *FCC*, 610 F 2d 838.

1979 *Berlin Communications* v. *FCC*, 626 F 2d 869.

1980 *CBS Inc.* v. *ASCAP*, 620 F 2d 930.

1984 *Buffalo Broadcasting Co.* v. *FCC*, 744 F 2d 217.

1985 *Quincy. Cable TV Inc.* v. *FCC*, 768 F 2d 1434.

Fabe, Maxine. 1979. *TV Game Shows.* Doubleday, NY.

Fallon, Norman, 1976, *Shortwave Listeners Handbook.* 2d ed. Hayden, Rochelle Park, NJ.

Fang, Irving E. 1977. *Those Radio Commentators!* Iowa State U. Press, Ames.

Faulk, John H. 1964. *Fear on Trial.* Simon and Schuster, New York.

FCC (Federal Communications Commission)

    Annual. *Annual Report.* Government Printing Office, Washington, DC.

    1939 *Investigation of the Telephone Industry in the United States.* Government Printing Office, Washington, DC.

    1941 *Report on Chain Broadcasting.* Government Printing Office, Washington, DC.

    1946 *Public Service Responsibilities of Broadcast Licenses.* Government Printing Office, Washington, DC.

    1979 (Children's Television Task Force). *Television Programming for Children.* 5 vols. FCC, Washington, DC.

    1980 *The Law of Political Broadcasting and Cable Casting: A Political Primer.* Government Printing Office, Washington, DC.

    1980 (Network Inquiry Special Staff). *New Television Networks: Entry, Jurisdiction, Ownership and Regulation. Final Report,* Vol. 1. *Background Reports,* Vol. 2. Government Printing Office, Washington, DC.

    1980 *Staff Report and Recommendations in the Low Power Television Inquiry.* FCC, Washington, DC.

    1984 *Equal Employment Opportunity Trend Report, Radio and Television* (30 Nov.).

    1985 *Cable TV Equal Opportunity Trend Report* (5 Feb.)

FCC (*FCC Reports,* 1st and 2d Series)

    1949 *Editorializing by Broadcast Licensees,* 13 FCC 1249.

    1952 *Amendment of Sec. 3.606 [adopting new television rules] . . . Sixth Report and Order,* 41 FCC 148.

1959 *Columbia Broadcasting System.* An Interpretive Opinion. 26 FCC 715.

1960 *En Banc Programming Inquiry.* Report and Statement of Policy. 44 FCC 2303.

1965 *Comparative Broadcast Hearings.* Policy Statement. 1 FCC 2d 393.

1966 *Contests and Promotions Which Adversely Affect the Public Interest.* Public Notice. 2 FCC 2d 464.

1968 *Broadcasting in America and the FCC's License Renewal Process: An Oklahoma Case Study.* 14 FCC 2d 1.

1969 *Network Coverage of the Democratic National Convention.* Letter. 16 FCC 2d 650.

1969 *Application . . . for Renewal of License of Station KTAL-TV, Texarkana, Tex.* Letter. 19 FCC 2d 109.

1969 *Complaints Covering CBS Program "Hunger in America."* Memorandum Opinion. 20 FCC 2d 143.

1970 *Comparative Hearings Involving Regular Renewal Applicants.* Policy Statement. 22 FCC 2d 424.

1970 *Nicholas Zapple.* Letter. 23 FCC 2d 707.

1970 *Complaint of the Committee for the Fair Broadcasting of Controversial Issues, Against Columbia Broadcasting System.* Memorandum Opinion and Order. 25 FCC 2d 283.

1970 *Amendment of Part 73 of the Commission's Rules and Regulations with Respect to Competition and Responsibility in Network Television Broadcasting.* Memorandum Opinion and Order. 25 FCC 2d 318.

1971 *Licensee Responsibility to Review Records Before Their Broadcast.* Public Notice. 28 FCC 2d 409.

1971 *Complaint Concerning the CBS Program "The Selling of the Pentagon."* Letter. 30 FCC 2d 150.

1972 *Cable Television.* Report and Order. 36 FCC 2d 143.

1972 *Complaint by Atlanta NAACP.* Letter. 36 FCC 2d 635.

1973 *Apparent Liability of Station WGLD-FM* [Sonderling Broadcasting] News Release. 41 FCC 2d 919.

1974 *Handling of Public Issues Under the Fairness Doctrine and the Public Interest Standard of the Communications Act.* Fairness Report. 48 FCC 2d 1.

1974 *Practices of Licensees and Networks in Connection with Broadcasts of Sports Events.* Report and Order. 48 FCC 2d 235.

1974 *Children's Television.* Report and Policy Statement. 50 FCC 2d 1.

1975 *Applications for Renewal of Star Stations of Indiana.* Decision. 51 FCC 2d 95.

1975 *Inquiry into Subscription Agreements Between Radio*

Broadcasting Stations and Music Format Service Companies. Report and Policy Statement. 56 FCC 2d 805.

1975 *Agreements Between Broadcast Licensees and the Public.* Report and Order. 57 FCC 2d 42.

1976 *Representative Patsy Mink et al. re WHAR . . . .* Memorandum Opinion and Order. 59 FCC 2d 987.

1976 *Development of Policy Re: Changes in the Entertainment Formats of Broadcast Stations.* Memorandum Opinion and Order. 60 FCC 2d 858.

1977 *Review of Commissions Rules and Regulating Policies Concerning Network Broadcasting by Standard (AM) and FM Broadcast Stations.* Report, Statement of Policy, and Order. 63 FCC 2d 674.

1977 *Application of Sponsorship Identification Rules to Political Broadcasts, Teaser Announcements, Government Entities, and Other Organizations.* Public Notice. 66 FCC 2d 302.

1978 *Application for License Renewal by WPIX, Inc. and Construction Permit by Forum Communications.* Decision. 68 FCC 2d 381.

1978 *Commission Policy in Enforcing Section 312(a)(7) of the Communications Act.* Report and Order. 68 FCC 2d 1079.

1978 *Complaints Against Station KVOF-TV by Council on Religion and the Homosexual, Inc.* Memorandum Opinion and Order. 68 FCC 2d 1500.

1979 *PTL of Heritage Village Church (WJAN-TV).* Memorandum Opinion and Order. 71 FCC 2d 324.

1979 *Objectionable Loudness of Commercial Announcements . . . .* Notice of Inquiry. 72 FCC 2d 677.

1979 *Deregulation of Radio.* Notice of Inquiry and Proposed Rule Making. 73 FCC 2d 457.

1979 *Children's Television Programming and Advertising Practices.* Notice of Proposed Rule Making. 75 FCC 2d 138.

1980 *Rules and Policies to Further the Advancement of Black Americans in Mass Communications.* Memorandum Opinion and Order. 76 FCC 2d 385.

1980 *Application of RKO General, Inc. (WNAC-TV), Boston, Mass., for Renewal of Broadcasting License.* Decision. 78 FCC 2d 1.

1980 *Application of Walton Broadcasting . . . for Renewal of License.* Decision. 78 FCC 2d 857.

1980 *Cable Television Syndicated Program Exclusivity Rules [and] Inquiry into the Economic Relationship Between Television Broadcasting and Cable Television.* Report and Order. 79 FCC 2d 663.

1981 *Application of Faith Center . . . .* Memorandum Opinion and Order. 84 FCC 2d 542.

1981 *Deregulation of Radio.* Report and Order. 84 FCC 2d 968.

1981 *Stereo Broadcasters Inc.* Decision. 87 FCC 2d 87.

1982 *AM Stereophonic Broadcasting.* Report and Order. 51 RR 2d 1.

1984 *Deregulation of Radio.* Second Report and Order. 96 FCC 2d 930.

1984 *Amendment of Part 73 of the Commissions Rules and Regulations to Eliminate Objectionable Loudness of Commercial Announcements and Commercial Continuity over AM, FM, and Television Broadcast Stations.* Memorandum Opinion and Order. 56 *Radio Regulation* 390.

1984 *Revision of Program Policies and Reporting Requirements Related to Public Broadcasting Licensees.* Report and Order. 98 FCC 2d 746.

1984 *Revision of Programming and Commercialization Policies, Ascertainment Reports and Program Log Requirements for Commercial Television Stations.* 98 FCC 2d 1076.

1985 *Cattle Country Broadcasting [KTTL-FM].* Hearing Designation Order and Notice of Apparent Liability. 58 *Radio Regulation* 1109.

1985 *Inquiry into . . . . the General Fairness Doctrine Obligations of Broadcast Licensees.* Report. 102 FCC 2d 143.

1985 *Application of Simon Geller.* Memorandum Opinion and Order. 102 FCC 2d 1443.

Federal Radio Commission. Annual. *Annual Report.* 1927–1933. Government Printing Office, Washington, DC.

Felix, Edgar. 1927. *Using Radio in Sales Promotion.* McGraw-Hill, New York.

Fenby, Jonathan. 1986. *The International News Services.* Schocken Books, New York.

Ferrall, Victor E., ed. 1980. *Yearbook of Broadcasting Articles.* 1959–1978. Federal Publications Inc., Washington, DC.

Ferris, Charles, et. al. 1983. *Cable Television Law: A Video Communications Guide.* 3 vols. Matthew Bender, New York.

Fessenden, Helen. 1940. *Fessenden: Builder of Tomorrow.* Coward-McCann, New York.

Feuer, Jane, et al., eds. 1984. *MTM 'Quality Television'.* British Film Institute, London.

Fink, Donald G., ed. 1943. *Television Standards and Practice . . . .* McGraw-Hill, New York.

———, and Lutyens, David M. 1960. *The Physics of Television.* Anchor Books, Garden City, NY.

Fischer, Stuart. 1983. *Kids' TV: The First 25 Years.* Facts On File, New York.

Fiske, Edward B. 1973. "The Oral Roberts Empire," *New York Times Magazine* (Apr. 22):14.

Fletcher, James, ed. 1981. *Handbook of Radio-TV Broadcasting: Research Procedures in Audience, Program, and Revenues.* Van Nostrand-Reinhold, New York.

———. 1985. *Squeezing Profits Out of Ratings: A Manual for Radio Managers, Sales Managers, and Programmers*. National Association of Broadcasters, Washington, DC.

Foley, Joseph M. 1979. "Mass Communication Theory and Research: An Overview," in Nimmo, Dan, ed. *Communication Yearbook 3*. Transaction Books, New Brunswick, NJ: 263–270.

FR (*Federal Register*)
1974 *Program Length Commercials*. 39 FR 4042.
1974 *The Public and Broadcasting: A Procedure Manual*. Rev. ed. 39 FR 32288.

F Sup (*Federal Supplement*)
1976 *Writers Guild et al. v. FCC*. 423 F Sup 1064.
1977 *CBS v. Stokely-Van Camp*. 456 F Sup 539.
1978 *U.S. v. NBC*. 449 F Sup 1127.
1979 *Universal City Studios v. Sony*. 480 F Sup 429.

Forbes, Dorothy, and Sanderson, Layng. 1980. *The New Communicators: A Guide to Community Programming*. Communications Press, Washington, DC.

Fornatale, Peter, and Mills, Joshua E. 1980. *Radio in the Television Age*. Overlook Press, Woodstock, NY.

Fowler, Mark S., and Brenner, Daniel L. 1982. "A Marketplace Approach to Broadcast Regulation," *Texas Law Review* 60 (February):207.

Fox, Stephen. 1984. *The Mirror Makers: A History of American Advertising and Its Creators*. Morrow, New York.

Frank, Peter. 1984. *Multichannel MDS: New Allocations, New Systems and New Market Opportunities*. National Association of Broadcasters, Washington, DC.

Frank, Ronald E., and Greenberg, Marshall G. 1980. *The Public's Use of Television*. Sage Publications, Beverly Hills, CA.

———. 1982. *Audiences for Public Television*. Sage Publications, Beverly Hills, CA.

Freeman, Roger L. 1981. *Telecommunications Transmission Handbook*. 2d ed. Wiley, New York.

Friedman, Leslie J. 1977. *Sex Role Stereotyping in the Mass Media: An Annotated Bibliography*. Garland Publishing, New York.

Friendly, Fred W. 1967. *Due to Circumstances beyond our Control . . . .* Random House, New York.

———. 1975. "What's Fair on the Air," *New York Times Magazine* (Mar. 30): 11–12, 37–48.

———. 1976. *The Good Guys, the Bad Guys, and the First Amendment: Free Speech vs. Fairness in Broadcasting*. Random House, NY.

Frost, J. M., ed. Annual. *World Radio-TV Handbook*. Billboard, New York.

Frost, S. E., Jr. 1937. *Is American Radio Democratic?* U. of Chicago Press, Chicago.

FTC (Federal Trade Commission)
1924 *Report on the Radio Industry*. Government Printing Office, Washington, DC.
1978 *Staff Report on Television Advertising to Children*. FTC, Washington, DC.

Garay, Ronald. 1984. *Congressional Television: A Legislative History*. Greenwood Press, Westport, CT.

Gates, Gary P. 1978. *Air Time: The Inside Story of CBS News*. Harper & Row, New York.

Geis, Michael L. 1982. *The Language of Television Advertising*. Academic Press, New York.

Gelatt, Roland. 1977. *The Fabulous Phonograph: 1877–1977*. 2d rev. ed. Macmillan, New York.

Gerbner, George. 1972. "Communications and Social Environment," *Scientific American* (September): 153–160.

———, et al. 1977. "The Gerbner Violence Profile . . .," *Journal of Broadcasting* 21 (Summer): 280–286.

———, et al. 1984. *Religion and Television: A Research Report by The Annenberg School of Communication . . . and the Gallup Organization . . .* U. of Pennsylvania, Philadelphia.

Gianakos, Larry J. 1978–1983. *Television Drama Series Programming: A Comprehensive Chronicle*. 4 vols. Scarecrow Press, Metuchen, NJ.

Gibson, George H. 1977. *Public Broadcasting: The Role of the Federal Government, 1912–1976*. Praeger Publishing, New York.

Gillespie, Gilbert. 1975. *Public Access Cable Television in the United States and Canada*. Praeger, New York.

Gillmor, Donald M., and Barron, Jerome A. 1984. *Mass Communication Law: Cases and Comment*. 4th ed. West, St. Paul, MN.

Ginsburg, Douglas H. 1979. *Regulation of Broadcasting: Law and Policy Towards Radio, Television and Cable Communications*. West, St. Paul, MN.

Gitlin, Todd. 1983. *Inside Prime Time*. Pantheon, New York.

Glatzer, Hal. 1984. *Who Owns the Rainbow? Conserving the Radio Spectrum*. Howard W. Sams, Indianapolis.

Glynn, Eugene D. 1968. "Television and the American Character," in Casty, Alan, ed., *Mass Media and Mass Man*. Holt, Rinehart and Winston Company, New York: 76–82.

Goldmark, Peter C., and Edson, Lee. 1973. *Maverick Inventor: My Turbulent Years at CBS*. Saturday Review Press, New York.

Gordon, Thomas F., and Verna, Mary E. 1978. *Mass Communication Effects and Processes: A Comprehensive Bibliography, 1950–1975*. Sage Publications, Beverly Hills, CA.

Graham, James M., and Kramer, Victor. 1976. *Appointments to the Regulatory Agencies: The Federal Communications Commission and the Federal Trade Commission*

(1949–1974). Report to Senate Committee on Commerce. Government Printing Office, Washington, DC.

Graham, John. 1983. *The Facts on File Dictionary of Telecommunications*. Facts on File, New York.

Grant, William. 1983. *Cable Television*. Reston Books, Reston, VA.

Great Britain, Committee on the Future of Broadcasting. 1977. *Report*. Cmnd. 6753 ["Annan Report"]. Her Majesty's Stationery Office, London.

Green, Timothy. 1972. *The Universal Eye: The World of Television*. Stein and Day, New York.

Greenberg, Bradley S. 1980. *Life on Television: Content Analysis of U.S. Television Drama*. Ablex, Norwood, NJ.

———. 1983. *Mexican-Americans and the Mass Media*. Ablex, Norwood, NJ.

———, and Parker, Edwin B., eds. 1965. *The Kennedy Assassination and the American Public: Social Communication in Crisis*. Stanford U. Press, Stanford, CA.

Greenberger, Martin, ed. 1985. *Electronic Publishing Plus: Media for a Technological Future*. Knowledge Industry Publications, White Plains, NY.

Greenfield, Jeff. 1977. *Television: The First Fifty Years*. Abrams, New York.

Gross, Ben. 1954. *I Looked and I Listened*. Random House, New York (expanded edition issued in 1970).

Gross, Lynne Shafer. 1986. *The New Television Technologies*. 2d ed. Wm. C. Brown, Dubuque, IA.

Grundfest, Joseph A. 1976. *Citizen Participation in Broadcast Licensing Before the FCC*. Rand Corporation, Santa Monica, CA.

Guimary, Donald L. 1975. *Citizen's Groups and Broadcasting*. Praeger, New York.

Hadden, Jeffrey K., and Swann, Charles E. 1981. *Prime Time Preachers: The Rising Power of Televangelism*. Addison-Wesley, Reading, MA.

Haigh, Robert W., et al., eds. 1981. *Communications in the Twenty-First Century*. Wiley-Interscience, New York.

Halberstam, David. 1979. *The Powers That Be*. Knopf, New York.

Hall, Jim. 1984. *Mighty Minutes: An Illustrated History of Television's Best Commercials*. Harmony Books, New York.

Hallin, Daniel C. 1986. *The "Uncensored War:" The Media and Vietnam*. Oxford U. Press, New York.

Hamelink, Cees. 1983. *Cultural Autonomy in Global Communications*. Ablex, Norwood, NJ.

Hammond, Charles M. 1981. *The Image Decade: Television Documentary 1965–1975*. Hastings House, New York.

Hancock, Harry. 1950. *Wireless at Sea: The First 50 Years*. Marconi International Marine Communication Co., Chelmsford, England.

Harlow, Alvin. 1936. *Old Wires and New Waves: The History of the Telegraph, Telephone, and Wireless*. Century, New York.

Harrell, Bobby. 1985. *The Cable Television Technical Handbook*. Artech House, Dedham, MA.

Harris, Paul. 1977. *Broadcasting from the High Seas: The History of Offshore Radio in Europe, 1958–1976*. Paul Harris Publishing, Edinburgh, Scotland.

Hayes, Thomas C. 1984. "Hollywood in Tumult, Booms," *New York Times* (29 Sep.): 19f.

Head, Sydney W. 1956. *Broadcasting in America: A Survey of Radio and Television*. Houghton Mifflin, Boston.

———. 1974. *Broadcasting in Africa: A Continental Survey of Radio and Television*. Temple U. Press, Philadelphia.

———. 1985. *World Broadcasting Systems: A Comparative Analysis*. Wadsworth, Belmont, CA.

Headen, R. S., et al. 1979. "The Duplication of Viewing Law and Television Media Schedule Evaluation," *Journal of Marketing Research*. 2: 29–36.

Heighton, Elizabeth J., and Cunningham, Don R. 1984. *Advertising in the Broadcast and Cable Media*. 2d ed. Wadsworth, Belmont, CA.

Henderson, Bruce. 1979. "How Residuals Checks Surprise Actors," *TV Guide* (Dec. 22): 3.

Hettinger, Herman S. 1933. *A Decade of Radio Advertising*. U. of Chicago Press, Chicago.

———, and Neff, Walter J. 1938. *Practical Radio Advertising*. Prentice-Hall, New York.

Hickey, Neil. 1976. "The Case of the Missing Viewers," *TV Guide* (May 8):4.

Hill, George H., and Davis, Lenwood. 1984. *Religious Broadcasting: An Annotated Bibliography*. Garland Publisher, New York.

Himmelstein, Hal. 1981. *On the Small Screen: New Approaches in Television and Video Criticism*. Praeger, New York.

———. 1985. *Television Myth and the American Mind*. Praeger, New York.

Hoggart, Richard, and Morgan, Janet. 1982. *The Future of Broadcasting*. Macmillan, London.

Hollowell, Mary Louise, ed. 1975. *Cable Handbook*. Communications Press, Washington, DC.

———. 1983. *The Cable/Broadband Communications Book, Volume 3, 1982–83*. Communications Press, Washington, DC.

Holman, Robert G. 1984. Personal Correspondence (Nov. 5) Daniels and Associates, Denver.

Hoover, Herbert. 1952. *Memoirs*. 3 vols. Macmillan, New York.

Horowitz, Susan. 1984. "Sitcom Domesticus: A Species

Endangered by Social Change," *Channels*. Sept./Oct.: 22 f.

Horsfield, Peter G. 1984. *Religious Television: The American Experience*. Longman, New York.

House CIFC (U.S. Congress, House of Representatives: Committee on Interstate and Foreign Commerce. Note: Committee was renamed Committee on Energy and Commerce in 1981.)

    1958 *Network Broadcasting*. Report of the FCC Network Study Staff. House Report 1297, 85th Cong., 2d Sess.

    1958 *Regulation of Broadcasting: Half a Century of Government Regulation of Broadcasting and the Need for Further Legislative Action*. 85th Cong., 2d Sess.

    1960 *Responsibilities of Broadcast Licensees and Station Personnel (Payola and Other Deceptive Practices in the Broadcast Field)*. Hearings in 2 parts. 86th Cong., 2d Sess.

    1963 *Broadcast Advertisements*. Hearings. 88th Cong., 1st Sess.

    1963, 1964, and 1965. *Broadcast Ratings: The Methodology, Accuracy, and Use of Ratings in Broadcasting*. Parts 1–3. 88th Cong., 1st Sess; Part 4, 88th Cong, 1st & 2d Sess.

    1971 *Subpoenaed Material re Certain TV News Documentary Programs*. Hearings. 92nd Cong., 1st Sess.

    1977 *Network Sports Practices*. Hearings. 95th Cong., 1st Sess.

    1977 *Options Papers*. 95th Cong., 1st Sess.

    1979 *The Communications Act of 1978: Hearings on H.R. 13015. 5 vols. in 7 parts. 95th Cong., 2d Sess.*

    1980 *The Communications Act of 1979: Hearings on H.R. 3333. 5 vols. in 8 parts. 96th Cong., 1st Sess.*

House CMMF (U.S. Congress, House of Representatives, Committee on Merchant Marine and Fisheries)

    1919 *Government Control of Radio Communication*. Hearings. 65th Cong., 3rd Sess.

    1924 *To Regulate Radio Communication*. Hearings. 68th Cong., 1st Sess.

Howard, Herbert H., and Carroll, S. L. 1980. *Subscription Television: History, Current Status, and Economic Projections*. National Association of Broadcasters, Washington, DC.

Howeth, L. S. 1963. *History of Communications-Electronics in the United States Navy*. Government Printing Office, Washington, DC.

IIC (International Institute of Communication). 1976 ff. *Broadcasting in . . .* [various countries, by various authors]. Routledge & Kegan Paul, London.

Independent Broadcasting Authority. Annual. *Guide to Independent Broadcasting* [title varies]. IBA, London.

Independent Thinking: An Overview of the Independent Television Industry. 1986. Frazier Gross & Kadlec, Washington, DC.

IRE (Institute of Radio Engineers). 1962. *Proceedings of the IRE*. 50 (May): entire issue on 50th anniversary, with articles covering 1912–1962.

Interactive Cable TV Handbook. 1984. Phillips Publications, Bethesda, MD.

Intintolli, Michael. 1984. *Taking Soaps Seriously: The World of Guiding Light*. Praeger, New York.

Irwin, Manley R. 1984. *Telecommunications America: Markets without Boundaries*. Quorum Books/Greenwood Press. Westport, CT.

Jamieson, Kathleen Hall. 1984. *Packaging the Presidency: A History and Criticism of Presidential Campaign Advertising*. Oxford U. Press, New York.

Johnson, Catherine E. 1979. *TV Guide 25 Year Index: By Author and Subject*. Triangle Publications, Radnor, PA.

Johnson, Joseph S., and Jones, Kenneth K. 1978. *Modern Radio Station Practices*. 2d ed. Wadsworth, Belmont, CA.

Johnson, Nicholas. 1970. *How to Talk Back to Your Television Set*. Little, Brown, Boston.

Johnson, William O., Jr. 1971. *Super Spectator and the Electronic Lilliputians*. Little, Brown, Boston.

Johnston, Donald F. 1982. *Copyright Handbook*. 2d ed. Bowker, New York.

Jolly, W. P. 1972. *Marconi*. Stein and Day, New York.

Jones, Kensinger, et al., 1986. *Cable Advertising: New Ways to New Business*. Prentice-Hall, Englewood Cliffs, NJ.

Jones, William K. 1979. *Cases and Materials on Electronic Mass Media Radio, Television and Cable*. 2d ed. Foundation Press, Mineola, NY.

Jowett, Garth. 1976. *Film: The Democratic Art*. Little, Brown, Boston.

Kaatz, Ronald B. 1982. *Cable: An Advertiser's Guide to the New Electronic Media*. Crain, Chicago.

Kahn, Frank J., ed. 1984. *Documents of American Broadcasting*. 4th ed. Prentice-Hall, Englewood Cliffs, NJ.

Kaltenborn, H. V. 1938. *I Broadcast the Crisis*. Random House, New York.

Katz, Elihu, et al. 1974. "Uses of Mass Communication by the Individual," in Davison, W. Phillips, and Yu, Frederick T.C., eds. *Mass Communication Research: Major Issues and Future Directions*. Praeger, New York: 11–35.

————, and Wedell, George. 1977. *Broadcasting in the Third World: Promise and Performance*. Harvard U. Press, Cambridge, MA.

Keith, Michael C., and Krause, Joseph M. 1986. *The Radio Station*. Focal Press, Stoneham, MA.

Kendrick, Alexander. 1969. *Prime Time: The Life of Edward R. Murrow*. Little, Brown, Boston.

Kiester, Edwin Jr. 1974. "That 'News' Item May Be a Commercial," *TV Guide* (Oct. 5): 10.

Kirkley, Donald. 1985. *Station Policy and Procedures: A Guide for Radio*. National Association of Broadcasters, Washington, DC.

Kittross, John M., ed. 1980. *Administration of American Telecommunications Policy*. 2 vols. Arno Press, New York.

Klapper, Joseph T. 1960. *The Effects of Mass Communication*. Free Press, New York.

Klein, Paul. 1971. "The Men Who Run TV Aren't That Stupid . . . They Know Us Better Than You Think," *New York* (Jan 25): 20.

Kleinfeld, Sonny. 1981. *The Biggest Company on Earth: A Profile of AT&T*. Holt, Rinehart & Winston, New York.

The Knowledge Industry 200, 1983 Edition: America's Two Hundred Largest Media and Information Companies. 1983. Knowledge Industry Publications, White Plains, NY.

Koenig, Allen E., ed. 1970. *Broadcasting and Bargaining: Labor Relations in Radio and Television*. U. of Wisconsin Press, Madison.

Kowet, Don. 1979. "Whose 'Truth' Can You Believe?" *TV Guide* (Sep. 22): 6.

_____. 1984. *A Matter of Honor: General Westmoreland versus CBS*. Macmillan, New York.

_____, and Bedell, Sally. 1982. "Anatomy of a Smear," *TV Guide* (May 29):10.

Krasnow, Erwin, et al. 1982. *The Politics of Broadcast Regulation*. 3rd ed. St. Martin's Press, New York.

_____, and Bentley, G. Geoffrey. 1983. *Buying or Building a Broadcast Station: Everything You Want–and Need–to Know but Didn't Know Who to Ask*. National Association of Broadcasters, Washington, DC.

Kraus, Sidney, and Davis, Dennis, 1976. *The Effects of Mass Communication on Political Behavior*. Penn State U. Press, University Park.

Kuhn, Raymond, ed. 1985. *The Politics of Broadcasting*. St. Martin's Press, New York.

Kutash, Irwin L., et al. 1978. *Violence: Perspectives on Murder and Aggression*. Jossey-Bass, San Francisco.

Land, Herman W., Associates. 1968. *Television and the Wired City*. National Association of Broadcasters, Washington, DC.

Landry, Robert J. 1946. *This Fascinating Radio Business*. Bobbs-Merrill, Indianapolis.

Lang, Kurt, and Lang, Gladys Engel. 1984. *Politics and Television Re-Viewed*. Sage Publications, Beverly Hills, CA.

_____. 1983. *The Battle for Public Opinion: The President, the Press, and the Polls During Watergate*. Columbia U. Press, New York.

Langley, Graham. 1983. *Telecommunications Primer*. Pitman Books, London.

Lapin, S. G. 1973. "Television Broadcasting," in *Great Soviet Encyclopedia*. Vol. 26: 484–486. Moscow.

Larson, James. 1984. *Television's Window on the World: International Affairs Coverage on the U.S. Networks*. Ablex, Norwood, NJ.

Lashner, Marilyn A. 1984. *The Chilling Effect in TV News: Intimidation by the Nixon White House*. Praeger, New York.

Lasswell, Harold D. 1952. "Educational Broadcasters as Social Scientists," *Quarterly of Film, Radio, and Television* 7: 150–162.

Lazarsfeld, Paul F., et al. 1944. *The People's Choice: How the Voter Makes Up His Mind in a Presidential Campaign*. Duell, Sloan & Pearce, New York.

_____ & Kendall, Patricia L. 1948. *Radio Listening in America*. Prentice-Hall, New York.

Le Duc, Don R. 1973. "Broadcast Legal Documentation: A Four-Dimensional Guide," *Journal of Broadcasting* 17 (Spring): 131–146.

_____. 1973. *Cable Television and the FCC: A Crisis in Media Control*. Temple U. Press, Philadelphia.

Leinwoll, Stanley. 1979. *From Spark to Satellite: A History of Radio Communication*. Scribner's, New York.

Lent, John A., ed. 1978. *Broadcasting in Asia and the Pacific: A Continental Survey of Radio and Television*. Temple U. Press, Philadelphia.

Lerner, Daniel, and Lyle Nelson, eds. 1977. *Communication Research: A Half Century Appraisal*. East-West Center, Honolulu.

Lesher, Stephan. 1982. *Media Unbound: The Impact of Television Journalism on the Public*. Houghton-Mifflin, Boston.

Lessing, Lawrence. 1956. *Man of High Fidelity: Edwin Howard Armstrong*. Lippincott, New York (Repr. Bantam Books, 1969).

Levin, Harvey J. 1971. *The Invisible Resource: Use and Regulation of the Radio Spectrum*. John Hopkins Press, Baltimore.

_____. 1980. *Fact and Fancy in Television Regulation: An Economic Study of Policy Alternatives*. Russell Sage Foundation, New York.

Levinson, Richard, and Link, William. 1981. *Stay Tuned: An Inside Look at the Making of Prime-Time Television*. St. Martin's Press, New York.

Lichty, Lawrence W., and Topping, Malachi, eds. 1975. *American Broadcasting: A Source Book on the History of Radio and Television*. Hastings House, New York.

Liebert, Robert M., et al. 1982. *The Early Window: The Ef-*

fects of Television on Children and Youth. 2d ed. Pergamon, New York.

Lindsey, Robert. 1983. "Home Box Office Moves in on Hollywood," New York Times Magazine (Jun. 12): 31–71.

Little, Arthur D., Inc. 1969. Television Program Production, Procurement, Distribution and Scheduling. Arthur D. Little, Cambridge, MA.

Lowry, Dennis. 1979. "An Evaluation of Empirical Studies Reported in Seven Journals in the '70s," Journalism Quarterly 56 (Summer): 262–268, 282.

Lowery, Shearon, and De Fleur, Melvin L. 1983. Milestones in Mass Communication Research: Media Effects. Longman, New York.

McCain, Thomas. 1985. "The Invisible Influence: European Audience Research," InterMedia (Jul./Sep.): 74–78.

McCavitt, William E., and Pringle, Peter K. 1986. Electronic Media Management. Focal Press, Stoneham, MA.

McCombs, Maxwell E., and Shaw, Donald L. 1977. The Emergence of American Political Issues: The Agenda-Setting Function of the Press. West Publishing, St. Paul, MN.

McCoy, Ralph E. 1968. Freedom of the Press: An Annotated Bibliography. Southern Illinois U. Press, Carbondale, IL.

———. 1979. Freedom of the Press: A Bibliocyclopedia Ten-Year Supplement (1967–1977). Southern Illinois U. Press, Carbondale, IL.

MacDonald, Dwight. 1953. "Theory of Mass Culture," Diogenes 3 (Summer): 5, 13–14.

MacDonald, J. Fred. 1979. Don't Touch That Dial! Radio Programming in American Life, 1920–1960. Nelson-Hall, Chicago.

———. 1983. Blacks and White TV: Afro-Americans in Television since 1948. Nelson-Hall, Chicago.

———. 1985. Television and the Red Menace: The Video Road to Vietnam. Praeger, New York.

McDowell, Edwin. 1979. "Texaco and the Met: A Long Marriage," New York Times (Mar. 10): 25.

McGillam, Clare D., and McLauchlan, William P. 1978. Hermes Bound: The Policy and Technology of Telecommunications. Purdue U. Office of Publications, West Lafayette, IN.

McGraw-Hill Encyclopedia of Electronics and Computers. 1983. McGraw-Hill, New York.

McGraw, Thomas K. 1984. Prophets of Regulation. Harvard U. Press, Cambridge, MA.

McGuire, Bernadette, and LeRoy, David J. 1977. "Audience Mail: Letters to the Broadcaster," Journal of Communication 27 (Summer): 79–85.

McLuhan, H. Marshall. 1964. Understanding Media: The Extensions of Man. McGraw-Hill, New York.

Maclaurin, W. Rupert. 1949. Invention and Innovation in the Radio Industry. Macmillan, New York.

McQuail, Denis. 1983. Mass Communication Theory: An Introduction. Sage Publications, Beverly Hills, CA.

———, and Windahl, Sven. 1981. Communication Models for the Study of Mass Communications. Longman, New York.

Madow, William G., et al. 1961. Evaluation of Statistical Methods Used in Obtaining Broadcast Ratings. House Report 193. 87th Cong., First Sess. Government Printing Office, Washington, DC.

Madsen, Arch. 1984. 60 Minutes: The Power and Politics of America's Most Popular TV News Show. Dodd, Mead, New York.

Magnant, Robert S. 1977. Domestic Satellite: An FCC Giant Step Toward Competitive Telecommunications Policy. Westview Press, Boulder, CO.

Mander, Jerry. 1978. Four Arguments for the Elimination of Television. Morrow, New York.

Marc, David. 1984. Democratic Vistas: Television in American Culture. U. of Pennsylvania Press, Philadelphia.

Marcus, Geoffrey. 1969. The Maiden Voyage. Viking, New York.

Marill, Alvin H. 1984. Movies Made for Television. Zoetrope, New York.

Marsh, Ken. 1974. Independent Video: A Complete Guide to the Physics, Operation, and Application of the New Television for the Student, the Artist, and for Community TV. Straight Arrow Books, San Francisco.

Martin, James. 1977. Future Developments in Telecommunications. 2d ed. Prentice-Hall, Englewood Cliffs, NJ.

———. 1982. Viewdata and the Information Society. Prentice-Hall, Englewood Cliffs, NJ.

Martin, L. John, and Chardhau, Anju Grover. 1983. Comparative Mass Media Systems. Longman, New York.

Matlon, Ronald. 1980. Index to Journals in Communication Studies Through 1979. Speech Communication Association, Annandale, VA.

Matusow, Barbara. 1983. The Evening Stars: The Making of the Network News Anchor. Houghton Mifflin, Boston.

Meadows, A. J., et al. 1982. Dictionary of New Information Technology. Kogan Page, London.

Meeske, Milan D. 1976, "Black Ownership of Broadcast Stations; An FCC Licensing Problem," Journal of Broadcasting 20 (Spring): 261–271.

Meringoff, Laurene. 1980. Children and Advertising: An Annotated Bibliography. Council of Better Business Bureaus, New York.

Metz, Robert. 1975. CBS: Reflections in a Bloodshot Eye. Playboy Press, Chicago.

———. 1977. The Today Show: An Inside Look . . . Playboy Press, Chicago.

Meyersohn, Rolf B. 1957. "Social Research in Television," in Rosenberg, Bernard, and White, David Manning, eds. *Mass Culture: The Popular Arts in America*. Free Press, Glencoe, IL: 345–357.

Meyrowitz, Joshua. 1985. *No Sense of Place: The Impact of Electronic Media on Social Behavior*. Oxford U. Press, New York.

Mickiewicz, Ellen P. 1981. *Media and the Russian Public*. Praeger, New York.

Midgley, Ned. 1948. *The Advertising and Business Side of Radio*. Prentice-Hall, New York.

Minow, Newton N. 1964. *Equal Time: The Private Broadcaster and the Public Interest*. Atheneum, New York.

———. 1985. "Being Fair to the Fairness Doctrine," *New York Times* (Aug. 27): A23.

MLR (*Media Law Reporter*). 1985. *Community Television v. Wilkerson*, U.S. Dist., Utah. 11 MLR 2217.

Murphy, Brian. 1983. *The World Wired Up: Unscrambling the New Communications Puzzle*. Comedia Publishing Group, London.

Murphy, Jonne. 1980. *Handbook of Radio Advertising*. Chilton, Radnor, PA.

NAB (National Association of Broadcasters, Washington, DC)
Annual. *Radio Financial Report*.
Annual. *Television Financial Report*.
Semiannual. *Broadcasting and Government*.
1973 *Standard Definitions of Broadcast Research Terms*.
1982 *Cuban Interference to United States AM Broadcasting Stations*.
1984 *Radio Employer Compensation and Fringe Benefit Report*.
1984 *Television Employer Compensation and Fringe Benefit Report*.
1984 *Broadcasting Bibliography: A Guide to the Literature of Radio and Television*. 2d ed.
1984 *NAB Legal Guide to FCC Broadcast Regulations*. 2d ed.
1985 *Profile: Broadcasting, 1985*.
1985 *Radio in Search of Excellence: Lessons from America's Best-Run Radio Stations*.

NCTA (National Cable Television Association). 1985. *Cable Television Salaries . . . National Averages*. NCTA, Washington, DC.

NAPTS (National Association of Public Television Stations). 1984. *Public Television and Radio and State Governments*. 2 vols. NAPTS, Washington, DC.

Naisbitt, John. 1982. *Megatrends: Ten New Directions Changing Our Lives*. Warner Books, NY.

National Institute of Mental Health. 1982. *Television and Behavior: The Years of Scientific Progress and Implications for the Eighties*. 2 vols. Government Printing Office, Washington DC.

National Science Foundation. 1976. *Social Services and Cable TV*. Government Printing Office, Washington, DC.

NTIA (National Telecommunications and Information Administration, U.S. Department of Commerce). Regularly Updated. *Manual of Regulations and Procedures for Federal Radio Frequency Management*. Government Printing Office, Washington, DC.

——— 1981. *Direct Broadcast Satellites: Policies, Prospects, and Potential Competition*. Government Printing Office, Washington, DC.

Nesson, Ron. 1980. "Now Television's the Kingmaker," *TV Guide* (May 10): 4.

Newcomb, Horace. 1983. *Television: The Critical View*. 3rd ed. Oxford U. Press, New York.

———, and Alley, Robert S. 1983. *The Producer's Medium: Conversations with Creators of American TV*. Oxford U. Press, New York.

Newsweek. 1963. "As 175 Million Americans Watched," (Dec. 9): 52.

New York Times, 1985. "And Now, the Media Mega-Merger." (Mar. 24): 3:1

Nielsen Company, A. C. 1978. *The Television Audience, 1978*. A. C. Nielsen Co., Northbrook, IL.

Nimmo, Dan, and Combs, James E. 1985. *Nightly Horrors: Crisis Coverage in Television Network News*. U. of Tennessee Press, Knoxville.

Nizer, Louis. 1966. *The Jury Returns*. Doubleday, New York.

Noam, Eli M., ed. 1985. *Video Media Competition: Regulation, Economics, and Technology*. Columbia U. Press, New York.

Noll, Roger, et al. 1973. *Economic Aspects of Television Regulation*. Brookings Institution, Washington, DC.

Nordenstreng, Kaarle. 1984. *The Mass Media Declaration of Unesco*. Ablex, Norwood, NJ.

Nye, Russel B. 1970. *The Unembarrassed Muse: The Popular Arts in America*. Dial, New York.

O'Connor, John E., ed. 1983. *American History/American Television: Interpreting the Video Past*. Ungar, New York.

Opportunities in . . . Broadcasting (1983); *. . . Cable Television* (1984); and *. . . Telecommunications* (1984). 3 vols. National Textbook Co., Lincolnwood, IL.

Osborn, J. Wes., et al. 1979. "Prime Time Network Television Programming Preemptions," *Journal of Broadcasting* 23 (Fall): 427–436.

O'Shaughnessy, Hugh. 1985. *Grenada: An Eyewitness Account of the U.S. Invasion and the Caribbean History That Provided It*. Dodd Mead, New York.

Owen, Bruce M. 1975. *Economics and Freedom of Expression: Media Structure and the First Amendment*. Ballinger, Cambridge, MA.

———, et al. 1974. *Television Economics*. Lexington Books, Lexington, MA.

Overman, Michael. 1978. *Understanding Sound: Video &*

Film Recording. Tab Books, Blue Ridge Summit, PA.

Paley, William S. 1979. *As It Happened: A Memoir.* Doubleday, New York.

Passer, Harold C. 1953. *The Electrical Manufacturers, 1875–1900.* Harvard U. Press, Cambridge, MA.

Passman, Arnold. 1971. *The Deejays.* Macmillan, New York.

Paterson, Richard. Annual. *TV and Video International Guide.* Tantivy Press, London.

Paulu, Burton. 1967. *Radio and Television Broadcasting on the European Continent.* U. of Minnesota Press, Minneapolis.

——. 1974. *Radio and Television Broadcasting In Eastern Europe.* U. of Minnesota Press, Minneapolis.

——. 1981. *Television and Radio in the United Kingdom.* U. of Minnesota Press, Minneapolis.

Pember, Don R. 1984. *Mass Media Law.* 3rd ed. Wm. C. Brown, Dubuque, IA.

Performing Arts Books: 1876–1981. 1981. Bowker, New York.

Pichaske, David. 1979. *A Generation in Motion: Popular Music and Culture of the Sixties.* Schirmer Books, New York.

Pierce, John R. 1981. *Signals: The Telephone and Beyond.* Freeman, San Francisco.

Ploman, Edward. 1982. *International Law Governing Communications and Information.* Greenwood Press, Westport, CT.

Polcyn, Kenneth A. 1973. *An Educator's Guide to Communication Satellite Technology.* Academy for Educational Development, Washington, DC.

Poltrack, David. 1983. *Television Marketing: Network, Local, and Cable.* McGraw-Hill, New York.

Pool, Ithiel de Sola, ed. 1977. *The Social Impact of the Telephone.* MIT Press, Cambridge, MA.

——. 1983. *Technologies of Freedom.* Harvard U. Press, Cambridge, MA.

Pope, Daniel. 1983. *The Making of Modern Advertising.* Basic Books, New York.

Post, Steve. 1974. *Playing in the FM Band.* Viking Press, New York.

Powers, Ron. 1977. *The Newscasters.* St. Martin's Press, New York.

——. 1984. *Supertube: The Rise of Television Sports.* Coward-McCann, New York.

PLI (Practising Law Institute, New York). Annual. *Communications Law.*

1985 *The New Era in CATV: The Cable Franchise Policy and Communications Act of 1984.*

Prentiss, Stan. 1983. *Satellite Communication.* TAB Books, Blue Ridge Summit, PA.

President's Study Commission on International Broadcasting ("Stanton Commission"). 1973. *The Right to Know.* Government Printing Office, Washington, DC.

Presidential Commission on Broadcasting to Cuba. 1982. *Final Report.* Government Printing Office, Washington, DC.

Quaal, Ward, and Brown, James. 1975. *Broadcast Management.* 2d ed. Hastings House, New York.

Quinlan, Sterling. 1979. *Inside ABC: American Broadcasting Company's Rise to Power.* Hastings House, New York.

RR (*Radio Regulation*): see under FCC.

Rader, Benjamin G. 1984. *In Its Own Image: How Television Has Transformed Sports.* Free Press, New York.

Radiofrequency Use and Management: Impacts from the World Administrative Radio Conference of 1979. 1982. Office of Technology Assessment, U.S. Congress. Government Printing Office, Washington, DC.

Ray, Michael L., & Webb, Peter H. 1978. "Advertising Effectiveness in a Crowded Environment." Preliminary Research Report. 78–113. Marketing Research Institute, Cambridge, MA.

Read, Oliver, and Welsh, Walter. 1976. *From Tin Foil to Stereo: Evolution of the Phonograph.* 2d ed. Sams, Indianapolis.

Read, William H. 1976. *America's Mass Media Merchants.* Johns Hopkins U. Press, Baltimore.

Reed, Maxine, and Reed, Robert. 1982. *Career Opportunities in Television and Video.* Facts on File, New York.

Reid, T.R. 1984. *The Chip.* Simon & Schuster, New York.

Rice, Jean, ed. 1983. *Cable TV Renewals & Refranchising.* Communications Press, Washington, DC.

Rivers, William L., et al. 1980. *Responsibility in Mass Communication.* 3rd ed. Harper & Row, New York.

Rivkin, Steven R. 1978. *A New Guide to Federal Cable Television Regulations.* MIT Press, Cambridge, MA.

Roberts, Donald F., and Bachen, Christine M. 1981. "Mass Communication Effects," in *Annual Review of Psychology:* 307–356.

Robinson, Michael J., and Sheehan, Margaret A. 1983. *Over the Wire and On TV: CBS and UPI in Campaign '80.* Russel Sage Foundation, New York.

Robinson, Thomas P. 1943. *Radio Networks and the Federal Government.* Columbia U. Press, New York.

Rogers, Everett, and Balle, Francis. 1985. *The Media Revolution in America & Western Europe.* Ablex, Norwood, NJ.

Roman, James. 1983. *Cablemania.* Prentice-Hall, Englewood Cliffs, NJ.

Roper Organization. 1985. *Public Attitudes Toward Television and Other Media in a Time of Change.* 14th Report in a Series. Television Information Office, New York.

Rose, Brian G. ed. 1985. *TV Genres: A Handbook and Reference Guide.* Greenwood Press, Westport, CT.

———. 1986. *Television and the Performing Arts: A Handbook and Reference Guide to American Cultural Programming.* Greenwood Press, Westport, CT.

Rose, C. B., Jr. 1940. *National Policy for Radio Broadcasting.* Harper, New York.

Rosen, Philip T. 1980. *The Modern Stentors: Radio Broadcasters and the Federal Government 1920–1934.* Greenwood Press, Westport, CT.

Routt, Edd, et al. 1978. *The Radio Format Conundrum.* Hastings House, New York.

Rowan, Ford, 1984. *Broadcast Fairness: Doctrine, Practice, Prospects.* Longman, New York.

Rowland, Willard. 1983. *The Politics of TV Violence: Policy Uses of Communication Research.* Sage Publications, Beverly Hills, CA.

Rubin, Bernard. 1967. *Political Television.* Wadsworth, Belmont, CA.

Rutkis, Denis S. 1976. "A Report on Simultaneous Television Network Coverage of Presidential Addresses to the Nation." (Jan. 12). Congressional Research Service, Washington, DC.

Sabine, Gordon A. 1980. *Broadcasting in Virginia: Benchmark '79.* Department of Communications, Virginia Polytechnic, Blacksburg, VA.

Sack, Robert D. 1980. *Libel, Slander, and Related Problems.* Practising Law Institute, New York.

Sadowski, Robert P. 1974. "Broadcasting and State Statutory Laws," *Journal of Broadcasting* 18 (Fall): 433–450.

Safran, Claire. 1980. "Children's Television: What Are the Best — and Worst — Shows?" *TV Guide* (Aug. 9): 2.

Sarnoff, David. 1968. *Looking Ahead: The Papers of David Sarnoff.* McGraw-Hill, New York.

Saudek, Robert. 1973. "Omnibus Was Like Running Five Broadway Openings Every Week," *TV Guide* (Aug. 11): 22.

Schaefer, R. Murray. 1977. *The Tuning of the World.* Knopf, New York.

Schiller, Herbert I. 1971. *Mass Communications and American Empire.* Beacon Press, Boston.

Schmidt, Benno C. 1976. *Freedom of the Press vs. Public Access.* Praeger, New York.

Schofield, Lemuel B. 1979. "Don't Look for the Hometown Touch," *TV Guide* (Apr. 14): 39.

Schonfeld, Reese. 1983. "Pop News: TV's Growth Industry," *Channels* (Sep/Oct): 33–38.

Schubert, Paul. 1928. *The Electric Word: The Rise of Radio.* Macmillan, New York.

Schultz, Richard H., and Godson, Roy. 1984. *Dezinformatisia: Active Measures in Soviet Strategy.* Pergamon-Brassey's, Washington, DC.

Scott, James D. 1977. *Bringing Premium Entertainment into the Home via Pay-Cable TV.* U. of Michigan Graduate School of Business Administration, Ann Arbor.

Seehafer, Gene F. and Laemmar, Jack W. 1959. *Successful Television and Radio Advertising.* 2d ed. McGraw-Hill, New York.

Senate CC (U.S. Congress, Senate Committee on Commerce. Title of Committee has varied.)

1930 *Commission on Communications.* Hearings. 71st. Cong., Second Sess.

1944 *To Amend the Communications Act of 1934.* Hearings. 78th Cong., First Sess.

1948 *Progress of FM Radio.* Hearings. 80th Cong., Second Sess.

1972 *Surgeon General's Report by Scientific Advisory Committee on Television and Social Behavior.* Hearings. 92nd Cong., Second Sess.

1980 *Amendments to the Communications Act of 1934.* Hearings. 96th Cong., First Sess.

Sendall, Bernard. 1982–1983. *Independent Television in Britain.* 2 vols. Macmillan Press, London.

Sethi, S. Prakash. 1977. *Advocacy Advertising and Large Corporations.* Lexington Books, Lexington, MA.

Settel, Irving. 1967. *A Pictorial History of Radio.* 2d ed. Gross & Dunlap, New York.

———. 1983. *A Pictorial History of Television.* 2d ed. Ungar, New York.

Shaffer, William Drew, and Wheelwright, Richard. 1983. *Creating Original Programming for Cable TV.* Communications Press, Washington, DC.

Shannon, Claude E., and Weaver, W. 1949. *The Mathematical Theory of Communication.* U. of Illinois Press, Urbana.

Shearer, Benjamin F., and Huxford, Marilyn. 1983. *Communications and Society: A Bibliography on Communications Technologies and Their Social Impact.* Greenwood Press, Westport, CT.

Shiers, George, and Shiers, May. 1972. *Bibliography of the History of Electronics.* Scarecrow Press, Metuchen, NJ.

Shooshan, Harry, ed. 1984. *Disconnecting Bell: The Impact of the AT&T Divestiture.* Pergamon, New York.

Shudson, Michael. 1984. *Advertising, The Uneasy Persuasion: Its Dubious Impact on American Society.* Basic Books, New York.

Shulman, Arthur, and Youman, Roger. 1966. *How Sweet It Was: Television—A Pictorial Commentary.* Shorecrest, New York.

Siepmann, Charles. 1946. *Radio's Second Chance.* Atlantic-Little, Brown, Boston.

———. 1950. *Radio, Television and Society.* Oxford U. Press, New York.

Signorielli, Nancy. 1985. *Role Portrayal and Stereotyping on Television.* Greenwood Press, Westport, CT.

Sikes, Rhea G. 1980. "Programs for Children: Public Television in the 1970s," *Public Telecommunications Review* 8 (Sep/Oct): 7.

Silvey, Robert. 1974. *Who's Listening? The Story of BBC Audience Research*. George Allen & Unwin, London.

Simmons, Steven J. 1978. *The Fairness Doctrine and the Media*. U. of California Press, Berkeley.

Singh, Indu B., ed. 1983. *Telecommunications in the Year 2000: National and International Perspectives*. Ablex, Norwood, NJ.

Singleton, Loy A. 1986. *Telecommunications in the Information Age*. 2d ed. Ballinger, Cambridge, MA.

Sklar, Robert. 1984. *Rocking America: How the All-Hit Radio Stations Took Over*. St. Martin's Press, New York.

Slide, Anthony. 1982. *Great Radio Personalities in Historic Photographs*. Dover, New York.

Smith, Anthony. 1973. *The Shadow in the Cave: The Broadcaster, His Audience, and the State*. U. of Illinois Press, Urbana.

———. 1980. *The Geopolitics of Information: How Western Culture Dominates the World*. Oxford U. Press, New York.

Smith, Bruce Lannes, et al. 1946. *Propaganda, Communication and Public Opinion*. Princeton U. Press, Princeton, NJ.

Smith, F. Leslie. 1974. "Hunger in America Controversy: Another View," *Journal of Broadcasting*. 18 (Winter): 79–83.

Smith, Myron J. 1984. *U.S. Television Network News: A Guide to Sources in English*. McFarland & Co, Jefferson, NC.

Smith, Richard A. 1985. "TV: The Light That Failed," *Fortune* (December): 78.

Smith, Robert R. 1980. *Beyond the Wasteland: The Criticism of Broadcasting*. Rev. ed. Speech Communication Association, Annandale, VA.

Smolla, Rodney A. 1986. *Suing the Press: Libel, the Media, & Power*. Oxford U. Press, New York.

Socolow, A. Walter. 1939. *The Law of Radio Broadcasting*. 2 vols. Baker, Voorhis, New York.

Spottiswoode, Raymond, ed. 1969. *The Focal Encyclopedia of Film and Television Techniques*. Hastings House, New York.

SRDS (Standard Rate and Data Service, Skokie, IL)
Monthly. *Spot Radio Rates and Data*.
Monthly. *Spot Television Rates and Data*.

Stedman, Raymond W. 1977. *The Serials: Suspense and Drama by Installment*. 2d ed. U. of Oklahoma Press, Norman.

Stein, Harry. 1979. "How '60 Minutes' Makes News," *New York Times Magazine*. (May 6): 28.

Steiner, Gary A. 1963. *The People Look at Television: A Study of Audience Attitudes*. Knopf, New York.

Stempel, Guido H., and Westley, Bruce H., eds. 1981. *Research Methods in Mass Communication*. Prentice-Hall, Englewood Cliffs, NJ.

Sterling, Christopher H. 1982. "Television and Radio Broadcasting," Chapter 6; and "Cable and Pay Television," Chapter 7 in Compaine, Benjamin, et al. *Who Owns the Media? Concentration of Ownership in the Mass Communications Industry*. 2d ed. Knowledge Industry Publications, White Plains, NY: 299–450.

———. 1984. *Electronic Media: A Guide to Trends in Broadcasting and Newer Technologies, 1920–1983*. Praeger, New York.

———, and Haight, Timothy R. 1978. *The Mass Media: Aspen Institute Guide to Communication Industry Trends*. Praeger, New York.

———, and Kittross, John M. 1978. *Stay Tuned: A Concise History of American Broadcasting*. Wadsworth, Belmont, CA.

Stone, Vernon A. 1978. "News Staff Size, Turnover, and Sources Surveyed," *RTNDA Communicator*. 32 (August): 8.

Straubhaar, Joseph D. 1982. "The Decline of American Influence on Brazilian Television," Paper presented at V Ciclo de Estudos Interdisciplinares da Comunicao, Sao Paulo (September).

Strong, William S. 1984. *The Copyright Book: A Practical Guide*. 2d ed. MIT Press, Cambridge, MA.

Sugar, Bert Randolph. 1978. *"The Thrill of Victory": The Inside Story of ABC Sports*. Hawthorn Books, New York.

Surgeon General, Scientific Advisory Committee on Television and Social Behavior. 1972. *Television and Growing Up: The Impact of Televised Violence*. Government Printing Office, Washington, DC.

Swerdlow, Joel. 1984. *Beyond Debate: A Paper on Televised Presidential Debates*. Twentieth Century Fund, New York.

Tannenbaum, Percy H., and Kostrich, Leslie J. 1983 *Turned-On TV/Turned-Off Votes*. Sage, Beverly Hills, CA.

Tannenwald, Peter. 1985. "Selling Off the Spectrum," *Channels* (July–Aug.): 41–43.

Taylor, John P. 1980. *Direct-to-Home Satellite Broadcasting*. Television/Radio Age, New York.

Tebbel, John. 1975. *The Media in America*. Crowell, New York.

———, and Watts, Sarah Miles. 1985. *The Press and the Presidency*. Oxford U. Press, New York.

TCAF (Temporary Commission on Alternative Financing for Public Telecommunications). 1983. *Final Report*. Federal Communications Commission, Washington, DC.

Technology & Economics, Inc. 1980. *The Emergence of Pay Cable Television*. 4 vols. NTIA, Washington, DC.

Tedford, Thomas L. 1985. *Freedom of Speech in the United States*. Southern Illinois U. Press, Carbondale.

Telecommunication Journal. 1980. "Telecommunications in the United States," 47 (June): 307–412 (special issue).

Telemedia. 1983. ''Where Does the Typical Station's Time Sales Dollar Come From?'' (Nov./Dec.): 27.

Television Age International. 1985. ''Worldwide TV Set Count,'' (February): 48–50.

Television and Behavior: Ten Years of Scientific Progress and Implications for the Eighties. 1982. 2 vols. Government Printing Office, Washington, DC.

''Television Surpasses Radio News in Survey,'' 1984. *New York Times* (Sep. 1): Y13.

Terry, Clifford. 1976. ''Vast Wasteland Revisited,'' *TV Guide* (Oct. 16): 4.

Thompson, Robert L. 1947. *Wiring a Continent: The History of the Telegraph Industry in the United States, 1832–66.* Princeton U. Press, Princeton, NJ.

Toffler, Alvin. 1980. *The Third Wave.* Morrow, New York.

Toll, Robert C. 1982. *The Entertainment Machine: American Show Business in the Twentieth Century.* Oxford U. Press, New York.

Truax, Barry. 1985. *Acoustic Communication.* Ablex, Norwood, NJ.

Tunstall, Jeremy. 1977. *The Media Are American: Anglo-American Media in the World.* Columbia U. Press, New York.

――――. 1984. *The Media in Britain.* Columbia U. Press, New York.

――――, and Walker, David. 1981. *Media Made in California: Hollywood, Politics, and the News.* Oxford U. Press, New York.

Turow, Joseph. 1981. *Entertainment, Education and the Hard Sell: Three Decades of Network Children's Television.* Praeger, New York.

――――. 1984. *Media Industries: The Production of News and Entertainment.* Longman, New York.

Tydeman, John, et al. 1982. *Teletext and Videotex in the United States: Market Potential, Technology, and Public Policy Issues.* McGraw-Hill, New York.

Tynan, Kenneth. 1979. *Show People: Profiles in Entertainment.* Simon & Schuster, New York.

Tyne, Gerald F. J. 1977. *Saga of the Vacuum Tube.* Howard W. Sams, Indianapolis.

Twentieth Century Fund. 1979. *A Free and Balanced Flow.* Lexington Books, Lexington, MA.

Udelson, Joseph H. 1982. *The Great Television Race: A History of the American Television Industry 1925-1941.* U. of Alabama Press, University, AL.

UNESCO (United Nations Educational, Scientific and Cultural Organization, Paris)

　Various Dates. *Communication Policies in . . .* [various countries, by various authors].

　Annual. *Statistical Yearbook.*

　1975 *World Communication: A 200 Country Survey of Press, Radio, Television, Film.* 5th ed.

　1979 *Statistics on Radio and Television, 1960–1976.*

　1980 *Many Voices, One World: Communications and Society Today and Tomorrow* (''MacBride Commission Report'').

US (*United States Reports*)

　1919 *Shenck* v. *U.S.* 249 US 47.

　1937 *FTC* v. *Standard Education Society.* 302 US 112.

　1940 *FCC* v. *Sander Bros. Radio Station.* 309 US 470.

　1942 *Marconi Wireless Telegraph Company of America* v. *U.S.* 320 US 1.

　1943 *NBC* v. *U.S.* 319 US 190.

　1949 *Terminiello* v. *Chicago.* 337 US 1.

　1951 *Dennis* v. *U.S.* 341 US 494.

　1959 *Farmers Educational Cooperative* v. *WDAY.* 360 US 525.

　1964 *New York Times* v. *Sullivan.* 376 US 254.

　1965 *FTC* v. *Colgate-Palmolive.* 380 US 374.

　1965 *Estes* v. *Texas.* 381 US 532.

　1968 *U.S.* v. *Southwestern Cable.* 392 US 157.

　1968 *Fortnightly Corp.* v. *United Artists Television.* 392 US 390.

　1969 *Red Lion* v. *FCC.* 395 US 367.

　1973 *CBS* v. *Democratic National Committee.* 412 US 94.

　1973 *Miller* v. *California.* 413 US 15.

　1974 *National Cable Television Association* v. *U.S. and FCC.* 415 US 336.

　1974 *Miami Herald* v. *Tornillo.* 418 US 241.

　1974 *Gertz* v. *Welch.* 418 US 323.

　1978 *FCC* v. *National Citizens Committee for Broadcasting.* 436 US 775.

　1978 *FCC* v. *Pacifica Foundation.* 438 US 726.

　1979 *Herbert* v. *Lando.* 441 US 153.

　1981 *Chandler* v. *Florida.* 449 US 560.

　1984 *Universal Studios* v. *Sony.* 464 US 417.

　1984 *FCC* v. *League of Women Voters of California.* 484 US＿＿. (104 S. Ct. 3106)

　1986 *City of Los Angeles* v. *Preferred Communications, Inc.* ＿＿ US ＿＿. (Slip Opinion 85–390).

USACPD (U.S. Advisory Commission on Public Diplomacy). Annual. *Report to the Congress and the President of the United States.* Government Printing Office, Washington, DC.

U.S. Bureau of the Census. 1935. *Radio Broadcasting.* Government Printing Office, 1935.

U.S. Commission on Civil Rights. 1977, 1979. *Window Dressing on the Set: Women and Minorities in Television.* 2 vols. Government Printing Office, Washington, DC.

U.S. Congress, House of Representatives. 1978. *Radio Laws of the United States.* Government Printing Office, Washington, DC (frequently revised).

USNCU (U.S. National Commission for UNESCO). 1982. "A Critical Assessment of U.S. Participation in UNESCO," Department of State Pub. 9297. Government Printing Office, Washington, DC.

Van Gerpen, Maurice. 1979. *Privileged Communication and the Press: The Citizen's Right to Know Versus the Law's Right to Confidential News Source Evidence*. Greenwood Press, Westport, CT.

Vaughn, Robert. 1972. *Only Victims: A Study of Show Business Black-listing*. Putnam, New York.

Warner, Charles. 1986. *Broadcast and Cable Selling*. Wadsworth, Belmont, CA.

Warner, Harry P. 1948. *Radio and Television Law*. Matthew Bender, Albany, NY.

————. 1953. *Radio and Television Rights*. Matthew Bender, Albany, NY.

Weaver, Sylvester L. 1955. "The Form of the Future," *Broadcasting-Telecasting* (May 30):56.

Webb, G. Kent. 1983. *The Economics of Cable Television*. Lexington Books, Lexington, MA.

Webster, James. 1985. "Program Audience Duplication: A Study of Television Inheritance Effects," *Journal of Broadcasting and Electronic Media* 29 (Spring): 121–133.

Webster, Lance, et al. 1983. *Advertising and Promotion*. Hastings House, New York.

Welch, Randy. 1985. "The Builder of Cable Empires," *Channels* (Jan./Feb.): 45.

Wenham, Brian, ed. 1982. *The Third Age of Broadcasting*. Faber and Faber, London.

Wertheim, Frank. 1979. *Radio Comedy*. Oxford U. Press, New York.

White, David M. 1950. "The 'Gate Keeper': A Case Study in the Selection of News," *Journalism Quarterly* 27 (Fall): 383–390.

White, Llewellyn. 1947. *The American Radio*. U. of Chicago Press, Chicago.

Whiteside, Thomas. 1985. "Cable," *The New Yorker* (May 20): 45; (May 27): 43; and (June 3): 82.

Whitman, Alden. 1973. "William Benton Dies Here at 73, Leader in Politics and Education," Obituary, *New York Times* (Mar. 3): 1.

Whitney, Dwight. 1974. "Cinema's Stepchild Grows Up," *TV Guide* (July 20): 21.

Williams, Christian. 1981. *Lead, Follow, or Get Out of the Way . . .* Times Books, New York.

Wilson, H. H. 1961. *Pressure Group: The Campaign for Commercial Television*. Rutgers U. Press, New Brunswick, NJ.

Wimmer, Roger, and Joseph Dominick. 1983. *Mass Media Research: An Introduction*. Wadsworth, Belmont, CA.

Winn, Marie. 1985. *The Plug-in Drug: Television, Children, and the Family*. 2d ed. Penguin Books, New York.

Wolfe, Charles H., ed. 1949. *Modern Radio Advertising*. Funk & Wagnalls, New York.

Wood, Donald N., and Wylie, Donald G. 1977. *Educational Telecommunications*. Wadsworth, Belmont, CA.

Woolery, George W. 1983–1984. *Children's Television: The First Thirty-Five Years, 1946–1981*. 2 vols. Scarecrow Press, Metuchen, NJ.

Yoakam, Richard, and Cremer, Charles. 1985. *ENG: Television News and the New Technology*. Southern Illinois U. Press, Carbondale.

Zoglin, Richard, and Ainslie, Peter. 1984. "Where's the Soaps," *Time* (Aug. 13): 96

Ziegler, Sharilyn K. and Howard, Herbert H. 1984. *Broadcast Advertising*. 2d. ed. Grid Inc., Columbus, OH.

Zuckman, Harvey, and Gaynes, Martin. 1983. *Mass Communication Law in a Nutshell*. West Publishing, St. Paul, MN.

Index

To the Student

We have made every effort to ensure that this edition of *Broadcasting in America* is a readable and useful resource. In addition to the main text, we have also published a *Study Guide* to aid you in learning this body of material. If you would like additional help, ask your instructor or bookstore manager to order the *Study Guide*, written by Norman Felsenthal of Temple University, that accompanies *Broadcasting in America*, Fifth Edition.

Each chapter of the *Study Guide* covers the parallel chapter in *Broadcasting in America* and is organized as follows:

1. Chapter Focus: gives an overview of the chapter in the text.
2. Capsule: summarizes each chapter in outline form; will help you to recall details and review.
3. Key Terms: exercises quiz you on the meaning and significance of important terms, names, and organizations mentioned in *Broadcasting in America*; answers appear at the back of the *Study Guide*.
4. Self-Test: fill-ins and true/false exercises allow you to test your understanding of the text chapter; answers appear at the back of the *Study Guide*.
5. Projects: encourage you to delve deeper into the broadcasting material discussed in each chapter and to develop your library and research skills.

Note from the Publishers

We are interested in your opinions of this textbook. When you have completed your reading, please take a moment to answer the questions below and mail your responses to Communications Editor, College Division, Houghton Mifflin Company, One Beacon Street, Boston, MA 02108. Thank you for helping us plan and improve future editions of *Broadcasting in America*.

1. In general, would you rate this textbook as excellent, above average, average, below average, or poor? _____
   Why? _____
   _____

2. Which chapters did you find the most helpful and why? _____
   _____
   _____
   Least helpful? _____
   Why? _____
   _____

3. What topics do you think should be added? _____
   _____
   Deleted? _____
   _____
   Given expanded treatment? _____
   _____
   Presented more clearly? _____
   _____

4. Which exhibits (photographs, diagrams, charts, boxed features, etc.) did you find particularly helpful or interesting? _____
   _____
   Which were confusing? _____
   _____

5. Any additional comments on *Broadcasting in America*? _____
   _____
   _____
   _____

6. Name of course for which you read *Broadcasting in America*, Fifth Edition:
   _____
   Did you take this course as a freshman, sophomore, junior, senior, or graduate student? _____

7. Your name? _____
   Name of your college or university? _____
   Name of your instructor? _____
   Thank you.